T0303256

Labiche & Co.

Fourteen One-Acts
by a French Comic Master

English Versions
by Norman R. Shapiro

PERFORMING BOOKS

DISTRIBUTED BY HAL LEONARD & APPLAUSE

A Performing Books Original

Labiche & Co: Fourteen One-Acts by a French Comic Master
Edited and translated by Norman R. Shapiro. Introduction by Norman R. Shapiro
Afterword: Finding the Funny: On Directing Farce by Michael Clark Haney

First Printing: 2010

ISBN: 978-1-55783-757-8

This Performing Books title is distributed to the trade by
The Hal Leonard Publishing Group and Applause Theatre Books
19 West 21st Street, Suite 201, New York, NY 10010

Publisher's Cataloging-in-Publication Data

Labiche, Eugène, 1815-1888.

Labiche & co. : fourteen one-acts by a french comic master / English versions by Norman R. Shapiro.—1st ed.—New York, NY : Performing Books ; dist. by the Hal Leonard Publishing Group and Applause Theatre Books, c2010.

p. ; cm.

ISBN: 978-1-55783-757-8

"Edited and translated by Norman R. Shapiro; introduction by Norman R. Shapiro; afterword: Finding the funny: on directing farce by Michael Clark Haney"—T.p. verso.

Contents: Bosom friends, or tit for tat / with August Lefranc—Mam'selle Frisette / with August Lefranc—The well-wooed wench, or beau's jests / "Dandré & Senneif"—The brat / with Marc-Michel—It's all relative / with Marc-Michel—Edouard and the chambermaid, or Hey-diddle-diddle / with Marc-Michel—Temper, temper! or A bee or not a bee / with Marc-Michel—Pater Omnipotens, or A suitor unsuited / with Marc-Michel—The unshakable suitor, or The matter at hand / with Alphonse Jolly—Barbara of Seville / with Marc-Michel—Smotherly love: a passion play / with Alfred Delacour—A nest egg well scrambled / with Edouard Martin—A slap in the farce / with Edouard Martin—A matter of wife and death.

1. French drama (Comedy)—19th century—Translations into English. 2. French farces—19th century—Translations into English. I. Shapiro, Norman R. II. Haney, Michael Clark. Finding the funny: on directing farce. III. Lefranc, Auguste, 1814-1878. IV. Marc- Michel, M., 1812-1868. V. Leveaux, Alphonse, b. 1810. VI. Delacour, M. (Alfred), 1815-1883. VII. Martin, Edouard, 1828- 1866. VIII. Title. IX. Title: Labiche and company.

PQ2321 .A6 2010
842/.8—dc22 0909

For Harry Shifman and Grete Friese,
with thanks for their talents
and their friendship

Publication of this book has been supported by a grant from the Thomas and Catharine McMahon Fund of Wesleyan University, established through the generosity of the late Joseph McMahon.

Contents

Introduction

It is a truism that all translators, by the very nature of their craft, are faced with choices. But translators of comic theater have to cope with even more than most. They can opt to remain close to the original, not only in plot-line—an obvious given—but also in individual character portrayals and idiosyncrasies, in "message," in setting—chronological, geographical, and social—in lexical tone, and even in linguistic humor to the extent that the differences from language to language permit. Or they can stray far afield from the original, making greater or lesser alterations in these elements, changing time and place, introducing new characters, toying with the idiom, and going so far as to re-work the medium itself by adding important visual effects and even including music and dance. In the latter cases they produce what it usually thought of as an "adaptation." Consider, for example, the many major (and minor) differences between Shakespeare's *The Taming of the Shrew* and Porter's *Kiss Me Kate.*

Those of us who choose to hew closely to the original texts we translate confront several choices as well. Should we conceal, or at least obscure, our presence in an effort to be utterly faithful to the author and translate as literally as possible, consistent with artistic, dramatic, and verbal integrity? Or should we allow our own sense of humor to dictate liberties with the language and with character quirks perhaps only hinted at in the original? In the former case, rigorous fidelity to the text may well produce a successful archival document of interest to literary and theatrical historians, but will it always—or ever—produce comedy? Will it, in short, be funny? The question may be a trifle banal in the face of so lofty a principle as literary exactitude, but when one is dealing with comedy it is hardly irrelevant.

The answer depends, of course, on the quality of the original and the accessibility, to audiences removed in time and space, of its "message," its character portrayals, and especially its idiom. Molière, for example, doesn't have to be "jazzed up" to be funny to present-day spectators. His plots are human and universal enough to cross the temporal and spatial divide more or less unaltered. So too his characters. And if liberties must occasionally (and judiciously) be taken to make his language and its humor speak to today's audiences, it is certainly unnecessary and, I think, sacrilegious to alter it in the extreme or to add gratuitously to it. Speaking for myself, I would cringe, in the interest of tonal consistency, before a version of any Molière comedy—other than a most intentional pastiche—in which, say, a typically 17th-century French fop, who maintains all his 17th-century-ness of character and language, were nonetheless to sound like a modern American or Brit, no matter how hilarious the result.

But not all comic theater of other times and places is as easily accessible as Molière's and his classical brethren's. Eugène Labiche (1815-1888) is a good case in point. Funny as are his bourgeois fathers, assertive wives, demure daughters, ambitious lovers, and a spate of other social fauna of varying comic stripe, all of whom actually present more variety than many commentators are willing to concede, his treatment of them, their foibles, and their language is not sacrosanct. So long as his plots are respected and the general lines of his dialogues are reproduced, I, as a translator, do not feel historically or dramatically constrained to transmit his texts verbatim. Other translators might. But for me, to do so would, in fact, be counterproductive. My obligation to him and his texts goes only so far, and it must be tempered by my no-less-imperious obligation to today's spectators: namely, to make them laugh. My approach to his comedies is something of a compromise between fidelity and freedom; fidelity, surely, to his plots and characters, but freedom to let them develop their dialogues in their imposed adopted tongue with more humor (I hope) than their 19th-century French counterparts would exhibit for us. If making them "accessible" means altering contemporary social allusions, recasting puns or adding new ones, exaggerating characters' comical personality traits and tics, or even tinkering with their very personas, so be it. It may even mean operating an occasional wholesale change.

A striking example of the latter operation is provided here by my version of *Barbara of Seville.* The egregious pun of the title in no way "translates" Labiche's *La Perle de la Canebière.* But since the flamboyant protagonist (Théréson in the original) is a native of Marseille, and since she frequently interjects a smattering of Provençal into her dialogue—more or less understandable to Labiche's French audiences but certainly not to mine—I decided to preserve her linguistic ambivalence by making her instead a less exotic but no less eccentric Spaniard. Once Marseille was transformed to Seville, with no harm to plot, or character, or details, her name eventually followed suit, as did the general carnage she commits on the English which, with disbelief appropriately suspended, represents her attempts at French.*

Clearly, then, readers and spectators looking for literal translations will not find them here. Nor, as in the preceding example, will they find all Labiche's titles or even all his characters' names scrupulously reproduced. I take the former liberty because most of his titles are, frankly, rather less inspired than the sprightly texts they accompany; whereas I take the latter to conform to those instances where the original French name suggests a specific meaning, or even where it might present pronunciation problems for Anglophone actors. What they will find here is a collection of Labiche's one-act comedies resulting, as with any translation, from my personal collaboration with them: his humor, indeed—and that of his frequent co-signers, whose contributions, impossible to dissect out exactly, should not be overlooked—but filtered generously through my own.

They will also find considerable variety. Theater historians, as I have suggested, often tend to declare that all Labiche's comedies are only variations on a theme; that of the bourgeois father trying to marry off his nubile but somewhat vapid daughter. That stereotype exists in these pages, to be sure, but readers and potential directors and actors who expect to find little more will be pleasantly disabused. On the contrary, variety, as I say, is the hallmark of these little comedies. Plot-wise, they range from the sentimentality of a *Mam'selle Frisette*—sentimental despite its farcical premise of an antagonistic man and woman occupying the same room unbeknownst to each other (she by night and he by day)—to the more robust and blatant farce of *Barbara of Seville, The Well-Wooed Wench,* and *Edouard and His Chambermaid.* Character-wise, they present, among their array of extravagant examples, the Latin-spouting father of *Pater Omnipotens,* who, uncharacteristically, does not want his

---

* A pleasant note is in order here. Originally I had chosen to make her a native of Barcelona, but my departmental secretary, a staunchly nationalistic Catalan lady, objected vigorously to her sporadic use of Spanish, maintaining that only Catalan would be appropriate. She refused to consider that, politically appropriate or not, that language simply wouldn't cross the footlights in an English version. I compromised by turning Barcelona to Seville, with its attendant changes.

daughter to marry at all; the over-protective mother in *Smotherly Love,* who harbors similar negative desires for her aggressively unromantic son; another atypical father, in *It's All Relative,* whose grotesque stepdaughter is anything but nubile in the Labiche mold and who stands in the way of his own marital ventures; the actor-suitor of *The Well-Wooed Wench,* whose virtuoso disguises win him his belle despite the objections of her actor-hating uncle; the usual parade of domestics in the comic tradition, but each individually nuanced in his or her own right; and, most outrageous of all, the headstrong seven-year-old in pigtails, anti-heroine of *The Brat,* a comedy that even sports a foulmouthed parrot. Not to mention the lovesick Texan millionaire of *A Matter of Wife and Death*... Enough variety, in short, to prove that Labiche, though often categorized, simplistically, as a writer of farce—perhaps owing to his acknowledged influence on the master of that supremely demanding genre, Feydeau—is far from harping on the same tune or exploiting one and only one comic vein. Eminent fabricator of farce though he was, to pigeon-hole him as such, as many theater historians blithely do, is to overlook much of his voluminous theater

And "voluminous" is certainly the word to describe it. Some ten years before his death, when Labiche had penned his last theater piece—probably *La lettre chargée*, translated here as *A Matter of Wife and Death*—he devoted himself to the publication of the fifty-seven comedies of his so-called *Théâtre complet*, prefaced by playwright Emile Augier (Paris, 1878-79). With that project his reading public would be denied, however, more than a hundred of the works that his Parisian theatergoing public had attended with delight over the years since 1838. Happily, a more recent collection of his *Œuvres complètes,* dating from 1966, lives up to its title, including even several of his previously unpublished comedies.

Unusually prolific, owing both to his own comic inventiveness and to his battery of collaborators—the "& Co." of my title: only a handful of his hundred-seventy-plus works were, in fact, signed without at least one—Labiche rarely knew a Paris theatrical season with fewer than a pair of his—or, often, their—plays on the boards. During his heyday, between 1845 and 1865, it was not uncommon for him to have six, seven, eight, or even nine (!) productions in a single year. Many if not most of these were *vaudevilles* in the French sense of the term—comedy interspersed with popular tunes provided with lyrics relating to the action—while several, more musically ambitious, were full-fledged comic opera libretti with scores by the likes of Léo Delibes and other lesser-known composers of the day. (Readers will notice that, given the evanescent nature of such tunes, as well as their dramatic irrelevance, I haven't seen fit to include them in the present versions.)

It is difficult if not impossible to dissect out the full extent of Labiche's collaborators' contributions. It seems reasonable to assume, however, that he was the prime architect of his comedies even if some-perhaps many—of the details were left to his dramatic confreres to provide. A master at depicting the concerns, pretensions, and affectations of the bourgeoisie in wittily appropriate dialogue, his plots are replete with character studies often worthy of high comedy as well as with those droll farcical entanglements that his disciple Feydeau would eventually manipulate to perfection, and on which, as I have said, much of Labiche's reputation is a little too one-sidedly based. His election to the Académie française in 1880 is proof enough of that exaggerated oversimplification. Surely that august body would never have allowed a "mere" *farceur* to sit in immovable honor among its immortals!

I am pleased to thank Glenn Young, for his confidence, and French Wall, Jamie Ciocco, and Ames Brown for their electronic wizardry in bringing this collection before the public. I have also been fortunate enough to attend performances of half my translations presented here, and have had the advantage of seeing what "worked" and what could stand improvement. My thanks to directors Michael C. Haney, Luke Jorgensen, and Sunil Swaroop, along with their casts of spirited, intuitively comic actors for giving me that opportunity and that pleasure. If seeing one's work take shape between two covers is fulfilling for any writer, a translator of theater can know a very special joy. There are, I think, few greater satisfactions for the translator than watching one's collaboration with the original author's text come to life, not merely on the printed page but before one's very eyes and ears. And, where comic theater is concerned, that satisfaction is amplified many fold by the laughter—from simple chuckle to guffawing belly-laugh—of an audience that "gets it" in all the right places.

I hope these modest comedies of Labiche, most of them little known today even in their native France, will reach out over a century and a half to provoke their share of such laughter, that essentially human—and essential—activity, of which there can never be too much.

Bosom Friends, or Tit for Tat

(L'homme de paille, 1843)

Eugène Labiche & Auguste Lefranc

*Characters**

DE CHAMVILLE, a rakish rogue intent on a socially advantageous marriage

DE CAMBIAC, an aristocratic gentleman, his supposed good friend

TOUPETTE, a foppish would-be poet

VAN GELDING, a notary

JULIEN, a domestic

MADAME DE LAJOIE, a charming and very sensible widow, quite well-off

ADELE, her maid

TWO MALE SERVANTS

---

* I reproduce the usual French style of the period, citing characters by gender, males first then females. Far from being an evidence of male chauvinism at a time when women ruled the footlights, the practice was especially useful to directors considering potential scripts.

Madame de Lajoie's elegantly furnished Parisian drawing room. Upstage center, the door to the rest of the apartment. In the left wall, upstage, the door to a bedroom; downstage, the door to the library. In the right wall, center, the door to madame's room. Next to it, downstage, an open window, appropriately curtained. Center stage, facing each other at an angle, two armchairs. Down left, a writing-table and chair. Hanging from the ceiling, up left, a bell-cord. Other tasteful furnishings—lamps, pictures, occasional chairs, etc.

At rise, MADAME DE LAJOIE *and* VAN GELDING, *the notary, are down left.* ADELE, *in maid's garb, is puttering about, listening as inconspicuously as possible.*

MADAME DE LAJOIE, *to* VAN GELDING: Well now, monsieur… I think that takes care of all the details of the contract. Please see to it that it's drawn up to the letter.

VAN GELDING: Certainly, madame… And I assume nothing will dissuade you from this marriage?

MADAME DE LAJOIE: Dissuade me? Heavens no! I realize that some people will think I'm perfectly mad…

VAN GELDING, *defensively*: Oh! Far be it from me to suggest… It's only that Monsieur de Chamville does have a reputation as… *(Hesitating.)* as something of a… How shall I say?…

MADAME DE LAJOIE, *with a laugh*: A young rake?

VAN GELDING: Well…

MADAME DE LAJOIE, *shrugging*: A mere trifle, monsieur! What could be less important? He's devoted, generous to a fault…

VAN GELDING: I suppose…

MADAME DE LAJOIE: And not affected in the slightest… Without a false bone in his body…

VAN GELDING, *nodding, apparently unconvinced*: Aha… *(Aside.)* If you think so…

MADAME DE LAJOIE: That's what I find so utterly fetching about him. Not to mention his family, monsieur… One of the oldest and noblest in all of France!

ADELE, *unable to resist*: Besides, it's not very pleasant being a widow.

MADAME DE LAJOIE: Adèle!

ADELE: Especially when that first husband of madame's was such a… Well, she deserves a better one to make up for him, believe me!

MADAME DE LAJOIE: Really, young lady…

ADELE: But it's true, madame! When I think of Monsieur de Lajoie I just get angry all over! It's all well and good that he had the decency to up and die, and let madame be rid of him once and for all! But then, to write a will that won't let her get married again for two whole years!… Poor Monsieur Van Gelding had his hands full, what with all those clauses, and codicils, and…

VAN GELDING, *aside*: I daresay!

ADELE: And all the debts, and all the lawsuits… A jungle… An absolute jungle!

VAN GELDING, *to* MADAME DE LAJOIE: I'm afraid she's right madame!

ADELE: Why, if that absolute stranger hadn't come along when he did, and lent madame a hundred thousand, I shudder to think…

VAN GELDING, *to* MADAME DE LAJOIE: The auction block madame!… Down to your very last handkerchief and your last stick of furniture!

MADAME DE LAJOIE: And believe me, I've never stopped blessing him. *(To* VAN GELDING.*)* Whoever he is, monsieur!... If only you would tell me, I could thank him myself for saving me from disaster.

VAN GELDING: Impossible, I'm afraid! I gave my word. And a notary's word—

MADAME DE LAJOIE, *interrupting*: Is his bond! I know... Especially a model notary like you, Monsieur Van Gelding.

VAN GELDING: Thank you, madame. I'm glad you appreciate—

MADAME DE LAJOIE, *returning to the business at hand*: So! This afternoon, then... Four o'clock... I'm sure you'll be prompt.

VAN GELDING: You can count on me, madame.

ADELE, *showing him out, upstage*: Monsieur...

VAN GELDING exits.

MADAME DE LAJOIE, *coming down right, standing by the window, impatiently*: Eleven o'clock, and still no sign of him! Really, Adèle, sometimes I just don't know what to make of that man!

ADELE: But madame knows that promptness is hardly one of Monsieur de Champville's virtues!... Especially when his friend, Monsieur de Cambiac, is in Paris...

MADAME DE LAJOIE: Alas!

ADELE: If madame doesn't mind my saying, she seems to have a powerful rival in that one!

MADAME DE LAJOIE: Please, Adèle! Spare me your words of wisdom! *(To herself.)* Of all days to be late... After waiting these two endless years... You would think that... that... *(The bell rings.)* Ah! *(To* ADELE.*)* Quick! Go see...

ADELE: And if it's the other one, madame? Monsieur Toupette? Suitor number two?

MADAME DE LAJOIE: That insufferable fop?... Heavens no!... If it is, I'm not at home!

ADELE: Very good, madame.

She exits, upstage.

MADAME DE LAJOIE, *listening to muffled voices offstage*: Ah! Thank goodness it's not... Today, of all days...

ADELE enters, followed by DE CHAMVILLE.

ADELE, *announcing*: Monsieur de Chamville... *(Wagging her finger at him.)* Tsk tsk!... One whole hour, monsieur! Madame has been sighing her heart out...

MADAME DE LAJOIE: Adèle!

DE CHAMVILLE: She has? I'm flattered!

MADAME DE LAJOIE, *to* DE CHAMVILLE, *archly*: Not true, Philippe! The child is an impertinent sot! *(To* ADELE.*)* How many times have I told you...

DE CHAMVILLE, *aside*: De Cambiac to the rescue... *(Aloud, to* MADAME DE LAJOIE, *dramatically.)* Ah, madame! Let me feel the full measure of your wrath! How richly I deserve it!... Oh yes! I do... I do...

MADAME DE LAJOIE: Well...

DE CHAMVILLE: And nothing you say... Nothing, dear lady, will prevent me from punishing the reprobate who caused me to affront you! Let me go see to it that the culprit pays, madame!

He moves upstage, as if to leave.

MADAME DE LAJOIE: But… Where are you going? You just arrived…

DE CHAMVILLE: Where? Off to slit my friend de Cambiac's scurvy throat, that's where!

MADAME DE LAJOIE: Again?

DE CHAMVILLE, *misunderstanding*: I… I don't believe I've ever slit it before, madame…

MADAME DE LAJOIE: No… I mean… Your friend de Cambiac? Again?

DE CHAMVILLE: Ah! My heart is powerless where that scoundrel is concerned!

MADAME DE LAJOIE: But… What ever did he do?

DE CHAMVILLE, *aside*: Damn! I haven't even invented a story! *(Aloud.)* Do, madame?… What did he do, that rapscallion? *(She gives an inquisitive look.)* Please! You mustn't ask! I'll not stoop to accusing him when he's not here to defend himself!

MADAME DE LAJOIE: But it must have been something dreadful…

DE CHAMVILLE: Please! Just be assured that he has me to thank for his freedom, madame! If not for me, he would have spent the night languishing in a prison cell.

MADAME DE LAJOIE: Oh my!

DE CHAMVILLE, *pressing his finger to his lips*: But really… I mustn't… Later, perhaps…

MADAME DE LAJOIE: As you wish… I must say that, under the circumstances, I not only excuse your tardiness. I even admire it…

DE CHAMVILLE: Oh?

MADAME DE LAJOIE: On a day like this, such a selfless good turn can only bring us luck!

DE CHAMVILLE: You're so right, Mathilde! I'm happy that you understand. Not many women would have such character…

MADAME DE LAJOIE: Well… *(Moving up to the armchairs, standing behind them, offhandedly.)* Ah! That reminds me, Philippe… It seems you were seen at the Opéra last evening.

DE CHAMVILLE: I was?

MADAME DE LAJOIE: And with a lady, they tell me…

DE CHAMVILLE, *aside*: Damnation! *(Aloud.)* A lady?

MADAME DE LAJOIE: Well… A woman, at least…

DE CHAMVILLE, *pretending to search his memory*: Ah, yes… I'd almost forgotten… His sister, Mathilde…

MADAME DE LAJOIE: "His"?

DE CHAMVILLE: Yes… de Cambiac's… He had promised to take her to hear that Jenny Lind person… The one they're all calling "The Sweetest Nightingale…" *(Aside.)* Or something… *(Aloud.)* But, wretch that he is, he much preferred to go off carousing with some of his worthless friends.

MADAME DE LAJOIE: Tsk tsk tsk!

DE CHAMVILLE: And he asked me… begged me, in fact… to take her in his place. I simply couldn't refuse.

MADAME DE LAJOIE: Too kind, monsieur…

DE CHAMVILLE, *with a gesture*: Pfff!… That's just the way I am. He knows I can't resist doing a favor, and he's only too willing to take advantage…

MADAME DE LAJOIE: Oh!… I do wish you would introduce me. He sounds utterly intriguing.

DE CHAMVILLE: Introduce you? To a scoundrel like that?

MADAME DE LAJOIE: Well, I thought…

DE CHAMVILLE: Why, the man is a… a bear! Totally without manners!… And a tongue that would make a sailor blush, Mathilde!

MADAME DE LAJOIE: But I—

DE CHAMVILLE: And a drunkard, to boot!… And a gambler!… *(MADAME DE LAJOIE's jaw drops in disbelief.)* With a temper!… Oh, what a temper! Believe me, nothing is safe from it.

MADAME DE LAJOIE: Goodness me!

DE CHAMVILLE: Wherever he goes… China…

MADAME DE LAJOIE, *misunderstanding*: He goes to China?

DE CHAMVILLE: He… No… I mean, he loves to smash it to bits! And glasses… And mirrors… And… And everything!

MADAME DE LAJOIE: Then why in heaven's name do you associate with such a creature?

DE CHAMVILLE: Ah! How can I explain it?… I know it makes no sense, and I blush to admit it, but… It's more powerful than I am.

MADAME DE LAJOIE: But…

DE CHAMVILLE: I saw him as a child… *(Feigning great sadness.)* A poor helpless child… When his father died… In my arms, Mathilde… Gasping his last… And his poor dear mother…

MADAME DE LAJOIE, *sadly*: Oh…

DE CHAMVILLE: And… And from that moment on I knew we would be inseparable. I was like a brother… In school… In the army… I tried to guide him, to lead him in the path of righteousness… *(Continuing, automatically.)* For His namesake…

MADAME DE LAJOIE, *puzzled*: For what?

DE CHAMVILLE, *correcting himself*: No, I mean… *(Dramatically.)* Bonds like those are not easily rent asunder!

MADAME DE LAJOIE: You're so right, Philippe! I never realized how noble… how selfless you were.

DE CHAMVILLE, *in a whisper, head bent*: Thank you…

MADAME DE LAJOIE, *continuing*: And I'll do my best to love your friend quite as much as you do, and… and to forgive him for all the precious moments when he steals you away from me!

DE CHAMVILLE: Ah…

MADAME DE LAJOIE: But do keep in mind that, until I actually set eyes on the… *(With a touch of irony.)* … the gentleman, I can only judge him by what you tell me. And I must say, he does sound rather frightful!

DE CHAMVILLE: Please! You can rest assured that, one of these days I'll lay him at your feet, Mathilde. Alive or dead…

MADAME DE LAJOIE, *taken aback*: Well, all things considered…

DE CHAMVILLE: In a manner of speaking, that is…

MADAME DE LAJOIE, *with a little laugh*: Indeed!… *(Changing the subject.)* Now then, about the contract… I've spoken to the notary. He's drawing it up as we speak, and he'll bring it round at four o'clock.

DE CHAMVILLE: Ah, Mathilde…

MADAME DE LAJOIE: And so, if you'll excuse me, I'll go pretty myself up a bit.

She moves toward her room, right.

DE CHAMVILLE: No need, my love! How can one improve on perfection?

MADAME DE LAJOIE: Come now, monsieur…

She exits.

DE CHAMVILLE, *alone, to himself, sighing*: Ah! So far so good… I must say, I have hardly a moment to myself these days! So many things to plan… So many lies… *(Reconsidering.)* Details, that is… An affair with a dancer at the Opéra to break off… The entire *corps de ballet* to set to rights… Heaven help me! It's almost too much for my poor shoulders to bear, and I would have had to stop courting the marquise a hundred times if fate hadn't thrown my friend de Cambiac in my path!… Well, not fate exactly… *(He takes a book from his pocket and holds it up.)* This delightful tome!… *The Key to Courtship: How to Woo and Win…* This is where I found him… *(Reading.)* "Be sure to invent a true and faithful friend, always by your side, devoted beyond belief, ever ready and willing to assume the blame for your faults, great and small. Do you need an excuse? He is there to provide it. Do you fail to keep a rendezvous with your mistress? It is he who provides the reason. Do you have a duel? It is his honor that you must defend…" *(Waving the book.)* Precious! Absolutely precious… *(Reading.)* "In short, your friend is a straw man who takes upon himself your shortcomings and preserves your good name at the expense of his own…" Brilliant!… And just what I needed!… Here I am, Madame de Lajoie's official suitor for these last two years… A husband-in-waiting you might say, with all the obligations and none of the rewards! Not a light yoke, I'm, afraid… At least, not until I invented de Cambiac! My faithful friend, my bosom companion par excellence, who gladly took upon himself every last peccadillo of my bachelor existence… Ah! *(Holding up the book.)* Tell me that's not a brilliant solution! *(He puts it back in his pocket, at the same time discovering a slip of paper.)* What the devil…? Oh yes… The summons… Sworn out by that idiot Toupette… Just because I owe him a few paltry thousand from some absurd card game, he thinks he's going to have me put away, under lock and key! Ha!… *(He rips up the paper.)* Besides, when he finds out that I'm marrying Mathilde… Like all the rest of them… *(Putting his finger to his lips.)* "Shhh! No one must know… Not until the contract is signed…" Well, it won't be long now…

ADELE appears up center, followed by JULIEN, in livery.

ADELE, *to* **JULIEN**: You see?

DE CHAMVILLE: What the…

ADELE: I told you he was here.

JULIEN, *holding out a letter, to* **DE CHAMVILLE**: A letter, monsieur… She said it was urgent!

DE CHAMVILLE: "She"? *(Reading the address.)* Ah yes… Of course… For my friend de Cambiac… *(He waves the pair off, and they exit, up center.)* Ha!… *(He opens the envelope, taking a second one from it, which he opens as well.)*

Her handwriting… How clever of me to tell him to bring all my letters here in an envelope marked "Monsieur de Cambiac"! Just in case… *(Reading.)* "You beast!…" *(Nodding.)* Yes, it's from her… *(Continuing.)* "So! I finally know the truth! You want to throw me over and marry someone else!" Now how on earth do you suppose… *(Continuing.)* "Well, you haven't seen the last of me! If, in one hour, you aren't here to explain your filthy trick, I'll hunt you down, wherever you are. Even in my rival's arms!…" Good God! That's all I need! *(Continuing.)* "Yours forever. Love, Olympe." Ha!… How the devil did she find out? Ah, women!… They always find out!… And she'll do it, too. I know her… I can see the scene now… *(He begins pacing back and forth.)* No, no! I've got to stop her, talk to her… Make her listen to reason… But how? I can't leave now. I just arrived… *(Looking toward the door, right.)* And Mathilde, "prettying herself up"… Getting ready for the signing… *(He continues pacing.)* If only… There must be… Ah! *(He stops.)* Why not? *(He goes to the writing-table, down left, sits down and writes.)* "My dearest… I have just received word from my friend de Cambiac and must absent myself briefly to fly to his side. Victim of a frightful accident…" *(Reflecting.)* What kind, I wonder?… Oh well, there's time to make one up… *(Continuing.)* "Victim of a frightful accident, it is, I fear, from his deathbed that he implores my presence. I pray that I am not too late. I shall return posthaste…" There! Perfect… *(Calling.)* Adèle…

TOUPETTE appears at the door, up center.

TOUPETTE, *entering, to himself*: Blast!… De Chamvillle…

DE CHAMVILLE, *noticing him*: Ah! Toupette… What a coincidence…

TOUPETTE: Oh?

DE CHAMVILLE: Yes… I was thinking of you just a moment ago.

TOUPETTE, *rather embarrassed*: Aha… The… The document…

DE CHAMVILLE: Quite… *(Calling.)* Adèle!… *(Aside, impatiently.)* Where is that… *(Aloud, to TOUPETTE.)* Yes… The document…

TOUPETTE: Well… I hope you understand… Legal niceties, after all… Formalities, don't you know…

DE CHAMVILLE, *casually*: Of course… Of course…

TOUPETTE: But as for the actual execution…

DE CHAMVILLE: Please! No need to discuss it now… We have time…

TOUPETTE: Ah…

DE CHAMVILLE, *changing the subject abruptly*: I say… Could I ask you to do me a favor and give this to Madame de Lajoie when she returns?

He hands him the note.

TOUPETTE: This…?

DE CHAMVILLE: I'm in something of a hurry, and I'm afraid the young lady is otherwise engaged!

TOUPETTE: Certainly… With pleasure…

DE CHAMVILLE: Thank you, my friend… *(With a wave.)* Au revoir…

He moves upstage, to the door.

TOUPETTE: No hard feelings at least…

DE CHAMVILLE: Heavens no!… Ta-ta… Ta-ta…

He exits.

TOUPETTE, *to himself*: "Ta-ta" indeed... Odd chap!... I must say, he's taking the matter rather well, all things considered... My suit, I mean... A simple precaution, given the situation... I said to myself: "This de Chamville is a randy sort... He won't let anyone tread on his toes! And when he learns that I'm courting the marquise de Lajoie, and that I have designs on her honor... Well, he'll challenge me to a duel, for sure... He could kill me, I just know it!" So... What to do?... Aha! *(Tapping his temple.)* Clever! Clever!... I had his signature on his note. He doesn't have a sou to his name... So! Not a sou?... So I sue!... *(Reflecting.)* So to speak... And now, if he learns about madame and me, and wants to vent his vicious revenge... Well, I take him to court and have him locked up for failure to pay! He can duel with his shadow! On the prison wall!

MADAME DE LAJOIE appears, upstage.

MADAME DE LAJOIE, *entering*: There, Philippe! I'm back... *(Looking for DE CHAMVILLE, to herself.)* Now where do you suppose... *(Noticing TOUPETTE, with a nod.)* Monsieur Toupette...

TOUPETTE: Greetings, O fairest of the fair... Belle marquise...

MADAME DE LAJOIE, *quickly, unimpressed*: Yes... Thank you... Tell me, you didn't see Monsieur de Chamville, by chance?

TOUPETTE: Ah, but I did, madame! The moment I came in...

MADAME DE LAJOIE: Oh?

TOUPETTE, *handing her the note*: And he asked me to give you this missive as he left.

MADAME DE LAJOIE: Left?... *(Reading it, aside.)* De Cambiac!... I should have guessed... *(Angrily.)* Really! That's simply too much! I never...

TOUPETTE: You seem a trifle perturbed, if I may say. Bad news, perhaps?

MADAME DE LAJOIE, *quick to deny it*: This? Certainly not! A passing acquaintance who was going to pay a visit, but... but...

TOUPETTE: But who is detained?

MADAME DE LAJOIE: Yes, quite... Circumstances...

TOUPETTE: Aha!... Well, on the other hand, madame... You were about to receive a visit that you hardly expected...

MADAME DE LAJOIE: I was?

TOUPETTE: From a consummate bore, if I may say... A visit that I was fortunate enough to be able to spare you... Thanks to a most remarkable adventure, and a clever stratagem of my invention...

MADAME DE LAJOIE: I see... *(With more than a touch of irony.)* Then you don't take kindly to consummate bores, monsieur?

TOUPETTE: Goodness, no! The minute I see one, I turn and run!

MADAME DE LAJOIE: And he follows you, no doubt. How ever can he resist?

TOUPETTE, *without appreciating her intent*: Why, thank you...

MADAME DE LAJOIE: Not at all... And you both arrive together...

TOUPETTE, *returning to the subject*: But do let me tell you what happened... My adventure, madame... I just ran a young man down in my coach!

MADAME DE LAJOIE: Oh my!

TOUPETTE: That is, not myself... When I say "I..." My horses, I mean... I had just left my solicitor's... A trifling matter... A friend who owes me... *(With a wave* *of the hand.)* But that doesn't matter… What matters, madame, is that I was coming to visit you, and I told my coachman not to spare the whip… *(Pausing, waiting for a reaction that doesn't come, emphasizing.)* I was coming to visit you, madame, and I told my coachman—

MADAME DE LAJOIE, *interrupting*: Not to spare the whip… And…?

TOUPETTE: Well… Just beyond the Place Royale, I hear a cry… I look outside and see a man sprawled out on the pavement. "What are you doing down there, monsieur?" I shout. "You're holding up traffic." But he didn't hear a word… He was unconscious…

MADAME DE LAJOIE: Tsk tsk tsk!

TOUPETTE: So I climb down and look, and I see that he's a very refined young man, the picture of quality… And I have him put into my coach, and I do all I can to bring him round. Like a mother, madame… Rubbing his hands, blowing in his face, slapping his cheeks… Well, when he finally comes to, he looks about and says: "Where am I?"

MADAME DE LAJOIE: I should think…

TOUPETTE, *continuing*: "Who are you?…" "Toupette," I tell him… And in no time we're becoming friends. It seems he was on his way hereabouts, so I offer to have him join me. On the way, he asks where I'm going. "To visit Madame de Lajoie," I tell him… "Madame de Lajoie!" he cries… "You know Madame de Lajoie?…" "Why, yes… Rather well…" "Ah, monsieur! My friend! How can I ever thank you for running me down!" *(Aside, to* MADAME DE LAJOIE.*)* My horses, that is… *(Aloud.)* "I'll let you introduce me!"

MADAME DE LAJOIE: How quaint!

TOUPETTE: Naturally, I refuse. If we had to introduce everyone we run down… But he insists, and pleads, and… And I begin to feel that I won't have a choice… That, want to or not, I'll have to bring him here…

MADAME DE LAJOIE: Indeed!

TOUPETTE: That's when I got an idea. My stratagem, madame… I know you'll find it delightfully droll.

MADAME DE LAJOIE: Aha…

TOUPETTE: Well, I pretend to say yes. But first, I tell him, I want to stop and have my coiffure refreshed a bit. Considering that I'm going to visit Madame de Lajoie, after all… So I have my coachman stop, and I tell the young man that I won't be long… That he should wait till I come back…

MADAME DE LAJOIE: And…?

TOUPETTE: And here I am! *(Proudly.)* Clever, don't you think?

MADAME DE LAJOIE: Terribly… And droll, monsieur…

TOUPETTE: I knew you would think so! Everybody tells me my sense of humor is simply—

MADAME DE LAJOIE, *interrupting*: But why didn't you bring him, monsieur?

TOUPETTE: Why?… But… It would have been a dreadful nuisance, madame. And besides, how could I be responsible for a young man I scarcely know? Even one from an excellent family… A de Cambiac, after all…

MADAME DE LAJOIE, *with a start*: De Cambiac?… Did you say…

TOUPETTE: Why yes… Do you know him?

MADAME DE LAJOIE: No... The name is familiar. I've heard tell of a young man, but I'm sure he can't be the one.

TOUPETTE: On the contrary, madame! There's no one else by that name in all of France. He's the last of his line... Or so he told me...

MADAME DE LAJOIE: A scoundrel, monsieur?... Who drinks, and gambles, and swears like a trooper? Is that your de Cambiac?

TOUPETTE: Well... I didn't notice... And I hardly know him well enough... But I suppose it's possible.

MADAME DE LAJOIE, *ignoring him, to herself*: Who else could it be?

TOUPETTE, *continuing*: Perhaps if I knew him better...

MADAME DE LAJOIE, *looking at the note, reading*: "Victim of a frightful accident..."

TOUPETTE, *continuing*: I only ran him down, after all... My horses, that is...

MADAME DE LAJOIE, *continuing, to herself*: A trifle exaggerated, but still...

TOUPETTE, *continuing*: It's not as if we frequent the same society...

MADAME DE LAJOIE, *continuing, to herself*: Of course it's his de Cambiac! No doubt about it!

TOUPETTE: So you understand, madame...

MADAME DE LAJOIE, *apostrophizing*: Well, I've got you now, monsieur!

TOUPETTE: I can only conjecture...

MADAME DE LAJOIE, *roused from her musing*: What?... You were saying...?

TOUPETTE: About his personal habits, that is...

MADAME DE LAJOIE: Yes... Yes, of course...

TOUPETTE: Besides... Enough about the young man... There are other matters—

MADAME DE LAJOIE, *interrupting*: Excuse me... *(She pulls the bell-cord.)* If you don't mind...

TOUPETTE, *to himself*: More pressing matters!...

ADELE appears, upstage.

ADELE: Madame?

TOUPETTE, *to himself*: I daresay it's time to press my suit...

He chuckles at his bon mot as MADAME DE LAJOIE goes up to ADELE and whispers in her ear.

ADELE: Very good, madame.

MADAME DE LAJOIE: You're sure that's clear? A young man in a coach...

ADELE: I'll do my best...

She exits.

MADAME DE LAJOIE, *to herself*: Now to get rid of him...

TOUPETTE: Madame... *(About to emote.)* For a long time now...

MADAME DE LAJOIE, *to herself*: But how?

TOUPETTE: A very long time...

MADAME DE LAJOIE, *joining him*: Yes... For a very long time you've been promising me a poem, monsieur. *(Feigning a pout.)* And here I am, still waiting...

TOUPETTE, *aside*: Is it possible? *(Aloud, enthusiastically.)* Ah, *belle marquise!* Your waiting is over! *(Taking a paper from his pocket and holding it out.)* I happen to have brought you my latest!

MADAME DE LAJOIE, *trying to conceal her displeasure*: Oh... Indeed!

TOUPETTE: And written just for you!

MADAME DE LAJOIE, *aside*: Of all things... *(Aloud, unconvincingly.)* What a pleasant coincidence!

She takes it and begins reading.

TOUPETTE: I daresay you'll find... If I may venture an opinion, madame... You'll find that it expresses... Rather timidly, to be sure... A sentiment that, though few the words, expands to fill the heart of the poet...

MADAME DE LAJOIE, *hypocritically*: How nobly expressed!

TOUPETTE: And, one would hope, the heart of his... his...

MADAME DE LAJOIE, *holding up the poem*: As charming as your verse, monsieur... Utterly charming...

TOUPETTE, *modestly*: Well...

MADAME DE LAJOIE: We must see to it that it's published. It will make all those professional poets gnash their teeth with envy!

TOUPETTE: Good! Let them gnash, madame!

MADAME DE LAJOIE: Though, if I'm not mistaken, this line, monsieur...

She points to a line in the text.

TOUPETTE: Yes...?

MADAME DE LAJOIE: It seems to have too many feet... More than the others, I mean.

TOUPETTE: Oh?... *(Counting on his fingers.)* Perhaps... But... *(Looking for a bon mot.)* That's only to let it run more quickly to your heart, madame! *(Chuckling.)* The more feet the better!

MADAME DE LAJOIE: I must say, monsieur, your gallantry knows no bounds! But still... I do think you would do well to touch it up a bit... Even if only in the name of perfection...

TOUPETTE: Well... If you think so...

MADAME DE LAJOIE, *motioning him toward the door, down left*: Come... You can sit in the library and be inspired to your heart's content.

TOUPETTE: Too kind... *(Aside.)* So far so good!

MADAME DE LAJOIE: You poets, after all...

TOUPETTE, *aside*: Ah! The power of genius... *(Aloud.)* I'll not be long, madame. *(He goes to exit, left, then comes back.)* I was just thinking... The young man... He's still waiting for me to return.

MADAME DE LAJOIE: Oh! I hardly think so. By now he will have got tired of waiting... *(Aside.)* Even for a poet! *(Aloud.)* You can be sure he's left...

TOUPETTE: Yes... I suppose... *(He approaches the door again, then turns round.)* Tell me... Is there a rhyming dictionary?

MADAME DE LAJOIE: Two, monsieur... You can use them both. *(Aside.)* For all the good it will do!

TOUPETTE: Aha... *(To himself.)* Yes... So far so good... The rest should be child's play.

He exits.

MADAME DE LAJOIE: A half-hour for each... That's an hour of freedom from that... that... *(With a shudder.)* Oh!

She exits, right. The stage remains empty. After a few moments, the door, upstage, opens and ADELE *enters, followed by* DE CAMBIAC.

ADELE: This way, monsieur…

DE CAMBIAC: But why all the mystery, mademoiselle? At least you can tell me—

ADELE, *interrupting*: Not a word…

DE CAMBIAC: But…

ADELE: My mistress will answer all your questions, I'm sure.

She exits, right, leaving the door open.

DE CAMBIAC, *alone*: Just like that!… Of all the… I swear, it's a Spanish drama, only without the cloak and dagger! Not yet, anyway… There I am, waiting an eternity in that idiot financier's coach, when, all of a sudden, a sweet young thing comes tugging at my sleeve and tells me: "Monsieur, my mistress wants to speak with you." "Who?" "She'll tell you…" "Where?" "Just come with me…" And I follow her here, and up a mysterious staircase into this apartment… Well, so be it! I may as well see the adventure through to the end. Better this than nothing!… And it's certainly better than sitting in that pompous fool's coach and letting him have a good laugh at my expense. Wherever he is!… *(Mimicking.)* "I'm going to visit Madame de Lajoie," he tells me… Of course! How could I be so stupid? A fool like that and an angel like her!… Ha!… And I believed him… Well, at least this drama will give me something else to think about. Something besides that vision of beauty that follows me everywhere I go… Oh! Madame de Lajoie! Madame de Lajoie!… To see you once is to yearn for you forever!… If only I knew the joy of setting foot in your abode… *(Listening.)* But… Someone's coming… I think… Yes… So… Finally an answer… *(He looks right, through the open door, awestruck.)* What?… No! It… It can't be!… It's…

MADAME DE LAJOIE *enters.*

MADAME DE LAJOIE: Ah, monsieur…

DE CAMBIAC, *agape, to himself*: Madame de… Madame de…

MADAME DE LAJOIE, *holding out her hand and approaching him*: At last we meet! I've been waiting for this moment…

DE CAMBIAC, *taking her hand, giving it a gentle kiss*: You… You have? *(Aside.)* She has? *(Aloud.)* I must say, madame…

MADAME DE LAJOIE: Please… *(Pointing to the armchairs, center.)* Won't you make yourself comfortable? You must still be a trifle upset after the accident.

DE CAMBIAC: You know, madame?… How—

MADAME DE LAJOIE, *wagging her finger*: Tsk tsk tsk!

DE CAMBIAC: But really… It was nothing…

MADAME DE LAJOIE, *sitting down, aside*: On his deathbed, indeed! *(Aloud, as* DE CAMBIAC *sits down in the other armchair.)* Perhaps a glass of brandy, to settle your nerves?

She gets up and goes to the bell-cord as if to ring.

DE CAMBIAC, *getting up and stopping her*: No, no… Really, madame… They're settled… I assure you…

MADAME DE LAJOIE: Very well, if you're certain… *(She sits down.)* Now then, Monsieur de Cambiac… *(Pointing to the other armchair.)* Please… *(He sits down.)* I trust that you'll pardon the somewhat mysterious manner in which I've brought you here. *(He gives a little shrug.)* I realized that you had your reasons for wanting to avoid our meeting, and I hoped to—how shall I say?—at least stir your curiosity.

DE CAMBIAC, *aside*: What? *(Aloud.)* Reasons, madame?… *(Rather formally.)* On the contrary! Your reproach is undeserved… I… I couldn't be more delighted… More ecstatic…

MADAME DE LAJOIE: Goodness me! *(She bursts out laughing.)* No offense, monsieur, but… Ha ha ha!…

DE CAMBIAC: Madame?

MADAME DE LAJOIE: You really are quite charming when you put on your airs! Ha ha ha!… "More ecstatic" indeed!

DE CAMBIAC, *aside*: My airs?

MADAME DE LAJOIE: If I didn't know you better, monsieur… Ha ha ha!… But you are a clever scoundrel!… As I've come to expect…

DE CAMBIAC: As you… Really… I—

MADAME DE LAJOIE, *getting down to business*: So! I think we understand one another, monsieur. Please feel free to be quite yourself. That's the first condition for a truce between us!

DE CAMBIAC: For a… But I don't recall that we were ever at war! As I said, my fondest desire has always been—

MADAME DE LAJOIE, *interrupting*: Yes, yes… Very good… Then let's leave it at that, shall we? As you know, Monsieur de Chamville and I are signing our marriage contract this afternoon.

DE CAMBIAC, *aside*: Oh?

MADAME DE LAJOIE: I had hoped that today, of all days, I might be able to enjoy his undivided attention, all things considered…

DE CAMBIAC: Yes, I should think…

MADAME DE LAJOIE: But it seems that his friendship for you, monsieur… His devotion, I might say…

DE CAMBIAC: His…

MADAME DE LAJOIE, *continuing*: Well, I'm sure I don't have to tell you! When he learned of your accident he left everything and went dashing off to see what he could do!

DE CAMBIAC, *nodding*: Aha… *(To himself.)* Damned if I understand…

MADAME DE LAJOIE: So it seems that, if I want to keep him by my side, the only way is to keep you here as well.

DE CAMBIAC: Me?

MADAME DE LAJOIE: I'm afraid that, for the likes of him, marriage is something of a prison, monsieur…

DE CAMBIAC: But a very pleasant one, I should think! With madame, I mean…

MADAME DE LAJOIE: There you go, being gallant again!… All the same, I have no illusions. Without his dear de Cambiac he'll be a most unwilling prisoner! With him, he'll scarcely feel the chains!… So! You accept?

DE CAMBIAC: I… I really don't know what to say, madame. *(To himself.)* How many a rogue would be only too willing…

MADAME DE LAJOIE, *with a little laugh*: And you promise to be my prisoner?

DE CAMBIAC: I must say, the prospect couldn't please me more! If... If you're sure that you know who I am, madame... Monsieur de Cambiac...

MADAME DE LAJOIE: Of course, my friend! Who else could you be?

DE CAMBIAC: Who else...? Of course...

MADAME DE LAJOIE: So! You're here, and you're staying! Come what may...

DE CAMBIAC, *aside*: Why not? *(Aloud.)* If it's your pleasure, madame... If you insist...

MADAME DE LAJOIE: It is, and I do! You give me your word?

DE CAMBIAC: My word as a gentleman!

MADAME DE LAJOIE: I accept! *(She gets up and points to the door, up left.)* There's your room...

DE CAMBIAC: My... *(Getting up.)* I'll have a room?

MADAME DE LAJOIE: It's my brother the colonel's, when he comes to Paris. I'm sure you'll find more than enough to drink...

DE CAMBIAC: Oh?

MADAME DE LAJOIE: And the best Turkish tobacco...

DE CAMBIAC, *about to protest*: But I...

MADAME DE LAJOIE: And a lovely little balcony that looks out on the Place Royale, and all the ladies walking back and forth. Until all hours... *(Suggestively.)* If you know what I—

DE CAMBIAC, *interrupting*: But madame... *(Aside.)* What does she think...?

MADAME DE LAJOIE: But first you'll have lunch, monsieur. *(With a little laugh.)* I want your prison to be as pleasant as it can be!

DE CAMBIAC: Oh, it will be! I'm sure...

MADAME DE LAJOIE: Just make yourself at home.

DE CAMBIAC: I will... I will...

He gives a little bow and exits, up left.

MADAME DE LAJOIE, *to herself*: He seems like such a charming fellow! Who would ever think he was such a... a roué?

DE CHAMVILLE appears, up center, obviously in a sweat.

DE CHAMVILLE, *entering, to himself*: Nowhere to be found!... Good God! If she's on her way here... *(Noticing MADAME DE LAJOIE.)* Ah, Mathilde...

MADAME DE LAJOIE: There you are, you naughty thing! Running off like that!

DE CHAMVILLE, *befuddled*: Yes... I...

MADAME DE LAJOIE: And you didn't even find your friend de Cambiac, now did you?

DE CHAMVILLE: I... Oh? How did you—

MADAME DE LAJOIE, *interrupting*: Goodness me! What a state you're in! *(Motioning to one of the armchairs.)* Come! Sit down...

DE CHAMVILLE, *waving off the suggestion*: No need... No need...

MADAME DE LAJOIE: You look as if you've been running over half of Paris!

DE CHAMVILLE: Well, not quite half...

MADAME DE LAJOIE: I must say, if you did nearly as much for me as you do for your friend...

DE CHAMVILLE: What could I do, Mathilde? The minute I heard that his life was in danger...

MADAME DE LAJOIE, *with a touch of irony*: Of course... And that he was tottering on the brink of death...

DE CHAMVILLE: Exactly!... I couldn't very well leave him there—

MADAME DE LAJOIE, *interrupting*: To totter by himself... Or teeter even...

DE CHAMVILLE: What kind of friend—

MADAME DE LAJOIE: Well, you can rest assured, Philippe. He's not teetering any more... Or tottering either... In fact, he really seems to be in perfect health.

DE CHAMVILLE, *puzzled*: What?

MADAME DE LAJOIE: Yes... Just a slight fall... Nothing serious... He's not giving it a second thought.

DE CHAMVILLE: He's... *(Aside.)* What?

MADAME DE LAJOIE: I'm sure you're wondering how I happen to know...

DE CHAMVILLE: Why, yes... I can't imagine—

MADAME DE LAJOIE: And that's not the only surprise, Philippe!

DE CHAMVILLE: It's not?

MADAME DE LAJOIE, *confidentially*: He's here!

DE CHAMVILLE: Who?

MADAME DE LAJOIE: Your friend de Cambiac!... He's here, Philippe! At this very moment...

DE CHAMVILLE, *agape*: He... He...

MADAME DE LAJOIE: Even though you seem to have sworn he would never set foot...

DE CHAMVILLE: De Cambiac? *(To himself.)* What kind of joke...

MADAME DE LAJOIE, *pointing, up left*: In there... Waiting for you...

DE CHAMVILLE: But...

MADAME DE LAJOIE, *as he opens his mouth from time to time, unable to speak*: By the sheerest of coincidences, Philippe... I'll tell you all about it. It's really terribly... Well, droll... But the important thing is that we're already the best of friends, he and I. I've even invited him to join us for lunch. I knew that would please you.

DE CHAMVILLE, finally succeeding in finding his voice: Please me...? Of course...

MADAME DE LAJOIE: Now then, I'll go to the kitchen and see to the details... "The way to a man's heart," as they say... *(As he stands transfixed, she moves up center, to leave.)* But goodness me! Don't just stand there! He's waiting for you... *(Gesturing him toward the door, up left.)* Go on!... Go on!...

She exits, up center, leaving DE CHAMVILLE alone, scratching his head.

DE CHAMVILLE, *coming down right*: Am I dreaming? De Cambiac? That figment of my imagination?... That creature that I invented one day, in a moment of madness, to take the blame for my follies!... Can it be that he's come to life?... Bah!... Impossible! Somehow she must have discovered my lie, and she's toying with me! Of course!... *(Looking up left.)* Then who...? In there...? Some adventurer, I suppose... Someone who learned about my ruse and decided to take advantage...

DE CAMBIAC appears at the door, up left, in a dressing gown.

DE CAMBIAC, *entering, to himself*: "Make yourself at home," she said… I mustn't dare disobey…

DE CHAMVILLE, *noticing him, aside*: Who in the name of…

DE CAMBIAC, *noticing him, aside*: Ah! The fiancé, I imagine…

DE CHAMVILLE, *scandalized, aside*: In a dressing gown?… Of all the…

The two exchange polite little nods.

DE CAMBIAC, *addressing him*: Do I assume that I have the honor of speaking to Monsieur de Chamville?

DE CHAMVILLE, *dryly*: Himself, monsieur…

DE CAMBIAC: Charmed to make your acquaintance… *(With a sharp little handshake.)* I trust you will forgive the rather informal attire, monsieur. Circumstances…

DE CHAMVILLE: No doubt…

DE CAMBIAC: But I'll not trouble you with the details.

DE CHAMVILLE, *sharply*: On the contrary! I'll thank you to do so! I think I have a right to know…

DE CAMBIAC: Certainly… And when you hear the curious adventure that brought me here, I assure you…

DE CHAMVILLE: First of all, I don't recall telling you my name…

DE CAMBIAC: You didn't, monsieur. I guessed.

DE CHAMVILLE: No matter… You seem to know it. And I should appreciate knowing yours.

DE CAMBIAC: What? Madame de Lajoie didn't tell you? She knows my name as well as she knows her own.

DE CHAMVILLE: Perhaps she did, perhaps she didn't. What she told me, monsieur, was that you were here. That you presented yourself…

DE CAMBIAC: Not quite "presented myself," monsieur… I was brought here… In a rather unorthodox manner, I might add.

DE CHAMVILLE, *losing patience*: Please! Let's not mince words! However you arrived here, you proceeded to pass yourself off as a certain Monsieur de Cambiac!

DE CAMBIAC: Quite! And for a particularly good reason…

DE CHAMVILLE, *sarcastically*: Oh? Do tell, monsieur!

DE CAMBIAC: In short, because that happens to be my name!

DE CHAMVILLE, *categorically*: Impossible! It can't be!

DE CAMBIAC: Oh? Should I cast doubt on the existence of the "de Chamville" clan as well?

DE CHAMVILLE: But you… You don't understand! "De Cambiac…" It's not a real name. It was invented… Made up… Out of whole cloth…

DE CAMBIAC, *piqued*: Aha? You think so?… Well, whole or in part, monsieur, I beg to differ. Go tell that to my father, Charles-François de Cambiac… And his father, Gustave-Edouard de Cambiac… And his, Gaston-Dagobert… For countless generations, monsieur!

DE CHAMVILLE: But—

DE CAMBIAC: All of whom bore it with dignity, pride, and honor!

DE CHAMVILLE: But I…

DE CAMBIAC: And all of whom would shudder were I accustomed to let the veracity of my statements be questioned more than once! A second time, monsieur, and…

DE CHAMVILLE, *aside*: Can it be?

DE CAMBIAC gives several imaginary dueling thrusts to make his point.

DE CAMBIAC: So! Please be advised!

TOUPETTE appears at the door, down left.

TOUPETTE: There!… *(Counting on his fingers.)* Every foot!… Perfect, down to the very last toe!

He chuckles at his bon mot.

DE CHAMVILLE, *approaching him*: Toupette!… Are you still here?

TOUPETTE: Oh, hello, de Chamville… I was just touching up an impromptu of sorts… For Madame de Lajoie… Perfecting it, you might say…

DE CAMBIAC, *recognizing him, surprised*: My goodness! The financier…

TOUPETTE, *to DE CAMBIAC*: Oh my! Is that…

DE CAMBIAC: The one in the coach!

TOUPETTE: Is that you, monsieur?

DE CHAMVILLE, *to TOUPETTE*: You know him?

TOUPETTE: Of course! Why wouldn't I… The last of the de Cambiacs… *(In a whisper.)* I almost killed him!

DE CHAMVILLE: You?

TOUPETTE: Why yes! I ran him down… My horses, that is…

DE CHAMVILLE, *to himself*: Then Mathilde must think… Oh my!… *(Aloud, to DE CAMBIAC.)* How frightful! *(To TOUPETTE.)* Tsk tsk tsk!… *(Aside.)* Best treat him carefully… If she ever finds out… *(Aloud, to TOUPETTE.)* Monsieur de Cambiac is one of my dearest friends!… A trifle young… A trifle headstrong…

DE CAMBIAC, *to himself*: Oh?

DE CHAMVILLE, *continuing*: But always ready to be of service when the need arises… *(To DE CAMBIAC, whispering.)* Please! Don't say anything… I'll explain…

TOUPETTE, *to DE CHAMVILLE*: Aha…

DE CAMBIAC, *aside*: Why the sudden change, I wonder…

TOUPETTE: I see… *(To himself.)* So… De Chamville must have brought him… *(To DE CAMBIAC.)* I trust we're none the worse for our little prank, monsieur.

DE CAMBIAC: Not at all!

DE CHAMVILLE, *to himself*: Toupette must have brought him…

DE CAMBIAC: Well now, dear friends… *(Aside.)* Whoever you are! *(Aloud.)* Since we all seem to be here, I trust you'll do me the honor of joining me for lunch. It shouldn't be long.

DE CHAMVILLE, *aside*: Joining him?

TOUPETTE, *aside*: Him?… Indeed!

DE CHAMVILLE, *aside*: Just who does he think…

TOUPETTE, *aside*: Even in that dressing gown!

DE CAMBIAC: Shall I tell madame you'll be staying?

DE CHAMVILLE, *to himself*: Careful, Philippe! *(To DE CAMBIAC.)* Tut tut, de Cambiac! One doesn't stand on ceremony with a dear friend like you!

He gives him a vigorous handshake.

TOUPETTE, *not to be outdone, shaking his hand too*: Tut tut, de Cambiac! One doesn't stand on ceremony… But alas! I'm obliged to decline. The comtesse de Vrillières is expecting me. A delightful child who is—how shall I say?—falling prey to my attentions…

DE CAMBIAC: Oh?

TOUPETTE: We're rehearsing Rameau.

DE CAMBIAC: Rameau?

TOUPETTE: She sings, I play the harp…

DE CHAMVILLE, *aside*: With much pluck, no doubt…

DE CAMBIAC, *to TOUPETTE*: As you wish, monsieur…

TOUPETTE, *to DE CAMBIAC:* Be good enough to tell madame that I've succeeded in retouching my impromptu. She can look forward to seeing it in all its perfection when I return.

DE CAMBIAC: Of course… With pleasure…

TOUPETTE: Now then, fellow rogues! Off to the wars! *(He gives a foolish little laugh.)* As they say… *(To DE CHAMVILLE, nodding.)* Monsieur… *(To DE CAMBIAC, nodding.)* Monsieur… *(Aside.)* Dressing gown indeed! Who does he think…

He exits, upstage.

DE CAMBIAC: Well now, monsieur… *(Coming down left.)* Since we seem to be alone… Perhaps you would be so good as to explain—

DE CHAMVILLE: I will indeed, monsieur! Because I have no doubt that I can count on your tact.

DE CAMBIAC: Of course…

DE CHAMVILLE, *joining him*: But first, I would ask you to forgive anything I said that might have offended you.

DE CAMBIAC, *with a casual wave*: Please! Think nothing of it. I assure you…

DE CHAMVILLE: Too kind… Too kind…

DE CAMBIAC: Though I must admit that my curiosity is getting the better of me, monsieur. Especially why Madame de Lajoie assumed, when I arrived, that I was your—if you'll pardon the expression—your bosom friend… I was about to disabuse her.

DE CHAMVILLE, *with a start*: You didn't, I hope?

DE CAMBIAC: Goodness no! When I saw how much pleasure it seemed to give her…

DE CHAMVILLE, *relieved*: Ah! Thank you!… Thank you, mon ami! *(Taking his hand and shaking it warmly.)* You're my guardian angel. My savior!

DE CAMBIAC: I am?

DE CHAMVILLE: You… You have no idea what I owe you, monsieur… And what you owe me…

DE CAMBIAC, *puzzled*: I beg your pardon?

DE CHAMVILLE: In a manner of speaking… The fact is, you'll never guess how often you came to my rescue, without even knowing of my existence. Any more than I knew of yours!

DE CAMBIAC: Oh?

DE CHAMVILLE, *continuing*: Or how often I saved you from the brink of death!… Or claimed to, at least…

DE CAMBIAC: But I never… What kind of nonsense…

DE CHAMVILLE, *taking the book from his pocket, handing it to him*: Here… This will explain it better than I can do…

DE CAMBIAC, *looking at the title*: *The Key to Courtship…*?

DE CHAMVILLE: Page thirty-five… In the middle…

DE CAMBIAC spends a moment perusing the passage in silence.

DE CAMBIAC, *with a smile*: And… And I'm that "true and faithful friend"? Is that what you're trying to tell me?

DE CHAMVILLE: Exactly!

DE CAMBIAC: But why me? Why a de Cambiac? Why not a… a Dupont, or a Lefèvre? Or a… a Petitfour de Camembert, for heaven's sake?

DE CHAMVILLE: Who can say? One day, I was trying to explain something to Madame de Lajoie. Something that really couldn't be explained, if you know what I mean… And that was the first name that sprang to my lips! Since then—

DE CAMBIAC: Since then the last of the de Cambiac line bears your shortcomings on his shoulders!

DE CHAMVILLE: Shortcomings, and worse, I'm afraid!

DE CAMBIAC: My, my…

DE CHAMVILLE: And I do beg your pardon, monsieur! But I had no way of knowing… I mean, how could I ever guess…?

DE CAMBIAC: Of course not… You couldn't… *(He reflects for a moment, then places the open book on the writing-table, down left, with a little laugh.)* Then I daresay our marquise has had occasion to form a rather unenviable opinion of me!

DE CHAMVILLE, *laughing*: Unspeakable, in a word!… And since I know that you are a gentleman who understands the follies of youth, I hope you will be willing—

DE CAMBIAC, *finishing his thought*: To continue playing my role! Right?

DE CHAMVILLE: Quite!

DE CAMBIAC: With pleasure! *(Aside.)* So much for my ancestors!

DE CHAMVILLE: Ah! Cher ami!… We may have met two years later, but our friendship will be just as fast as I said it was two years before! And just a deep!

He holds out his hand.

DE CAMBIAC, *grasping it*: Just as deep!

TWO SERVANTS enter, upstage, carrying a table with four settings, food, and wine, which they place down right. They exit for a moment and return with four chairs, which they place around the table, then leave.

DE CHAMVILLE, *aside, during the preceding*: Once I'm married, au revoir, monsieur!

DE CAMBIAC, *aside, likewise*: If he thinks I believe him…

DE CHAMVILLE, *aloud*: But first I'd best give you a few details about yourself, monsieur. If not, you might—

MADAME DE LAJOIE enters, upstage, interrupting.

MADAME DE LAJOIE: Luncheon is served, messieurs! *(Gesturing toward the table, right.)* Come!… *(Noticing* DE CAMBIAC *in the dressing gown.)* Ah, monsieur… I see that you're making yourself quite at home…

DE CAMBIAC: Why yes… To please you, madame… *(Pointing up left.)* Your brother's room, and all…

MADAME DE LAJOIE: Of course… Of course…

DE CHAMVILLE, *under his breath*: The scoundrel!

MADAME DE LAJOIE, *looking around*: Oh… And Monsieur Toupette?… I almost forgot about the dear boy. *(Pointing down left.)* I left him in the library… *(Crossing down left, as if to call him, sarcastically:)* Delving deep into the wonders of his inspiration…

DE CAMBIAC, *stopping her*: Toupette?… He said he had to leave. Something about a countess…

DE CHAMVILLE: And a harp, if I recall…

MADAME DE LAJOIE, *aside*: Thank goodness!

She goes upstage and pulls the bell-cord.

DE CHAMVILLE: And someone named Ramón… A Spaniard I imagine… *(With a shrug.)* Whatever…

The TWO SERVANTS *return, upstage.* MADAME DE LAJOIE *gestures to them to remove one of the chairs and settings from the table.*

MADAME DE LAJOIE, *as they do so*: He must have lost patience… *(Hypocritically.)* Tsk tsk tsk!… Now I'll never see what he did with those extra feet of his!

DE CHAMVILLE *and* **DE CAMBIAC**, *looking at one another, quizzically, together*: Oh?

MADAME DE LAJOIE: No matter… *(Gesturing them to the table.)* Come… Luncheon is waiting.

DE CAMBIAC, *taking her by the hand*: Ah, madame! A hand that would make the king of France lose his senses!… *(Kissing it, to* DE CHAMVILLE.*)* With your permission, mon ami…

DE CHAMVILLE, *under his breath*: Snake in the grass!

MADAME DE LAJOIE, *aside*: So gallant! Who would ever think…

They approach the table.

DE CAMBIAC, *rushing to hold the chair for her*: Permit me…

DE CHAMVILLE, *likewise*: I insist…

MADAME DE LAJOIE: Really, messieurs…

DE CAMBIAC: Please…

After considerable give-and-take, they are all finally seated, with MADAME DE LAJOIE *facing the audience,* DE CAMBIAC *to her right and* DE CHAMVILLE *to her left.*

MADAME DE LAJOIE, *to* DE CAMBIAC, *as she begins serving*: You must be very hungry, monsieur, after all you've been through this morning.

DE CHAMVILLE, *pouring the wine, to* DE CAMBIAC: To your health!

DE CAMBIAC, *to* DE CHAMVILLE: And to yours, my friend… *(Sipping.)* Excellent wine… A Bordeaux… 1836, if I'm not mistaken…

DE CHAMVILLE, *to* MADAME DE LAJOIE: There's nothing he doesn't know about wine, Mathilde…

MADAME DE LAJOIE, *to* DE CAMBIAC: Is Bordeaux your favorite, monsieur?

DE CAMBIAC: I wouldn't say my absolute favorite…

MADAME DE LAJOIE: Oh?

DE CHAMVILLE, *quickly*: He likes them all! And the stronger the better!

DE CAMBIAC: What?

DE CHAMVILLE: The more alcohol, the more he likes them! *(To* DE CAMBIAC.*)* She knows, my friend!

DE CAMBIAC, *puzzled*: She does?

DE CHAMVILLE: About your life… Among the dregs of society… The cabarets, day and night…

DE CAMBIAC, *suddenly remembering his role*: Oh! The dregs! The deepest dregs!

MADAME DE LAJOIE, *to* DE CAMBIAC: Yes, monsieur… I know all about it.

DE CAMBIAC: Yes… Well… *(As* DE CHAMVILLE *holds out a plate to him, he accidentally knocks it on the floor, smashing it.)* Oh my… *(To* MADAME DE LAJOIE.*)* I'm terribly sorry… I don't know how…

DE CHAMVILLE, *to* MADAME DE LAJOIE, *in a whisper*: It's beginning, Mathilde… The china…

MADAME DE LAJOIE, *to* DE CAMBIAC: Please, monsieur… Feel free… *(Calling.)* Adèle… *(To* DE CAMBIAC.*)* We have at least a dozen more for you…

DE CAMBIAC: A dozen?… You must think I'm terribly clumsy…

ADELE appears, upstage.

ADELE, *at the door, arranging her clothing, somewhat in disarray*: Madame?

MADAME DE LAJOIE, *pointing to the broken dish*: Please…

ADELE: Very good, madame.

She exits.

MADAME DE LAJOIE, *to* DE CAMBIAC, *as the three of them pick at their food*: Clumsy?… Not at all… Just a trifle—how shall I say?—impetuous, monsieur!… Monsieur de Chamville has told me all about your… your…

DE CHAMVILLE: Everything…

MADAME DE LAJOIE, *continuing*: So please… You needn't hold back…

DE CAMBIAC: Oh…?

MADAME DE LAJOIE, *to* DE CHAMVILLE, *whispering*: It's the cheap china. No harm…

DE CHAMVILLE, *to* DE CAMBIAC: Go on, my friend! Smash as much as you like.

DE CAMBIAC: What?

DE CHAMVILLE: Feel free!

MADAME DE LAJOIE: Feel free!… I insist…

DE CHAMVILLE: Since madame insists…

DE CAMBIAC, *aside*: Damn! *(Aloud, to* MADAME DE LAJOIE.*)* Anything to please…

He proceeds to smash one or two more plates on the floor, and to fling a few out the window, next to him. As DE CHAMVILLE *and* MADAME DE LAJOIE *erupt in gales of laughter,* ADELE *enters with dustpan and broom.*

ADELE, *noticing the added debris*: Oh my… More?

She sweeps it up.

MADAME DE LAJOIE, *to* DE CAMBIAC: You find it amusing, monsieur?

DE CAMBIAC: Me? Not especially… But you do, I see…

DE CHAMVILLE, *to* DE CAMBIAC: At your age, my friend, you should really be settling down. It's time you were acting more… Well, mature…

While they are speaking, ADELE, *not having a receptacle, goes behind the table and, when the others are not looking, empties the dustpan out the open window.*

ADELE, *aside*: There!

She exits, upstage.

DE CHAMVILLE, *to* DE CAMBIAC, *continuing*: You should even do like me! Get married… There's nothing like a wife, my friend…

DE CAMBIAC, *gazing lovingly at* MADAME DE LAJOIE: Ah yes… I must say, the thought has entered my mind. If only a certain person…

MADAME DE LAJOIE: Oh? A friend of your sister's, no doubt?

DE CAMBIAC, *about to object*: My sis… *(As* DE CHAMVILLE *gestures to him to be careful what he says.)* No, no… My sister has no friends.

MADAME DE LAJOIE: Tsk tsk tsk!

DE CAMBIAC: She doesn't know a soul. And not a soul knows her.

MADAME DE LAJOIE: Poor child…

DE CAMBIAC: Why, it's almost as if she didn't exist…

ADELE *appears at the door, upstage.*

ADELE, *announcing*: Monsieur Van Gelding, madame…

DE CAMBIAC, *to himself*: Good God, what a lunch!

MADAME DE LAJOIE, *to* ADELE, *getting up and moving upstage*: Back so soon?

DE CHAMVILLE *stands up.*

ADELE: Yes, madame. I asked him to wait in the library.

DE CAMBIAC, *standing up, aside*: The notary? Already?

MADAME DE LAJOIE, *to* DE CHAMVILLE: You go see him, Philippe. He must want to go over some of the details with you.

DE CHAMVILLE, *hesitating*: But…

MADAME DE LAJOIE: Then all we'll have to do is sign. No need to wait till four o'clock…

DE CHAMVILLE, *aside*: And leave him here, alone with her?

DE CAMBIAC, *to* DE CHAMVILLE: She's quite right, you know…

DE CHAMVILLE: Yes, but… *(Aside.)* He's sure to put his foot in his mouth!

MADAME DE LAJOIE, *waving him off*: Go on… Go on…

She pulls the bell-cord.

DE CHAMVILLE, *to* DE CAMBIAC, *whispering*: For heaven's sake, be careful what you say!

DE CAMBIAC, *whispering*: Don't worry. I know my role.

DE CHAMVILLE, *joining* MADAME DE LAJOIE: I'll only be a moment… *(As* MADAME DE LAJOIE *moves down right, back to the dining table, aside.)* Damnation! Of all times…

He exits, down left, as ADELE *enters, upstage.*

MADAME DE LAJOIE, *to* ADELE, *pointing*: The table and chairs, Adèle…

ADELE: Very good, madame…

She exits, upstage.

MADAME DE LAJOIE, *to* DE CAMBIAC: Well now, monsieur… I must say you seem to be growing accustomed to your captivity! *(Pointing to the armchairs.)* Please…

DE CAMBIAC: More than accustomed, lovely lady! *(As she sits down in the chair to the right.)* Your presence is such a joy, that… *(Sitting down in the chair to the left.)* that I would gladly surrender a lifetime of freedom for one day, one hour of a prison like this!

The TWO SERVANTS *enter, upstage, and remove the table and chairs during the ensuing dialogue.*

MADAME DE LAJOIE: Heavens, monsieur! You do know how to turn a phrase! *(Aside.)* For someone whose tongue could make a sailor blush!

DE CAMBIAC: The truth speaks for itself, madame!

MADAME DE LAJOIE, *with a little laugh*: Ha!… So you say… But I'm sure that, if the truth be known, you wish the contract were signed already, and that you were free to leave!

DE CAMBIAC, *quick to reply*: Not true, madame! Not at all!… No, no, no!… I couldn't be happier, just to be here… Just to see you, to speak to you… *(Growing more lyrical.)* Just to breathe the very air you breathe…

MADAME DE LAJOIE: Good heavens!

DE CAMBIAC, *continuing*: Why, I shudder to think that, in just a few hours, that pleasure will disappear… Vanish, forever…

MADAME DE LAJOIE: But why should it, monsieur? On the contrary… It seems to me that you can enjoy it whenever you like. As my husband's bosom friend… And me along with him…

DE CAMBIAC: Ah no!… Impossible!… Once you become his wife, he will have seen the last of me!

MADAME DE LAJOIE: But why?

DE CAMBIAC: Why, you ask?… Why?

MADAME DE LAJOIE: Yes! Why?

DE CAMBIAC: Why?… Why?… Because once he becomes your husband, I'll loathe the very sight of him! My life will have lost its meaning, madame, and I'll live out my days in loneliness and despair!

MADAME DE LAJOIE: Good heavens! I fail to see… Can your friendship for him be so demanding? Can you really be so jealous of me, monsieur?

DE CAMBIAC: Of you?… Ha ha! Not at all, madame… Of him!… *(Aside.)* God help me!

MADAME DE LAJOIE, *shocked, with a start, aside*: What?

DE CAMBIAC: Of him, I tell you!… Watching him enjoy his treasure of virtue… His wealth of beauty… What might have belonged to another, if only…

MADAME DE LAJOIE: You?

DE CAMBIAC, *continuing*: If only my boundless devotion… My limitless love, madame…

MADAME DE LAJOIE, *unable to believe her ears*: Love?… You, Monsieur de Cambiac?… A man who… *(At a loss for words.)* A… A… You must be joking!

DE CAMBIAC, *standing up*: Joking?

MADAME DE LAJOIE: I… I don't know what to say…

As DE CAMBIAC *falls to his knees before her,* TOUPETTE *enters, upstage, unannounced and unnoticed.*

DE CAMBIAC: Please, madame! I beg you to forgive this outburst of passion... But every minute is precious when one has only a day...

TOUPETTE, *agape, transfixed, aside*: Goodness me!

He crouches down and hides behind the chair just vacated by DE CAMBIAC.

DE CAMBIAC, *continuing*: A day...? An hour...?

MADAME DE LAJOIE: You... You're serious...

DE CAMBIAC: If only you knew... Since that fateful night when my gaze first fell upon you... At Madame de Sérigny's ball...

MADAME DE LAJOIE: You were there?

DE CAMBIAC, *continuing*: So beautiful... So gracious... And the minuet, madame... Your hand gently grazing mine...

MADAME DE LAJOIE: You?

DE CAMBIAC, *continuing*: Ah! If only you might have felt the passion in my breast... Known the one desire that has haunted me since that moment...

TOUPETTE, *hidden, aside*: What?

MADAME DE LAJOIE, *standing up, angrily*: Enough, monsieur!... How can you... Oh! For shame!... You! Philippe's dear friend... His bosom companion... After all he's done for you... His kindness, his selflessness... To betray him in such an utterly shameless fashion!

DE CAMBIAC, *getting to his feet*: But madame... If you only knew...

MADAME DE LAJOIE: I do, monsieur! I know all I have to know! I know that you are the cad and the bounder that he told me you were! And worse!

DE CAMBIAC: Madame...

MADAME DE LAJOIE: To think so little of me... To think I would listen to your vulgar... Your unspeakable... Your... Oh! For shame, monsieur!

She storms out, down left.

DE CAMBIAC, *following her*: But madame... *(As she slams the door in his face.)* In the name of all that's holy...

He opens the door as if to follow her.

MADAME DE LAJOIE, *poking her head in*: For shame!

She slams the door shut.

DE CAMBIAC: Damnation!... Oh!... And I can't even tell her the truth! If she knew how he was deceiving her... And with how many others!... Ah, but she loves the wretch! How can I destroy her illusions if they make her happy?

TOUPETTE, *still hidden, listening intently, aside*: What?

DE CAMBIAC: No, de Cambiac!... Noblesse oblige!... It's time for you to leave. It was a lie that brought you here. Let your silence whisk you away... Best you try to forget...

He exits to his room, up left, as TOUPETTE, *manages to remain hidden.*

TOUPETTE, *standing up and looking around, cautiously*: Of all things... The young viper!... And to think... I warmed him in my bosom... *(Coming down right.)* Slapped his cheeks... Blew in his face... And no sooner did he open his eyes, than... Oh! No doubt about it!... He's a rival for her affections! And a dangerous one at that!... Young, charming, well put together... And de Chamville?... When he finds out, I can just imagine… Because he's the one who brought him here, after all… Me?… I knew he was trouble from the beginning. The minute I ran him down… My horses, that is… *(DE CHAMVILLE appears at the door, upstage.)* Ha! Speak of the devil…

DE CHAMVILLE, *entering*: Ah, Toupette…

TOUPETTE: Monsieur…

DE CHAMVILLE, *looking around*: I say… Where is the marquise? And my friend de Cambiac?

TOUPETTE: Your friend?… Ha ha ha! You think he's your friend, that one?

DE CHAMVILLE: Do I think…? *(Aside.)* Does he suspect?

TOUPETTE: I just saw… *(Sarcastically.)* …your friend, monsieur, at Madame de Lajoie's feet!

DE CHAMVILLE: What?… At her—

TOUPETTE, *continuing*: And saying things that I would never dream of saying… Not even to any of the women who have fallen prey to my attentions!… Scandalous things, monsieur…

DE CHAMVILLE: You… You saw him…?

TOUPETTE: With my very own eyes!… Both of them!

DE CHAMVILLE: Both your eyes?

TOUPETTE: Both him and her, monsieur!

DE CHAMVILLE, *furious*: That snake!… That… That… Of all the… Oh! I'll get my revenge!

TOUPETTE: Yes! We certainly will!

DE CHAMVILLE: "We"?… What difference does it make to you?

TOUPETTE: What difference indeed!… Would you have me be insensitive to the distress of a friend? His pain, his woe… Come, come now, monsieur!

DE CHAMVILLE, *angrily*: Leave my pain and woe to me, thank you! I'll take care of them myself!

TOUPETTE: Oh… I… I only thought…

DE CHAMVILLE, *musing for a moment, suddenly slapping his forehead*: Ah! Of course!… That explains this vile poem I just found in the library.

He takes the original version of TOUPETTE's poem from his pocket and holds it up.

TOUPETTE, *aside*: Ayyy! The first one… With the extra feet…

DE CHAMVILLE: He's the one who wrote it, for sure! *(Beside himself.)* A love poem for her, damn it! *(Apostrophizing.)* Well, we'll see about that, de Cambiac! You traitor!… Walk in my tracks, will you?… Oh! My revenge will be terrible, you… you…

TOUPETTE, *aside*: Heaven help me! What if he finds out…? *(Aloud.)* Come now, monsieur… Perhaps the poet's intentions were honorable. Who can say?

DE CHAMVILLE: The poet? Him?… A child could have written better!

TOUPETTE: Oh?… Well…

DE CHAMVILLE: And as for his intentions, you saw him yourself! You just said so…

TOUPETTE: I know, but… Frivolous as his behavior was… Perhaps it was just a momentary lapse… A flash of romantic fancy… Inspiration… At our age, don't you know?

DE CHAMVILLE: Our age, monsieur?… Yours and mine?

TOUPETTE: No… Mine and his…

DE CHAMVILLE, *sarcastically*: Aha… No doubt!…

TOUPETTE: Besides…

DE CHAMVILLE: Yes, of course! You're defending him because it was you who brought him here in the first place!

TOUPETTE: What?… Me?… Not at all! It was you!

DE CHAMVILLE: What are talking about? He was here when I arrived!… It was you, for God's sake!

TOUPETTE: But I left him in my coach… My stratagem, remember?… It was you…

DE CHAMVILLE: But I don't even know the man!

TOUPETTE: What? I thought—

DE CHAMVILLE: And you told me how you met. How you ran him down on the street…

TOUPETTE: My coach, monsieur! Not me… My horses…

DE CHAMVILLE: And you knew so much about him… Last of his line…

TOUPETTE: But I thought you and he… I thought you were friends for the last twenty years!

DE CHAMVILLE: Wrong! I mistook him for someone else!

TOUPETTE: Then… Then the man is a nobody! A fraud!

DE CHAMVILLE: An unprincipled adventurer!

TOUPETTE: Or a Gypsy…

DE CHAMVILLE: A Bohemian…

TOUPETTE: Without so much as a guitar!

DE CHAMVILLE: Well, we'll just see… *(Brandishing the poem.)* We'll see what he has to say about this… this rubbish!

TOUPETTE, *alarmed*: W-W-What are you going to do? *(Aside.)* If de Cambiac tells him he didn't write it…

DE CHAMVILLE, *dramatically*: Toupette…

TOUPETTE: Monsieur?

DE CHAMVILLE: The author of these lines is going to perish by my hand!… A duel, Toupette! *(TOUPETTE gives a noticeable shudder.)* A duel to the death!… And you'll be my second!

TOUPETTE: Your second?

DE CHAMVILLE: My second!

TOUPETTE, *nodding rather tentatively*: But first… Let me go get the weapons…

DE CHAMVILLE: My blade is quite sufficient!

TOUPETTE: Yes, but… Only one?… What if it breaks? We need several… To the death, after all… *(Aside.)* Good heavens! What am I going to do? *(Aloud.)* Wait here… I'll be back…

He exits, upstage.

DE CHAMVILLE, *alone, down right*: What a frightful situation! A man I should treat as a friend is my enemy. And, in the midst of it all, if the marquise learns the truth… Who can say? Perhaps he told her already. Why not? "In love and war…" Oh! The wretch…

DE CAMBIAC appears at the door, up left, without the dressing gown.

DE CAMBIAC, *entering, mumbling to himself, going toward the door, upstage:* Enough is enough! No need for long, drawn out farewells…

DE CHAMVILLE, *as he is about to exit:* Monsieur!

DE CAMBIAC, *stopping at the door:* Monsieur?

DE CHAMVILLE: After your disgraceful behavior, my friend…

DE CAMBIAC, *aside:* He knows…

DE CHAMVILLE, *continuing, approaching him:* …I trust you will not oblige me to tolerate your presence a moment longer.

DE CAMBIAC, *aside:* Can't the idiot see I'm leaving? *(Aloud, sarcastically.)* Do I take it, my friend, that you are the master of the establishment, free to dispense hospitality or to refuse it?

DE CHAMVILLE: Master or not, I find your presence here most disagreeable. And if my words are not enough to convince you…

DE CAMBIAC: What? You're threatening me?… You dare—

DE CHAMVILLE: I am indeed, monsieur! Consider yourself insulted, and in no uncertain terms!

DE CAMBIAC: Oh! How base… How unworthy… Need I remind you that, in our world, an affront demands certain swift reparations…

DE CHAMVILLE: Precisely!… Into the garden then… And the sooner the better!

DE CAMBIAC: My sentiments exactly, monsieur! *(Aside.)* So be it!

DE CHAMVILLE: A duel to the death…

DE CAMBIAC: To the death… *(To himself.)* Without her, what's the difference?

MADAME DE LAJOIE appears at the door, down left.

DE CHAMVILLE *and* **DE CAMBIAC,** *noticing her, together: Ah…*

MADAME DE LAJOIE, *to DE CHAMVILLE:* We're waiting for you, Philippe.

DE CHAMVILLE, *shaking DE CAMBIAC's hand, to keep up appearances:* Dear friend!

DE CAMBIAC, *likewise:* Bosom companion!

MADAME DE LAJOIE, *aside, with a sneer toward DE CHAMVILLE:* Hypocrite!

DE CHAMVILLE, *affecting a smile for her benefit, whispering to DE CAMBIAC:* Don't think I don't loathe the very sight of you, you traitor!

MADAME DE LAJOIE, *to DE CHAMVILLE:* Come, come… The witnesses are here…

ADELE appears at the door, upstage.

ADELE, *to DE CHAMVILLE:* A lady to see monsieur… I asked her to wait in the sitting-room.

DE CHAMVILLE: To see me?

ADELE: Something about an oil-lamp, I thought she said…

DE CHAMVILLE, *aside:* Good God! Her!… Olympe!… *(Aloud.)* I can't imagine… *(To MADAME DE LAJOIE.)* Excuse me, Mathilde… I'll just be a moment…

He exits, upstage.

MADAME DE LAJOIE, *to herself:* Now who do you suppose…

DE CAMBIAC, *to MADAME DE LAJOIE:* No doubt you are surprised, madame, to find me still here…. If Monsieur de Chamville hadn't stopped me…

MADAME DE LAJOIE, *coldly*: Your whereabouts are no concern of mine, I assure you! And if Monsieur de Chamville is still blind to your vices… If his friendship for you—

DE CAMBIAC, *interrupting*: His friendship? *(With a sardonic laugh.)* Ha ha ha!… Please, madame!… If only you knew the truth, you would find me far less deserving of your reproach. But, cruel as it is, I have no choice but to bear it. No explanations, no complaints… One day, perhaps, it will all become clear, and you will regret that you judge me so harshly!

MADAME DE LAJOIE, *to herself*: What ever can he mean?

DE CAMBIAC: Farewell, madame… Be happy with your new husband. I have no other wish, and no other regret.

> *TOUPETTE enters quickly, upstage, carrying a variety of swords, sabers, etc. under his arm.*

TOUPETTE, *noticing them, aside*: Again?… *(Aloud, to MADAME DE LAJOIE.)* Don't listen to him, madame!

MADAME DE LAJOIE: Toupette!

TOUPETTE: Don't listen! For heaven's sake!… The man is an impostor…

DE CAMBIAC: I'm what?

TOUPETTE, *continuing*: Thank goodness I got here in time to save you! Everything he says… Everything he does is a falsehood, madame!

DE CAMBIAC: I beg your pardon?

TOUPETTE: I'm not even sure he's the one I ran down this morning!… My horses, that is… *(To DE CAMBIAC.)* Did I?… Are you the one?

DE CAMBIAC: What are you…

TOUPETTE, *rattling the swords at him*: Who are you, monsieur? You've been here all morning, but do I know you?

DE CAMBIAC: Know me…?

TOUPETTE: No! Does madame? Does anyone? Who are you?… Tell me! Tell us!

MADAME DE LAJOIE, *to TOUPETTE*: But Monsieur de Chamville, monsieur—

TOUPETTE: Monsieur de Chamville met him this morning for the very first time!

MADAME DE LAJOIE: What?

TOUPETTE: He told me so himself!

DE CAMBIAC, *to TOUPETTE, with a great sigh of relief*: Ah!… Thank you! Thank you! Thank you, my friend!

TOUPETTE, *puzzled*: What?

DE CAMBIAC: You've just told her what I could never tell her! *(To MADAME DE LAJOIE.)* The confidence that my honor wouldn't let me reveal… The secret…

MADAME DE LAJOIE: But his utter devotion… Your displays of friendship…

DE CAMBIAC: Pretense, madame!… Sham…

TOUPETTE, *rattling the swords*: Shame, you mean!

DE CAMBIAC, *continuing*: He made me promise…

MADAME DE LAJOIE, *aside*: Oh! The treachery… I'm beginning to see…

TOUPETTE, *to MADAME DE LAJOIE*: But that's only half the story, madame! *(To DE CAMBIAC.)* I'm sorry, monsieur, but why should I be silent? *(To MADAME DE LAJOIE, pointing at DE CAMBIAC.)* This man, who dared fill your ears with words of love, on bended knee... This very man who dares to accuse Monsieur de Chamville... *(To* DE CAMBIAC.*)* Ha!... *(To* MADAME DE LAJOIE, *continuing.)* Even as he pressed his suit before you, he was receiving love letters from a dancer at the Opéra!

DE CAMBIAC: I was what...?

TOUPETTE, *awkwardly reaching into a pocket and removing the outer envelope and the letter from Olympe to de Chamville, holding them up*: Like this one, madame!... I found it on the floor in your sitting-room, not moments ago... *(To* DE CAMBIAC, *sarcastically.)* Tsk tsk tsk!... How careless! Tsk tsk tsk!

DE CAMBIAC: But that's impossible!

TOUPETTE: Oh? *(Showing him.)* I think the address is clear enough: "To Monsieur de Cambiac..." And the billet doux, no less so, my friend! *(To* MADAME DE LAJOIE, *handing them to her as* DE CAMBIAC *reaches for them.)* This will show you how "impossible" madame...

DE CAMBIAC: But I have no idea...

MADAME DE LAJOIE, *reading*: "Olympe..." *(To herself.)* That woman... "Oil-lamp" indeed!... *(To* DE CAMBIAC.*)* Have you ever seen this letter, monsieur?

DE CAMBIAC: Never! I swear... It couldn't have been meant for me! On my honor...

TOUPETTE: Your honor!... Ha!

MADAME DE LAJOIE, *to herself, musing*: Unless... Could it be that the envelope was a ruse?... That his entire friendship, in fact... That there really was no Monsieur de Cambiac until this morning? *(To* DE CAMBIAC.*)* But why, monsieur? I don't understand...

DE CAMBIAC, *noticing the open book on the writing-table, down left, pointing*: Perhaps you can find the answer in that book of his... Page thirty-five, as I recall...

TOUPETTE, *aside*: Book? What book?

DE CAMBIAC: In the middle...

TOUPETTE lays the swords down on the armchairs and draws closer to the table, inquisitively, as MADAME DE LAJOIE picks up the book, finds the page, and begins reading.

MADAME DE LAJOIE: "Be sure to invent a true and faithful friend..."

Her jaw drops as she continues in silence.

TOUPETTE, *aside*: Is this a time to read, I ask you?

MADAME DE LAJOIE, *aloud*: "In short, your friend is a straw man..." *(Aside, aghast, at a loss for words.)* Oh! The... The wretch! He... I don't believe it! He...

VAN GELDING appears at the library door, down left. As DE CAMBIAC notices him, he reacts with a start, and tries to keep out of sight.

VAN GELDING, *to* MADAME DE LAJOIE: Everything is ready for the signing, madame. Almost, that is... Everything but the names...

He goes and sits down at the writing-table, down left, about to write.

MADAME DE LAJOIE, *to* VAN GELDING: Wait, monsieur... Not yet...

VAN GELDING: Oh?... *(Catching sight of* DE CAMBIAC, *he puts on his pince-nez to examine him more closely, and leers at him.)* I say... Is that you, Monsieur de Cambiac? Are you here as a witness? You...

DE CAMBIAC, *flustered*: Am I... No, monsieur... I...

VAN GELDING, *to* MADAME DE LAJOIE: Then I take it monsieur has finally decided to reveal his identity?

MADAME DE LAJOIE: What?

DE CAMBIAC, *to* VAN GELDING: Please!…

VAN GELDING, *embarrassed*: Oh… I beg your pardon!… I thought you must have told her that it was you who—

DE CAMBIAC: Shhh! For heaven's sake!

MADAME DE LAJOIE, *to* DE CAMBIAC, *suspecting*: You?… *(To* VAN GELDING.*)* Him, monsieur…? Who what…?

VAN GELDING, *to* MADAME DE LAJOIE: You mean, he hasn't told you? Oh my… I assumed… Seeing him here, I mean…

MADAME DE LAJOIE: Told me…?

VAN GELDING, *as* DE CAMBIAC *tries desperately to signal him to be quiet*:: That he was the one… Two years ago… When the marquis… Well, when he went to his eternal reward… *(Aside.)* Such as it is…

MADAME DE LAJOIE: What?

VAN GELDING: The one who saved you from disaster…

MADAME DE LAJOIE, *to* DE CAMBIAC: Monsieur de Cambiac!… Are you… Did you… Is it possible?

TOUPETTE, *aside*: Is what possible? *(Aloud.)* Will somebody please tell me…

MADAME DE LAJOIE: What a noble heart! What a generous soul!

TOUPETTE: Him?

MADAME DE LAJOIE, *continuing, aside*: And that liar, Philippe… Oh! *(Aloud, to* DE CAMBIAC.*)* You were right, monsieur! I regret already that I judged you so harshly!

DE CAMBIAC: Ah, madame…

TOUPETTE, *aside*: And what about me? *(Aloud, to* MADAME DE LAJOIE.*)* Madame… I thought I proved… *(Aside, with a gesture of despair.)* Blast!

DE CHAMVILLE appears at the door, upstage.

DE CHAMVILLE, *entering, aside*: Poor Olympe!… So gullible!… But at least I got rid of her… *(Aloud.)* Sorry to have kept you all waiting…

MADAME DE LAJOIE, *to* DE CHAMVILLE: And that woman, monsieur? Just now…

DE CHAMVILLE: Oh… It… *(Pointing to* DE CAMBIAC.*)* His sister… *(To* DE CAMBIAC.*)* It was your sister, my friend.

DE CAMBIAC: It was?

DE CHAMVILLE, *offhandedly*: She wanted to tell me how much she enjoyed the concert…

MADAME DE LAJOIE, *aside*: The cheek!… The gall!

DE CHAMVILLE: Too bad she couldn't stay…

MADAME DE LAJOIE, *aside*: Just what does he take me for?

She goes and stands at VAN GELDING's right.

DE CHAMVILLE: But I'm all yours now… *(To* VAN GELDING.*)* We're ready to begin, monsieur.

VAN GELDING, *preparing to write*: The name of the groom?

DE CHAMVILLE, *moving toward him*: Philippe-Auguste de Chamville…

MADAME DE LAJOIE, *to* DE CHAMVILLE: Pardon me, monsieur… You're not the one he's speaking to!

DE CHAMVILLE: Mathilde…?

TOUPETTE, *aside*: Oh joy! Then it's me! I'm the one! *(Approaching* VAN GELDING.*)* Achille-Fortuné Toupette, monsieur… *(Spelling.)* A-C-H-…

MADAME DE LAJOIE, *to* TOUPETTE: Neither are you, monsieur!

TOUPETTE: What? How can that be?… Then, who…

MADAME DE LAJOIE, *to* DE CAMBIAC, *coyly*: Haven't you anything to say?

DE CAMBIAC: Madame, if I dared think…

MADAME DE LAJOIE: Dare, monsieur!

DE CAMBIAC: But…

MADAME DE LAJOIE: Have you forgotten your name!

DE CHAMVILLE: Him?

TOUPETTE: Bah!

DE CHAMVILLE, *to* MADAME DE LAJOIE: What does this mean?

MADAME DE LAJOIE: It means that I've learned the truth, monsieur. That my heart's first choice has proven himself unworthy…

TOUPETTE, *aside*: But what did I do? I thought…

MADAME DE LAJOIE, *continuing*: And that his place has been taken by another, more deserving…

DE CHAMVILLE, *aside*: Damnation! She knows…

MADAME DE LAJOIE, *sarcastically*: And one whom you certainly will approve of yourself, monsieur… *(Pointing to* DE CAMBIAC.*)* Your dear, dear friend… Your bosom companion…

DE CHAMVILLE, *aside*: The wretch!

> DE CAMBIAC, *taking the pen from* VAN GELDING, *gives it to* MADAME DE LAJOIE *with one hand, and, with the other, leads her over to the table, where they both sign the contract.*

TOUPETTE, *aside*: After all I told her!… And still she wants him!… The… The woman is a pervert!

DE CHAMVILLE, *whispering, to* DE CAMBIAC: You may choose your weapon, monsieur!

DE CAMBIAC, *whispering*: Swords, my friend… *(Pointing to the array on the armchairs.)* There are several to choose from…

MADAME DE LAJOIE, *overhearing*: A duel!… Good heavens! I should have guessed…

TOUPETTE: Wait!… No! Not a duel!… *(Taking a document from his pocket and waving it at* DE CAMBIAC.*)* You can't kill him! He owes me money!

DE CAMBIAC, *examining the document*: Yes… So I see… *(To* VAN GELDING.*)* Monsieur, be so kind as to pay the gentleman what Monsieur de Chamville owes him.

DE CHAMVILLE: I refuse!

TOUPETTE, *quickly*: I accept!

DE CHAMVILLE: But my honor—

DE CAMBIAC, *to* DE CHAMVILLE: And now, monsieur, any time you choose…

MADAME DE LAJOIE: But you mustn't… *(To* DE CAMBIAC.*)* I can't let you…

DE CHAMVILLE, *to* DE CAMBIAC: I could have pardoned an honorable rival, monsieur… But one who abuses a confidence…? A sacred trust…?

DE CAMBIAC, *with a start*: Me… ? Never, monsieur! You're mistaken. I didn't!

DE CHAMVILLE: You didn't?

MADAME DE LAJOIE, *to* DE CHAMVILLE: He didn't! *(Pointing.)* It was Toupette!

DE CAMBIAC: Toupette!

DE CHAMVILLE: Toupette?… But that poem… That ridiculous poem that I found in the library?

MADAME DE LAJOIE: Toupette!

DE CAMBIAC: Toupette!

DE CHAMVILLE: You mean…

TOUPETTE, *echoing automatically*: Toupette! Toupette!… *(Aside.)* Damned if I understand…

DE CHAMVILLE, *to* TOUPETTE: Idiot! *(To* DE CAMBIAC.*)* Then a duel is out of the question! If you're not the one…

MADAME DE LAJOIE, *with a sigh of relief*: Ah…

DE CHAMVILLE, *to* DE CAMBIAC: I'm sorry, monsieur, but I really can't kill you… It just wouldn't be right.

DE CAMBIAC: Oh well…

TOUPETTE: Bah! *(Aside.)* One of these days… When she comes to her senses…

DE CHAMVILLE, *aside*: Besides, I still have Olympe, sweet child. *(To* DE CAMBIAC.*)* No hard feelings, mon ami… Dear de Cambiac! *(With a laugh.)* Just like before!

DE CAMBIAC, *likewise, shaking his hand*: Just like before! Dear de Chamville!

TOUPETTE: But I thought… I was sure…

MADAME DE LAJOIE: Philippe, you devil…

TOUPETTE: Blast!… Why did I have to go and run him down this morning?

DE CAMBIAC: Your horses, that is…

DE CHAMVILLE: Your horses…

MADAME DE LAJOIE: Your horses, monsieur…

Everyone except TOUPETTE *bursts out laughing as* DE CAMBIAC *takes her hand and kisses it, and the curtain falls.*

CURTAIN.

Mam'selle Frisette

(Frisette, 1846)

Eugène Labiche & Auguste Lefranc

Characters

GABRIEL GAUTIER, a young baker's apprentice with a past

FRISETTE, a rather plain young woman, mother of an adopted infant

MADAME MÉNACHET, a meddlesome, penny-pinching housekeeper

[**BAGALOUCHE,** an offstage man's voice]

A furnished room in a middle-class rooming-house. One half is papered blue; the other half, yellow. Each half has a door, up center, to the outside corridor. Only the one to the left is used; the other is obstructed by a tall coat rack. On the latter, a woman's simple coat and bonnet. Up right, a curtained bed, lying horizontally, with bedclothes in disarray. Close by the bed, an end-table with a washbasin and a pitcher of water. On the floor, next to it, a woman's bag. A little downstage of the bed, a table and chair. On the table, a plate, and a salt shaker and sugar bowl, both almost empty. In the wall, down right, a window. In the same wall, up right, a door, leading to another room. Between them, right center, a fireplace with tongs and a basket of logs. On the wall above it, a mirror; in front of it, a small desk with paper, pen, and ink. In the opposite wall, down left, a door to another alcove. Next to it, center, another fireplace, also with appropriate furnishings. On each mantelpiece, a vase. Under the one on the left, a key. Also on the mantelpiece, left, a pin cushion with several long pins, and a tablecloth, neatly folded. Up left, two small chairs. Other chairs, here and there, with various items of feminine attire.

At rise, FRISETTE *is primping in front of the mirror, right. After a moment, there is a knock, up center.*

BAGALOUCHE'S VOICE, *outside*: Mam'selle Frisette!… Mam'selle…

FRISETTE, *aside*: Oh my! *(Aloud.)* Yes? What is it?

BAGALOUCHE'S VOICE: Sorry to bother you… It's me, mam'selle… Bagalouche…

FRISETTE: Again? What is it this time?

BAGALOUCHE'S VOICE: Same as before… Like always… You know…

FRISETTE, *impatiently*: No, no, no! How many times do I have to tell you?

BAGALOUCHE'S VOICE: But your aunt said she was sure that… She thought that if I—

FRISETTE: And I'm telling you she's wrong! She can think what she likes! Now please! Leave me alone!

BAGALOUCHE'S VOICE: Oh well… Au revoir, mam'selle… I'll come back later…

FRISETTE, *aside, sarcastically*: Yes, I'm sure you will!

BAGALOUCHE'S VOICE: After you've thought it over…

FRISETTE, *aside*: Good heavens!

BAGALOUCHE'S VOICE: After you've had time…

He can be heard heavily tramping down the stairs.

FRISETTE: Oh! Did you ever… Stubborn? Some people… I've told him twenty times if I've told him once… "You're bothering me, young man!… Really, it's nothing personal. Marriage is simply not for me! I know that your intentions are pure as the driven snow…" *(Imitating.)* "Oh yes, mam'selle! Purer, even!…" *(In her own voice.)* "But you're a man! And I hate men! Every last one! So there!" *(Going to the window, down right, opening it and taking a few deep breaths.)* No matter! He never stops trying. He even hunts me down at work. At my aunt's… Making my lace… And always with the same refrain… *(Imitating.)* "I'll come back later… After you've thought it over…" *(Going back to the mirror.)* Three months, for goodness' sake! How long does he think I'm thinking! Thank you just the same!… *(Talking to her reflection.)* Your freedom is too precious, Frisette. Let them talk about you all they like. No man is worth your independence. And certainly not that one!

MADAME MENACHET enters, up center, with a feather duster in one hand and a bowl of café au lait in the other.

MADAME MENACHET: Up already, mademoiselle?

She puts the café au lait on the table.

FRISETTE: I'm afraid so, madame. I didn't sleep a wink.

MADAME MENACHET: Was it something you ate?

FRISETTE: No. Something I dreamt... I dreamt I got married.

MADAME MENACHET: Now there's a pretty dream for you!

She comes over and gives a few finishing touches to FRISETTE's attire.

FRISETTE: A nightmare, you mean!

MADAME MENACHET: Oh?... But I moved the pillow, just like you asked me...

FRISETTE: Yes, well...

MADAME MENACHET, *dusting here and there*: After all, I don't know all your habits yet, mademoiselle... Only three days that you've been here... But you'll see... Once I do, I'm sure you'll be pleased.

FRISETTE: No doubt...

MADAME MENACHET: Why, I'll come in at seven and light the fire... Since you leave at eight, I mean... Because I'm sure you want it nice and warm in the morning. And at night, before you go to bed... Because, when you go to bed—

FRISETTE: Not at all, madame!

MADAME MENACHET: Oh?

FRISETTE: In fact, I wish you would be careful and not use so much firewood. *(Pointing left and right.)* With two fireplaces, it just seems to disappear. Really, there's no need...

MADAME MENACHET: Aha...

FRISETTE: And the same with my candles...

MADAME MENACHET: Of course, mademoiselle... I'll be careful.

FRISETTE: Please see that you are. *(Picking up the sugar bowl, looking at it in surprise.)* And the sugar... Good heavens! Where does it go?

She scrapes a spoonful out of the bowl and pours it into her coffee.

MADAME MENACHET: You must use more than you think. Like my Baptiste, mademoiselle... Sometimes he just keeps pouring it in until I make him stop.

She continues puttering about as FRISETTE takes a few sips, takes her coat from the coat rack, then goes to the mirror and puts it on.

FRISETTE: And while I think of it...

MADAME MENACHET: Mademoiselle?

FRISETTE: Pardon me for asking but... You don't smoke, do you?

MADAME MENACHET, *shocked*: Me? I beg your pardon!

FRISETTE: Because last night, when I came back the room absolutely reeked of tobacco. I thought perhaps...

MADAME MENACHET, *aside*: Oh my!

FRISETTE: These days, one never knows...

She takes a few more sips.

MADAME MENACHET, *embarrassed*: No... But I assure you...

FRISETTE: One would almost think that while I was at work—

MADAME MENACHET, *quickly*: Ha! I know what it is! Of course… It's… It's the neighbor, upstairs. Him and his pipe…

FRISETTE: Upstairs?

MADAME MENACHET: Yes… And since smoke rises…

FRISETTE, *sarcastically*: His comes down just for me! I see…

MADAME MENACHET: No, it… I mean… I mean… Buildings nowadays… They're just not what they used to be. And the drafts, don't you know! And rooming-houses in particular… Everybody says so… *(Eager to change the subject, as FRISETTE continues drinking.)* Why don't you get your own place, mademoiselle?

FRISETTE: Why?… More easily said than done, I'm afraid… Crocheting lace for thirty sous a day, with a wet nurse to pay, month after month… Do you think I have anything left?

MADAME MENACHET, *sympathetically*: I know… I know… *(Commiserating.)* The infant, poor thing… Tsk tsk tsk!… What a nice thing to do, mademoiselle…

FRISETTE: Yes, well… *(Going over to the mirror, arranging her curls.)* Oh, my!… Where is that hairpin? *(Pointing left.)* Be a dear, madame… The black one…

MADAME MENACHET, *crossing left and taking a pin from the pin cushion on the other mantelpiece, returning and giving it to her*: This one?

FRISETTE: Thank you… *(Arranging it, as MADAME MENACHET returns to her dusting.)* There… *(Picking up her bag by the bed.)* Well, I'll be on my way…

She takes her bonnet from the coat rack, puts it on, and takes a few more sips.

MADAME MENACHET: Very good, mademoiselle… Give the little one a big kiss for me.

FRISETTE, *about to leave, sniffing with a grimace*: And don't close the window! Not until all the smoke goes back to his room!… *(Thinking out loud.)* No doubt I'll cross him on the stairs… I always do!

MADAME MENACHET, *overhearing*: "Him," mademoiselle?

FRISETTE: That wretched person upstairs… He's always coming up just as I'm going down. Every morning, like clockwork…

MADAME MENACHET, *a little embarrassed*: Aha…

FRISETTE: Vile creature that he is! Even without his pipe! Always mumbling insults under his breath… "Bah! Women!… How I hate them!"

MADAME MENACHET: And that bothers you, does it?

FRISETTE: Me? Not a bit! Men are all alike. If they all disappeared from the face of the earth… Believe me, madame. They're not to be trusted… None of them!

MADAME MENACHET: Even my Baptiste?

FRISETTE: Is he a man?

MADAME MENACHET: I should hope so! I think I would know by now if—

FRISETTE: Then that's all there is to it! *(Taking the few last sips, gesticulating with the bowl.)* Sooner or later, he'll cheat on you, madame…

MADAME MENACHET: He will?

FRISETTE: They can't help it. It's their nature.

MADAME MENACHET: And isn't there anything I can do?

FRISETTE: Of course! Become a widow! *(She slams the bowl down on the table.)* There's no other way!

She exits, up center.

MADAME MENACHET, *alone*: My, my… Did you ever see… ? Cheat? My Baptiste? The very idea… Besides, who could he find to cheat with? *(She laughs.)* I must say, she certainly does hate men!… Become a widow! Ha!… *(She goes about picking up the various articles belonging to* FRISETTE.*)* Say what you want, it's not every day you have two tenants for the same room! But what could I do? *(Coming downstage.)* Three days ago she comes and asks me if we have a room to rent…"I'm desperate," she tells me… "Of course!" I tell her… Well, we didn't, but in this business you never turn down a client! So I said to myself: "What if I put her in number seven? The one that the baker's apprentice is in… He works all night and only comes home in the morning. She works all day and only comes home at night. It will do until number ten is empty." It shouldn't be long. Old Monsieur Plouque is on his last legs. He probably won't last the week. So… A perfect arrangement, and everybody's happy… *(She returns to picking up* FRISETTE*'s things.)* Only, I really should ask Monsieur Gautier not to smoke so much! Him and that blasted pipe of his… *(Beginning to move down left, stopping abruptly.)* No, no… Her door… *(Pointing down left.)* Not his!… *(Shaking her head.)* That would never do! *(She exits, up right, for a few moments, then returns without the articles, closes the door, locks it, and places the key under the vase on the mantelpiece, right.)* God in heaven! If they suspected… *(Remembering.)* Ah! The bed… *(She goes up right.)* Mustn't forget to move the pillow! *(She puts the pillow at the foot of the bed.)* He likes his head down there, and she likes hers up here… Lucky they're not married!

She makes up the bed. A moment later, GAUTIER *enters, up center.* MADAME MENACHET *quickly and clumsily hides the coffee bowl in her bosom.*

GAUTIER, *stopping, casting a haughty, disparaging look up center, to himself*: Bah! That woman again!… There ought to be a law… No women allowed within a hundred feet of a man!… Two hundred feet!… *(Coming downstage.)* Vixens! Every last one of them!… Vampires, that's what they are! Bloodsuckers! Up to no good… No good at all!

MADAME MENACHET, *dusting here and there, overhearing*: None of us, monsieur?

During the following exchange, he moves nervously about the room, sitting on all the chairs, jumping up, etc.

GAUTIER: I beg your pardon?

MADAME MENACHET, *with as much coquettishness as she can muster*: Are we all so terrible?

GAUTIER: All what, madame?

MADAME MENACHET: All the… the fair sex, monsieur!

GAUTIER: Ah… Hmm… *(Aside.)* Fair?… Ha! *(Aloud.)* Well… *(Aside.)* All those that matter!… *(Aloud.)* Most, madame!… Present company excepted, of course…

MADAME MENACHET: Of course…

GAUTIER: And ugly as sin, to boot!… Vile…*(With a shudder.)* Yeccch!… *(Pretending to spit.)* Ptui!… Ptui!… If I had my way, I'd make them all suffer. I'd get rid of them all! Every last one… Present company excepted…

MADAME MENACHET: Of course… You said that…

GAUTIER: Yes… That's what I would do!

MADAME MENACHET, *upstage*: That's what you say now… But if you fell in love…

GAUTIER, *jumping up*: In love? In love?... Me? *(Standing right, before the mirror.)* Gabriel Gautier?... Surely you jest, madame! *(Primping.)* I may be a handsome devil... But love? Quite out of the question!

MADAME MENACHET: Oh? I would think—

GAUTIER: Don't! It's not becoming!... True, I enjoy attracting their attention... The tarts!... Seeing them gaze at me with their longing glances... Hungering after me... Suffering!... Yes, suffering!... That's what they deserve! Every one of them!... Present company excepted...

MADAME MENACHET, *sarcastically*: Thank you, I'm sure...

GAUTIER, *joining her, upstage*: By the way, madame... Speaking of which... Who is that atrocious little hussy who is always coming down just as I'm coming up?

MADAME MENACHET, *uneasy*: Who?

GAUTIER: The one who leers suggestively at me as we pass on the stairs...

MADAME MENACHET: Her?... Oh... A tenant, monsieur...

GAUTIER: Yes, well... An ugly one, I must say! There should be a law...

MADAME MENACHET: Ugly? Mademoiselle Frisette?

GAUTIER, *grimacing*: Pouah!

MADAME MENACHET: Maybe if you'd look at her you wouldn't think so!

GAUTIER: Look at her?... Come, come, madame! I should look at her? I should affront my eyeballs with the sight of an ugly female, when there are so many less unpleasant things that deserve my attention?

MADAME MENACHET: But she's—

GAUTIER, *interrupting*: Ugly!... Now not another word, or I'll give you my notice!

MADAME MENACHET, *with a shrug*: Well... *(Aside.)* In that case... *(Aloud.)* Now that you mention it, she is rather... plain.

GAUTIER: Plain?...No! Ugly, I tell you!... Just plain ugly...

MADAME MENACHET: If you say so... *(Coming right, to the mirror, dusting.)* Of course, that's what you say about all of them...

GAUTIER: Quite! I loathe them all!

MADAME MENACHET: And it... *(Hazarding an opinion.)* It wouldn't just be because one of them...

GAUTIER, *sharply, approaching her*: One of them?

MADAME MENACHET: Because one of them sent you packing?

GAUTIER, *pacing up and down*: Me? Sent me...? Ha ha ha!

MADAME MENACHET: Isn't that what you told me?

GAUTIER: Don't be absurd!

MADAME MENACHET: Some featherbrain, you said...

GAUTIER: Enough! Not another word!... Let's not talk about it!... I... It... *(Stamping his foot, suddenly changing his tune.)* Yes, by God! Let's!... Let's!... I want to! I enjoy it!

MADAME MENACHET: Oh?

GAUTIER: It's invigorating! It stirs the blood!... It... *(Stopping, stamping his foot again.)* Yes! I loved her!...Ha ha ha! What a fool!... And I was even going to marry her!... Me! Can you imagine?... Me, Gabriel Gautier... And that... that...

MADAME MENACHET: I know...

GAUTIER: Then one day... The hussy... The jade...

MADAME MENACHET: I know, monsieur...

GAUTIER: One day I found the proof...

MADAME MENACHET: You told me...

GAUTIER, *continuing, oblivious to her objections*: The proof that she had another... Some wretch by the name of... By the name of... *(Trying to recall.)* Edgar?... Edmond?...

MADAME MENACHET, *correcting*: Edouard, monsieur...

GAUTIER: Quite! Edouard!... A vulgar peasant!... A vile nobody, madame!... So I washed my hands of her! "We're finished!" I told her... And I never laid eyes on her again! Who knows what became of her? They told me she was dead!... Of remorse, no doubt!

MADAME MENACHET, *under her breath*: I'm sure...

GAUTIER: Well, so much for that one!... But the others? All the rest?... Bah!... Attila the Hun couldn't hate them more! Every last one...

MADAME MENACHET: Really, monsieur... Don't you think you're being a little—

GAUTIER, *stamping his foot*: Enough! Or I give my notice!

MADAME MENACHET, *aside*: My oh my!... *(Aloud, sarcastically.)* As long as present company is excepted...

She turns and exits, up center, shaking her head.

GAUTIER, *alone, watching her go*: Old witch!... You can bet she was quite the vamp in her day!... Before the Flood!... Well now... Time for breakfast... *(He reaches into the inner pocket of his jacket, takes out a loaf of bread, and puts it on the table.)* I can't complain that it isn't fresh! I baked it myself! *(He reaches into each trouser pocket and takes out two small packages, unwraps them, and puts the contents on the plate on the table.)* And my pickled feet!... Mmm! Pigs' feet!... Delicious!... With a little salt and pepper... *(He picks up the salt shaker, about to use it, but stops in disbelief.)* What? Empty? It can't be. I just filled it. *(Scratching his head.)* At least, I thought I did. *(With a yawn.)* Bah! Breakfast can wait... First things first... A little nap will clear my head... *(He goes up to the bed and sits down on it, jumping up quickly with a cry.)* Ayyy!... What in blazes...? *(Picking something up.)* A hairpin?... A woman's... *(Apostrophizing, toward the door, up center.)* Really, madame! I'll thank you not to leave your vulgar little trinkets lying about! *(To himself.)* Did you ever... She'll hear from me!... *(Yawning.)* After my nap...

He pulls the curtain closed. The stage remains empty. After a few moments, FRISETTE enters, up center, still carrying her bag and holding a letter.

FRISETTE, *placing the bag down on one of the chairs, left, to herself*: Of all things... What nasty news, poor angel! *(Looking the letter over.)* His wet nurse is ill and they'll have to bring him here! *(Pocketing it, apostrophizing.)* Well, at least I'll have you with me, precious! And not only on Sunday!... I'll just have to do my work here I'm afraid. *(She takes her crocheting from her bag and lays it on the other chair, left.)* Auntie will understand when I explain... *(Taking a loaf of bread and a large salami from her bag.)* But breakfast first... *(She goes over to put them on the table, but stops, surprised.)* What?... Pigs' feet?... Who's... *(Looking up center.)* Oh! Madame Ménachet!... No! I don't believe it! Eating here? In my room?... Of all the... Well, we'll see about that! *(She puts her food and bag down, takes the other loaf and the pigs' feet, and places the latter in the wash basin and the* *former on the pitcher, replacing them on the plate with her own food.)* Of all the ill-bred… So much for your feet, madame!… Now then, my knife and fork… *(Looking around.)* Ah…

Taking the key from under the vase, right, going to her room, up right, she unlocks the door, exits, and pulls it shut, loudly, obviously in bad humor.

GAUTIER, *wakened by the sound, still behind the curtain*: Come in!… Who's there?… *(Pulling the curtain aside, getting up, to himself.)* I could have sworn someone knocked… *(Going over to the table.)* What… *(Holding up the salami.)* Where did this come from? I don't remember… *(He looks around and sees the pigs' feet in the wash basin and the loaf of bread on the pitcher.)* And my pigs' feet!… My… Damn! More of that old hag's little tricks!… Who does she think she is? Just because I know her sex for what it is!… Her sex? Ha!… Maybe fifty years ago… Even then… *(He mimes choking the salami, angrily, then throws it out the open window, down right, along with* FRISETTE*'s bread.)* So much for her! *(Moving the table and chair center and placing them at an angle.)* There!… Now for my food!… *(Apostrophizing, toward the door, up center.)* My food, madame!… Like a gentleman… *(He takes the table cloth from the mantelpiece, left, and spreads it out on the table, placing the pigs' feet on the plate and his bread beside it, then looks around, mumbling.)* And my napkin… And my knife and fork… *(Looking down left.)* Ah, of course…

He takes the key from under the vase on the mantelpiece, left, opens the door, down left, exits, and closes it. At the same time, FRISETTE *returns, up right, with a napkin, knife, and fork.*

FRISETTE, *approaching the table, in surprise*: The table cloth?… When did I… And just look at that! *(Putting the things down and straightening out the table, noticing the pigs' feet.)* What?… Her pigs' feet? Again?… Is this her idea of a joke? *(Facing the door, up center.)* Well, madame! It's not mine! *(She takes the pigs' feet and goes to the window, down right, about to throw them out.)* Here's what I think of your disgusting feet!

Just as she is about to fling them out the window, GAUTIER *enters, down left, with his utensils.*

GAUTIER, *seeing her maneuver*: What?… Stop!

FRISETTE, *letting them fly*: So there!

GAUTIER: What are you—

FRISETTE, *slamming the window shut, turning*: What? Who… *(Shocked.)* A man!

GAUTIER: A woman!

FRISETTE: In my room!

GAUTIER: In mine!

FRISETTE: Mine!

GAUTIER: Mine!

FRISETTE: Mine, I tell you!

GAUTIER: Nonsense! I've paid my rent! *(He pulls a piece of paper from his back trouser pocket, brandishing it.)* See? I have my receipt!

FRISETTE, *going to her bag, doing likewise*: And I have mine!

GAUTIER, *angrily*: I'll thank you to leave, woman!

FRISETTE, *approaching, menacingly*: Well, we'll see about that!

GAUTIER, *backing away, eager to avoid contact*: Please! Keep your distance! *(Calling.)* Madame!... Madame Ménachet! *(To FRISETTE.)* A hundred feet!... Two hundred feet!...

FRISETTE, *replacing the paper, calling*: Madame Ménachet!

GAUTIER, *likewise, calling louder*: Madame Ménachet!

FRISETTE, *pointing up center, at the top of her voice*: Out!

GAUTIER, *pointing with his knife and fork*: Out!

FRISETTE, *calling*: Madame!

GAUTIER, *calling*: Madame!

MADAME MENACHET appears at the door, up center.

MADAME MENACHET: What's all the fuss?... *(Seeing them together, with a start.)* Ayyy!... *(At a loss for words.)* I... I...

GAUTIER: You...

He slams the knife and fork down on the table.

FRISETTE: You...

Each one seizes her by one arm and they drag her bodily down center.

MADAME MENACHET: I... I see you've met...

FRISETTE *and* **GAUTIER**: *Oh!*

MADAME MENACHET, *babbling*: You... You know each other... How nice...

GAUTIER, *pointing to FRISETTE*: Please explain that, madame!

FRISETTE, *pointing to GAUTIER*: And that!... What is it?

GAUTIER, *continuing*: And what is it doing in my room?

FRISETTE: In mine! In mine!

MADAME MENACHET: Please!... It's—

GAUTIER: Mine!

MADAME MENACHET, *pointing to GAUTIER*: His...

GAUTIER, *to FRISETTE*: See?

MADAME MENACHET, *pointing to FRISETTE*: And hers...

FRISETTE, *to GAUTIER*: See?

MADAME MENACHET: It's both...

FRISETTE, } *thunderstruck, together*: { Both?...What?
GAUTIER, } { What?...Both?

MADAME MENACHET, *shaking herself free*: If you let me explain...

GAUTIER: Please do!

FRISETTE: I wish you would!

She moves the table and chair back to their original position.

MADAME MENACHET: You see... It's... It's really very simple. There... There used to be a wall... *(Pointing.)* There...

FRISETTE: And that isn't there now!

GAUTIER, *to MADAME MENACHET*: Then I'll thank you to have it put back!

MADAME MENACHET: But...

FRISETTE: Immediately, madame!

MADAME MENACHET: But… You can just imagine it's there… *(With a gesture, cutting the room in half.)* Can't you?

FRISETTE: Oh! Of all the…

GAUTIER: Imagine it, indeed!

FRISETTE: The proprietor will hear about this, madame!

GAUTIER, *stamping his foot*: I'm giving my notice!

MADAME MENACHET, *first to one, then the other*: Please!… Mademoiselle… Monsieur… He… He'll fire me!… Please! If you could just wait a little while… Number ten will be vacant! *(Aside.)* I'll put Plouque in the cellar. He'll never know the difference.

FRISETTE: I'll take it!

GAUTIER: So will I!

MADAME MENACHET: What? Both of you?… Then why bother…

FRISETTE: No! It's mine!

GAUTIER: Fine! If you insist! *(Stamping his foot, announcing like an auctioneer.)* Sold! *(Aside.)* To the disagreeable female with the ugly hat!… *(Aloud, to FRISETTE.)* I hope you'll both be very happy!

MADAME MENACHET: If you'll just be patient, mademoiselle… *(To GAUTIER.)* You too, monsieur… *(To FRISETTE.)* I'll let you know as soon as the room is ready.

FRISETTE: Yes! See that you do!

GAUTIER: And the sooner the better!

They push her bodily out the door, up center, and slam it shut.

FRISETTE: Of all things…

GAUTIER, *coming down right, pacing up and down, angrily, to himself*: Disgusting!

FRISETTE, *to herself*: Did you ever…

GAUTIER: A woman! In my room!

FRISETTE, *down left, aside*: A man! In my room!… Oh!

GAUTIER: I'd better wash my hands!

He stops at the basin and proceeds to do so.

FRISETTE: Lovely!… Simply lovely!

GAUTIER, *pacing again, aside*: You'll see… My liver…

FRISETTE, *aside*: How long is he going to keep pacing?

GAUTIER, *aside*: The shock will be too much for it!

FRISETTE, *aloud, to GAUTIER*: Really, monsieur… *(Sarcastically.)* I hope you don't intend to honor me with your presence much longer!

GAUTIER, *pacing*: Certainly not!

FRISETTE: Especially since you seem to have a passion for exercise! I should think you would prefer to do it out of doors!

GAUTIER: It's raining, mademoiselle.

FRISETTE: Oh? Let me give you an umbrella! I insist…

She makes a move toward the door, up right.

GAUTIER, *stopping her*: Don't trouble yourself! I'm not leaving… But please… If you have somewhere to go…

FRISETTE, *aside*: Ha! If he thinks I'm going to leave him here…

She takes off her coat and bonnet, puts them on the coat-rack, and returns to the table.

GAUTIER: Don't stand on ceremony!

FRISETTE: That's quite all right... *(Sitting down.)* I'm staying!

GAUTIER, *stamping his foot*: So am I! *(He crosses left and sits down on the chair with her crocheting.)* Ayyy! *(Jumping up.)* Pins! Needles!... *(Flinging the crocheting onto the other chair, by her bag.)* What next?

FRISETTE: I'll thank you not to... Oh!

As she crosses left and retrieves it, placing it in her bag, he takes his pipe from a pocket, lights it, and begins puffing ostentatiously.

GAUTIER: This should help pass the time until the room is ready.

FRISETTE: What?... Oh no!... No, no, no!...*(She opens the window, down right.)* Not that... that...

GAUTIER: What are you doing? It's freezing!

FRISETTE: Too bad!

She sits back down at the table.

GAUTIER: Then I have no choice but to get into bed and under the covers.

He stands up, puts his pipe down on the table, and begins to take off his jacket.

FRISETTE, *scandalized*: In my bed, monsieur?

GAUTIER: No, mine!

FRISETTE: Mine, I said!

GAUTIER: Then in ours, mademoiselle!

FRISETTE: Oh! Bite your tongue, you... you...

GAUTIER, *taking the pipe and puffing great clouds of smoke at her as they talk*: Ah! Of course!... How crass of me not to realize... No doubt you're waiting for your lover, mademoiselle... Some vile scoundrel...

FRISETTE, *coughing*: My...

GAUTIER: Some vulgar churl...

FRISETTE: Oh!... I'll... I'll have you know... I'm a virtuous young woman, monsieur!

GAUTIER: Of course... Of course...

FRISETTE: I have principles... Morals...

The door, up center, opens, and MADAME MENACHET *appears.*

GAUTIER: Ah! Is number ten ready?

MADAME MENACHET, *ignoring him, to* FRISETTE: Someone to see you, mademoiselle...

GAUTIER, *trying to attract her attention*: I say...

MADAME MENACHET, *continuing*: With the baby... All wrapped up in a cradle, the little doll...

FRISETTE: Already?

She moves up center, joins MADAME MENACHET, *and they both exit briefly.*

GAUTIER: Baby indeed!... *(Apostrophizing.)* Well, "virtuous young woman"! So much for your principles and morals... *(Emphasizing.)* mademoiselle!

MADAME MENACHET *and* FRISETTE *reenter, carrying the cradle. In it, the baby can be heard whimpering and whining.*

FRISETTE: There, there, precious... There, there, my little angel...

They put the cradle down, center.

GAUTIER: On no! That's the limit! *(To* FRISETTE, *angrily.)* I didn't rent the cheapest... *(Quickly correcting himself.)* ...the most economical room in the house to have it overrun with things like that! *(Pointing.)* Dirty, loud, ugly things, mademoiselle!... *(Approaching the cradle.)* Will you please... *(As* FRISETTE *stops him in his tracks, to the baby.)* Be quiet, you!

FRISETTE: Don't you dare, monsieur! You lay a hand on my... You dare touch him, and—

GAUTIER: Get it out! *(Stamping his foot.)* Out! Out, you hear me? There's no room for the two of us!

MADAME MENACHET: You can leave if you like, monsieur!

GAUTIER: Oh?... Oh, can I now? *(Brandishing his receipt again.)* I've paid my rent! I'll leave when I'm good and ready! Or when number ten is good and ready! *(Aside.)* Old witch!

FRISETTE, *to* MADAME MENACHET: Don't mind him, madame... Come... We'll take my little angel inside.

They pick up the cradle and carry it off, up right, shutting the door.

GAUTIER, *calling after her*: Yes!... Please do!

He blows one last puff of smoke in her direction, then taps the pipe out in the fireplace, right, and sits down at the table. Throughout the following scene, the baby can be heard offstage, whimpering sporadically.

GAUTIER: Bah!... Women, women, women!... *(As* MADAME MENACHET *enters, up right.)* Faithless hussies! Liars, every one of them!...

MADAME MENACHET, *overhearing*: Present company excepted, monsieur!

GAUTIER: Present... Who asked you? *(Pointing right.)* She has the cheek to pretend to be an unblemished, virtuous, innocent young thing! With a baby, no less!... You see, madame? It's just as I was saying...

MADAME MENACHET: Oh? *(Giving him tit for tat.)* And who asked you? What difference does it make...

GAUTIER: What difference?... To me? No difference at all! It just goes to prove that I was right when I told you—

MADAME MENACHET, *interrupting*: And what if the baby isn't hers, monsieur?

GAUTIER: What if what?

MADAME MENACHET: What if the baby isn't hers, I said!

GAUTIER: Ha ha ha!... *(Mimicking.)* "You lay a hand on my... on *my* little angel..."

MADAME MENACHET: So?

GAUTIER: So, I think I can understand the language when I hear it!

MADAME MENACHET: The language, maybe, monsieur... But not the story!

GAUTIER: Story? What story?

MADAME MENACHET: Hers!

GAUTIER, *incredulous*: Pfff!

MADAME MENACHET: Yes, monsieur. It's her baby... But only because she adopted the little dear...

GAUTIER: Pfff!

MADAME MENACHET: Don't "pfff" me, monsieur! I'm telling you… It was an orphan… Like she told me… When her cousin Philomèle passed away, poor thing…

She crosses herself.

GAUTIER, *suspecting*: Philomèle?

MADAME MENACHET: Philomèle Dubois, I think…

GAUTIER, *jumping up*: What?… Did you say…

MADAME MENACHET, *ignoring his surprise*: So you see how wrong you are! Say what you want about women, monsieur… Present company excepted… That one is a jewel! A gem!… And it won't hurt you to spend a few more hours under the same roof!

She exits, up center.

GAUTIER: My God! Is it possible?… That child… *(Pacing.)* Philomèle's?… No, no… "Dubois" is such a common name… There must be dozens… It… It can't be!… *(Stopping to reflect.)* But "Philomèle"? *(Stamping his foot.)* God in heaven! It… It must be hers! *(Struck by an obvious thought.)* But then… Who…? No!… Me?… Oh… *(Reconsidering.)* Or the other one… That Edgar… Edmond… *(Babbling.)* That…That Edouard… Whatever… It… It must be his… I mean… He must be… He's the one she cheated on me with. Or even someone else!… If she cheated with one, she could have… Why not? Women, after all…

FRISETTE'S VOICE, *offstage, right*: There, there, Gabriel… Don't cry, my little angel…

GAUTIER: Gabriel?… *(Stammering.)* Ga… Ga… *(Shocked.)* Oh! He has my name! They gave him…That means… *(Going upstage.)* Oh! That proves it! That means he… That child… *(Coming back down.)* Why not? It's possible… I… I'll have to find out… Make sure… I'll figure out the dates… Subtly, of course…

FRISETTE enters, up right, and goes over to her bag, still on the chair, left.

GAUTIER: Ah! Mademoiselle… *(FRISETTE, ignoring him, takes a doll from her bag.)* Mademoiselle… *(Clearing his throat to attract her attention.)* Ahem… Ahem… *(As pleasantly as possible, as she continues to ignore him.)* I say… *(Noticing the doll.)* Is he old enough to play with dolls?… Of course, he must be… *(As she moves up right.)* How old did you say he was?

FRISETTE, *stopping at the door, finally acknowledging his presence, archly*: I didn't, monsieur!

GAUTIER: No… That's true… *(To himself.)* Subtly, Gabriel… Subtly… *(Aloud.)* And who is the father, mademoiselle?

FRISETTE, *turning*: Oh! How dare you, monsieur!… What concern is that of yours?

GAUTIER: It… It's just that… It seemed to me just now… When I saw him… Something about his chin… The dimple… *(Quickly covering his chin.)* I… I thought it looked familiar. Like someone's I used to know… A friend… I thought perhaps I knew the father.

FRISETTE, *confronting him*: Well, if you did, monsieur, you knew the scum of the earth!

GAUTIER, *aside*: Of course! Edouard!

FRISETTE, *continuing*: And if I had him here… *(She takes a pin from her hair and plunges it into the doll.)* That… That wretch! That… Gautier!

GAUTIER, *with a start, clutching his chest*: What? *(Aside.)* Oh my!… *(Aloud.)* What did you say?

FRISETTE: Nothing… Not a thing…

GAUTIER: Sorry, I…I thought you said… You mentioned a name… A friend of mine… *(With a casual wave.)* An acquaintance, that is… A baker…

FRISETTE: A monster, monsieur!

GAUTIER: Well…

FRISETTE: A heartless monster, who abandoned his child!… A baby!

GAUTIER: But… But perhaps he had a reason. Perhaps—

FRISETTE: A reason? To leave its mother helpless?

GAUTIER: You never know… I mean… Perhaps she was unfaithful!

FRISETTE: Philomèle? Impossible! She didn't have an unfaithful bone in her body…

GAUTIER: But…

FRISETTE: Besides, why am I telling you?

GAUTIER: Please… Go on… Don't stop…

FRISETTE: Why? What business is it of yours? *(She turns her back.)* I don't even know you!

GAUTIER: But… But we live together… That is…

FRISETTE, *wheeling about*: Monsieur!

GAUTIER: And… And he… My friend Gautier… He told me the whole story…

FRISETTE: Oh yes! A pack of lies, I'm sure! *(Approaching him.)* Well, now you'll hear the truth, monsieur!… Just as they were about to be married… Philomèle and that friend of yours…

GAUTIER: An acquaintance… Just an—

FRISETTE: He pretends he has to leave on important business. The wedding will have to wait… And she loves him so much… She finds him so irresistible…

GAUTIER, *aside, fatuously*: Well…

FRISETTE: …that she actually believes him! She actually trusts the swine to keep his word! And she sends for her brother to come to the wedding…

GAUTIER, *aside*: Her brother?

FRISETTE: Poor, innocent lamb!

GAUTIER: Who, her brother?

FRISETTE: Philomèle, monsieur! Poor gullible fool…

GAUTIER: And… And this brother of hers… What did you say his name was?

FRISETTE: I didn't!… But it was Edouard, if that's any concern of yours.

GAUTIER, *shocked, aside*: My God! *(Aloud, stammering.)* It… It…

FRISETTE, *sarcastically*: And it still is, I suppose…

GAUTIER, *on whom the irony is lost*: Her brother…

FRISETTE: Well, the other one never did come back! But that shouldn't surprise you if he's a friend of yours, monsieur!

GAUTIER: An acquaintance… Only—

FRISETTE: Just like the rest of you! You're all the same!

She pulls the hairpin from the doll and crosses to the mantelpiece, left.

GAUTIER, *as she places it in the pincushion, aside, pacing*: Then… There's no doubt! If he was her brother, that makes me… That means I'm… I must be… I… I had a baby… Of all things!… Now what? *(As* FRISETTE *crosses back, up right, aloud, pointing to the door.)* Oh!… Can I give the little doll a kiss?

FRISETTE, *misunderstanding*: What? *(With a shrug, holding out the doll to his lips.)* If you like… *(Aside.)* Odd chap!

GAUTIER, *recoiling*: What?… No, no! *(Pointing.)* The child… That little doll!

FRISETTE: So you can frighten him, monsieur?

GAUTIER: Can't I just take a peek?

FRISETTE: But I thought you couldn't stand the… *(Emphasizing.)* the "dirty, loud, ugly little things!"

GAUTIER: Me? What ever gave you that idea?

FRISETTE: "What ever" indeed!

GAUTIER: I adore them!

FRISETTE, *aside*: Very odd… *(Aloud.)* Well, just a peek… *(Opening the door a crack.)* Shhh! He's sleeping…

GAUTIER, *pulling the door open, about to go in, admiringly*: Oh!

FRISETTE, *stopping him*: Shhh!… Please!… *(Shutting the door.)* You'll wake him, for heaven's sake!

GAUTIER: Just a little kiss…

FRISETTE: Really, monsieur! *(Aside.)* What ever has got into him?

GAUTIER, *stamping his foot, aside*: Damnation!

FRISETTE: Please!

GAUTIER: A little peck on the cheek isn't going to wake him!

He goes to open the door.

FRISETTE, *stopping him*: Don't…

GAUTIER: But… He takes after his father…

The baby can be heard beginning to whimper again, and continues to do so throughout the scene.

FRISETTE: Oh! You see?

GAUTIER: He's a heavy sleeper…

FRISETTE: What are you… Who?

GAUTIER: My… My acquaintance… That Gautier fellow… He sleeps like a log! It's common knowledge…

FRISETTE: Don't mention his name!

GAUTIER: But what if… I mean, it could happen, you know…

FRISETTE: What? What could happen?

GAUTIER: What if… *(Pointing to the door, up right, with his pipe.)* What if little Gabriel… What if his father… It's possible, you know…

FRISETTE, *losing patience*: What is possible, monsieur?

GAUTIER: What if his papá suddenly came back to claim him? A father has rights…

FRISETTE: Not that one, my friend!

GAUTIER, *gesticulating*: But he does! Of course he—

FRISETTE, *sharply*: He doesn't!

GAUTIER: But…But…

FRISETTE: There are no "buts"! It's the law, monsieur! When Philomèle passed away… When that poor little angel was left all alone…

GAUTIER, *touched*: Oh…

FRISETTE: When I saw him reaching out his tiny hands… Reaching out to my heart…

GAUTIER: Tsk tsk tsk!

FRISETTE: I had no choice! I said to myself: "Frisette…" That's my name, monsieur… "Frisette, you have no choice. He's an orphan now, and fate has placed him on your path. From now on you're his mother."

GAUTIER: You…

FRISETTE: And no one can take him from me. Not even that monster of a father of his!

GAUTIER: But… But…

FRISETTE: So let your friend Gautier—

GAUTIER: Acquaintance, mademoiselle…

FRISETTE: Yes, well… Let him put that in his pipe and smoke it!

She turns on her heel and exits quickly, up right. Throughout the rest of the scene the baby's offstage whimpering gradually subsides.

GAUTIER, *alone*: Damnation! *(He is about to stamp his foot but looks toward the door and thinks better of it.)* Shhh!… *(Crossing left, on tiptoes.)* Damn! Damn! Damn!… Now there's a situation for you! I have a son and I don't have a son! I find him and I lose him, all at the same time! Of all the… But what can I do? How can I prove… A father, after all… No doubt who's the mother!… Legally, that is… Yes, she has the law on her side, and she knows it. *(Pacing, left.)* Still, I can't desert my child. My own flesh and blood… It's not like before… I mean, how was I to know?… But now… Now that I do… I can't let a stranger keep him, whatever the law says! Not now that I've found him… *(Crossing right.)* Not now that I… Oh! Not now that I'm willing… *(He places his hand tentatively on the doorknob.)* No, I mustn't… Shhh!… Shhh!… She'll have my head! *(He retreats, up right, and sits down at the table.)* If only there were some way… If only… *(After a moment of silent musing.)* Eureka! *(Jumping up.)* There is!… Of course there is! *(Pointing up right.)* Me… Her… Why not?… She's a woman, I know, but… *(Repressing a grimace.)* So what? For my son?… A little self-sacrifice… A little suffering… *(To himself.)* Why not, Gabriel? That's the only way… For your son, old man! Your son!… *(Downstage, pacing back and forth.)* Ah! But how? That's the question!… How do I win her heart? What if my charm falls on deaf ears? What if she resists?… It's not likely, but it's possible, after all… Perhaps with a poem?… Bah!… A serenade or two?… *(At the window, down right, looking out.)* No! Too many neighbors… They would think it was for them… A fancy loaf of bread?… *(Reflecting for a moment.)* No, not very romantic… A dinner? With violins?… A dozen oysters?… But what if she doesn't like them? It's possible… Some people… *(Down right.)* Wait! I've got it!… Flowers!… Of course!… But where, this time of day?… *(Looking out the window.)* Ah! *(Taking the tongs from the fireplace, right.)* The neighbor won't mind if I borrow them for a while. Besides, it's in a good cause! *(He leans out the window and plucks some unseen flowers with the tongs.)* There…

As he comes down right, FRISETTE enters, up right, and crosses left.

FRISETTE, *aside*: Finally! He's asleep…

GAUTIER, *turning and noticing her*: Ah!

He replaces the tongs.

FRISETTE, *continuing*: Now if he'll only stay that way while I do my work…

GAUTIER, *awkwardly holding out the flowers to her*: Mademoiselle, if I may…

FRISETTE, *taken aback*: What?

GAUTIER: If you permit me… This token of my esteem…

FRISETTE: This what?

GAUTIER: This… These… It's a bouquet… Flowers, mademoiselle…

FRISETTE: I know what they are! But why, monsieur…

GAUTIER: A symbol… A tribute to your goodness…

FRISETTE: My…

GAUTIER: Your virtue, mademoiselle… Your kindness…

FRISETTE: Oh… *(Unable to hold back a laugh.)* Ha ha ha!

GAUTIER, *laughing along with her*: Ha ha ha! *(To himself.)* She's making fun of me!

FRISETTE: Did you ever…

GAUTIER, *to himself*: No matter… Go to it, Gabriel!

He thrusts the flowers into the vase on the mantelpiece, right.

FRISETTE: Flowers? For me?

GAUTIER: I thought they would make our room… *(Catching himself.)* Your room… A little cozier, mademoiselle…

FRISETTE: Of all things! *(Sarcastically.)* How gallant!

He takes the pitcher, up right, and pours some water into the vase.

GAUTIER, *aside*: I'm just no good at this sort of thing!

He replaces the pitcher and puts the vase noisily back on the mantelpiece.

FRISETTE: Shhh!… Please!… After all my trouble…

GAUTIER, *listening for a moment*: There!… He's asleep… *(Trying to make conversation.)* He certainly sleeps a lot, mademoiselle. *(Trying again, despite her silence.)* Is… Is that all he does?

FRISETTE: Like any baby his age, monsieur…

She crosses left, takes her lace from the chair, sits down, and begins her crocheting.

GAUTIER, *noncommittal*: Of course… Of course… *(Casually dragging the chair, up right, toward her.)* And he must be a little doll, I'm sure!

FRISETTE, *crocheting*: I should say! All plump and pink… Like a little cherub!

GAUTIER: My, my… *(Aside, flustered.)* My son… Plink and pump…Plunk and… *(Aloud.)* Is that work you're doing, mademoiselle?

FRISETTE: I daresay… The bills don't pay themselves, monsieur! It's either work or starve… Myself and my son!

GAUTIER: Of course… Of course… Another mouth to feed…

FRISETTE: No matter… I would work all night if I had to.

GAUTIER, *touched*: Oh!… *(Aside.)* Poor thing! *(Aloud.)* Really, mademoiselle… *(Aside.)* Tsk tsk tsk! *(Aloud.)* I had no idea… Who would have guessed…? Such a noble gesture… *(Aside.)* Tsk tsk tsk!

FRISETTE: Noble? Not at all…

GAUTIER: To adopt that poor, helpless little soul… To sweat and slave for him, day and night… When other people… *(Sitting down, awkwardly.)* Other people as young and… and as pretty…

FRISETTE: Please, monsieur—

GAUTIER: No, no! You are!… And they wouldn't, mademoiselle… They would rather fritter away their time in the dancehalls!… In the theaters, in the cafés… With this lover and that… *(Stopping her with a gesture as she is about to object.)* No, mademoiselle! You work day and night, without thinking of yourself. Without thinking how you might destroy your health… Ruin your eyes… Turn them all red… *(Moving the chair a little closer.)* Very nice eyes, I must say…

FRISETTE: Oh?

GAUTIER, *staring at them*: Strange! Not long ago I couldn't look at them. And now…

FRISETTE, *looking at him*: And now, monsieur?

GAUTIER: Now I… I can't seem to stop…

FRISETTE, *aside*: Oh my!

GAUTIER, *aside*: Damnation! Was I blind?

FRISETTE, *a little uneasily*: Monsieur…

GAUTIER, *suddenly*: Mademoiselle! May I ask you something?

FRISETTE: If you like…

GAUTIER: Have you… Have you ever thought of getting married?

FRISETTE: Me? Heavens no!

GAUTIER: Well, you should! *(She gives him a quizzical look.)* If you'll pardon the liberty!… Because… Because, when a pretty, young woman… *(Bumbling.)* When a pretty, young woman is… is so young and… and so pretty…

FRISETTE, *softly*: Monsieur…

GAUTIER: And so intelligent, and… And so kind… Well, you shouldn't save all that for… *(Struggling to find an apt comparison.)* for the king of Denmark, for goodness' sake!

FRISETTE: Heavens! I don't even know him!

GAUTIER: No… I didn't suppose… *(Reiterating.)* You should share it with a husband! A good, solid French husband, mademoiselle!

FRISETTE, *with a wry little laugh*: Ha ha!… There's only one problem, I'm afraid…

GAUTIER: What?

FRISETTE: A little one…

GAUTIER: Where?

FRISETTE, *pointing right*: There…

GAUTIER: The child? *(Getting up.)* The little cherub?… A problem?… Au contraire!… Au contraire, mademoiselle! You don't know what you're saying.

FRISETTE, *getting up*: What? You think…

GAUTIER, *getting up*: Think?… I know!… There are men who don't care a rap about gossip…

FRISETTE: Not at the beginning, perhaps... But later... When they throw it up in your face...

GAUTIER, *misunderstanding*: Throw up?... Why should anyone—

FRISETTE: When they keep thinking the worst, I mean... Tattling... Spreading nasty rumors...

GAUTIER: Bah! If you love the child...

FRISETTE: Love him? With all my heart, monsieur...

GAUTIER: Then, if for no other reason than to give him a father... It might not seem like much, but... A father is a useful thing to have, mademoiselle. Maybe not right now, but later, when he grows up... When he wants to make his way in the world... Unless you have a name, people look at you as if... As if you're nothing... A nobody...

FRISETTE, *reflecting*: I'm afraid you're right...

GAUTIER: Besides, how can you raise him all by yourself? No offense, but... *(Pointing to the crocheting in her hands.)* Certainly that can't support the two of you!

FRISETTE, *proudly*: On a good day I make two whole francs, monsieur!

GAUTIER: Ha ha ha! Two francs!... Try living on that! Try raising him to be more than a... a potter's apprentice! If he's lucky!

FRISETTE: Oh... Poor little thing!

GAUTIER: But if you add to it what a husband earns... A good, honest worker, with a trade... Like a... Like a butcher... Or a baker...

FRISETTE: Or a candlestick maker, monsieur...

GAUTIER: No... Something important... Something people need... *(As if reflecting, with a nod.)* Yes... A baker, mademoiselle...

FRISETTE: Perhaps...

GAUTIER: Why then, who knows what he might become? There's no limit. He could be a... a magistrate... A statesman...

FRISETTE, *impressed*: Oh...

GAUTIER: A dentist, even!

FRISETTE: Yes, I suppose...

GAUTIER: I don't suppose... I know!... I'm not telling you to jump into the arms of the first man who comes your way! But... But if you just happen to find a nice, honest young man... With a good trade... Well, believe me, mademoiselle, you shouldn't waste any time!

FRISETTE: Oh!... I... I'll think about it, monsieur...

GAUTIER: Yes, you think!... And while you're thinking, I'm going to go get my pay... *(Emphasizing.)* For a week of honest work!... At a good trade, mademoiselle... Because I've got an idea. A wonderful idea... *(As he moves up center.)* Au revoir, Mademoiselle Frisette... We'll talk some more later...

FRISETTE: Au revoir, Monsieur... Monsieur... ? Why, I don't even know your name...

GAUTIER: Later... *(Hurrying.)* No time to chat... *(Aside.)* Damn! How do I tell her?

He exits.

FRISETTE, *alone*: He's right… Everything he says… He makes such good sense. Not like Bagalouche, poor thing…

MADAME MENACHET enters, up center.

MADAME MENACHET: Mademoiselle… Number ten is all ready… Any time…

FRISETTE: Ah!… Thank you, madame… I hope it was no trouble.

MADAME MENACHET: None at all, believe me… *(Aside.)* Upstairs? Downstairs?… Plouque can't tell the difference!

FRISETTE, *stopping her as she is about to leave*: Oh, madame… Something else… That young man… The one who lives here with me…

MADAME MENACHET: Mademoiselle!

FRISETTE, *flustered*: I mean… The one who sleeps in my bed… *(Quickly.)* When I'm not in it…

MADAME MENACHET: So?

FRISETTE: How well do you know him?

MADAME MENACHET: How well…?

FRISETTE: Yes… Is he… Does he… *(MADAME MENACHET gives her a blank look.)* What I mean is, does he have principles?

MADAME MENACHET: Him? I should say!… A real gem, mademoiselle… Pays his rent right on time… Only one fault, if you really want to know…

FRISETTE, *aside*: A fault? *(Aloud.)* What ever can it be?

MADAME MENACHET, *mysteriously, looking around to be sure no one is listening*: He doesn't like women, mademoiselle!

FRISETTE, *relieved*: Oh…

MADAME MENACHET: Can't stand the sight of them… *(As an afterthought.)* Except for me, that is.

FRISETTE: Well, if that's all… *(Aloud.)* But he seems so pleasant. A trifle odd, but… Why, just now—

MADAME MENACHET: Ha! Don't let him fool you!

FRISETTE: What?

MADAME MENACHET: It's a sham, mademoiselle! He's poison to our sex… Yours and mine!

FRISETTE: But…

MADAME MENACHET, *as an afterthought*: Well, yours at least…

FRISETTE: But I assure you—

MADAME MENACHET: Like a snake, mademoiselle… Sometimes he makes believe, but you can't trust him! Like a viper…

FRISETTE: But—

MADAME MENACHET: That's what he is!

FRISETTE: But what ever makes you think… How do you know?

MADAME MENACHET: He told me so himself! Just this morning he was saying: "If I had my way…" That's what he said… "If I had my way, I'd make them all suffer! I'd get rid of them all! Every last one…"

FRISETTE: How frightful!

MADAME MENACHET, *continuing*: "Present company excepted…"

FRISETTE: And he said that? *(Pointing to the upstage door.)* Him?... You're not thinking of someone else?

MADAME MENACHET: Please! I know my tenants!... Him!... Gautier...

FRISETTE, *with a start*: Gau... *(With a cry.)* What?... Did you... You didn't say "Gautier"?... You didn't—

MADAME MENACHET: Why not? That's his name... Gabriel Gautier!

FRISETTE, *aside*: Good Lord!... So that's what he's after!... Of course! It's so clear! So perfectly...Oh! Well! We'll see about that! *(Aloud.)* Madame Ménachet, please be so good as to take all my things upstairs! My clothes, my belongings... Everything!

MADAME MENACHET: Mademoiselle?

FRISETTE: Nothing will keep me in this room another minute! *(Pushing her up right, toward the door.)* Everything, you understand?

MADAME MENACHET: Whatever you say... *(Aside.)* Now what's got into her, I wonder...

She exits, mumbling.

FRISETTE, *angrily, to herself*: Oh!... That turnabout, all of a sudden... *(Coming down left, imitating.)* "Besides, how can you raise him all by yourself?..." How, indeed!... Well, thank you just the same! I don't need any help from you!... All that sweetness and light... Just so he can beat a path to his son!... And me? No more than a convenient excuse... A means to an end!... *(She strides up center, apostrophizing at the door.)* Well, monsieur, that's precisely what it is! The end!... The end of your little game! *(Coming right, to the mirror, addressing her reflection.)* You poor fool, Frisette! How could you think... Look at you... He almost convinced you... *(Examining her reflection, sadly.)* Still, if I don't get married... If I stay a spinster lady... No! An old maid!... What he said was true. *(Looking toward the door, right.)* My poor little angel... What kind of dreadful life will he have? And it will all be my fault! *(Crossing left, angrily.)* Well, he's not the only man in the world! Why shouldn't I marry someone else? If I want to... There's always Bagalouche... He would have me in a minute! And... *(Trying to be enthusiastic.)* And he's a good, honest young man! And... And he loves me! Sincerely, I mean... Not like... *(Determined, going to the mantelpiece, right.)* I know... I'll write him a note. Yes, that's what I'll do... And the next time he comes knocking... If he's willing to have me and my Gabriel too... To give him his name... It's not much of a name, but it's better than nothing. And better than "Gautier"!... *(She sits down at the desk and begins to write.)* "Monsieur... I would consider your kind proposal of marriage on one condition. Namely, that you declare my Gabriel to be your son. Sincerely..." There! Short and to the point... So much for you, Monsieur Gautier!

As she stands up, a knock is heard at the door, up center.

BAGALOUCHE'S VOICE: Mam'selle!... Mam'selle Frisette!

FRISETTE: Oh!... *(To herself.)* Speak of the devil... *(Aloud.)* Yes?

BAGALOUCHE'S VOICE: It's me... I'm back!... Have you thought yet?

FRISETTE: I'm still thinking...

BAGALOUCHE'S VOICE: About saying yes?

FRISETTE: Perhaps...

BAGALOUCHE'S VOICE, *delighted*: "Perhaps"? You mean... Maybe?

FRISETTE: Yes… But only on one condition…

BAGALOUCHE'S VOICE, *eagerly*: I accept! I accept!

FRISETTE: But you don't even know—

BAGALOUCHE'S VOICE: I don't have to! I accept!

FRISETTE, *opening the door a crack and handing the unseen* BAGALOUCHE *the note*: Here, monsieur… Read this… The terms of the marriage contract…

She closes the door.

BAGALOUCHE'S VOICE, *ecstatically*: Ah! Mam'selle Frisette!… Mam'selle…

He can be heard mumbling as he reads.

FRISETTE: Well?

BAGALOUCHE'S VOICE: Ah! Mam'selle! You've made me the happiest man in the world!

FRISETTE: You understand?

BAGALOUCHE'S VOICE: I accept! I accept!

FRISETTE, *sighing*: Thank you, Monsieur Bagalouche…

BAGALOUCHE'S VOICE: Please! Call me "Constantine"!

FRISETTE, *sadly*: Constantine…

BAGALOUCHE'S VOICE: Now I'll run off and sign the papers. To make everything legal… But don't worry, I'll be back! I'll be back!… Ah! Mam'selle Frisette… *(As his voice trails off down the stairs.)* Mam'selle Frisette…

FRISETTE: At least that one really loves me! *(Looking at her reflection.)* So?… Madame Bagalouche!… It's not the prettiest name… But at least my son will have one. And that's all that matters…

GAUTIER *enters, up center, with his arms full of various objects.*

GAUTIER, *happily*: Mademoiselle!

FRISETTE, *jumping up*: Oh!

GAUTIER: Don't get up… It's only me… With a few little things for… *(Motioning toward the door, up right.)* for him… See? *(Holding them up, one by one, and laying them on the table.)* A baby bottle… A rattle… A little stuffed monkey… A drum… A copy of *What Every Young Man Should Know*… For later, of course… *(Holding up a chamber pot.)* And for now…

FRISETTE, *approaching him*: But monsieur…

GAUTIER: I know it's not proper to accept gifts from strangers. But since they're for him… And since I'm not going to be one for long…

FRISETTE: What? One what?

GAUTIER: There! I've said it!… Oh well… I was bound to let it out sooner or later, mademoiselle… Will you marry me?

FRISETTE, *startled*: Will I… *(Recovering her aplomb.)* Impossible, monsieur!… Now that I know who you are! You needn't—

GAUTIER, *flustered*: You… You mean… You know…

FRISETTE: Everything, Monsieur Gautier!

GAUTIER, *dejected*: Oh… Then… I understand, mademoiselle… I understand how you must detest me! How you must never want to lay eyes on me again!… How you… How you… *(Crossing to a chair, left, and sitting down.)* Oh…

(Nodding, sadly.) I understand... Just when I realized how much I... *(Turning aside, softly.)* how much I love you...

FRISETTE, *aside*: What?

GAUTIER: It took me a while, but... I thought I could make you happy. Both of you, mademoiselle... But... *(Melodramatically.)* It just wasn't meant to be!

FRISETTE, *aside*: Good heavens! Is it possible?

GAUTIER, *sighing*: Well... That's that, I'm afraid... *(Standing up.)* Let's say no more about it... *(Pointing right.)* Or about him... Besides, he'll do better without me in his life... To ruin it the way I've ruined so many others...

FRISETTE, *about to object, weakly*: But monsieur...

GAUTIER: Keep him... Take care of him... Love him... *(Dejectedly, moving to leave.)* Farewell!

FRISETTE, *aside*: Oh...

GAUTIER, *stopping at the door*: Just promise me that I can come and see him from time to time...

FRISETTE, *touched*: Monsieur...

GAUTIER: Even bring him a trinket now and then...A little pittance from my savings... For him... For you...

FRISETTE: But...

GAUTIER: At least that will give me an excuse to see you...And brighten my days, mademoiselle!

FRISETTE, *aside, delighted*: Can it be? He really loves me! *(Aloud.)* Monsieur...

GAUTIER, *approaching her*: Please?

FRISETTE: Really, Monsieur Gautier... You... You're a very fine young man, and... I would be honored to...

GAUTIER: "To"... ? "To"...?

FRISETTE, *coming downstage, to herself, changing her tone*: What am I saying? I can't... Bagalouche is already signing the papers!

GAUTIER, *insistently*: "To," mademoiselle?

FRISETTE, *continuing, aside*: I... I can't leave him with my Gabriel and no wife! It wouldn't be right! *(Aloud, to* GAUTIER.*)* I'm sorry, monsieur... Terribly sorry, believe me... But I simply cannot marry you.

GAUTIER: Oh!... *(Stamping his foot.)* Why?... Tell me, mademoiselle...

There is a knock at the door, up center.

BAGALOUCHE'S VOICE: Mam'selle Frisette! Mam'selle Frisette!

FRISETTE: Oh!

GAUTIER, *aside*: Who the devil...?

BAGALOUCHE'S VOICE: I went to sign the papers...

FRISETTE: Oh my! I... I know...

BAGALOUCHE'S VOICE: But they told me I couldn't! They said... They said somebody else already signed them!

FRISETTE, *hopefully*: What?... But...

BAGALOUCHE'S VOICE: Somebody with an armful of junk and... and a chamber pot, mam'selle!

GAUTIER, *aside*: Junk?... My word!...

FRISETTE: But who?

GAUTIER, *aloud*: Can't you guess?

FRISETTE, *to GAUTIER*: You… You mean… You?

GAUTIER, *taking the chamber pot from the table and holding it up, as if in a toast*: To my son, mademoiselle!… Our son!

FRISETTE: Oh!

GAUTIER: And a lucky thing I got there when I did! There seems to be quite a demand today for babies!

BAGALOUCHE'S VOICE: Is somebody in there with you, mam'selle?

FRISETTE: Why, yes…

GAUTIER, *in a deep voice*: I'm her dressmaker, monsieur! For a fitting…

FRISETTE, *to GAUTIER, in a whisper*: Monsieur!

BAGALOUCHE'S VOICE: Oh… Well, then… I'll come back…

GAUTIER, *in the same voice*: Regards to the family!

BAGALOUCHE'S VOICE, *as his voice trails off*: I'll come back…

FRISETTE: Poor thing!

GAUTIER: Are you sorry that I got there first?

FRISETTE, *quickly*: Certainly not!… *(Softly.)* I mean… I'm free now, monsieur…

GAUTIER: So am I, mademoiselle!… And being free is all well and good. But…

FRISETTE: But…?

They draw close to each other

GAUTIER: But not being free is even better, don't you think?

FRISETTE: Oh yes!

GAUTIER, *with a gesture*: In a nice little room…

FRISETTE: With two beds…

GAUTIER: Two?

FRISETTE: Well…

GAUTIER: When one of them is a cradle!

They draw even closer but separate quickly as MADAME MENACHET enters suddenly, up right, carrying all of FRISETTE's belongings.

MADAME MENACHET, *noticing their move*: Ah!… *(To FRISETTE, approaching, slyly.)* Will you still be wanting number ten, mademoiselle?

FRISETTE: Of course!

MADAME MENACHET: Oh… I thought… For how long? A month? Two weeks?

FRISETTE: Well, that depends… *(To GAUTIER, in a whisper.)* Will it take us a month to get married, monsieur?

GAUTIER, *whispering*: Oh, less! Even less!

FRISETTE, *to MADAME MENACHET*: For two weeks, madame…

MADAME MENUCHET, *aside*: Then Plouque can go back…

GAUTIER, *taking FRISETTE aside, delighted*: Ah! Mademoiselle Frisette…

MADAME MENACHET, *continuing*: If he lasts that long…

GAUTIER, *continuing*: What can I say?

FRISETTE: Just don't say you have to go off on important business, and that the wedding can wait!

GAUTIER: Never!... Never!... *(Taking her hands in his.)* And, in the meantime...

FRISETTE: Monsieur?

GAUTIER: I'll... I'll come up to salt my feet... *(She gives him a quizzical look.)* My pigs' feet, mademoiselle... *(Going to the table, holding up the salt shaker.)* You didn't leave me any!

FRISETTE: Oh dear!... And you'll come every Sunday and visit your... our son...

GAUTIER: I will! I will!

FRISETTE: Well then, I think it's time you gave him a little kiss!

GAUTIER: Don't you think I should start with my wife? After all...

MADAME MENACHET, *agape, dropping all the items, aside*: His wife?

FRISETTE, *pushing him aside, wagging her forefinger*: A month, monsieur! And not until!

GAUTIER, *good-naturedly*: Bah! If you insist... *(Going upstage, to MADAME MENACHET.)* In that case...

MADAME MENACHET: But I thought you hated women, monsieur!

GAUTIER: Present company excepted!

He hugs her and plants a huge kiss on her lips. Suddenly the baby can be heard crying offstage.

MADAME MENACHET, *wiping her mouth with her sleeve*: Monsieur!

GAUTIER, *to FRISETTE*: So there!

FRISETTE, *holding out her hand to him*: Monsieur...

GAUTIER, *kissing it*: Mademoiselle...

They exit, up right, arm in arm.

MADAME MENACHET, *watching them go, hands on hips*: I never... Of all things... Of all things...

The baby can be heard cooing and gurgling contentedly, as the curtain falls.

CURTAIN.

The Well-Wooed Wench, or Beau's Jests

(Les prétendus de Gimblette, 1850)

"Dandré & Senneif"*

*__Paul Dandré:__ collaborative pseudonym of Eugène Labiche, Marc-Michel, and Auguste Lefranc; **Senneif:** pseudonym of Charles-Matharel de Fiennes

Characters

MACASSOU, an impecunious innkeeper in the provinces, near Lyon

RAOUL, his estranged nephew and talented member of an acting troupe

COUNT POPINOFF
DON RAMÓN
MODESTE BACHEFOLLE } supposed suitors

BARNABÉ, Macassou's sentimental domestic

FLOUPETTE, his niece, impatient to find a husband but not willing to compromise her principles

A country inn. Up center, a double door opening out to the road. In the right wall, up and down, two doors; the former, leading to the kitchen, the latter, to Floupette's room. Down left, a curtained alcove leading to the corridor off of which are the sleeping-rooms. Up right, against the wall, a sideboard, with a scraggly broom leaning against it. Up left, facing the side wall, a desk and chair. On it, a pen and inkwell, a mirror, and a vase with flowers. Near it, and close to the right wall, a standing coatrack with a man's coat hanging on it. Two dining tables with chairs, midstage right and down left. On one of the chairs of the stage right table, a woman's apron. Down right a floor plant. Other appropriate furnishings.

At rise, MACASSOU *is alone on stage.*

MACASSOU, *calling*: Barnabé!

BARNABE'S VOICE, *offstage, left*: What?

MACASSOU: Get in here! *(Under his breath.)* Lazy good-for-nothing!

BARNABE, *entering, left, grumbling*: Bah!

MACASSOU: How much can one man sleep? Even you!

BARNABE, *down center*: But I didn't get a bloody wink! *(Pointing left.)* Because of that one… The one who came in at three in the morning…

He yawns.

MACASSOU: A guest?

BARNABE: What else? Of course, a guest!

MACASSOU: Where did you put him?

BARNABE, *pointing left*: In number nine…

MACASSOU, *nodding*: Aha… And what is he like?

BARNABE: Nothing special…

MACASSOU: Young? Old?

BARNABE: Youngish, I guess… And pretty tired, if you ask me… Three in the morning, after all…

MACASSOU: Did he have bags?

BARNABE, *misunderstanding*: Under his eyes?

MACASSOU: Under his… *(Impatiently.)* Under his arms, idiot!

BARNABE: His arms? *(Aside.)* Funny place to have them… *(Aloud.)* Who knows? *(Going to the coatrack, up left, holding up the coat.)* He was wearing this…

MACASSOU: He was… No, you fool! Bags… Baggage… A trunk!

BARNABE: Oh… Yes, a big one… And heavy…

MACASSOU: And did he give you his name?

BARNABE: He didn't give me a thing! Not even a tip!

MACASSOU: Did he say what he wanted? Why he was here?

BARNABE: Did he say…? I'll say he did…

He pauses, yawning.

MACASSOU, *waiting*: Well?

BARNABE: Talk, talk, talk!… He wanted to know all about you. And mam'selle…

MACASSOU: My niece? Ha! Then he must be a suitor!

BARNABE: Another one?

MACASSOU: Day in, day out…

BARNABE, *aside*: But at three in the morning…

MACASSOU, *calling toward the door, down right*: Floupette!... Floupette!

FLOUPETTE appears at the door. BARNABE casts a tender glance in her direction.

FLOUPETTE: Yes, uncle dear?

MACASSOU: There's another one!

FLOUPETTE, *resigned*: There is?

MACASSOU: Yes! *(Pointing left.)* Number nine... *(As BARNABE heaves a quiet sigh.)* Another one...

FLOUPETTE, *coming downstage*: But... I think you're wrong. I've been counting. He must be number twelve. This month, I mean... So far...

MACASSOU: What?

FLOUPETTE, *beginning to count on her fingers*: First there was—

MACASSOU, *interrupting*: No, no, no!... Room number nine! Room...

FLOUPETTE, *naively*: Oh... Well... Nine or twelve... What's the difference?

BARNABE, *under his breath, with a shrug*: Three?

FLOUPETTE, *to MACASSOU, continuing*: Besides, I don't know why they bother! You always send them packing! There's never been a single one—

MACASSOU: Of course I do! But not before they've eaten, and drunk, and... and paid their bill! *(To BARNABE.)* Has this one had lunch?

BARNABE: Not yet...

MACASSOU: Well, go warm up the stew.

BARNABE: But he didn't order stew.

MACASSOU: So? That's what we're serving... Rabbit stew à la Macassou... And don't forget the spices. A few weeks don't help the flavor.

BARNABE, *aside*: Damn! Him and his rabbit stew!... And for all my bloody rivals!

He exits up right, grumbling, and with a longing glance at FLOUPETTE.

FLOUPETTE, *to MACASSOU*: But uncle dear, what if the gentleman doesn't like rabbit stew?

MACASSOU, *joining her, downstage*: So much the better! He'll pay for it anyway, and we'll save it for the next ones. And they'll pay for it too! That's what innkeeping is all about!

FLOUPETTE: Oh... I thought it was to serve the traveler...

MACASSOU: Well? That's what I'm doing! I'm serving them rabbit stew.

FLOUPETTE: But... The same one?

MACASSOU, *ignoring her objection*: And anyway, it's not to serve the traveler. It's to serve the innkeeper.

FLOUPETTE: Oh...

MACASSOU: And to fill his pockets!... Because mine need filling! Thanks to that new railroad from Paris to Lyon...

FLOUPETTE: The railroad?

MACASSOU: Why, it almost ruined my clientele!

FLOUPETTE: It did?

MACASSOU: The trains would whisk the travelers past...Toot toot! Toot toot!... The same ones who always used to stop before...Drink... Stay the night...

FLOUPETTE: Eat the stew...

MACASSOU: Spend their money... Now they would just go flying by, without a station to stop at for miles around... And taking your dowry with them, Floupette!

FLOUPETTE: Oh my! I didn't know...

MACASSOU: But that wasn't going to stop your uncle! Oh no!... *(Tapping his forehead.)* What did he do?... I'll tell you what I did... I hired three traveling salesmen... Three of my best clients...Well, former clients... And I have them go spread the word as far as they can, that rich old Macassou, the innkeeper, has a pretty, young niece to marry off, with a dowry as beautiful as she is!

FLOUPETTE: But uncle dear! I don't have—

MACASSOU: No... Not yet... But all the more reason to say that you do! They come, they settle in... They do their best to please you. They eat, they drink. The money flows like the wine... It's an endless parade of suitors!

FLOUPETTE: I know, but—

MACASSOU: And when they finally decide to ask me for your hand... "Never!" I tell them! Then I give them the bill... They pay... And off they go!

FLOUPETTE: Oh...

MACASSOU: Now that's what I call running an inn! And that's how all the suitors I say "No!" to now are giving you a dowry for the one I'll tell "Yes!"... Some one of these days...

FLOUPETTE: But uncle dear... I don't like when you keep saying "No!" to all of them! Really... I'm beginning to—

MACASSOU, *interrupting*: Now, now, Floupette... Just a little bit longer... Two years... Maybe three...

FLOUPETTE: Oh!

MACASSOU: The longer you wait, the richer you're going to be!

FLOUPETTE: Yes! And the older!

MACASSOU, *unable to deny her logic*: Well... Maybe a little...

FLOUPETTE: And nobody will want me! The parade will be over! I'll be old...

MACASSOU: Nonsense!... *(Emphasizing.)* Er... Only er...

FLOUPETTE: I beg your pardon? *(Aside.)* Er...?

MACASSOU: Older, Floupette!... But certainly not old!... No woman is ever old if she's rich! *(With a little laugh.)* The richer you get, the younger you're going to be!

FLOUPETTE, *not convinced*: Well... At this rate, uncle dear, by the time I'm thirty I'm sure I'll be nursing!

MACASSOU: Come, come... Let's not exaggerate! Just leave it all to me. I know what I'm doing.

FLOUPETTE, *with a sigh*: I hope so...

MACASSOU: And anyway, whose fault is it? If that wretched cousin of yours...My sister's son—

FLOUPETTE: Raoul?

MACASSOU: If he had known how to behave...

FLOUPETTE, *angrily*: Please, uncle dear! Don't even mention his name! I hate him! I can't bear the thought of him!... I—

MACASSOU: My sentiments exactly!

FLOUPETTE: After the way he acted… I would die an old maid sooner than marry that… that beast!

MACASSOU: Me too!… If I were you, I mean… You're absolutely right!

BARNABE enters, up right, with a casserole of food and an empty wine bottle, placing them on the table, down left.

BARNABE: The stew, monsieur.

MACASSOU, *to BARNABE*: Good!… Now, set the table so that everything is ready the minute he comes in. The white tablecloth… The clean one… The good silverware… And let's not forget our manners!

BARNABE, *as he goes to the sideboard, up right, taking out the items mentioned, as well as a napkin and a glass, under his breath*: Bah!

Without removing the casserole and bottle from the table, he goes about setting it, not without considerable difficulty, all the while gazing longingly at FLOUPETTE.

MACASSOU, *continuing, to FLOUPETTE*: I don't have to tell you how to act, Floupette. All smiles… Keep him happy…

FLOUPETTE: Yes, uncle dear.

MACASSOU, *moving up left*: Because the happier they are, the less they worry about how much they're spending! *(Fingering the coat on the coatrack.)* And, by the looks of it, this one shouldn't worry at all! *(Going right, taking the apron from the back of the chair, holding it out to her.)* Here! Put this on…

FLOUPETTE: But that's the one I wore for the other eleven!

MACASSOU: So? Why not wear it for the twelfth? When it's all worn out I'll buy you a new one.

BARNABE stands gazing at FLOUPETTE with the glass by his face.

BARNABE, *aside, heaving a breathy, romantic sigh*: Haaa!

MACASSOU, *noticing him*: What are you doing?

BARNABE, *caught up short, wiping the glass with the napkin*: Just cleaning the glass… It's got spots… *(He breathes on it several more times, intentionally, wiping it as he does.)* There!

MACASSOU, *catching sight of the empty wine bottle, holding it up*: What the… *(To BARNABE.)* Idiot! You forgot to put the wine in the Château-Lafitte bottle! *(Handing it to him, aside.)* Château Lafitte or "Château Macassou"? They never know the difference! *(Aloud, to BARNABE.)* Now go fill it and be quick about it!

BARNABE, *under his breath*: Bah!

As he goes up left, to the sideboard, to comply, a loud sigh is heard offstage.

FLOUPETTE: My goodness! What was that?

MACASSOU, *pointing left*: Him!… He's up, and he must be coming in. Ready? A nice big smile…

RAOUL appears at the curtained alcove, left.

RAOUL, *to MACASSOU*: Good morning, uncle!

MACASSOU, *taken aback*: What?

RAOUL, *to FLOUPETTE*: Cousin dear!

MACASSOU: You!

FLOUPETTE: Raoul!

RAOUL, *to MACASSOU*: Come! Let me give you a nice big hug!

MACASSOU, *pushing him away*: Don't you dare!

RAOUL, *to FLOUPETTE, holding out his arms*: Floupette?

BARNABE places the newly-filled bottle on the table, down left.

FLOUPETTE, *to RAOUL*: Oh! Keep your distance!

MACASSOU, *to BARNABE, pointing*: Take away the stew!

RAOUL, *putting his coat on*: Just a minute! I haven't eaten...

MACASSOU: And you won't! Not at my expense, you... you...

FLOUPETTE: The very idea!

RAOUL: What? *(To MACASSOU.)* Is that any way to welcome an artiste? *(To FLOUPETTE.)* Your dear little Raoul...

FLOUPETTE, *scandalized, crossing right*: My dear—

MACASSOU, *to RAOUL, replying*: Too gentle a way, monsieur! *(To BARNABE, pointing up right, at the broom handle leaning against the sideboard.)* Barnabé... The broom!

BARNABE: It's broken. There's almost nothing left but the handle.

MACASSOU: That's quite enough! *(Pointing to the casserole.)* And take that back to the kitchen!

BARNABE, *taking it, aside*: Bah!

He exits, up right.

RAOUL, *crossing right, joining FLOUPETTE, to MACASSOU, as the latter replaces the wine in the sideboard*: But uncle dear... What's the matter?

MACASSOU: The matter? *(Aside.)* Him!... Instead of a paying client! *(Aloud, to RAOUL.)* You ask me... *(To FLOUPETTE.)* He asks me what's the matter! Did you ever...

FLOUPETTE, *to RAOUL*: What are you doing here, monsieur? Why did you come?

RAOUL: Why?... Why, to marry you, of course!

MACASSOU: Oh no!... *(Laughing archly.)* Ha ha ha!... Marry her? Just like that?... Ha ha ha!... Oh no, monsieur! I refuse! I don't give my consent!

RAOUL: But... *(To FLOUPETTE.)* Since we were children... Even before! *(To MACASSOU.)* It's been all arranged. *(To FLOUPETTE.)* Besides, I love you!

MACASSOU: Well, I'm disarranging it!

RAOUL: And I'm in a hurry. *(To MACASSOU, taking a sheet of paper from his pocket.)* Here, uncle... *(Very matter-of-fact.)* Sign this...

MACASSOU, *taking it*: This what?

RAOUL: The marriage contract...

MACASSOU: Oh?... This is what I think of your marriage contract!

He crosses left and begins as if to rip it up.

RAOUL, *following him, stopping him*: No! Don't—

MACASSOU: You're right! I'm sure I can find some use to put it to! *(He puts it into his back pocket, with a tap on his rear.)* The nerve!... An actor, and he wants to marry my niece! *(To RAOUL.)* Never, monsieur!

RAOUL, *aside*: We'll see about that!

FLOUPETTE, *approaching him*: It's your own fault, you know! You shouldn't have spurned me when you had your chance!

RAOUL: "Spurned" you?... What ever do you—

FLOUPETTE: Two years ago, monsieur!

MACASSOU: When they built the railroad... And she didn't have a dowry... And the inn almost fell to pieces...

RAOUL, *puzzled*: It did?... Was it hit by a train?

MACASSOU, *sarcastically*: Ha ha ha!... Of course! Play dumb!

RAOUL: Besides, when I thought of a career... *(To MACASSOU.)* A profession, uncle... Well... The inn was simply... out!... I couldn't see myself spending my life in a... a chophouse...

MACASSOU: Oh!

RAOUL: A... A tavern... *(With a sweeping gesture.)* I mean, this...

MACASSOU: A chophouse, indeed!

RAOUL, *to FLOUPETTE*: But surely you must realize why I left, Floupette! How could I marry you before I made a name for myself?

FLOUPETTE: Oh?

RAOUL: My fame... My fortune...

MACASSOU, *aside*: Fortune?

RAOUL: That's why I joined the troupe...

MACASSOU: Yes! A troupe of traveling actors!... Ne'er-do-wells, one and all... Ha! *(Aside.)* Fortune, my foot!

FLOUPETTE, *to RAOUL*: For shame, monsieur!

RAOUL: But that was my calling!

MACASSOU: Well, you shouldn't have answered!

FLOUPETTE, *to RAOUL*: Your calling?... Oh yes!... Those actresses! Those tarts!... Calling you to go chase them!

MACASSOU: Those brazen hussies!

FLOUPETTE: Anything with a skirt!

MACASSOU: Or without one! I know their type...

RAOUL, *turning to MACASSOU*: But that's not true! *(To FLOUPETTE.)* I never... *(To MACASSOU.)* Besides, I don't play young lovers. *(To FLOUPETTE.)* Only character roles...

FLOUPETTE: That's all well and good! At least your roles have character...

MACASSOU, *to RAOUL*: Which is more than you can say for yourself, monsieur!

FLOUPETTE, *continuing*: But you spurned me once, and you won't have a chance again!

MACASSOU: Here, here!

RAOUL: But Floupette... Down deep, you love me! I'm sure... You must...

FLOUPETTE: Well, you're wrong! I don't!... Down deep, or anywhere else! So there!

RAOUL, *pointing to MACASSOU*: I know! It's my pot-swabbing uncle who's turning you against me!

MACASSOU: Monsieur!

RAOUL: And if you listen to him, you'll be an old maid, mark my words! Your life will be nothing but skewers and... *(Turning an imaginary handle.)* and spit!

FLOUPETTE, *misunderstanding*: Monsieur!

RAOUL: A scullery wench... *(Very dramatic.)* Our Lady of the Ladle...

FLOUPETTE: Oh my…

RAOUL: The Vestal of the Soup Tureen!

MACASSOU, *to RAOUL, scandalized*: Hold your tongue, you… you actor!

RAOUL: Whatever you say, Milord of the Galley!

MACASSOU, *to FLOUPETTE*: Don't listen to him, Floupette! I'm expecting a new lot of suitors this very afternoon!

RAOUL, *to FLOUPETTE*: You'll see! They won't come… *(To MACASSOU.)* They won't!

MACASSOU: They will! *(Aside.)* They have to! The stew won't keep much longer.

RAOUL, *to MACASSOU*: You'll see… *(To FLOUPETTE.)* You'll see…

BARNABE appears at the door, up center.

BARNABE, *to MACASSOU, waving a letter*: For you!… It just came.

MACASSOU: A letter? *(Joining him upstage, perusing it.)* Ah! From my friend Doghidou!

BARNABE remains upstage, observing the ensuing action and casting more tender glances at FLOUPETTE.

FLOUPETTE: Who?

MACASSOU: Doghidou… Doghidou the toothpick salesman… Listen… *(To RAOUL, scornfully.)* You too!… *(Reading.)* "My dear Macassou… Success! I've managed to flush out three game birds for your niece's inspection…" *(To FLOUPETTE.)* He does a lot of hunting…

RAOUL, *to FLOUPETTE, softly*: Foul suitors, I'm sure…

MACASSOU, *continuing to read*: "They should be perching in your vicinity as you read these lines…"

RAOUL, *aside*: Hmm!

MACASSOU: That means today… *(To RAOUL.)* You see? *(To FLOUPETTE.)* I told you… *(Continuing to read.)* "The first is a Russian gentleman…"

FLOUPETTE: Oh my…

MACASSOU: "Count Popinoff… Rich beyond belief…" *(Under his breath.)* Aha!

RAOUL, *to FLOUPETTE, softly*: Don't count on it!

MACASSOU: "The second, a Spanish nobleman… Don Ramón Mayonéz y Bearnéz y Olandéz y…" *(Nodding.)* Et cetera, et cetera… "…who owns half the vineyards in Andalucía…" *(Aside, admiringly.)* Ay ay ay!…

RAOUL, *to FLOUPETTE, softly*: No doubt some seedy drunkard…

MACASSOU, *continuing*: "And the third, Monsieur Modeste Bachefolle… Only son of the richest farmer this side of Avignon… Wheat, barley, rye…"

RAOUL, *to FLOUPETTE, softly*: He'll go against your grain, believe me…

MACASSOU, *coming downstage, brandishing the letter, victoriously, to RAOUL*: You see? That's what I call suitors! Real ones, monsieur! *(To FLOUPETTE, in a whisper.)* And eaters, by the sound of it… *(Aside.)* We may even have to cook up more stew!

RAOUL: But that's impossible! *(Seizing the letter.)* Let me see that! *(To MACASSOU.)* Just as I thought! April fool! April fool!… This letter is a joke!

MACASSOU: Ha ha!… In September?

RAOUL: Then September fool! *(With a shrug.)* What's six months…

MACASSOU: You're insane, monsieur! Even for an actor…

RAOUL, *perusing the letter, aside*: What's this? A postscript?... *(Crossing right, reading in a whisper, as* MACASSOU *takes* FLOUPETTE *aside, leading her left, tapping his temple.)* "But you'd better not plan on any one of them, old man. They're all very married and just passing through town!" Idiot!... "So no sense in their applying for the position..." *(Stopping, far right, suddenly struck by a thought.)* Ah! Wait!... What a brilliant idea!... But of course! Of course!... Why not?

He stuffs the letter into his pocket.

MACASSOU, *crossing right, to* RAOUL: Well? Are you convinced?

RAOUL: Completely, uncle dear!

MACASSOU: Good! Then... *(Pointing up center.)* There's the door! You're wasting my time. *(Aside.)* And he's not even drinking! *(To* BARNABE.*)* Barnabé!... My nephew's trunk...

BARNABE *exits, left.*

RAOUL: You mean... You're asking me to leave? Your sister's only child?

MACASSOU: Everyone is entitled to make one mistake, monsieur!

RAOUL: You're throwing me out?

MACASSOU: In a word!

RAOUL, *aside, counting on his fingers*: Well... Four actually... *(Aloud.)* Like a nobody?

MACASSOU: No! Like the cad that you are!

FLOUPETTE, *aside*: Poor thing!

RAOUL, *to* MACASSOU: I'm warning you! I'll be back! *(To* FLOUPETTE.*)* Don't you worry!

BARNABE *reenters with the trunk.*

MACASSOU, *pointing*: Out!

FLOUPETTE, *aside*: Tsk tsk tsk!

RAOUL, *to* MACASSOU: Without even a hug?

MACASSOU: Out!

RAOUL, *to* FLOUPETTE: Or a kiss?

MACASSOU, *beginning to lose his temper*: Out, I said! *(With a sneer.)* Actor!... And you can forget about Floupette, understand?

RAOUL, *moving to leave*: Forget about her? *(To* FLOUPETTE.*)* Forget? *(To* MACASSOU.*)* When she's going to be my wife? Don't be absurd!

MACASSOU: Never! And that's final!

FLOUPETTE, *to* RAOUL, *unconvinced*: He's right, you know...

BARNABE, *still up center, with a longing look in her direction, aside*: Then maybe... Ah! Why not...?

FLOUPETTE, *to* RAOUL: That's final! *(Aside.)* I suppose...

RAOUL: We'll see... We'll see...

He exits, up center. BARNABE *follows him with the trunk.*

MACASSOU, *center, watching them leave*: Young scoundrel!

FLOUPETTE: Do you think he'll come back?

MACASSOU, *joining her, down center*: He wouldn't dare!

FLOUPETTE: I don't know... Nothing would surprise me.

MACASSOU: Well, if he does...

FLOUPETTE: If he does, uncle dear, he'd better find me married! If not…

MACASSOU: Patience! Patience!… We have plenty of time, Floupette!

FLOUPETTE: Oh? Not if you keep saying "No!" to all my suitors!… Because everyone in town… Well, I would hate to tell you how they're all making fun of you!

MACASSOU: Making fun? Of me?

FLOUPETTE: Saying that, when a suitor comes, you welcome him with open arms… But that, when he asks for my hand, he gets a meatball instead…

MACASSOU: Well, they can't eat your hand!

FLOUPETTE, *continuing*: …and a finger to boot! Pointing to the door!… But only after he's paid his bill, of course!

MACASSOU: Really, Floupette…

FLOUPETTE, *crossing right, rather petulantly*: My cousin is right! I'll be an old maid…

MACASSOU, *following her*: Now, now… No need to get angry… The toothpick salesman is sending us three today. My friend Doghidou… You heard what he said.

FLOUPETTE: Yes, well… Picking a suitor isn't as easy as picking teeth! And, even if I like one, you're bound to refuse! I don't know why we bother—

MACASSOU: But I told you… Your dowry…

FLOUPETTE: Old maids don't need one!

MACASSOU: But surely I can refuse two of them at least!

FLOUPETTE: Yes… But no more than two! And I'll be the one to decide!

MACASSOU: Very well… If you insist… Two for me, and one for you, Floupette!… And all three for the rabbit stew and the "Château Macassou"!… Let's not forget to make them eat and drink their fill!

FLOUPETTE: And the one I choose? The one I'm going to marry?

MACASSOU: Well, your future husband we can spare, I suppose… But the other two are fair game!

BARNABE appears at the doors, up center, whimpering and rubbing his backside.

BARNABE, *entering*: Oh!… Of all the…

MACASSOU, *joining him, center*: What?… What is it, Barnabé?

FLOUPETTE, *to BARNABE*: What ever is the matter?

BARNABE, *to MACASSOU*: That nephew of yours… *(To FLOUPETTE.)* Your cousin, mam'selle… I carried his trunk to The Purple Pelican. Just next door, but still… *(Rubbing his backside more vigorously.)* Oh! My… My…

MACASSOU, *impatiently*: "But"…? But what?… He didn't give you anything for your trouble?

BARNABE: Oh yes! He gave me…

MACASSOU: A franc?

BARNABE, *continuing*: …a good kick! *(Turning around, exhibiting a footprint on the seat of his trousers.)* That's what he gave me!

FLOUPETTE: Good heavens!

MACASSOU: What? He dared… The… The blackguard dared attack my livery? He dared lay a hand on the symbol of my establishment?

BARNABE: Not his hand...

FLOUPETTE: But why?

MACASSOU, *aside*: Oh! Something is afoot!

BARNABE: When we get next door, he goes "Whoa... Whoa..." Like he's talking to an ass... So I put down the trunk, and I ask him: "Well? Don't you have a little something to give me?" And he goes: "Oh, but I do!" And he tells me: "Turn your back! Damned if I want you to see where I keep my money!" So I do like he says... And... And bam!... *(Rubbing his backside.)* This is what he gives me!

MACASSOU: And you let him? You took it?

BARNABE: Who had time to argue?

MACASSOU: You just stood there, dolt? You let somebody bring dishonor to The Golden Giraffe? And in front of The Purple Pelican, no less?... Oh! You... You imbecile! You...

BARNABE: But...

MACASSOU: "But, but, but..." No "buts," you hear?... Turn around! *(BARNABE turns around and he gives him a swift kick.)* There, you idiot!

BARNABE: Ay, ay, ay!

FLOUPETTE, *trying to intercede*: Uncle dear...

MACASSOU: That should teach him!... And in front of the competition... Did you ever...

FLOUPETTE: Oh! Poor thing!

BARNABE, *to FLOUPETTE*: Thank you, mam'selle... *(Aside.)* Maybe she'll kiss it and make it better!

FLOUPETTE: Tsk tsk tsk!

BARNABE, *gazing at her, sighing*: Ahhh...

MACASSOU: What are you bellowing about?

BARNABE, *trying to conceal his emotion*: I'm worried! "That's for now," he tells me... Your nephew, I mean... "You'll get the rest later!"

FLOUPETTE, *to MACASSOU*: Oh! You see? He is coming back! *(Unable to conceal her enthusiasm.)* I knew it!

MACASSOU: Well, we'll just see about that!... Barnabé! *(Pointing up right.)* The broom!

BARNABE, *getting it, under his breath*: Bah!

MACASSOU, *pointing up center*: You stand guard at the door! And as soon as you see him coming—

BARNABE, *interrupting*: I run out and give him a whack in the rear!

MACASSOU: Or anywhere you like!

FLOUPETTE, *aside*: Good heavens!

MACASSOU: Just make sure you keep him out!

> *BARNABE goes to the doors, up center, opens them a crack and stands at the ready, looking out.*

BARNABE: Don't worry...

MACASSOU, *mumbling to himself*: Come back, indeed! Of all the nerve...Who does he think—

BARNABE, *suddenly*: Look!... Look!

MACASSOU: What?

FLOUPETTE, *to BARNABE*: Do you see him?

BARNABE, *peering out*: Not him, but… Someone else… With a beard… And ugly… And he's dressed like an undertaker!

MACASSOU: Ah!… One of Doghidou's suitors… It must be…

FLOUPETTE, ASIDE: Oh my…

BARNABE: Should I give him a whack?

MACASSOU: Certainly not! *(To FLOUPETTE.)* Are you ready?

FLOUPETTE: Yes, uncle dear.

MACASSOU: Now smile… And you're wearing your yellow apron? *(Admiringly.)* Very nice… Just right… *(As an afterthought.)* Wait! We need to have a signal.

FLOUPETTE: What ever for?

MACASSOU: So I'll know what you think… If you don't like one of them, you take off the apron, and… Voilà!… I'll know that's it's all right to feed him till he bursts, and then show him the door! Agreed?

FLOUPETTE, *unenthusiastically*: If you think so…

MACASSOU, *going up to the doors, looking out*: Ah! It must be the count! I can tell by his medals!

> *He withdraws and takes a position, center, as POPINOFF, in full dress and bemedaled, enters and stands for a moment at the door. He has a long beard, and is the very picture of Russian angst and despondency.*

POPINOFF, *with a thick accent*: So?… Good day… *(To BARNABE.)* Moussyor… I count…

BARNABE: Me too… *(To prove the point.)* One, two, three…

MACASSOU, *to BARNABE, under his breath, pushing him out of the way*: Dolt!… *(To POPINOFF.)* May I help you, monsieur?

POPINOFF: Da! You help… *(Holding out his hand.)* Count Popinoff…

BARNABE, *returning to his post, aside*: Bah!

MACASSOU, *shaking his hand*: Delighted, I'm sure…

POPINOFF: Moussyor… I here… I here…

MACASSOU, *scratching his head*: Oh?… What do you hear, Your… *(Hesitating, uncertain how to address him.)* Your—

POPINOFF: No! No "hear"… I here!… *(Pointing to the floor.)* Here! I come here!

MACASSOU, *still scratching*: Aha…

POPINOFF, *noticing him, curiously*: You hev nits, moussyor?

MACASSOU: I beg your pardon?

POPINOFF: Nits… You hev?

MACASSOU: Nits?… Hardly!… Just a mild itch…

POPINOFF: Ach! Nyet!… Nits!… *(Pointing to FLOUPETTE.)* She your nits, da?

MACASSOU: My… Oh! Oh, yes!… My niece… *(Introducing.)* Floupette… His… His Countship… *(To himself.)* His Countenance?

> *FLOUPETTE curtsies.*

POPINOFF: Da! I come for her meet.

FLOUPETTE: For what?

POPINOFF, *to FLOUPETTE*: For you meet… I here…

MACASSOU: To meet her… Yes! Of course…

POPINOFF: Because I so sed… Bozhe moy! Is mosh tromble for to live! *(Loudly.)* Aaaaach!

FLOUPETTE: Oh my…

POPINOFF: I strongle… I strongle…

FLOUPETTE, *misunderstanding*: Can I get you a glass of water?

POPINOFF: Vater?… For vy, vater?

FLOUPETTE: I thought… *(Putting her hand to her throat.)* You just said…

POPINOFF: "I strongle," is vat I say… I strongle for to live! For to find raisin… Good raisin for to live… But no find…

MACASSOU, *trying to sound sympathetic*: I'm sorry to hear that.

POPINOFF: Da! Every ting bleck!…

FLOUPETTE: Bleak?

POPINOFF: Blik? *(Correcting her.)* Bleck!…Bleck!… Day bleck, night bleck…

MACASSOU: Ah, black… Well, yes… Nighttime does tend to—

POPINOFF: Sun bleck, moon bleck… Life bleck, moussyor!… *(Confidentially.)* I have big collie.

FLOUPETTE: Oh? I love animals!

MACASSOU, *to* POPINOFF: Beg pardon?

FLOUPETTE, *looking around*: Did you bring him?… Her…?

POPINOFF: Her? Him?… Vat you talk?… I bring who?

FLOUPETTE: Your collie… Your dog… You said…

POPINOFF: Vat you talk, dog?… Mellow collie… Big mellow collie… I so sed…

FLOUPETTE, *suddenly understanding*: Aha… Your…You….

POPINOFF: I bore…

MACASSOU: Oh? Not at all, count! You're very interesting.

FLOUPETTE, *to* MACASSOU, *explaining*: His melancholy… He's bored…

POPINOFF: Big bore…

FLOUPETTE: Very bored…

POPINOFF: Is vat I say, nyet?

MACASSOU, *nodding*: Well… Almost…

POPINOFF: No ting vat I do help… No ting…

FLOUPETTE: Tsk tsk tsk…

POPINOFF: I buy hose… Pretty bleck hose…

MACASSOU, *aside*: Why on earth…? *(Aloud, to* POPINOFF.*)* You mean… Stockings?… Or a… a hose?

He mimes watering something with a hose.

POPINOFF: Vid big mozzle…

MACASSOU: Ah… I think you mean "nozzle." A… A hose with a—

POPINOFF, *interrupting, categorically*: Nyet!… Mozzle… Full vid big teet…

FLOUPETTE, *thoroughly confused*: What?

POPINOFF, *pointing to his teeth*: Big teet in hose's mozzle… And doctor tell me: "You go ride, you feel better!" So I poot seddle, and go for to ride.

FLOUPETTE, *suddenly understanding*: Ah! Your... *(To MACASSOU.)* His horse!... He means...

MACASSOU: Oh!

FLOUPETTE, *to POPINOFF*: Your horse...

POPINOFF: Da! *(To MACASSOU.)* Is vat I say, nyet?

MACASSOU: Well... Not exactly...

POPINOFF: And every ting I try... Every ting!... But no ting help. No ting... No ting...

FLOUPETTE: Tsk tsk tsk...

POPINOFF: So I go tek nose... Big nose... Strong, heavy nose... *(FLOUPETTE and MACASSOU look at each other, quizzically.)* And poot inside, head... Poot nose around nook...

He mimes pulling tightly on a noose.

FLOUPETTE: Oh! That's terrible! You didn't!

POPINOFF: Da! I do!... But ach!... Go "paf!"

FLOUPETTE *and* **MACASSOU**: "Paf"?

POPINOFF: "Paf!"... Nose brek. Vat to do? Vat to do?... Still big bore... Still mellow collie... No ting help. No ting!... *(Shaking his head in depressed resignation.)* Nyet, nyet, nyet...

MACASSOU, *motioning him to a chair at the table, down left*: Please, count... Won't you have a seat?

POPINOFF, *with a wave of the hand*: Nyet... I sit, I sed... I stend, I sed... I go bed, I sed... I get op...

FLOUPETTE, *to MACASSOU, in a whisper*: Really, uncle dear...

POPINOFF, *continuing*: I sed... I sed...

MACASSOU, *to POPINOFF*: Perhaps if Your Countenance had a nice lunch... *(To BARNABE.)* Barnabé!... The rabbit stew!

POPINOFF, *stopping BARNABE, who has begun to move up right, toward the door*: Ach! Nyet, moussyor!... Raw bit, no for stew... Raw bit, for borsh'ch! Bit borsh'ch...

MACASSOU, *not understanding*: For...?

POPINOFF: Borsh'ch!... *(Insisting.)* Borsh'ch!

BARNABE: God bless you!

POPINOFF, *to MACASSOU*: You hev maybe... How you say?... You hev big beerd?

MACASSOU: Beard?... Why no... *(Feeling his chin.)* As you can see... Why do you ask?

POPINOFF: No beard... Big beerd... Mek loud "clook"... *(MACASSOU and FLOUPETTE look at each other, nonplussed.)* "Clook clook..." *(He flaps his arms up and down.)* Big beerd... "Clook clook..."

MACASSOU, *suddenly comprehending*: Ah! A bird... You mean, like a chicken...

POPINOFF: Nyet!... Chicken, smoll... *(Holding out his arms.)* Big... Big...

FLOUPETTE: An ostrich?

POPINOFF, *ignoring her suggestion*: Like in prism... Prism gourd...

MACASSOU, *scratching his head, aside*: What in the name...

BARNABE: He wants to eat a gourd?

POPINOFF, *to* MACASSOU: Prism gourd! Prism gourd!… In prism, vat you coll gourd?

FLOUPETTE, *to* MACASSOU: I think he means a prison guard.

POPINOFF: Da, da!… Vat you coll?

MACASSOU: A turnkey?

POPINOFF: Da!… Det vat I vant! Tournkey… Stuff vid chassnoot!

MACASSOU: Aha!… Turkey, with chestnut stuffing… That's no problem…

BARNABE, *approaching, to* MACASSOU, *in a whisper*: But we don't have any turkey…

MACASSOU, *in a whisper*: Then kill the rooster, damn it!

BARNABE, *in a whisper*: And we have no bloody stuffing!

MACASSOU, *in a whisper, angrily*: Then stuff it with the stew! *(Aloud, to* POPINOFF, *as pleasant as can be.)* Very good… If that's what you want… Turkey with chestnut stuffing it is!

BARNABE, *to* MACASSOU, *in a whisper*: But…

MACASSOU, *to* BARNABE, *in a whisper*: Or your goose is cooked, idiot!

BARNABE, *as he moves toward the door, up right, shaking his head, aside*: Bah!

POPINOFF, *stopping him*: Nyet… You give to me heddeck…

BARNABE, *under his breath*: I don't care for you either!

POPINOFF, *continuing*: Da! Better maybe you give fish… Nice piss… Nice piss broil heddeck…

BARNABE: Broiled what?

FLOUPETTE, *timidly venturing a suggestion*: Haddock, I think…

POPINOFF: Da! Is vat I say, nyet?

FLOUPETTE: Well…

POPINOFF, *to* BARNABE, *continuing*: Vid gorlink!… No to forget… Big gorlink… Big…

FLOUPETTE, *aside*: Oh my!

BARNABE, *to* POPINOFF, *sarcastically*: With pleasure…

FLOUPETTE, *softly, to* MACASSOU: Really, uncle dear…

POPINOFF, *to* BARNABE: Nyet… No vid pleasure… Vid gorlink!

BARNABE: Of course… *(Aside, mimicking.)* Mush gorlink! *(To* MACASSOU, *in a whisper.)* We have no fish, monsieur. The cat ate the last of it.

MACASSOU, *in a whisper*: Well, go catch one! Anything with fins, if you know what's good for you! The man is a millionaire!

FLOUPETTE, *overhearing*: But uncle…

BARNABE, *aside*: Bah!

He exits, up right, shaking his head.

POPINOFF, *putting his arm around* MACASSOU, *coming down left*: So, Moccassin…

MACASSOU, *gently correcting*: Macassou…

POPINOFF: Ach!… Better I like Moccassin… It mean some ting. Vat mean Macassou? *(*MACASSOU *gives a shrug of resignation.)* So… You know for vy I here… For vy I come to you pitifool inn…

MACASSOU: Piti… I think you mean "beautiful," count.

POPINOFF: Nyet… *(Looking around, categorically.)* Pitifool… Pitifool…

MACASSOU: Oh… Well…

POPINOFF: Da!… Is Doghidou…

MACASSOU: My friend…

POPINOFF: He say: "Count, you so sed. For vy you no merry, like me…"

MACASSOU: Yes… Doghidou is a merry soul!

POPINOFF, *correcting*: Nyet! No merry… Merry!… "For vy you no merry? For vy you no tek vife?"

MACASSOU: Ah!… "Why don't you marry…?"

POPINOFF: Is vat I say, nyet?

MACASSOU: Well…

POPINOFF, *continuing*: "You go see friend Moccassin…"

MACASSOU: Macassou…

POPINOFF: Better I like Moccassin… *(Continuing.)* "He hev nits… Pretty nits… Pouflette…"

FLOUPETTE, *sharply*: Floupette, monsieur!

POPINOFF: Da! Fouplette…

MACASSOU, *to FLOUPETTE, mimicking*: Is vat he say, nyet?

POPINOFF, *on whom the sarcasm is lost, continuing*: "And you go…" How you say?… Like… Like tailor…

MACASSOU: Oh?

POPINOFF: Da… "You mek suit," he say… "Mek suit." Maybe vedding suit he mean… So! I come… I here… I see pretty nits.

MACASSOU, *whispering, to FLOUPETTE*: For heaven's sake, smile! He's worth millions, you hear?

POPINOFF, *inspecting her*: Da… Da… *(To FLOUPETTE.)* Please for to open mout, pretty nits…

FLOUPETTE: What?

As she utters the exclamation, POPINOFF peers in at her teeth.

POPINOFF: Now tourn… For to let me see beck…

As FLOUPETTE demurs, MACASSOU turns her around bodily before POPINOFF's ogling gaze.

FLOUPETTE, *under her breath*: Oh! I never…

POPINOFF: Da!… Is good…*(To MACASSOU.)* I tek… *(To FLOUPETTE.)* Come, Loufpette… Ve merry…

FLOUPETTE, *out of patience*: Floupette, if you don't mind!

POPINOFF: Nyet! I no mind…

MACASSOU, *to POPINOFF*: Just like that?… *(Chuckling.)* I didn't know Russians could come to a boil so fast!

POPINOFF: Boil?… Boil?… Nyet! I no hev boil! Bozhe moy!… For vy you tink… Vere you tink I hev…? I big bore, da! Onheppy, sed… Bot no hev boil!… Boil? *(Grimacing.)* Yechhhh!

MACASSOU: No… I didn't mean—

POPINOFF, *spitting on the floor in disgust*: Tfoo! Tfoo!… For vy you tink—

MACASSOU: I… I meant—

POPINOFF: Ach! Boil… Tfoo!

MACASSOU: You're very hot-blooded, count. Very passionate…

POPINOFF: Da!… Bot no hev boil!… Only, no vant for to be sed oll alone! Enough be sed oll alone already! And doctor say sem ting like Doghidou… "For you, best meditsin? Vife!"

FLOUPETTE: Medicine?

POPINOFF: "You merry… You get rid bleck bile… You no more sed, no more big bore… No more onheppy."

FLOUPETTE: And that's why you want me to marry you? For your bile?

POPINOFF, *nodding*: Bleck… Bleck…

FLOUPETTE: How flattering!

POPINOFF: Da!… You good meditsin! I tek… *(Smiling.)* I tek tree, four time itch day, maybe!… Ha ha ha!

MACASSOU, *forcing a laugh*: Ha ha ha!

POPINOFF: Tree, four time… *(Giving him a good-natured poke.)* Ha ha ha!

FLOUPETTE, *to MACASSOU, in a whisper*: Oh?

POPINOFF, *suddenly serious*: Ach!… Det fourst time I leff! Count Popinoff leff!… *(To FLOUPETTE.)* You see, pretty nits? You very good meditsin for count!

MACASSOU, *in a whisper, to FLOUPETTE*: Laugh, for heaven's sake!

POPINOFF: Bleck bile go "poof!"

MACASSOU, *to FLOUPETTE, continuing*: The man is a millionaire! *(To POPINOFF, enthusiastically.)* Count…

POPINOFF: Moussyor?

MACASSOU: We're immensely honored by your proposal, and…

FLOUPETTE, *aside*: Oh no!

MACASSOU, *continuing*: And I'm delighted to tell you…

FLOUPETTE, *aside*: No, no, no!

She whips off her apron.

MACASSOU, *suddenly*: …that I have to refuse.

POPINOFF, *taken aback, sharply*: Vat?… For vy to refuse?

MACASSOU: Because… *(Looking for an excuse.)* My niece is in love!

POPINOFF: Da!… Vid me… Pretty nits, in love vid me! *(To FLOUPETTE.)* So for vy you no merry?

MACASSOU: Not exactly, count… With… With someone else…

POPINOFF: Else? Else?… How can be dis ting? Else?

FLOUPETTE: Yes! It's true! *(Quick to exaggerate.)* And I'm signing the marriage contract this very day, in fact…

POPINOFF: Nyet!

MACASSOU: Da!… *(Correcting himself.)* I mean, "yes"… At two o'clock…

POPINOFF: Is no true!

MACASSOU: Yes! It is!

POPINOFF: Nyet! I bet is no true!

MACASSOU: What?

POPINOFF: I bet pretty nits no sign contreck today! No two clonk today!… No et oll, today!… No et oll! No never!

MACASSOU: But I assure you—

POPINOFF: Nikagdá!… Never!… Nyet, nyet, nyet!

MACASSOU, *aside*: Stubborn! *(Aloud.)* Oh? And you really want to wager?

POPINOFF: Veger?… Vat mean "veger"?

MACASSOU: You really want to bet?

POPINOFF: Da!… Bet…

MACASSOU: How much?

POPINOFF: Tventy tousand franc!

MACASSOU: That Floupette won't say "I do"? Today, by two o'clock?

POPINOFF: Da!… I do, I do!…

MACASSOU: You…?

POPINOFF: Da! I vant bet…

MACASSOU: And if you lose?

POPINOFF: I lose? I pay!… Bot is good for me… Is good! It mek for to smile. It mek for to leff. It good for pess time. I no bore now…

MACASSOU, *aside*: Damn! *(To FLOUPETTE, in a whisper.)* If I win, Floupette…

FLOUPETTE, *in a whisper*: But uncle dear… That's absurd!

MACASSOU, *in a whisper*: Not at all! Doghidou promised two more suitors. At least one of them is sure to… suit you!

POPINOFF: So?

MACASSOU: Agreed!… Your twenty thousand francs if I win, and… and my inn, if I lose! *(Aside.)* It's not worth five hundred, with all the mortgages!

FLOUPETTE, *whispering, to MACASSOU*: Really, uncle…

POPINOFF, *to MACASSOU*: So… Now… Give to me hen!

MACASSOU: Hen?… I thought we said haddock…

POPINOFF, *extending his hand*: You hen… Ve shek…

MACASSOU: Ah! My… Of course…

They shake hands.

POPINOFF: So!… Now you give to me food!

MACASSOU: Are you hungry, Your Highness?

POPINOFF: Nyet… Is for to pess time only… Ontil clonk strike two!… You give to me private room, da? I no like for to eat in poblink.

MACASSOU: Of course, of course!… *(Pointing left.)* Number seven… You can have it all to yourself. I'll see that you're served… Bon appétit!

POPINOFF: Da!… *(Taking his watch from his vest pocket and consulting it.)* Ach!… Is time fourst for to axercise.

MACASSOU: Exercise, Your Grace?

POPINOFF, *replacing his watch*: Da! Doctor tell me, always before eat, I dence!

MACASSOU: Oh?

POPINOFF: Like so…

With utter seriousness, he proceeds to do a spirited Cossack dance before the startled gaze of MACASSOU and FLOUPETTE.

FLOUPETTE, *aside*: Good heavens!

POPINOFF, *after several moments, consulting his watch again, stopping*: Is finish now, dence... So, I eat... Please for to bring!

He exits left, through the alcove.

MACASSOU, *to FLOUPETTE*: That should help his appetite! *(Calling.)* Barnabé!... Luncheon for number seven!

BARNABE enters, up right, carrying a casserole of food.

BARNABE: Right away...

MACASSOU: And don't forget the wine! Lots of wine! *(To FLOUPETTE.)* Pure profit!

BARNABE takes the bottle from the sideboard.

BARNABE, *to himself*: Bloody rival!... Bah!

He exits left. The sound of knocking on a door is heard offstage.

POPINOFF'S VOICE: Da?

BARNABE'S VOICE: Your lunch!

POPINOFF'S VOICE: Ach!... So...Spaseebo!

MACASSOU, *to FLOUPETTE*: Twenty thousand francs, Floupette!... Now you have three hours to find a husband and sign a marriage contract!

FLOUPETTE, *beginning to demur*: But uncle... Three hours... I don't know...

MACASSOU: Besides, you're in a hurry! You said so yourself. By two o'clock you'll be married, and my fortune will be made!

FLOUPETTE: But...

MACASSOU: But what?... It's only a husband! How much time do you need! They're like melons, Floupette! Why go feeling and poking to see which one is the ripest?... Just close your eyes and take your pick! Chances are you'll get a good one!

FLOUPETTE: Really...

MACASSOU: Because, if I lose... *(Realizing the possibility.)* Good God! What am I saying?... If I lose... The inn... My life... Everything, Floupette! Everything I've worked for...

FLOUPETTE: I know, but...

MACASSOU: Don't do this to me! Please!... Not to me... Not to your uncle... Your mother's only brother... Your godfather...

FLOUPETTE: But...

MACASSOU: But? But? But?... Why always "but"...?

FLOUPETTE, *on the verge of tears*: I only know, uncle dear, that I'll simply never marry a man I don't love! Never!

She puts on her apron, turns on her heel, and exits, up right.

MACASSOU, *alone*: Ay ay ay!... What does love have to do with it? Where did she get such ideas? Not from her mother, I'm sure!... *(He begins pacing up and down.)* And if Doghidou's other suitors don't come? What will I do?... And even if they do, what if she doesn't like them? Look at the count! A millionaire! But all she cares about is love! As if love can buy money!... Damn!... I can't very well put up posters... "Wanted! A rich husband!"... And the inn... Good God! I could lose the inn! Everything!... What the devil was I thinking? *(Stopping, upstage.)* Of course, if I win... *(At the doors, up center, looking out.)* No one!... *(Consulting his watch.)* And time is flying!

BARNABE enters, left, with the casserole.

BARNABE, *aside*: Bah! *(Holding out his empty hand, disgustedly.)* Nothing!

MACASSOU: You?

BARNABE, *aside*: Well, at least he didn't kick me!

MACASSOU: What's that?

BARNABE: Number seven's lunch… *(Aside.)* What does it look like?

MACASSOU: Why isn't he eating it?

BARNABE: He said he'd rather starve… At least, I think that's what he said.

MACASSOU, *joining him, down left, inspecting it*: What on earth did you give him?

BARNABE: I did like you said. I tried to catch a fish, but all I got was a bunch of minnows. I told him they were baby haddock.

MACASSOU: A millionaire, and he's not eating!… You idiot!

BARNABE: But he's drinking the wine…

MACASSOU: You imbecile!

BARNABE: Besides, I can't help it. I've got other things on my mind. My heart just isn't in it.

MACASSOU, *hands on hips*: Oh? And where is it, may I ask?

BARNABE: I… I…

MACASSOU, *mimicking*: Ay ay ay!… What? What, you dolt?

BARNABE, *hesitating*: I… I'm in love!

MACASSOU: You?… With what? Who's the happy victim?

BARNABE: If… If I tell you… No… I can't… Mam'selle… No! You'll hit me, for sure!

MACASSOU, *aside*: Good God! Not Floupette?

BARNABE: I can't…

MACASSOU, *reflecting for a moment, to himself*: But… Why not? He's one more at least.

BARNABE: Please, monsieur…

MACASSOU, *aside*: And twenty thousand francs… And the inn…

BARNABE: Don't make me…

MACASSOU, *aside*: Beggars can't be choosers! *(Aloud.)* Who? Tell me!

BARNABE: But…

MACASSOU: That's an order!

BARNABE: It's… *(He puts the casserole on the table, down right.)* It's… *(He holds his arm against his face to protect himself.)* It's Mam'selle Floupette!… *(Aside, expecting the worst.)* Ayyy!

MACASSOU, *aside*: Bravo!

BARNABE, *aside*: He didn't hit me!

MACASSOU: Barnabé! *(Opening wide his arms.)* Son!… Nephew!

BARNABE, *surprised*: What? You mean… You don't mind?

MACASSOU: Mind…? Why should I mind?

BARNABE: I thought…

MACASSOU: You're young!… And quick-witted… *(Aside.)* As an ass! *(Aloud.)* And handsome… *(Aside.)* As a baboon!

BARNABE: Oh! Thank you!

MACASSOU: So! Go to it!… What more could she ask for?

BARNABE: Are you sure?

MACASSOU: As long as you can make her say "I do!" by two o'clock… *(Pointing, down right.)* She's in her room. Go on! Go on!… Don't waste another minute!

BARNABE: Well…

As he turns to leave, MACASSOU *stops him.*

MACASSOU: Wait!… *(Aside.)* God, he's a fright! She'll never… *(Aloud, pointing to a chair at the table, right.)* Sit down… Let me pretty you up a little. Not that you need it, but…

During the ensuing exchange, POPINOFF *enters and, unseen by them tiptoes, quietly out, up center.*

BARNABE, *sitting*: Me?

MACASSOU, *aside*: How do I begin? *(Fussing with* BARNABE's *hair.)* Ah!… A few nice little curls here and there… *(Pulling and twisting, in desperation.)* On top… On the sides…

BARNABE, *as he looks more and more like a haystack*: Ayyy!… It hurts!

MACASSOU: Nonsense! What do you know?

BARNABE: But you're pulling it all out…

MACASSOU: There!… *(Standing back and pretending to admire his handiwork.)* Very nice!… She'll love it! *(Taking the mirror from the sideboard, handing it to him.)* See?

BARNABE, *looking at his reflection*: Well… I don't know…

MACASSOU: It's the latest style. From Paris!

BARNABE: If you're sure…

MACASSOU *replaces the mirror and takes a flower from the vase.*

MACASSOU, *putting it in his buttonhole, he takes off his jacket and gives it to* BARNABE: Here! Wear this…

BARNABE, *beside himself*: Oh!… *(Putting it on, pricking up his ears.)* I think I hear her!

MACASSOU: She's coming… I'll leave you two alone.

BARNABE, *losing courage*: But… But…

MACASSOU: Now go to it! Do your best! Just remember, if she doesn't adore you by two o'clock, you're fired!

He exits, up right.

BARNABE, *alone*: Oh my! Oh my!

He picks up the casserole, absentmindedly, as FLOUPETTE *enters, up right.*

FLOUPETTE, *to herself, musing*: Poor Raoul!

BARNABE, *to himself*: Maybe she'd like something to eat…

FLOUPETTE, *continuing*: No matter how I try, I simply can't put him out of my mind!

BARNABE, *stirring the casserole, continuing*: A little haddock à la Macassou…

FLOUPETTE, *continuing*: I'm afraid he was right. I do love him! I do…I do…

BARNABE, *aside*: Now or never! *(Aloud, to* FLOUPETTE, *still stirring, approaching her.)* Mam'selle…

FLOUPETTE, *startled*: Oh!… *(Looking him up and down.)* Good heavens! *(Laughing.)* Is that you, Barnabé?

BARNABE: I… I… *(She gives him a questioning look.)* I just wanted to say…

FLOUPETTE: Yes…? To say…

BARNABE: That… That I hope you're well…

FLOUPETTE: Why, yes… Quite well, thank you…

BARNABE turns aside with an emotional shudder.

BARNABE, *stirring more and more vigorously*: And… And I wanted to ask you…

FLOUPETTE: Yes…?

BARNABE, *aside*: Oh my! *(Aloud.)* If… If…

FLOUPETTE: What ever is the matter, Barnabé? *(Aside.)* Is he ill?

BARNABE: The matter, mam'selle? *(With exaggerated passion.)* Did you ask me what's the matter?… You?

FLOUPETTE, *beginning to lose patience*: Yes! Me! *(Looking around, aside.)* Who else? *(Aloud.)* What did you want to ask me?

BARNABE, *intimidated, holding the casserole out under her nose*: If… If you wouldn't like a taste…

FLOUPETTE, *turning aside, with a grimace*: Pouah!… Certainly not! *(Waving him away.)* Now please…

She turns her back and begins to move off.

BARNABE: No… Wait… I have to ask you… Before two o'clock…

FLOUPETTE: What?

BARNABE: I have to… You have to… We… We…

He gets down on his knees, stirring the casserole emotionally.

FLOUPETTE, *angrily*: Barnabé! What ever are you doing?

BARNABE: I… I'm stirring, mam'selle!… See? I'm stirring…

As FLOUPETTE is about to react, the doors, up center, fly open, and DON RAMON appears, a swaggering, mustachioed Spanish grandee.

DON RAMON, *striding downstage, calling, in a thick Castilian accent*: Ho ho ho!… Garthón!… I thurst! I thurst!

Noticing BARNABE, still on his knees, he gives him a kick.

BARNABE, *jumping up*: Ayyy!

FLOUPETTE, *aside*: Who in heaven's name…

DON RAMON, *to BARNABE*: You peón, sí?… You surve me, no? I thurst, I tell you!

BARNABE: Careful, monsieur! What do you think—

DON RAMON, *exaggerating his pronunciation*: Silenthio, peón!… Or I step on you, like bog on groon!

BARNABE, *aside*: Oh! *(To FLOUPETTE.)* I'll show him! *(To DON RAMON.)* I dare you!

DON RAMON: You dare?… Ho ho ho!… You dare?… Tourn roon, you!

BARNABE, *accommodatingly, turning round*: Like this?

DON RAMON: Sí… Like so… Perfecto! Sí sí!… *(He gives him another kick, but harder.)* You see? You see?

BARNABE: Ayyy!… *(Calling.)* Help!… Help!

MACASSOU enters, up right.

MACASSOU, *impatiently*: What?... What is it?

BARNABE, *pointing*: He kicked me! That... That bloody...

DON RAMON, *to* BARNABE: Now you annoonth me, peón!

BARNABE: Twice... And hard! *(Rubbing his backside.)* Right here...

DON RAMON, *continuing*: Ees tine... *(Waiting a moment.)* So?... Caramba! You annoonth...

BARNABE: But I don't even know your—

DON RAMON, *interrupting, to* MACASSOU: Ees I am Don Ramón Mayonéz y Bearnéz y Olandéz y...

MACASSOU, *interrupting*: Ah!... Of course... We were expecting you! *(To* FLOUPETTE.*)* Weren't we, Floupette?

FLOUPETTE, *unenthusiastically*: I suppose so, uncle dear.

MACASSOU, *to* DON RAMON, *putting his arm around him*: Come...

BARNABE, *to* MACASSOU: And what about me?

MACASSOU: Out of the way!

BARNABE: What?... But he—

DON RAMON: You hear? Out of way!... Sí, sí!... Go, go! *(To* MACASSOU.*)* An you, señor... You Papá Cacassou?

MACASSOU: Yes... No... That is... "Ma"... "Ma"...

DON RAMON: You Mammá Cacassou?... How ees...?

MACASSOU: No... Papá... Papá...

DON RAMON: Mammá Papassou?

MACASSOU: No... Papá Macassou... "Maca"... "Maca"...

DON RAMON: Ah so! Ah so!... Sí, sí... I see... But... "Maca"... "Caca"... Ho ho ho! *(Giving him a sharp poke in the belly.)* What deeference?

MACASSOU, *aside*: Ouf!... *(To* DON RAMON.*)* Well... *(Rubbing his stomach, aside.)* Good-natured devil... *(Aside.)* You're just in time for lunch... *(Emphasizing.)* ... señor!

DON RAMON: Ah! Bueno!... I honger... I thurst...

MACASSOU, *to* BARNABE: Barnabé! The rabbit stew...

DON RAMON: No, no!... Rabbeet, no! Ees always cat, I theenk!... No me gusta! No, no!... *(To* BARNABE.*)* I take eenstead filette mignonne, weeth moshroon... Beeg! Beeg!

MACASSOU, *aside*: Damn! He must be worth millions!

DON RAMON, *as* BARNABE, *still holding the casserole, hesitates*: So? *(Menacingly.)* Why you no go? Why you no get?

BARNABE: I... *(Protecting himself with the casserole.)* Don't you touch me! *(To* MACASSOU, *in a whisper.)* We don't have any of that!

MACASSOU, *in a whisper*: Well, find something, damn it! Something expensive! Or—

BARNABE: I know! My goose is cooked...

DON RAMON, *overhearing*: Goose?... No, no!... No goose! Feather make for to sneeze... *(Illustrating.)* Atchoom!... Atchoom!

BARNABE shrugs and moves up right.

BARNABE, *aside*: Bah!

He exits.

MACASSOU, *to* DON RAMON: And would you care for a nice bordeaux, señor? A bottle, perhaps?… One of our finest…

DON RAMON: No! Bordeaux ees peess of cat I theenk! Cat what you poot een stew!… Ho ho ho!… No, no!… No bordeaux!… *(Calling.)* Garthón!… Breeng bottle wheesky an two beeg glass, por favor!

MACASSOU: But…

DON RAMON waits a moment expectantly, then continues.

DON RAMON, *impatiently*: So? Where ees peón?

FLOUPETTE, *aside*: The man is an absolute drunkard!

DON RAMON, *to* MACASSOU: Ees no peón?… Why he no cone?

FLOUPETTE, *continuing*: Raoul was right!

DON RAMON, *to* MACASSOU: So, you breeng! You!

MACASSOU: Of course… *(He goes to the sideboard, rummages, and returns with a bottle and one glass.)* I hope this will do… *(Aside.)* It came with the inn!

DON RAMON: Bueno! *(Taking the bottle.)* An you? You dreenk too!

MACASSOU: No… Thank you just the same… Nothing stronger than lemonade for me…

DON RAMON, *with a sneer*: What you say? Limonada?… Ho ho ho!… I say you dreenk? You dreenk!… I no dreenk alone!

MACASSOU: That's very kind of you, but—

DON RAMON: Eef I take wife, ees so to have oncle who dreenk weeth me! Sí, sí! You dreenk!

MACASSOU: It's just that—

DON RAMON: Ees jus no theeng! Breeng glass for you, or I go! I no stay!

MACASSOU, *going up to the sideboard and taking another glass, under his breath*: Anything to humor him… *(Rejoining him.)* There…

DON RAMON: Bueno! *(Pointing to* FLOUPETTE.*)* An leettle one… She dreenk too, jes?

FLOUPETTE: I'm afraid not, monsieur… She doesn't drink whisky.

DON RAMON, *disillusioned*: Oh… *(With a note of resignation.)* Bueno… Bueno… Ees woman! She dethide… *(Filling both glasses to the brim, to* MACASSOU.*)* So… Jus you, jus me… Tcheen tcheen, papá!

MACASSOU, *aside*: Good God! I can't drink all that!

DON RAMON, *clinking glasses, pointing at* FLOUPETTE: To hur! To hur!

FLOUPETTE, *sarcastically*: You're too kind!

DON RAMON, *pretending to drink, to* MACASSOU: So? Why you wait? Dreenk! Dreenk!

MACASSOU takes a big, reluctant gulp.

MACASSOU, *gagging and grimacing*: Pfahhh!

DON RAMON: More? *(Filling his glass, without giving him time to object.)* Jes!… More!

MACASSOU: No, no!… Really… Lemonade…

DON RAMON: One glass only make seeck!

MACASSOU, *aside*: And two glass make dead!

DON RAMON, *clinking glasses*: Tcheen tcheen, oncle!... To hur! To hur!... *(Pointing to FLOUPETTE.)* Again!

MACASSOU, *aside*: Why did I have to bet with that Russian?

DON RAMON: So?... Why you wait?... Porqué? Porqué?

MACASSOU: Of course... To her! To her!... *(He takes another gulp.)* Damn!

As inconspicuously as possible, he pours the rest into the floor plant, down right.

DON RAMON, *pretending to drink down his glass*: Bueno! *(Smacking his lips.)* Ees good! So! *(He too, surreptitiously, pours his drink into the plant.)* Now I ready for beezness! *(To MACASSOU.)* You eentroduth, jes?... Ees tine I meet bride!

FLOUPETTE, *aside*: Oh?

MACASSOU: I should say!... Floupette...Let me present—

FLOUPETTE, *softly*: No need... I know... Don Ramón Et Cetera, Et Cetera, Et Cetera...

DON RAMON, *to MACASSOU*: Ah! Flupeta! Flupeta!... She ees peetcher!

MACASSOU: A pitcher?

DON RAMON: Sí!... Peetcher of health... An peetcher of beauty!... An fooll, like peetcher... Peetcher of fine vino!

FLOUPETTE: How flattering, monsieur!

DON RAMON: Please to call "Don Ramón"! *(Without giving her a chance to react.)* Now I talk aboot me, jes? Wife should know hosban before she say "Jes!," no?... Ees true, jes?... Sí, sí? *(To MACASSOU.)* Ees true, no?

FRISETTE, } *together, mimicking*: { Oh, jes!... Sí! Sí!
MACASSOU, } { Oh, sí... Jes! Jes!

DON RAMON: Sí!... So I tell... *(Pretending to be drunk.)* For me, I always be fooll!

FLOUPETTE, ASIDE: Jes... Jes...

DON RAMON: Be fooll weeth one theeng!... Weeth wheesky... Weeth vino... Weeth thervetha... *(He gives the word 'cerveza' the Castilian pronunciation, almost in FLOUPETTE's face.)* Thervetha, thervetha, thervetha!

MACASSOU, *trying to be witty, as FLOUPETTE wipes her face with her sleeve*: Actually, señor, those are three things... Whisky, wine...

DON RAMON, *ignoring him, sitting down at the table, down right*: Becose, for me, ees always to dreenk, dreenk, dreenk!... Life ees to dreenk! *(Pounding the table, calling.)* Garthón! *(To MACASSOU.)* An for you also, papá? For you also ees to dreenk?

MACASSOU, *to FLOUPETTE, in a whisper*: He certainly has spirit!

FLOUPETTE, *to MACASSOU, in a whisper, emphasizing*: Spirits, uncle dear!

DON RAMON, *calling again*: Garthón!... *(After a moment, to MACASSOU.)* Peón no cone, papá! *(Getting up.)* So! Eenstead I keess bride!... Ho ho ho! *(To FLOUPETTE.)* Cone here, Flupeta!

FLOUPETTE, *recoiling*: Please, monsieur...

DON RAMON: Please to call "Don Ramón!" *(Approaching her.)* Cone... Cone... When ees weddeeng, leettle one?

FLOUPETTE: Really... I...

MACASSOU, *to DON RAMON, trying to intercede, timidly*: Perhaps you shouldn't... Perhaps she doesn't know if she—

DON RAMON, *interrupting, angrily*: Sí! Sí!… She no know? No know?… Sí, sí!

MACASSOU: She…

DON RAMON: Sí, sí!

MACASSOU: She…

DON RAMON: Sí! Sí! She know!… Ho ho ho!… She know! She know!…Sí, sí!!

MACASSOU: She…

DON RAMON: Sí, sí! *(To FLOUPETTE, menacingly.)* She no know? No know?…Sí, sí!

MACASSOU: She…

DON RAMON: Sí, sí!

FLOUPETTE, *trembling with fright*: I… Really, monsieur…

DON RAMON, *shouting, insistently*: Please to call "Don Ramón," I tell!

FLOUPETTE: Really, Don Ramón, I…

She takes refuge behind the table, right.

DON RAMON, *to FLOUPETTE*: So! You no like? *(To MACASSOU.)* You no like Don Ramón?

MACASSOU: I like! I like!… *(Aside.)* He's out of his mind!

DON RAMON: Aha! So!… Eef you like, so for why you say "No"…?

MACASSOU: But I didn't… I haven't… I mean, I never said "No"… I haven't said a thing!

DON RAMON: Oh?

MACASSOU: Besides, I have twenty thousand reasons to say "Yes, " for heaven's sake! It's Floupette… It's up to her…

DON RAMON, *to FLOUPETTE, who is still cowering behind the table*: You, leettle one! You hear? Ees op for you! So! You tell me… You tell Don Ramón… Bot be carefool what you tell! Don Ramón no like bad news! *(Growing more and more agitated.)* Ees very bad, bad news! Make anngry, bad news! Make want to keell someone!

MACASSOU, } *together*: { God!
FLOUPETTE, } { Heavens!

DON RAMON, *continuing, to FLOUPETTE*: So! You tell true… You love me, jes?

FLOUPETTE, *aside, trembling*: Goodness me!

DON RAMON: Ees jes? Ees jes?

FLOUPETTE, *trying to sound convincing*: Why, of course I do, monsieur…

DON RAMON, *out of patience*: Please to call—

FLOUPETTE, *quickly*: Don Ramón! Don Ramón!… I do!… Very much! Can't you tell? *(Aside.)* Oh! What a vile brute!

DON RAMON, *to MACASSOU*: You see? She worsheep me, Flupeta! Ees always so! You hear what she say?… "Very moch! Very moch!"

MACASSOU, *flabbergasted, to himself*: Who would ever think…? *(Aloud.)* She does?… *(To FLOUPETTE.)* You do? *(Aside.)* Then I'll win! I'm saved! The twenty thousand francs are mine!

DON RAMON, *to FLOUPETTE*: So! I ask… For when ees weddeen?

FLOUPETTE: My uncle knows my feelings… *(Emphasizing.)* Don Ramón…

DON RAMON: Ah, bueno! You no forget thees tine!

FLOUPETTE, *continuing*: I leave all the details to him. *(She takes off the apron, holds it up, and shakes it in front of* MACASSOU.*)* I'm sure he'll give you your answer!

MACASSOU, *aside*: Damn! She took it off!

FLOUPETTE: Now, if you'll excuse me…

She throws the apron down on a chair and exits, down right.

DON RAMON, *to* MACASSOU, *insistently*: So? So? So?… What ees anssouer, papá?

MACASSOU, *turning toward the door, down right, apostrophizing, aside*: Thank you! *(Aloud, to* DON RAMON.*)* The answer… *(Stammering.)* The…The…

DON RAMON, *growing more and more impatient*: Sí! Sí!… The! The!…

MACASSOU: Well…

DON RAMON: Ees more better you no make anngry, mi amigo!

MACASSOU, *as agreeably as possible*: Of course not! I wouldn't dream… Not you, Don Ramón!… A gentleman… A friend…

DON RAMON: Ees I no be only frien, papá! Soon I be nephew!… Sobrino, no? Sí! Sobrino!

MACASSOU: Sí, sí… *(Stammering over the word.)* "So… so…"

DON RAMON: So?… You tell when ees weddeen, no?

MACASSOU, *trying to hedge*: As a matter of fact… I was just thinking…

DON RAMON: We go make contrack, jes? Now! Now!… Thees minoot, no? Or else…

He begins flailing his fists about over his head.

MACASSOU: Ayyy! *(Frightened, calling.)* Barnabé! Barnabé!

BARNABE comes running in, up right.

BARNABE, *bumping into* DON RAMON: What is it?

DON RAMON: Peón!

He stomps on his foot.

BARNABE: Ayyy! My corns!… What do you think you're—

DON RAMON, *taking both* MACASSOU *and* BARNABE, *each under one arm*: Bueno! I take peón too! He be weetness…

BARNABE, *struggling*: Witness?

MACASSOU, *struggling*: But… My dear Don Ramón…

DON RAMON drags them both up center, as they voice their vociferous objections :

BARNABE, } *together*: { What?…Take your hands off me, you…
MACASSOU, } { But… For heaven's sake… Where do you think…

DON RAMON, *as they continue to object*: Cone! Cone!… We go for make contrack! Bot furst we go fine more wheesky! An thervetha!… Then we go for make contrack!

BARNABE, *as they reach the doors, up center*: Help!

MACASSOU: Don Ramón!… Will you please…

As DON RAMON *tries to drag them out the door, they each hit against the jambs and he drops them, staggering out, mumbling incoherently.* BARNABE *picks himself up and runs off, up right.*

MACASSOU, *alone, up center*: Good heavens!

DON RAMON'S VOICE, *offstage*: Ouf!

A MAN'S VOICE, *offstage*: Watch where you're going, you clumsy ass!

MACASSOU, *peeking out*: Oh my!

DON RAMON'S VOICE: Ass? Ass?… Caramba! Who be ass?… Ho ho ho! I show you ass!

MACASSOU: Now what?

DON RAMON'S VOICE: I show…

The sounds of a scuffle ensue, with appropriate exclamations, shouts, and threats.

MACASSOU, *shutting the doors*: If I'm lucky the gendarmes will drag him off, and that will be the end of it! *(With a sudden realization.)* Damn! He didn't even pay for the whisky! Or the stew he didn't eat!… *(Coming downstage.)* Why does Doghidou have to have such vile taste?… *(Moaning.)* My twenty thousand francs… Pffff!… My inn… My… *(Shaking his head.)* My, my, my!… Popinoff… Don Ramón… One as bad as the other… *(Going up center, looking out.)* Well, at least he's gone!… And still no sign of the third one, whatever his name is! *(Taking out his watch and consulting it.)* Good God! Look at the time!… *(Pacing back and forth.)* So what? He's probably the worst of the lot!… It's a damned conspiracy, that's what it is! A plot to make me lose The Golden Giraffe… *(Stopping at the table, right, and taking the apron from the chair.)* Why did I make that foolish bet? What was I thinking?… She puts it on, she takes it off!… On, off… On, off… *(Putting it back on the chair.)* Not that I blame her!… Where did he ever find them? *(As if having a conversation.)* "Really, my friend! Is this the best you could do? A crazy Russian and a drunken Spaniard?…" "But they're rich, Macassou! They're worth millions!…" Yes!… And soon the count will have my inn, to boot! *(He sits down at the table, right, dejectedly.)* Oh! My life! My life!… One foolish bet… One imbecile of a friend… *(Aside.)* Dumb toothpick salesman!… *(Aloud.)* And it's all turning to… to… *(As if addressing his friend.)* Doghidou!… Doghidou!… What have you done to me?

There is a soft knock at the doors, up center. MACASSOU *cocks his ear, listening, unsure that he has heard it. After a moment there is another.*

MACASSOU: Come in!

The doors open and BACHEFOLLE *pokes his head in, tentatively.*

BACHEFOLLE: Monsieur Macassou, please?

MACASSOU: Yes, yes… I'm Macassou… May I ask…

BACHEFOLLE: May I come in, monsieur?

MACASSOU: Of course! Of course…

BACHEFOLLE *enters and stands up center. He is dressed rather like Little Lord Fauntleroy, with thick glasses, and carrying a small package under his arm.*

BACHEFOLLE: Much obliged, monsieur…

MACASSOU: Did you want to have lunch? We have a fine rabbit stew today. And a Château Lafitte, 1825…

BACHEFOLLE: No… No, monsieur…

MACASSOU: Oh?… Then…

BACHEFOLLE: My name is Modeste Bachefolle.

MACASSOU, *jumping to his feet*: Bachefolle?… *(Joining him.)* Ah! Come in!…Do come in!

BACHEFOLLE, *as* MACASSOU *puts his arm around him and leads him downstage*: I wouldn't have disturbed you, monsieur, but—

MACASSOU: Please! Not at all!

BACHEFOLLE, *continuing*: But papá said I should come.

MACASSOU: Yes, yes! I know!... What a pleasure, my friend!... Please! Make yourself at home! You're saving my life!

BACHEFOLLE, *quizzically*: I am?

MACASSOU, *aside*: Charming! I like him! *(Aloud, offering him a chair, right.)* Here... *(Reaching for his package.)* Let me take that...

BACHEFOLLE: Oh! Be careful, monsieur!

MACASSOU: Is it fragile?

He lays it carefully on the table, right.

BACHEFOLLE: Oh! I should say! They're shells... For mam'selle... The one papá said I should come and visit...

MACASSOU, *aside*: Sweet child!

BACHEFOLLE: I picked them up along the river.

MACASSOU: Ah? And what are they for?

BACHEFOLLE: Why, to play with... When we're married, mam'selle and me...We'll have to do something to pass the time, monsieur.

MACASSOU: Of course! *(Enthusiastically, under his breath.)* Damn! He's perfect!

BACHEFOLLE, *overhearing him, drawing back, shocked*: Oh!... You swore, monsieur!

MACASSOU: I did?

BACHEFOLLE: I'm leaving!

MACASSOU: What?... No, no! You can't!... I... I never swear! That... That just slipped out! *(Aside.)* Good God! She'll have to wipe his... his nose!... *(Aloud.)* Please! Don't go...I'll introduce you to my niece.

BACHEFOLLE: Does she swear?

MACASSOU: No! Never!... She's... She's sweet and pure as a newborn lamb! You'll see...

BACHEFOLLE: Because, if she does...

He shudders.

MACASSOU: You'll see... *(Calling, as* BACHEFOLLE, *as inconspicuously as possible, moves up left and sits on the chair by the desk.)* Floupette!... Floupette!...

FLOUPETTE *enters, down right.*

FLOUPETTE: Yes, uncle dear?

MACASSOU, *joining her, softly*: Number three is here! *(Taking the apron from the chair.)* Quick! Put it on...

FLOUPETTE, *about to object*: But really, I...

MACASSOU: Here... Let me... *(He ties it around her waist.)* There!... *(Aloud.)* Floupette, my love... Let me present... *(Looking around for* BACHEFOLLE.*)* Where the devil... *(Noticing him folding a large piece of paper.)* Monsieur... What are you doing?

BACHEFOLLE: Making a hat, monsieur...

MACASSOU: Oh? What for?

BACHEFOLLE: To play soldier...

MACASSOU, *to* FLOUPETTE: Delightful chap! *(To* BACHEFOLLE.*)* Come closer, young man… *(To* FLOUPETTE.*)* Don't worry… He's tame… *(To* BACHEFOLLE, *pointing to a chair at the table, right.)* Please… Sit here…

BACHEFOLLE: If… If you're sure I may…

He gets up, comes right, timidly, and sits down, as MACASSOU *leads* FLOUPETTE *left, speaking to her in a confidential whisper.*

MACASSOU: So? What do you think?

FLOUPETTE: I suppose he might do… *(Sighing.)* He reminds me a little of Raoul…

MACASSOU: Nonsense! Your cousin is a lout! The scum of the earth!… An actor, for goodness' sake!

FLOUPETTE, *sighing*: I know…

MACASSOU: This one is a gem. A diamond in the rough!… Listen! You'll see… *(To* BACHEFOLLE.*)* Young man…

BACHEFOLLE: Monsieur?

MACASSOU: Stand up!… *(He complies.)* Come here… *(To* FLOUPETTE, *in a whisper, as* BACHEFOLLE *takes several cautious steps in their direction.)* See? He's already trained. *(To* BACHEFOLLE.*)* Very good! Now talk… This is Floupette… Your intended… Tell her something.

BACHEFOLLE, *to* FLOUPETTE, *turning his back to her*: Mam'selle… Papá is the richest farmer this side of Avignon, and I'm his only son…

MACASSOU, *to* BACHEFOLLE: What are you doing?

BACHEFOLLE: I'm proposing to her, monsieur.

MACASSOU: With your back turned?

BACHEFOLLE: Papá always says you should never look a young lady in the eye.

MACASSOU: He says you… The ones you're not marrying, maybe! But… Come now, turn around!

BACHEFOLLE: If you're sure I ought to…

MACASSOU: I'm sure!

BACHEFOLLE *turns around.*

FLOUPETTE, *aside*: Poor thing!

MACASSOU, *to* BACHEFOLLE: So!… Start again… But face to face this time!

BACHEFOLLE, *standing in front of* FLOUPETTE, *looking down at the ground, repeating mechanically*: Mam'selle… Papá is the richest farmer this side of Avignon, and I'm his only son. He raises…

MACASSOU, *interrupting*: That's not important. Get to the point!

BACHEFOLLE, *losing his train of thought*: He raises… He… *(To* MACASSOU.*)* See? You made me forget! *(To* FLOUPETTE, *beginning again.)* Mam'selle… Papá is the richest farmer this side of Avignon, and… and… *(He takes the sheet of paper that he had folded into a hat, unfolds it, and hands it to* MACASSOU.*)* Help me, monsieur!… *(Continuing, as* MACASSOU *follows along on the paper.)* And… And…

MACASSOU, *prompting him*: "And I'm…"

BACHEFOLLE: And I'm his only son. He raises wheat, barley, and rye. And that makes me a very fine prospect…

MACASSOU, *approving*: Good!… Very good!

BACHEFOLLE, *continuing, searching his memory*: Your daughter is very pretty…

MACASSOU, *correcting him*: My niece...

BACHEFOLLE, *repeating*: Your daughter is very pretty, and...

MACASSOU: You mean my niece...

BACHEFOLLE: That's not how I learned it, monsieur!

MACASSOU, *with a shrug*: Never mind!

BACHEFOLLE: Your daughter is very pretty, and papá says that I love her.

FLOUPETTE, *aside*: "Papá says"...?

BACHEFOLLE, *continuing*: So I have the honor, monsieur, of asking you for her hand in marriage so I can take her back to the farm as soon as possible... Your obedient servant... Sincerely yours, Modeste Bachefolle...

MACASSOU: Very good!... *(He gives him back the paper.)* Well done!

BACHEFOLLE: Papá is the richest farmer this side of...

MACASSOU: You already said that part!

BACHEFOLLE: Oh...

MACASSOU, *taking out his watch, looking at it*: And we don't have time to hear it again! *(Aside.)* A memory like a sieve!... But as long as he remembers how to sign his name... *(He gives him a little peck on the forehead.)* Dear boy...

BACHEFOLLE, *offering his forehead to* FLOUPETTE: And mam'selle too!

MACASSOU, *wagging his finger at him*: Tsk tsk tsk! Not yet... After all...

BACHEFOLLE: But mammá always gives me a kiss when I recite well.

MACASSOU: Yes, but... *(To* FLOUPETTE.*)* I told you he was a gem!

FLOUPETTE: But uncle dear...

BACHEFOLLE, *to* MACASSOU: What should I tell papá, monsieur?

MACASSOU: Well, I... *(He and* FLOUPETTE *exchange glances, the latter obviously undecided, then proceed to discuss the question in hushed whispers.)* Floupette?...

FLOUPETTE: I... I don't know...

MACASSOU: Please...

FLOUPETTE: I mean... He's not that awful Count Popinoff or Don Ramón, but...

MACASSOU, *aloud, to* BACHEFOLLE: My niece wants just a few moments to consider your flattering proposal. *(Pointing up left.)* In the meantime, you can sit down...

BACHEFOLLE: Oh, good! I can make another hat!

He sits down at the desk, up left, takes a sheet of paper out of his pocket, and begins folding it assiduously, utterly absorbed and oblivious to the following exchange.

MACASSOU: Please, Floupette! You can't say "No!" this time! Your poor uncle will be ruined!

FLOUPETTE: But...

MACASSOU: You don't want that, do you?

FLOUPETTE: But marriage is forever! And that's a long time, uncle dear!

MACASSOU: I know, but... You just said so yourself. He's not Don Ramón... He's not the count... So what if he's... Well, a little...

FLOUPETTE: A little simple!

MACASSOU: It's better for a husband not to be too bright!

FLOUPETTE: Besides, I don't know if I would be happy with him...

MACASSOU, *insisting*: You would! You would!

FLOUPETTE: …even though he does look like my cousin Raoul a little…

MACASSOU: Your… Please! Don't say that! Don't even mention that wretch's name! That blackguard!… That brute!… I'm begging you, Floupette! Modeste is perfect! Marry him! I don't have much more time…

FLOUPETTE: Oh…

MACASSOU: I… Please! For me!… For us!… For The Golden Giraffe!

FLOUPETTE, *wavering*: Oh… I… *(Just as she seems about to acquiesce.)* No! I'm sorry, uncle dear, but it's bigger than I am!… I can't do it! I simply can't!

She begins to untie the apron.

MACASSOU, *stopping her*: No! Stop!… Think what you're doing!

FLOUPETTE, *having difficulty*: Oh!… There's a knot…

MACASSOU: There! You see? It's fate!… Whether you love him or… or not!

FLOUPETTE, *weakly*: But…

MACASSOU: You're right… It's bigger than you are! And bigger than me!

FLOUPETTE: But…

MACASSOU: It's… It's your destiny! *(To* BACHEFOLLE*, without waiting for her reply.)* Young man!… Modeste!

BACHEFOLLE, *looking up from his paper hat*: Monsieur?

MACASSOU: You can tell your papá that it's all arranged! She's going to be your wife!

FLOUPETTE, *softly*: But uncle dear…

MACASSOU, *continuing*: Come… Kiss her! Kiss me!… Kiss everyone!… I'm saved! *(Deliriously happy, as* BACHEFOLLE *comes down and joins them.)* I'm saved!… Saved, you hear?

FLOUPETTE, *aside*: Poor thing! *(Sighing.)* If it makes him happy…

Dejected, she wipes a tear or two and stands, hanging her head.

MACASSOU: Saved, you hear?… Damn!

BACHEFOLLE, *reacting*: Oh!… Monsieur, you—

MACASSOU, *quickly*: I didn't say that! I didn't!… Now come… We have just enough time to take care of the contract. *(Looking at his watch.)* With a half-hour to spare…

BACHEFOLLE, *to* MACASSOU: But I can't, monsieur… Not now…

MACASSOU: What?… "Not now"? "Not—"?

BACHEFOLLE: No…

MACASSOU: Why not?

BACHEFOLLE: I have to watch the one-thirty train go by. The one from Lyon… If I miss it… Oh! I mustn't! *(Moving up center.)* Bye bye…

MACASSOU: Wait! You can't leave…

BACHEFOLLE: But I have to! It's almost time…

MACASSOU: I know! That's what I mean!

BACHEFOLLE: It will be coming any minute!

MACASSOU: All right! All right!… Just be sure you come right back! *(Muttering under his breath.)* He has to watch the train! Good God in heaven!

BACHEFOLLE, *overhearing him, stopping at the doors, up center, jaw agape*: Oh!…

MACASSOU, *realizing his faux pas*: I didn't say that! I didn't... Now go! And come right back, you hear?

BACHEFOLLE: Yes, monsieur... *(As he is about to leave, he stops.)* Oh, I almost forgot... *(Holding out the paper hat.)* Papá asked me to give you this letter.

MACASSOU: But it's a paper hat!

BACHEFOLLE: Well... It was a letter... He said it's all about the wedding.

FLOUPETTE, *aside, sighing*: Oh my... Oh my...

MACASSOU, *taking the paper and unfolding it, to* BACHEFOLLE, *impatiently*: Yes!... Now go!... Go! Go! Go!

BACHEFOLLE, *to* FLOUPETTE: When we're married, mam'selle, we can watch the trains together!

He exits.

MACASSOU, *to* FLOUPETTE, *heaving a sigh of relief*: At last!... As soon as he comes back... Ah! Twenty thousand francs... *(Taking a few steps left, toward the alcove.)* So there, Count Popinoff!... And the inn is still mine! *(To* FLOUPETTE, *who is still standing mournfully to one side, down right.)* I'll never forget what you're doing for me, Floupette! You'll see! I promise... *(Calling.)* Barnabé!... Barnabé!

BARNABE *enters, up right.*

BARNABE: What is it?

MACASSOU: Go tell the count that I want to see him! *(Gloating.)* And tell him to bring his money!

BARNABE, *aside*: Bah!

He exits, left.

MACASSOU, *looking at his watch*: Twenty-five minutes! *(Noticing the letter he still has in his hand.)* What's this...? Ah! His father's letter...

FLOUPETTE: What does it say, uncle dear?

MACASSOU: We'll soon find out... *(Reading.)* "Monsieur... Marriage is a sacred institution..." *(Spoken, sarcastically.)* How profound!... *(Reading.)* "...and if the soil is to be fertile..." *(Spoken.)* Farmer!... *(Reading.)* "...'Straight is the furrow that will bring forth its grains,' as the good book tells us..." *(Spoken, aside.)* It does?

FLOUPETTE: I never knew...

MACASSOU: Of course it does! *(Reading.)* "That is why I must tell you that, in spite of his innocent air, my son has a vice..."

FLOUPETTE: What?

MACASSOU, *continuing*: "He loves the fair sex..."

FLOUPETTE, *putting her hand to her mouth, shocked*: Oh, uncle dear...

MACASSOU, *continuing*: "...if you will pardon the expression..." *(Spoken.)* Of course!... So?... He's a gigolo...

FLOUPETTE: He is?

MACASSOU: There are worse faults!

FLOUPETTE: But... I thought he was a Frenchman...

MACASSOU: No, child... A... A lecher... *(She gives him a quizzical little look.)* If that's his only vice... In my younger days, even I was know to... *(With a gesture.)* Pfff!

FLOUPETTE: But...

MACASSOU, *reading*: "...and it pains me to tell you that he is a shameless rake!"

FLOUPETTE: A rake?

MACASSOU, *trying to make a joke*: Ha ha!... A farmer's son, after all... *(Reading.)* "What's more, he loves them so much that he has two children..."

FLOUPETTE, *aghast*: What?

MACASSOU: Two...? *(Aside.)* God in heaven! Now she'll never... *(Aloud.)* Well, that just proves that he... that he... *(Embarrassed.)* You know what I mean...

FLOUPETTE, *angrily*: Yes! That he's a hypocrite!... A two-faced, lying hypocrite!... Oh! I never...

MACASSOU: Please, Floupette!... Don't let a little thing like that spoil your marriage! Your... My—

FLOUPETTE: A little thing? A little... Two little things you mean!... No! Never!

MACASSOU, *desperate*: But men always have them! They have to... It's... It's...If nobody did, why... Who would come to the inn? Who would spend money?... Men have to have children!

FLOUPETTE: That's all well and good, but I'll never have his!... I... I'd rather die an old maid! So there!

MACASSOU, *ready to tear his hair*: Oh!... I'm ruined! I'm finished!... I...

BARNABE comes running in, left.

BARNABE, *to MACASSOU*: You'll never guess!... The count—

MACASSOU, *not listening, furious*: Damn him! He... I... Him and his paper hats!

BARNABE, *continuing*: He's not—

MACASSOU, *still ignoring him*: After everything I've done... To lose like this... At the very last moment!... No contract! No marriage!

BARNABE, *trying to get a word in edgewise*: But—

FLOUPETTE, *trying to calm him*: Please, uncle dear...

MACASSOU: No money!... No inn!... *(Suddenly struck by a thought.)* Wait!... Ah! What an idea!... Yes, yes! There's still hope!... Raoul's contract... *(Feeling all his pockets.)* Where did I... *(He takes the contract from his back pocket and thrusts it into her hands.)* Quick! Sign this!... He already has...

FLOUPETTE: What?

MACASSOU, *taking her up left, to the desk, and handing her the pen and ink*: Better him than no one!

BARNABE: But—

FLOUPETTE: But—

MACASSOU: Quick! Quick!

Thoroughly confused, she signs it. MACASSOU does likewise.

BARNABE: But I'm trying to tell you—

MACASSOU, *ignoring him*: Ha!... *(As he kisses the contract and holds it up, waving it back and forth.)* Signed, sealed, and delivered!

The doors, up center, suddenly fly open and RAOUL strides in.

RAOUL, *seizing the contract from MACASSOU's hands*: Thank you, uncle!

BARNABE, *aside*: Damn!

MACASSOU, *to RAOUL*: You!

FLOUPETTE, *obviously happy to see him*: Oh!

RAOUL, *to MACASSOU*: I told you I'd be back! *(With a Russian accent.)* Ach! Dat mek me so heppy!

MACASSOU *and* **FLOUPETTE**: *What?*

RAOUL, *to MACASSOU, scratching his head, as FLOUPETTE, speechless, stands gaping at them*: You have nits, da?

MACASSOU: You… I…

RAOUL: And I have mellow collie…

MACASSOU: But…

RAOUL: So!… I dence before lonch!

He does a few quick steps of his Cossack dance.

FLOUPETTE, *clapping*: Oh!

MACASSOU: But… I can't believe… *(RAOUL gives a little shrug.)* And… My twenty thousand francs? My bet?

RAOUL, *in his own voice*: I'm afraid you'll have to collect it from His Countenance!

MACASSOU: Of all the…

RAOUL, *to BARNABE, with a Spanish accent*: Peón! You annoonth!… Caramba! You annoonth, jes?

MACASSOU, *flabbergasted*: What? Don Ramón?… You?

RAOUL: Sí, sí, señor!

MACASSOU: It… It can't be…

RAOUL, *to FLOUPETTE, timidly*: Mam'selle… Papá is the richest farmer this side of Avignon…

MACASSOU: And Bachefolle too?

RAOUL, *continuing*: …and I'm his only son.

MACASSOU: Goddamn!

RAOUL: Oh! You swore!

MACASSOU: Damn! Damn! Damn!

RAOUL, *pretending to move upstage*: I'm leaving!

MACASSOU: All three?… But, how? You couldn't have… It's impossible…

RAOUL: Not for an artiste… Just another role… *(As an afterthought.)* Or three…

MACASSOU: And you think I'm going to give you Floupette after that?

RAOUL, *waving the contract*: Signed, sealed, and delivered, uncle! You can't take back your signature!

MACASSOU: Oh? And why not? They do it all the time in business! Every day—

FLOUPETTE, *interrupting*: But I'm not in business, uncle dear! And when I sign my name… *(Giving RAOUL her hand.)* I keep my word!

RAOUL, *tenderly*: Ah! Floupette!

FLOUPETTE: Ah! Raoul!

MACASSOU, *mimicking*: Ah! Ah! Ah!… *(Aside.)* The scoundrel! I can thank my sister…

BARNABE, *aside*: What does she see in him when she could have me?

MACASSOU: Her and her one mistake!

BARNABE, *to MACASSOU*: What should I do with the haddock à la Macassou?

MACASSOU, *angrily*: I don't give a… Eat it!

BARNABE: Thank you! *(Aside.)* I'd rather starve!

MACASSOU: Just be sure you save the stew! You never know when we might have guests! *(With a withering look at* RAOUL.*)* And now that I'm keeping the inn…

RAOUL, *to* MACASSOU: That reminds me, uncle… About the wedding dinner… I'm sure you'll want to have one for us!

MACASSOU: Oh? You think…

RAOUL: I mean, she is your niece!… And I am your nephew…

MACASSOU: Yes! Aren't you! *(Looking heavenward, under his breath.)* Sister dear!

RAOUL: Nothing too fancy…

MACASSOU: Well… On one condition…

RAOUL: That is?

MACASSOU: That you give me a ticket for your very next play…

RAOUL: Why? I didn't think you cared for the theater!

MACASSOU: To throw tomatoes at you, damn it! *(Aside.)* Young scoundrel!

FLOUPETTE, *laughing*: Tsk tsk tsk! Uncle dear…

RAOUL chuckles and exchanges loving glances with her.

BARNABE, *to* MACASSOU, *softly*: But we don't have any!

MACASSOU: Well, you'd better go get a bushel if you know what's good for you! Because, if you don't—

BARNABE: I know… I know… My goose is cooked!

RAOUL, *with his Spanish accent*: No no!… No goose! Feather make for to sneeze!

MACASSOU, *shaking his head in resignation*: Of all things! An actor!

FLOUPETTE: Raoul!

RAOUL: Floupette!

BARNABE, *aside*: Bah!

He exits, up right.

MACASSOU, *muttering*: An actor… An actor…

Hands on hips, he stands watching RAOUL and FLOUPETTE embrace, as the curtain falls.

CURTAIN.

The Brat

(Une fille bien gardée, 1850)

Eugène Labiche & Marc-Michel

Characters

PHILIPPE, a domestic not overly encumbered by scruples

DAGOBERT, a cavalry officer with an eye for the ladies

THE BARONESS, an attractive widow and devoted mother

CHANTAL, her seven-year-old-in-pigtails with a will of her own and no lack of energy

NANETTE, Philippe's female counterpart, the Baroness's maid, scheming but harmless

An elegantly furnished drawing room. Upstage center, a curtained alcove with a child's bed. In the upstage wall, left, a door leading outside to a vestibule. In each wall, left and right center, a door, the former leading to the baroness's room, the latter, to Nanette's. Down left, an open window, opening out onto a small balcony with a parrot and cage. Close to it, an armchair and end table. Down right, a fireplace with a mirror on the wall above it. On the mantelpiece, a long feather duster and a vase with flowers. Near it, another armchair and end table. A life-sized doll is draped over the back of the chair. Between the fireplace and the stage right door, a vanity table and small chair, facing the wall. On the table, a journal, writing materials, and assorted flasks and jars. In a drawer, more flasks. In the up left corner, a small table and chair. On it, Nanette's sewing and a lighted candelabra. Rugs, pictures, etc.

At rise, NANETTE *is closing the alcove curtains. From time to time boisterous music—cancans, polkas, and the like—can be heard, ostensibly coming from the floor below.*

NANETTE, *sighing, in obvious ill humor, to herself*: Damnation! Asleep at last!… Blasted little pest!… Children? *(With a gesture.)* Pfff!… Especially that one… Spoiled?… "Spoiled" isn't the word! *(Toward the alcove.)* If you were my child, believe me… *(Mimicking.)* "I don't want to go to bed! I don't want to…" *(In her own voice.)* I don't care what you want, you little—

THE BARONESS, *hurriedly entering, left, in evening dress—gown, shawl, hat—interrupting*: Did you put her to bed, Nanette?

NANETTE, *caught short, suddenly all smiles*: Oh yes, madame! *(Lifting a corner of the alcove curtains.)* See? Fast asleep… Like a little angel!

THE BARONESS, *joining her*: Just look at her! The picture of innocence! *(*NANETTE *heaves a hypocritical little sigh.)* My little cherub…

NANETTE, *heaving another*: Cherub!… That's the word… It's like I was saying, madame…

THE BARONESS, *blowing a kiss*: Sleep tight, treasure.

NANETTE, *likewise*: Sleep tight, little lamb.

THE BARONESS, *putting on her gloves, coming down right, examining herself in the mirror*: Poor dear… Wheezing and coughing all the livelong day… She just hasn't been herself.

NANETTE, *hypocritically*: Tsk tsk tsk!

THE BARONESS: And here I am… Simply, utterly obliged to go running off to their silly old soirée, when I should be here with my precious Chantal, nursing her back to health.

NANETTE, *aside*: Nursing? A seven-year-old?

THE BARONESS: What a bore!

PHILIPPE, *in footman's livery—uniform and hat—appears at the door, up left.*

PHILIPPE, *clearing his throat, to* THE BARONESS: Begging the baroness's pardon… *(Coughing.)* But madame is hitched…

THE BARONESS: I'm what?

PHILIPPE, *coming down to the open window, left, pointing outside*: The horses, madame… *(Coughing.)* They're hitched and ready to depart, if I may say… *(Under his breath.)* Damn!

NANETTE: Shhh! You'll wake mademoiselle!

The music becomes very raucous.

THE BARONESS: If that horrid music downstairs doesn't wake her first!

NANETTE: Quite, madame...

She and PHILIPPE begin unconsciously keeping time with the music.

THE BARONESS, *continuing*: That... That...

PHILIPPE, *coughing*: Moulin Bleu, madame...

THE BARONESS: What's the matter, Philippe? Are you ill?

PHILIPPE: Madame needn't be concerned. *(Coughing.)* It's only my lungs.

THE BARONESS, *to NANETTE*: Please, Nanette! Shut the window! The poor boy will catch his death in that draft.

NANETTE: Very good, madame...

PHILIPPE, *to THE BARONESS*: Madame is too kind.

THE BARONESS, *as NANETTE moves to comply*: Of all the neighbors to have downstairs! The Moulin Bleu, indeed!

NANETTE, *as she is about to pull the window shut*: Oh my! *(Bringing the parrot cage in from the balcony.)* I almost forgot to bring it in...

THE BARONESS: Please, Nanette! "Him"!... How many times do I have to tell you? Little Raoul is not an "it"!

NANETTE, *leaving the window open and handing the cage to PHILIPPE, who holds it at arm's length*: Very good, madame...

PHILIPPE, *to THE BARONESS*: If madame has no objection, and if I may allow myself to venture a suggestion regarding her little Raoul...

THE BARONESS: And that is...?

PHILIPPE: And that is, with all due respect, that she refrain from leaving her parrot so close to the premises of a public dance hall, madame...

THE BARONESS: Oh?

PHILIPPE: Unless she wants it... *(Coughing, as NANETTE gives him a little nudge.)* Unless she wants him to develop a vocabulary that would make a sailor blush...

THE BARONESS: Goodness me! Do you think...?

PHILIPPE: Think?... I know, madame!... Why, only yesterday, as I was attempting to engage him in casual conversation, he saw fit to address me in a manner that... Well...

THE BARONESS: That what, Philippe?

PHILIPPE: That called into question my mother's honor...

THE BARONESS: Oh!

PHILIPPE: My sainted mother, madame...

NANETTE: He didn't!

PHILIPPE, *continuing*: ...and the conditions of my birth, if I may say...

He crosses right and places the cage on the end table by the armchair.

THE BARONESS: Poor dear!

PHILIPPE, *misunderstanding*: Madame is too kind.

THE BARONESS, *between PHILIPPE and NANETTE*: I... What?... No, no... Raoul... My poor little Raoul...

PHILIPPE: Ah... I thought...

Suddenly the parrot begins cackling: "Awk awk!... Stupid bastard!... Stupid bastard!... Awk awk awk!..."

THE BARONESS, *shocked*: What?

PHILIPPE: Madame sees what I mean.

THE BARONESS: Well, we'll just have to find him a better place in the morning! It's not his fault, poor thing. *(To* NANETTE.*)* I do love him so...

NANETTE: Of course, madame...

THE BARONESS: And I wouldn't give him up for all the tea in China!

NANETTE: Certainly not...

THE BARONESS: After all, he was the very last gift my dear deceased husband gave me...

NANETTE: Tsk, tsk tsk...

THE BARONESS: The late baron de Flochepette... *(*PHILIPPE *lifts his hat and bows deeply.)* Before he died...

NANETTE: Yes... *(Aside.)* I would imagine...

THE BARONESS, *continuing, as* PHILIPPE *replaces his hat*: Master of the Holy Order of Saint Christopher... *(*PHILIPPE *repeats his move.)* Commander of the Venerable Knights of King Ferdinand... *(Turning to* NANETTE, *as* PHILIPPE *repeats his move.)* Third degree, Nanette... With the sash...

NANETTE, *with feigned admiration*: Tsk tsk tsk!

THE BARONESS, *continuing, to* PHILIPPE: Supreme Head of Saint John the Baptist Order of the Blade... *(As* PHILIPPE *repeats once again.)* And Honorary Seneschal of the Order of Saints Peter, Paul, and Mary... *(To* NANETTE.*)* In Rome, Nanette... *(To* PHILIPPE.*)* The Vatican...

NANETTE, *as* PHILIPPE *takes off his hat, places it over his heart, and bows again, not without a little difficulty*: Tsk tsk tsk!

THE BARONESS: Thank you... I appreciate domestics who know how to show respect. *(Looking heavenward.)* And I'm sure he would too...

PHILIPPE, *rubbing his back*: I'm sure, madame... *(Coughing.)* I'm sure... *(Replacing his hat, aside.)* Damn!

THE BARONESS, *as* NANETTE, *moving up left, takes her sewing from the table*: Really, Philippe... *(Going to primp in front of the mirror, as* NANETTE *sits down in the armchair, down left.)* You simply must take care of that cough. It seems to be getting worse.

PHILIPPE: Madame is too kind. But she needn't worry. It will disappear in time.

THE BARONESS: Yes, and you with it, Philippe! Especially if you stand out in the cold until four o'clock in the morning!

PHILIPPE: One does what one's profession demands, madame.

THE BARONESS: Well, I simply wouldn't forgive myself!

PHILIPPE: I appreciate madame's concern.

THE BARONESS: And where would I ever find another?... No, no... I'll have Gustave take your place tonight. You need your rest.

PHILIPPE: Madame's breast is flowing with the milk of human kindness, if I may say...

Suddenly the parrot cackles: "Awk awk!... Madame's breast... Awk awk awk!... Madame's breast!..."

THE BARONESS: Raoul!

NANETTE, *under her breath*: Both of them…

THE BARONESS, *to PHILIPPE*: Tomorrow we simply must find him another place. *(To NANETTE.)* And as for you, child… *(Surprised.)* Good heavens, still sewing? At this hour?

NANETTE: Idle hands are the devil's workshop, madame! I can't stand sitting and doing nothing.

PHILIPPE, *still coughing, crossing quickly to the other armchair, down right, rubbing it vigorously with his handkerchief*: Nor can I, madame…

THE BARONESS, *to PHILIPPE*: Please! You needn't… Not now… *(To NANETTE.)* You too, Nanette… Both of you…

PHILIPPE, *continuing to rub, not to be outdone*: But madame… *(Sententiously.)* The bread of idleness tastes bitter on the tongue. *(She gives him a quizzical look.)* It's a proverb.

NANETTE, *aside*: Oh?

PHILIPPE: My sainted mother always used to quote it.

THE BARONESS: Aha… Still… I insist… It's late, and tomorrow is another day. *(Aside.)* What absolute jewels! The two of them! *(Aloud, getting ready to leave.)* Now, please…

NANETTE, *putting the sewing down on the end table, getting up*: Well, only because madame insists…

THE BARONESS, *crossing up left, to NANETTE*: Just be sure to leave your door open. In case she wakes up… *(Stopping at the door.)* Oh… And don't forget her medicine. Two spoonfuls at midnight…

NANETTE: Madame can rest assured…

THE BARONESS: You're a jewel, Nanette!

NANETTE: What wouldn't I do for the child! I love her like my own.

PHILIPPE, *again, not to be outdone*: Me too… Like my very own…

NANETTE: An angel, madame…

PHILIPPE: An archangel… An archangel…

THE BARONESS, *delighted*: How true! *(Aside.)* Utter jewels… *(Aloud.)* Well, I leave her in your hands. *(With a little wave.)* Ta ta…

> *As she is about to exit, PHILIPPE runs up to take a candelabra and accompany her out.*

PHILIPPE, *coughing*: If madame will permit me…

THE BARONESS: Heavens, no, Philippe! You'll catch your death!

PHILIPPE, *with a little bow, not nearly as deep as before*: Madame is too kind…

> *THE BARONESS exits. NANETTE and PHILIPPE stand for a moment listening at the door, then move to the window and look out. Horses' hooves and a carriage can be heard going off into the distance.*

NANETTE: Gone!

PHILIPPE, *taking off his hat and placing it on the end table by the armchair, down left, loosening his collar and unbuttoning his jacket*: At last!… I thought she'd never leave!

NANETTE: Her and that dead husband of hers! The baron de Floche… de Ploche…

PHILIPPE: De Focheplette…

NANETTE: De Flechepotte…

PHILIPPE: Whatever! And when the cat's away… Till dawn, Nanette!

NANETTE: The mice will play! *(Reconsidering.)* Or they would, if you weren't so sick…

PHILIPPE: Sick? Me? *(Thumping his chest.)* Ha ha ha! Silly child!… Hook, line, and sinker!… You too, I see!

NANETTE: But… Your cough?… I thought—

PHILIPPE: Tsk tsk, tsk!… Bad! Bad!… Thinking rots the brain, my sweet. Just listen and learn. The only time I cough is when I swallow the wrong way.

NANETTE: You mean… Just now? When you came in…

PHILIPPE: Exactly… I was, if I may say, attempting to form a considered opinion of madame's new cognac.

NANETTE: Oh!

PHILIPPE: And just between us, Nanette, it's not fit to be drunk! The old one is much better. But there I was, about to compare, when all of a sudden I hear madame's voice, and… Well, rather than get nabbed I had to cut the test short.

NANETTE: Poor Philippe…

PHILIPPE, *with a gulp*: And… Down the wrong way!

He mimics gagging.

NANETTE: Tsk tsk tsk!

PHILIPPE: But, no harm… *(Thumping his chest again.)* Still fit as a fiddle… *(Taking her around the waist.)* As you can see…

NANETTE: Careful! Don't break your strings!

PHILIPPE, *ignoring her remark, continuing*: And ready to enjoy this night to the fullest!

NANETTE: Oh? *(Coyly.)* Just what did you have in mind?

PHILIPPE: Why… I thought, maybe a nice little supper…

NANETTE, *pushing him away*: Bah! That's all you ever think about! Your stomach…

PHILIPPE: Don't you?

NANETTE: My belly, yes… But not my stomach!

The music downstairs begins again.

PHILIPPE: Listen!… *(He tries to give several energetic kicks in rhythm.)* Damn! Doesn't it make you want to kick up your heels?

NANETTE: Well… Not too high… I'm not wearing garters!

The parrot cackles again: "Awk awk awk!… Garters! Garters!… Awk awk awk!"

PHILIPPE: Ha! Don't be a prude!… *(He takes her hands and begins dancing clockwise around the room with her.)* La la la la la…

NANETTE, *reluctantly going along, stopping as they reach the alcove*: Shhh!… We'll wake her…

PHILIPPE, *pulling her down left*: Not if we're not here, we won't!

NANETTE: Not here? *(Pushing him away.)* What are you talking about?

PHILIPPE: Not if we go downstairs… To the Moulin Bleu… You and me…

NANETTE: To the… *(Not averse to the idea.)* Do you think we should?

PHILIPPE: Why not?

NANETTE, *pretending to ruminate*: Well… I can't think of a single reason!

PHILIPPE: Neither can I!

NANETTE: Especially because my friend Claudine is going to be there...

PHILIPPE: Claudine?... The one with... with... *(Miming an ample bosom.)* And freckles?... That Claudine?

NANETTE: That Claudine...

PHILIPPE, *aside, smacking his lips*: Mmm!... Yum yum!

NANETTE: With her cousin Dagobert, the corporal... *(Aside.)* Now there's a man! No supper for him!

PHILIPPE: The corporal?

NANETTE, *aside*: He has better things to do!

PHILIPPE: But last week he was a sergeant. How did he change ranks?

NANETTE: He didn't... She changed cousins.

PHILIPPE: Ah yes! Dear Claudine... *(He turns aside and repeats his suggestive mime.)* So? We're going?

NANETTE: We're going!

PHILIPPE: Good! Go put on something fancy.

NANETTE, *crossing right, to her room*: I'm on my way! *(Suddenly stopping at the door.)* But... *(Joining him, down left, pointing upstage.)* What about her?

PHILIPPE: Bah! Children sleep like logs. We'll come up between polkas and give her the medicine.

NANETTE, *after a brief hesitation, slapping her thigh*: Damnation!... Why not! *(With a note of sarcasm.)* If I may say...

PHILIPPE takes her hands and dances her around, counterclockwise.

PHILIPPE, *singing*: La la la la la...

NANETTE, *stopping him in front of the alcove*: Shhh! *(Whispering.)* Not so loud!

PHILIPPE, *whispering*: You're right!

He takes her hands and they continue, singing along in muted tones.

NANETTE, *as they reach the door, right, mimicking the baroness*: Ta ta!

She exits, as the parrot pipes up: "Awk awk!... Ta ta! Ta ta!... Awk awk awk!"

PHILIPPE: Enough, damn it! *(He retrieves his hat and lays it over the cage.)* There!... And now to make myself beautiful... More beautiful, I mean... For Claudine! *(He sits down at the vanity table and opens a jar.)* First, some of my best brilliantine... Well, the baroness's, that is... But it may as well be mine. *(Smelling it.)* Mmm!... Violet!... *(He scoops out a quantity, rubs it between his hands, and slicks it over his hair.)* A little more? *(He repeats the action and, when finished, licks his hands.)* Delicious! *(He gets up and goes to the mirror above the fireplace.)* Perfect!... Almost... *(He twists a little curl on each of his temples.)* There! Irresistible!... Sorry, corporal! Your hours are numbered... If I may say...

He replaces the jar on the vanity and sits down.

CHANTAL'S VOICE, *yawning*: Aaaah...

PHILIPPE, *opening the drawer*: What is it, Nanette? *(Rummaging.)* Aha! Rouge?... *(Holding up the jar.)* You mean, the baroness...? *(Feigning shock.)* She doesn't!... *(He puts it down and continues rummaging.)* Now, where is my cologne?

CHANTAL'S VOICE: Aaaah!...

PHILIPPE, *impatiently*: I said, "What is it, Nanette?" *(Finding a flask.)* Ah! Here we are… *(Smelling it.)* Mmm! Good enough to drink, I bet! *(He soaks his handkerchief with it and, seeing almost none left, gulps down the rest.)* Delicious!

CHANTAL'S VOICE, *again, but louder*: Aaaah!… Mammá!

PHILIPPE, *aside*: Son of a… The brat! She's up… *(He goes up to the alcove and listens quietly for a moment.)* Not for long, thank heavens.

CHANTAL'S VOICE, *again*: Mammá!… Mammá!

PHILIPPE: Damn!… Again?

CHANTAL sticks her head out from between the curtains.

CHANTAL: Oh!… Stealing mammá's cologne!… Naughty, naughty!

PHILIPPE, *aside*: Blast!… *(Aloud.)* Nothing of the kind, mademoiselle!… *(Coming down right.)* I was tidying up… Just tidying up…

He replaces the flask in the drawer, shuts it, and crosses left.

CHANTAL: Come here!

PHILIPPE, *approaching her, embarrassed, with hypocritical respect*: Is their something I can do for mademoiselle?

CHANTAL: Closer!

PHILIPPE, *complying*: Aha…

CHANTAL: I want to talk to you.

PHILIPPE: Mademoiselle is too kind.

CHANTAL: What time is it, Philippe?

PHILIPPE: Late… Very late…

CHANTAL: Where is mammá?

PHILIPPE: Madame is out for the evening.

CHANTAL: And Nanette?

PHILIPPE: Mademoiselle Nanette is in bed… Off in dreamland, if I may say…

CHANTAL: Oh, there's no such place!

PHILIPPE, *ignoring her remark*: And, if I may allow myself to venture a suggestion…

CHANTAL: Be quiet!

PHILIPPE: Very good, mademoiselle.

CHANTAL: Now give me my doll!

PHILIPPE, *about to object*: But…

CHANTAL, *petulantly*: What?

PHILIPPE: Very good, mademoiselle.

He goes down right and retrieves the huge doll draped casually over the back of the armchair.

CHANTAL, *as he takes it to her*: Never mind! I don't want it! *(With an imperious gesture.)* You can go now! Get out!

PHILIPPE: Very good, mademoiselle.

CHANTAL, *as he moves down right*: Wait!… Come back!

PHILIPPE, *obeying, aside*: Damn brat! Make up your mind!

CHANTAL: I'm going to get up…

She pulls her head in behind the curtains.

PHILIPPE: What did she say? *(Crossing up left, flinging the doll onto the chair by the door.)* That's all I need! Did you ever...

As he continues grumbling under his breath, CHANTAL *appears from the alcove. She is wearing a long nightshirt.*

CHANTAL: See?

PHILIPPE: Son of a... *(Aside.)* And Nanette, getting dressed up... And Claudine, downstairs... *(Aloud.)* May I remind mademoiselle that it's time she was asleep!

CHANTAL: I know! *(With a note of scorn.)* In dreamland!

PHILIPPE: Quite...

CHANTAL: Yes, you may...

PHILIPPE, *after a pregnant pause*: Well?

CHANTAL, *categorically*: Well, Philippe... At midnight it's mammá's birthday, and I'm going to wait up for her so I can recite the little poem you taught me.

PHILIPPE, *aside*: Of all the... *(Controlling his temper, bending over and addressing her calmly.)* But mademoiselle... If mademoiselle goes back to bed, like a good little lady, I'll wake her up the minute madame returns.

CHANTAL, *sniffing*: Oooh! You smell awful!

PHILIPPE, *aside*: Damn!

CHANTAL: See? I knew you were stealing mammá's cologne! *(Shaking her finger at him.)* Tsk tsk tsk!

PHILIPPE, *at a loss*: But—

CHANTAL, *interrupting*: Never mind... Now we're going to play... *(*PHILIPPE *heaves a sigh of resignation.)* So! Tell me a story!

PHILIPPE: But... I really must remind mademoiselle that it's very, very late!

CHANTAL, *stamping her foot*: I don't care! Tell me a story, Philippe... Or I'll cry. And I'll tell on you!

PHILIPPE, *quickly taking her by the hand*: Yes, well... Once upon a time there were three little pigs...

CHANTAL: Not that one!

PHILIPPE: And a big, bad wolf...

CHANTAL, *giving him a little punch in the belly*: Not that one, I said!

PHILIPPE: Three bears, then... A father bear—

CHANTAL: No! I know that one too!

PHILIPPE, *bending over as if to let her jump on his shoulders*: Fine! Then I'll give mademoiselle a nice ride around the room!

CHANTAL, *pushing him away*: I don't want a ride! I want a story!

PHILIPPE: But... *(Aside.)* Stubborn brat!

CHANTAL: I know what! We'll play store!... You wait here...

She runs off, left, into the baroness's room.

PHILIPPE: But...

CHANTAL *returns with a fan, a parasol, and a handbag hanging from her arm.*

CHANTAL: There!

PHILIPPE: What in the name...

CHANTAL, *pointing to the armchair, down left*: Now go sit down!... You be the owner. I'll be the customer.

PHILIPPE, *resisting*: But...

CHANTAL, *poking him repeatedly in the stomach with the fan, backing him up*: Go on!

PHILIPPE, *falling into the armchair*: Blast!

CHANTAL: Bonjour, madame.

PHILIPPE: But mademoiselle...

CHANTAL, *putting on an air*: Please, madame! Not "mademoiselle"! I'll have you know I'm Madame... Madame Ducharme!... Oh! This heat! *(Fanning herself.)* It's simply, utterly stifling, don't you think?

She opens the parasol and twirls it about.

PHILIPPE: Really, mademoiselle...

CHANTAL, *angrily*: Please, Philippe! I just told you... Now we'll have to start all over! *(Pretending.)* Bonjour, madame.

PHILIPPE: Does mademoiselle mean me?

CHANTAL, *losing patience*: Of course I do! You're the owner, and... and... Oh! *(Beginning again.)* Bonjour, madame.

PHILIPPE, *playing along, unenthusiastically*: Bonjour, madame...

CHANTAL: I'd like to look at your hats. But only the chic ones, if you don't mind...

PHILIPPE, *sharply*: I'm sorry, but the store is closed!

CHANTAL: Then open it! *(Menacingly.)* Open it this very minute, or I'll cry!

PHILIPPE, *resigned*: Fine! It's open... See? *(Muttering under his breath.)* Little...

CHANTAL: I want something utterly elegant... The *eleganter* the better!... With little silk rosebuds... And a veil, of course... Something for when I attend the races, don't you know... With my husband, the duke...

PHILIPPE: Of course... *(Aside.)* Why not a prince while you're at it!

CHANTAL: Do you have one?

PHILIPPE: Certainly, madame...

CHANTAL, *correcting him*: Duchess!

PHILIPPE: Certainly, duchess... *(Sarcastically.)* My *elegantest*, if I may say...

He gets up and takes his hat from on top of the parrot cage and holds it out.

CHANTAL: But it's beige, madame... I simply detest beige! I wanted one in mauve!

PHILIPPE, *replacing it, and picking it up again, pretending*: Like this, ma... *(Catching himself.)* Duchess?

She hands him the parasol, which he closes as she takes the hat and tries it on.

CHANTAL: Oh! It's simply exquisite! Utterly fetching!

PHILIPPE: And it's you, duchess! Utterly...

CHANTAL, *fanning herself*: Oh, it is! It is!

PHILIPPE, *with a sigh of relief, stepping out of character*: There!... Now I think it's time for bed.

He takes the hat and places it on the end table by the armchair, down left.

CHANTAL, *ignoring his remark*: Your turn, Philippe...

PHILIPPE: What?

CHANTAL, *handing him the fan and the handbag*: Now you be the customer... I'm the owner...

She sits in the same armchair.

PHILIPPE: But… Really, mademoiselle…

CHANTAL: Hurry up… I'm waiting…

PHILIPPE, *resigned*: Of course… *(Aside.)* At this rate they'll close and I'll miss Claudine! *(He slips the handbag over his arm, opens the parasol, and lopes over to* CHANTAL, *pretending grotesquely.)* Bonjour, madame.

CHANTAL: Oh! Can it be?… Why, marquise! What an honor!… The marquise is pretty as a picture this morning! Fresh as a daisy…

PHILIPPE, *exaggeratedly coy*: Too kind, madame…

He takes his pipe out of his pocket.

CHANTAL: And to what do I owe… *(Noticing the pipe, as* PHILIPPE *feels his pockets for his tobacco.)* Oh! Does Your Marquiseship smoke tobacco?

PHILIPPE, *aside*: When I can find it!

CHANTAL: How utterly quaint! *(Shaking her head, as* PHILIPPE, *unsuccessful, puts the pipe back in his pocket.)* Tsk tsk tsk!…

PHILIPPE, *aside*: Blast!

CHANTAL: Now then, what did the marquise have in mind? Something terribly chic? Perhaps with a plume or two?

PHILIPPE, *in his own voice*: A pack of rough-cut Turkish broadleaf… Good and strong!

CHANTAL, *dropping her character, not understanding*: What?… What kind of hat is that, Philippe?

PHILIPPE, *in character again*: And a slug of cognac, madame…

CHANTAL: But…

PHILIPPE: Ah! You don't have any?… Well, in that case I'd better try somewhere else.

He moves toward the door, up left.

CHANTAL, *jumping down from the armchair*: Wait! Where is the marquise going?

PHILIPPE: To meet my husband… He's waiting by the lamppost.

CHANTAL: Oh? And what is the marquis doing these days?

PHILIPPE: Why, he's a doctor… And terribly busy!… I mustn't keep him waiting. *(Aside.)* Enough is enough!

He turns to leave, up left.

CHANTAL: A doctor?… Oh! Please… Go get him! *(She crosses right, toward the other armchair.)* Please!… *(Convincingly.)* The pain!… You simply have no idea… Oh! The pain!

She sinks into the chair.

PHILIPPE, *taking her seriously, stopping at the door*: What? *(He lays the handbag, the fan, and the parasol on the chair, up left, next to the doll, and rushes over to her.)* What is it? What…

CHANTAL, *laughing*. Nothing, silly!… We're going to play doctor!

PHILIPPE, *angrily*: Now just one minute!… *(Aside.)* How much longer… *(With forced good humor.)* If mademoiselle doesn't mind my saying…

CHANTAL, *sighing*: Ah! Doctor!… Thank heavens you've come!… Oh…

PHILIPPE: No… No more… Really…

CHANTAL, *continuing*: My poor nerves!… They're simply in such a state… I'm sure it's my liver! It is, isn't it, doctor?

PHILIPPE, *aside*: Well, we'll see about that!

CHANTAL, *continuing*: I mean, what else could it be?… Oh!… I do think I'm going to swoon…

PHILIPPE, *very professionally*: Stick out your tongue, madame… *(She complies.)* My, my… *(Shaking his head.)* Tsk tsk tsk!… Bad… Very bad… *(As* CHANTAL, *beginning to tire, yawns in his face.)* And you're yawning. Bad sign… Very bad… *(Pretending to take her pulse, as she yawns repeatedly.)* Pulse?… *(Shaking his head.)* Tsk tsk tsk… Bad, madame… Very bad…

CHANTAL, *sleepily*: But… What can I do?… Can you give me a *subscription* for it?

PHILIPPE: A… No… No *subscription* necessary, madame… Only rest… Lots and lots of rest…

CHANTAL, *beginning to doze off:* Oh… Thank you, doctor! I feel ever so much better… *(Gradually falling asleep.)* And… And do thank the marquise for sending you… The mar… The…

She begins snoring lightly.

PHILIPPE: At last!

He lifts her up and, careful not to wake her, takes her to the alcove and puts her into bed. A moment later, NANETTE *enters, right, in a fancy silk dress, and wearing a shawl.*

NANETTE: Are you ready?

PHILIPPE, *joining her*: Shhh!

NANETTE: What's the matter?

PHILIPPE, *pointing to the alcove*: She woke up…

NANETTE: She didn't!

PHILIPPE: Oh yes she did! And I thought I'd never get her back to bed! You should have seen what she had me doing!… "Beige?"… "Mauve!"…

NANETTE: What?

PHILIPPE: On second thought, I'm glad you didn't!… "It's *you*, madame… Utterly!…"

NANETTE: What on earth…?

PHILIPPE: Every time I tried to tell her a story—

NANETTE, *losing patience*: Never mind! Tell me later… If we don't hurry they'll close before we get there!

She crosses to the armchair, down left.

PHILIPPE: And we'll miss Claudine!

NANETTE: And her cousin!

She puts her feet on the armchair one after the other, and buttons her shoes.

PHILIPPE: Two minutes and we're out the door…

He puts his feet on the other armchair, right, wiping them with his handkerchief.

NANETTE: Even less…

PHILIPPE: Just time for a little polish… *(Aside.)* You never know… *(Aloud, admiring his shoes.)* There!… As shiny as the gold piece madame is going to give me!

NANETTE: You?… What for?

PHILIPPE: For the poem I wrote…

NANETTE: A poem?… You?

PHILIPPE: For her birthday tomorrow… Mademoiselle is going to recite it over a bouquet of roses. Do you want to hear it?

NANETTE: Not if it takes more than a minute…

PHILIPPE: Not even…

NANETTE, *reluctantly*: Well… *(Turning toward the open window, aside.)* I smell a corporal on the loose…

PHILIPPE: Listen… Imagine she's reciting it.

"Accept these rosebuds on this special day,
Your birthday, if we listen to the rumors.
May your day be as lovely, bright, and gay,
Full of the scents that fill your fragrant bloomers."

NANETTE, *quizzically*: Do we say "bloomers"?

PHILIPPE: Why not? They're buds, aren't they? And buds bloom… So…

NANETTE: I suppose… *(Aside, disdainfully.)* Pffff!

PHILIPPE, *aside*: She wishes I wrote it for her, poor thing!

NANETTE, *aside*: As silly as he is ugly!

PHILIPPE, *aside*: But she's no Claudine…

NANETTE, *aside*: He's no Dagobert!

Just then, DAGOBERT can be heard, apparently downstairs, signaling up to the open window.

DAGOBERT'S VOICE: Pssst! Nana!… Pou-pi-doup! Pou-pi-doup…

PHILIPPE: What on earth…?

NANETTE, *aside*: Speak of the devil… *(Aloud, to PHILIPPE.)* There's Dagobert now!

PHILIPPE: Who?

NANETTE: Dagobert… Claudine's cousin…

PHILIPPE: You mean, you know this corporal of hers?

NANETTE, *aside*: Why, I do believe he's jealous! *(Aloud.)* Well… *(Coyly.)* We've met…

PHILIPPE: And you recognize his… his "pou-pi-doup"? *(Aside.)* Or whatever…

NANETTE: He has a very special little "pou-pi-doup," Philippe. I'd know it anywhere.

PHILIPPE, *aside*: No doubt…

NANETTE: Now please, let's go… *(Aside.)* Before he leaves!

PHILIPPE, *at the door, up left, standing aside to let her pass*: After you…

As they are about to exit, CHANTAL, fully dressed, emerges from the alcove.

CHANTAL: Wait a minute! *(As PHILIPPE and NANETTE freeze in their tracks.)* You're forgetting me!

NANETTE *and* **PHILIPPE**: What?

CHANTAL: I want to go too!

NANETTE: Come here this instant! And take off those clothes!

CHANTAL sticks out her tongue and utters an appropriately disrespectful sound.

PHILIPPE: Did you ever…

CHANTAL: I want to go!… I want to! I want to!

PHILIPPE: Go? Go where?

CHANTAL: To the Moulin Bleu… With the two of you…

PHILIPPE, *feigning ignorance*: The Moulin Bleu?… What's that? *(To NANETTE.)* Do you know what she means?

NANETTE: Me? Not a bit…

PHILIPPE, *muttering*: Moulin… Moulin…

CHANTAL: Liars! Don't you know it's naughty to lie?

PHILIPPE, *trying to be conciliatory*: But mademoiselle… Perhaps mademoiselle was dreaming…

CHANTAL: Oh? *(Pointing to NANETTE.)* Then why is she all dressed up?

NANETTE: Dressed up?

CHANTAL, *to PHILIPPE*: Is she dreaming too?

NANETTE: Who?

CHANTAL: You!

NANETTE: Me?

CHANTAL, *to PHILIPPE, pointing*: Her!… Why is she wearing that fancy dress?

PHILIPPE: That?… Why… To go to bed, mademoiselle… To sleep in… That's a nightgown.

Once again DAGOBERT can be heard signaling from downstairs.

DAGOBERT'S VOICE: Pssst!… Pou-pi-doup!… Pou-pi-doup!

CHANTAL: There! You hear that?

PHILIPPE: That?

NANETTE, *shrugging her shoulders, to PHILIPPE*: That?

CHANTAL: That "Pssst!… Pou-pi-doup! Pou-pi-doup!"

NANETTE: Oh, that…

PHILIPPE, *to CHANTAL*: Yes! That's the Bogey Man! The one who comes and gobbles up little children who… who won't go to bed!

NANETTE: And who want to go to the Moulin Bleu!

PHILIPPE: That's right!

NANETTE, *calling out toward the open window*: Never mind, Monsieur Bogey Man! She'll be good! You can go!

PHILIPPE, *likewise*: She'll go back to bed…

CHANTAL, *hands on hips*: Don't be stupid, you two! It's Dagobert…

PHILIPPE, } *together*: { What?… Who?
NANETTE, } { Who?… What?

CHANTAL, *sarcastically*: I'd know his little "pou-pi-doup" anywhere! *(As NANETTE and PHILIPPE react.)* Don't think that, just because my eyes are shut, I've got to be asleep!

PHILIPPE, *aside*: Oh! If she was my child… If only…

CHANTAL: So? Are you going to take me with you? Yes or no?

PHILIPPE, *very properly*: A de Flochepette? At the Moulin Bleu?… Never!

CHANTAL: Then I'll cry!

PHILIPPE, *offering her his handkerchief*: As mademoiselle wishes... *(Turning away, aside.)* Little brat!... *(Aloud, to* CHANTAL.*)* I have several others if she needs them.

NANETTE: Oh!

CHANTAL, *with a pretended sigh of resignation*: Well, if that's how it is...

PHILIPPE: It is...

CHANTAL: Then I'll simply have to go to bed, now won't I?

NANETTE and PHILIPPE exchange victorious glances.

PHILIPPE, *replying*: If I may say...

CHANTAL: Oh well... Ta ta, Nanette... Bonsoir, Philippe... *(Calling toward the open window as the other two heave sighs of relief.)* You too, monsieur!... Bonsoir, corporal! *(To NANETTE and PHILIPPE.)* Enjoy yourselves...

NANETTE, *aside*: Did you ever...

PHILIPPE, *shaking his head*: If only...

CHANTAL, *as if having an afterthought*: Of course, I probably won't fall asleep right away. I have to write a little poem for mammá, you know...

NANETTE, *laughing*: A poem, mademoiselle?

CHANTAL: For her birthday tomorrow...

PHILIPPE, *laughing, aside*: Has mademoiselle forgotten mine so soon?

CHANTAL, *continuing*: Yes... About a certain footman who drinks her new cognac and uses up all her cologne...

PHILIPPE, *aside*: Good God!

CHANTAL, *continuing*: And a certain maid who thinks she can wear mammá's silk stockings!

NANETTE: Oh!

PHILIPPE, *aside, miming a strangling motion*: If only...

CHANTAL: Of course, it won't have any rosebuds in it. Or any fragrant bloomers... But then again, it won't cost mammá a thing. She'll save her shiny gold piece...

Suddenly the parrot cackles: "Awk awk!... Fragrant bloomers! Fragrant bloomers!... Awk awk awk!"

NANETTE, *to PHILIPPE, whispering*: What do we do now?

PHILIPPE, *replying, likewise*: Damned if I know!

CHANTAL, *as if deciding to exit*: Oh well... Have a good night, Philippe.

PHILIPPE, *aghast*: Mademoiselle is too kind...

CHANTAL: Bonsoir, Nanette... *(Moving upstage.)* I really must go to bed... I simply, utterly must...

PHILIPPE, *to NANETTE, drawing her down right a little*: Listen... I was thinking...

NANETTE: Oh?

CHANTAL, *overhearing, stops in her tracks and tiptoes behind their backs to listen.*

PHILIPPE: I've got an idea.

NANETTE: What? Tell me, for heaven's sake!

PHILIPPE: Well... I mean... There's really no reason not to take her with us.

NANETTE: To the Moulin Bleu?

PHILIPPE: Why not? It's a fine place for a child...

NANETTE, *quick to agree*: Nice bright lights…

PHILIPPE: Good music… Lots of people…

NANETTE: Dancing… Having a good time…

PHILIPPE: She'll see how grown-up young ladies behave!

NANETTE: And maybe it will tire her out…

PHILIPPE: And she'll sleep better… Agreed?

NANETTE: Agreed!

Just as they are about to turn around, CHANTAL *scurries back to the alcove.*

PHILIPPE, *joining her*: Mademoiselle has convinced us.

CHANTAL, *feigning ignorance*: Oh? What on earth about?

PHILIPPE: We've decided to take her with us.

CHANTAL, *indifferently*: I don't know, Philippe… It's so terribly late… And a de Flochepette, after all…

The music grows louder and more boisterous.

NANETTE, *aside*: She's going to make us beg her, the little…

She continues muttering under her breath.

PHILIPPE, *to* CHANTAL: Ah! How can mademoiselle resist the lovely music?

CHANTAL: Well… If it will make you happy… I suppose…

PHILIPPE, *aside, controlling his anger*: Oh! If only… If only…

NANETTE: Then off we go!… *(To* PHILIPPE, *in a whisper.)* As long as we get her back before madame… She'll never suspect…

PHILIPPE, *whispering a reply*: Please! *(He crosses himself.)* The very thought… *(Aloud.)* Moulin Bleu, here we come!

He and NANETTE *take* CHANTAL *by the hand and lift her bodily, moving up left, to the door. As they arrive,* NANETTE *stops suddenly.*

NANETTE: Wait! We'll need the key to get back in.

PHILIPPE: Where is it?

NANETTE, *pointing right*: Over there… On the mantelpiece…

PHILIPPE, *motioning them out*: Go on… I'm right behind you. *(As* NANETTE *and* CHANTAL *exit, he runs over to the fireplace, singing to the music and fitting his words to the notes as best he can.)*

The key, the key… We're going to find the key…
It's over here, she said… Let's see… Let's see…

(He looks all over the mantelpiece.) But where, damn it! *(Looking high and low.)* The key… The key… *(Just then, the parrot begins to cackle once again: "Awk awk… The key, the key… Where, damn it? Awk awk awk…")* Son of a bitch!… If there's a key here… *(The parrot continues: "Awk awk awk… It's not up my—") (Covering the parrot's last word.)* I'll eat my hat! *(As the parrot continues cackling.)* Where the devil did she put it? *(Going over to the window, calling out.)* Nanette!… Nanette!… *(About to close the window.)* Damn!… There she is… And that must be her famous Dagobert. But no Claudine?… And no key!… Well, to hell with the key! I'll leave the door unlocked. What's the harm? We won't be gone long. *(As he turns to leave, up left, one can hear the trotting of horses' hooves on the cobblestones, approaching.)* What?… *(Looking out the window, not believing his eyes.)* Good God in heaven! It can't be!… It's… It's madame!… But it's too early… She said… She… *(Not knowing which way to turn.)* And the brat… Her empty bed… *(Struck*

by an idea.) What if I… No… She's sure to come and kiss her good night… I mean me, that is! *(He shudders.)* No, thank you! *(Suddenly noticing the doll, on the chair, up left.)* Ah!… Why not?… It's just the right size, and… *(Taking it to the alcove and putting it under the covers.)* And if I cover it up… There!

THE BARONESS'S VOICE, *offstage*: Thank you, Gustave. You can put up the horses.

PHILIPPE: She'll never guess…

He comes down right and begins vigorously rubbing the same chair as before with his handkerchief, as THE BARONESS *enters.*

THE BARONESS, *throwing her shawl on the chair by the door, surprised*: Philippe? Is that you?

PHILIPPE, *polishing*: Of course… As madame can see… *(At a loss for words.)* Bonsoir, madame…

THE BARONESS: But… Why on earth… Are you still—

PHILIPPE: Madame?

THE BARONESS: How long are you going to keep polishing that chair, Philippe?

PHILIPPE: We want to make it shine, madame. "The bread of idleness—"

THE BARONESS: I know… Your sainted mother's proverb… But it's almost midnight. You're going to wear yourself out. And you're not well…

He gives a shrug and stops polishing.

PHILIPPE: Begging madame's pardon, but… I thought she had an engagement this evening… A fête of some kind…

THE BARONESS, *sighing*: Oh, I did… A very dreary kind, Philippe… With dozens of strangers I never saw in my life and will never see again!

PHILIPPE, *beside himself, not sure what he is saying*: How nice for madame!

THE BARONESS: Nice?… An utter bore, you mean!

PHILIPPE: Yes… Yes, that's what I meant… A bore…

THE BARONESS: Thank heavens there were so many…

PHILIPPE: Yes… So many boring people… How nice…

THE BARONESS, *hardly listening to him*: Just in and out… I was able to run off, and no one was any the wiser.

PHILIPPE: No one, madame…

THE BARONESS: Besides, I was simply too uneasy. I never should have left the child. Not when she wasn't herself…

PHILIPPE, *quickly*: The child… Yes! She's still here, madame. Believe me…

THE BARONESS, *with a little laugh*: Of course she is… Where else—

PHILIPPE: Of course!

THE BARONESS, *seeming to hear a noise coming from the alcove, listening*: Do you hear that? I think she's stirring. The little angel probably hasn't slept a wink.

PHILIPPE, *petrified*: Oh no, madame… Oh yes, I mean… She has!… Mademoiselle sleeps like a top! Madame knows how she sleeps…

THE BARONESS: No matter… I'll have a look. *(Crossing down right, to the vanity table, taking the bottle of medicine and a spoon.)* Besides, it's almost time for her medicine. I may as well…

PHILIPPE, *quickly heading her off*: But madame needn't bother… She isn't thirsty… *(Growing more frantic.)* I know… She told me…

THE BARONESS: She did? When?

PHILIPPE: A little while ago… *(Backing up to the alcove.)* I tried to give it to her, but she told me: "No! I'm not thirsty! Go away! Go away!" Her very words, madame…

THE BARONESS: Well, thirsty or not, she has to take it! I know she has a mind of her own, but still…

She continues to move upstage.

PHILIPPE: Then madame should let me…

THE BARONESS: Really, Philippe…

PHILIPPE, *putting his ear against the curtains, pretending to hear*: What? Mademoiselle wants me to give her the medicine now? Her nice little Philippe? *(To* THE BARONESS.*)* That's what she said, madame. *(Pretending.)* Very well… But only if she promises to go right back to sleep! *(Listening.)* Agreed?… Fine!… *(To* THE BARONESS.*)* See? Madame needn't trouble herself…

THE BARONESS, *smiling*: "A mind of her own" is right!

PHILIPPE: Children, madame! *(She hands him the bottle and spoon, then goes left, to the vanity, takes out her hatpins, removes her hat, her gloves, and lays them down on her shawl as* PHILIPPE, *at the alcove, curtains slightly apart, pretends to address the child.)* That's right, mademoiselle… A nice big swallow… *(Making sure that* THE BARONESS *isn't looking, he takes a gulp himself.)* There! Now that wasn't so terrible, was it? *(Taking another, aside.)* Mmm! Not bad! *(Pretending, aloud.)* And just one more… *(Taking another, aside.)* If I knew how good it was before…

THE BARONESS, *at the vanity, calling out*: You see, treasure? Was that so awful?

PHILIPPE, *trying to imitate the child's voice*: Oh no, mamma!… Oh no…

She begins to move up toward the alcove.

THE BARONESS: Goodness me! How hoarse she is, poor thing!

PHILIPPE, *closing the curtains, gesturing her back*: It's just because she's half asleep, madame… Has madame ever heard me when I wake up in the middle of the night?

THE BARONESS, *ironically*: Not that I recall, Philippe!

PHILIPPE: Because, if she has, she knows what I mean.

He makes several hoarse grunts to prove his point.

THE BARONESS: Yes, no doubt…

PHILIPPE, *coming down to join her*: Now I think we should let her keep her promise. Mademoiselle needs her sleep.

THE BARONESS: You're absolutely right! What ever would I do without you?

PHILIPPE: Madame is too kind… *(Growing more and more uneasy.)* And I think we should go to bed too, madame…

THE BARONESS, *taken aback*: You think…

PHILIPPE, *not realizing his gaffe*: Tomorrow is another day, if I may say…

THE BARONESS, *chuckling*: Yes… Quite…

PHILIPPE, *waiting for her to leave*: Indeed… *(Aside.)* What is she waiting for?

THE BARONESS, *as she stands by the mirror, inspecting herself*: Please, Philippe… Gustave is seeing to the horses. You're excused… You may go to bed.

PHILIPPE: Me?… No, no!

THE BARONESS, *surprised at his reaction*: What?

PHILIPPE, *recovering his aplomb*: I mean… Of course… *(Sputtering.)* Madame is too… Madame is… Madame… *(Aside.)* Good God!

THE BARONESS, *aside*: What ever is the matter with him? *(Aloud.)* But please… First call Nanette.

PHILIPPE, *stammering*: Na… N-N-Na… N-N-Nanette, madame?

THE BARONESS: Yes! Nanette!… *(Aside.)* What in heaven's name… *(Aloud.)* Yes, I want her to help me undress.

PHILIPPE: But madame… I can… If madame needs someone… I can…

THE BARONESS, *shocked*: What?

PHILIPPE: I… I mean… I'll see if I can find her.

THE BARONESS: Yes, please do! *(Aside.)* It can't be just his lungs.

PHILIPPE, pretending to look for NANETTE, stands by her open door, right, calling softly.

PHILIPPE: Nanette… Nanette… *(He crosses up left, to the door, opens it, and repeats his call.)* Nanette… *(To THE BARONESS.)* She doesn't seem to be—

Just at that moment, NANETTE enters, up left, without seeing THE BARONESS.

NANETTE, *to PHILIPPE*: Well? *(PHILIPPE stands agape.)* We're waiting…

PHILIPPE: But… *(Pointing to THE BARONESS.)* Shhh!

THE BARONESS: Did you say something, Philippe?

NANETTE, *terrified, aside.* Ayyy!

She quickly takes off her shawl, crosses right, and throws it into her room.

THE BARONESS, *noticing her*: Ah, there you are… *(To PHILIPPE.)* Thank you, Philippe.

NANETTE: Madame? I thought… Was there something…

THE BARONESS: My hair, Nanette… *(Pointing to her hat and gloves, on the chair by the vanity.)* I want you to put away my things, then come back and brush it out.

NANETTE: Of course, madame… Right away…

She picks up the items and disappears for a moment out the door, left, returning as THE BARONESS sits down at the vanity. As NANETTE begins taking the pins out of her hair, she and PHILIPPE exchange frantic whispers.

PHILIPPE: And the child?

NANETTE: Downstairs…

PHILIPPE: Where?

NANETTE: By the orchestra… On the left…

PHILIPPE: Good!

NANETTE: On Claudine's lap… Hurry!

PHILIPPE dashes out, up left.

THE BARONESS, *without turning round*: You can go now, Philippe. *(Muttering.)* How many times must I tell him?

NANETTE, *undoing her coiffure with trembling fingers, trying to be calm*: Monsieur Philippe has left, madame.

THE BARONESS, *muttering*: At last… You would think… *(Catching a glimpse of her sleeve.)* Goodness me! Is that your new dress you're wearing?

NANETTE, *stammering*: Y-Yes, madame… I… I was trying it on to… to see where the seamstress has to take it in a bit.

THE BARONESS: Does it really need… *(Suddenly, looking over the articles on the vanity.)* Oh! Look, Nanette! Someone has been into my things! *(Opening the drawer.)* Why, they're all… Who on earth…?

NANETTE: The child, madame… This afternoon… She… She was playing house.

THE BARONESS, *laughing*: Little devil!… Has she been good while I was gone?

NANETTE: Oh yes! Good as gold!… A… A little angel…

THE BARONESS: And did she cough?

NANETTE: Not once, madame.

THE BARONESS: Well,. I'm certainly glad of that! Poor dear! She's such a delicate little thing! I'm happy to have a jewel like you to look after her.

NANETTE: I… Yes, madame… I…

THE BARONESS: Now do be quick and brush me out. I want to go give her a hug and a kiss before I go to bed.

She takes a journal from the vanity and reads here and there as NANETTE *begins brushing her long locks.*

NANETTE, *uneasy, looking to see if there are any signs of* PHILIPPE: But… But madame shouldn't hurry! It… It's not good for the hair to hurry. And madame's is so lovely… *(Aside.)* Where is he? *(Aloud.)* She really must brush it at least a hundred times if she wants it to shine. Even two hundred… *(Looking toward the door, up left.)* Or three…

THE BARONESS: Really that much?

The door, up left, opens slowly and PHILIPPE, *obviously in a state, tiptoes down right, crouching behind* NANETTE. *The two whisper hurriedly as* NANETTE *attempts to reply as well to* THE BARONESS. *The latter becomes more and more absorbed in her reading.*

NANETTE, *answering* THE BARONESS: So they say, madame… *(Whispering, to* PHILIPPE.*)* Well?

PHILIPPE, *whispering*: No Claudine! She left!

THE BARONESS, *to* NANETTE: Are you counting?

NANETTE, *aloud*: Fifty-eight… Fifty-nine… *(Whispering, to* PHILIPPE.*)* And the child?

PHILIPPE, *whispering*: Sitting with four cavalry officers… They're feeding her cherry brandy!

NANETTE, *whispering*: Good God!

THE BARONESS, *to* NANETTE: I think one hundred will be sufficient, Nanette…

NANETTE, *whispering, to* PHILIPPE: Why didn't you bring her back? *(Aloud, to* THE BARONESS.*)* If madame thinks so…

PHILIPPE, *whispering*: They wouldn't trust me…

THE BARONESS, *to* NANETTE: Or I'll fall asleep before you finish…

PHILIPPE, *whispering*: You'll have to go get her yourself. They know you…

NANETTE, *whispering, showing him the mass of hair she is brushing*: And this?

PHILIPPE, *whispering*: Let me… *(He takes the hair in his hands.)* Now hurry…

NANETTE *rushes out without a sound.* PHILIPPE *begins brushing, doing his best, in every manner of awkward position, to avoid being seen, as* THE BARONESS, *reading, turns her head accordingly from side to side.*

THE BARONESS, *beginning to nod and yawn*: Careful, Nanette! You're pulling… *(PHILIPPE grimaces and continues, very gently, as she puts down the journal.)* That's better… *(Yawning.)* Much better… *(PHILIPPE, still contorting to keep from being seen, keeps brushing, all the while anxiously looking toward the door. All of a sudden she cries out in pain.)* Ayyy!

PHILIPPE, *jumping back, under his breath*: Blast!

THE BARONESS, *wriggling about*: A pin or something… In my blouse, Nanette…

PHILIPPE, *aside*: Son of a…

THE BARONESS: Please! Get it out!… *(PHILIPPE, not knowing what to do, looks toward the door in utter despair.)* Please! *(Finally, making up his mind, he places his hand, tentatively, into her blouse.)* Farther down… On the side… Oh!… *(As he resolutely plunges his hand still farther.)* Ah!… *(Sighing.)* Ah!… That's better…

PHILIPPE, *pulling a round cotton wadding from her blouse, gaping at it in disbelief, aside*: Oh!… She doesn't!… Not madame…

The door, up left, opens and NANETTE enters gingerly, coming down and replacing PHILIPPE, taking the hair in her hands. PHILIPPE shows her the wadding, indicating with a gesture how he retrieved it, and stuffing it in his pocket. Then he crouches down behind her, out of sight.

THE BARONESS, *turning slightly*: Thank you, Nanette.

NANETTE: Don't mention it, madame.

She begins brushing. THE BARONESS yawns, beginning to doze, as PHILIPPE and NANETTE again exchange frantic whispers.

PHILIPPE: Well?

NANETTE: Not a soul… The place is shut tight!

PHILIPPE: And the officers?

NANETTE: Not a trace…

PHILIPPE: Where do you suppose…

NANETTE: The Café Alhambra?

PHILIPPE, *with disgust*: Not that vile… They wouldn't…

NANETTE: Who knows?

PHILIPPE: Maybe the barracks?

NANETTE: Good God!… Well, go look! Go find her! *(As PHILIPPE, on all fours, crawls to the door, up left, under her breath.)* Heaven help us!

PHILIPPE creeps out quietly.

THE BARONESS, *with a yawn*: I think that will do, Nanette.

NANETTE: But… But it's only ninety, madame… If… If madame wants her hair to shine…

THE BARONESS: Then ten more and be done with it. I'm much too tired… *(As NANETTE continues, as slowly as possible, THE BARONESS prepares to get up, readjusting her clothing. Suddenly.)* Oh!

NANETTE: Madame?

THE BARONESS, *standing*: Where is… What did you do with my… my "little deceiver," Nanette?

NANETTE: Madame's… Me, madame?

THE BARONESS: Yes! I know it was… where it was supposed to be, when I came in… I'm utterly sure…

NANETTE, *pretending to look high and low*: I… I'll find it, madame…

THE BARONESS: And it's not something I want to leave lying about…

NANETTE: Madame can rest assured…

THE BARONESS: I certainly hope so!

NANETTE, *giving her a lighted candelabra*: Does madame need me for anything else?

THE BARONESS, *with a wide yawn*: No, no, Nanette… Thank you… You can go to bed. *(She is about to go to her room, left.)* I simply can't stay awake another minute!

NANETTE, *aside, with a sigh of relief*. At last!

THE BARONESS stops suddenly.

THE BARONESS: Oh! What ever was I thinking!

She puts down the candelabra and goes up to the alcove.

NANETTE: Madame?

THE BARONESS: I almost forgot… I was going to go to bed without giving my Chantal a big hug and a kiss!

NANETTE, *aside*: God help us!

THE BARONESS, *lifting the curtain and placing her hand on the doll*: Oh! Poor treasure! She's as cold as ice! *(NANETTE stands agape as THE BARONESS, taking her shawl from the chair by the door, lays it on the bed.)* There!… Now we'll be nice and warm! *(Giving the doll a little kiss.)* Sleep tight, angel!

NANETTE, *transfixed, aside*: She's back?… But… But…

THE BARONESS, *taking the candelabra*: Good night, Nanette.

She goes left, to her door.

NANETTE, *stammering*: G-G-Good night, m-madame…

THE BARONESS, *stopping*: Is something wrong?

NANETTE, *forcing a smile*: Wrong, madame?… N-No… Wh-What could be wrong?

She forces a laugh.

THE BARONESS, *with a little shrug*: She's as strange as he is!

She exits.

NANETTE, *going toward the alcove*: How in the name of…

Just then, PHILIPPE enters, excited and out of breath, makes sure that NANETTE is alone, and joins her, down left.

PHILIPPE: Nowhere!… Everything, closed up, tight as a clam… Not a sign of her…

NANETTE: But she's back! She's here!

PHILIPPE: She's what?

NANETTE: Madame just kissed her good night!

PHILIPPE: She… Where?

NANETTE, *pointing*: In her bed!

PHILIPPE: Oh?… *(He runs up to the alcove and seizes the doll.)* Yes! So I see! *(Brandishing it, with a loud, angry shout, flinging it to the floor.)* Aaaargh!

NANETTE, *horrified*: Oh, my God!

THE BARONESS enters, left. PHILIPPE quickly picks up the doll and hides it behind his back.

THE BARONESS: What on earth was that? Is the house falling down?

PHILIPPE, *innocently*: "That," madame?

THE BARONESS: That noise...

PHILIPPE: Begging madame's pardon, but... My cough... It's getting worse...

THE BARONESS: You could wake a regiment, Philippe!

PHILIPPE, *looking at* NANETTE: A regiment?

NANETTE, *looking at him*: A regiment?

THE BARONESS, *to* PHILIPPE: Here... *(Turning toward the alcove.)* Let me give you some of her medicine. It's done wonders for the child.

PHILIPPE: No, no... Madame needn't be concerned. I'll be fine with a little rest.

THE BARONESS: Well? Why aren't you in bed? I told you...

He comes down right and begins frantically polishing the same chair as before, still hiding the doll behind his back.

PHILIPPE: I... I thought...

THE BARONESS, *flabbergasted*: Again?

PHILIPPE: Just one spot, madame... One last spot...

THE BARONESS, *aside*: I never!... *(To* PHILIPPE.*)* Please! Go to bed! *(Aside.)* Both of them... What on earth is their problem?

She exits to her room.

NANETTE, *terrified*: You're mad! What have you done?

PHILIPPE: Just broken her nose... It can be fixed with a little glue.

He throws the doll into her hands.

NANETTE: This... You mean... This is what madame just kissed good night?

PHILIPPE: In the flesh!... But tomorrow, in the daylight...

NANETTE, *at a loss for words*: Oh!

PHILIPPE: When I think that, at this very moment, she may be in a barracks with a pack of drunken cavalry officers!... A de Flochepette, Nanette!

NANETTE: Impossible! The regiment was leaving for Fontainebleau at midnight. They told me so themselves!

PHILIPPE: Good God! Then... What have they done with her?

NANETTE: Poor thing!

PHILIPPE: Poor little thing!

He falls exhausted into the armchair, down right.

NANETTE, *falling into the armchair, down left*: Poor sweet, little thing!... Lost... Lost for good...

PHILIPPE: Poor mademoiselle!

NANETTE: Poor darling mademoiselle!

PHILIPPE: Poor dear, darling mademoiselle!

NANETTE: What do we do now?

PHILIPPE: I can only think of one thing...

NANETTE: What?

PHILIPPE, *getting up*: Let's get out of here while we can!

NANETTE, *getting up*: Before madame finds out...

She runs to her room, right, disappears for a moment, then returns with her shawl and without the doll.

PHILIPPE: And the sooner the better…

NANETTE, *having second thoughts*: But… Our money… Madame owes us—

PHILIPPE: Forget it! I'd rather go on living.

NANETTE: Of course… If not, how would we spend it?

She grabs his arm and they move quickly up left.

PHILIPPE, *stopping at the door*: But at least we should leave her a note, don't you think?

NANETTE: You're right… So it doesn't come as a complete surprise… *(She points to paper, pen, and inkwell on the vanity.)* Go ahead… You write better than me.

PHILIPPE: Well… *(Sitting down and writing.)* "Your dear Baroness-ship…"

NANETTE: Poor madame…

PHILIPPE: "It is with hearts heavy with sorrow that we dip our pen in our tears…" *(Dipping the pen in the inkwell and scratching out the last word, continuing.)* "… our bitter tears…"

NANETTE, *on the verge of tears*: Yes… "bitter" is better…

PHILIPPE: "…to inform madame that we are obliged to leave her employ…"

NANETTE, *sighing*: Ah…

PHILIPPE: "…haunted by our remorse…" *(Dipping his pen and scratching out the last word, continuing.)* "…our deep remorse…"

NANETTE, *nodding*: Yes… "Deep"…

PHILIPPE: "… at having lost…" *(To NANETTE.)* "Misplaced"?… "Mislaid"?

NANETTE: "Mislaid," I think…

PHILIPPE: "… at having mislaid an object dear to her tender heart…" *(NANETTE begins to sob.)* "… dearer than any other… "

NANETTE: Oh! The poor little thing!… I loved her so!

PHILIPPE, *sobbing*: No more than I did!… How many times did I say: "Oh, if only she was mine!" *(With a sigh, continuing.)* "We know it's our fault, but we are honorable domestics. That is why madame can use the money she owes us, for posters and the reward…"

NANETTE: But… She just paid us yesterday.

PHILIPPE, *shrugging*: Still… Every little bit… *(Continuing.)* "Yours truly, madame's humble, obedient, and unhappy servants…" *(Correcting.)* "… former servants…" *(Signing with an ostentatious flourish.)* "Philippe…" *(To NANETTE, giving her the pen.)* Now you… *(She writes out her name with obvious difficulty.)* That's that… *(He folds the paper and writes the name.)* "To the Baroness de Flochepette…" *(Sobbing, he places it on the end table, down left.)* There! She'll see it in the morning when she comes out.

NANETTE, *sobbing*: Such a good mistress…

PHILIPPE, *likewise*: Always so kind…

NANETTE: Always so generous…

PHILIPPE: So free with her cognac… *(Sobbing, he goes to his pocket for his handkerchief and pulls out the cotton wadding.)* Ah!… Her… Her… I'll leave it with the letter. *(Placing it on the table.)* At least she won't lose everything all at once. Us and that too…

NANETTE: Come, Philippe…

PHILIPPE: Let's be on our way… Ah! it breaks my heart…

NANETTE: I know… I know…

As they move upstage, CHANTAL, *can be heard outside the upstage door.*

CHANTAL'S VOICE: Forward… March!

PHILIPPE *and* **NANETTE**, *looking at each other, agape*: It's her!

The door flies open and DAGOBERT *enters, in uniform, with* CHANTAL *on his shoulders.*

CHANTAL: Company… Halt! One, two!

NANETTE: Mademoiselle!… Dagobert!… *(To* DAGOBERT.*)* You… You found her!

DAGOBERT: I never lost her, goddammit!

PHILIPPE: How can we ever thank you!… We…

He and NANETTE, *overcome, jabber and gesticulate in a flurry of appropriate exclamations: "You… ," "She.… ," "We thought…," etc.*

NANETTE, *to* DAGOBERT: How can we ever…

PHILIPPE: Our honor, my friend… You've saved our honor!

DAGOBERT, *as* PHILIPPE *lifts* CHANTAL *from his shoulders and puts her down*: I have?

CHANTAL, to DAGOBERT, *obviously a little tipsy*: Thanks for everything, old fart…

As NANETTE *and* PHILIPPE *look at each other, not sure if they have heard correctly, she runs to the fireplace, takes the long feather duster from the mantelpiece, straddles it, and begins galloping around the room.*

DAGOBERT: Quite a kid!… She had us all in stitches… The others wanted to take her with them to Fontainebleau…

PHILIPPE, *with a shudder*: My God!

DAGOBERT: But I didn't think—

NANETTE: Thank heavens, Dagobert! *(To* PHILIPPE.*)* Fontainebleau!

PHILIPPE: With a company of cavalry officers?

He crosses himself.

DAGOBERT: If not for me…

NANETTE: Just for that, I owe you a nice big kiss…

DAGOBERT: One kiss from the lady, coming right up!

She kisses him.

PHILIPPE: Me too, comrade!

DAGOBERT, *holding him off*: Comrade? You?

PHILIPPE, *pointing to their uniforms*: Of course… You're in service… And so am I…

He is about to fling his arms around DAGOBERT*'s neck.*

DAGOBERT: My ass you are!

He gives him a good-natured poke in the ribs.

PHILIPPE: Oh!

CHANTAL, *stopping down right, at the vanity*: Garçon! One cherry brandy!

NANETTE: Mademoiselle…

PHILIPPE, *to* DAGOBERT: You… You've gotten her drunk!

CHANTAL *begins galloping again.*

DAGOBERT: My ass!… It's good for her… It'll make her grow!

NANETTE, *chasing her, as DAGOBERT looks on, laughing*: Mademoiselle…

PHILIPPE, *to NANETTE*: Catch her!

NANETTE: I'm trying!

CHANTAL, *mocking*: Na-na!… Na-na!…

PHILIPPE, *to NANETTE*: We've got to get her back before—

NANETTE, *to CHANTAL*: Please…

CHANTAL: Garçon! My cherry brandy?

NANETTE: Mademoiselle… *(About to grab her.)* It's time for bed!

CHANTAL, *escaping*: Bed my ass!

PHILIPPE: What? *(To DAGOBERT.)* She's swearing, goddammit!… A de Flochepette, swearing!

NANETTE, *still chasing*: We've got to go to bed, mademoiselle!

CHANTAL: Go by yourself!

NANETTE: Oh!

CHANTAL: Garçon!… Garçon!

PHILIPPE: Shhh!… For God's sake!… *(To NANETTE.)* She'll wake madame!

NANETTE, *finally catching CHANTAL, who jumps up on the armchair, right, dropping the feather duster on the seat, with a grimace*: Pouah!… She stinks of tobacco!

CHANTAL, *pointing to DAGOBERT*: He taught me to smoke!

PHILIPPE, to *DAGOBERT*: You what?

DAGOBERT, *still standing next to PHILIPPE*: So? It makes their teeth grow!

He gives him another poke.

PHILIPPE: Oh!… *(To NANETTE.)* Don't let her go! *(He goes to the vanity, finds a bottle that still has something in it.)* This should take care of it…

He douses CHANTAL with its contents.

CHANTAL, *stamping her foot on the chair*: That's not my cherry brandy, goddammit!

She jumps down and begins galloping around again, with NANETTE and PHILIPPE in pursuit.

DAGOBERT, *laughing, urging her on*: Giddy-ap! Giddy-ap!

CHANTAL, *echoing*: Giddy-ap! Giddy-ap!

NANETTE: Please!… Shhh!…

PHILIPPE, *to NANETTE*: Catch her! For God's sake…

As CHANTAL knocks over the armchair, down left, THE BARONESS calls out from her room.

THE BARONESS'S VOICE: Nanette!… Are you in there?

PHILIPPE, *terrified*: Ayyy! *(To DAGOBERT.)* You hear?

NANETTE, *not knowing where to turn, to PHILIPPE*: Hide her! Quick!

PHILIPPE manages to grab CHANTAL, dragging her off, right, pushing her into NANETTE's room.

CHANTAL, *as she exits*: Garçon! My—

PHILIPPE *slams the door and returns.*

DAGOBERT: Time to go!

He plants a kiss on NANETTE. *As he dashes out, up left, slamming the door, the door to* THE BARONESS'*s room opens and* THE BARONESS, *in a nightgown, appears on the threshold.*

PHILIPPE, *as he sees her*: Not a second too soon!

He comes down to the armchair, right, takes out his handkerchief, and begins vigorously polishing it again. At the same time, NANETTE *picks up the feather duster.*

THE BARONESS: Goodness me! What ever is going on? Is the house on fire?

NANETTE, *stammering*: N-N-No, madame…

She absentmindedly begins dusting PHILIPPE.

THE BARONESS, *to* PHILIPPE, *noticing that he is still polishing*: Again?… What on earth…? You're going to wear out that chair, Philippe!

PHILIPPE, *not knowing what to say*: Madame is too kind… *(Babbling.)* She… It… I… I want it to shine, madame…

THE BARONESS: I know, but… *(Noticing the other armchair, knocked over, and other signs of* CHANTAL'*s rampage.)* What?… What happened? Why is everything… Oh!… Why is my furniture—

PHILIPPE: We were just tidying up, madame…

THE BARONESS, *aside*: He's out of his mind!

CHANTAL *is heard giving the door, right, several loud kicks.*

PHILIPPE, *aside*: Damn!

He gives several loud coughs to cover the noise.

THE BARONESS: What was that?

PHILIPPE: Just my lungs… Madame needn't be concerned.

There are several more kicks, even louder.

THE BARONESS: There's someone in there!

NANETTE: It's… It must be the plumber, madame… Upstairs…

THE BARONESS: At this hour? What do you take me for? *(*NANETTE *and* PHILIPPE *open their mouths as if to reply, but nothing comes out.)* Well, we'll just see about that! The plumber, indeed! *(She strides up to the door and opens it.* CHANTAL *steps out.)* Chantal!

CHANTAL, *jumping up and down, clapping her hands*: Mammá!

THE BARONESS: And all dressed! *(She moves left, obviously disturbed.)* But… It's after midnight! Will somebody please explain…

NANETTE, *stammering*: M-Madame…

THE BARONESS: And in her best dress, of all things!… *(To* NANETTE.*)* What is the meaning of this?

NANETTE: Yes, well… As madame can see… Mademoiselle is wearing her nice pink dress…

CHANTAL, *to* THE BARONESS: And I put it on all by myself, mammá!

NANETTE: I mean… That is…

PHILIPPE, *suddenly inspired*: Ah…

THE BARONESS, *to* NANETTE: I can see what she's wearing! But will you please tell me why!

Taking advantage of a moment when her back is turned, PHILIPPE *quickly snatches up the flowers on the mantelpiece and hides them behind his back.*

PHILIPPE, *to* THE BARONESS: Begging madame's pardon, but... Can't she guess?

THE BARONESS, *turning to him, archly*: Guess?... No! I'm afraid I can't! Of all things...

PHILIPPE, *with a silly smile*: Why... The party, madame...

THE BARONESS: Party? What party?

PHILIPPE *wags the flowers back and forth behind him so that* NANETTE *can see them. Taking the hint, she seizes them and puts them into* CHANTAL*'s hands, as* PHILIPPE *replies.*

PHILIPPE: Madame's party... For her birthday... It was going to be a surprise.

THE BARONESS: My...

She stands speechless.

PHILIPPE: And mademoiselle wanted to be the first... The little angel!... Isn't that so, Nanette?

NANETTE: Oh, yes! *(To* THE BARONESS.*)* It's just like he says, madame! *(Aside.)* Brilliant!

THE BARONESS, *smiling*: Then that's why you two were acting so strangely! I couldn't imagine... My birthday! Did you ever...

NANETTE *and* PHILIPPE *urge* CHANTAL *left, toward* THE BARONESS.

PHILIPPE, *whispering in her ear*: Go ahead... "Happy birthday!"... Give her the flowers... Tell her...

CHANTAL, *holding them out*: Happy birthday, mammá!

THE BARONESS, *taking them*: Why, thank you...

PHILIPPE *and* **NANETTE,** *aside*: Saved!

THE BARONESS, *taking* CHANTAL*'s hand and leading her up left, sitting down*: Thank you, you dear little... *(She is about to give her a kiss, but stops short, sniffing.)* Goodness me! What is that vile smell! *(To* CHANTAL.*)* Where ever have you been, child?

PHILIPPE, *aside*: Damn! The tobacco...

NANETTE: It's... It's...

PHILIPPE, *to* THE BARONESS: It's toilet water, madame...

THE BARONESS: I daresay!

PHILIPPE: Perfume, that is...

THE BARONESS: Perfume?

PHILIPPE: For the party...

THE BARONESS: That foul stench?

PHILIPPE: Madame knows what thieves perfumers are nowadays!

THE BARONESS: Oh?

PHILIPPE: They make it from ground up sheep heads. It's common knowledge...

THE BARONESS: Good heavens!

PHILIPPE, *aside, to* NANETTE: Saved again!

THE BARONESS, *to* CHANTAL: And you mean, treasure... You mean you got up just to wish me a happy birthday?

CHANTAL: Oh no, mammá! I got up to go to the Moulin Bleu...

THE BARONESS, *shocked, to* NANETTE *and* PHILIPPE: What?

They stand aghast for a long moment.

PHILIPPE, *finally, bursting out laughing*: Ha ha ha!... The Moulin Bleu... *(Aside, to* NANETTE.*)* Laugh, damn it!

NANETTE, *laughing*: The Moulin Bleu!... Ha ha ha!

CHANTAL: And I had so much fun!

PHILIPPE, *laughing uproariously, to* THE BARONESS: Imagine, madame! She... She dreamt that she went to the Moulin Bleu, and... and there's no way to convince her that it was only a dream! What a child!

THE BARONESS, *joining in the laughter*: What a dream, you mean! *(To* CHANTAL.*)* And just what did you do at the Moulin Bleu, precious?

CHANTAL: Well... I drank cherry brandy... And...

PHILIPPE, *laughing*: Ha ha ha!... *(Aside, to* NANETTE, *who has stopped laughing.)* Laugh, damn it!

NANETTE: Ha ha ha!

PHILIPPE: Cherry brandy!... Ha ha ha!... What a child!... She has an answer for everything! *(To* NANETTE, *sarcastically.)* She drank cherry brandy!

CHANTAL, *approaching him*: Well I did! So there! *(To* THE BARONESS.*)* With a lot of soldiers... And we danced, and danced...

PHILIPPE, *laughing, to* NANETTE: Soldiers, no less!

CHANTAL: And...

PHILIPPE, *to* THE BARONESS: Why not sailors while she's at it! *(Aside, to* NANETTE.*)* Laugh!

CHANTAL: And...

NANETTE: Ha ha ha!

CHANTAL: And they took me to their *racks...*

THE BARONESS: Their what?

CHANTAL: Their *racks...* Their *bare racks...*

PHILIPPE, *laughing*: Their barracks!... Ha ha ha! What a child!

CHANTAL: And Corporal Dagobert gave me a piggy-back ride... And he brought me here...

PHILIPPE, *splitting his sides*: Ho ho ho!... *(To* NANETTE.*)* Corporal Dagobert, no less!... A piggyback ride...

NANETTE: Ha ha ha!

PHILIPPE: Did you ever...

THE BARONESS, *laughing*: She gets her imagination from the baron. My late husband...

NANETTE: Aha...

PHILIPPE, *to* THE BARONESS: I'm sure...

NANETTE, *aside, to* PHILIPPE: For heaven's sake, change the subject!

The laughter gradually subsides.

PHILIPPE, to CHANTAL: Now mademoiselle... It's time to recite the nice little poem we learned. *(Whispering in her ear.)* "Accept these rosebuds on this special day..."

THE BARONESS: A poem?

PHILIPPE: A surprise for madame... To go along with the flowers...

THE BARONESS, *to* CHANTAL: You learned a poem, angel?

PHILIPPE: One of mine, madame…

THE BARONESS: Oh? I didn't know you were a poet, Philippe!

PHILIPPE: Well… *(To* CHANTAL, *coaxing.)* Go ahead… You remember…

CHANTAL, *reciting*:

"We love our horses, proud to ride astride 'em…"

PHILIPPE: What?

NANETTE, *aside*: Good heavens! The cavalry officers…

CHANTAL, *continuing*:

"With sabers out, and ready for a fight!…"

PHILIPPE, *aside, to* CHANTAL: That's not the one!

CHANTAL, *giving him a poke*: Stop! You're making me forget…

PHILIPPE: But…

THE BARONESS, *to* PHILIPPE: Let her finish, Philippe! *(To* CHANTAL.*)* Go on, treasure…

CHANTAL, *beginning again*:

"We love our horses, proud to ride astride 'em,
With sabers out, and ready for a fight!"

PHILIPPE, *under his breath*: God help me!

CHANTAL, *continuing*:

"We love our ladies, and we love to ride 'em,
With sabers stout, drawn out the livelong night!"

THE BARONESS, *shocked*: What?

CHANTAL, *proudly*: There!

PHILIPPE, *to* THE BARONESS: But… But madame… That's not the one! I… I don't know where she could have learned it! *(To* CHANTAL.*)* Please! Mademoiselle should recite the one I taught her!

CHANTAL begins marching back and forth, in military fashion, with appropriate gestures and salutes.

THE BARONESS, *to* PHILIPPE: Well, no harm… *(Laughing.)* She's too young to understand it! *(Suddenly noticing* CHANTAL*'s demeanor.)* I say… What's that she's doing?

NANETTE, *replying quickly*: It's… It's a dance, madame. The latest step…

PHILIPPE, *to* CHANTAL, *still trying to get her ear*: The poem, mademoiselle…

THE BARONESS, *to* NANETTE: Oh?

NANETTE: Everyone in high society is doing it.

THE BARONESS: I didn't know… *(To* CHANTAL, *as she joins her, mimicking her steps.)* Like this, treasure?

PHILIPPE, *to* CHANTAL, *still trying*: The poem…

THE BARONESS, *to* NANETTE: But who on earth taught her?

PHILIPPE, *to* CHANTAL: Please, mademoiselle… *(Grabbing her as she marches past.)* The one with the flowers…

NANETTE, *to* THE BARONESS, *replying*: Who?… Why… I did, madame! For madame's birthday…

PHILIPPE, *to* CHANTAL, *coaxing*: Go on…

THE BARONESS: I'll have her do it at my soirée tomorrow. She'll be all the rage!

CHANTAL, *reluctantly stopping, as* THE BARONESS *attempts a few more steps, to* PHILIPPE: Oh… *(To* THE BARONESS, *reciting.)*

"Accept these rosebuds on this special day,
Your birthday, if we listen to the rumors.
May your day be as lovely, bright, and gay,
Full of the scents that fill your fragrant bloomers."

THE BARONESS, *applauding*: Charming!… Simply, utterly charming! *(To* PHILIPPE.*)* And you wrote that, Philippe? All by yourself? For me?

PHILIPPE: Yes, madame… I taught her the poem and Nanette taught her the dance. Just for madame's birthday…

THE BARONESS: Oh! As I always say… You two are jewels! Absolute jewels! How can I ever thank you? *(*PHILIPPE *gives a noncommittal shrug.)* I know!… Wait here…

She crosses left with CHANTAL, *and they both exit briefly to her room.*

PHILIPPE, *to* NANETTE: How much do you want to bet? A gold piece for each of us!

NANETTE: But my conscience… I feel so guilty…

PHILIPPE: Then you can give me yours! My conscience can handle it!

THE BARONESS *and* CHANTAL *return.*

THE BARONESS, *to* PHILIPPE *and* NANETTE, *pressing a coin into their hands*: There! *(As* CHANTAL *stops by the end table, left.)* That's for being so utterly devoted… And for taking such wonderful care of my little—

CHANTAL, *interrupting, noticing the letter*: Mammá! Mammá!… Look! *(Waving it.)* A letter…

THE BARONESS, *going over, taking it from her*: For me?

PHILIPPE, } *together, under their breath:* { Oh God!
NANETTE, } { Ayyy!

CHANTAL, *waving the cotton wadding*: With this, mammá… This…

THE BARONESS, *appalled*: Give me that! *(She grabs it, hides it down her bosom.)* Of all the… *(Opening the letter, reading.)* What?… But I don't… *(To* NANETTE *and* PHILIPPE.*)* Leaving?… What ever does this mean?… *(Reading.)* "… mislaid an object dear to her tender heart… Dearer than any other…"

NANETTE, *stammering*: W-W-We th-thought…

THE BARONESS: Did you lose something?

NANETTE: Well… In fact…

CHANTAL *has ambled up right. During the following dialogue, she casually takes a cigar from her pocket, lights it, and, unseen by the others, begins to take a few puffs.*

THE BARONESS: But what?… Tell me…

PHILIPPE, *standing next to the end table, down right, looks at the parrot cage and gets a sudden inspiration.*

PHILIPPE, *aside*: Ah!

As surreptitiously as possible, he takes the parrot from the cage and desperately tries to stuff it into his jacket, without success.

NANETTE: The truth is, madame… We… We lost madame's…

THE BARONESS, *impatiently*: My what?

PHILIPPE quickly puts the parrot in his hat and puts the hat on his head.

NANETTE: Madame's dear little—

PHILIPPE, *finishing the sentence*: Raoul! Her dear little Raoul!

THE BARONESS: My parrot? *(Relieved.)* Is that all?… Goodness me! I couldn't imagine… Much as I love the little darling…

PHILIPPE, *squirming*: Yes, madame… *(Aside.)* Damn him! He's pulling out my hair!

THE BARONESS, *getting ready to go to her room*: Well… Enough excitement for one night…

NANETTE, *aside, to PHILIPPE*: If she only knew!

THE BARONESS, *to PHILIPPE*: Tomorrow you can post some notices. He can't have gone very far, the dear. I'll give a fifty-franc reward. I'm sure someone will bring him back and claim it.

PHILIPPE: I'm sure, madame… Someone… *(He gives NANETTE an unobtrusive little nudge.)* I'm sure…

THE BARONESS, *to CHANTAL, without noticing the cigar*: Come along, Chantal… You're going to sleep with me…

PHILIPPE, *suddenly seeing the cigar, and snatching it from her lips, aside*: Oh! If only she was mine…

THE BARONESS, *to CHANTAL*: Now no more bad dreams, right? *(Laughing.)* No Moulin Bleu, no cherry brandy…

CHANTAL: But mammá…

THE BARONESS: No piggy-back rides…

PHILIPPE, *aside*: Little brat!

THE BARONESS and CHANTAL cross left.

NANETTE, *calling after them as they reach THE BARONESS's door*: Happy birthday, madame!

PHILIPPE: Happy birthday!… Happy birthday!

THE BARONESS and CHANTAL exit and shut the door. PHILIPPE and NANETTE stand sighing with relief for a moment, as the former puffs contentedly on the cigar. As the two shake hands in victory, the parrot can be heard cackling: "Awk awk awk!… Happy birthday!… Fragrant bloomers!… Awk awk awk!… Little brat…. Little brat…."

CURTAIN.

It's All Relative

(Les suites d'un premier lit, 1852)

Eugène Labiche & Marc-Michel

Characters

TRÉBUCHARD, a bachelor in his early forties, well-off and desperate to get married

PRUDENVAL, the father of Trébuchard's latest fiancée, something of a hypochondriac

PIQUOISEAU, a military man, given to alcohol, dashing but not very bright

CLAUDINE, Prudenval's beautiful but willful young daughter, Trébuchard's fiancée

MATHILDE, Trébuchard's aging and quite unattractive stepdaughter by a previous marriage

DELPHINE, Trébuchard's easily flustered maid

Trébuchard's well-furnished salon. A door, up left, set diagonally into the corner, leads to the outside; another door, similarly set up right, leads to other rooms of the apartment. In the upstage wall, two open French doors looking out on a small balcony, whose railing, above the street, is visible. Two other doors, down left and down right, lead, respectively, to Mathilde's and Trébuchard's rooms. Near the upstage wall, to the left of the balcony, a coatrack with Mathilde's hat and shawl, and Trébuchard's hat and coat. On the upstage wall, to the right of the balcony, a cuckoo clock. Down right, a little serving-cart or table, with bottles, glasses, a carafe of wine, an ashtray, etc. Behind it, on the wall down right, a mirror. Midstage left, two armchairs facing the audience and at a slight angle to each other. Down left, a table. Other furniture— lamps, chairs, loveseat, pictures, etc.— here and there.

At rise, DELPHINE *is out on the balcony with dustpan and broom.*

DELPHINE: Damnation! Not again!... Butts, butts, butts!... Every day... *(Pointing and counting, half under her breath.)* One, two... Five, six, seven... Eleven, twelve... Fourteen! *(With a sigh of disgust.)* Fourteen of his damn cigar butts! *(She gives a look up at the window of the floor above, hands on hips, shaking her head.)* Oh! *(Carefully sweeping up the butts into the dustpan.)* Some people!... They just don't care where they throw their trash!... Tsk tsk tsk!... I never...

She proceeds to empty the dustpan over the railing, into the street, still shaking her head, as TREBUCHARD *enters, down right, overhearing her complaint.*

TREBUCHARD: You never what, Delphine? What's the matter this time?

DELPHINE, *at the threshold*: The matter, monsieur? *(Pointing to the balcony.)* That! That's the matter! *(*TREBUCHARD *gives a quizzical look outside.)* Fourteen this morning!... Fourteen more cigar butts...

TREBUCHARD, *suddenly comprehending*: Oh...

DELPHINE: Fourteen, monsieur!

She puts the dustpan and broom aside, against the rear wall, and indicates "Fourteen" with the fingers of both hands: ten and four.

TREBUCHARD: Yes, I heard you.

DELPHINE: It's a disgrace, that's what it is!

TREBUCHARD: I must say he's improving! Yesterday it was only a dozen.

DELPHINE, *grumbling to herself*: If he thinks all I have to do...

TREBUCHARD: Who the devil does he think he is? Officer or not... Since when is my balcony that idiot's private ashtray! I mean, some of my best friends are soldiers, but still...

DELPHINE: At this rate, monsieur, by the end of the year... Well, monsieur can just imagine...

TREBUCHARD: Quite!... Perhaps I should have a word with him.

DELPHINE, *to herself*: High time, if you ask me!

TREBUCHARD, *going out onto the balcony*: Yes, I think a brief tête-à-tête would be in order. *(Looking up to the floor above.)* You, up there... Monsieur... Mon capitaine...

DELPHINE, *to herself, reacting to his remark*: You can say that again!

TREBUCHARD, *after a brief pause, repeating*: Monsieur... Mon capitaine...

DELPHINE, *misunderstanding, to* TREBUCHARD, *excusing herself*: Oh no, monsieur… I didn't mean…

PIQUOISEAU'S VOICE: Who's calling?… What is it?

TREBUCHARD: Down here, monsieur… Your neighbor, Trebuchard…

PIQUOISEAU'S VOICE: So? What do you want?

TREBUCHARD: Well, it's just that… I thought I'd suggest, if it's not too much to ask… Nothing against the military, mind you… I'm in the reserves myself… But I thought, perhaps… If you could manage to stop flicking your cigar butts down here…

PIQUOISEAU'S VOICE: Oh? And why's that?

TREBUCHARD: Why? *(Aside.)* Why indeed! *(To* PIQUOISEAU.*)* Because they're filthy, that's why! It's disgusting! Throw them somewhere else, why don't you!…

PIQUOISEAU'S VOICE: Like where, for example?

TREBUCHARD: I don't care. Anywhere… The street…

PIQUOISEAU'S VOICE: What? And hit somebody? Some officer maybe?

TREBUCHARD, *losing patience*: Oh…

He comes inside and moves downstage.

PIQUOISEAU'S VOICE: Where the blazes were you brought up?

DELPHINE, *stepping out onto the balcony, to* TREBUCHARD: Fifteen, monsieur!

She comes back in and stands at the threshold.

TREBUCHARD, *turning*: What?

DELPHINE: One more. *(Pointing.)* Just now…

TREBUCHARD: That does it! *(Stalking outside.)* All right… *(Calling up to* PIQUOISEAU.*)* You leave me no choice, my friend. I'm going to report you to your commanding officer!… Tomorrow… First thing…

He comes back inside.

PIQUOISEAU'S VOICE: Go fry an egg! I *am* my commanding officer!

TREBUCHARD, *to* DELPHINE: What did he say?

DELPHINE: I think he told monsieur to go fry an egg.

TREBUCHARD, *furious*: He… Oh! Is he still up there?

DELPHINE *goes out and looks.*

DELPHINE, *returning*: No, monsieur. He's gone back in.

TREBUCHARD: Lucky for him! Of all the… Oh!… *(Calming down.)* As if I didn't have other things on my mind…

DELPHINE: Yes, monsieur.

TREBUCHARD: More important than that… that… *(He sighs.)* Tell me, Delphine…

DELPHINE: Monsieur?

TREBUCHARD, *downstage, looking around almost surreptitiously, in a whisper*: Did you do what I told you? Did you pack my bag?

DELPHINE: Yes, monsieur. It's all packed and ready to go. *(Pointing down right.)* Right inside monsieur's door…

TREBUCHARD: Shhh! Not so loud!… *(Nodding toward* MATHILDE*'s door, down left.)* She's not supposed to know.

DELPHINE: No, monsieur.

TREBUCHARD: Not a word, you understand?

DELPHINE: Yes, monsieur. Not a word…

TREBUCHARD, *forefinger to lips*: Please… *(He takes a few steps, moving left.)* Is she still in bed?

DELPHINE: Oh no, monsieur. She's already slapped me twice this morning… And called me a "crouton" or something… Four times, I think…

TREBUCHARD: Oh?

DELPHINE: On account of her corset… But it's not my fault if it won't lace up, monsieur. I pulled it as tight as I could, but…

She shrugs.

TREBUCHARD: I know… I know…

DELPHINE, *after a brief pause, as if struck by a new thought*: Does monsieur want me to tell her that he's going to Lyon?

TREBUCHARD, *with a start*: Do I… No, no! For goodness' sake! What did I just say? Not a word, you understand?

DELPHINE: Yes, monsieur. Not a word.

TREBUCHARD: I'll write to her when I get there. No long, drawn-out good-byes, thank you!

DELPHINE: Then monsieur won't be taking her with him?

TREBUCHARD: Taking her… Certainly not! How many times do I… That's all I need!

DELPHINE: And he expects me to stay here with her? The whole time? Just me and her?

TREBUCHARD: Of course.

DELPHINE: But monsieur knows how afraid she gets when she's alone.

TREBUCHARD: Well, she won't be alone. You'll be with her.

DELPHINE: Maybe so… But she's afraid when the two of us are alone together…

TREBUCHARD: Bah! Just because she's my daughter… I can't wrap her up like a… a papoose, and drag her everywhere I go! No, I'm better off leaving her here, Delphine… Before she even knows I'm gone…

DELPHINE: But she'll hit me, monsieur, like she always does.

TREBUCHARD: Then hit her back. You're old enough to take care of yourself, I daresay!

DELPHINE: Yes, monsieur. *(Aside.)* And so is she!

As she goes about her business tidying up the room, the door, down left, opens and MATHILDE *appears, pulling on her gloves. She is a portly, middle-aged woman.*

DELPHINE, *aside*: Damn! Speak of the devil…

MATHILDE, *coming in, to* TREBUCHARD: Good morning, papá!

TREBUCHARD, *aside*: "Papá!" God in heaven! *(To* MATHILDE.*)* Good morning, mademoiselle…

MATHILDE, *drawing back, a little piqued*: "Mademoiselle," papá?… Is something wrong?… I hope you're not angry with your little Mathilde…

TREBUCHARD, *aside*: My little... *(Aloud.)* Angry?... Why should I be... Not at all... *(Forcing himself:)* daughter dear. *(Aside.)* Ugh!

MATHILDE: Good! Because... *(Hesitating.)* I have something to ask you.

TREBUCHARD: Oh?

MATHILDE: Yes... If I may.

TREBUCHARD: Of course you may! What is it?

MATHILDE: It's just that I would like to go out this morning...

TREBUCHARD, *impatient*: So? Who's stopping you? Go...

MATHILDE: Well, if you're sure... If I have your permission, papá...

TREBUCHARD: My per... By all means, mademoi... *(Correcting himself.)* daughter dear... Please!... Anywhere you like! *(Aside.)* For as long as you like!

MATHILDE: Aren't you going to ask me where? Don't you even want to know?

TREBUCHARD, *beginning to lose his composure*: Who gives a... *(Taking a deep breath, very properly.)* Why yes, my child... *(He turns aside with a grimace, then continues.)* Do tell papá where you're going this morning.

MATHILDE: To the florist's...

TREBUCHARD: I see...

MATHILDE: To buy some flowers...

TREBUCHARD, *aside*: How quaint!

MATHILDE: Tulips, I think...

TREBUCHARD: An excellent choice... Yes, do go buy some tulips... *(Looking at his pocket watch.)* And take as long as you like. Four hours... Five, six, seven...

MATHILDE: Oh? Aren't you coming with me, papá?

TREBUCHARD: With you?... No... Sorry! I'm busy... Very busy...

MATHILDE: Too busy for me?

TREBUCHARD: It's... I... It's important! *(Looking for an excuse.)* I'm... I... I'm expecting my tailor...

MATHILDE: Oh yes! Very important! *(Pouting.)* Never mind, I know. You don't have to make excuses.

TREBUCHARD: Excuses?

MATHILDE: You think I'm a nuisance, don't you?

TREBUCHARD: I never said—

MATHILDE: And you'd like to get rid of me, papá! Go on, admit it!

TREBUCHARD: But—

MATHILDE: Well, you can, you know. There's a very easy way.

TREBUCHARD, *suddenly interested, drawing closer*: There is?

MATHILDE: Yes. *(Matter-of-fact.)* Find me a husband.

TREBUCHARD, *let down*: Oh yes, of course... *(Aside.)* Just like that! Move the Rock of Gibraltar! *(To MATHILDE.)* Yes, well... We'll see... I'll look...

MATHILDE: Thank you, papá.

TREBUCHARD, *aside*: Don't ask me where! *(To MATHILDE.)* Only not today. I'm busy.

MATHILDE: I know... With your tailor...

TREBUCHARD: So... You go buy your tulips. Delphine will go with you.

DELPHINE, *down right, pricking up her ears*: I will?

MATHILDE: But papá, do you think it's safe? Entrusting me to a domestic? I mean, with all those men out there, ready to take advantage of a poor, defenseless woman…

DELPHINE, *under her breath*: Defenseless? Ha!

TREBUCHARD: Really, I wouldn't worry. At night you might have a problem, but not in broad daylight.

MATHILDE: Are you sure?

TREBUCHARD: Trust me… I assure you… *(Aside.)* As long as they can see you…

MATHILDE: Well…

TREBUCHARD, *going over to the coatrack, up left, and handing her her shawl, but leaving her hat*: Here! *(Urging her toward the door, up left.)* Now hurry, or I'll be… *(Catching himself.)* Or you'll be late.

MATHILDE, *putting on the shawl*: Late? Late for what?

TREBUCHARD: For the tulips… The best ones always get sold before noon. It's common knowledge… *(Motioning to* DELPHINE *to accompany her.)* Delphine…

MATHILDE: Oh, I didn't know…

DELPHINE *moving reluctantly toward the door, up left*: Well, if I have to…

MATHILDE, *giving her a push in passing*: Come on, cretin! Come on!…

DELPHINE: I'm coming! *(Aside, to* TREBUCHARD.*)* See, monsieur?

TREBUCHARD, *aside, to* DELPHINE: Well, hit her back, I told you. You have my permission.

MATHILDE, *at the door*: Bye-bye, papá…

TREBUCHARD, *turning his back on her, very offhand*: Bye-bye… Bye-bye…

MATHILDE: Don't I even get a kiss?

TREBUCHARD, *approaching her, reluctantly*: Of course. What was I thinking! *(He gives her a grudging peck, then turns his head aside.)* Ptui! *(Aside.)* Like kissing my grandmother!

MATHILDE: Bye-bye… *(To* DELPHINE, *giving her another poke.)* Go on! Go on!

DELPHINE: Damnation!

TREBUCHARD watches them disappear out the door, then goes to the coatrack and puts on his coat.

TREBUCHARD, *coming downstage, to the audience*: Well, now you've seen her… Oh yes, I know what you're thinking. *(Affecting another voice.)* "Your daughter, monsieur?… You expect me to believe that that rather… mature individual…" *(In his own voice.)* I know… I know… She's fifty if she's a day! *(In the other voice.)* "Whereas you, monsieur…" *(In his own voice.)* Me? A mere twenty-nine… Give or take… *(Sighing.)* Yes, it's absolutely absurd… Absurd, but true… And all because… *(He shakes his head.)* Ah! When I think of it… All because… *(Looking at his watch.)* I still have five minutes. Let me tell you the story… The whole ugly story, from the beginning. *(Crossing right.)* I was born… *(Reconsidering.)* No… No need to go back that far. Everyone gets born sooner or later, I suppose… Anyway, my parents were rich, but… Well, stingy, to put it mildly… *(Ambling upstage.)* Which didn't help me much with my studies, I can tell you!… Five long years of medicine… *(Taking the broom and using it as a billiard queue, miming.)* And billiards!… Yes, billiards and medicine… *(Laying the broom aside and coming downstage.)* Two very expensive fields of academic endeavor! Especially when you haven't a sou to your name! *(He looks at his watch.)* Well, to make a long story short, one morning I got up… "Time to take stock of the situation," I told myself… And not very pretty! Nothing but debts, debts, debts! Nine thousand eight hundred thirty francs and seventy-five centimes, to be precise… On the credit side, not much… Two clay pipes and a pack of cigarette papers… And no tobacco, I might add… Well, just as I'm getting ready to go back to bed, there's a little knock at the door… "Come in, come in…" *(Moving up left, toward the coatrack.)* And in comes old widow Dufour, of all people… The one who runs my favorite bistro in the Latin Quarter… For months I'd been paying my tabs with nothing but lustful and provocative glances… *(He demonstrates, gazing soulfully at the coatrack, still topped with MATHILDE's hat.)* Not exactly coin of the realm, you understand, but since she didn't object… She even tried to give me change in kind! Which was something to see, believe me!… Anyway, there she is. In the flesh… Such as it was… "Monsieur Trébuchard…" And she's all trembling and out of breath… From climbing up to my seventh-storey garret, I imagined… But no, not quite… "Monsieur Trébuchard," she tells me, "I've come to inform you that I have assumed all of your financial obligations. Now all of your debts are mine." "Well, that's a nice arrangement," I answered. "Very considerate, I must say. How can I ever thank you?" "I'm afraid you misunderstand," she went on. "I've bought them, monsieur. Now it's me you owe… And at twenty percent per annum." *(Addressing the coatrack.)* "But madame, I'm afraid…" "No buts, monsieur…" "But…" *(Imitating her displeasure.)* "For years you've been toying with my affection…" "I have?" "…and now I'm offering you my hand." *(With a grimace, to the audience.)* Good God! Not her hand, or anything else! No thank you! *(To the coatrack.)* "Ah, madame, what a pleasure… If only I could accept… But I've taken a vow of chastity, and I'm about to become a monk." *(To the audience.)* I don't think she believed me… "My hand, monsieur, or prison. It's up to you. Take your choice…" Well, all things considered… *(He comes down center.)* So I wound up in prison… With my two clay pipes and my cigarette papers… And still no tobacco!… The first month, no problem… I passed the time training a couple of spiders and writing vicious quatrains about old widow Dufour. But the second month… *(He looks at his watch.)* Let me tell you… Tobacco or not tobacco, that is the question!… Frankly, I couldn't stand it. "After all," I asked myself, "can she really be so bad?… Old, ugly, yes… And dried up like a prune… But maybe, if I keep her buttoned up to the chin…" So I sent her a note. "My love, come save me from this craving deep within me: this longing to fill my lungs…" *(Correcting himself)* "…my heart… This longing to fill my heart with warm billows of joy!" Not terribly original… But, of course, it worked… A week later we were man and wife. More or less, that is… Because, actually, that night—our wedding-night, so to speak—I bribed my reserve commander to put me on active duty. Then and there… No deferment… For as long as he liked… *(He goes over to the bottles, down right, and pours himself a drink from the carafe.)* Two years later… Tsk tsk tsk!… I was a widower… *(He raises his glass heavenward in an unspoken toast and takes a sip.)* Just one minor complication: the dear departed left me her amazon of a daughter… *(With a nod toward the door, up left.)* From a previous marriage, thank you!… And fifty in the shade!… And who keeps calling me "papá"… In front of my ladyfriends, damn it!… And whines all day that I should take her out for a walk!… A walk? Along the boulevard, with that…

that mammoth on my arm? Can't you just see it? *(He lays down his glass and moves left, laboriously, as if dragging a heavy weight, tipping an imaginary hat to imaginary passers-by.)* "Monsieur… Madame…" If only I could get rid of her!… But how in heaven?… I would if I could. It's not that I haven't tried!… But she clings… And clings… Like a vine!… Poison ivy… *(He mimes trying to disentangle himself.)* Damn!… *(Sitting on the arm of one of the chairs, left.)* I even tried marrying her off to a friend… Gaston Billetdoux… Well, he used to be a friend… Before the duel, that is… He claimed I insulted him by just suggesting it… Not that I blame him… *(Getting up, pacing left and right.)* I wouldn't mind so much if she kept her bad luck to herself… If she stayed an old maid for the rest of her life… But no! *(Stopping down center.)* Let me tell you… Me… Hector Trébuchard… Seven engagements, and all of them up in smoke!… That's right, seven… Nipped in the bud, thanks to her. Would you believe it?… It's not that I don't make an excellent impression… Au contraire, I assure you… The minute they see me, if I do say so myself… It's always the same tune… *(Imitating several voices.)* "What a charming young man!…" "Did you see his lovely teeth?…" "And so witty, so clever…" "And he's still got all his hair!…" Fine!… But then I introduce my daughter, bless her heart! And… *(With a wave.)* Pfffft! The kiss of death! That's that! No more! Fini!… *(Moving right.)* Well, that's why, this time, I'm not taking any chances, understand? Tell me I'm a bounder, and a cad, and a sneak… Tell me I'm not a good father. I don't care!… I'm off to change my luck with the beautiful number eight! Far off! All the way to Lyon this time… Where no one knows a thing about the bane of my existence… And where they'll never find out!… That I'm a widower, yes… No harm in that. But nothing about my daughter!… By this time next Saturday I'll be the proud and happy husband of Mademoiselle Claudine Prudenval… Ravishing creature… Innocent, young… Only eighteen years old… *(Picking up his drink and toasting.)* "To your health and long life, Madame Trébuchard!…" At last! *(He drinks.)* And no children by a previous marriage, thank you!… *(Raising the glass again.)* "And to Monsieur Prudenval, my new father-in- law!…" A pleasant enough chap, all things considered… *(He finishes the drink and puts down the glass.)* He wanted to make the wedding here in Paris, heaven help us! Lucky for me I was able to talk him out of it. Seven is enough! This is one wife my sweet little cherub won't frighten off!… When it's over I'll send her a wedding announcement, and invite her to vacate the premises. On the spot!… Oh, no need to feel sorry… With old widow Dufour's millions… *(Reconsidering.)* Well, some of them, that is… *(He looks at his watch.)* Damn! Look at the time!… My bag… I'll miss my train…

He runs off, down right, and returns a moment later with his valise.

PRUDENVAL'S VOICE, *offstage*: Thank you, my good man… We'll just go right in.

TREBUCHARD: What? That voice… Don't tell me… It can't be… *(Running to the balcony and peering over the railing.)* Good God in… It is!… *(Running back in, still carrying the valise, not knowing which way to turn.)* Prudenval and his daughter!… The two of them! Here!… But… Oh! I should have known better than to trust that… that…

The door, up left, opens and PRUDENVAL enters, followed by CLAUDINE. He has an umbrella dangling from his arm and is carrying several valises and an assortment of packages. She is wearing a hat and carrying a parasol.

PRUDENVAL, *taking* TREBUCHARD *for a domestic*: Good morning, monsieur. Please announce us to your… *(Realizing his error.)* Oh! I say!… You are your… *(With a silly little laugh.)* I mean…

TREBUCHARD: Monsieur…

PRUDENVAL: It's you… Trébuchard…

TREBUCHARD, *backing into the room as the pair advance*: Quite…

PRUDENVAL: Because for a minute I thought…

TREBUCHARD, *babbling*: Yes… No…

PRUDENVAL: But it's you…

TREBUCHARD: Yes… Yes… So it seems…

PRUDENVAL, *trying to hold out his arms, but obviously encumbered*: Son!

TREBUCHARD: Monsieur!

PRUDENVAL: No, no!… Please!… "Father!"

TREBUCHARD, *down center, putting down his valise but making no move to relieve* PRUDENVAL *of his*: Yes… Of course… *(Under his breath.)* Whatever…

PRUDENVAL: And… *(Turning, trying unsuccessfully to point to* CLAUDINE.*)* And my daughter…

TREBUCHARD: Yes… Your… My…

CLAUDINE, *with a little curtsy*: Monsieur!

TREBUCHARD, *aside*: Damn! Five minutes sooner, and…

CLAUDINE, *to* TREBUCHARD: You must be surprised to see us!

PRUDENVAL, *aside*: I wish he would tell me to put these things down!

TREBUCHARD, *to* CLAUDINE: Well…

PRUDENVAL, *to* TREBUCHARD: We've come from Lyon.

TREBUCHARD: No! What a coincidence! I was just on my way there! *(Picking up his valise.)* Come! We'll all go back together!

He moves hurriedly up left.

PRUDENVAL, *following him*: Go back?

CLAUDINE: Back? Why on earth…?

PRUDENVAL, *to* TREBUCHARD: Don't be silly! Why go back? *(Trying to gesture.)* Now that we're here… *(Aside.)* I do wish he would tell me…

CLAUDINE, *to* TREBUCHARD: You didn't expect us, did you?

PRUDENVAL, *to* TREBUCHARD: But I hope you're not angry…

TREBUCHARD, *to* CLAUDINE: Expect you…? *(To* PRUDENVAL.*)* Angry? *(To* CLAUDINE.*)* Well, I… *(To* PRUDENVAL.*)* Why should I be angry? It's just that I thought—

PRUDENVAL, *coming down center, interrupting*: I know… I know…

TREBUCHARD: I mean, the wedding… I thought it was all agreed… Lyon…

PRUDENVAL: And it was, son. You're right. Only… *(To* CLAUDINE, *up left.)* You tell him, ma petite…

CLAUDINE: No, no, papá. You!…

PRUDENVAL: But since it was your idea…

TREBUCHARD, *suddenly noticing* MATHILDE'*s hat on the coatrack, aside*: Good God! She forgot her hat…

CLAUDINE, *coming down left, to* PRUDENVAL *as* TREBUCHARD *stuffs the hat under his arm*: I know, but you can explain it much better.

PRUDENVAL: Well…

TREBUCHARD, *aside*: What if she comes back for it?

He goes over to the balcony and peers out.

PRUDENVAL, *to* CLAUDINE: If you think so… *(To* TREBUCHARD.*)* You see, son, it's my condition…

TREBUCHARD, *pacing uneasily between the balcony and the door, up left*: Yes… I see… Your… *(Stopping.)* What condition?

PRUDENVAL: Why, the same one as before. You remember…

TREBUCHARD: I do?

PRUDENVAL: The one I told you about in Lyon, each time you came to visit…

CLAUDINE, *to* TREBUCHARD: You remember, monsieur. Each time…

TREBUCHARD, *at the balcony, offhand*: Aha… Yes… That…

PRUDENVAL: Because… Well frankly, son, it's getting worse.

TREBUCHARD, *peering out, preoccupied*: Yes… That's nice…

PRUDENVAL, } *together*: { What?
CLAUDINE, } { Monsieur?

TREBUCHARD, *realizing his gaffe*: Oh… "Worse… Getting worse…" I thought you said…

PRUDENVAL: Yes, much worse…

TREBUCHARD: Tsk tsk tsk!

PRUDENVAL: You see, every time I eat… It's like a dull ache… Or maybe more like an itch… But inside… *(Trying in vain to indicate the location.)* Inside… *(As an afterthought.)* In fact, even when I don't eat…

TREBUCHARD, *stealing an anxious glance over the balcony*: Tsk tsk tsk!

PRUDENVAL, *shrugging*: Who knows what it is? Do I? *(Shaking his head, then with a nod in* CLAUDINE*'s direction.)* Does she? *(Shaking his head.)* And my doctor?… No idea!

TREBUCHARD: Tsk tsk tsk! Tsk tsk tsk!

CLAUDINE, *to* TREBUCHARD: So I told him, monsieur…

PRUDENVAL: That's right. It was her idea. She said: "You really should go see a doctor in Paris!"

CLAUDINE, *to* TREBUCHARD: I was right, monsieur, wasn't I?

TREBUCHARD: Of course, mademoiselle! No question! *(Aside.)* Much obliged!

PRUDENVAL: Anyway, since we're here… Well, we may as well kill two birds with one stone, as they say.

TREBUCHARD: Yes. As they say…

CLAUDINE, *crossing right, to* TREBUCHARD: Besides, I've always wanted to be married in Paris. It's so much more chic…

TREBUCHARD, *still very preoccupied, continues to steal glances out the balcony.*

PRUDENVAL: And even if it does cost much more than in Lyon… *(With a nod toward* CLAUDINE.*)* She's worth it, don't you think?

TREBUCHARD, *hardly listening*: I'm sure… If you say so…

PRUDENVAL: If *I* say so, son?

TREBUCHARD, *catching himself:* Oh, her!... *(Pointing to* CLAUDINE.*)* You mean her!... Certainly she's worth it! Every sou! Every centime, monsieur!

PRUDENVAL, *correcting:* Please!... "Father..."

TREBUCHARD: Yes... Of course...

PRUDENVAL: And we'll spare no expense, believe me. The best food, the best wine... Champagne... Pâté, caviar... All that sort of thing... And oysters... Lots of oysters...

TREBUCHARD: Oh?

PRUDENVAL: Yes. The doctor thinks they may be good for my condition.

TREBUCHARD: Aha... *(Under his breath.)* Good for your itch, I'm sure!

PRUDENVAL, *approaching* TREBUCHARD, *up center:* Well son, now that that's settled... I say... Would you mind if I put these things down?

TREBUCHARD: Why bother? We're leaving!... Come, I'll take you to the hotel. *(Hurrying toward the door, up left, beckoning.)* There's a lovely one only a half-day's walk from here.

PRUDENVAL: Hotel?... Don't be silly! We don't need a hotel! We'll just stay here with you.

TREBUCHARD, *freezing:* You will?

PRUDENVAL, *coming down left:* Of course! We don't mind...

CLAUDINE, *still down right, with a little pout, to* TREBUCHARD: Unless you think we would be in the way, monsieur.

TREBUCHARD: In the way? Not at all... My pleasure, mademoiselle! I was going to suggest... *(Stealing a look at* MATHILDE'*s hat under his arm, aside.)* Oh my!... *(Coming down center, between the two, to* CLAUDINE.*)* It's just that I thought you might be more comfortable...

CLAUDINE: Because, if you don't have the room... With the baby and all, that is...

PRUDENVAL *gives a knowing little chuckle.*

TREBUCHET, *to* PRUDENVAL: Baby? (To CLAUDINE.) What baby?

PRUDENVAL: Oh, you're a sly one, you are, son!

TREBUCHARD: I am?

PRUDENVAL: Not telling us about your daughter...

CLAUDINE: That's right...

TREBUCHARD, *thunderstruck, to* PRUDENVAL: Daughter... *(To* CLAUDINE.*)* Baby... *(Aside.)* God in heaven! *(Beginning to babble.)* My... My...

PRUDENVAL, *good-naturedly:* Because, I have my sources, you know!

TREBUCHARD: My... My...

CLAUDINE: Besides, I think it's charming!

TREBUCHARD, *to* PRUDENVAL, *innocently:* You mean... I didn't tell you?

CLAUDINE: I simply adore babies!

TREBUCHARD, *to* CLAUDINE: Oh?

CLAUDINE: And so does papá!

PRUDENVAL: Yes, as long as they don't grow up! *(With a little laugh.)* After five, they're insufferable!

TREBUCHARD, *aside*: And after fifty?

PRUDENVAL, *to TREBUCHARD*: Where is she, son?

TREBUCHARD: She… She's… *(With a vague gesture, down left.)* still asleep.

PRUDENVAL: So late?

CLAUDINE, *to TREBUCHARD*: Is she weaned yet, monsieur?

TREBUCHARD: Is she… Almost… We're trying…

PRUDENVAL: And teeth?… Does she have any?

TREBUCHARD: Oh, a mouthful… Forty… Fifty…

CLAUDINE, } *together*: { What?
PRUDENVAL, } { How many?

TREBUCHARD, I mean, four or five…

CLAUDINE: Oh, she must be simply precious! I can't wait to give her a big hug and kiss! I'll dress her up and play with her… And teach her to blow kisses!… She'll be my little doll…

TREBUCHARD: Yes… *(Aside.)* I can just see it!

CLAUDINE, *pointing to PRUDENVAL's packages*: You see, monsieur? We've brought her some presents. I even knitted her a darling little bonnet, all by myself. All pink and white…

PRUDENVAL, *to TREBUCHARD, trying to indicate one of them*: And guess what I brought her.

TREBUCHARD: Don't tell me… You knitted her some booties.

PRUDENVAL, *on whom the sarcasm is lost*: No… I got her a giant gingerbread man.

TREBUCHARD: How thoughtful!

PRUDENVAL: And that's not all…

TREBUCHARD: You shouldn't have, monsieur.

PRUDENVAL: Please!… "Father!"

TREBUCHARD: Yes… Of course…

PRUDENVAL: After all, I'll be her grandfather… In a manner of speaking…

TREBUCHARD: In a manner…

CLAUDINE: Oh, I do hope she gets up soon!

TREBUCHARD: Yes… Well… In the meantime I'll show you to your rooms. *(To PRUDENVAL, gesturing.)* Please… This way…

CLAUDINE: I simply can't wait!

> *TREBUCHARD retrieves his valise and shows CLAUDINE out the door, up right. PRUDENVAL hangs back, midstage.*

PRUDENVAL, *watching CLAUDINE and TREBUCHARD exit, shuffling his packages*: I say, son… Oh well, no harm… *(He puts the valises and umbrella down on the floor, and the packages, on the table, down left.)* There!… *(Heaving a sigh and stretching.)* Well now, off to my room…

> *He picks up the packages, valises, and umbrella again, and begins crossing up right to go out. As he reaches the door, MATHILDE enters, up left, followed by DELPHINE, who is carrying three pots of flowers.*

MATHILDE, *to* DELPHINE: Careful, clumsy! *(Menacingly.)* If you dare drop them…

DELPHINE: Don't worry! *(Under her breath.)* Blasted crouton!

PRUDENVAL, *noticing* MATHILDE, *aside*: Hmm! Now who's that, I wonder?

MATHILDE takes off her shawl and drapes it over the coatrack.

MATHILDE, } *noticing* PRUDENVAL, *aside*: { Oh… A man!
PRUDENVAL, } { Who the devil?

PRUDENVAL, *coming center, to* MATHILDE: I say… I take it you're looking for Monsieur Trébuchard?

MATHILDE: And to whom do I have the pleasure—

PRUDENVAL, *managing a little bow*: No, no… Please!… The pleasure is all mine!

MATHILDE: Too kind…

PRUDENVAL: Not at all…

MATHILDE, *joining him, center*: Now then… Monsieur…?

PRUDENVAL: But really, I'm not… Not me…

MATHILDE: Not you?… I beg your pardon?

PRUDENVAL: No, I'm not… I'm Prudenval… From Lyon… I've just arrived.

MATHILDE, *still confused, with an inquisitive cock of the head*: Monsieur?

PRUDENVAL: But I'll be happy to call him… *(With a nod toward the armchairs, left.)* If you would like to take a seat… *(Going up right, calling.)* Trébuchard!… Trébuchard!…

MATHILDE, *to* DELPHINE, *who has been watching, up left*: Delphine! Don't stand there gaping! Take these flowers to my room!

PRUDENVAL, *overhearing, aside*: Her room?

MATHILDE, *to* DELPHINE: Well, you heard me!

PRUDENVAL, *aside*: One of the family, no doubt! *(Calling.)* Trébuchard!

DELPHINE, *grumbling*: I'm going…

MATHILDE, *to* DELPHINE: Go on! *(Giving her a push out the door, down left.)* And be careful!

DELPHINE exits.

PRUDENVAL, *who has been scrutinizing* MATHILDE, *suddenly struck by a thought, aside*: Of course!… His mother!… Same nose, same chin… The other one must be the wet nurse. *(The door, down right, opens, and* TREBUCHARD *enters. He has removed his coat.)* Ah! There you—

TREBUCHARD: What do you— *(Noticing* MATHILDE, *aside.)* Good God! Mathilde! *(Aloud, stammering.)* Ma… Ma… You're back!

PRUDENVAL, *aside*: "Mammá!"… I guessed it!

MATHILDE, *still at the door, down left, to* TREBUCHARD: Yes, And you were right. The tulips were all gone.

TREBUCHARD, *distraught, hardly listening*: Aha…

MATHILDE: I never realized that by noon… Well, I had to settle for geraniums. Three pots…

TREBUCHARD, *as* PRUDENVAL *comes down right, standing to his right*: Yes… Fine… Geraniums… *(Aside.)* Has she told him?

PRUDENVAL, *to* TREBUCHARD, *softly*: Your mother is quite a woman… For her age…

TREBUCHARD, *confused, aside*: She is? *(To* PRUDENVAL.*)* Who told you?

The following exchanges are delivered in whispers until otherwise indicated.

PRUDENVAL: No, no… *(With a nod toward* MATHILDE.*)* Madame… Your mother…

TREBUCHARD: My who?

PRUDENVAL: I guessed right away… You're the spit and image!

MATHILDE *comes right and stands beside* TREBUCHARD, *to his left.*

TREBUCHARD, *to* PRUDENVAL: Aha… My… Yes… *(To* MATHILDE.*)* Please! Go to your room!

MATHILDE, *to* TREBUCHARD: Who is that gentleman?

TREBUCHARD: A… A dear friend… *(Desperately.)* My… My tailor!

PRUDENVAL, *to* TREBUCHARD: Introduce me, son, won't you?

TREBUCHARD: Who? Me?.. To… To…

MATHILDE, *trying in vain to attract* PRUDENVAL*'s attention, aloud*: Monsieur…

PRUDENVAL, *to* TREBUCHARD, *whispering*: Your mother…

MATHILDE, *to* PRUDENVAL, *archly*: Monsieur… I hate to complain, but those buttons on monsieur's last vest…

PRUDENVAL: Please?

MATHILDE: Well, they really leave something to be desired, don't you think?

TREBUCHARD, *to* PRUDENVAL, *still in a whisper*: It's nothing… Ignore her…

PRUDENVAL, *to* TREBUCHARD, *whispering*: Aren't you going to introduce me?

TREBUCHARD, *whispering*: Of course! Give me a chance! *(Aside.)* Good God in heaven! *(To* MATHILDE, *aloud.)* I'd like you to meet Monsieur Prudenval… *(Whispering.)* Now please! Go to your room!

PRUDENVAL, *to* MATHILDE: Delighted, madame!

MATHILDE, *under her breath*: "Madame?"

PRUDENVAL: I brought a giant gingerbread man, you know… All the way from Lyon…

MATHILDE: You what?

PRUDENVAL: And toys for the baby…

TREBUCHARD, } *together*: { Ayyy!
MATHILDE, } { The baby?

PRUDENVAL: Anyway… *(To* MATHILDE, *managing to extend his right hand in front of* TREBUCHARD.*)* Grandpapas and grandmammas should always be friends, don't you—

TREBUCHARD *quickly seizes his hand and shakes it vigorously.*

MATHILDE, *to* PRUDENVAL: I beg your pardon?

PRUDENVAL, *to* TREBUCHARD: What are you—

TREBUCHARD, *to* MATHILDE: It's a proverb! You know…

PRUDENVAL, *overhearing, aside*: It is? *(To* MATHILDE, *clumsily trying to hold out his snuffbox.)* I say… May I give you a pinch, madame?

MATHILDE, *not noticing his offer*: Monsieur!

TREBUCHARD, *to MATHILDE, whispering*: Please! Go to your room!

PRUDENVAL, *to MATHILDE*: Sorry... *(Aside, with a shrug.)* I thought maybe she sniffed...

MATHILDE, *to TREBUCHARD, whispering*: Really, papá! Your tailor—

TREBUCHARD, *to MATHILDE, clapping his hand over her mouth*: Shhh! Shhh! *(Pushing her toward the door, down left, whispering.)* Not now!... Please! Not now!...

MATHILDE, *at the door, to PRUDENVAL, with a very proper nod*: Monsieur...

She turns to leave.

PRUDENVAL: Madame... *(As she disappears out the door.)* Delighted to...

TREBUCHARD, *with a sigh, aside*: My God, what a nightmare!

He sits down in one of the armchairs, left, fanning his brow.

PRUDENVAL, *to himself*: Yes, quite a woman... Well seasoned, but still... *(Moving left, to TREBUCHARD, trying to match the gesture to the word, good-naturedly.)* Naughty, naughty, son!

TREBUCHARD: Hmm?

PRUDENVAL, *with a nod toward the door through which she has just left*: Madame... Mammá... You never told me you had a mother...

TREBUCHARD: Oh? It must have slipped my mind.

PRUDENVAL: That makes two little secrets...

TREBUCHARD: Two? *(With a tinge of irony.)* Mammá, and...?

PRUDENVAL: And the baby...

TREBUCHARD: Yes... Of course... The baby...

PRUDENVAL: I say... Does she play whist?

TREBUCHARD: The baby?

PRUDENVAL: No, no... Mammá...

TREBUCHARD: Oh, like a trooper!

PRUDENVAL: Delightful woman!... *(Aside.)* Do troopers play whist?

TREBUCHARD: Yes, delightful... Quite...

PRUDENVAL: Well, son... If you don't mind, I'm going to freshen up... Before I go see the doctor...

He takes a few steps up right.

TREBUCHARD, *getting up*: Yes... Don't let me keep you...

PRUDENVAL, *stopping*: About my condition... A specialist from the university... *(TREBUCHARD nods.)* You see, every time I eat... In fact, even when I don't eat...

TREBUCHARD, *subtly urging him toward the door, up right*: Yes, by all means, go see him. It sounds rather serious.

PRUDENVAL: I'm afraid so too. Oh well... *(Nodding toward the door.)* This way, right?

TREBUCHARD: Yes, all the way down... *(Opening the door for him.)* As far as you can go... *(Aside.)* Only not far enough!

PRUDENVAL, *halfway out the door, returning*: Oh, and be sure to tell mammá what a pleasure it was to make her acquaintance! We'll play a spirited game of whist tonight and I'll tell her about my condition.

TREBUCHARD: Yes… I know she'll be delighted, monsieur.

PRUDENVAL, *again halfway out and returning:* No, no… Please—

TREBUCHARD, *cutting him off:* Father!

PRUDENVAL: "Papá!"… Please… "Papá!"

He exits.

TREBUCHARD, *unnerved, gesturing alternately toward the doors, up right and down left:* Papá!… Mammá!… Mammá!… Papá!… Damn his whist! And damn his "condition"!… God in heaven, what's next? *(Coming down center.)* They're sure to want to see her! And when they do… When the "baby" turns out to be a… a fifty-year-old colossus!… Pffft! Good-bye number eight!… *(He begins pacing right and left.)* If there were only some way… *(With a glance toward MATHILDE's room, down left.)* She's right… If only I could find her a husband… Maybe marry her off to some traveling salesman… One who would haul her halfway around the world… The farther the better… Like, say, Tibet!… Anywhere, just to get her out of my hair… Before I tear it all out by the roots! At the rate I'm going, I'll be bald before I'm… *(Stopping, down right, with a noncommittal shrug.)* thirty… Give or take…

At that moment there is a noise of something falling on the balcony and breaking.

PIQUOISEAU'S VOICE: Goddammit!

TREBUCHARD: What the devil…?

PIQUOISEAU'S VOICE: My favorite pipe!

TREBUCHARD, *looking up at the ceiling:* Again? *(Going to the balcony.)* That… That… *(Stepping out, surveying the damage.)* His cigars aren't enough? Now he's got to throw his pipe?… I never… *(Calling up.)* Monsieur!

PIQUOISEAU'S VOICE, *ignoring him:* Just when I had it all nice and broken in…

TREBUCHARD: "Broken in," my foot!… Just plain broken, monsieur! And all over my balcony! *(After a pause, getting no reaction, calling.)* Well?

PIQUOISEAU'S VOICE, *finally replying:* You again? What is it this time?

TREBUCHARD: "What is…" Monsieur! It's your pipe…

PIQUOISEAU'S VOICE: It was, you mean… A damn good one, too… Goddamn sonofabitch!

TREBUCHARD: Monsieur! Hold your tongue! *(As an afterthought.)* I have a daughter…

PIQUOISEAU'S VOICE, *sarcastically:* Oh, pardonnez-moi! *(Repeating the oath, but this time ostensibly holding his tongue between his fingers.)* Gaw-gang thung-a-the-thith!… *(With mock solicitude.)* Is that better?

TREBUCHARD: Oh!… *(At a loss for words.)* Go fry an egg! *(Coming back inside, under his breath.)* Barbarian!… I wish I could teach him a lesson!… *(Coming down left.)* Something really awful… Like some medieval torture!… Something ancient and disgusting… Something… *(Looking at MATHILDE's door, suddenly inspired.)* Eureka!… *(Pointing to the door, then to the ceiling, then clasping his hands together.)* Of course! Why not?… Kill two birds with one stone… *(Glancing toward the door, up right.)* As they say… *(Running out onto the balcony, calling up.)* Monsieur!… Monsieur!… Mon capitaine…

PIQUOISEAU'S VOICE: Now what?

TREBUCHARD, *in the most gracious of tones*: Monsieur… I wonder… Would you do me the honor of coming down a moment?

PIQUOISEAU'S VOICE: Should I bring my saber, or would you rather duel with pistols?

TREBUCHARD, *with affected good humor*: Ha ha!… No… Nothing like that, monsieur. I have something terribly important to tell you.

PIQUOISEAU'S VOICE, *still rather snidely*: Well, my egg isn't done yet… But if you insist…

TREBUCHARD, *coming back inside, down right, rubbing his hands*: What a perfectly, absolutely brilliant idea! Why didn't I think of it sooner?… An army man, after all… Here today, and who knows where tomorrow? They get sent all over… One day to the next… Who can say where he'll take her? Africa, if I'm lucky… Or India even…

> *PIQUOISEAU appears at the balcony, feet first, ostensibly climbing down from the floor above. He is in uniform, with a handsome mustache and goatee, but rather disheveled and smoking a pipe.*

PIQUOISEAU, *stepping inside*: So?

TREBUCHARD: What…? Oh… You could have used the door, monsieur.

PIQUOISEAU: This was faster. I didn't want to keep you waiting… So, what is it?

TREBUCHARD, *terribly polite, approaching him*: Please… Make yourself comfortable… *(Gesturing toward the armchairs, left, as PIQUOISEAU comes down center.)* Won't you have a seat, mon capitaine…? *(PIQUOISEAU remains standing and blows a puff of smoke in his face.)* Yes, well… *(With a cough.)* As I was saying… I just wanted to let you know how sorry I am about our… our little disagreement…

PIQUOISEAU, *curtly*: Apologies accepted!

TREBUCHARD, *aside*: Not a promising beginning!… *(As PIQUOISEAU turns to leave, holding him back, aloud.)* And… And I wanted to tell you how often I've thought to myself… With you up there in the window… Smoking cigar after cigar, and pipe after pipe… *(PIQUOISEAU blows another puff.)* Day after day… How often I've thought: "Now there's a fine young officer… A fine young French officer… Pride of the cavalry…"

PIQUOISEAU: Infantry…

TREBUCHARD: Infantry…

PRUDENVAL, *blowing another puff, apparently unimpressed*: So?

TREBUCHARD, *continuing*: "There he is, sitting up there, all by himself… Alone… All alone…"

PIQUOISEAU: I'm waiting for La Destinée…

TREBUCHARD: Aha!… Of course! I knew you had the soul of a poet, monsieur!

PIQUOISEAU: What, "poet"?… That's her name, Désirée La Destinée… She's a dancer at the Alhambra.

TREBUCHARD: Oh…

PIQUOISEAU: Dances naked… Without a stitch…

> *He blows another puff in TREBUCHARD's face, and will continue to smoke intermittently throughout the rest of the scene.*

TREBUCHARD, *with affected jocularity*: Sly devil, you!

PIQUOISEAU: Well, if that's all you had to say…

He turns upstage to leave.

TREBUCHARD: Wait!

PIQUOISEAU, *stopping, brusquely*: Now what?

TREBUCHARD: I was wondering… I wanted to ask you… I take it you're not married?

PIQUOISEAU: You take it right!

TREBUCHARD, *aside*: Good!… *(Aloud.)* And tell me… Your regiment… Is it staying in Paris long?

PIQUOISEAU: Two more weeks… Then Algeria…

TREBUCHARD, *aside*: Even better!

PIQUOISEAU: Why? Who wants to know?

TREBUCHARD: Oh… No reason… Just making conversation… *(Aside.)* It's not Tibet, but still… *(Putting his arm around PIQUOISEAU's shoulders and gesturing toward the bottles, down right.)* May I offer you a drink?… A glass of beer, perhaps?

PIQUOISEAU: Beer?…Never touch it…

TREBUCHARD: Oh?

PIQUOISEAU: Bad for the liver!… I only drink rum.

TREBUCHARD, *going over to the serving-cart, very accommodating*: Then rum it is! I just happen to have a bottle of the best! Straight from Jamaica… *(Pouring two glasses.)* And I can't think of anyone I'd rather drink it with…

He returns to PIQUOISEAU and gives him a glass.

PIQUOISEAU: Much obliged…

TREBUCHARD, *indicating the armchair, left*: Please… Make yourself at home. *(PIQUOISEAU sits down as TREBUCHARD raises his glass in a toast.)* To your health, monsieur!

They clink glasses and drink. TREBUCHARD sits in the other chair, to PIQUOISEAU's right.

PIQUOISEAU: Hmm! Not bad!

He drinks again.

TREBUCHARD: Nothing but the best for the artillery, mon capitaine!

PIQUOISEAU: Infantry…

TREBUCHARD: Infantry…

PIQUOISEAU, *raising his glass*: To La Destinée!

TREBUCHARD: To La… Yes, well… *(Clinking.)* Monsieur!

PIQUOISEAU drinks.

PIQUOISEAU, *raising his glass*: And to all the lovely young ladies!

TREBUCHARD: Yes… *(Aside.)* And one of the others!

PIQUOISEAU finishes his glass.

PIQUOISEAU: Not bad at all…

TREBUCHARD, *getting up and taking the empty glass*: Please, let me…

PIQUOISEAU: If you insist…

TREBUCHARD, *going over to the bottle and refilling it*: I do… I do… *(Returning to PIQUOISEAU, with another toast.)* To marriage!

PIQUOISEAU, *raising his glass*: To… *(Stopping.)* Well, I wouldn't go that far!

He drinks anyway.

TREBUCHARD, *still standing by his chair*: Why not, monsieur? A man of your age… In the prime of life… Dashing… Debonair… Distinguished…

PIQUOISEAU, *toasting*: To me!

He drinks.

TREBUCHARD: And handsome…

PIQUOISEAU, *falsely modest*: Well…

TREBUCHARD: Yes indeed!… I like your face!

PIQUOISEAU: And I like your rum. That makes us even.

He finishes his glass.

TREBUCHARD, *going over to the serving-cart and putting down his own glass*: In fact, now that I think of it… *(As if struck by a sudden inspiration.)* You know… I have just the perfect woman for you, monsieur!

PRUDENVAL: For me?… Not bloody likely, thank you!

He holds out his empty glass.

TREBUCHARD, *not noticing, aside*: Hmm! It's not going to be easy! *(Aloud, ambling upstage as he speaks.)* Mature… Solid…

PIQUOISEAU, *waving his glass*: Monsieur…

TREBUCHARD: Dynamic…

PIQUOISEAU: Pssst!

TREBUCHARD: Talented…

PIQUOISEAU, *aside*: Goddamn!

He gets up, crosses right, and refills the glass himself.

TREBUCHARD, *at the balcony*: And when I say "talented," my friend…

PIQUOISEAU: Does she dance naked at the Alhambra?

TREBUCHARD: No… *(Aside.)* Good God! The very thought… *(Aloud.)* She draws…

PIQUOISEAU, *crossing back to his chair, under his breath*: What? Flies?

TREBUCHARD: And plays the piano… *(Continuing, very matter-of-fact, as PIQUOISEAU sits down and drinks.)* And she comes with a dowry of a hundred thousand francs.

PIQUOISEAU, *choking and spitting, jumping up*: Sonofabitch! A hundred thousand…?

TREBUCHARD: In round figures…

PIQUOISEAU: Did you say…?

TREBUCHARD: A hundred thousand… Yes…

PIQUOISEAU finishes his glass in one gulp.

PIQUOISEAU: You know, it's not nice to try to fool the army!

TREBUCHARD: Word of honor, monsieur!

PIQUOISEAU: You mean, I could be marrying a hundred thousand francs?

TREBUCHARD: Quite…

PIQUOISEAU, *sitting down, nonplussed*: But… But…

TREBUCHARD: Please, monsieur. No more "buts"… *(Glancing at the balcony.)* So to speak…

PIQUOISEAU: Goddamn! For that kind of woman… *(Raising his glass.)* To hell with La Destinée!

He goes to drink but sees that the glass is empty.

TREBUCHARD, *coming downstage, joining him*: I assume, monsieur, that a gentleman of your discernment doesn't insist on a—how shall I say?—on a ravishing beauty…

PIQUOISEAU, *with a gesture*: Pfff… Not ravishing… No… *(Aside.)* For a hundred thousand!

TREBUCHARD: Or on a mere callow child…

PIQUOISEAU: No… No…

TREBUCHARD, *sitting down in his chair*: Good… Because…

PIQUOISEAU, *jumping up, suspicious*: Wait a bloody minute!… You're not trying to marry me off to just any old hag, are you?

TREBUCHARD, *affecting injured innocence*: Certainly not, monsieur! *(Aside.)* Not just *any*… *(Aloud.)* Certainly not!

PIQUOISEAU, *sitting down*: Well…

TREBUCHARD, *getting up and crossing right, to get the rum*: Believe me, my friend… *(Returning and refilling* PIQUOISEAU*'s glass.)* She's not just one of your everyday beauties…

PIQUOISEAU: No…

TREBUCHARD: Just another pretty face…

He crosses right, picks up his glass, and pours himself a drink.

PIQUOISEAU: I'll drink to that!

He drinks.

TREBUCHARD, *drinking, aside*: So will I! *(Aloud.)* More in the classic mould, you might say… Stately… Strong features… Bold… Aggressive, if you know what I mean…

PIQUOISEAU: Aha…

TREBUCHARD: Especially her profile… Classic, monsieur… Classic… *(Under his breath.)* Like the Trojan Horse!… *(Aloud.)* Mind you, she's no Venus de Milo… *(Searching for another apt comparison.)* No "Winged Victory"…

PIQUOISEAU: Oh? You mean she's got arms and a head?… Well that's a start…

TREBUCHARD, *putting down his glass and crossing left*: "Arms and a…" *(With an embarrassed little chuckle.)* Very good!… Yes, she has arms, and a head, and…

PIQUOISEAU, *having second thoughts*: Well, still… I don't think…

TREBUCHARD, *approaching him, very matter-of-fact*: And a hundred thousand francs…

PIQUOISEAU, *convinced*: So? Where is the little lady?

TREBUCHARD: "The little…" Oh, I don't know if I would exactly call her "little"…

PIQUOISEAU: That's all right. I like them nice and tall.

TREBUCHARD: Well, let's say "substantial"…

PIQUOISEAU: And you wouldn't be trying to fool me, now… You did say a hundred thousand…

TREBUCHARD: Right…

PIQUOISEAU: And a new wife to boot…

TREBUCHARD: Quite… *(Aside.)* At least, never used…

PIQUOISEAU: Well… It sounds good to me. If you're sure… A whole hundred thousand…?

TREBUCHARD: Not one centime less!… Now you stay right here. Don't move… I'll go get her… *(He goes toward MATHILDE's door, down left, but stops at the threshold and turns.)* Oh, wait… *(He returns to PIQUOISEAU, takes his empty glass, and goes over to the serving-cart and puts it down.)* There!… *(He crosses back to MATHILDE's door but stops again.)* Monsieur… Your pipe…

PIQUOISEAU: So? What about it?

TREBUCHARD: I think, perhaps, you should put it out. Don't you?

PIQUOISEAU: Out? Out where? *(Pointing to the balcony.)* Out there?… I thought you didn't like—

TREBUCHARD, *cutting him off*: No, no… Out… Just out… Stop smoking it, I mean. First impressions, you know…

PIQUOISEAU: Oh… Out… Well, if you think so…

TREBUCHARD, *turning to leave*: I'll just be a minute.

He exits. PIQUOISEAU blows one more hearty puff.

PIQUOISEAU: Goddamn! Who ever would have thought…? A hundred thousand francs!… And my pay besides… If I invest it right… I can even afford a son… Maybe two… Why not? One for the cavalry and one for the infantry… Or the other way round… Unless one of them is a girl… *(Reflecting.)* Or the other… *(Getting up and crossing right.)* Or both of them, goddammit!… *(He pours himself another drink.)* No, they wouldn't dare!… *(He gulps it down.)* Well… *(He taps his pipe in the ashtray by the bottles and puts it in his pocket, then suddenly catches sight of his reflection in the mirror.)* Attention! *(He gives a smart salute.)* Like he said… "Dashing… Debonair… Distinguished…" It's the uniform! Whoever she is, the poor thing probably saw me on my balcony one day and just couldn't resist… *(Practicing his greeting, striking a variety of poses, with different tones of voice, nods, gestures, etc.)* Mademoiselle… Mademoiselle…

TREBUCHARD enters, down left, holding MATHILDE by the hand, as PIQUOISEAU continues.

TREBUCHARD, *to MATHILDE, whispering*: Come, come… Up straight… Head up, head up…

PIQUOISEAU, *still facing the mirror, posing*: Mademoiselle…

TREBUCHARD, *to MATHILDE, still whispering, pushing her head to one side*: And show him your classic profile!

PIQUOISEAU, *continuing*: Mademoiselle…

TREBUCHARD, *aside*: Half as much is twice as good!

PIQUOISEAU, *twirling his mustache, seductively*: Mademoiselle… *(Turning.)* Mademoi… *(Catching sight of MATHILDE, who is about to turn her face to him.)* Ouf!… *(Aside.)* Sonofabitch! That's her?

TREBUCHARD turns MATHILDE's head aside and brings her toward PIQUOISEAU.

TREBUCHARD, *as diffidently as possible, introducing*: Monsieur… Mon capitaine… Mademoiselle Mathilde Trébuchard, my… *(Clearing his throat.)* my daughter…

PIQUOISEAU, *aside*: His daughter?… *(Joining them down center, to* TREBUCHARD, *whispering..)* You must have got a goddamn early start!

MATHILDE, *to* PIQUOISEAU, *about to face him*: Monsieur…

TREBUCHARD, *turning her head aside, then to* PIQUOISEAU, *in a whisper*: A hundred thousand francs, remember?

MATHILDE, *to* PIQUOISEAU, *about to face him again*: Delighted to make your… *(*TREBUCHARD *turns her head aside.)* acquaintance, I'm sure…

TREBUCHARD, *to* MATHILDE, *in a whisper*: Please! Profile, I said… *(To* PIQUOISEAU, *in a whisper.)* Say something, for heaven's sake!

PIQUOISEAU, *to* MATHILDE: I… I… I… *(Aside.)* Ayayay! *(To* TREBUCHARD, sotto voce.*)* She's no chicken, that's for sure!

MATHILDE, *to* PIQUOISEAU, *about to face him again*: Monsieur?

TREBUCHARD, *turning her head aside again, this time holding it with his hand, to* PIQUOISEAU, *in a whisper*: Well?

> *He will keep* MATHILDE*'s head turned aside throughout the rest of the scene until otherwise indicated, reacting quickly to any attempt on her part to look squarely at* PIQUOISEAU.

PIQUOISEAU, *to* MATHILDE: I… I… *(To* TREBUCHARD, *whispering.)* I can't… I… I…

TREBUCHARD, *to* MATHILDE: You see how overcome he is with emotion? *(To* PRUDENVAL.*)* Aren't you, monsieur?

PIQUOISEAU: I… I…

TREBUCHARD, *to* PIQUOISEAU, *saluting with his free hand*: Aye aye, mon capitaine!… Aye aye! *(To* MATHILDE.*)* You see?… *(To* PIQUOISEAU.*)* Very touching! *(To* MATHILDE.*)* Very touching, indeed!…

PIQUOISEAU, *about to protest*: That is…

MATHILDE, *to* TREBUCHARD: I should say!

TREBUCHARD, *to* PIQUOISEAU, *in a whisper*: A hundred thousand! *(Aloud.)* But the time has come… *(To* MATHILDE, *grandiloquently.)* Yes, the time has come, daughter dear… *(Aside.)* God help me!… *(Aloud, to* MATHILDE.*)* The time has come to let you try your wings… To let you fly from the paternal nest…

MATHILDE, *to* TREBUCHARD, *moved*: Yes, papá…

PIQUOISEAU, *under his breath*: Fly? She'll fall like a bloody rock!

TREBUCHARD, *continuing*: …and into the arms of a fine, upstanding soldier… *(Gesturing.)* Our distinguished Captain…

PIQUOISEAU, *aside*: And dashing… And debonair…

TREBUCHARD, *hesitating*: Captain… *(To* PIQUOISEAU, *in a whisper.)* Quick! What's your name?

PIQUOISEAU, *whispering in reply*: Piquoiseau!

TREBUCHARD: Captain Piquoiseau…

MATHILDE, *aside*: What a lovely name!

TREBUCHARD, *continuing*: …whose heart is utterly filled to overflowing…

MATHILDE, *aside, musing*: "Madame Piquoiseau…"

TREBUCHARD, *waxing eloquent*: A young man devoted to the service of his country… To the values of hearth, and home, and family… Always sitting on his balcony, deep in thoughtful meditation…

PIQUOISEAU, *aside*: Me?

TREBUCHARD: Peacefully watching the passing parade…

MATHILDE, *to PIQUOISEAU*: Oh, monsieur! I love parades!

TREBUCHARD: Kind, considerate, good-natured… A twinkle on his lips and a cigar in his eye… *(Correcting.)* That is… A twinkle in his eye and a cigar… *(Correcting again.)* I mean, a twinkle in his eye and a smile on his lips…

PIQUOISEAU, *aside*: Bla-bla-bla!

TREBUCHARD, *turning, to MATHILDE*: A smile of hope and a heart full of passion…

PIQUOISEAU, *to TREBUCHARD, in a whisper*: Now wait just one minute!

TREBUCHARD, *ignoring him, to MATHILDE, still keeping her head turned*: Look at him! See how he trembles with desire… How he quivers with expectation!…

MATHILDE, *trying unsuccessfully to face PIQUOISEAU*: I can't…

PIQUOISEAU, *to TREBUCHARD, in a whisper, objecting*: I said—

TREBUCHARD, *to PIQUOISEAU, in a whisper, insisting*: A hundred thousand, damn it! *(To MATHILDE.)* How he waits for your answer…

PIQUOISEAU, *aside*: What in blazes was the question?

TREBUCHARD, *to MATHILDE, continuing*: The answer that he yearns for, that will fill his life with joy!

MATHILDE, *sighing*: Oh… *(To PIQUOISEAU, emotionally.)* Papá's word is my command, monsieur. I accept!

TREBUCHARD, *disguising his voice*: O ecstasy!… O rapture!… *(To MATHILDE.)* Did you hear? He said: "O rapture!"

MATHILDE,	*together:*	He did?
PIQUOISEAU, *aside*,		I did?

TREBUCHARD, *to PIQUOISEAU, whispering again*: Go on!… The iron's hot!… Strike!… Strike, for heaven's sake…

PIQUOISEAU: But… *(To TREBUCHARD, whispering back.)* And you're sure it's a hundred thousand?

TREBUCHARD, *replying, still in a whisper*: Yes!… Now go ahead! Quick! Before she changes her mind…

PIQUOISEAU: Well… *(To MATHILDE.)* Mademoiselle, I have the honor…

TREBUCHARD, *with a sigh of relief, letting MATHILDE's face go and clasping his hands in a gesture of victory, aside*: At last!

MATHILDE, *to PIQUOISEAU, finally turning toward him, full face, quickly*: Yes, yes!… I accept, I told you…

PIQUOISEAU, *getting a good look, aside*: Ouf!… *(To MATHILDE.)* I… I… That is… *(Moving right, toward the bottles, as if tempted to pour himself a drink.)* I think I should sleep on it…

MATHILDE: Sleep?… But it's only noon!

TREBUCHARD, *following PIQUOISEAU, turning, to MATHILDE*: It's an expression!

PIQUOISEAU, *resisting the rum, but seizing the excuse*: What? Noon?… Already? *(Looking at his watch.)* Five minutes to twelve?… I'll be late for my billiards…

MATHILDE, *moving right, to* PIQUOISEAU: Monsieur…

PIQUOISEAU: With the major…

TREBUCHARD, *to* PIQUOISEAU: But monsieur…

PIQUOISEAU, *crossing up left*: The general…

TREBUCHARD, *following him*: Mon capitaine… *(To* MATHILDE.*)* See how excited he is?

PIQUOISEAU, *at the door*: The field marshal… Mustn't keep him waiting!

TREBUCHARD, *to* PIQUOISEAU, sotto voce: Two hundred thousand! *(Turning, to* MATHILDE.*)* The ecstasy… The rapture…

MATHILDE, *calling to* PIQUOISEAU: I accept, monsieur! I accept…

She begins to follow as PIQUOISEAU *disappears out the door.*

TREBUCHARD, *stopping her*: No, no! You stay here!… I mean, go to your room! And stay there, for God's sake!… Leave your fiancé to me!

He exits, running, on PIQUOISEAU*'s heels.*

MATHILDE, *to herself*: My fiancé!… *(She sits in the armchair, far left.)* Handsome devil! *(Twirling an imaginary mustache and stroking an imaginary goatee.)* Papá was right. He certainly is distinguished!… *(As if hitting on the adjectives out of the blue.)* And dashing… And debonair… *(Musing.)* "Madame Piquoiseau…" Yes, monsieur… I accept…

PRUDENVAL *and* CLAUDINE *enter, up right. He is still wearing his coat, and is carrying several children's toys and a giant gingerbread man. She is holding a pink and white knitted baby bonnet.*

PRUDENVAL: Come… She must be awake by now.

CLAUDINE: I certainly hope so! I simply can't wait…

PRUDENVAL: Even an infant doesn't sleep all day!

MATHILDE, *noticing them, aside*: Oh… That awful tailor again…

PRUDENVAL, *noticing her*: Ah… *(To* CLAUDINE, *whispering.)* Her grandmother… Plays an excellent game of whist, I hear… I'll introduce you… *(Approaching* MATHILDE, *left, as* CLAUDINE *comes down right, with a little bow.)* Madame…

MATHILDE, *still seated, replying coldly*: Monsieur… *(Aside.)* "Madame" indeed!

PRUDENVAL, *unobtrusively taking out his snuffbox*: I say… May I give you a pinch?

MATHILDE, *aside*: Again? *(Aloud, to* PRUDENVAL.*)* Certainly not, monsieur! *(Aside.)* The man is some kind of pervert!

CLAUDINE *clears her throat to remind* PRUDENVAL *of her presence.*

PRUDENVAL: Ah, yes… *(To* MATHILDE, *indicating* CLAUDINE.*)* Madame, my daughter…

MATHILDE, *coldly*: Yes… I see… *(Nodding toward* CLAUDINE, *emphasizing the salutation.)* Mademoiselle…

CLAUDINE, *down right, gives a little curtsy.*

PRUDENVAL, *continuing*: Mademoiselle Prudenval… From Lyon… The intended…

MATHILDE: I beg your pardon?

PRUDENVAL: His intended…

MATHILDE: "Intended"?.. "His"?.. Whose?

PRUDENVAL: Why, monsieur's… Your son…

MATHILDE, *offended*: My son?… My… What son? I have no son!

CLAUDINE, *joining* PRUDENVAL, *center*: What?

PRUDENVAL, *to* MATHILDE: Of course you do! *(To* CLAUDINE.*)* She does!

CLAUDINE: Of course!

PRUDENVAL, *to* MATHILDE: The vest… The buttons… You know… *(Emphasizing.)* Your son!

MATHILDE: Monsieur! I'll have you know I'm not married!

CLAUDINE: Oh!…

PRUDENVAL, *to* MATHILDE: Not… *(Confused.)* But… Then…

MATHILDE: Not quite, that is… Almost…

PRUDENVAL: Oh… *(Apologetically.)* Please, madame… Mademoiselle… Really… I thought… *(Gesturing toward* CLAUDINE.*)* That is, we… I mean, we just assumed…

MATHILDE: Monsieur?

PRUDENVAL: That you must be the grandmother…

MATHILDE, *jumping to her feet*: Grandmother? Me?

CLAUDINE, *to* MATHILDE: Please excuse us, madame…

PRUDENVAL, *to* MATHILDE: It was a natural mistake…

MATHILDE, *to* PRUDENVAL: Oh? And just why, may I—

PRUDENVAL, *interrupting, eager to change the subject*: I say… Is the tot awake yet?

CLAUDINE, *to* MATHILDE: Yes, madame… Can we see her?

MATHILDE: Tot? Tot?… Awake?… What tot?

PRUDENVAL, *aside*: Not very bright, whoever she is! *(To* MATHILDE.*)* His daughter, madame!

CLAUDINE: The baby!

MATHILDE, *to* CLAUDINE: What baby? *(To* PRUDENVAL.*)* Whose daughter?

PRUDENVAL: Why, Monsieur Trébuchard's… My son-in-law…

MATHILDE, *to* PRUDENVAL: "Monsieur…" Your… His… But monsieur, *I'm* his daughter!

PRUDENVAL drops everything but the gingerbread man.

PRUDENVAL, } *together:* { You?
CLAUDINE, *backing away, down right,* } *together:* { What?

MATHILDE, *with a little bow, emphasizing*: Mademoiselle… Mathilde Trébuchard…

CLAUDINE: You? *(Aside.)* What kind of baby…

PRUDENVAL, *picking up the toys* : But… But… How can that…? Oh my!… *(Holding out the toys and the gingerbread man.)* And here I brought you all these… Brought her, I mean… That is…

He lays the toys down on the table, down left, still holding the gingerbread man.

CLAUDINE: Indeed!

PRUDENVAL: Oh well… *(He takes a healthy bite, joining* CLAUDINE*, right.)* And my daughter, who knitted her… Who knitted you… Her…

MATHILDE: What?

CLAUDINE, *moving up right and quickly stuffing the bonnet into a pocket*: Oh… Nothing! I assure you…

PRUDENVAL, *returning to* MATHILDE: But really, madame… Mademoiselle… It's just that… You do seem a good deal… well... older than your father. *(Attempting a gallantry.)* That is, not quite as young…

MATHILDE, *sitting down, left, coyly*: Yes… Well, perhaps a little…

PRUDENVAL, *sitting down in the other armchair*: But… I mean, even a little… You have to admit, it is rather unusual…

CLAUDINE, *aside*: Rather!

PRUDENVAL: …to say the least!

MATHILDE, *to* PRUDENVAL: Papá was mammá's second husband, monsieur.

PRUDENVAL: Her second… *(Suddenly comprehending.)* Oh, then… You mean…

MATHILDE, *still eager to justify herself*: I was younger than the first.

PRUDENVAL: Monsieur… "Papá"… *(Nodding.)* Aha… *(To* CLAUDINE.*)* That explains it! Understand?… Monsieur Trébuchard…

CLAUDINE, *stiffly*: Yes, papá, I understand!

PRUDENVAL, *standing up, suddenly struck by a novel thought*: I say… That means… *(Approaching* CLAUDINE*, with a little chuckle, turning, to* MATHILDE.*)* That means you're going to be my daughter's daughter, aren't you!

MATHILDE, *standing up*: Me?

CLAUDINE: Oh no she isn't!

PRUDENVAL, *center, to* CLAUDINE: But of course she is, Claudine!… You're marrying her father, aren't you? It's only logical… *(With a little laugh.)* Mammá!

CLAUDINE: "Mammá" indeed!

PRUDENVAL: Of all things! *(To* MATHILDE.*)* It will make quite a story for the newspapers when we get home!

The cuckoo begins to strike twelve.

CLAUDINE: Oh, will it? *(Under her breath.)* Well, we'll see about that!

PRUDENVAL: Ah! Noon!… It's time I left… *(To* CLAUDINE.*)* The doctor's hours are from twelve to two. *(Moving up left, as if to leave, but returning center, to* MATHILDE.*)* My condition, you know… Every time I eat… *(Going to leave again, but returning, to* MATHILDE.*)* Or even when I don't…

MATHILDE: I see…

CLAUDINE, *to* PRUDENVAL: I'll come with you, papá…

She begins to cross left, toward the door.

PRUDENVAL: No, no… Please… You just stay here and chat with your new daughter.

CLAUDINE, *furious*: Papá!

PRUDENVAL, *moving again toward the door, to* CLAUDINE: After all, you should get to know her…

CLAUDINE: Really! I hardly think…

PRUDENVAL, *returning, to* MATHILDE, *offering her what is left of the gingerbread man*: Oh, here… You may as well…

MATHILDE: Thank you just the same…

PRUDENVAL, *placing it on the table, down left, and pointing to the toys, to* MATHILDE: And if there's anything here you would like…

MATHILDE: You're too kind!

PRUDENVAL: Well, I'll be on my way. *(He moves again toward the door; then, reaching for his snuffbox, returning, to* MATHILDE.*)* And you're sure I can't give you a little pinch, mademoiselle…?

MATHILDE: Monsieur! Please!…

She turns in a huff and exits to her room, down left.

PRUDENVAL, *with a shrug*: I say… *(To* CLAUDINE.*)* Well… Bye-bye, ma petite… Au revoir…

He exits, up left.

CLAUDINE, *fuming, going down left, glaring at* MATHILDE*'s door*: Oh! Of all the… *(Crossing right.)* Did you ever…? My daughter indeed! That… That… I'll be the laughingstock… I can hear my friends now: "Can we help you change her diapers?…" Oh! Monsieur Trébuchard!… That liar! *(She stamps her foot.)* Not weaned yet, my foot!… Why, he never would have told me! Not until it was too late! *(Glowering at the door, up left.)* And papá, who thinks that it's simply too funny! And that I should be delighted!… *(Crossing back, left.)* Well, it isn't, and I'm not! *(Hands on hips.)* And I won't have it! So there!… *(Turning on her heel and crossing up right, toward the door.)* The wedding is off! The minute papá comes back…

TREBUCHARD enters, up left, without noticing CLAUDINE.

TREBUCHARD, *coming down left, aside*: Damn!… More time to decide, he tells me!… How much time does a man need?

CLAUDINE, *turning, noticing him*: Well! There you are, Monsieur Trébuchard!

TREBUCHARD, *surprised, turning*: What…? Ah! Mademoiselle… Claudine… *(Somewhat at a loss for conversation.)* Are you settled?

CLAUDINE: Yes, but not for long, thank you!

TREBUCHARD: Oh? *(Gesturing toward the door, up right.)* It's not too small, I hope?

CLAUDINE: Hardly, monsieur!… *(Emphasizing.) It* is too big!… And too old, if I may say so!

TREBUCHARD: What? Your room?

CLAUDINE: No, monsieur! Your baby! The one you're still trying to wean, if I remember… We've just met…

TREBUCHARD: You… *(Aside.)* Good God! She told them!

CLAUDINE, *coming center*: I'm sure you understand, monsieur, that under the circumstances our marriage is quite out of the question!

TREBUCHARD: What?… But…

CLAUDINE: I have no desire to hear a grown woman…

TREBUCHARD: But—

CLAUDINE: …a very grown woman, monsieur, I might add…

TREBUCHARD: But—

CLAUDINE: …call me her "mammá!"

TREBUCHARD: But… But…

CLAUDINE, *coming down center*: And I don't think you can blame me! If I had known before…

TREBUCHARD: But.. You don't have to worry! I'm having her sent off to Algeria… You'll never see her!…

CLAUDINE: You're what?

TREBUCHARD: Yes… I've found her a husband… It's all arranged… Well, almost…

CLAUDINE: Oh? So that I can become a grandmother? Thank you! You're much too kind!

TREBUCHARD, *with a little laugh, despite his dismay*: Well, I don't think there's very much danger of that! Considering…

CLAUDINE: No, but it's possible! And as long as there's a chance…

TREBUCHARD: But—

CLAUDINE: I'm sorry, monsieur. My mind is made up! The wedding is off!

She turns and moves toward the door, up right.

TREBUCHARD, *following her*: Don't say that! Please!… What do you want me to do? I can't very well strangle her!

CLAUDINE, *stopping at the door, sarcastically*: In her cradle? Hardly!… Or give her up for adoption either, I imagine!

TREBUCHARD: Quite… So you see…

CLAUDINE: But that's none of my concern. I only know I will never marry the man who turns me into that woman's mother! Of all things…

TREBUCHARD: But—

CLAUDINE, *opening the door*: Never, monsieur!… Never, never, never!

She exits and slams the door.

TREBUCHARD, *watching her leave, distraught, then coming down left*: "Never, never, never!"… Of course! Just like all the rest!… One through seven… No matter what I do… No matter how hard I try… This time, I thought… But no! I should have known… *(Pacing left and right.)* Oh for the good old days… When they still had human sacrifice!… Before we went and made laws about such things… Before we got civilized… *(Stopping.)* And had fifty-year-old daughters! *(Pacing again.)* My cross to bear… Damn rope around my neck… Thorn in my side… Pain in my… *(Stopping, down center.)* But… *(With a shrug.)* Who can blame her? A daughter old enough to be her mother…? It's humiliating! It's revolting! It's… It's grotesque!… *(Echoing CLAUDINE.)* "Never, never, never!…" *(Pacing again.)* Well, damn, damn, damn! What am I supposed to do? I can't make them change places! I can't just wave a magic wand and make Mathilde the mother and Claudine the daughter! I can't just… *(Stopping in his tracks, down center, struck by a sudden inspiration.)* Wait a minute! Why not?.. Why can't I?… Of course I can! *(Pointing up right.)* Prudenval!… Of course! They're made for each other!… Like Philemon and Baucis… *(Searching.)* Jason and Medea… Scylla and Charybdis… He's a widower, isn't he? He must be looking for some sweet young thing... *(Reconsidering.)* Some mature, devoted creature... Someone to mend his meals and cook his stockings... I mean... *(With a gesture.)* Whatever... Well, anyway, I suppose even Mathilde could learn... And to play whist too... *(Moving up right.)* Besides, why shouldn't he suffer a little? Am I the only one...? *(At the door, determined.)* That's it! That's the answer! Piquoiseau can go hang! Who needs him?... My father-in-law... That's the son-in-law I need!... Now if only I can convince him... *(Noticing* PRUDENVAL *entering, up left.)* Speak of the devil...

PRUDENVAL, *at the door, obviously disgruntled, aside*: Bother! Some people...

TREBUCHARD: Ah! There you are, son...

PRUDENVAL, *aloud*: Please?

TREBUCHARD, *correcting himself*: Father... Papá!...

PRUDENVAL, *crossing down right*: Did you ever see...?

TREBUCHARD, *coming down center, very solicitously*: You seem upset, papá. Is something wrong? Did the doctor—

PRUDENVAL, *interrupting*: Wrong? I'll say there's something wrong!... Can you imagine...? A doctor, of all people... Did you ever...?

TREBUCHARD: What did he say?

PRUDENVAL: Nothing! Not a blessèd word!

TREBUCHARD, *with hypocritical interest*: Oh? Really?... The doctor...?

PRUDENVAL: He wasn't there! Can you believe it? A doctor who tells you: "Office hours from twelve to two..." And when you get there...

TREBUCHARD, *contemplating him, aside*: How do I begin?

PRUDENVAL: When you ring the bell, some flunky opens the door and tells you: "I'm sorry. The doctor is in Dijon. He's been there since Sunday and there's no telling when he'll be back."

TREBUCHARD, *aside*: I can't just say: "Father, I want you to marry my daughter!"

PRUDENVAL, *continuing*: It's a scandal!... Now I'll have to wait until tomorrow and go look for another doctor. Did you ever...?

He moves left, behind TREBUCHARD, *toward the armchairs.*

TREBUCHARD, *with mock compassion*: Tsk tsk tsk! You're right... I never...

PRUDENVAL: And in the meantime, it's getting worse... My condition, that is... The ache...

TREBUCHARD: Yes, the itch... Tsk tsk tsk!

PRUDENVAL: I say... I don't suppose you would know a good specialist... One who doesn't go running off to Dijon when he has office hours in Paris?

TREBUCHARD: A specialist? *(Aside.)* Hmm! Maybe... *(Aloud.)* Not a specialist exactly... But... *(With false modesty.)* Well, actually, I have had some experience along those lines myself... If you like...

PRUDENVAL: You? A doctor?

TREBUCHARD: No, not quite... Though I did study medicine, mind you... Five years... *(Aside.)* Between billiard games... *(Aloud.)* Besides, my father was a veterinarian. You can't imagine how much I learned....

PRUDENVAL, *impressed*: Aha!

TREBUCHARD: Once I helped him give birth to a litter of pigs...

PRUDENVAL: I say!... Your father—

TREBUCHARD: Cows... Goats...

PRUDENVAL: Unusual...

TREBUCHARD: Horses... I always had my hand in it...

PRUDENVAL: Yes, I should think...

TREBUCHARD: So, of course, if I can be of any help, monsieur...

PRUDENVAL: No, no... Please!...

TREBUCHARD, *quickly correcting himself*: Papá... Papá... *(Continuing.)* If my modest talents can be of some use...

PRUDENVAL: Indeed!... I didn't realize... Shall we sit down? *(He sits in the armchair, left.)* You see, it's very strange, but every time I eat...

TREBUCHARD, *sitting in the other chair, facing him*: Yes... And even when you don't...

PRUDENVAL: Oh? You can tell?

TREBUCHARD, *nodding*: Quite...

PRUDENVAL: Do you want to see my tongue? *(He sticks out his tongue.)* Aaaah!

TREBUCHARD: Not especially, thank you... Do you want to see mine?

He sticks his out too.

PRUDENVAL: Oh... It's just that my doctor in Lyon always begins that way.

TREBUCHARD: Yes... *(Nodding, very professorial.)* They do that in Lyon... But in Paris... *(Taking out his pocket watch.)* Here... Let me take your pulse. *(Reaching across.)* Hmm!

PRUDENVAL: Well?

TREBUCHARD: Very interesting... It seems to be beating... Not too well, but at least—

PRUDENVAL, *alarmed, interrupting*: It's my liver, isn't it!

TREBUCHARD: No...

He stands up and percusses PRUDENVAL*'s chest and back several times in a very doctor-like manner.*

PRUDENVAL: What is it, then?

TREBUCHARD: Tsk tsk tsk!

PRUDENVAL: Well?

TREBUCHARD, *sitting down again*: Do you mind if I ask you a few personal questions?

PRUDENVAL: No... Please... *(Anxiously.)* But—

TREBUCHARD: Tell me, when you see a pretty woman, what's the first thing you want to do?

PRUDENVAL: Well... Like anybody else... Play a hand of whist... But—

TREBUCHARD: Aha... Bid or no-bid?

PRUDENVAL: Bid, of course... But—

TREBUCHARD: Yes, just as I suspected...

PRUDENVAL: But—

TREBUCHARD: A classic case... I'm afraid what you've got, my friend, is a severe case of "widower's peritoneum." I've seen a lot of them.

PRUDENVAL: In cows and goats?

TREBUCHARD, *solemnly*: A peritoneum is a peritoneum, monsieur!

PRUDENVAL: I didn't even know I had one! Where is it?

TREBUCHARD: Oh… *(With a vague gesture.)* Here and there…

PRUDENVAL: But—

TREBUCHARD: Tell me… Exactly how old were you when you got married, if I may ask?

PRUDENVAL: Why… Twenty-nine…

TREBUCHARD: Exactly?

PRUDENVAL: Well… Twenty-nine years and nine months…

TREBUCHARD: Aha…

PRUDENVAL: And a few days, I think…

TREBUCHARD: Bad… Bad… Much too young…

PRUDENVAL: You're right. Marriage doesn't agree with me.

TREBUCHARD, *quickly*: Don't say that! Of course it does! *(Aside.)* It has to!

PRUDENVAL: My wife was a fine woman, and all that. But enough is enough! Never again!

TREBUCHARD: "Never…" *(Standing up.)* You don't know what you're saying! *(He proceeds to percuss him again, more energetically.)* Just as I thought. It's getting worse!

PRUDENVAL: I say… This "widower's peritoneum"… Is it serious?

TREBUCHARD, *turning around and moving right, dramatically*: Fatal… Very…

PRUDENVAL, *sinking into the chair*: Oh…

TREBUCHARD: Worse than fatal… *(Turning back, quickly.)* But only if you don't follow my instructions to the letter…

PRUDENVAL: What? Anything!

TREBUCHARD: No… You won't want to… Never mind…

PRUDENVAL: I will! I will!

TREBUCHARD: What's the use? You won't do it…

PRUDENVAL: But I will, I tell you!

TREBUCHARD: My friend, the only cure is to get married again… And soon!

PRUDENVAL: Oh my!

He jumps up and begins running up left.

TREBUCHARD: Wait a minute! Where are you going?

PRUDENVAL: Back to Lyon… To find someone…

TREBUCHARD: But—

PRUDENVAL, *at the door, up left*: I don't know a soul here in Paris!

TREBUCHARD: Yes you do! Yes you do!

PRUDENVAL: I do?

The door, down left, opens and MATHILDE *appears at the threshold.*

TREBUCHARD, *pointing to her*: Her! *(Running to join her.)* Mathilde!

PRUDENVAL, *crossing down right, aside*: His daughter?

TREBUCHARD, *to* MATHILDE, *whispering*: Stand up straight and turn your head! *(Aloud, solemnly.)* My child, the time has come to give your hand in marriage!

MATHILDE, *standing in profile, delighted*: It has? Oh…

She begins to turn her head to face him.

TREBUCHARD, *pushing her head back to the side, whispering*: Please!… *(Aloud.)* And here, my sweet, is the happy bridegroom!

He takes a few steps back and the two look at each other.

MATHILDE, } *together*: { His tailor?
PRUDENVAL, } { Oh!…

TREBUCHARD, *between them, approving, aside*: Voilà!

MATHILDE, *to TREBUCHARD, whispering*: Isn't he a little old?

PRUDENVAL, *to TREBUCHARD, whispering*: Really son, I don't think…

TREBUCHARD: Like Scylla and Charybdis!

MATHILDE, *objecting*: But… *(To PRUDENVAL.)* I'm sorry, monsieur. But as flattered as I am at your gallant proposal, I'm afraid I simply cannot accept…

TREBUCHARD: What?

PRUDENVAL, *with an indifferent shrug*: Aha… Well…

TREBUCHARD: Mathilde! What are you saying?

MATHILDE, *to PRUDENVAL, dramatically*: You see, monsieur, I've been promised to another…

TREBUCHARD, *to MATHILDE*: Piquoiseau?… Don't be silly!

PRUDENVAL, *to MATHILDE*: Fine… Fine… I understand…

TREBUCHARD, *to PRUDENVAL*: No you don't. *(Whispering.)* What do you mean: "Fine… Fine…"? It's not fine at all! What about your peritoneum?

PRUDENVAL, *to TREBUCHARD*: Oh my! You're right! I wasn't thinking…

The following exchanges, until PIQUOISEAU's entrance, are delivered sotto voce.

TREBUCHARD, *to MATHILDE*: Your Piquoiseau is a cad and a bounder! He's having an affair with Désirée La Destinée!… She dances naked!

MATHILDE, *to TREBUCHARD*: That's not true!

PRUDENVAL, *looking askance at MATHILDE, aside*: If I have to, I have to…

TREBUCHARD, *to MATHILDE*: And he's a soldier, Mathilde! Who knows where they'll send him off to? He'll take you away from me!… *(With mock emotion.)* I couldn't bear it, ma petite!

MATHILDE, *to TREBUCHARD*: Don't worry, papá. I'll write…

PRUDENVAL, *aside*: My health, after all…

TREBUCHARD, *to MATHILDE*: Besides, he doesn't love you! You'll see, he won't come back!

MATHILDE, *to TREBUCHARD*: Yes he will! My heart tells me…

TREBUCHARD, *to MATHILDE*: Your heart!

PRUDENVAL, *aside*: My peritoneum…

PIQUOISEAU is heard approaching in the wings.

PIQUOISEAU'S VOICE, *singing*:

Wine, wine,
Fruit of the vine,
Nectar divine,

O won't you be mine…

TREBUCHARD, *aside*: Damn!

MATHILDE, *to* TREBUCHARD: There! You see, papá? I told you!

PIQUOISEAU *enters, up left.*

DELPHINE, *moving up left to greet him*: Mon capitaine…

PIQUOISEAU: I'm back, and I've made up my mind…

TREBUCHARD: And you refuse!

PIQUOISEAU: Says who? *(Whispering into* TREBUCHARD*'s ear.)* For a hundred thousand francs?… Or two hundred thousand, wasn't it? *(Coming down left, to* MATHILDE*, still in profile, standing to her right.)* Mademoiselle… I have the honor…

MATHILDE, *as demurely as possible*: Monsieur…

TREBUCHARD, *moving behind* MATHILDE *and forcibly turning her face toward* PIQUOISEAU*, holding it, aside*: Oh no you don't…

PIQUOISEAU, *getting a good long look*: Ouf! *(Aside.)* Sonofabitch! It's worse than I remembered! *(Aloud.)* On second thought… *(To* TREBUCHARD*.)* You're right! I refuse!

MATHILDE, *angrily*: Oh!

PIQUOISEAU, *aside*: Even two hundred thousand! *(Moving right and pouring himself a glass of rum.)* I'd never live it down! *(Drinking, with a shudder.)* Brrr!

He moves toward the door, up left.

MATHILDE: The cad!

TREBUCHARD, *rubbing his hands, aside*: The bounder!

PRUDENVAL, *still down right, looking toward* PIQUOISEAU: What did he say?

MATHILDE: Nothing! *(Moving right, extending her hand to* PRUDENVAL*, graciously.)* Monsieur Prudenval… My hand… I accept…

PRUDENVAL, *unenthusiastic*: Ah… Well, I suppose… *(Looking for something to say.)* I say, mademoiselle… May I give you a little pinch?

He reaches for his snuffbox.

DELPHINE, *misunderstanding, coyly*: Well, if you really think you should…

PRUDENVAL, *offering*: Help yourself.

MATHILDE: Oh!… A pinch… You mean…

She takes a pinch with a little laugh, and sniffs. PRUDENVAL *does likewise.*

TREBUCHARD, *down left, sighing, aside*: Free at last! *(He joins his hands together in mock reverence and looks heavenward.)* Thank you…

As he blows a kiss toward the ceiling, the door, up right, opens and CLAUDINE *enters, with hat and parasol, followed by* DELPHINE*, who is carrying all the valises.*

CLAUDINE, *to* PRUDENVAL: Come, papá! We're ready to leave…

She stops, center, as DELPHINE *gives the valises to* PRUDENVAL*, down right, and retreats up left beside* PIQUOISEAU*.*

TREBUCHARD: Leave? *(To* CLAUDINE*.)* Don't be absurd! Everything is all arranged…

MATHILDE, *with a clumsy little curtsy, to* CLAUDINE: That's right, mammá!

CLAUDINE, *furious*: Again?

TREBUCHARD, *far left, to* MATHILDE: No, no, no, Mathilde! Not "mammá!"… Now it's "daughter dear"… "Daughter…"

MATHILDE, *grudgingly, to* CLAUDINE: Daughter dear…

CLAUDINE: What?.. "Daughter…"? Who?

TREBUCHARD, *to* CLAUDINE, *gesturing toward* MATHILDE: May I present the new Madame Prudenval-to-be… *(Whispering.)* You didn't want her for a daughter, so you've got her for a mother!

CLAUDINE, *turning to* PRUDENVAL: But… Papá?…

PRUDENVAL: Say hello to your new mammá, Claudine… *(Whispering.)* I have to… For my condition… For my peritoneum…

CLAUDINE: Your…

TREBUCHARD, *overhearing, to* PRUDENVAL: Tsk tsk! No secrets, son!

PRUDENVAL, *aside*: "Son"? Me?… *(Reflecting for a moment.)* I say… He's right!

TREBUCHARD, *to* CLAUDINE, sotto voce, *pointing to* MATHILDE: You see? Now she's the one who'll be the grandmother!… As often as you like!

CLAUDINE, *coyly*: Why, Hector, whatever do you mean?

TREBUCHARD: Well, we have time to discuss such things…

> *He gives a broad wink to the audience, Then, crossing right, he fills three glasses with rum, gives one to* PRUDENVAL, *goes up left and gives one to* PIQUOISEAU, *and returns down left to* CLAUDINE.

PIQUOISEAU, *during the preceding, to* DELPHINE: Say, haven't I seen you before? Don't you dance naked at the Alhambra?

DELPHINE: No, monsieur… *(Tweaking his mustache.)* But I can learn…

PIQUOISEAU: I'll drink to that!

> *He drinks.*

DELPHINE, *toasting*: To the bride and groom… *(To* PRUDENVAL.*)* Papá!… *(To* MATHILDE.*)* Mammá!

MATHILDE: "Mammá"? Me?.. Oh my…

PRUDENVAL, *correcting* TREBUCHARD, *toasting in turn*: Don't you mean "the brides and grooms," monsieur?

TREBUCHARD, *quickly, to* PRUDENVAL: No, no… Please! Not "monsieur!" Just call me "father," son!

PRUDENVAL: Well, now that you mention it…

> *He and* TREBUCHARD *drink.*

PIQUOISEAU, *scratching his head*: "Father… Son… Papá… Mammá…" What the blazes…?

PRUDENVAL, *pointing toward* TREBUCHARD: He's marrying my daughter and I'm marrying his!

TREBUCHARD, *pointing toward* PRUDENVAL: So my father-in-law is going to be my son-in-law, monsieur!

CLAUDINE, *pointing toward* TREBUCHARD: You see, papá is marrying his daughter, so she's going to be my mother!

MATHILDE, *pointing toward* TREBUCHARD: And I'm going to be my papá's mother-in-law, monsieur!

DELPHINE, *to* PIQUOISEAU: Understand?

PIQUOISEAU: Not a goddamn word!

DELPHINE: Stupid crouton!

PRUDENVAL: I say…

The couples begin to explain once again, all talking at once, as the curtain falls on their explanations.

CURTAIN.

Edouard and the Chambermaid, or Hey-Diddle-Diddle

(Edgard et sa bonne, 1852)

Eugène Labiche & Marc-Michel

Characters

EDOUARD BEAUDELOCHE, a young dandy on the verge of marriage

VEAUVARDIN, his none-too-bright future father-in-law

THE NOTARY, an inflexible professional

MADAME BEAUDELOCHE, Edouard's socially-conscious mother

JEANNETTE, Veauvardin's daughter and Edouard's blandly unimpressive intended

FLORESTINE, Madame's ambitious chambermaid, given to backstairs adventure

GUESTS

Madame Beaudeloche's elegant Parisian drawing-room. Up center, a fireplace with shovel, poker, etc., and smoldering logs. On the mantelpiece, a mirror, a clock, lighted candelabra, and, at one end, a clothes-brush. Close by, hanging from the ceiling, a bell-cord. On the hearth, to the right, a basket of firewood. In front of the fireplace, left and right, an armchair; on the one to the right, a lady's shawl and a magazine; and, on the one to the left, a man's hat. In the angled corners, up right and left, opening onto the grand salon, tall double doors, hung on the inside with drapes gathered up in the middle. Right center, against the side wall, another armchair; close by it, a footstool. In the walls, down right and left, a door; the former, leading to Edouard's room, the latter, to other rooms of the apartment and the outside. Next to each door, against the wall, a small table and chair. Other appropriate furnishings: carpet, pictures, lamps, plants, etc.

At rise, FLORESTINE, *in maid's garb, is arranging the articles on the mantelpiece.* MADAME BEAUDELOCHE, *in street clothes, enters from the salon, up left.*

MADAME BEAUDELOCHE: I'll be rather late this evening, Florestine. (*Primping at the mirror.*) Please be sure to light the fire in my room and see that everything is in order when I return.

FLORESTINE: Madame can count on me.

MADAME BEAUDELOCHE: I know I can. You have a good head on your shoulders. Not like the others…

FLORESTINE: Thank you, madame.

MADAME BEAUDELOCHE: And serious as the day is long!… Not flighty like the rest of them… Not always waiting to go running off… Always work, work, work!… I must say, I'm more than satisfied.

FLORESTINE, *modestly*: I do what I can to please madame.

MADAME BEAUDELOCHE: And you do! You do!… Believe me, you won't be sorry… How old are you, child?

FLORESTINE: Twenty-three, madame.

MADAME BEAUDELOCHE: Well, I'll find you a husband! Just leave it to me! And a good one, too…

FLORESTINE: Oh! I can wait. I'm in no hurry.

MADAME BEAUDELOCHE, *with an incredulous little laugh*: What?

FLORESTINE: I'd really rather go on working for madame.

MADAME BEAUDELOCHE, *to herself*: A gem!… An absolute jewel!… (*Aloud, with a note of irony, moving toward her.*) And that fireman I saw in the courtyard last night, Florestine? I would have sworn he was looking for something… Or someone…

FLORESTINE, *defensively*: The fireman?

MADAME BEAUDELOCHE: Rather a handsome devil…

FLORESTINE: He… He was looking for a fire, madame! The… The neighbor next door… Her stew was burning, and… and…

MADAME BEAUDELOCHE: Aha…

FLORESTINE: And… (*Changing the subject.*) What shawl will madame be wearing?

MADAME BEAUDELOCHE, *pointing to the shawl on the armchair, up right*: That one… (*Moving left.*) Oh! One more thing… Don't forget to change the drapes.

FLORESTINE: Drapes, madame?

MADAME BEAUDELOCHE, *pointing to the double doors, up left and right*: Those... They're an absolute disgrace. (*Coming downstage.*) Now, be a dear and see if Monsieur Edouard is ready.

FLORESTINE, *hesitating, lowering her eyes*: Me, madame?

MADAME BEAUDELOCHE: Please...

FLORESTINE: But... Go into a young man's bedroom? While he's there!... I don't know...

MADAME BEAUDELOCHE, *with a smile*: Quite right, child!... (*To herself, moving toward the door, down right.*) No! Not like the others!... (*Aloud, calling.*) Edouard!... Are you ready?

EDOUARD'S VOICE: Coming, mammá...

MADAME BEAUDELOCHE, *calling*: Hurry! We'll be late...

EDOUARD appears at the door, elegantly dressed, wearing white gloves and a blue cravat.

EDOUARD: Here I am...

MADAME BEAUDELOCHE: Let me look at you... (*To FLORESTINE.*) What do you think, Florestine? Handsome, isn't he, this son of mine!

FLORESTINE, *lowering her eyes*: I... I wouldn't know, madame.

MADAME BEAUDELOCHE, *continuing her inspection*: But... What on earth... A blue cravat?

EDOUARD: But—

MADAME BEAUDELOCHE, *interrupting*: Blue, Edouard?... What ever were you thinking?

EDOUARD: Blue sets off my complexion, mammá. I thought...

MADAME BEAUDELOCHE: Nonsense! (*Taking it off his neck, handing it to FLORESTINE.*) Be a dear, Florestine... Go fetch a white one...

FLORESTINE: Very good, madame.

She exits, down right.

EDOUARD, *objecting*: A white cravat! A white cravat!... Why always a white one...

MADAME BEAUDELOCHE: Now, now...

EDOUARD: It makes me look like a bloody oyster, for heaven's sake!

MADAME BEAUDELOCHE: Please, Edouard! (*Very properly.*) A future notary has to think of appearances.

EDOUARD: Bah!

MADAME BEAUDELOCHE: Today of all days!... One doesn't sign a marriage contract with Mademoiselle de Veauvardin in a blue cravat! It simply isn't done!

EDOUARD: Shhh! Please!...

MADAME BEAUDELOCHE: What?

EDOUARD: No need to let the help know our business!

MADAME BEAUDELOCHE: My, my! Aren't we the secretive ones!

FLORESTINE enters, down right, with a white cravat.

FLORESTINE, *giving it to him*: Monsieur's cravat...

EDOUARD, *coldly*: Thank you, I'm sure...

MADAME BEAUDELOCHE, *to FLORESTINE*: Help him put it on, child.

FLORESTINE: Very good, madame.

She complies.

EDOUARD: Really! I'm perfectly capable of—

MADAME BEAUDELOCHE: Now, now… (*To* FLORESTINE.) Monsieur has to be especially handsome today.

EDOUARD, *clearing his throat loudly in an effort to cover her words*: Ahem! Ahem! (*As* FLORESTINE *finishes the task, still coldly.*) Much obliged! (*Looking at himself in the mirror, aside.*) I look like a fool!

MADAME BEAUDELOCHE: By the way, Florestine… Has the florist delivered the rosewood flower-box yet?

FLORESTINE: A flower-box, madame?

MADAME BEAUDELOCHE. Yes… The one Monsieur Edouard ordered yesterday…

EDOUARD, *clearing his throat again*: Ahem! Ahem!

FLORESTINE: I'm afraid I haven't seen it.

MADAME BEAUDELOCHE: Well… (*To* EDOUARD.) We can stop by his shop and check. We absolutely must have it today. Mademoiselle Jeannette is counting on it, the dear…

EDOUARD, *continuing*: Ahem! Ahem!

MADAME BEAUDELOCHE, *holding out her arm to him*: Come…

EDOUARD: Yes, mammá…

He takes his hat from the armchair, up left.

MADAME BEAUDELOCHE, *stopping short*: Oh!… My bracelets… Good heavens! Where is my head today! I'll just be a moment… (*Taking the clothes-brush from the mantelpiece.*) Florestine… Brush monsieur's hat while you're waiting.

She exits, down left.

FLORESTINE, *taking the hat and beginning to brush it*: Very good, madame…

EDOUARD, *objecting*: But I can—

FLORESTINE, *planting herself squarely in front of him, hands on hips, imperiously*: And just where do you think you're going?

EDOUARD, *timidly*: What?

FLORESTINE: Over my dead body!

EDOUARD: Florestine!

FLORESTINE: And who is this Mademoiselle Jeannette?

EDOUARD, *muttering*: Who?… (*With a shrug.*) No idea…

FLORESTINE: Oh? No idea?… And we give a rosewood flower-box to someone we don't know?

EDOUARD: What does that prove?… In society lots of people don't know each other, but… but that doesn't mean they can't give each other a flower-box now and then. Even rosewood… It happens all the time in society.

FLORESTINE: I don't care! (*Brushing the hat vigorously against the nap without realizing it.*) You're not going anywhere! Understand?

EDOUARD: Really, Florestine…

FLORESTINE, *stamping her foot*: No!… I won't have it!

EDOUARD: But—

FLORESTINE: No! No! No!

MADAME BEAUDELOCHE *enters, down left, wearing her bracelets.*

MADAME BEAUDELOCHE: There!

FLORESTINE, *aside*: Damnation!

MADAME BEAUDELOCHE: I'm ready...

FLORESTINE, *to* EDOUARD, *suddenly very subservient, handing him his hat, all disheveled*: Monsieur's hat ...

EDOUARD, *coldly*: Much obliged, mademoiselle. (*Putting it on and looking at himself in the mirror, aside.*) Good God!

MADAME BEAUDELOCHE, *without looking at him*: Come, come, Edouard...

EDOUARD: Yes, mammá... I'm coming! (*He looks alternately at her and at* FLORESTINE, *who is mechanically arranging articles on the table, down left; then, suddenly, shrieking.*) Oh!... Ayyy!... Ayyy!

MADAME BEAUDELOCHE,	*together*:	Son?
FLORESTINE,		What?

EDOUARD, *clutching his cheek, crouching in apparent pain*: My tooth! My tooth!... Ayyy!

MADAME BEAUDELOCHE: Good heavens! Not again?

EDOUARD: Oh! The pain!... It's killing me!

FLORESTINE, *feigning sympathy*: Oh! Poor monsieur...

She brings the armchair from the left of the fireplace, center stage.

EDOUARD, *whispering to her*: Save your breath!

FLORESTINE: I think he should sit down...

MADAME BEAUDELOCHE, *to* EDOUARD: How odd!... It seems to be happening to you more and more...

EDOUARD, *sitting down*: Yes... Whenever I want to go out...

MADAME BEAUDELOCHE: And when my dentist comes to examine you, he can't find a thing!

EDOUARD: Of course not! It's nerves, that's why!... Nerves...

MADAME BEAUDELOCHE, *suddenly noticing the disheveled state of his hat*: Good heavens, Edouard! What ever have you done to your hat?

She takes it off his head and examines it.

EDOUARD, *trying to hold it back*: It's nerves!... Like my teeth...

MADAME BEAUDELOCHE: Nerves?... Your hat?

EDOUARD: I mean...

MADAME BEAUDELOCHE: Really, son!...

EDOUARD, *with a wave of the hand*: Whatever...

MADAME BEAUDELOCHE: Are you sure it's not your head, dear boy? Pain can do that, you know...

She goes down right and puts the hat down on the table.

EDOUARD, *looking at* FLORESTINE: I... I think it's getting better... Maybe if I went out and got some fresh air... (*As he gets up* FLORESTINE *gives him a pinch.*) Ayyy!... No, no!... It's worse... Much worse!

He sits back down.

MADAME BEAUDELOCHE: Poor dear!... What ever are we going to do?

She moves upstage.

FLORESTINE, *taking a little flask from her pocket, offering it to* EDOUARD: Perhaps if monsieur took a little sip of this... It's a new *elixitive...* Dr. Wong's...

EDOUARD, *coldly*: Thank you just the same.

FLORESTINE: From China... It does wonders for toothache...

EDOUARD, *under his breath*: Toothache be damned!

FLORESTINE: And cramps, and things...

EDOUARD, *to* FLORESTINE, *muttering*: I don't like being made to look like a bloody fool!

MADAME BEAUDELOCHE, *coming back, taking a large handkerchief from her pocket, standing behind the armchair and knotting it under* EDOUARD*'s chin*: There!... Nice and tight!... That should help...

EDOUARD, *aside*: Lovely! The picture of the perfect fiancé...

MADAME BEAUDELOCHE, *to* EDOUARD: You just rest... And keep warm... And when you're feeling better, come meet me at Mademoiselle de Veauvardin's—

EDOUARD, *interrupting*: Shhh!

MADAME BEAUDELOCHE, *to* FLORESTINE: I'm leaving monsieur in your care, Florestine!

FLORESTINE: I'll do my best, madame.

MADAME BEAUDELOCHE: Now then... (*Pointing up right.*) Be a dear and take my shawl out to the coach... (*To* EDOUARD.) I'll tell them that you'll be along shortly.

EDOUARD: God willing! (*Aside.*) And Florestine!

FLORESTINE, *aside*: We'll just see about that!

She takes the shawl and follows MADAME BEAUDELOCHE *out, down left.*

EDOUARD, *getting up, angrily*: Damn! Of all things... This is really getting to be a bore!... A toothache every time she snaps her fingers!... (*Ripping off the kerchief, holding it up.*) And this!... (*He stuffs it into a pocket.*) And... And... (*At a loss for words.*) No! I... She... Oh!... (*Calming down.*) That will teach me to... to diddle with a domestic!... Believe me, if I had it to do over again... (*Taking his hat and smoothing it down, going to the mirror and putting it on.*) And it's all my tailor's fault, the peasant! (*Examining himself.*) Two years ago... While I was studying law... One day he brings me a new jacket... I go to button it up, and... (*Snapping his fingers.*) Just like that! One of the buttons... Pffft!... (*He throws up his hands in disgust.*) You might know... At that very moment Florestine comes by... (*He takes off the hat, speaking to it.*) "Mademoiselle... Would you be so kind as to sew this button on for me?..." "Of course, monsieur..." And that was the beginning... Her hair, brushing against my chin... Smelling of brilliantine... Lavender, I think... Mammá's, of course... But on her, well... On her shiny black locks... Ah! I couldn't resist. One two three, I... (*Kissing the hat.*) I kissed her!... Yes, damn it all! (*He lays the hat down on the armchair, center.*) It just goes to show... A young man should never let anyone but his mother sew on his buttons! Especially when he's studying law... And with a tailor like mine!... A chambermaid is all well and good, but... It's the sort of thing that clings to you, and won't let you go!... And with chapped hands... No gloves... And fingers all black and blue... And scuttling about all morning with big ugly slippers... On her feet, I mean, not her hands... No! That's not for me! Give me a pretty young widow... A good musician, with a sense of humor... And an income of at least eighty thousand a year!... That's what a young man should go after! Even if they can't sew on buttons... (*Taking out his pocket watch.*) Oh my! Four thirty already… And the signing is at five… No two ways about it… I've simply got to get past her somehow! (*As* FLORESTINE, *returning, appears at the door, down left.*) Ah!… Courage, Edouard!

FLORESTINE *enters.*

EDOUARD, *determined, addressing her*: I'd like a word with you, mademoiselle. (*Returning the armchair to its original position, up left.*) We really have to talk…

FLORESTINE, *casually*: Oh?… Don't tell me you're going to pout!

EDOUARD: I'll not dignify that remark with a reply, mademoiselle. I'll only tell you that your… your demands have become… how shall I say?… exceedingly vexatious!

FLORESTINE, *puttering about the table, down left, ignoring him, humming to herself*: Tra-la-la… Tra-la-la…

EDOUARD: Really! Obliging me to pretend to have a toothache every day… Keeping me prisoner in my own home… Throwing obstacles in my path when I have matters of the utmost—

FLORESTINE, *interrupting*: Really! You look so stupid when you try to use big words!

EDOUARD: Mademoiselle! I'll thank you to…

FLORESTINE, *humming*: Tra-la-la… Tra-la-la…

EDOUARD, *aside, discouraged*: "Tra-la-la" indeed!… That's what I get… (*As* FLORESTINE *takes the magazine from the armchair, up right, and sits down.*) Well, at least she's in a good mood. Maybe I should just come right out with it and tell her. It's not a crime to get married, after all! And she'll find out sooner or later… (*Aloud, cajoling.*) Florestine… Florestine, treasure…

FLORESTINE, *flipping the pages, casually*: Yes?

EDOUARD: Did you ever think… Did it ever occur to you that… that…

FLORESTINE: That…?

EDOUARD: …that one day I might decide to… get married?

FLORESTINE: Bah! Don't be silly! (*Laughing.*) Married! You?

EDOUARD, *rather piqued*: I beg your—

FLORESTINE, *interrupting*: Twenty-five is much too young!

EDOUARD: Oh!

FLORESTINE: You're still wet behind the ears! You should wait until you're weaned!

EDOUARD, *muttering, aside*: Vulgar creature! (*Aloud.*) But I assure you… If… If the right young lady came along… Just *if*, mind you… The right one, I mean…

FLORESTINE, *getting up, putting down the magazine, approaching him.* What are you trying to… (*Standing in front of him, hands on hips.*) Are you serious?

EDOUARD, *intimidated*: Serious?… Well… A little… That all depends…

FLORESTINE: It wouldn't be that Mademoiselle Jeannette, now would it?

EDOUARD, *quick to reply*: Mademoiselle who?

FLORESTINE: Because, if it is… Believe you me, I'll find her! And, when I do, it won't take me long…

EDOUARD: To… To what?

FLORESTINE: To tell her a thing or two! That's what!

EDOUARD, *shuddering, aside*: Heaven help me! (*Aloud.*) You mean… (*Forcing a little laugh.*) You thought… Me?… And Jeannette de Veauvardin?… Ha ha ha!… Have you ever seen her?

FLORESTINE: No…

EDOUARD: A faded little redhead… And… And with a wooden leg, to boot…

FLORESTINE: What?

EDOUARD, *getting confused*: Yes!… Rosewood… That's why mammá promised her a rosewood flower-box… You see? (*Aside.*) What on earth am I saying?

FLORESTINE: Then why this talk about getting married, all of a sudden?

EDOUARD, *at a loss for a moment*: Why?… Why, to… to test you! To see if you really love me… Because… (*Suddenly.*) Florestine! I'm jealous!

FLORESTINE: What?

EDOUARD: You'll never know how jealous I am!

FLORESTINE: You?

EDOUARD: There! I've told you… Now you know.

FLORESTINE: Of who, for goodness' sake?

EDOUARD: Who?… Who?… (*Aside.*) Oh my!… (*Struck by an idea.*) Ha!… That's right! Try to play innocent!

FLORESTINE: But…

EDOUARD, *sternly*: Please be good enough to tell me who that fireman was… The one I saw coming down the backstairs this morning!

FLORESTINE, *flustered*: Fireman?… I… I can't imagine…

EDOUARD: Oh? (*Dramatically.*) Faithless creature!… (*Aside.*) Now I've got her!

FLORESTINE, *recovering her aplomb*: Unless you mean the neighbor's son… On the top floor…

EDOUARD: Oh?

FLORESTINE: He brings him his milk every morning. And, come to think of it… Yes, he is a fireman, now that you mention it.

EDOUARD: Aha…

FLORESTINE: I'm sure… So you see, silly… You have no reason to be jealous! No reason in the world…

EDOUARD, *with a shrug, aside*: Who cares?

He takes his hat from the armchair, up left.

FLORESTINE, *stretching and yawning*: Ahhh… I can't stand on my feet another minute…

She sprawls out on the armchair, up right.

EDOUARD, *aside*: Of all the… Mammá's favorite chair!

He moves to leave, down left.

FLORESTINE, *mimicking his mother*: Be a dear, Edouard, and put a wooden leg on the fire…

EDOUARD, *startled*: A what?

FLORESTINE, *realizing her gaffe*: A log… Another log…

EDOUARD, *taken aback*: You want me…

FLORESTINE: It's a trifle chilly, don't you think?

EDOUARD, *changing his tone*: Of course, treasure… (*He puts the hat down again on the armchair, up left.*) A log… (*Going up to the basket of logs by the hearth and removing one.*) Of course… (*Putting it on the fire, catching sight of the clock, aside.*) Heaven help me! Four forty-five!… (*Aloud.*) Florestine… Love…

FLORESTINE, *almost dozing*: Hmm?

EDOUARD: I'll be back shortly…

He moves down left, as if to leave.

FLORESTINE: Oh? Where are you going?

EDOUARD: I… I'm going to vote… The polls close at five o'clock sharp, and I—

FLORESTINE, *interrupting*: Vote?… Why bother?

EDOUARD: But… It's my civic duty!

FLORESTINE, *ignoring his remark*: Be a dear, Edouard, and bring me the stool…

EDOUARD: Stool?… What stool?

FLORESTINE, *pointing to the footstool by the chair against the wall, right center*: That one…

EDOUARD: Of course… (*Aside, bringing the footstool over and placing it down to the left of the armchair.*) For this I needed a white cravat!

FLORESTINE, *stretching out, with a sigh of satisfaction*: Ahhh!

EDOUARD: There!… Now… (*Shaking her hand.*) I'll be back shortly.

FLORESTINE, *holding his hand*: No, no! Don't go… (*Pulling him with one hand, tapping the stool beside her with the other.*) Here!… Come sit down here, beside me.

EDOUARD: But… The polls, Florestine… (*Unable to resist her tugging, sitting down on the stool.*) My civic duty…

FLORESTINE: See? What could be cozier! Sitting by the fire… Just the two of us…

EDOUARD, *impatiently*: Yes… (*Aside.*) What indeed!

FLORESTINE: Not like last night… When you left me here, all by myself… (*Emphasizing.*) All alone…

EDOUARD, *aside*: No doubt!…

FLORESTINE: Tell me… Where did you go?

EDOUARD: Last night?… Why… (*Aside.*) Good God! My fiancée's… (*Aloud.*) To… To the opera… I went to the opera.

FLORESTINE, *very matter-of-fact*: Oh? What did you see?

EDOUARD: I saw… Why, I saw something by… by Rissoni… Charming… Utterly charming…

FLORESTINE: Rissoni…? You mean Rossini, love! Even I know that!

EDOUARD: Of course! (*Trying to get up.*) Now really… I've got to go vote! I'll be back shortly…

FLORESTINE, *pulling him back down, coaxingly*: Don't go, Edouard!… Please! Stay here with me!

He falls to his knees on the stool.

EDOUARD, *aside*: Damn!

FLORESTINE: What was it about?… I love operas…

EDOUARD, *aside*: Just my luck!

FLORESTINE: Please… Tell me…

EDOUARD, *jumping up, pulling away, coming downstage*: But Florestine!... The polls... I don't have time...

FLORESTINE, *following him, insisting*: Just a little...

EDOUARD: It... It was about a barber...

FLORESTINE: From Seville?... Figaro?

EDOUARD: Yes... Yes, that's it... And he goes down to hell to rescue his wife...

FLORESTINE: What?

EDOUARD: Or something like that...

FLORESTINE: No, no, no! You've got it all mixed up! That's Offenbach...

EDOUARD, *aside*: Off a what? (*Aloud.*) Well, it was all in Italian. What do you expect?... And I slept a lot...

FLORESTINE: Silly!

EDOUARD: Now please!... I've got to go vote. They're closing any minute...

FLORESTINE, *suddenly*: Oh! I almost forgot...

EDOUARD: Now what?

FLORESTINE: The drapes... (*Pointing up left and right.*) Madame told me to change them.

EDOUARD: Well? Go ahead...

He moves down left as if to leave.

FLORESTINE: But I can't reach... Please, love! Go get the ladder...

EDOUARD: Not now!

He exits.

FLORESTINE, *calling after him*: But I need it!... Edouard!... It's too heavy for me! Please!... Edouard!

EDOUARD'S VOICE: I heard you!... Just a minute, damn it all! (*He reenters with a ladder, muttering to himself.*) For this I needed a white cravat!

He places the ladder against the double door, up right.

FLORESTINE: There!... Now, while you take them down I'll go get the other ones.

EDOUARD: What? Me?...

FLORESTINE: Go on...

EDOUARD: Not on your life! I'm afraid of heights.

FLORESTINE, *laughing*: Heights?... That?

EDOUARD: But Florestine...

FLORESTINE: Go on, go on!... And hurry...

She exits, up left.

EDOUARD, *angrily, climbing up a few rungs*: Of all the... This is what happens when you diddle with a domestic, damn it! Believe me, if I had it to do over again...

FRANÇOIS appears at the door, down left.

FRANÇOIS, *announcing*: Monsieur de Veauvardin!

EDOUARD, *up the ladder, aside*: Good God! Jeannette's father...

He takes the kerchief from his pocket and hastily knots it under his chin.

VEAUVARDIN, *entering, doffing his hat, jovially*: Now then, where is this young son-in-law of mine?

He puts his hat down next to EDOUARD*'s, on the armchair, up left.*

EDOUARD, *clutching at his jaw*: Ayyy!

VEAUVARDIN, *continuing*: A trifle under the weather, they tell me…

EDOUARD: Ah! Monsieur…

VEAUVARDIN, *noticing him*: I say, son…

EDOUARD: How nice of you to come…

VEAUVARDIN: What the devil are you doing up there?

EDOUARD: It's for my toothache!

VEAUVARDIN, *aside*: Up a ladder?

EDOUARD: Heights help ease the pain… (*Babbling.*) Something about the blood…

VEAUVARDIN, *aside*: Odd!… But who knows?

EDOUARD: The distance it has to travel…

VEAUVARDIN, *aside*: Science, after all…

EDOUARD, *moaning*: Oh!… Ayyy!…

VEAUVARDIN: What a bother! (*Climbing up the ladder behind him.*) Today, of all days… When we're signing the—

EDOUARD, *looking anxiously up left, groaning, to cover his comments*: Ayyy!… Oh!… Please, not so close! It might be contagious…

VEAUVARDIN: You think so?… (*Climbing down, aside.*) A toothache?… (*Scratching his head, coming down center, aloud.*) Tell me, have you ever tried this magnetism everyone is talking about?

EDOUARD: You believe in that?

VEAUVARDIN: I should say I do!… Why, the things I've seen, with my very own eyes… Two weeks ago, for example… I had a devil of a headache. The kind I always get when I think too hard…

EDOUARD: Aha… (*Under his breath.*) Indeed!

VEAUVARDIN, *continuing*: I just happened to have the name of a certain Madame… (*Searching his memory.*) Madame… Something-or-Other… An expert, they told me… So I went to see her. And there she was, sitting in the middle of the room… Dark… Very dark… The room, I mean… And she was in a trance!… Eyes closed… (*He shuts his eyes and makes some mysterious passes.*) An honest-to-goodness trance, believe me… (*At this point,* EDOUARD*, losing patience, climbs down the ladder, unseen by* VEAUVARDIN*, and goes up left, to the double door, anxiously peering through the drapes.*) Well, she takes my hand, and before I can say a word… Before I even open my mouth, she says: "You're pregnant, madame… In nine months you'll be better!"

EDOUARD: And twenty francs lighter, I'm sure!… She was a quack, monsieur!

VEAUVARDIN, *addressing the ladder, where he thinks* EDOUARD *is still perched*: Do you think so, son?

EDOUARD: I daresay!

VEAUVARDIN, *coming downstage*: Well, perhaps… But there are others!… The ones with the fluid…

EDOUARD, *aside*: Bah!

VEAUVARDIN: And with second sight… They can find things…

EDOUARD, *aside*: Like your purse!

VEAUVARDIN: All kinds of things…

EDOUARD, *joining him, center, looking at his watch, impatiently*: Really, monsieur…

VEAUVARDIN, *ignoring him*: Yes! That's the kind I'm looking for… High and low… They're not easy to find…

EDOUARD, *sarcastically*: Maybe you should ask one to find one for you…

VEAUVARDIN, *ignoring him*: That's the kind I want!

EDOUARD: You?… (*Moving to the door, down left.*) What on earth for? (*Opening the door, calling.*) François!

VEAUVARDIN: Shhh! It's a secret!

EDOUARD: Quite all right… I'm not curious…

FRANÇOIS appears at the door.

FRANÇOIS: Monsieur?

EDOUARD, *pointing to the ladder*: Get that out of here!

FRANÇOIS: Very good, monsieur.

He carries the ladder off, down left.

VEAUVARDIN: But I can tell you…

EDOUARD: Good!… You can tell me on the way…

He picks up the two hats from the armchair, up left.

VEAUVARDIN: It's all because of my pigs… On my farm… In the country…

EDOUARD, *baffled*: Your pigs?

VEAUVARDIN: Yes… They gave me the most ingenious idea. And a lucrative one, I don't mind telling you… It was the twenty-seventh of last September, as I recall… (*EDOUARD looks impatiently at his watch.*) One of my prize hogs turned up a pair of the most perfectly lovely truffles…

EDOUARD, *waving his watch at him*: Monsieur… It's getting late. Don't you think—

VEAUVARDIN, *interrupting*: But damned if the little bugger didn't gobble them up!… "One of the hazards of truffle-hunting," I told myself…

EDOUARD: Please…

VEAUVARDIN: And then it hit me!

EDOUARD, *sarcastically*: The hog?

VEAUVARDIN, *ignoring him*: "What if I didn't need pigs to go find them?" I asked myself. "What if I got a medium?"

EDOUARD: A medium what?

VEAUVARDIN: No… That's what they call them… The real ones… The ones with second sight…

EDOUARD: Aha…

VEAUVARDIN: She could find the truffles. And you can be damned sure she wouldn't eat them! I could give her a generous five percent, and still make a handsome profit!

EDOUARD: Indeed!

VEAUVARDIN: I've been looking all over for one…

EDOUARD, *aside*: One who wouldn't tell you that you're pregnant…

VEAUVARDIN: …and believe me, when I find her…

EDOUARD, *putting on his hat and pulling* VEAUVARDIN*'s down around his ears*: Don't you think it's time we were going?

VEAUVARDIN: Going, son?… Where?

EDOUARD: Where? (*Trying not to lose patience.*) To sign the marriage contract, for heaven's sake!

VEAUVARDIN: The… Oh! That's right… I didn't tell you… We're signing it here.

He takes off his hat and puts it back on the armchair.

EDOUARD, *with a start*: We're what?

VEAUVARDIN: Yes… The notary is coming, and all the guests…

EDOUARD: But… No!… They can't… (*Aside.*) Good God!

VEAUVARDIN: Your mother didn't think we should. But you're not feeling well after all, and I thought…

EDOUARD, *nodding, aghast*: You thought…

VEAUVARDIN: Like they say: "If the mountain won't come to my helmet…"

EDOUARD, *nodding*: Your helmet…

VEAUVARDIN: So I insisted…

EDOUARD, *groaning*: Oh…

VEAUVARDIN: What's the matter, son?

EDOUARD: Nothing… Nothing… I couldn't be more delighted.

FRANÇOIS appears at the door, down left.

FRANÇOIS, *to* EDOUARD: A number of people with monsieur's mother, monsieur… I didn't get all their names.

EDOUARD: Yes… (*Waving him off.*) Thank you…

FRANÇOIS exits.

VEAUVARDIN: See? Right on time…

EDOUARD, *looking up left, anxiously, aside*: And Florestine… With the drapes…

MADAME BEAUDELOCHE enters, down left, followed by JEANNETTE, who hangs back, and several guests and musicians in evening clothes.

MADAME BEAUDELOCHE: Edouard, love!… I think you should thank all our guests for being so thoughtful.

EDOUARD, *taking off his hat and fiddling with it, awkwardly*: Yes… Of course… (*Babbling.*) If my helmet won't go to the mountain… (*Chuckling.*) That is…

THE GUESTS look at one another, simultaneously mumbling appropriate exclamations: "His helmet…?," "What did he say?," "What was that?," etc.

MADAME BEAUDELOCHE: Edouard?

EDOUARD: Yes… Yes… (*To* THE GUESTS, *pompously.*) How good of you all… Please accept my thanks… My *farthelt…* (MADAME BEAUDELOCHE *gives a start.*) Heartfelt… My heartfelt thanks… And my *gutter attitude…*

MADAME BEAUDELOCHE: What?…

EDOUARD: My utter gratitude for your consideration…

THE GUESTS mutter comments like "Curious…," "Is it only his tooth?," etc.

MADAME BEAUDELOCHE, *softly*: Please, Edouard…

EDOUARD: Come… (*Anxiously.*) Shall we all go into the salon?

MADAME BEAUDELOCHE, *to* EDOUARD, *whispering*: Mind your tongue! And for heaven's sake, say something to your fiancée! You haven't opened your mouth…

She joins THE GUESTS.

EDOUARD: Of course!… (*To* VEAUVARDIN.) Mademoiselle… How kind of you… (*Realizing his mistake.*) Sorry… (*Crossing left, to* JEANNETTE.) Mademoiselle… How happy I am… How terribly happy… Come… Shall we go into the salon?

VEAUVARDIN: Good idea!… We can play a spirited game of whist until the notary arrives.

Everyone but EDOUARD *exits, up right, closing the double door.*

EDOUARD, *pacing nervously*: Now what? (*Looking up right.*) All those people in there, and the notary on his way… (*Looking up left.*) And Florestine, with her drapes… Ah! If only I had it to do over again!… She'll never believe that Jeannette has a wooden leg! And she'll start screaming and making a bloody scene in front of them all!… Damn! I wish the earth would swallow me up! (*As* FLORESTINE *enters, up left, carrying the drapes.*) Ayyy!

FLORESTINE, *moving toward the door, up right*: What?… You didn't take down those drapes?

EDOUARD, *aside*: Or swallow *her*…

FLORESTINE: I thought I—

EDOUARD, *heading her off, trying to keep her away from the door*: I… I tried… But the higher I went, the more jealous I felt. Heights can do that to you… Something about the blood… So…

FLORESTINE: So?

EDOUARD: So I went to vote… (*Struggling to keep her away.*) There's nothing like voting to make a man feel proud… And take his mind off his problems…

FLORESTINE, *trying to reach the door*: Please Edouard…

EDOUARD, *throwing his arms around her, desperately*: Oh! Florestine!… Never have I loved you the way I love you now!

FLORESTINE: What's got into you?

EDOUARD: Ah! If only we two… (*Romantically.*) If only I could sweep you up and take you away… Away from all this… Off to the country… Just you, just me…

FLORESTINE: A trip to the country, Edouard?… That's a wonderful idea!… When?

EDOUARD: Today! Tonight!… Now!

FLORESTINE: Now?

EDOUARD: This minute!… It's a surprise… I didn't want to tell you, but you guessed it! For your birthday…

FLORESTINE: My… But that's not for two months!

EDOUARD: So? A little headstart… Why not?

FLORESTINE: You're right… Why not?… But where?

EDOUARD, *blurting out the first name that comes to his mind*: Strasbourg!

FLORESTINE: What? That would take hours…

EDOUARD: Of course… Neuilly, then… For a nice fish dinner…

FLORESTINE: And an omelette with rum!

EDOUARD: Rum?

FLORESTINE: Rum!

EDOUARD: Yum yum!

FLORESTINE, *still carrying the drapes*: Come… Come…

EDOUARD, *resisting*: Not just like that!... Not together...

FLORESTINE: Why not?

EDOUARD: Because... Because... People will see us! Tongues will wag! You know how people talk, Florestine! I'm thinking of your reputation.

FLORESTINE: Then how?

EDOUARD: You take the next train... We'll meet at the bridge... The one over the Seine... On the left, understand? Whichever one gets there first will wait for the other.

FLORESTINE: Aha...

EDOUARD: Agreed?

FLORESTINE: Oh, yes!

EDOUARD: There! Are you happy?

FLORESTINE, *squeezing his hand, enthusiastically*: Happy?... I'm absolutely *ecstitic!*

She moves down left, as if to leave.

EDOUARD, *aside*: *Ecstitic,* indeed!... Spoken from the bosom!

FLORESTINE, *returning*: I know! I'll wear my lilac shawl and my new pink bonnet!

EDOUARD: What more could I ask!

FLORESTINE, *holding out the drapes*: And these can wait until we come back...

She exits, down left.

EDOUARD, *calling after her*: The bridge at Neuilly!... Don't forget... On the left... The one who gets there first... (*Sighing, as she shuts the door.*) At last!... Free! Free! Free!... (*He cavorts about in delight, clicking his heels, etc.*) Tra-la-la-la-la-la!... Free at last!... (*He jumps up on the armchair, up right, continuing to express his pleasure.*) Ah!... *Ecstitic!*... Absolutely *ecstitic!*

VEAUVARDIN appears at the doors, up right, and notices him perched on the chair.

VEAUVARDIN, *aside*: Again?

EDOUARD, *aside*: Damn! Veauvardin...

VEAUVARDIN: I say, son... What are you doing up there?

EDOUARD, *clutching at his jaw*: Ayyy!... The pain!... The pain!

VEAUVARDIN: Oh?

EDOUARD: The height, monsieur...

VEAUVARDIN: Odd!... Who would ever think that standing on a chair...

EDOUARD. *stepping down*: I know... But modern science...

VEAUVARDIN, *reproachfully*: Besides, monsieur... I left my game of whist in the middle to come have a word with you.

EDOUARD: Aha...

VEAUVARDIN: And only an urgent matter could make me do that!

EDOUARD: About your pigs?

VEAUVARDIN: About my daughter!

EDOUARD: Oh?

VEAUVARDIN: I must say, you're not being very attentive to her! You haven't said a word... I find it most distressing!

EDOUARD: Ah, but...

VEAUVARDIN: First I find you up on a ladder… Then on a chair… Really! That's no way to court a young lady!

EDOUARD: But—

VEAUVARDIN: At least, not my daughter!

EDOUARD: I tried to explain…

VEAUVARDIN: I know! I know!… Your tooth… But if it hurts so much you should have it pulled out! I'll take you to my dentist.

EDOUARD: Thank you, but… No need… In fact, even as we speak, it seems to be getting better… (*Aside.*) Now that my pain is on her way to Neuilly!… *(Aloud.)* Yes… Much better… (*He takes off the kerchief and stuffs it into his pocket.*) You see? The height… I was right.

VEAUVARDIN: Good! Then keep in mind what I told you… Because my daughter is beginning to notice it too. She finds you… Well, a trifle cool, monsieur…

EDOUARD: Cool? Me?

JEANNETTE appears, up left.

JEANNETTE, *taking a few steps into the room, to VEAUVARDIN*: Papá… It's your turn to deal.

EDOUARD, *whispering, to VEAUVARDIN*: Leave us alone… I'll take care of it!

VEAUVARDIN, *whispering*: Yes! Please do… Go to it! And for the love of heaven, don't go climbing on any more furniture!

He exits, up left, with surreptitious gestures of encouragement.

EDOUARD, *to himself*: Ha! Cool?… Well, we'll just see how cool I am!

He bounds up behind JEANNETTE and plants a loud kiss on one side of her neck.

JEANNETTE, *startled*: Oh!

EDOUARD, *with several mechanical little bows*: Mademoiselle!… Will you accord me the honor of the first polka?

JEANNETTE, *curtsying*: With pleasure, monsieur! (*Aside.*) How curious!

EDOUARD, *aside*: So! I'm a trifle cool, am I?

He kisses her the same way, on the other side of her neck.

JEANNETTE, *jumping back*: Again?

EDOUARD, *bowing several times, as before*: And a waltz, mademoiselle?… A nice little waltz?

JEANNETTE: With pleasure… But you needn't trouble to invite me for the others. I'm afraid my card is already quite full. (*Aside.*) Thank goodness!

EDOUARD: I suspect, mademoiselle, that you find me rather cold.

JEANNETTE: Oh?

EDOUARD: Rather reserved, I might say…

JEANNETTE: Why… Why no…

EDOUARD: Aha… I thought… I don't know why, but…

JEANNETTE, *changing the subject*: I'm so happy to see that you're no longer in pain, monsieur.

EDOUARD: But I am, mademoiselle! I am!… The pain of love! The pain of passion! (*He takes her hands and covers them with kisses.*) The pain of not being able to express—

JEANNETTE, *trying to pull free*: Excuse me, monsieur…

EDOUARD, *aside*: What sweet little hands!

JEANNETTE, *still trying*: My… My dance card…

EDOUARD, *aside*: And with gloves!

JEANNETTE, *still trying*: I promised…

EDOUARD, *aside*: No black and blue, chapped fingers, I'll bet!

JEANNETTE, *aside*: What ever has got into him?

EDOUARD, *aside*: And those dainty feet!… No big ugly slippers… (*Passionately, aloud.*) Ah! Mademoiselle…

JEANNETTE: Please! The musicians are waiting. I promised…

At that moment, FLORESTINE *enters, down left, in shawl and bonnet, carrying a closed umbrella. She stands for a moment, shocked, unseen by the other two, then flings the shawl angrily onto the table, down left, and sits on the chair next to it, quietly seething.*

EDOUARD, *continuing, passionately*: At this moment of moments… As we prepare to join our lives as one…

JEANNETTE, *resisting*: Please…

EDOUARD: …in the bonds of holy matrimony…

JEANNETTE: You're wrinkling my cuffs…

EDOUARD: I look at you and… and every other woman becomes a pale imitation… A faded wench… A vulgar little chambermaid…

FLORESTINE, *aside*: Oh!

JEANNETTE: I… I think they're calling me, monsieur. (*Finally breaking free, with a nod.*) I'm so happy to see that you're feeling ever so much better.

EDOUARD: You are? You angel!

JEANNETTE: Yes!… Ecstatic!

She exits, up left.

EDOUARD, *without seeing her leave, aside*: "Ecstatic"!… (*Emphasizing.*) "Tat…" No "tit" for "tat"… "Ecs*tat*—" (*He turns to kiss her again, and notices* FLORESTINE, *leering at him.*) Good God!

FLORESTINE, *quickly getting up, throwing her bonnet down on the table*: Well now, monsieur!

EDOUARD, *stammering*: Wh-What… What are you… Why aren't you on your way to Neuilly?… To the bridge?… You're supposed to wait… The one who gets there first…

FLORESTINE, *angrily*: I came back—

EDOUARD: To spy on me!

FLORESTINE: To get my umbrella!

She brandishes it at him.

EDOUARD, *ignoring her explanation, furiously*: Like a… a…

FLORESTINE: A faded wench, monsieur? A vulgar little chambermaid?

EDOUARD, *at a loss for words*: Oh!

FLORESTINE: And what do I find? You!… (*Pointing up left.*) And her!

EDOUARD: Her?… Who?

FLORESTINE, *shaking the umbrella at him*: After all you told me! After all you said!… My birthday!… The fish dinner!…

EDOUARD: Florestine!

FLORESTINE: The omelette with rum!... Oh!

She makes a move up right, as if to exit.

EDOUARD, *beside himself*: No!... You mustn't!... (*He grabs the umbrella and bars her path.*) I forbid you... (*Threatening her with it.*) I forbid you to take another step!

FLORESTINE, *terrified*: Oh my God!

EDOUARD: Not another step!... (*Pointing down left.*) Now go! You hear me?... Go! Or I'll... I'll...

FLORESTINE: Help!... I... Oh...

She falls, fainting, into his arms.

EDOUARD: What?... She... Oh my!... (*Shaking her.*) Florestine!... Don't do this to me!... I... I was only joking!... I...

MADAME BEAUDELOCHE'S VOICE, *offstage*: Florestine!... Florestine!

EDOUARD, *panicking, calling out*: Just a moment! (*To himself.*) They'll all come looking... And the contract... I can't sign it like this! Dear God! I... Where can I... What can I...

He paces up and down with FLORESTINE in his arms, and still clutching the umbrella. After a moment he stops and opens it, holding it as if to try to hide her. Just then FRANÇOIS appears, down left.

FRANÇOIS, *announcing*: The notary, monsieur...

He exits.

THE NOTARY, *entering, noticing EDOUARD with FLORESTINE in his arms under the open umbrella*: My heavens!

EDOUARD, *to THE NOTARY, thrusting the umbrella into his hands*: Not a word, or I'll strangle you! Understand?

He exits to his room, down right, hauling FLORESTINE off and leaving THE NOTARY petrified and confused.

THE NOTARY: What did he say?

MADAME BEAUDELOCHE enters, up left.

MADAME BEAUDELOCHE, *calling*: Florestine!... (*Seeing THE NOTARY.*) Ah! I'm glad you're here...

THE NOTARY, *frightened*: Madame!

MADAME BEAUDELOCHE, *noticing the open umbrella*: Is it raining, monsieur?

She looks quizzically up at the ceiling.

THE NOTARY: I... I didn't see a thing! I don't know anything about it!

He dashes out, up right, throwing the open umbrella down on the armchair, right, as he passes.

MADAME BEAUDELOCHE, *alone, puzzled*: What in heaven's name...

VEAUVARDIN appears, up left.

VEAUVARDIN, *calling*: Edouard!... We're waiting... (*To MADAME BEAUDELOCHE, joining her.*) Pardon me, madame... You haven't seen that son of yours, have you?

MADAME BEAUDELOCHE, *pointing upstage*: I thought he was in there with all of you...

VEAUVARDIN: No... We want the dear boy to favor us with a song, but he's nowhere to be found.

MADAME BEAUDELOCHE: Curious...

VEAUVARDIN: He must be standing on a piece of furniture somewhere.

MADAME BEAUDELOCHE: I beg your pardon?

EDOUARD enters, down right, without seeing them, obviously distraught, and carrying a bucket of coal.

EDOUARD, *to himself*: Bloody leech! (*Mimicking.*) "You'll be sorry when I *sphinxiate* myself with the fumes!..." (*In his own voice.*) Better get rid of the coal, or she just might try!

VEAUVARDIN, *to EDOUARD*: Ah! There you are!

EDOUARD, *aside*: Good God!

He hides the bucket behind his back.

MADAME BEAUDELOCHE, *to EDOUARD*: Where were you, Edouard?

EDOUARD, *casually*: Oh... Nowhere special... Here and there...

VEAUVARDIN, *to EDOUARD, taking his free arm*: Come...

EDOUARD: Where?

VEAUVARDIN, *pointing upstage*: In there, of course!

MADAME BEAUDELOCHE, *to EDOUARD*: In the salon, son...

VEAUVARDIN: We're all waiting for you to sing...

EDOUARD: What?

MADAME BEAUDELOCHE, *misinterpreting his exclamation*: Oh... Anything... *Ave Maria* would be nice... You do it so beautifully.

VEAUVARDIN: And my daughter will accompany you on the piano.

EDOUARD: But I—

MADAME BEAUDELOCHE, *interrupting*: Come, come, Edouard! You're not going to make us beg you! (*Jokingly.*) You temperamental artiste, you!

EDOUARD, *still awkwardly struggling to keep the bucket out of sight*: Not at all... It's just that...

MADAME BEAUDELOCHE: Then do be a dear and hurry... In the meantime the gentlemen would like to indulge in a few hands of poker. Are the chips in your room?

She moves right, toward his door.

EDOUARD, *leaving VEAUVARDIN and rushing to stand in her way, frantically*: No!... Not in there!... They're not!... (*Pointing to the little table, down left.*) There!... In the table...

VEAUVARDIN, *aside*: Is he going to jump up on it?

MADAME BEAUDELOCHE, *taken aback*: Oh?... (*To EDOUARD.*) No need to get upset...

She crosses left to the table and goes rummaging about in the drawer, finding the chips. JEANNETTE appears, up left.

JEANNETTE, *to EDOUARD*: Monsieur... We're all waiting for your song.

EDOUARD: With pleasure!... In a moment... (*Aside.*) *Ave Maria?* With a bucket full of coal?

VEAUVARDIN, *to EDOUARD*: Monsieur... Son...

EDOUARD, *to JEANNETTE*: Right away... (*To VEAUVARDIN.*) Here! Take this!

He thrusts the bucket into his hands.

VEAUVARDIN, *aghast*: What?... I say...

JEANNETTE, *who hasn't seen the preceding, to* EDOUARD: Well?

EDOUARD: With pleasure... With pleasure...

He follows her out, up left.

VEAUVARDIN, *staring at the bucket, nonplussed*: Coal?

MADAME BEAUDELOCHE, *turning around, noticing it*: What in heaven's name is that?

During the following exchange, the muffled sounds of Schubert's Ave Maria. *with piano accompaniment, can be heard coming from the salon.*

VEAUVARDIN, *agape*: I have no idea!

MADAME BEAUDELOCHE: Where did you get it?

VEAUVARDIN: I... I don't know! It... It just appeared...

MADAME BEAUDELOCHE: Do you find it chilly?

VEAUVARDIN: Me?... No... Not particularly...

MADAME BEAUDELOCHE, *with a shrug*: Well?

VEAUVARDIN, *with a shrug*: Well?

MADAME BEAUDELOCHE, *aside*: The man is a lunatic! (*Aloud, calling.*) Florestine!... Florestine!... (*Aside.*) I hope it doesn't run in the family at least.

She exits, down left.

VEAUVARDIN, *alone*: What the devil am I supposed to do with it? And in evening clothes, no less!... (*Looking at his soiled gloves.*) And my gloves!... All smudged...

THE NOTARY enters, up right.

THE NOTARY, *to* VEAUVARDIN: Monsieur... I've been asked to invite you to join in a game of poker.

VEAUVARDIN: I'd be delighted... (*Thrusting the bucket into his hands.*) Here! Take this!...

He dashes off, up left. While the double door is open, the last few bars of the song can be heard, followed by muffled applause as it is closed.

THE NOTARY, *flustered*: "Take this!..."? This what? (*Looking at the bucket with disgust.*) This... What does he think a notary is? A domestic?

As he goes about, upstage, unsure how to get rid of it, EDOUARD *enters, up right, unseen by* THE NOTARY, *whose back is turned to him..*

EDOUARD, *calling offstage*: Yes... Thank you... (*Coming down left, to himself, excitedly.*) There are two more verses, but enough is enough! *Ave Maria,* indeed!... While that poor child is swooning her heart out...

THE NOTARY, *opening the door, down right, to himself*: Perhaps in here...

EDOUARD, *to himself*: Maybe if I can put her to bed...

He turns and begins crossing right, to his room.

THE NOTARY, *noticing* FLORESTINE *inside, shouting*: Good Lord!

EDOUARD, *surprised to see him*: What? You again?

THE NOTARY: A woman!

EDOUARD, *threatening*: Not a word, or I'll strangle you! Understand?

He exits quickly, down right, and slams the door shut.

THE NOTARY, *alone, scandalized*: In all my thirty years as a notary, I never... Never!... All the best homes! All the best families!... The finest food and drink!...

And here they want to strangle me!… And what do they give me?… (*Holding up the bucket.*) Coal!… I never… (*Alarmed, as* EDOUARD *appears at his door.*) Oh my!…

He runs off, exiting down left, still carrying the bucket.

EDOUARD, *entering cautiously, aside*: Shhh… (*To himself.*) Well, at least she's better… The smelling salts didn't do much good. Or the glass of water in the face… But when I told her a monstrous lie, she came right around!… "The marriage is off!" I said… "Off!… Canceled!…" (*Mimicking.*) "Oh? And why?…" I didn't know what to say… So I blurted out: "Her wooden leg has termites, Florestine! It's disgusting!" (*Down left, calling offstage.*) François!…

FRANÇOIS'S VOICE: Monsieur?

EDOUARD: The bed-warmer… Bring it in here… (*Continuing, to himself.*) Anyway, she believed me. The simple child!… Now to get her upstairs… Up to her garret… But first I have to warm her bed. She's freezing, poor thing!… I forgot to shut the bloody window!… And who can blame me? After all this… (*With a sigh.*) Then I can go sign the contract in peace! Tomorrow is another day… I'll worry about it when it comes… (*Shaking his head.*) Oh! If only I had it to do over again…

FRANÇOIS appears at the door, down right, with a bed-warmer.

FRANÇOIS, *puzzled, holding it out*: Monsieur?

EDOUARD, *taking it and waving him off*: Very good… (*As FRANÇOIS exits, scratching his head.*) You can go!… (*Looking about to make sure that he is alone, he goes up to the fireplace and puts several shovelfuls of embers into the pan.*) It's the least I can do, considering… (*Sighing.*) Ah! If only…

JEANNETTE'S VOICE, *offstage*: Yes, papá… I'll go find him…

Muted polka music can be heard coming from the salon.

EDOUARD, *with a start*: What?

He hides the bedwarmer behind his back as JEANNETTE appears, up right.

JEANNETTE, *entering*: Well, monsieur? I'm waiting…

EDOUARD, *aside*: Dear God! (*Awkwardly.*) You are?… What for?

JEANNETTE: For our polka! Remember?

EDOUARD: Poker?… But I don't know how… I've never played…

JEANNETTE: What?

EDOUARD: Whist, if you insist… (*With a silly little laugh.*) Ha ha!… It rhymes… But no poker…

JEANNETTE: Our polka!… Our polka, monsieur! (*Taking her dance card from her bosom and holding it up, impatiently.*) You invited me, you know!

EDOUARD: For… For the second one, mademoiselle…

JEANNETTE: No, no! Not the second one… The first!

EDOUARD: Aha… That's… The one before the second one, you mean…

JEANNETTE, *holding out her hand*: Come, or we'll miss it!

EDOUARD: But I thought… (*The bed-warmer hits the back of his legs, and he lets out a shriek of pain.*) Ayyy!

JEANNETTE, *misinterpreting his exclamation*: You thought you what, monsieur?

EDOUARD, *rubbing one leg against the other, hopping about, aside*: Damn!

JEANNETTE: I told you… The first one!

VEAUVARDIN appears, up left.

VEAUVARDIN, *standing in the doorway, to EDOUARD*: Well?

EDOUARD, *taking a bewildered JEANNETTE around the waist with his free hand, transforming his little hops into awkward polka steps, dancing her down right as far from VEAUVARDIN as he can, humming*: Tra-la-la-la…

VEAUVARDIN: What the devil are you two doing?

EDOUARD, *dancing in place*: Why… Can't you see?… I'm… We're practicing our polka…

VEAUVARDIN, *tapping his forehead, aside*: Polka?… Dotty!… (*Aloud, to EDOUARD, approaching him.*) Come, come!… You'll do just fine!

EDOUARD: Right away, father! (*He dances JEANNETTE upstage; as they pass in front of VEAUVARDIN, he thrusts the bed-warmer into his hands.*) Here! Take this!

He and JEANNETTE go dancing out, up right.

VEAUVARDIN, *staring at it, flabbergasted*: Is someone sick?

MADAME BEAUDELOCHE enters, down left.

MADAME BEAUDELOCHE, *to herself*: Where can she be? It's simply not like her! (*Looking at the doors, upstage.*) And the drapes?… Oh! After I told her expressly…

VEAUVARDIN, *approaching her*: Madame…

MADAME BEAUDELOCHE, *noticing the bed-warmer*: Goodness me! What are you doing with that?

VEAUVARDIN: I… I'm sure I don't know!

MADAME BEAUDELOCHE: First a bucket of coal, and now… Is this some kind of joke, monsieur?

VEAUVARDIN: Really! I have no idea… But I'm certainly going to ask him!

He strides up to the double door, up right.

MADAME BEAUDELOCHE, *calling after him*: Wait!… Not in there!… Not with that!

VEAUVARDIN, *ignoring her, calling, as he exits*: Monsieur!… Son!…

MADAME BEAUDELOCHE, *shaking her head*: An absolute lunatic!

FLORESTINE, without her bonnet, enters, down right, behind her back.

FLORESTINE, *to herself*: Where can he be?… (*Noticing MADAME BEAUDELOCHE.*) Oh my…

She quickly crosses left, trying to avoid being seen.

MADAME BEAUDELOCHE, *catching sight of her, impatiently*: Ah! There you are, Florestine! Where on earth…? I've been calling you for an hour.

FLORESTINE: I didn't hear, madame.

MADAME BEAUDELOCHE: It's your place to hear me, whenever I call you!

FLORESTINE: Yes, madame.

MADAME BEAUDELOCHE: Even if you don't.

FLORESTINE: Very good, madame.

MADAME BEAUDELOCHE: Now listen very carefully. In a little while we're going to sign the contract.

FLORESTINE: What contract?

MADAME BEAUDELOCHE: Monsieur Edouard's marriage contract…

FLORESTINE: But… That's impossible… It's called off…

MADAME BEAUDELOCHE: Called off?

FLORESTINE: The termites… I thought… On account of the—

MADAME BEAUDELOCHE: Are you out of your mind? Why on earth would we call it off?

FLORESTINE, *aside, fuming*: Oh! The liar!…

MADAME BEAUDELOCHE: Now then, Florestine… As soon as everything is ready to be signed… When all the guests are in here…

FLORESTINE, *under her breath*: The swine!

MADAME BEAUDELOCHE, *continuing*: I'll ring, and you'll go fetch the wedding basket…

FLORESTINE, *aside*: Oh!

MADAME BEAUDELOCHE, *pointing left*: It's in my boudoir. Under the vanity… And you'll bring it here! But not until you hear the bell… It's a surprise, understand?

FLORESTINE: Oh yes, madame! (*Aside.*) It certainly is…

MADAME BEAUDELOCHE: In the meantime you'll pass the refreshments. (*Pointing left.*) The drinks and the platters of fruit are in the pantry.

FLORESTINE: Very good, madame…

MADAME BEAUDELOCHE: Just be sure not to let anyone take too many. We weren't expecting…

FLORESTINE: Of course, madame… (*Aside.*) Surprise, my foot! I'll give him a real surprise, that… that…

She continues muttering as she exits, down left. As the polka music in the salon comes to a stop. EDOUARD *appears, up left.*

EDOUARD, *calling offstage, with a little bow*: Thank you, mademoiselle! You polka divinely… (*Coming downstage, aside.*) Now to find that bed-warmer… (*Noticing* MADAME BEAUDELOCHE.) Oh!… Mammá…

MADAME BEAUDELOCHE: Bravo, Edouard! You're being the perfect gentleman! Just one thing… Be a dear and invite your fiancée's aunt to dance. If not, she'll just stand there in the corner and keep eating!

EDOUARD, *very agreeably*: Of course, mammá! (*Aside.*) And drinking!

He goes up left, as if to leave.

MADAME BEAUDELOCHE: Thank you, son…

She exits, up right. As he sees her leave, he turns around and hurries back down.

EDOUARD, *to himself*: I have better things to do than drag that old hag over the floor! (*Looking all over.*) Where on earth did he put it?

VEAUVARDIN *enters, up left, still carrying the bed-warmer.*

VEAUVARDIN, *to himself*: If what the notary says is true… No, I can't believe it! A woman? In my son-in-law's bedroom? Today of all days?

EDOUARD, *noticing him*: Ah!… Just what I was looking for…

He seizes the bed-warmer by the pan.

VEAUVARDIN, *resisting*: Let go, monsieur!

He moves right, toward EDOUARD*'s room.*

EDOUARD: Where are you going?

VEAUVARDIN: Into your bedroom, that's where!

EDOUARD, *alarmed*: No, no! You mustn't!

VEAUVARDIN: Oh?

EDOUARD: It... It hasn't been swept! The dust is an inch thick!... It's... Come back later... Tomorrow...

VEAUVARDIN: Let go, I said!... Let go!...

As they tug back and forth on the bed-warmer, the pan comes off in EDOUARD*'s hands, and the handle remains in* VEAUVARDIN*'s. The latter, staggering, exits into the room, down right.*

EDOUARD, *throwing the pan into the fireplace, resigned*: Ay ay ay!... That's that!... The end!... (*Falling in a heap on the armchair, up left.*) My marriage, up in smoke... Good God, what a day!... And all because of my tailor! (*He clutches his head.*) Oh! My head...

FLORESTINE *enters, up left, carrying a platter of fruit.*

FLORESTINE: Well, well!

EDOUARD, *shocked, jumping up*: What?... You...?

FLORESTINE, *sarcastically*: What have we here?

EDOUARD, *pointing to his room*: But... Just now, you were...

FLORESTINE, *under her breath*: Swine!

EDOUARD: Then he won't... (*Delighted.*) Ah! Florestine! Kiss me!... (*Reflecting for a moment.*) On second thought—

FLORESTINE, *coldly, interrupting*: So! When is the wedding?

EDOUARD: I... I told you... It's called off... Canceled...

FLORESTINE: Oh? (*Looking upstage.*) Is that why everyone is celebrating in there?

EDOUARD, *aside*: God!

FLORESTINE, *holding up the platter*: Is that why I'm serving refreshments? Is that—

EDOUARD, *quickly*: Of course!... They're... They're celebrating the cancellation. It's a... a cancellation party! (*As she places the platter down on the table, down left.*) Everyone in society has one when a wedding is called off!

FLORESTINE, *hands on hips, standing in front of him*: Just what do you take me for?

EDOUARD: Florestine...

FLORESTINE: In fifteen minutes they're going to sign your marriage contract!

EDOUARD, *feigning surprise*: They are?

FLORESTINE: And the second I hear the bell, I'm bringing in the wedding basket!

EDOUARD: I say... That's very good of you...

FLORESTINE, *ignoring him*: But that's not all! (*She takes a small photograph from her pocket.*) Do you recognize this swine?... This pig?...

EDOUARD, *shocked*: Ayyy!... My picture! The one—

FLORESTINE: Yes! The one you gave me... With your "undying love," I think you said...

EDOUARD, *reaching for it*: Florestine!... Please... (*She pulls it back.*) It... It was just a memento... This newfangled photography... You know...

FLORESTINE: Oh? Well, just imagine what everyone will think when I show it to them!

EDOUARD: You wouldn't... You... Please, Florestine! I'll give you back your letters...

FLORESTINE: Bah!

EDOUARD: Your nice little love letters... (*Aside.*) With all the nice little mistakes!... (*Aloud.*) The ones you wrote me when you were visiting your aunt in the country...

FLORESTINE, *aside*: Yes... Dear old aunt Gustave!

EDOUARD, *reaching*: Please...

FLORESTINE: No, no, no!... It's a surprise they want, and it's a surprise they're going to get! The second I hear the bell...

EDOUARD: Then what?

FLORESTINE: Then I'll go right up to Monsieur... Monsieur Whatever-His-Name-Is... And I'll show him this! And I'll tell him about us! About you, and me... And your "undying love!"

EDOUARD, *aside*: Good God!

FLORESTINE: And I'll tell him to ask you for all the... the vile, *assorted* details!

EDOUARD, *begging*: Florestine!... Wouldn't you like a lovely new shawl? The best that twenty-nine francs can buy?

FLORESTINE: No!

EDOUARD: And fifty centimes...?

FLORESTINE: No!

EDOUARD: Pure wool?

FLORESTINE: No!

EDOUARD: From the best shop in Paris?... Thirty francs?... Forty?

FLORESTINE: No, no, no!... If you had just told me the truth...

EDOUARD: I will! Right now!... The absolute truth, Florestine...

FLORESTINE: Now doesn't count!... Before!... Instead of that *cockeyed bull* story! Off to Neuilly... To the bridge... (*Mimicking.*) "The one who gets there first..." (*Angrily.*) Oh!... (*Moving toward the door, down left, apostrophizing.*) Ring! I'm ready!... Ring!

EDOUARD, *following her*: Forty francs, fifty centimes...?

FLORESTINE, *at the door, ignoring him*: Ring! Ring! Ring!

She retrieves the platter and storms out.

EDOUARD, *calling after her*: With a silk fringe...? (*Alone.*) Damn!... You try to be nice to the help... Treat them like human beings... Even give them your picture... And do they appreciate it?

VEAUVARDIN appears at the door, down right, hiding FLORESTINE's bonnet behind his back.

VEAUVARDIN, *calling to him*: Monsieur Beaudeloche!

EDOUARD, *under his breath*: Lovely! Now him!

VEAUVARDIN: I'd like a word with you.

EDOUARD: Any one in particular?

VEAUVARDIN: Monsieur... I am a father...

EDOUARD: Yes... I suspected...

VEAUVARDIN: And I love my daughter.

EDOUARD: I'm sure... I'm sure...

VEAUVARDIN, *showing him the bonnet*: Would you be good enough to explain what this was doing in your room, monsieur? (*Emphasizing.*) Your bedroom!

EDOUARD, *aside*: Damn!… Hers… (*To* VEAUVARDIN, *aloud.*) Why, it's… it's…

VEAUVARDIN: A bonnet!… Yes! Your chambermaid's, monsieur!… On your night table, no less!

EDOUARD, *innocently*: Oh?

VEAUVARDIN: Next to your bed, if I may say…

EDOUARD: Well…

VEAUVARDIN: And I'll thank you to explain how it got there!

EDOUARD: Really… It's quite simple…

VEAUVARDIN: I'm listening!

EDOUARD: She… That poor child… She… She has a nasty habit… A character flaw, you might say…

VEAUVARDIN, *sharply*: Go on!

EDOUARD: She… She forgets…

VEAUVARDIN: Her clothes?

EDOUARD: She… (*Aside.*) Give me time to think, damn it! (*Aloud.*) She… She leaves them lying anywhere… Wherever they fall…

VEAUVARDIN, *sarcastically*: How convenient!… Even in your bedroom?

EDOUARD: Anywhere!… Everywhere!… It's terribly annoying…

VEAUVARDIN: Even at night?

EDOUARD: Even… (*Suddenly struck by an idea, emphatically.*) Especially at night!… Because she… she walks in her sleep! (*Aside.*) That's it!… (*Aloud.*) Especially when she's in one of her trances!

VEAUVARDIN, *pricking up his ears*: Her trances?… Did you say—

EDOUARD: Yes! She has the power… The fluid!

VEAUVARDIN: She does?

EDOUARD: Oh yes!… Second sight… Third even…

VEAUVARDIN, *ecstatically*: Oh!

EDOUARD: Think of all the truffles she could find!

VEAUVARDIN: Where is she now?

EDOUARD, *pointing upstage*: In there… Serving the fruit…

VEAUVARDIN: Ah!

He runs up to the bell-cord.

EDOUARD: What are you doing?

VEAUVARDIN: I'm going to ring for her, so she can show me…

EDOUARD, *stopping him*: Ring?… No, no! You mustn't! (*Aside.*) She'll bring that bloody picture! (*Aloud, holding him back.*) Don't ring, whatever you do!

VEAUVARDIN: Oh? Why not?

EDOUARD: It… It will wake her… You mustn't…

VEAUVARDIN: But I can't very well magnetize her from here!

EDOUARD: Oh?… (*Inspired.*) Why not? (*Aside.*) Maybe… (*Aloud, dramatically.*) Monsieur de Veauvardin… You are about to witness one of the miracles of modern science!

VEAUVARDIN: I am?

EDOUARD: We… You and I… are going to magnetize that young woman… (*Pointing upstage.*) And through the wall!

VEAUVARDIN: Bah!

EDOUARD: We're going to command her to come in here…

VEAUVARDIN: Impossible…

EDOUARD: And that's not all! We're going to concentrate on an object… Any object!… And we'll make her bring it to us!

VEAUVARDIN: Fine!… A nice plump Smyrna fig!

EDOUARD, *waving off the suggestion*: Ha!… Too simple!… Much too simple… That wouldn't prove anything! Her platter of fruit, after all… It could be a coincidence…

VEAUVARDIN: Well…

EDOUARD, *pretending to try to think of something difficult*: I've got it!… My picture!… Yes! That's it!

VEAUVARDIN: I'd rather have a fig…

EDOUARD, *aside*: I don't give a… (*Aloud.*) There's one of those newfangled photography things in the cupboard. A picture of me… The third drawer on the left… Under the table linen… Way in back… Way, way in back…

VEAUVARDIN: Monsieur Beaudeloche… If you… If I…

EDOUARD: We… We, monsieur…

VEAUVARDIN, *pointing up left*: If we can make her come through those doors with your picture…

EDOUARD: We can! (*Very matter-of-fact.*) She'll have to open them first, of course…

VEAUVARDIN, *impressed*: If we can do that, monsieur, my daughter is yours! No questions asked!

EDOUARD: Now then… (*Placing him up left, a few feet from the doors, facing them.*) You stand here…

VEAUVARDIN: Like this?

EDOUARD: Perfect!… Just one thing… When she gives you the picture, send her out right away!

VEAUVARDIN: Oh? Why is that?

EDOUARD: The fatigue… It… It tires her out terribly. Using all that fluid, you understand… She'll probably start to babble, and say all kinds of wild things she won't even know she's saying…

VEAUVARDIN: My, my…

EDOUARD: The fluid can do that.

VEAUVARDIN: Thank you for warning me!

EDOUARD: Good!…. Now close your eyes and… and concentrate on your fluid.

VEAUVARDIN: *My* fluid?… I thought she was the one with the fluid.

EDOUARD: She… You… Me… All of us!

VEAUVARDIN: Aha…

EDOUARD: I'll help you… (*He stands behind him.*) Concentrate!… Concentrate!

VEAUVARDIN, *making exaggerated magnetic passes toward he door, aside*: Maybe if I concentrate on a nice plump Smyrna fig…

EDOUARD, *duplicating his gestures*: Come, mademoiselle!… The picture… The picture… In the cupboard… (*After a few moments, to* VEAUVARDIN.) I feel her presence… Don't you?

VEAUVARDIN: I… I think so… A little…

EDOUARD: Yes… Definitely…

VEAUVARDIN: Come, mademoiselle…

EDOUARD, *making sure* VEAUVARDIN*'s eyes are closed*: I'm sure…

He reaches over and pulls on the bell-cord, ringing several times.

VEAUVARDIN: What was that?

EDOUARD: Next door, monsieur… Don't stop! Don't stop!…

VEAUVARDIN, *redoubling his magnetic passes*: Come, mademoiselle!… Come…

The double door, up right, opens and MADAME BEAUDELOCHE *appears.*

MADAME BEAUDELOCHE, *calling back into the salon*: This way, everyone… We're ready…

EDOUARD, *aside*: Damn!… The bell… I forgot…

MADAME BEAUDELOCHE *enters, followed by* JEANNETTE, THE NOTARY, *and all* THE GUESTS.

MADAME BEAUDELOCHE, *noticing* VEAUVARDIN, *still making his passes toward the door, up left*: What on earth… (*To* EDOUARD, *as the others mutter to one another in astonishment.*) What ever is he doing?

EDOUARD, *with a shrug*: I have no idea… I was wondering myself.

MADAME BEAUDELOCHE, *calling*: Monsieur de Veauvardin!…

VEAUVARDIN: Shhh!… She's coming… I can feel her presence…

MADAME BEAUDELOCHE: What?

The double door, up left, opens and FLORESTINE *appears.*

VEAUVARDIN, *jumping back*: There! You see?

EDOUARD, *aside*: Good God! Now what?

MADAME BEAUDELOCHE, *to* FLORESTINE: And the wedding basket, child?

VEAUVARDIN, *trying to silence her*: Shhh!

MADAME BEAUDELOCHE: Couldn't you find it? In my boudoir—

VEAUVARDIN, *more energetically*: Shhh! I told you!… For heaven's sake! She's been magnetized…

As all THE GUESTS *turn to one another with appropriate expressions of bewilderment, surprise, etc.,* EDOUARD *approaches* FLORESTINE.

EDOUARD, *whispering*: Florestine…

VEAUVARDIN: Quiet! Or she'll lose the fluid!

MADAME BEAUDELOCHE, *to* VEAUVARDIN: Nonsense, monsieur!

FLORESTINE, *to* EDOUARD, *whispering*: No!… It's no use asking…

MADAME BEAUDELOCHE, *under her breath*: An absolute lunatic!

FLORESTINE, *to* EDOUARD, *whispering*: Not even with a silk fringe!

EDOUARD, *to* FLORESTINE: But…

FLORESTINE, *whispering*: You're going to pay, you swine!

VEAUVARDIN, *to* MADAME BEAUDELOCHE: Nonsense, is it? Well, we'll see… (*Turning to* FLORESTINE, *solemnly.*) Mademoiselle… Be good enough to tell us why you came in here just now!

FLORESTINE: Why…? To show you the… the biggest pig in all of France!

VEAUVARDIN: What? (*To* EDOUARD.) Did she say "fig"?

EDOUARD, *whispering, to* VEAUVARDIN: Your fig! You see?

VEAUVARDIN, *jubilant*: I did it! I… I really… (*To all* THE GUESTS.) You see? You didn't believe me…

EDOUARD, *quick to agree*: He did! He did!… (*Very matter-of-fact.*) And now I think we should all—

VEAUVARDIN, *to* FLORESTINE: Well? Where is it?

FLORESTINE: Where is what, monsieur?

VEAUVARDIN: My fig… My Smyrna fig… The one you brought me, in the trance… With the fluid! (THE GUESTS *turn to one another with puzzled looks, and mutter appropriately.*) Through the wall… All that fluid…

THE NOTARY, *picking up the open umbrella, still lying on the armchair, up right, and holding it up:* Is something leaking?

VEAUVARDIN, *to* FLORESTINE, *continuing*: Yours… Mine… (*Pointing to* EDOUARD.) His…

FLORESTINE, *taking her umbrella from* THE NOTARY, *closing it, to* VEAUVARDIN: Fig? What fig?

VEAUVARDIN: My plump—

FLORESTINE, *interrupting*: I'm here to show you the pig who betrayed me! (*Dramatically.*) The swine who *smyrned* my love…

EDOUARD, *forcing a laugh*: Ha ha!… *Smyrned* indeed! (*To* THE GUESTS.) Who *smyrned* her!… Ha ha!

VEAUVARDIN, *laughing, to* THE GUESTS: Poor innocent child!

> THE GUESTS *continue muttering appropriately throughout the following exchanges.*

EDOUARD, *to* FLORESTINE, *whispering*: Florestine! I beseech you…

VEAUVARDIN, *to* FLORESTINE: And who is this cad who could… (*Emphasizing.*) *smyrn* the likes of such a pretty young thing?

FLORESTINE: You want to know, do you? (*To* THE GUESTS.) You all want to know who treated my heart like a meaningless *truffle?*

VEAUVARDIN, *pricking up his ears*: Truffle?… Did she say—

EDOUARD, *to* VEAUVARDIN, *beside himself*: She means "trifle"… She—

VEAUVARDIN, *to* FLORESTINE: Mademoiselle…

FLORESTINE: Well, I'll tell you! (*Shaking the umbrella at* EDOUARD.) Yes… I will!

VEAUVARDIN, *to* FLORESTINE: Did you say…

EDOUARD, *in desperation*: Florestine! I forbid you—

VEAUVARDIN, *to* FLORESTINE: Did you say…

> THE GUESTS *buzz in astonishment.*

FLORESTINE, *with a sneer*: Ha ha ha!… He forbids me! (*To* VEAUVARDIN, *taking a photograph from her pocket, handing it to him.*) Here, monsieur! Look at the wretch!

EDOUARD, *collapsing onto the armchair, up left, aside*: Ayyy!

VEAUVARDIN, *to* FLORESTINE: The picture?… (*Without looking at it..*) The one in the third drawer? Under the table linen? (*He makes some awkward mystical passes at her.*) Way back?… (*To* EDOUARD.) *Your* picture, you said!… You?… (*To* FLORESTINE.) You mean… (*Pointing to* EDOUARD.) Him?… He's the… My—

EDOUARD: No, no!… It's a coincidence… (*As* THE GUESTS *continue to voice their puzzlement.*) She has no more fluid!… (*To* FLORESTINE.) You have no more—

MADAME BEAUDELOCHE, *to* VEAUVARDIN: Monsieur! Will you please explain…

JEANNETTE: Yes… Please, papá…

VEAUVARDIN, *brandishing the picture, still without looking at it*: The wretch, whose picture I hold in my hand… The unprincipled cad who would trifle with this poor child's affection…

EDOUARD, *aside*: God help me!

VEAUVARDIN: …is none other than… (*Finally looking at it, surprised.*) … than… a fireman? (*Aside.*) My word!

EDOUARD *jumps to his feet as* THE GUESTS *utter a simultaneous "What?"*

FLORESTINE, *aside*: Damnation! Wrong pocket!

EDOUARD, *to* FLORESTINE, *in a whisper, a trifle piqued*: Who?… That fireman?… The one—

FLORESTINE, *to* EDOUARD, *in a whisper*: I decided to save your skin. Don't ask me why!

EDOUARD, *relieved, aside*: Sweet child!… (*He reaches into his pocket, aside.*) And here… Your letters… Now we're even!

He hands her a thick packet.

FLORESTINE, *looking at it, aside*: Money? (*Agape.*) There must be hundreds…

EDOUARD, *aside*: Damn! Wrong pocket!

VEAUVARDIN, *rather embarrassed*: Well now… I think it's time we were getting back to the business at hand! We have a marriage to arrange!

EDOUARD, *aside*: An expensive one, damn it!

VEAUVARDIN, *with a little laugh*: And that's no truffle!

MADAME BEAUDELOCHE, *to* JEANNETTE: And you know what, daughter dear? I'll even give you Florestine as a wedding present.

EDOUARD, *aside*: What?

MADAME BEAUDELOCHE: She's an absolute gem.

EDOUARD, *trying to object*: But…

MADAME BEAUDELOCHE, *continuing*: Serious as the day is long!… Not flighty, like the rest of them…

EDOUARD: But…

MADAME BEAUDELOCHE, *continuing*: That way we can keep her in the family!

EDOUARD: But we can't… We… I mean—

MADAME BEAUDELOCHE: Why not, Edouard?

EDOUARD: Because… Because she's getting married…

FLORESTINE: Me?

EDOUARD: To her fireman…

FLORESTINE: I…

EDOUARD, *whispering*: Marry him, or I'll strangle you! (*Aloud, pleasantly.*) Aren't you, Florestine?

FLORESTINE: I... I...

EDOUARD, *to MADAME BEAUDELOCHE*: See?... "Aye aye! Aye aye!" (*To THE GUESTS, with a shrug.*) Or maybe he's a sea captain. One or the other...

MADAME BEAUDELOCHE, *to FLORESTINE*: That handsome devil?... See? I knew there was something between you two! The neighbor's stew indeed!

FLORESTINE: But...

MADAME BEAUDELOCHE: And just to thank you for being such a dear, I'll take care of your dowry!

FLORESTINE: Oh, madame! Thank you... But...

MADAME BEAUDELOCHE, *pointing, good-naturedly*: But only if you change those drapes! How many times do I have to tell you!

VEAUVARDIN. *to FLORESTINE*: And I'll give you five percent of all the truffles you find!

> *THE GUESTS look at one another quizzically, with questions like: "What is he talking about?" "Five percent of what?" "What ever does he mean?" etc.*

JEANNETTE, MADAME BEAUDELOCHE, *and* **THE NOTARY**, *together*: Truffles?

EDOUARD, *to VEAUVARDIN*: I told you... Her fluid has dried up. No more fluid! Not a drop...

THE NOTARY, *holding out his upturned palm, looking up at the ceiling*: Oh?

EDOUARD, *to VEAUVARDIN, continuing*: You'll be lucky if she finds you a bloody potato!

> *THE GUESTS repeat their bemused mumbling.*

JEANNETTE, MADAME BEAUDELOCHE, *and* **THE NOTARY**, *together*: A potato?

EDOUARD: Just a little pleasantry... Between father and me! (*To THE NOTARY.*) Now what say we sign that contract!

THE NOTARY: Well, if you're sure... (*Under his breath.*) Truffles?... A bloody potato?... I never... In all my thirty years...

> *THE GUESTS all shout agreement with exclamations like "We're sure!" "Yes, we are!" "It's about time!" etc. THE NOTARY, still mumbling, crosses down left, to the little table, sits down, and prepares his papers. As THE GUESTS, MADAME BEAUDELOCHE, VEAUVARDIN, and JEANNETTE all gather round, EDOUARD and FLORESTINE hang back a bit.*

EDOUARD, *suddenly examining his jacket*: Oh my! (*To FLORESTINE.*) Mademoiselle... I say... I seem to have lost a button. Would you be so kind...

VEAUVARDIN, *calling*: We're waiting, son...

MADAME BEAUDELOCHE, *calling*: Stop diddling, Edouard!

EDOUARD: Right away, mammá... I'm coming... Right away...

> *He turns and casts one last look at FLORESTINE. Then, as THE GUESTS voice their encouragement, he joins them, down left, as the curtain falls amid their happy shouts.*

> *CURTAIN.*

Temper, Temper!, or A Bee or Not a Bee

(Un monsieur qui prend la mouche, 1852)

Eugène Labiche & Marc-Michel

Characters

BÉCHAMEL, a middle-aged widower

JOLICŒUR, his long-time friend and would-be traveling companion

ANTOINE DE BEAUJOLAIS, an elegant but eccentric young Parisian

PHILIPPE, Béchamel's outspoken domestic, almost part of the family

DOMINIQUE, Beaujolais's domestic and groom

CÉCILE, Béchamel's beautiful young daughter

A drawing room in the country. In the upstage wall, center, a door opening out, with occasional chairs on both sides. In each of the angled corners, up right and left, a door, opening out onto other rooms. In the stage left wall, center, an open window looking out onto the garden. Downstage left, a pedestal table with two chairs, facing each other. On the table, a bell and embroidery. Center stage, a loveseat. Stage right, center, against the wall, another table and chair. Other appropriate furnishings—carpet, lamps, pictures, etc.

At rise, it is forenoon. PHILIPPE *is seated at the pedestal table, down left, reading the newspaper aloud, not without difficulty.*

PHILIPPE, *reading*: "Alas, the fact remains, and bears frequent repetition: society, shaken to its very foundation, is rotten to the core…" *(Nodding.)* True… True… *(Reading.)* "And, if asked to offer a solution, we recuse ourselves and simply hold our tongues…" *(Spoken.)* "Recuse" my foot! Talk simple, damn it!… Then why scribble all this claptrap?… This… *(Reading.)* "France Since the Revolution…"

JOLICŒUR *appears at the door, upstage.*

JOLICŒUR, *entering*: Philippe, my good man…

PHILIPPE, *without budging*: Oh… It's you.

JOLICŒUR, *somewhat taken aback*: Why, yes…

PHILIPPE: Well, make yourself at home. *(Reading.)* "France Since the Revolution…" Of all the—

JOLICŒUR, *coming down center, interrupting*: Excuse me… If you don't mind…

PHILIPPE: Monsieur?

JOLICŒUR: Monsieur Béchamel…? Do you know where he is?

PHILIPPE: Of course I do. He's in his room. Where else would he be? *(Calling.)* Monsieur… Monsieur…

BECHAMEL'S VOICE, *offstage right*: What is it?

PHILIPPE: Your friend is here. Get a move on!

BECHAMEL'S VOICE: I'm coming…

PHILIPPE, *to* JOLICŒUR: He's coming.

JOLICŒUR: Yes… So I gather… *(As* PHILIPPE *returns to his paper.)* Ah! I see you have today's newspaper.

He reaches for it but PHILIPPE *pulls it away.*

PHILIPPE: Yes… *(Grumbling.)* And I'm still reading it!

JOLICŒUR: Oh…

PHILIPPE, *shaking his head, reading*: "France Since the Revolution…"

BECHAMEL *appears at the door, up right, wearing a beret.*

BECHAMEL, *entering*: Ah! Jolicœur… How nice to see you! *(Coming down center, joining him.)* Will you join me for lunch?

JOLICŒUR: Impossible! At two o'clock I have to take my pills. On an empty stomach…

BECHAMEL: Pills? You're not ailing, I hope?

JOLICŒUR: Heavens no! *(Thumping his chest.)* The Rock of Gibraltar, if I do say so myself!

BECHAMEL: Then why—

JOLICŒUR: Just a precaution… The guidebook says that, when you're going to take a trip—

BECHAMEL: A trip? You?... Where? When?

JOLICŒUR: Italy, old chap... Florence, Rome, Venice...

BECHAMEL: But...

JOLICŒUR: I leave in three days for *il paese del sole...*

BECHAMEL: What? Shame on you!... Italy? Without me?

PHILIPPE, *impatiently, getting up and brandishing the paper, aside*: Idiots!... "France Since the Revolution..." Bah!

JOLICŒUR, *to BECHAMEL*: You?

PHILIPPE sits down on the chair on the other side of the table.

BECHAMEL, *to JOLICŒUR*: But you promised to wait....

PHILIPPE, *aside, still grumbling*: What garbage they print!

JOLICŒUR, *to BECHAMEL*: Wait? For you? *(Laughing sarcastically.)* Ha ha ha!... I've been waiting for almost twenty years already! If you think I'm going to wait for twenty more...

BECHAMEL: But whose fault is that? We almost left once...

JOLICŒUR: Yes... In our bachelor days!

BECHAMEL, *nostalgically*: Almost...

JOLICŒUR: The tickets were bought... We're ready to leave...

BECHAMEL, *nodding*: And suddenly I get married! Not exactly my idea, but still...

JOLICŒUR: And you ask me to wait a month, for your honeymoon.

BECHAMEL: It was the least I could do!

JOLICŒUR: So, of course, I say yes. Goodbye tickets!... But it's only money... And what's a month? I could wait.

BECHAMEL: And my honeymoon, after all...

JOLICŒUR: But in no time your wife has a... a bun in the oven!... Wearing her apron high, old chap!

BECHAMEL: So...? Whose fault...?

JOLICŒUR: Not mine, I'm sure!

PHILIPPE, *getting up, grumbling, going upstage and sitting on the chair to the left of the door, aside*: Damn! *(Reading.)* "France Since the Revolution..." Did you ever...

JOLICŒUR, *to BECHAMEL*: So you ask for more time...

BECHAMEL: But I couldn't very well leave the country before I met my child. Before I gave it a hug, at least...

JOLICŒUR: Of course not! So, again, bye-bye tickets! Money? Pfff!

BECHAMEL, *nodding*: Pfff!

JOLICŒUR: Your daughter arrives... You give her a hug... And I say: "Well, now we can leave! Are you ready?" And what do you tell me? *(Mimicking.)* "Let's wait until she's weaned..." Then: "Let's wait until she teethes..." Then: "Let's wait until she finishes school..." So! Wait, wait, wait!... I'm still waiting.

BECHAMEL: Good old Jolicœur!

JOLICŒUR: Yes! "Old..." And getting older... And poorer... I can't spend my life buying tickets... I mean—

BECHAMEL: This time, mon ami, just a few more days... I promise! Just give me a few more days, and we're on our way!

JOLICŒUR: Oh? What for? What is it now?

BECHAMEL, *confidentially*: If you must know, it's Cécile… *(Putting his forefinger to his lips.)* I'm marrying her off!… There! Now you know.

PHILIPPE, *getting up and coming down left, to the table, sitting on the chair to the right, still grumbling*: Of all the damn trash… *(Reading.)* "France Since the Revolution…"

JOLICŒUR, *to* BECHAMEL: What? Another marriage? Is that all you people do?

BECHAMEL: But, my Cécile…

JOLICŒUR: You're sure you won't want to wait to give your grandchild a little hug?

BECHAMEL: Please, Jolicœur! The husband I've chosen is a man of honor! I'm sure he can wait.

JOLICŒUR, *wryly*: No doubt! So were you!

BECHAMEL, *ignoring his remark*: In fact, I'm surprised I haven't heard from him yet. He's had more than enough time… *(Coming down left.)* Philippe!

PHILIPPE, *without looking up*: Monsieur?

BECHAMEL: A letter didn't come for me this morning, did it?

PHILIPPE: Yes, monsieur.

BECHAMEL: It did?… Then why on earth didn't you… *(Impatiently.)* Where is it?

PHILIPPE: In my pocket… *(Nodding toward his right pocket.)* That one…

BECHAMEL, *reaching out*: Well?

PHILIPPE, *without budging*: Take it… Just leave my pipe.

BECHAMEL, *reaching into his pocket, taking out the letter*: Thank you!… *(Opening it.)* Ah! It is! *(To* JOLICŒUR.*)* My son-in-law to be!

PHILIPPE, *getting up, moving upstage, aside*: Enough is enough! *(Aloud, to* BECHAMEL.*)* Monsieur…

BECHAMEL, *scanning the letter*: Hmm?

PHILIPPE, *to* BECHAMEL: I'm quitting! *(Aside.)* I can't take any more…

BECHAMEL, *hardly listening*: Of course…

PHILIPPE, *aloud*: Back to the country, where they write important things…

BECHAMEL: Whatever you say…

PHILIPPE: Whose cow got married… Whose daughter had calves…

BECHAMEL: Philippe?

PHILIPPE: I mean… *(Waving the paper.)* Damn fools!… "France Since the Revolution" my foot…

He exits, up center.

JOLICŒUR, *watching him leave*: Not in a very good mood, your domestic!

BECHAMEL: Philippe?… Oh, don't mind him! He's my godson. Like one of the family… *(Finishing the letter.)* Ah! Bravo, Jolicœur! *(Joining him center, holding it up.)* It's all arranged! He accepts!

JOLICŒUR: "He," Béchamel?

BECHAMEL: Hollandez… The lawyer… He accepts the conditions. They're as good as married! He's coming today to discuss it over lunch.

JOLICŒUR: And how does she feel about it? After all…

BECHAMEL: Cécile?… I haven't told her, but she's met him. Believe me, she'll be delighted! Why shouldn't she be? A lawyer… And a rich one…

JOLICŒUR: Good! Then when do we leave?

BECHAMEL: Well, today is the first. She'll be married on the fifteenth. And on the sixteenth—

JOLICŒUR, *finishing his sentence*: We clear out our bowels…

BECHAMEL, *not sure he has heard correctly*: We what?

JOLICŒUR: The guidebook says… When you're going to take a trip… You have to be sure—

BECHAMEL: Fine! If you insist… *(Aside.)* His bowels, not mine! *(Aloud, to JOLICŒUR.)* And on the seventeenth—

JOLICŒUR: We leave!

BECHAMEL: Exactly! *(Carried away.)* Ah! Italy!… Rome! Florence!…

JOLICŒUR: Venice!… The canals, the gondolas…

BECHAMEL: The signoras, the signorinas…

JOLICŒUR: And we'll take our flannel pajamas. The nights can be chilly.

BECHAMEL: If you say so, Jolicœur!

JOLICŒUR: Not me… The guidebook…

BECHAMEL: Aha…

JOLICŒUR: Good! Then it's decided! I'll go reserve the tickets. But I'm warning you, old chap… This is the last time! Put me off again, and—

BECHAMEL: No problem, mon ami! *(He holds up the letter.)* Hollandez says yes, I told you… Cécile will jump for joy! I marry her off, and…

JOJLICŒUR: And the next day, off we go! Agreed?

BECHAMEL: Agreed!

They shake hands.

JOLICŒUR: Ah! Venezia la bella! *(Muttering as he turns to leave.)* Roma… Firenze… *(Stopping at the door, up center, to BECHAMEL.)* Arrivederci!

BECHAMEL: Arri… Aver… Avider… *(Laughing.)* Whatever…

JOLICŒUR: The signoras… The signorinas…

He exits, still muttering happily.

BECHAMEL, *looking at the letter, then taking out his pocket-watch and consulting it as the clock strikes twelve*: He'll be here in less than an hour, I imagine. Just enough time to have a chat with Cécile… *(CECILE appears at the door, up left.)* Ah… Speak of the—

CECILE, *coming center*: Papá… Do you have the key to the pantry? There are no more macaroons for dessert.

BECHAMEL: The dessert will have to wait. I have something more important than macaroons to discuss.

CECILE: You do? *(Aside.)* What ever can it be?

BECHAMEL: My child… *(Motioning her to sit down on the loveseat.)* The moment has come for a serious and solemn talk.

CECILE: It has? *(Aside.)* Goodness me!

She sits down.

BECHAMEL, *sitting down beside her, gravely*: Cécile… Have you ever thought that one day you might take a husband?

CECILE: Oh yes, papá! All the time!

BECHAMEL: Well… The hour has struck…

CECILE: I know. It's just noon…

BECHAMEL: No, no… I mean… The time has come! The time to get married…

CECILE, *clapping her hands*: Oh, papá! Is he nice?

BECHAMEL: Who?

CECILE: My fiancé! The young man!

BECHAMEL, *aside*: Young?… Well… *(Aloud.)* A perfect match… Serious, stable…

CECILE, *with a little pout*: Oh…

BECHAMEL: With a good business head on his shoulders… And he owns a hundred and eight shares of Pyrenees Gypsum. An excellent investment…

CECILE: That's not what I mean, papá! What does he look like?… Is he blond? Does he have a mustache?

BECHAMEL, *getting up*: He… He looks like a lawyer. Because that's what he is… A very distinguished lawyer…

CECILE: Oh?

BECHAMEL: And one that you know… At least, you've met him.

CECILE: I have?

BECHAMEL: Yes… Can't you guess?

CECILE: No… I'm afraid—

BECHAMEL: Well, it's… it's… You're going to be delighted, Cécile… It's Hollandez!

CECILE, *recoiling*: What?… *(Standing up.)* Hollandez?

BECHAMEL: Why yes… What's the matter?

CECILE: But… But… Thank you just the same, papá!… "Mademoiselle Béchamel" is bad enough! *(Mimicking.)* "Oh! I just love your sauce! Will you give me the recipe?"

BECHAMEL: Cécile…

CECILE, *continuing*: But "Madame Hollandaise…" No! Thank you just the same!

BECHAMEL: But he spells it D-E-Z!

CECILE: I don't care! You can't hear how it's spelled!

BECHAMEL: Really, Cécile…

CECILE: Besides, he's not young at all!

BECHAMEL: Cécile…

CECILE: And he's cross-eyed! *(Looking for a convincing argument.)* He sings off-key…

BECHAMEL: He does?… I don't see…

CECILE: We could never sing duets! *(Continuing.)* And he's bow-legged, papá!… And… And he's always talking Latin!

BECHAMEL: But… The glorious language of Cicero…

CECILE: I don't care! If that's what I wanted I would marry Cicero himself!

BECHAMEL: Well…

CECILE, *at a loss for words*: And… And he… And I…

BECHAMEL: Please, Cécile! Just think…

PHILIPPE appears at the door, up center.

PHILIPPE: Monsieur…

BECHAMEL: What is it?

PHILIPPE: There are two horses outside...

BECHAMEL: What?

PHILIPPE: And some man is on one of them.

BECHAMEL: Hollandez?

CECILE, *aside*: Oh my!

PHILIPPE, *disdainfully*: And his domestic is on the other. He says he wants to talk to you.

BECHAMEL: His domestic?

PHILIPPE: The man... *(Holding out a calling-card.)* His card, monsieur...

BECHAMEL, *reading*: "Antoine de Beaujolais..." Who on earth...?

PHILIPPE: And he says he's in a hurry. He can't wait.

BECHAMEL: Very well! Show him in... *(Aside.)* Of all times...

PHILIPPE, *calling offstage*: All right, you... You can come in! *(ANTOINE appears at the door, up center, stopping at the threshold.)* Come on! Come on!

ANTOINE enters. He is dressed in elegant riding attire—jacket, white vest, white gloves, black cravat—and carrying a riding-crop in one hand and his cap in the other.

ANTOINE, *to PHILIPPE, with a sneer*: I say... I should think you might announce me in a rather less cavalier fashion! *(Aside.)* Boor!

PHILIPPE, *under his breath*: Bah!

ANTOINE, *under his breath*: Bah!

BECHAMEL, *approaching ANTOINE, taking off his beret*: Excuse me, monsieur... To what do I owe the honor...

ANTOINE, *taking off his gloves, putting them in a pocket*: Monsieur Béchamel?

BECHAMEL, *nodding*: At your service... But, may I ask—

ANTOINE, *nodding*: Charmed, I'm sure... *(Noticing CECILE.)* And mademoiselle is your daughter, I presume? *(Bowing.)* Permit me to offer her my profuse and profound respects.

CECILE, *with a little bow*: Monsieur... *(Aside.)* My, my! Isn't he polite!

She sits at the table, down left, striking a coy pose, and begins embroidering.

BECHAMEL, *to ANTOINE*: I believe you wanted to speak with me, Monsieur... *(Looking at the card.)* Monsieur Beaujolais...

ANTOINE: De... De...

BECHAMEL, *looking at the card again, correcting*: Monsieur de Beaujolais... "De..."

ANTOINE: Quite... I've come all the way from Paris. On horseback, I might add...

BECHAMEL: Yes... So I see...

ANTOINE: Very bracing, despite the distance... Good exercise, monsieur... For myself and my horse as well...

BECHAMEL, *beginning to grow impatient*: I'm sure... But if you don't mind...

PHILIPPE, who has been watching with curiosity, gives a shrug and moves left, by the open window.

ANTOINE: Of course! Of course! *(Assuming a more formal tone.)* Monsieur, I have the pleasure of apprising you... If I may take the liberty, that is...

He stops for a dramatic pause.

BECHAMEL: Yes! Do, by all means…

ANTOINE: Of apprising you, monsieur…

He stops again.

BECHAMEL: Go on…

PHILIPPE, *to ANTOINE*: Apprise him, for the love of—

ANTOINE, *to PHILIPPE, interrupting*: I beg your pardon, lackey! *(To BECHAMEL.)* Of apprising you…

PHILIPPE, *aside*: Lackey, my foot!

ANTOINE: …of a most unpleasant and utterly distasteful occurrence…

BECHAMEL: Oh?

CECILE, *aside*: What ever can he mean?

ANTOINE, *continuing*: One you will find as disagreeable as I…

PHILIPPE, *nodding, aside*: As disagreeable as you…

BECHAMEL, *to ANTOINE*: Go on…

PHILIPPE, *aside*: Maybe even more!

ANTOINE, *clearing his throat, assuring himself that he has an audience*: Three months ago, monsieur… One lovely spring evening… *(Lyrically.)* The purple shadows spreading over the horizon were flecked with the sun's last lingering rays of gold…

BECHAMEL, *taking out his watch and looking at it*: Monsieur…

ANTOINE: Of course! Of course! *(Continuing.)* I was walking along the boulevard… In front of the Café du Midi…

BECHAMEL, *nodding*: Aha…

ANTOINE: The Café du Midi, monsieur… In Paris…

BECHAMEL: Yes… I know it well…

Out of patience, he puts his beret back on his head.

ANTOINE, *looking him up and down for a moment with a sneer, apparently shocked by his impoliteness, and pointedly putting on his cap, continuing*: All of a sudden, a friend of mine comes by. Before my very eyes… Naturally, I remove my hat to greet him. *(He takes off his cap.)* I'm extremely well-bred, monsieur…

BECHAMEL: I don't doubt it… And the distasteful occurrence?

PHILIPPE, *aside*: Damn chatterbox!

ANTOINE, *seeing that BECHAMEL is leaving on his beret, putting back his cap*: I'm coming to it.

BECHAMEL: Aha…

ANTOINE: So, as I said, I remove my hat. But, instead of returning my courtesy… *(With a look.)* My elementary courtesy, monsieur… The wretch just keeps walking…

PHILIPPE, *approaching him*: Tsk tsk tsk!

ANTOINE, *to PHILIPPE*: Excuse me, my friend! I'm not accustomed to relating my adventures to the help! *(To BECHAMEL.)* Right past me! Without so much as a glance in my direction…

BECHAMEL: Yes… I see… But—

ANTOINE: As you can imagine, I was cut to the quick, and I went running after him. As anyone would do, under the circumstances…

BECHAMEL, *nodding, bemused*: And…?

ANTOINE: A moment later, I was grasping him by the coattails. He stops, monsieur, and turns around… I take one look, and who do you suppose is standing there in front of me?

BECHAMEL, *impatiently*: Your friend! Who else…?

ANTOINE, *with a victorious little laugh*: Ha ha ha! Not at all!… An absolute stranger!… I had made a mistake!

BECHAMEL: Aha… *(Aside.)* Why on earth…

ANTOINE, *continuing*: Well, he looks me in the eye, and he asks me: "Who the devil are you?…" Naturally, I tell him the truth. "I'm the gentleman who just greeted you in front of the Café du Midi…" "But I don't know you," he tells me…

BECHAMEL: And…?

ANTOINE, *continuing*: "I don't know you either. But that didn't stop me from greeting you, monsieur. And very politely, I might add! Now then, are you going to return my greeting? Yes or no?" "Go jump in the lake!" he tells me… So, you can see, he's not only impolite, but he's stupid as well! What lake? There's not a lake for miles around…

BECHAMEL, *aside*: How much longer…

ANTOINE: "You're a boor," I tell him. *(To BECHAMEL.)* Because anyone who doesn't take off his hat and return a greeting is a boor! A common, ill-bred boor, monsieur…

CECILE, *to herself*: I must say, he's different!

ANTOINE, *continuing*: Unless he isn't wearing one, that is… In which case… Well, to make a long story short…

BECHAMEL's jaw drops in obvious doubt.

CECILE, *to herself*: I like him!

ANTOINE: As I was saying… We stand there exchanging several disagreeable epithets.

CECILE, *to herself*: Oh yes! I do!

ANTOINE, *continuing*: You might not think I know any, monsieur…

BECHAMEL, *with a casual wave*: Pfff!

ANTOINE: But I assure you… Well, as soon as a crowd has gathered, I seize him by the throat, and I tell him: "This should teach you to have some manners, my friend! *(Shaking the imaginary individual.)* There's a right way and a wrong way to behave in society!"

BECHAMEL: Very interesting, monsieur… But I still don't quite see…

ANTOINE: I'm getting to the point… *(Offended.)* Unless, of course, I'm boring you…

BECHAMEL: No, no…

ANTOINE: If I am, I can leave.

PHILIPPE: No, please… Go on!

ANTOINE, *to PHILIPPE, sarcastically*: You're much too kind! *(Aside.)* He's beginning to get on my nerves, this domestic! *(Aloud, to BECHAMEL.)* Well, believe it or not… Two days later… On March 27th… Or was it the 28th?

BECHAMEL: Yes, yes… Whenever…

ANTOINE: Now that I think of it, it may have been the 29th… Because the next day was the 30th… Or was it?

BECHAMEL, *aside*: Good God!

He turns the chair across from CECILE facing center, and sits down on it, impatiently.

ANTOINE, *going up center, taking the chair to the left of the door, placing it next to BECHAMEL, facing forward, and, sitting down, continuing*: Yes, I'm sure… Well, on the 29th, can you guess what happened? *(Before BECHAMEL has a chance to react.)* I was watering my hounds, monsieur, when, all of a sudden, a gentleman appeared… If I may use the term loosely… If I had known he was a process-server I'd have set them on him, for sure!

BECHAMEL, *nodding*: Aha…

ANTOINE: At any rate, I found myself summoned to appear before the tribunal to answer a charge of aggravated assault and attempted murder!

PHILIPPE: No!

ANTOINE: And all because that ill-bred imbecile didn't take off his hat!… So! What do you think of that?

BECHAMEL: I think it's… *(Aside.)* Rather long! *(Aloud, to ANTOINE.)* It's outrageous, monsieur!

He stands up and moves up left.

PHILIPPE, *coming down and sitting on the chair just left by BECHAMEL, to ANTOINE, familiarly*: If you ask me, it's hilarious! All that for a goddamn hat!

ANTOINE, *standing up, replying, archly*: But I did not ask you, my friend! And I'll thank you to go and jump in the lake!

PHILIPPE: Ha ha!… What lake?

ANTOINE, *to BECHAMEL*: Your flunky is rather familiar, don't you think?

BECHAMEL, *to ANTOINE*: My… Philippe?…

PHILIPPE, *to ANTOINE, laughing*: There isn't a lake for miles around! *(Taking ANTOINE's chair, replacing it upstage, and coming back down beside him, aside.)* You said so yourself!

BECHAMEL, *to ANTOINE*: He's part of the family!

ANTOINE: Yes… Well, he's not part of mine… *(Approaching BECHAMEL, up left.)* At any rate, monsieur… When one has an encounter with the law, the first thing one does… *(Noticing that PHILIPPE, following behind him, is listening, he casts an annoyed look at him and moves away, behind the loveseat.)* The first thing one does is to find oneself a lawyer… *(Waiting for a reaction.)* Which is precisely what I did… The first one who came my way… *(Pausing again, expectantly, as BECHAMEL consults his watch without a word.)* If I'm boring you, monsieur, I can leave.

PHILIPPE: No, no…

BECHAMEL: Please… Go on…

ANTOINE: If you insist… *(Sarcastically, to PHILIPPE.)* Both of you… *(To BECHAMEL.)* When we arrive before the bench, my lawyer stands up. Vile creature that he was!… I use the expression advisedly!… "Vile creature…" To put it mildly…

He stops as he notices BECHAMEL distractedly scratching the sleeve of his jacket.

BECHAMEL, Yes… I'm listening…

ANTOINE, *annoyed*: Are you sure? I can wait until you finish your toilette, if you prefer…

BECHAMEL, *holding up the sleeve*: It's nothing… Just a bit of sealing wax…

ANTOINE: Oh? (*Aside, looking up at the ceiling.*) Wax the ceiling, do they?

BECHAMEL: Monsieur…

ANTOINE, *aside*: How elegant…

BECHAMEL: You were saying…

ANTOINE, *aloud, continuing*: Yes, as I was saying… My vile creature of a lawyer recounts the events… Down to the last detail… He waves his hands in every direction… Reads scraps of paper… Spouts Latin at every turn…

BECHAMEL, *growing more impatient*: Yes… Yes…

ANTOINE: And incorrectly, I might add… Utterly atrocious pronunciation…

BECHAMEL: No doubt, monsieur…

ANTOINE, *continuing*: Well, so far so good… He had a right to do his little act before the judges. But then, all of a sudden, what does he do? (*Without giving BECHAMEL a chance to reply.*) I'll tell you what he does, monsieur! He points his finger at me, and he shouts: (*Mimicking.*) "No, Your Honors! My client is no wild beast, thirsting to glut on the blood of humankind! He is no murderer!… A madman? Yes!… A featherbrain? No doubt!… A fuss-pot? I agree…"

CECILE, *aside*: A fuss-pot?

ANTOINE, *continuing*: "Disagreeable, ill-mannered…" (*In his own voice, to BECHAMEL.*) Ill-mannered, monsieur! Me!… Did you ever…? (*Mimicking.*) "An ill-tempered blackguard who would bite your head off at the slightest provocation… Indeed… Indeed…" And he went on in that manner for three-quarters of an hour! And they laughed, monsieur!… Laughed… (*Imitating.*) "Ha ha ha!… Ha ha ha!…"

CECILE, *aside, laughing, as BECHAMEL and PHILIPPE laugh as well*: I should think…

ANTOINE, *angrily*: Like a pack of hyenas… Braying like donkeys!

PHILIPPE, *laughing, aside*: Make up your mind, damn it!

ANTOINE, *continuing*: In a vulgar and thoroughly tasteless display!

PHILIPPE, *aside*: Which was it? Donkeys or hyenas?

ANTOINE, *to BECHAMEL, as he and the others try to control themselves*: Quite like your own at this moment, if I may say…

BECHAMEL: I… I beg your pardon… I—

ANTOINE, *coldly*: Yes, well… I was acquitted. I won my case.

CECILE *and* **PHILIPPE**, *together: Oh?*

BECHAMEL, settling down: Aha?… Well, I'm sure that made you happy…

ANTOINE, indignant: Happy? To listen to a cackling lout, whom I'm paying by the hour, insult me by the minute? Rip me up and down?… Besmirch my good name?…

BECHAMEL: But you won your—

ANTOINE, *interrupting*: Happy? (*With a sarcastic little laugh.*) Ha ha!… I was furious!

PHILIPPE, *aside*: Idiot!

ANTOINE: Fit to be tied, monsieur… So I run to confront him. And he stands there, smiling… Like this… (*Mimicking, with a grin.*) "Well, mon ami…" (*In* *his own voice.)* "Ami?… Ami?… Here! Take your fifty francs, you… you wretch! You'll pay, understand?"

BECHAMEL: What?… Your lawyer… The one…

CECILE, *standing up*: The one who won—

ANTOINE: Won? Won?

PHILIPPE: Won!

BECHAMEL: The one who won your acquittal…

ANTOINE: My acquittal be damned!

CECILE, *putting her hand over her mouth*: Oh my…

ANTOINE, *snapping his fingers*: A fig for my acquittal!… So I give him my card, and a few days later we meet on the field of honor! Yesterday, in fact…

BECHAMEL, *aside*: A duel? *(To PHILIPPE, in a whisper.)* Now he'll never shut up! Why on earth did you let him in?

PHILIPPE, *whispering*: Let him talk! I'm enjoying it!

BECHAMEL, *whispering*: Maybe you are… But Hollandez will be here any minute…

ANTOINE, *coming round in front of the loveseat, assuming a dueling stance*: We take our places… Assume the stance…

BECHAMEL, *to ANTOINE*: But monsieur…

ANTOINE, *gesturing appropriately*: We cross swords… Tic tac! Tic tac!…

CECILE: Oh…

ANTOINE: My adversary turns… And voilà!… I plunge my blade—

CECILE: Good heavens!

BECHAMEL: Into his heart?

ANTOINE: No, no… Into his buttocks… Buttock, that is… One… The right one…

PHILIPPE, *aside*: The wrong one, you mean!

ANTOINE: I told you, he turned around…

BECHAMEL: Aha…

ANTOINE, *satisfied that he has now finished his story*: So!… *(To BECHAMEL.)* There you are, monsieur! The whole truth and nothing but the truth… Nothing to do now but take my leave… With my respects… *(Taking off his cap, to CECILE, with a nod.)* Mademoiselle… *(Noticing that BECHAMEL doesn't take off his beret, he puts his cap back on and gives him a little wave.)* Monsieur…

> *He moves upstage, glowering at PHILIPPE as he passes, and arrives at the door, up center.*

BECHAMEL, *as he begins to exit, calling*: Monsieur! Wait!

ANTOINE, *turning*: I beg your pardon?

BECHAMEL: You… You came all the way from Paris…?

ANTOINE: Yes… *(Taking a step or two toward him.)* And on horseback…

BECHAMEL: And just to tell me about your trial? And your duel?

ANTOINE: Precisely!

BECHAMEL: But… But why? Is there something I should know? Something I've missed…

ANTOINE: Is there… *(Suddenly slapping his forehead.)* Ah! You're right, monsieur… I seem to have omitted a detail.

BECHAMEL, *aside*: Good God! Not another story…

ANTOINE: About my lawyer… My adversary…

BECHAMEL: Yes… Yes…

ANTOINE: …who turned around…

BECHAMEL: Go on!… Please!

ANTOINE: Monsieur Hollandez, monsieur… Your son-in-law elect!

BECHAMEL, } *together*: { What?
CECILE, } *together*: { Good heavens!
PHILIPPE, } *together*: { Goddamn!

BECHAMEL, *furious*: And you dare show your face? You dare cross my threshold, still dripping with his blood?

ANTOINE, *examining himself, aside*: Dripping…?

BECHAMEL: For shame!

ANTOINE: At any rate, no need to be concerned… He'll be up and about in three months, they tell me… More or less…

CECILE *and* **BECHAMEL**, *together*: Three months!

ANTOINE, *solemnly*: I asked him if he had any final requests… Well, semi-final… "Get on your horse," he said, "since I can't get on mine…"

BECHAMEL: But…

ANTOINE, *in his own voice*: Under the circumstances… *(Continuing.)* "Go visit my future father-in-law, Monsieur Béchamel. Explain that I'm unable to join him for lunch tomorrow… Because of my—"

PHILIPPE, CECILE, and BECHAMEL interrupt in rapid succession.

PHILIPPE: But…

CECILE: But…

BECHAMEL: But…

ANTOINE, *continuing*: "…my nasty scratch…"

PHILIPPE, *continuing*: …three months…

CECILE, *continuing*: …that's frightful…

BECHAMEL, *continuing*: I'd better write him a note, poor chap! As a balm to his wound…

ANTOINE, *aside*: If he sits on it, perhaps! *(Aloud, to BECHAMEL.)* Most considerate, monsieur… I'll be happy to see that he receives it, if you like.

BECHAMEL: Thank you… I'll just be a minute. *(Moving up right, shaking ANTOINE's hand in passing.)* Ah! What a barbaric custom, these duels! When will we wipe it from the face of the earth?

He exits quickly, up right, as CECILE, following, stops at the door.

ANTOINE, *thinking he is replying to BECHAMEL*: A noble thought, monsieur… *(He holds out his hand.)* Worthy of a noble heart…

PHILIPPE, *grasping his hand*: Still… Wounding his son-in-law…

ANTOINE, *realizing his mistake, pulling his hand away with a shout*: You?

PHILIPPE: "Elect," that is… But…

ANTOINE: Go jump in the lake!

PHILIPPE, *continuing*: ...it wasn't very nice!

ANTOINE: I'll be happy to help you find one!

PHILIPPE, *shaking his head, as he moves up center*: Tsk tsk tsk!... Not nice... Not nice at all, monsieur...

He exits.

ANTOINE, *up center, to himself*: How he does get on my nerves, that domestic!

CECILE, up right, approaches him.

CECILE, *timidly*: Monsieur...

ANTOINE, *taking off his cap*: Mademoiselle... *(To himself.)* No doubt a well-chosen reproach from the fiancée...

CECILE: That wound... Is it serious?

ANTOINE: Hardly! And not very noble either, I'm afraid! It's not a scar he'll be able to wear with pride!

CECILE, *with a refined little laugh*: No...

ANTOINE: If I may say, mademoiselle... You must find me rather... Well, something of a brute...

CECILE, *quickly replying*: Oh no! Not at all, monsieur!

ANTOINE: But your marriage, I mean... Postponed like this... You must be—

CECILE, *interrupting, categorically*: Delighted!

ANTOINE, *surprised*: Oh?

CECILE: Really, monsieur!... A fifty-year-old... And who's cross-eyed...

ANTOINE: Yes, but... Only in one eye... The left, if I recall... The side by the heart...

CECILE: Still, I really would prefer someone who isn't cross-eyed at all!

ANTOINE: Oh? I say...

CECILE: Not at all, monsieur!

ANTOINE, *aside*: She was looking at me!

CECILE, *continuing*: In either eye...

ANTOINE, *continuing, aside*: I could swear... She... *(Aloud, to CECILE.)* Mademoiselle... I accept... *(As CECILE makes an almost imperceptible little gesture.)* ...your appreciation and your thanks... I'm happy to have been of service. Unintentionally, but still...

CECILE, *with a bow*: Monsieur...

ANTOINE, *returning the bow, more deeply*: Mademoiselle... *(Aside, moving right, as she moves up left, toward the door.)* Charming young thing!

CECILE, *aside*: What a pleasant young man! *(Aloud, bowing to him again.)* Monsieur...

ANTOINE, *bowing even more deeply*: Mademoiselle...

CECILE, *to herself*: If only...

She exits, up left, sighing as she goes.

ANTOINE, *alone, watching her leave, to himself*: That's one little lady who could turn this bachelor's head!... Bah! No marriage for me, I'm afraid! *(Taking his watch from a pocket, looking at it impatiently.)* How long is he going to take to write that letter? *(Beginning to pace.)* Seventeen times I've tried, and each one… *(With a wave.)* Pfff! Up in smoke… And always because of the father, thank you!… I certainly have a knack!… Nothing but grumps and grouches… Without a patient bone in their bodies… *(Interrupting his train of thought, looking toward the door, up right, impatiently.)* How long is that imbecile going to take? *(Continuing.)* Why couldn't they be like me? Easygoing… Calm… Always in control… Take the other day, for example… *(Stopping, down center.)* There I was, walking along Rue du Coq… In the rain… And behind me I hear a woman saying to her husband… At least, I suppose he was… "Why didn't you take an umbrella, you idiot?" Yes, he must have been her husband… And he says: "An umbrella? Please! Nothing makes a man look more like a fool!" A fool! That's what he said… And who was carrying one? I was!… So I ask you… A problem? Well, it could have been… And a serious one!… But I didn't say a word… Always in control… Cool, calm, and collected… *(Moving up right, glaring at the door.)* Damnation! Where is that Béchamel? What does he take me for? Some vulgar merchant, selling my wares? I go out of my way to bring him some news… Nice unpleasant news… And he keeps me here, cooling my heels! *(Growing angrier by the minute.)* Because that's what he's doing… Anyone who would receive me the way he did… No manners at all! That's his problem! Putting his beret back on, and as obvious as you please!… Still, I didn't say a word! Always in control! *(Stamping his foot.)* Always, goddammit! Always, you hear me?

DOMINIQUE enters, up center, his cap on his head.

DOMINIQUE, *thinking the remark is meant for him, puzzled*: Monsieur?

ANTOINE, *still cap in hand, angrily, to DOMINIQUE*: I thought I told you to go water the horses.

DOMINIQUE: I wanted to tell monsieur—

ANTOINE, *interrupting*: Young man! Your cap…

DOMINIQUE: Monsieur?

ANTOINE: I find it rather odd that it is still on your head, while mine is in my hand!

DOMINQUE, *naively*: Oh, I don't mind. Monsieur can put his on if he wants.

ANTOINE: Are you trying to irk me? *(Aside)* Control… Control… *(Aloud.)* Take it off, this instant!

DOMINIQUE, *complying*: Yes, monsieur.

ANTOINE: Now then, you were saying…

DOMINIQUE: The horses are ready. Whenever monsieur would like to leave…

ANTOINE, *to himself, annoyed*: And that letter of his? *(Looking up right.)* "A minute," he said!… *(Aloud.)* Dominique!

DOMINIQUE: Monsieur?

ANTOINE: Count to sixty…

DOMINIQUE: Count…?

ANTOINE: To sixty, I said!… To twenty, three times…

DOMINIQUE, *embarrassed*: Very good, monsieur… *(He begins counting on his fingers.)* One, two, three…

When he arrives at "ten" he sits down, takes off a shoe, and begins to take off the stocking.

ANTOINE, *appalled*: What are you doing?

DOMINIQUE: Monsieur said to twenty…

ANTOINE: Never mind! Never mind!… Put them back on!

DOMINIQUE, *complying, standing up*: Yes, monsieur.

ANTOINE, *to himself, looking up right as he paces, impatiently*: Where the devil… Is that any way to treat a guest? *(Aloud.)* Dominique!

DOMINIQUE: Monsieur?

ANTOINE, *putting on his cap, pulling it down, sharply, over his ears*: Come! *(In a huff.)* We're leaving!

DOMINIQUE, *doing likewise*: Very good, monsieur…

They exit, up center, leaving the door ajar. A moment later, BECHAMEL *enters, up right.*

BECHAMEL, *coming center, waving a letter*: Terribly sorry to keep you… I… *(Looking around.)* Now where do you suppose…? Hmm! He couldn't wait another minute? *(Going to the window, left, looking out.)* Bah! There he goes, galloping off… Oh well… I'll send it by post. At least, no more stories!

JOLICŒUR *enters, up center.*

JOLICŒUR: There!

BECHAMEL: Ah! Jolicœur…

JOLICŒUR, *joining him, down left*: It's done!

BECHAMEL: It is?… What is?

JOLICŒUR: Our tickets… I've just sent a wire to Paris to reserve them.

BECHAMEL: Ah…

JOLICŒUR: With my deposit… Eighty-three francs…

BECHAMEL: But… But Jolicœur, mon ami… I… That is… It's impossible… I can't leave now…

JOLICŒUR, *unable to believe his ears*: What?

BECHAMEL: Not for three months… The wedding… It has to be postponed… My son-in-law turned around!

JOLICŒUR: What are you talking about?… "Turned around"? You mean he changed his mind? Got cold feet?

BECHAMEL: No… His feet had nothing to do with it… In his duel… Monsieur de Beaujolais's sword got him right in the… *(Pointing.)* Right in the—

JOLICŒUR: Did you say "Beaujolais"? Antoine de Beaujolais?

BECHAMEL: Yes… He just left… Do you know him?

JOLICŒUR: Know him? Of course I do! He was a tenant of mine for two years. A delightful fellow… Always paid his rent in advance! I'm so sorry I missed him…

BECHAMEL: Oh? And why is that?

JOLICŒUR: Nothing… Just an idea that I've had running around my head… *(*BECHAMEL *gives him an inquisitive look.)* If you must know, I thought he would make a perfect match for your daughter.

BECHAMEL: Him?… Come now! The man is as bizarre as… Him?

JOLICŒUR: Beaujolais?… Nonsense! I don't know anyone more agreeable, more easygoing, more… He paid his rent in advance, I tell you!

BECHAMEL: Funny… Who would think… Why, to talk to him… *(Suddenly interested.)* And is he socially… How should I say…?

JOLICŒUR: You mean, is he rich?

BECHAMEL: Well… I wouldn't put it that way…

JOLICŒUR: Put it any way you like. Have you ever seen that magnificent building next to the Oriental Baths, in Paris?

BECHAMEL, *musing*: The Oriental Baths… The… You mean the big one?

JOLICŒUR, *nodding*: His!

BECHAMEL, *impressed*: You're right! He would make a perfect match for Cécile! Next to the Oriental Baths, indeed!… Blast! Why didn't I invite him to stay for lunch? Table conversation… One thing leads to another… *(Suddenly.)* Ah! But what about Hollandez?

JOLICŒUR: Too bad! It's his loss.

BECHAMEL: Exactly! Who told him to go and turn around? Anyway, I can't ask my daughter to wait for three whole months! And besides, she doesn't love him. He's bow-legged… And he has no ear…

JOLICŒUR, *shocked*: What? None at all? A lawyer…? How does he argue his cases in court?

BECHAMEL: How… *(Realizing his misunderstanding.)* For music… No ear for music…

JOLICŒUR: Oh… That's all well and good, but… Our tickets are reserved.

BECHAMEL: Eighty-three francs…

JOLICŒUR: Ah! Think… If she marries him, in a few weeks we step out of the train and set foot on the soil of Italia!

BECHAMEL, *enthusiastically*: Rome! Venice!… Ah! Venezia la bella!… *(Suddenly changing his tone.)* But what are we talking about? He left… We lost our chance!

The door, up center, opens and ANTOINE *appears, carrying an enormous armful of flowers.*

ANTOINE, *calling into the wings*: Wait for me, imbecile!

He takes a few steps inside.

BECHAMEL *and* **JOLICŒUR**, *together*: Him!

BECHAMEL *takes off his beret.*

ANTOINE, *to* BECHAMEL, *coldly, making a point to tap his cap solidly on his head*: Believe me, monsieur… I hardly expected to find you! I assumed you would still be composing your endless missive!

BECHAMEL: My what?

ANTOINE, *ignoring the question, holding out the flowers*: Here! Take these! My arms are tired…

BECHAMEL: For me? *(Turning to* JOLICŒUR.*)* How sweet!

ANTOINE: Not unless this is your saint's day and your name is Brigitte!

BECHAMEL: I beg your—

ANTOINE: I just came galloping back to tell you… My horse, that is… He came galloping… To tell you… me, that is… that my domestic is a consummate scoundrel!

BECHAMEL, *puzzled*: To tell me that…

ANTOINE, *pointing left, toward the garden, sarcastically* : That he seems to have ravaged your garden in order to present a bouquet to his lady fair! One Brigitte… The wretch!

BECHAMEL: You mean… You came back just for that?

He lays the flowers on the table, down left.

JOLICŒUR, *to ANTOINE*: How considerate, monsieur! *(To BECHAMEL, nodding.)* Typical!... Typical!

ANTOINE, *noticing him*: Ah! Monsieur Jolicœur!... How nice to see you, cher ami! Tell me, do you still have the same concierge? A most disagreeable fellow, as I recall... *(To BECHAMEL, not waiting for an answer.)* And now, monsieur... If you deign to receive my humble salutations... I shall be on my way.

He gives a curt little bow and moves upstage, as if to leave.

BECHAMEL, *to JOLICŒUR, in a whisper*: He's leaving...

JOLICŒUR, *to BECHAMEL, in a whisper*: Stop him!

BECHAMEL, *calling, as ANTOINE reaches the door*: Monsieur de Beaujolais!

ANTOINE, *stopping*: Monsieur?

BECHAMEL: Come now... Certainly you'll join us for lunch? We have a delicious leg of lamb left over from last week.

ANTOINE, *coming down, approaching him, sarcastically*: I assure you, monsieur... Nothing would give me greater pleasure than to join you for your distinguished leftovers...

JOLICŒUR: You accept?

ANTOINE: But unfortunately I must decline.

JOLICŒUR, *disappointed*: Oh...

BECHAMEL, *to ANTOINE*: Is it because I didn't send you a formal invitation?

ANTOINE: Hardly, monsieur... *(Aside.)* Who knows how long it would have taken him to write it!

BECHAMEL: Because, if you refuse, I'll have to assume that you're easily offended!

ANTOINE, *dismissing the idea*: Easily offended? Me?... Ha ha ha!

BECHAMEL, *joining in the laughter*: Ha ha ha!...

JOLICŒUR joins in, and the three of them laugh for a few moments.

ANTOINE, *to BECHAMEL*: I am always totally in control of my emotions, monsieur!

BECHAMEL: I'm sure...

JOLICŒUR: No doubt...

ANTOINE: Always in control... And to prove it, I accept!

BECHAMEL: Fine!

He gives him a good-natured little jab in the belly.

ANTOINE, *drawing back, aside*: My word!

BECHAMEL: That's what I wanted to hear!

JOLICŒUR, *to BECHAMEL, in a whisper*: See? I told you...

BECHAMEL, *to JOLICŒUR, in a whisper*: He's a gem!

ANTOINE, *aside*: Hmm!... Whispering... Probably wondering if I'll eat too much...

BECHAMEL, *to JOLICŒUR, still in a whisper*: You try to sound him out...

JOLICŒUR, *likewise*: Me?

BECHAMEL, *continuing*: In the meantime I'll go prepare Cécile.

ANTOINE, *aside*: Still whispering? How rude! *(Aloud, to BECHAMEL, archly.)* Really, monsieur... If I'm in the way...

BECHAMEL: Not at all!... *(Turning to leave, up left.)* I'll just be a minute.

ANTOINE, *aside*: Again?

BECHAMEL: I'll leave you with my old friend Jolicœur. Yours too, he tells me... He assures me that your morals are impeccable, monsieur!

ANTOINE, *aside*: My morals?

BECHAMEL: Of course, I didn't doubt it for an instant!

ANTOINE, *aside*: Did he think I might steal the silverware? *(Aloud, nodding, as* BECHAMEL *reaches the door, up left.)* Monsieur...

BECHAMEL, *returning his nod*: Monsieur...

He exits. ANTOINE, *finally removing his cap, goes to the table, right, and puts it down, along with his riding-crop.*

JOLICŒUR, *down center, somewhat uncomfortably*: Well now, my friend—

ANTOINE, *interrupting, joining him*: Tell me, Jolicœur... Be frank! Was I wrong? Was I ill-advised to accept?

JOLICŒUR: Wrong?... Heavens no! Béchamel is a delightful fellow!

ANTOINE: Oh?... I must say... I find him a trifle unpleasant.

JOLICŒUR: Unpleasant? Béchamel?

ANTOINE: Quite!... In fact, even more than a trifle...

JOLICŒUR: I can't imagine why. The man is a prince! Sincere... Forthright... Not a pretentious bone in his body... And charming to a fault...

ANTOINE: Like me, you mean...

JOLICŒUR: Exactly! Like you, Beaujolais! You put your finger on it!

ANTOINE: Strange... I could have sworn... He seemed rather...

JOLICŒUR: In fact, it's because the two of you are so much alike that I've got an idea!

ANTOINE: Oh?

JOLICŒUR, *putting his arm around him and leading him upstage*: Just between us, monsieur... Antoine... Have you ever given any thought to getting married?

ANTOINE, *suspicious*: Why do you ask? *(Aside.)* Does he know about my seventeen times, I wonder?

JOLICŒUR: Because, no offense, my friend... But you're getting something of a paunch!

ANTOINE, *offended, stepping aside*: Oh?... As long as I'm not getting yours, cher ami...

JOLICŒUR, *following him*: And your hair is turning... Well... Gray, as a matter of fact...

ANTOINE, *aside*: Did they invite me to lunch just to tell me that?

JOLICŒUR, *putting his arm around him again*: Believe me, Antoine... When we reach middle age...

ANTOINE, *pulling away*: What?

JOLICŒUR: ...there's nothing like marriage to keep us from getting older!

ANTOINE: Really, monsieur... *(Sarcastically.)* Your little joke is the essence of wit and good taste, but—

JOLICŒUR: Little joke? What joke? I'm not joking, Beaujolais! I'm talking about a charming young thing. Here, in this very house... *(Pointing up left.)* His daughter!

ANTOINE: Yes. I've seen her...

JOLICŒUR: Oh? And what do you think?

ANTOINE, *coming down left*: Please, monsieur. Your humor eludes me.

JOLICŒUR, *following him*: But I'm serious, for heaven's sake!

ANTOINE: You are?

JOLICŒUR: Look... It's none of my business, and I certainly haven't the right... But just between us... Her father likes you!

ANTOINE, *ironically*: Yes... I can tell!

JOLICŒUR: And I think it's safe to say that a proposal would not be... Well, unfavorably received!

ANTOINE, *astonished*: A proposal?... You mean... You're serious? A proposal...

JOLICŒUR: What have I been saying?

ANTOINE, *crossing right, delighted*: Ah! Me?... Married?... *(To himself.)* After seventeen attempts... And each one... Pffft!... *(Aloud.)* Damnation!... Zut alors!

JOLICŒUR, *following him*: What's wrong?

ANTOINE, *ecstatic*: Wrong?... Nothing! It... It... It couldn't be righter... *(Correcting himself.)* More right... Less wrong...

JOLICŒUR: Then you're interested?

ANTOINE: That's not the word! I'm... I... She's a vision of loveliness! A... A sight to behold...

JOLICŒUR: Indeed...

ANTOINE: I came in... I beheld her!... And that's just what I said to myself... "Damnation!... Zut alors!" *(Changing his tone.)* I say, Jolicœur... Could you lend me a white cravat?

JOLICŒUR: What on earth for?

ANTOINE: To make my proposal!

JOLICŒUR: Not so fast!... And anyway, I don't just happen to have one.

ANTOINE: Of course... Of course...

JOLICŒUR: It's not something I carry around!

ANTOINE: No... Of course...

JOLICŒUR: So, you think she'll do?

ANTOINE: Do? I should say she'll do! With me the young ladies always do! It's their fathers that don't!

JOLICŒUR: Ah! No problem with Béchamel... You and he will get along famously, I assure you.

ANTOINE: Besides, when he acts like a boor I'll pretend not to notice! With a daughter like that... *(Taking JOLICŒUR's hands in his.)* Ah! Cher ami!... *(Kissing his hands.)* Jolicœur... Jolicœur...

JOLICŒUR, *pulling away*: Monsieur...

ANTOINE: Why did I ever leave your house? What was I thinking?... Tell me, have you anything to rent?

JOLICŒUR: Why yes! A lovely bachelor apartment...

ANTOINE: Fine!... *(After a moment of reflection.)* I don't want it! I won't be needing it...

JOLICŒUR: No, I shouldn't think... So, should I go fetch Béchamel?

ANTOINE: Indeed! I should say! By all means!... *(Moving upstage, as* JOLICŒUR *begins crossing up left.)* Tell him that I know how crass and crude he is... That he has no manners...

JOLICŒUR, *stopping in his tracks*: What?

ANTOINE: But that it doesn't matter! He's a father-in-law! That's all that counts! *(Pushing him toward the door, up left.)* Go on!... Go on!

JOLICŒUR: I'm going...

He exits.

ANTOINE, *alone, up center*: Married!... Me!... And all because that idiot Hollandez didn't take off his hat!... Talk about luck!... Now he's flat on his back. *(Reflecting.)* Well, on his side... Because... And me? I'm going to get married. That should teach him! Fifty years old, and he dares to cross swords with a Beaujolais! *(Coming downstage, confidentially.)* Not that I'm exactly a Beaujolais nouveau... I'm forty, after all... *(Looking around, making sure no one has heard.)* Shhh!... I didn't say that!... Besides, if they ask me, I'll tell them thirty... Well, thirty-three... Not a day more... I may not be as rich as he is, but... And anyway, I want to be loved for myself, not for my money. Marriage isn't a business! It's... It's...

The door, up left, opens and PHILIPPE *enters.*

PHILIPPE, *coming down, to* ANTOINE, *giving him a sudden nudge*: Hey, you!

ANTOINE: I beg your pardon? *(Aside.)* Churl!

PHILIPPE, *pointing up right*: You've really got them excited in there!

ANTOINE, *pulling back*: I what?

PHILIPPE: You and that big building of yours in Paris... Next to the Oriental Baths, or something...

ANTOINE: What?... Who told you...

PHILIPPE: That's all they can talk about! You and your building...

ANTOINE, *appalled*: Oh? And what about me? What are they saying—

PHILIPPE, *continuing*: ...and that it must bring in a good twenty-two thousand five hundred francs a year...

ANTOINE: And me? What about me?

PHILIPPE: ...and that you're probably even richer than Hollandez!

ANTOINE, *aside*: Damnation!

PHILIPPE, *nudging him again*: So, don't worry! If you ask me you're as good as married. *(Turning upstage, aside.)* Who cares which one? It's champagne either way!

He exits, up center.

ANTOINE, *piqued, beginning to pace back and forth, in a huff*: Oh! Very nice! It's my building that she's marrying! I just happen to come along with the property! A stone, a tile... A handful of plaster... That's all I am... Next to the Oriental Baths, indeed! *(Stopping up right.)* And I'm supposed to accept that, am I? *(Very dignified.)* No, Beaujolais! You cannot!... You must not!... You will not!

BECHAMEL, CECILE, *and* JOLICŒUR *enter, up left.*

BECHAMEL, *in a whisper, to* CECILE, *who is carrying her embroidery*: I'm so happy you think so too, Cécile…

JOLICŒUR, *whispering, to* BECHAMEL: So! It's agreed… I'll go tell him…

He crosses right, to ANTOINE.

BECHAMEL, *to himself*: Yes… He's a gem! *(To* CECILE, *whispering.)* Come, let's sit down. *(He takes a newspaper from his pocket, pointing to the chair to the left of the pedestal table, down left.)* You sit there and make believe you're embroidering.

CECILE, *whispering*: Yes, papá.

She sits down.

JOLICŒUR, *whispering, to* ANTOINE: It's all arranged, mon ami.

BECHAMEL, *to* CECILE, *continuing, still in a whisper*: And I'll pretend to be reading the paper…

He sits down on the other side of the table.

ANTOINE, *to* JOLICŒUR, *replying*: Oh?

JOLICŒUR: All you have to do is talk to Béchamel…

ANTOINE: Aha… *(Aside.)* Well, we'll see!

JOLICŒUR: And ask him officially…

ANTOINE *crosses right, approaching* BECHAMEL.

BECHAMEL, *to* CECILE, *whispering*: Here he comes… Don't look!

She lowers her eyes and begins embroidering.

ANTOINE, *to* BECHAMEL: Monsieur…

BECHAMEL, *getting up, fumbling to take off his beret*: Monsieur?

ANTOINE, *categorically*: This part of the country is really quite fertile. The subsoil seems rather porous…

BECHAMEL, JOLICŒUR, *and* CECILE *look at each other, exchanging bewildered glances.*

BECHAMEL, *whispering, to* CECILE: You're embarrassing him… You'd better leave!

CECILE, *whispering*: Yes, papá…

She gets up, puts down her embroidery, gives ANTOINE *a wan smile, and exits, up left.*

JOLICŒUR, *whispering, to* ANTOINE: She's gone. Now you can ask him.

He joins BECHAMEL.

ANTOINE, *to* BECHAMEL: Monsieur…

BECHAMEL: Monsieur?

ANTOINE: This part of the country is really quite fertile. The subsoil…

BECHAMEL, *whispering, to* JOLICŒUR: It's you…

ANTOINE, *continuing*: …seems rather porous…

BECHAMEL, *whispering, to* JOLICŒUR: You're embarrassing him… You'd better leave!

JOLICŒUR, *whispering, to* ANTOINE: What are you waiting for? Go on! Don't be shy!

He exits, up center.

BECHAMEL, *to* ANTOINE: There! He's gone. Now you can talk! I'm listening, monsieur.

ANTOINE: They tell me the alfalfa crop is becoming more important by the day.

BECHAMEL, *with a quizzical look*: Pardon me, but... I thought... Monsieur Jolicœur assured me that...

ANTOINE, *coldly*: That what?

BECHAMEL, *shocked*: That... That... *(Shaking his head.)* Nothing...

ANTOINE, *sarcastically*: What ever could he have assured you, I wonder!

He thrusts his hands in his pockets and casually ambles about, humming.

BECHAMEL, *to himself*: Then it's me... I'm embarrassing him... Who else could it be?

He turns on his heel, shrugging, and exits, up center.

ANTOINE, *alone, taking his cap and riding-crop from the table, right*: That should teach them! My building indeed! I still have my pride! *(Crossing left, to the window, calling out.)* Dominique! The horses!

CECILE enters, up left.

CECILE, *aside*: He must have spoken to papá by now. *(Catching sight of ANTOINE.)* Oh!... Pardon me, monsieur... *(Coming down left, pointing.)* My embroidery...

ANTOINE: Mademoiselle... What a pleasure to see you...

CECILE, *aside*: He's going to propose!

ANTOINE, *continuing*: ...and bid you a most respectful adieu!

CECILE: What? Are you leaving?

ANTOINE: Yes... Some work is being done on my building... *(Emphasizing, sarcastically.)* My building, mademoiselle... In Paris... Next to the Oriental Baths! The big one...

CECILE: And that's why you have to leave? *(Offended.)* Well, please don't let me keep you, monsieur!

ANTOINE: But it's no great loss! Only the façade is in stone... The rest is all wood.

CECILE: I beg your pardon?

ANTOINE: And not very elegant wood at that! I'm sure you'll find better! Bigger, too... And higher...

CECILE, *aside*: What ever can he mean?

ANTOINE: But as I take my leave, mademoiselle, permit me to wish you all the wealth you deserve...

CECILE: The wealth?

ANTOINE: May you marry a whole street!... A whole city block...

CECILE: Really, monsieur—

ANTOINE: ...with shops that rent for much more than my modest apartments!

CECILE: Your apartments? What apartments?

ANTOINE: In my building... Next to the... *(Emphasizing.)* Oriental Baths...

CECILE, *surprised*: You own a building, monsieur?

ANTOINE: Ha ha!... As if you didn't know, mademoiselle...

CECILE: But... But I didn't... I assure you...

ANTOINE: You didn't?... You... Do you swear?

CECILE, *putting her hand to her mouth*: Oh... Swear, monsieur? Never!... If I tell you...

ANTOINE: Yes!... I believe you! I do... I... Still, do you swear you didn't know?

CECILE: I... *(Hesitating.)* If I must... *(With determination.)* Yes, I swear!

ANTOINE, *ecstatically*: Oh! You angel! You... *(To himself.)* She didn't know... *(To CECILE.)* You didn't know... You didn't?

CECILE: No! I didn't know...

ANTOINE: You didn't! *(Beside himself.)* No, no... You didn't...

He gives her a hug.

CECILE, *stepping back, alarmed*: Monsieur!

ANTOINE: Forgive me... I lost control... Really, it's the very first time...

CECILE: Well...

ANTOINE: Ah! Now I'll go ask your father for your hand, mademoiselle! *(Taking her hand.)* Your sweet, dainty hand...

CECILE, *surprised*: You mean... You haven't asked him yet?

ANTOINE: No... I... He... We had other things to talk about... Alfalfa and... and porous subsoil, and...

CECILE: Papá?

ANTOINE: But before I do... *(Rather formally.)* Permit me to make certain of your feelings in my regard. *(Posing.)* I'm thirty-two years old... *(Aside.)* Bah! What's one year! *(Aloud.)* People tell me that I'm rather witty... So often, in fact, that I have to assume it's true... As for my appearance... It's quite as you see it! I wouldn't venture an opinion...

CECILE, *embarrassed*: No...

ANTOINE: What did you say?

CECILE: Nothing... I...

She lowers her eyes.

ANTOINE: Nothing? *(Aside.)* I must say, she's a trifle cold! *(Aloud.)* Mademoiselle... *(Aside.)* I might have hoped for more enthusiasm! *(Aloud.)* May I flatter myself to infer that you are not entirely ill-disposed toward my person?

CECILE, *confused*: Ill... No... Of course not...

ANTOINE, *misinterpreting her remark*: No? You mean, you are?

CECILE: That is... You—

ANTOINE: And I suppose I have your hateful father to thank for your attitude!

CECILE: My... What attitude?... Not at all, monsieur! Papá would never try to influence my choice.

ANTOINE: Aha!... *(Offended.)* Then it's quite clear, mademoiselle! It is you who find me... How shall I say?... You and you alone who refuse... I see... *(Going to the window, calling.)* Dominique! The horses!

CECILE, *impatiently*: Please! Let your horses be! Who said I refuse...

ANTOINE: But... You mean?... You don't?

CECILE: Monsieur...

ANTOINE: One word then... Just one... That's all I ask!

CECILE: Really, Monsieur Beaujolais...

ANTOINE, *correcting*: De... De...

CECILE: Monsieur de Beaujolais...

ANTOINE: Besides, marriage is only a ceremony. It doesn't prove a thing! Be frank, mademoiselle... Like me... Frank and straightforward... I'm not afraid to speak the truth! And the truth is… The truth is, I love you! There! I said it! I love you!… That should put your mind at ease… Now, tell me…

CECILE: What can I say, monsieur? *(Coyly.)* I scarcely know you…

ANTOINE: Know? What is there to know? *(Posing.)* Mademoiselle, I'm forty… *(Catching himself.)* Thirty-two years old… *(Aside.)* I hope she didn't hear that! *(Aloud.)* People tell me that I'm rather witty…

CECILE: Can you sing, monsieur?

ANTOINE, *enthusiastically*: Indeed! And quite well, I daresay!

CECILE, *clapping her hands*: Oh! Then we can sing duets!

ANTOINE: With the greatest of pleasure… Even now, if you like…

CECILE: Now?

ANTOINE: Why not?

CECILE: Very well… I'll go fetch my music.

She moves up left.

ANTOINE, *crossing right, to himself*: Some kind of test, I imagine…

He places his cap and riding-crop back on the table, right.

CECILE: Don't go… I'll just be a minute…

ANTOINE: Aha… *(Aside.)* If her minute is like her father's… *(Aloud.)* Then I trust I'll know in a minute, mademoiselle!

CECILE, *at the door, up left*: Know, monsieur?… Know what?

ANTOINE, *approaching her*: Your feelings in my regard…

CECILE, *enthusiastically*: Oh yes! I'm sure you will!

ANTOINE: Ah!

He gives her another sudden hug.

CECILE, *drawing back*: Monsieur!

ANTOINE, *aside*: Damnation! *(Aloud.)* That's the second time I've lost control!… To lose control once can be excused! But to lose it a second time?… It's the first time I've lost it a second time, mademoiselle!

CECILE, *coyly*: I forgive you!

She exits quickly, up left.

ANTOINE, *alone, up left, ecstatic*: Ah! What an angel! What an absolute angel! A veritable treasure-trove of love… A gold mine… A… Ah me! Ah me!

As he stands blowing kisses toward the door, up left, BECHAMEL *appears at the door, up center.*

BECHAMEL, *entering, to himself*: I simply don't understand… Jolicœur told him plain as day to talk marriage. *(Noticing* ANTOINE *blowing kisses.)* What the devil…? *(Aloud, calling.)* Monsieur!

ANTOINE, *turning, seizing him by the throat*: Ah! Monsieur! Monsieur! Monsieur! Your daughter is an angel! I have the honor of requesting her hand…

BECHAMEL, *struggling*: Ayyy!… Let me go…

ANTOINE, *shaking him*: Her hand, monsieur… In marriage…

BECHAMEL: It's yours! *(Aside.)* And all the rest…

ANTOINE, *letting him go*: Ah! Thank you! Thank you!

BECHAMEL, *aside*: Odd chap!

ANTOINE, *aside*: So much for the proposal!

BECHAMEL, *aside*: First he's not interested, and then he almost chokes me!

ANTOINE: Now then, what else do we have to do?

BECHAMEL: Well, as long as you ask... There's the matter of the marriage contract...

ANTOINE: No problem! I agree... To everything!

BECHAMEL: Good! So do I... *(Aside.)* Delightful fellow! *(Aloud, giving him a good-natured poke in the belly.)* You know? *(Poking him again.)* I like you!

ANTOINE: You do? *(Aside.)* Strange tic... *(He gives* BECHAMEL *three quick jabs in the belly.)* Shall we get on with it then? Your daughter is waiting... We're going to make music.

BECHAMEL: Oh? *(Misinterpreting his remark, aside.)* Here? Now?

ANTOINE: If you have no objections...

BECHAMEL: Just like that?

ANTOINE: Sing duets...

BECHAMEL: Ah!... Please... I insist...

He winks at him broadly and gives him another little poke.

ANTOINE: I say... *(He gives* BECHAMEL *three more quick little jabs.)* So... About the contract... You were saying...

BECHAMEL: Just one thing...

ANTOINE, *ignoring him*: But first, monsieur... A few well-chosen words to acquaint you with my life...

BECHAMEL: I don't think... Really, you needn't—

ANTOINE, *continuing to ignore his objections*: My father was Swiss.

BECHAMEL: In cheese?

ANTOINE: Hardly!

BECHAMEL: Chocolate?

ANTOINE: Please, monsieur! Do I look like a mere grocer's son?

BECHAMEL: I didn't mean—

ANTOINE, *rather curtly*: My family left France under Louis the Fourteenth.

BECHAMEL: Aha...

ANTOINE: The Sun King, monsieur...

BECHAMEL: Yes...

ANTOINE: 1643 to 1715...

BECHAMEL, *repressing a yawn*: Indeed...

ANTOINE, *annoyed*: For reasons I needn't go into...

BECHAMEL: No... You needn't...

He tries again, less successfully.

ANTOINE: Am I boring you, monsieur?

BECHAMEL: No, no... Please!

ANTOINE: Because, if I am...

BECHAMEL: Go on... I'm all ears!

ANTOINE: My great-grandfather settled in France, manufacturing clocks.

BECHAMEL: Cuckoo?

ANTOINE, *annoyed*: Not in the slightest!

BECHAMEL, *misunderstanding*: What?

ANTOINE: At least he didn't have a preposterous tic, monsieur!

BECHAMEL: I beg your pardon? *(ANTOINE gives him three quick jabs in the belly. Aside.)* Again?

ANTOINE: No matter... *(Continuing.)* And in no time he was worth millions! Needless to say, his fortune—

BECHAMEL, *giving a monstrous yawn*: Aaaah!

ANTOINE, *stopping abruptly*: Very well! I've finished!

BECHAMEL: Oh?

ANTOINE, *aside*: Where did he learn his manners?

BECHAMEL: And they tell me you own a building, monsieur...

ANTOINE, *aside*: Again?... *(Aloud.)* Yes! I own a building! *(Annoyed.)* A very large building!... In Paris, monsieur!... Next to the Oriental Baths... *(Under his breath.)* If, by some remote chance, you were unaware...

BECHAMEL: So I'm told... And how many stories?

ANTOINE, *aside*: Imbecile! *(Aloud.)* Three... Each one on top of the other...

He begins pacing nervously.

BECHAMEL: Three? That's not very many...

ANTOINE, *sharply*: No... I'll have five more added as soon as possible!

BECHAMEL, *taking him seriously*: Ah... In brick, perhaps?

ANTOINE, *raising his voice*: Brick... Stone... Cement...

BECHAMEL: What's the trouble?

ANTOINE, *almost shouting*: Stucco...

BECHAMEL: Did I say something...

ANTOINE: No trouble!... No trouble at all!

BECHAMEL: Oh... *(With a shrug.)* I thought... *(Continuing his train of thought.)* Any mortgages?

ANTOINE, *curtly*: None!

BECHAMEL, *to himself*: I must have said something... *(Aloud.)* And solid, monsieur? Well built?

ANTOINE, *stopping, right*: By the Romans!... A hundred ten meters wide... Four shops on the ground floor, twenty-one apartments... And a mezzanine, monsieur! Even a mezzanine!... Now, if we might discuss something else...

BECHAMEL, *aside*: Like cuckoo clocks? *(Aloud.)* What, for instance?

ANTOINE: "What?" *(Losing patience, approaching him.)* It seems to me, my friend, that if I were marrying off my daughter, I would be talking about something besides laying bricks! It's the height of vulgarity! *(Turning aside disgustedly, as if spitting on the floor.)* Ptui! Ptui!

BECHAMEL: What?

ANTOINE, *punctuating each word with a less-than-good-natured poke*: Nothing! Nothing! Nothing!

BECHAMEL, *beginning to lose his temper, aside*: Oh!

ANTOINE, *hands on hips*: Monsieur Béchamel! I love your daughter! I told you... I agree to everything!

BECHAMEL, *raising his voice*: "Everything"? What "everything"? I'm not asking you for anything! I agree! I thought I made that clear!

ANTOINE, *sarcastically*: Oh yes! Of course! How delightful!... You agree, because I own a building! How very flattering!

BECHAMEL: But... What do you expect? If you didn't have a sou to your name, you can be bloody well sure I wouldn't!

ANTOINE: Ha! Thank you! Now it all comes out!

BECHAMEL, *angrily*: You're welcome! *(Wiping his brow.)* Damn it all!

ANTOINE: Then if someone came by with a pocketful, monsieur... Two buildings... Three...

BECHAMEL: Two buildings in his pocket?

ANTOINE: You know what I mean...

BECHAMEL, *shouting*: What?... What? What?... Buildings!... What buildings?

ANTOINE: Please, monsieur! Control yourself!

BECHAMEL: Bah!

ANTOINE: Like me... *(Very calmly.)* You don't see me flying off the handle...

BECHAMEL: For an hour that's all you can talk about! *(Wiping his brow again.)* Your building!... Your shops, your apartments.... Your... Your mezzanine! *(Aside.)* Damn it!

He takes off his jacket and lays it on the chair, by the table, right.

ANTOINE, *aside*: Good grief! He's undressing! *(Aside, as* BECHAMEL *joins him, fanning himself.)* Does he think I'm a bath attendant? *(Aloud.)* Just a moment... *(Taking off his jacket, aside.)* What's good for the goose...

BECHAMEL: Are you warm?

ANTOINE: No, monsieur... Actually I find it rather chilly. But if this is how one discusses a marriage contract here... Who am I to... *(Laying the jacket on one of the chairs, down left.)* There!... I trust we're ready? *(Sarcastically.)* Or shall I remove my trousers too?

BECHAMEL: No!... And yes, we're ready! *(Aside.)* Bloody odd if you ask me!

ANTOINE: Now then... The property... Separate or communal? I'm quite agreeable to either arrangement.

BECHAMEL: So am I! I told you! How many times... *(Aside, impatiently.)* Doesn't he listen? *(Aloud, calling.)* Philippe!... Philippe!

ANTOINE, *crossing right, aside*: At least he could close the blasted window!

PHILIPPE *pokes his head in the door, up center.*

PHILIPPE, *to* BECHAMEL: Monsieur?

BECHAMEL: A pen and ink, and some sheets of paper... *(In a whisper.)* The cheap ones...

PHILIPPE *leaves.*

ANTOINE, *sneezing*: Atchoo!... *(Waiting, expecting* BECHAMEL *to say something: then, sarcastically.)* Thank you, monsieur! You're much too kind!

BECHAMEL, *raising his voice*: What?... Again?... Because I didn't say "God bless you!"...? *(Archly.)* Fine!... God bless you!... There! Are you happy?

ANTOINE: It seems to me, monsieur...

PHILIPPE *reappears.*

PHILIPPE, *entering, to* BECHAMEL, *handing him the paper, pen, and ink*: Here… *(Aside.)* Shirtsleeves? The two of them? *(Aloud.)* Is this enough?

BECHAMEL: Fine! Fine!… *(Placing the things on the table, down left, as* PHILIPPE *shrugs and takes off his jacket; to* ANTOINE.*)* So! Let's get down to business, shall we? *(Handing him the pen.)* Here…

ANTOINE, *taking it, standing between the wall and the table*: With pleasure!… You see? I'm very reasonable…

BECHAMEL, *standing across from him, impatiently*: Yes… Now write… *(With a little shiver, looking toward the window, aside.)* Damnable draft!

He crosses right, taking his jacket from the chair, and puts it on.

ANTOINE, *sitting down*: Whatever you say, monsieur… *(Noticing* BECHAMEL, *aside.)* Aha…

He stands up and puts his jacket on.

PHILIPPE, *up left, aside*: Now what?

BECHAMEL, *to* ANTOINE: Are you cold?

ANTOINE: No, monsieur… Actually, I'm rather warm. But please, don't mind me… If this is the way one does it here…

He sits down again, as PHILIPPE *puts his jacket back on and stands watching.*

BECHAMEL, *returning left, sitting down on the other chair*: I think we said that you were bringing a sum of twenty-two thousand five-hundred francs. Am I correct?

ANTOINE: Five-hundred twenty-three, to be exact…

BECHAMEL: Yes… And that's all… You have nothing else…

ANTOINE: I have sixty-two francs in my pocket, monsieur. And nine sous in a jar in my secretary drawer.

BECHAMEL *gives an impatient sigh.* ANTOINE *does likewise.*

BECHAMEL: Yes… And I'm giving my daughter a dowry of thirty thousand francs.

ANTOINE: Oh?

BECHAMEL: The yearly income from my—

ANTOINE, *interrupting*: No!… Oh no!

BECHAMEL: What?

ANTOINE: I'm bringing twenty-two thousand five hundred twenty-three francs! And I will not accept one sou more than that!

BECHAMEL: I beg your—

ANTOINE, *pounding the table with his fist*: No, no, no! Absolutely not!… It's… It's unheard of, monsieur!

BECHAMEL: But…

ANTOINE: My pride… My honor…

BECHAMEL, *shouting*: Now look here! I'll give my daughter a dowry of as much as I like!

ANTOINE, *standing up*: No you won't!

BECHAMEL, *standing up as* ANTOINE *sits down*: Yes I will!

ANTOINE, *standing up, as* BECHAMEL *sits down*: No, monsieur!

BECHAMEL, *standing up, as* ANTOINE *sits down*: Yes, monsieur!

PHILIPPE, *coming down to the table, to* ANTOINE, *in a whisper*: Don't be a fool! Take it!

ANTOINE, *turning to him, sharply*: You?... Lackey!... Churl!... *(To* BECHAMEL.*)* I make no demands whatever, monsieur! But one sou more than me, and I'll send it all off to feed the starving Poles!

BECHAMEL, *furiously*: Good God! He's not a son-in-law! He's a... a cactus!... A burr!... *(Searching for a comparison.)* A... A bumblebee, damn it! All he can do is buzz about and sting!

ANTOINE, *just as furiously*: What? *(To* PHILIPPE.*)* What did he say?

PHILIPPE, *laughing*: He said you're a bee!... A burr...

ANTOINE, *misunderstanding*: A boor?

PHILIPPE: That too!... But he said "burr"... And you sting!

ANTOINE: Oh! *(Sniffing.)* I do not! You... You...

He gives him a resounding slap.

PHILIPPE: Ayyy!

BECHAMEL: No! That's too much!... I never...

ANTOINE, *glaring at* PHILIPPE: Of all the impudent louts...

PHILIPPE: Me? But I was only—

CECILE *appears, up left, with a roll of music.*

CECILE, *entering*: What in heaven's name...

BECHAMEL, *in a rage*: No! That's the last straw! *(Approaching* PHILIPPE.*)* To dare lay a hand on my godson! And in this house!... *(To* ANTOINE.*)* Monsieur! Here's your contract!

He rips it up and flings the pieces on the floor.

CECILE, *aside*: Oh my! *(To* ANTOINE.*)* Monsieur! What ever did you do?

BECHAMEL *and* PHILIPPE *exit, up right, in a huff.*

ANTOINE, *pacing angrily, to himself*: So! Number eighteen...

CECILE: Please, tell me what happened! I go off to fetch my music, and—

ANTOINE: Ha! If it's music you wanted... You should have been here just now! The beating of drums and the clashing of cymbals... Fortissimo furioso!

CECILE, *puzzled*: Monsieur?

ANTOINE: And not a sweet little wedding-march, believe me! *(Under his breath.)* A madman!... A monster!

CECILE, *overhearing*: Who...?

ANTOINE, *suddenly*: Mademoiselle! I adore you... *(With a little bow.)* But I beg to inform you that you have seen the last of me! *(At the window, calling.)* Dominique!

CECILE: Are you leaving?

ANTOINE: As fast as my horse's hooves can carry me!... After the unspeakable way your father has treated me... Calling me a burr!... A bumblebee!... Really, mademoiselle! Do I buzz about like a bee?

CECILE: Of course not! But I'm sure he didn't mean anything by it!

ANTOINE: Then let him apologize! *(Waving his fist.)* An apology!... An apology!

CECILE: Please! Let me talk to him. I'll make him listen to reason. Just promise not to leave until I return...

ANTOINE: I promise! *(Aside.)* An apology! And a civil tongue, damn it!

CECILE: I'll just be a moment...

She leaves the music on the table, down left, then crosses, up right, and hurriedly exits.

ANTOINE, *alone*: Ah!... An angel... An absolute angel... And with a father like that? No! How can it be?... He's not! He can't be!... Science won't allow it!... Do grizzly bears sire delicate gazelles! Do porcupines father kittens? Do... Bah! We wouldn't have butterflies if we didn't have caterpillars!... *(Questioning his observation.)* Or something like that... *(To himself.)* And you have to give up an angel like her?... Why?... Just because her father is a bear? *(Stamping his foot.)* No! You can't be that stupid!... You can't! You can't!... *(Shouting, addressing an imaginary accuser.)* Stupid? Me?... Antoine de Beaujolais? *(Looking around.)* Who said that?... *(Realizing it was himself.)* Oh...

JOLICŒUR appears at the door, up right.

JOLICŒUR, *entering, to ANTOINE*: Mon ami...

ANTOINE: Ah! Monsieur...

JOLICŒUR, *approaching*: I'm afraid I've come on a difficult mission. I've just left Béchamel...

ANTOINE: Does he want to apologize?

JOLICŒUR, *hesitating*: Not quite... He... He asked me to tell you that you are free to leave.

ANTOINE, *in a subdued tone of voice*: Aha... So... *(At the window, calling.)* Dominique!... *(He crosses right and retrieves his cap and riding-crop; then, hesitating, coming back down, to himself.)* But I promised her I would wait...

JOLICŒUR: Believe me, I had nothing to do with it!

ANTOINE, *calmly*: I understand perfectly, monsieur.

JOLICŒUR: I couldn't be more upset... *(Aside.)* A man who always paid his rent... *(Aloud.)* Come, I'll see you out...

ANTOINE, *sitting down on one of the chairs, down left*: So!... *(Casually.)* Tell me about your concierge...

JOLICŒUR: My... Excuse me, but I don't think you understand...

ANTOINE: You asked me to take my leave...

JOLICŒUR: And instead, you take a seat!

ANTOINE, *romantically*: I prefer to wait until the moon hides her face, and evening wafts its gentle breezes...

JOLICŒUR: How poetic! *(Aside.)* And Béchamel says this man is a brute! Did you ever...?

CECILE appears at the door, up right.

CECILE, *to ANTOINE*: I've spoken to him, monsieur...

ANTOINE, *getting up*: And he wants to apologize?

CECILE: No...

ANTOINE: Very well...

Putting his cap and riding-crop under his arm, he takes his gloves from his pocket and puts them on.

CECILE: You slapped his godson, monsieur...

ANTOINE, *archly*: I did indeed!

CECILE, *continuing*: ...and he'll forgive you only on one condition.

JOLICŒUR: A condition?

ANTOINE, *to JOLICŒUR*: Ha ha ha, monsieur!… A condition, for a de Beaujolais! Ha ha ha! *(To CECILE.)* And that is…?

CECILE: Oh, there's no point in telling you… You'll never—

ANTOINE: Come, come!… Let me hear Monsieur Béchamel's… *(Emphasizing, scornfully.)* condition!

CECILE: He… He says that you should… *(Stopping, shaking her head, disheartened.)* But you wouldn't…

ANTOINE: "Should"?… Wouldn't what, mademoiselle?

CECILE, *softly*: Apologize, monsieur… To Philippe…

ANTOINE, *scandalized*: To a flunky? A lackey? A… A domestic?… Never!

JOLICŒUR: Of course not! He's out of his mind to suggest—

CECILE, *to ANTOINE*: That's his final word, monsieur!

ANTOINE: Ha ha ha!… His final word?… *(To JOLICŒUR.)* His final word, indeed!… *(To CECILE.)* This is what I think of is final word! *(He stamps his foot on the floor and pretends to spit.)* Ptui! Ptui!

JOLICŒUR: A domestic! Really!

ANTOINE, *to CECILE*: Apologize?… To him?… When he called me a bee?… Ha ha ha!… And a burr?… Because he did, you know!… *(Brandishing his riding-crop.)* No! This is what he deserves!

CECILE: But…

ANTOINE: No, no!

JOLICŒUR: Apologize to a domestic? Did you ever…?

ANTOINE: No, no, no!

JOLICŒUR: Even a godson!

ANTOINE: His condition is unacceptable! *(To himself, proudly.)* Unacceptable, Beaujolais!

JOLICŒUR: I'll see that your horses are ready, monsieur.

ANTOINE: You're too kind!

JOLICŒUR: Apologize, indeed! *(Shaking his head.)* Tsk tsk tsk!

He exits, up center. CECILE follows him, stopping at the door.

ANTOINE, *gazing at her, aside*: Poor child! It breaks my heart… To think how it must be breaking hers… *(Sighing.)* Ah… With her beauty and my character, what children we could have made! *(Aloud, approaching her.)* Mademoiselle…

CECILE, *lowering her eyes*: Monsieur…

ANTOINE, *coming down left, taking the roll of music*: We'll not be needing this, I'm afraid.

CECILE, *wistfully*: I'm afraid not…

ANTOINE: Pity… Pity… We could have made lovely music.

CECILE: But… It's not my fault, you know. Nothing would have pleased me more.

ANTOINE: I know… I know… *(Moving up, toward her.)* If not for your father… And that imbecile, Philippe!

CECILE: Please! He's one of the family, monsieur!

ANTOINE: Your father…? Yes, I—

CECILE: Philippe!

ANTOINE: Oh… So be it! *(Emotionally.)* But… But this is not good-bye. Our paths will cross again. And in a far better place…

CECILE, *raising her eyes heavenward*: Ah…

ANTOINE: I'll see to it that they do… *(After a pause.)* This winter… In Paris…

CECILE: Monsieur?

ANTOINE: At the artists' ball, mademoiselle… *(On the verge of tears.)* And you'll save the first waltz for me!

CECILE: Oh yes!

ANTOINE: And the first polka… And the first mazurka…

CECILE: I will! I will!

ANTOINE: And… And all the others! Every one of them!

CECILE: Oh yes!

She begins weeping softly.

ANTOINE: Are you crying, mademoiselle? *(Encumbered by his cap and riding-crop, he awkwardly takes her in his arms.)* Cécile?… Can it be? You're shedding those tears for me?

CECILE, *softly*: Monsieur…

ANTOINE, *ecstatically*: For me!… Oh joy! Oh rapture!… *(He kisses her.)* Ah!… *(Suddenly.)* Let him ask me to do anything! *(Putting on his cap.)* Let him tell me to… to walk through Place Vendôme with a melon on my head!… Anything, mademoiselle!… But apologize? To that… that…

CECILE: If you loved me, monsieur—

ANTOINE: What?… If I… How can you doubt it?… You'll see! I'll have my man go pick one! *(Going to the window, calling.)* Dominique!… *(To CECILE.)* A big fat one!

CECILE, *drying her eyes*: Wouldn't it be simpler just to speak to Philippe?

ANTOINE, *returning to her*: To a flunky? A domestic?… A nobody?

CECILE: Precisely, monsieur… That makes it so unimportant…

ANTOINE: Oh? You think so?… My honor?… Unimportant?… *(To himself.)* She does have a point…

CECILE: Just think, if we were married…

ANTOINE, *sighing*: Ah…

CECILE: Think how happy we would be…

ANTOINE, *aside*: Oh my…

CECILE: Just think, monsieur!

ANTOINE: I… I know! I know!… *(Beginning to weaken.)* I… I… *(Resisting.)* No!… No! I can't!… I—

CECILE: Even for me?… It would prove how much you love me.

ANTOINE, *aside*: Damnation!

CECILE, *begging*: Please!… Please… *(Pointedly.)* Antoine!… I would never forget! I would spend my whole life just thinking of ways to love you!

ANTOINE, *weakening again*: You would?

CECILE: To thank you for your sacrifice!

ANTOINE: Well… *(Resisting again.)* No!

CECILE: I would! I would!

ANTOINE, *with an obvious struggle*: Bah!... *(Suddenly.)* Where is that miserable—

CECILE: You mean, you will?

ANTOINE: I'm not promising. But I'll do my best... I'll try...

At that moment, PHILIPPE appears, up center.

PHILIPPE, *approaching, to ANTOINE, curtly*: Your horses are ready!

CECILE, *to ANTOINE, softly*: Try!...

ANTOINE, *making a supreme effort, aside*: God help me!... *(Aloud, to PHILIPPE, in an angry tone, motioning to him with his riding-crop.)* Come here, you!

PHILIPPE, *seeing the crop, misinterpreting his intentions, alarmed*: Ayyy! *(Turning on his heel.)* Help!... Help!

He dashes out, up center, slamming the door behind him.

ANTOINE: What?... I try to apologize, and he runs away? *(Calling.)* Come back, you! Come back!

He dashes out in hot pursuit.

CECILE, *going to the window, looking out*: Good heavens! He's chasing him through the garden!... But Philippe is too fast... *(Appalled.)* Oh my! He's trampling my melons... Poor little things!... Oh!... Careful! The fountain... Don't fall in!... *(Relieved.)* Oh! That was close... No! He'll never catch him... *(Calling.)* Stop, Philippe!... Stop!... He only wants to... Now where did he disappear—

PHILIPPE comes running in, up left, panting.

PHILIPPE, *crossing right, stops briefly, leaning against the chair*: Help!... Help!

CECILE: Really! He only wants to—

ANTOINE, comes running in, up left, out of breath.

ANTOINE, *crossing, to PHILIPPE, brandishing his crop*: You... You...

PHILIPPE: Ayyy!

He dashes up left, exiting and slamming the door.

ANTOINE, *panting*: Enough is enough! I can't...

He falls in a heap onto the chair, right.

CECILE, *aside*: Tsk tsk tsk!... Poor dear!

ANTOINE: The wretch!... *(To CECILE.)* You see? I tried! You can't say I didn't try...

CECILE: Just stay right there, monsieur... I'll talk to him and send him in.

She exits, up left.

ANTOINE, *to himself, still out of breath*: Damn it all! He'd better hurry! I must say, I'm losing my enthusiasm by the minute!... Ha! Apologize to a domestic... Indeed!

DOMINIQUE appears, up center.

DOMINIQUE: Excuse me, monsieur, but I thought we were leaving.

ANTOINE: Ah! *(Getting up, struck by an idea.)* Dominique! Come here... *(To himself.)* I can practice on him!

DOMINIQUE, *overhearing, aside*: Practice what on me?

ANTOINE: Dominique, my friend... I... *(Stopping.)* No... Wait... First, tell me that I'm a burr!

DOMINIQUE: A boor, monsieur?

ANTOINE: No! A burr!... Tell me that I'm a burr, and that I buzz about like a bee!

DOMINIQUE: But…

ANTOINE: That's an order, Dominique!… Then I'll apologize… Go on!

DOMINIQUE, *approaching him, with a shrug*: Monsieur is a burr!… There!… *(ANTOINE gives him a swift kick in the shins.)* Ayyy!

ANTOINE: That one doesn't count… Tell me again… And that I buzz about like a bee…

DOMINIQUE: But…

ANTOINE: Go on! Go on!… Then I'll apologize…

DOMINIQUE: Monsieur is a burr! *(ANTOINE tries in vain to control himself, and gives him another kick.)* Ayyy!

ANTOINE: Again!… You see? That kick wasn't as hard… I'm getting used to it!… Go on! Again… And that I buzz--

DOMINIQUE: No, thank you!

He limps up to the door, up enter, and exits.

ANTOINE, *alone*: Ah! That helped… I almost think I can do it. *(Looking up left.)* I thought she said she was going to send him in… *(He goes to the table, down left, takes the bell and rings several times.)* Ah! Love, love, love!… Who would ever think… *(He rings again and again, but no one appears.)* Well? Is he going to make me ring all day? And to apologize, damn it!

He rings the bell furiously. PHILIPPE finally appears, up left, standing timidly at the door.

PHILIPPE: You rang?

ANTOINE, *calmly*: Yes… Come in! Come in! *(Pointing up center with his riding-crop.)* I practiced on Dominique… Just now…

PHILIPPE, *not daring to enter*: But… *(Pointing to the crop.)* That…

ANTOINE: Quite right!… *(He puts the crop under his arm.)* There! You see? *(Showing his hands empty.)* Now then, Philippe… My dear Philippe… *(Aside.)* Good God! What am I saying?… A lackey, who called me… *(Aloud.)* I may have been a trifle sharp with you just now…

PHILIPPE: Well…

ANTOINE: But… But… *(With great effort.)* Would you accept… Would you… *(Aside.)* Vulgar brute!… *(Aloud.)* My dear Philippe… Would you accept… *(Gritting his teeth.)* My… *(Aside.)* Ugh!… *(Aloud.)* My… apologies?

PHILIPPE, *very properly*: That depends how you ask me.

ANTOINE, *exploding*: What?

PHILIPPE: If you ask me real nice…

ANTOINE, *beside himself, seizing him by the throat*: You will, damn it! You will!

PHILIPPE: Ayyy!

ANTOINE, *as PHILIPPE continues reacting loudly*: You'll accept them, do you hear?

PHILIPPE: Help!… Police!

ANTOINE, *accompanying each exclamation with a whack of the crop on his shoulders*: You wretch!… You lackey!… You flunky!… You… You chattel!

BECHAMEL and CECILE enter, up right, and JOLICŒUR, up center.

BECHAMEL: Philippe!

CECILE,	*together:*	What on earth…
JOLICŒUR,		What's the trouble?

ANTOINE, *aside*: Damnation!

BECHAMEL: What's wrong?

ANTOINE, *to* PHILIPPE, *in a whisper*: Five hundred francs if you keep your mouth shut!

PHILIPPE, *rubbing his shoulders*: Ayyy!

ANTOINE, *continuing, in a whisper*: And smile! *(To* BECHAMEL.*)* You're interrupting, monsieur! I was just beginning to apologize…

CECILE, *to* BECHAMEL: You see, papá? I told you…

BECHAMEL: Now that's something I've got to see!

ANTOINE, *to* PHILIPPE, *still whispering*: Smile, damn you!

BECHAMEL, *sitting down on the loveseat*: Up close! *(To* ANTOINE.*)* Please… Go on! *(To* PHILIPPE.*)* Don't let me interrupt…

JOLICŒUR, *to* ANTOINE, *on one side of him, in a whisper*: Don't give in…

ANTOINE, *turning to him*: No… I…

CECILE, *to* ANTOINE, *on the other side, in a whisper*: Please!… For me… For us…

ANTOINE, *turning to her*: Yes… I…

BECHAMEL, *to* ANTOINE: I bet you five francs you won't!

ANTOINE: I will!… *(Not knowing which way to turn.)* I… *(To* PHILIPPE, *approaching him.)* Monsieur Philippe… *(Aside, wiping the sweat from his brow with his sleeve.)* Good God! I'm burning up!… *(Aloud, to* PHILIPPE, *affecting a formal air.)* As one gentleman to another… *(Trying desperately to resist making threatening gestures with the riding-crop.)* I… I… *(To* JOLICŒUR, *in a whisper, handing it to him.)* Please! Take this before I use it!

JOLICŒUR, *complying*: But…

ANTOINE, *continuing, aloud, to* PHILIPPE: As one gentleman to another… *(Aside.)* Ugh!… *(Extending his hand.)* Your hand, monsieur…

PHILIPPE, *hesitating*: Well… *(Finally giving him his hand, which* ANTOINE, *unable to control himself, squeezes in a vise-like grip, grimacing.)* Ayyy!

He pulls his hand free.

ANTOINE, *whispering to him*: Smile, damn it!… Five hundred francs… *(To* BECHAMEL, *as* PHILIPPE, *shaking his hand in pain, attempts to force a smile.)* There, monsieur! As I told you…

BECHAMEL: You call that an apology? Really!

CECILE, *to* ANTOINE, *coyly*: Please, Antoine…

ANTOINE, *aside*: Damnation! *(Summoning up all his will power, to* PHILIPPE.*)* Monsieur Philippe… *(Uttering each word with a supreme effort.)* I… I… *(Aside.)* Oh!… *(Aloud, continuing.)* I humbly request that you… *(Glaring at* BECHAMEL.*)* that you… *(Aside.)* No! I can't do it!

CECILE: Go on!

ANTOINE, *continuing*: …that you accept… *(Aside.)* God help me!

CECILE: Yes! Go on! Don't stop now!

ANTOINE, *to* JOLICŒUR, *in a whisper, putting his hands behind his back*: Please! Hold my hands! Tight!... Don't let them go!

JOLICŒUR, *complying*: Bah!

ANTOINE, *continuing, to* PHILIPPE: That you accept this expression... of my heartfelt... *(Through clenched teeth.)* apology!... *(With a sigh.)* Ohhh! *(His hands still immobilized, giving* PHILIPPE *a sharp kick in the shins, unseen by the others, in a whisper.)* Smile, I said!

CECILE, *clapping*: Ah!... Finally!

BECHAMEL: Bravo! Bravo!... Now that's more like it!

JOLICŒUR, *under his breath*: Coward!

He moves off, right.

BECHAMEL, *getting up, to* ANTOINE, *handing him some coins*: Well I've lost my five francs. But in a good cause... *(Emphasizing.)* Son!... My daughter is yours!

CECILE, *to* ANTOINE: How can I ever thank you!

ANTOINE: Oh... I'll think of something...

CECILE *takes him aside and continues expressing her pleasure.*

JOLICŒUR, *to* BECHAMEL: And now I hope we can go pack our bags!

CECILE, *overhearing*: What?

JOLICŒUR: At last!

ANTOINE, *to* BECHAMEL: Are you going somewhere... *(Emphasizing.)* Father?

BECHAMEL: To Italy... *Il paese del sole!*

JOLICŒUR: The land of the sun!

BECHAMEL: With my dear friend Jolicœur!... But not until after the wedding, of course!

JOLICŒUR: Immediately after! *(To* ALPHONSE.*)* Before he has a grandchild that he simply has to hug!

BECHAMEL *gives a hearty laugh.*

ANTOINE, *to* JOLICŒUR: Monsieur?

JOLICŒUR: Or that has to be weaned... Or out of school...

CECILE, *to* BECHAMEL, *quizzically*: Papá?

JOLICŒUR: Or married!

ANTOINE, *to* BECHAMEL: And you're taking Philippe, of course?

BECHAMEL: Why, no...

ANTOINE, *his lips frozen in a smile, gives* PHILIPPE *several unseen kicks and pokes.*

ANTOINE, *to* PHILIPPE, *in a whisper, before he has time to react*: Smile, damn it! Smile!... *(Aloud, to* BECHAMEL*)* Then he can come and work for me!

JOLICŒUR: What a generous offer!

ANTOINE, *aside*: And I can throw him off the roof of my beautiful building!

PHILIPPE, *in a whisper, to* ANTOINE: And my five hundred francs?

ANTOINE, *in a whisper, giving him* BECHAMEL's *coins*: Here! Take five on account... *(Aside.)* Or drown him next door, in the Oriental Baths!... *(Aloud.)* Dear, dear Philippe... *(Aside.)* Temper, temper...

He and CECILE *embrace as* PHILIPPE *goes limping off, exiting up center.*

JOLICŒUR *and* BECHAMEL *shake hands on a job well done.*

JOLICŒUR: To Italy...
BECHAMEL: To Italy...
JOLICŒUR: To Rome...
BECHAMEL: And Florence...
JOLICŒUR: And Venice...

They continue as the curtain slowly falls.

BECHAMEL: The canals...
JOLICŒUR: The gondolas...
BECHAMEL: The signoras...
JOLICŒUR: The signorinas...

CURTAIN.

Pater Omnipotens, or A Suitor Unsuited

Mon Isménie!, 1852

Eugène Labiche & Marc-Michel

Characters

OCTAVE PETITFOUR, a middle-aged widower and overprotective father

ADELBERT RUMPSKINNE, a magistrate from Brussels, latest in a long line of suitors

GRISELDE, Petitfour's wealthy spinster sister, impressed by her own importance

VITRUVIA, Petitfour's young daughter, eager to find a husband despite her father's objections

CHIQUETTE, a cheeky maid

A middle-class drawing-room. Upstage center, French doors leading to the rest of the apartment. Angled corners, up right and left, each with a curtained door. The one up right leads to the dining-room, the one up left opens onto a small terrace. Next to it, in the up left wall, a window, and a small chair close by. Right center, the door to Petitfour's room, opening inward. Left center, the door to Rumpskinne's, likewise opening inward. Upstage of the latter, a small chair, close to the wall, placed so that when the door is open it is still visible. Down right, against the wall, a small desk with writing paraphernalia. Down left, a table. On it, an empty vase. Midstage right, an armchair; midstage left, a loveseat. Other appropriate furnishings—carpet, candelabra, pictures, etc.

At rise, CHIQUETTE *is vigorously brushing a morning-coat and trousers with a clothes brush.*

CHIQUETTE, *musing*: Now that's what I call quality!… Just the suit that would suit a suitor… And I should know, believe me! How many have we had, the last two years?… One after another… And each one… *(Brushing.)* Brushed off like the one before!… It's a shame, if you ask me. Nice young sprouts, all of them… They show up, fresh as a daisy… Full of beans… And after a couple of days… Pfff! Monsieur throws them out on their ear, like yesterday's *pommes frites*!… Really!… And Mademoiselle Vitruvia, poor thing… *(Sighing.)* Still single, and not a prospect in sight… *(She lays the clothes neatly on the chair by the door, left.)* Except for this one… For all the good it will do him… *(Looking toward the door.)* Still fast asleep, I suppose… And who can blame him? *(She goes about the room tidying up.)* That awful night train from Brussels… It can wear out the best of them… Well, he won't be staying long! *(Shaking her head.)* Today monsieur will show him Notre Dame. And tomorrow, a boatride on the Seine… Next day, back to the station!… Bye-bye! Bon voyage!… And another one bites the dust… Tsk tsk tsk!… Next!… Next!

The door up right opens and PETITFOUR *enters.*

PETITFOUR: Chiquette…

CHIQUETTE: Oh!… Was there something monsieur wanted?

PETITFOUR: Yes! A cup of good strong coffee!… I didn't sleep a wink.

CHIQUETTE: Tsk tsk tsk!…

PETITFOUR: And I've been up since the crack of dawn.

CHIQUETTE: Monsieur's liver again?

PETITFOUR, *ignoring her question*: Is he still asleep?

CHIQUETTE: Who, monsieur?

PETITFOUR, *pointing left*: Him! Monsieur… *(Unsure of the name.)* Monsieur… Van Rump…

CHIQUETTE: The young sprout from Brussels?

PETITFOUR: Almost noon, and—

CHIQUETTE, *interrupting*: I guess so, monsieur…

PETITFOUR: You guess? Didn't you go in?

CHIQUETTE: Just to get his clothes and give them a good brushing… After all, all night in the train…

PETITFOUR: Well, what do you think of him? Ugly, isn't he!

CHIQUETTE: Really, monsieur… I didn't look… He was in bed…

PETITFOUR: Idiot! In bed or not! You're supposed to look. How else can you tell?

CHIQUETTE: Besides, monsieur… I've given up the flesh. *(Crossing herself.)* Since I had my vision…

PETITFOUR, *under his breath*: Vision… *(To* CHIQUETTE.*)* Does he snore at least? Like a saw?

CHIQUETTE: I wouldn't know.

PETITFOUR: Does he wear a woolen nightcap? Knotted under his chin?… And with a tassel?

CHIQUETTE: I told monsieur… I didn't look.

PETITFOUR: Bah! What good are you! *(Waving her off.)* Get out of here! You're useless!… Absolutely useless!

CHIQUETTE: My vision, monsieur…

She exits, up right, crossing herself as she goes.

PETITFOUR: Her vision!… *(He heaves a sigh.)* If anyone was going to have a vision, why couldn't it be my Vitruvia? I'd be done with all these damnable suitors, once and for all!… No more boatrides on the Seine… No more visits to Notre Dame… No more young scoundrels, every other week! All with the same idea… To take my Vitruvia away from me… My little *puella*, the light of my life… How dare they even think such a thing?… *(Mimicking.)* "But she's twenty-four years old, Octave! It's high time she was married!" If Griselde had her way I'd have married her off at twelve!… Twenty-four, indeed!… I got married at thirty-eight, and even then I was too young! But try telling that to the youth of today!… *O tempora, o mores!*… Nothing but a band of thieves, out to rob me of my little Vitruvia!… *(Pacing back and forth, gesticulating, stopping every so often to make a point.)* Why can't they leave us in peace? Do I invite them? Do I shout from the rooftops: "*Venite omnes!*… Come one, come all!"… It's incredible!… You spend your life raising a beautiful little flower. You nurture it, you water it, you protect it from the cold. Just so you can have it all to yourself… Nothing too good for it… The best of everything… *(Pacing.)* You give it English lessons… Even Latin… You teach it music, and geography, and astronomy… And then, one fine day, some nobody comes calling. Someone you never met, from who knows where?… He gets off the train and makes himself at home. And the next thing you know he's walking off, arm in arm, with your precious flower, and telling you: "I hope you don't mind, monsieur!… We'll try to come visit on Sundays, if we have time…" Very nice… First you're a *paterfamilias*, and then you're a Sunday dinner… If they have time!… No! It's a scandal! There ought to be a law!… *(Pacing.)* I remember the first one… "I have the honor of requesting your daughter's hand, monsieur…" Ha ha! Her hand, indeed!… It was my foot he got! The wretch!… And you know where!… The only problem is, she wants to get married! She actually wants to!… At twenty-four, God help us!… And the tears… You wouldn't believe… The weeping, and the wailing… What can I do? I've tried to take her mind off of it. I thought her singing lessons would help… Bah! Her teacher was a handsome devil, and you can imagine… So now I just let them come, and I hope they'll be monsters. Or at least that they'll have plenty of faults… Even little ones… I don't care… Because, no matter how little, I scratch till I find them. And then: "Thank you so much for coming, monsieur. What a shame you can't stay!… *(Dejected.)* Until the next one!… *(Looking left.)* Like the buffoon in there… The one who came last night… It's my sister who went and invited him, of all things!… A rich old maid… My sister, that is… And no children… I mean, of course not… So this one I have to treat with kid gloves!…

Well, we'll see about this Monsieur Van Rump of hers! *(Looking at his watch.)* Eleven-thirty indeed!… There's one fault already… He sleeps too late!… Well, it's time I started scratching… I'm sure I can find some big ones! *(Noticing the clothing on the chair.)* Ah! His coat… What say I have a look? Didn't Tacitus say: "It is oft in the pocket of his toga that we find the secret of a man's passions…"? Or was it Suetonius?… No matter… Let's see… *(As he approaches the chair, about to take the coat, the door, left, opens, and an arm reaches out, quickly seizes it, and shuts the door.)* Ah! The scoundrel!… Never mind… I'll scratch till I find something!

VITRUVIA enters, up right.

VITRUVIA: Good morning, papá…

PETITFOUR, *joining her*: Good morning, my child! *(Giving her a kiss.)* My sunflower of the dawn!… My heliotrope!… My—

VITRUVIA, *interrupting*: Is it true what Aunt Griselde told me, papá?

PETITFOUR: Told you?… What?

VITRUVIA: That a new suitor arrived last night?… From Brussels…

PETITFOUR, *sadly*: I'm afraid so, treasure… Not quite what we ordered, but…

VITRUVIA: Ordered, papá?

PETITFOUR: In a manner of speaking… We wanted a soprano aria, and they sent us a baritone solo… With tuba obbligato!

VITRUVIA: "They," papá?… An aria?

PETITFOUR: A metaphor, my love… Not at all what you would like… Take my word… Not at all…

VITRUVIA: But… But you say that about every… *(Searching for the word.)* every metaphor who comes calling!

PETITFOUR: Because it's always true! They're all the same. Every last one of them… Not for you… Not for my Vitruvia…

VITRUVIA: But…

PETITFOUR: Besides, child… We're alone…

VITRUVIA: But…

PETITFOUR: You can tell me the truth…

VITRUVIA: Papá?

PETITFOUR: Do you really want to get married so badly? Do you really want to leave your poor little pater?

VITRUVIA: But… I'm twenty-four years old! I—

PETITFOUR, *interrupting*: Bah! Your aunt Griselde is forty-nine! Does she want to get married?

VITRUVIA: But she… But I… *(Sulking.)* I don't want to be an old maid for the rest of my life! *(Pointing left.)* And maybe this metaphor…

PETITFOUR: I doubt it… *(Under his breath.)* Not when I get through scratching…

VITRUVIA: Have you seen him? How old is he?

PETITFOUR: Who knows? *(Sarcastically.)* I didn't have time to count his teeth!

VITRUVIA: Really, papá! He's not a horse, you know!

PETITFOUR: Quite! The horse is a noble beast, whereas… whereas our Monsieur Van Rump…

VITRUVIA, *correcting*: Rumpskinne, papá!... Auntie says his name is...

PETITFOUR, *interrupting, with a wave of the hand*: Whatever...

VITRUVIA: See? You don't even know his name, and you're already finding fault!

PETITFOUR: Finding fault? Me?... Bah! Nothing of the kind...

VITRUVIA: But you said...

PETITFOUR: I... I'll love him like my son... My very own son!... There! Is that better?

VITRUVIA: Like the son you don't have?... You can't fool me, papá! I wasn't born yesterday!

PETITFOUR: I'm only thinking of you, Vitruvia! I just want to see you happy!

VITRUVIA: So do I!... And married!... I want to see me married!

PETITFOUR: I know... In time... *Festina lente*... *(Muttering.)* Stubborn child! *(Aloud.)* All in due time...

VITRUVIA: But why isn't it "due time" now, papá? Why wasn't it last month? Or the month before? *(Wheedling.)* Papá dearest... I know you want what's best for me. But I'm not getting any younger!

PETITFOUR, *caressing her*: Listen to her, will you!... A baby, and all she can talk about is a husband!

VITRUVIA: Besides, Aunt Griselde says you hate all my metaphors...

PETITFOUR: She what?

VITRUVIA: ...and that none of my suitors will ever suit you.

PETITFOUR: Me?... But that's absurd! You know how I practically scour the countryside to find them! Why, we've had eight so far this year, and it's only August! That's one a month! Any other young lady would be delighted!

VITRUVIA: Yes, papá... But you send them all away!

PETITFOUR, *hardly listening*: And if this one has as many bad habits as the rest, I have another one ready and waiting in the wings.

VITRUVIA: You do?

PETITFOUR: Yes... Oscar de Buzenval... So you see... My sister doesn't know what she's talking about! *(Aside.)* An ugly little runt... All covered with hair...

VITRUVIA, *relenting*: Well...

PETITFOUR, *under his breath*: Like a black widow spider... *(As an afterthought.)* Black widower, I mean...

VITRUVIA: And is he nice, papá?

PETITFOUR: De Buzenval? Nice?... Why, he's absolutely charming... And he speaks English! *(Aside.)* Like a Chinaman, but sill... *(Aloud.)* Think of the lovely conversations you can have!... And he's much handsomer than Griselde's... Griselde's Rumpskinne... With that debauched, hangdog look of his... *(He looks left and gives a little shudder of disgust.)* Why, anyone would think he never slept. At least, not at night!...

VITRUVIA: But... I thought you didn't know him... You said—

PETITFOUR, *interrupting*: I don't... But I caught a glimpse of him last night. And believe me... *(Grimacing.) Eheu, filia mea!...*

VITRUVIA: But what do you expect? All night in the train, papá... It must have been the trip...

PETITFOUR: No... *(Categorically.)* It's vice and riotous living, Vitruvia!

VITRUVIA: Riotous living? A Belgian?

PETITFOUR: Why, debauchery is written all over his face!

VITRUVIA: There! You see?… You're doing it again… *(On the verge of tears.)* You just don't want me to get married! Ever… That's all…

She begins sobbing quietly.

PETITFOUR, *embracing her*: But I do… I do… It's just that… that…

VITRUVIA: That what, papá?

PETITFOUR: Aren't you perfectly happy here? With me?

VITRUVIA: Yes, but…

PETITFOUR: Then what more could you want?

VITRUVIA, *aside, sighing*: Oh!

PETITFOUR: You'll see! I'll send for all the soprano arias you like… Without tuba obbligato… You'll be able to sing from morning to night. And I'll find you another teacher… *(Aside.)* A woman, this time…

VITRUVIA: But there's more to life than music!… And besides, I'd rather sing duets!

PETITFOUR, *aside*: Stubborn child!

GRISELDE enters, up right, obviously in a state, calling back offstage.

GRISELDE: And the best china, understand?… And the silverware…

PETITFOUR, *to GRISELDE*: My goodness! How fancy!… What's the occasion, sister dear? Why all the fuss?

GRISELDE: Fuss?… Don't be absurd… Nothing is too good for dear Adelbert!

PETITFOUR: "Adel…" who?

GRISELDE: Adelbert… *(Motioning toward the door, left.)* Monsieur Rumpskinne… I hope he likes pig's brains. What do you think?

PETITFOUR: Think? About what?

GRISELDE: Pig's brains… A Belgian, after all…

PETITFOUR: I'm afraid I have no idea…

GRISELDE: Oh!… What good are you, Octave! Do I have to do everything myself?

PETITFOUR: But I can't very well go wake the young man up and say: "Excuse me, monsieur, but do you like pig's brains?" *Domine Deus!* He'd pull his nightcap over his mouth and curse like a sailor!

He proceeds to mumble a few indistinguishable sounds.

GRISELDE: Please! Not in front of the child!

PETITFOUR: And I wouldn't blame him!

VITRUVIA, *to PETITFOUR, rather shocked*: His nightcap, papá? *(To GRISELDE.)* You mean, he wears a nightcap?

PETITFOUR: Does he?… I'll say! With a long tassel, to boot…

VITRUVIA, *grimacing*: Oh!

PETITFOUR: Chiquette told me… She saw him… *(He gives a little shudder of disgust.)* "Quite a sight," she said! "Monsieur can't imagine…" *(Looking left, under his breath.)* So much for you, my friend!

GRISELDE: Really! Is that any way to make fun of your son-in-law?

PETITFOUR: My… Pardon me, sister dear! Aren't you rushing things a bit? *(Under his breath.)* Son-in-law indeed!

GRISELDE, *solemnly*: Now look, Octave…

PETITFOUR: You were saying…?

GRISELDE: I shouldn't have to remind you that I enjoy a very comfortable fortune…

PETITFOUR: No… I mean, yes… You shouldn't…

GRISELDE: …and that, young as I am, and fit…

PETITFOUR, *aside*: For what, *mehercules!*

GRISELDE: …I've decided to sacrifice myself and my posterity… the fruit of my loins…

PETITFOUR, *aside*: *Miserere!*

GRISELDE: …in order to insure the future of my niece.

VITRUVIA, *touched*: Auntie dear…

GRISELDE, *continuing, dramatically*: Yes… I am willing to remain a flower unpicked… A fair bloom unplucked…

PETITFOUR, *aside*: *Cum grano salis!*

GRISELDE: But only on one condition!… And that is, that I see this dear young child happily married…

PETITFOUR: Of course, Griselde! Of course!… There's nothing I want more!

VITRUVIA, *to PETITFOUR*: Papá?

PETITFOUR, *continuing*: But you have to admit… First she has to find a husband. I mean, without one—

GRISELDE, *interrupting, categorically*: And so I have, Octave! *(Pointing left.)* Young Monsieur Rumpskinne is a perfect gentleman… Patient, docile, unassuming…

PETITFOUR, *under his breath*: Like an ass!

GRISELDE: Sober… With no vices… Virtuous to a fault…

PETITFOUR, *aside*: We'll see about that!

GRISELDE: The perfect match! I guarantee it.

VITRUVIA, *enthusiastically, to GRISELDE*: Oh, auntie…

PETITFOUR, *with a note of sarcasm*: What more could we ask?

GRISELDE, *to PETITFOUR*: And I hope that you won't treat him as shabbily as all the others!

PETITFOUR: Shabbily?… I beg your—

VITRUVIA: Yes, papá! All the ones you sent away, for no reason at all…

PETITFOUR, *to VITRUVIA*: No reason…? All those fortune-hunters?… Why, the last one, Monsieur de Coquauvin, said your dowry was too small! Can you imagine…

GRISELDE: Oh! Octave! That's not true!

PETITFOUR: On my honor!… *(Mimicking.)* "It's simply not enough, monsieur! Why, I'd be the laughing-stock…"

GRISELDE, *to PETITFOUR*: I heard every word!… The door was open, and… and I heard every word!

PETITFOUR, *abashed*: Oh?

GRISELDE: Even when he offered to marry her with no dowry at all!

VITRUVIA: What?

GRISELDE, *to* PETITFOUR: And you said he would never do… That Vitruvia found him unattractive… That's what you said, Octave!

VITRUVIA: That I what?

GRISELDE: Don't deny it! I was right outside the door.

VITRUVIA: Oh, papá! You didn't!

GRISELDE: I heard you…

VITRUVIA: Unattractive? Monsieur de Coquauvin?

PETITFOUR, *aside*: Oh my!… Caught *in flagrante delicto! (Aloud, to* GRISELDE.*)* But… You must have misunderstood…

VITRUVIA, *to* PETITFOUR: You mean, that's why he… Oh!

GRISELDE: I heard every word!

PETITFOUR: So? I exaggerated a little! Besides, the man is an absolute libertine! You have no idea what things I found out about him!

GRISELDE: Things?

VITRUVIA: What things?

PETITFOUR: Things… Things I wouldn't say in front of two ladies… *(Waving them both off.)* Go out, and I'll explain…

GRISELDE: Now look here, Octave! You're not fooling me for one minute! This time I'm going to watch you like a hawk!

VITRUVIA: So am I, papá!

GRISELDE: You won't pull the wool over my eyes again!

VITRUVIA: Or mine…

GRISELDE: Adelbert Rumpskinne is a model of virtue… Pure as the driven snow…

PETITFOUR: Yes, well… All I ask is that we look at the facts…

VITRUVIA: Of course, papá…

PETITFOUR: The cold, hard facts… *(To* GRISELDE.*)* Cold as the driven snow, sister dear…

GRISELDE: Of course, Octave… *(As the door, left, opens.)* Ah!… Shhh! Shhh!… Here he is…

VITRUVIA, *to* PETITFOUR, *in a whisper*: Oh! He's handsome!

PETITFOUR, *to* VITRUVIA, *likewise*: Please… Appearances are deceiving. He just looks handsome…

GRISELDE, *approaching* RUMPSKINNE, *who is still hidden by the open door*: Ah, monsieur… *(To the others.)* Permit me to introduce Monsieur Adelbert Rumpskinne…

RUMPSKINNE, *stepping forward, with a little bow*: Bachelor of Arts…

GRISELDE: My brother, Monsieur Octave Petitfour…

PETITFOUR, *correcting*: De Petitfour…

RUMPSKINNE, *continuing*: Diplomate in Civil and Criminal Law, chief clerk in the offices of Maître Gottferdeck, Brussels'… most celebrated solicitor…

He gives his heels a little click.

PETITFOUR, *returning his bow, coldly*: Charmed, monsieur… *(Aside.)* I was right…

GRISELDE: And my niece, Vitruvia…

PETITFOUR, *aside*: A face that reeks of riotous living!

GRISELDE, *continuing*: Mademoiselle Petitfour…

PETITFOUR, *whispering to* GRISELDE, *with a little nudge*: De… De…

VITRUVIA, *curtsying*: Monsieur…

RUMPSKINNE, *gallantly*: I thought I was going to Paris. But I see that I erred, and came to Paradise instead!

VITRUVIA, *coyly*: Oh, monsieur…

GRISELDE, *charmed at the bon mot*: What a delightful thought, monsieur! And so terribly witty… Paradise… Paris…

PETITFOUR: Yes… And old as the hills! I heard it years ago.

RUMPSKINNE, *aside*: Blast! I thought I made it up in the train!

GRISELDE, *to* RUMPSKINNE: I trust, monsieur, that we will have the pleasure of your company for a few days.

RUMPSKINNE: Ah, madame…

GRISELDE, *correcting him*: "Mademoiselle," monsieur…

RUMPSKINNE, *to* GRISELDE: Yes… Mademoiselle… *(Gazing, enraptured, at* VITRUVIA.*)* I can safely say that the wildest of wild horses will not drag me willingly from this oasis of loveliness. This pleasure-dome of beauty…

GRISELDE, *impressed*: Oh!

RUMPSKINNE, *continuing, clutching at his chest, poetically*: Be still, my heart!

PETITFOUR, *looking down at his shoes, under his breath*: Be still, my foot!

GRISELDE, *to* RUMPSKINNE: I didn't know you were a poet, monsieur.

VITRUVIA, *to* RUMPSKINNE: Are you a musician too?

RUMPSKINNE, *falsely modest*: Well… I've been known to tootle a bit on the flute.

VITRUVIA, *clapping*: Oh! Then you can play with me!

RUMPSKINNE, *momentarily misunderstanding*: I can?

VITRUVIA: I sing, monsieur.

RUMPSKINNE: Oh…

VITRUVIA: I'm a soprano.

RUMPSKINNE: Ah! The very thought…

VITRUVIA: And I can sing a high E flat!

RUMPSKINNE, *as if most impressed*: Oh! E flat!… So beautiful, and she can sing a high E flat!… Oh, the joy…

VITRUVIA: What's your favorite key, monsieur? Mine is F sharp minor.

RUMPSKINNE: Key?… Any key… As long as it's the key to your heart, mademoiselle!

GRISELDE: What a delightful thought, monsieur!

PETITFOUR: Yes… And even older than the hills…

RUMPSKINNE: Oh?

PETITFOUR, *under his breath*: Idiot!

RUMPSKINNE, *aside*: I thought I made that one up too in the train…

GRISELDE, *to* PETITFOUR, *in a whisper*: What do you think of him?

PETITFOUR, *replying in a whisper*: He's knock-kneed, for heaven's sake… And a nincompoop to boot!

GRISELDE, *replying, angrily*: Oh! You'll never change! *(To* RUMPSKINNE.*)* I hope you weren't too cold last night, monsieur.

RUMPSKINNE: Cold? Not at all… As long as my head is covered…

GRISELDE, *with a little laugh*: Yes… So we heard…

RUMPSKINNE: "Cold the night but warm the head, man lies cozy in his bed."

VITRUVIA: Oh?

RUMPSKINNE: It's a Flemish proverb, mademoiselle…

VITRUVIA: But…

RUMPSKINNE: Freely translated…

VITRUVIA: For a young man… I mean, don't you find it terribly unattractive?

RUMPSKINNE: Unattractive?… Why… What?

GRISELDE: A woolen nightcap… For an old man, perhaps… But—

RUMPSKINNE, *interrupting*: Heavens, no! A madras foulard… *(To* GRISELDE.*)* They're terribly chic, mademoiselle. Everyone is Brussels wears one.

VITRUVIA: Oh?

GRISELDE: But I thought…

VITRUVIA: We distinctly heard…

GRISELDE, *looking daggers at* PETITFOUR: We were told, monsieur…

PETITFOUR, *self-defensively*: Chiquette!… It was Chiquette!… *(Aside.)* Damn! *Flagrante delicto* again!

GRISELDE: Well, no matter… *(To* RUMPSKINNE.*)* Now then, monsieur… I should think you must be hungry.

RUMPSKINNE: Please… No hurry on my account…

GRISELDE: I'll go see to lunch.

She goes up right, to the door.

RUMPSKINNE, *calling after her as she exits*: I'm perfectly happy to sit here and chat with my dear Monsieur de Petitfour… And mademoiselle…

PETITFOUR, *coldly*: Impossible! We were just on our way to the cellar, monsieur…

VITRUVIA: But papá…

PETITFOUR: For a bottle of wine… *(Aside.)* The cheapest one I have… *(To* VITRUVIA.*)* Come, come…

VITRUVIA: Yes, papá…

As RUMPSKINNE *gives a little bow, she and* PETITFOUR *exit, up center.*

RUMPSKINNE: Well now… *(He sits down on the loveseat.)* So far so good… Though I must say monsieur doesn't seem overly fond of me!… I can't imagine why… It can't be my clothes. The very best in Brussels!… Or anything I said… Still, the minute I open my mouth… The minute I utter a delightful bon mot.… *(Mimicking.)* "Old as the hills, monsieur!…" Indeed! He makes me feel like a perfect fool! And everyone knows I'm nothing of the kind! Not even almost perfect!… Not even just a little… Oh well, at least mademoiselle seems won over. *(Thrusting his thumbs into his vest pockets, fatuously.)* And who can blame her?… Both mademoiselles, in fact… But especially the daughter! *(Looking toward the door, up right.)* Because the other one… Thank you just the same!… Ah, Vitruvia!… Rosy cheeks… The picture of health… A thing of beauty!… What perfect specimens our children are going to be! Her looks, my wit… *(Feeling something in one of the pockets.)* What… ? *(Taking out a medallion.)*

Ah yes... The miniature I bought at the flea market last week... *(Holding it up, admiringly.)* A bargain at nine gilders... They wanted fifteen, but... *(Mimicking.)* "It's Cleopatra, monsieur!..." "But I didn't think anyone knew what she looked like." "They don't... That's why it's so valuable..." *(Struck by an idea, standing up.)* I know! I'll give it to her... "One beauty to another, mademoiselle..." That should impress her! *(He puts it back in his pocket.)* It will make up for my... Well, for my little faults... If she ever discovers them, that is... Because I do have a couple... Exactly two!... The first one... Ah, the first one is my... *(Hesitating.)* How shall I say?... My weakness for the fair sex... My overwhelming passion... *(He sighs.)* Let a beautiful woman look at me in a... a certain way... Let her lips part, and her sweet voice whisper "Adelbert... Adelbert..." Oh! *(Shuddering.)* I cease to be a man... A mere mortal, I mean... And suddenly I turn into a seething volcano. A flood of molten lava just waiting to erupt... *(Calming down, heaving a sigh.)* And the second one, you wonder?... Vice number two?... Ah! A social aberration... A foul, vile habit... *(Taking a snuffbox from his other vest pocket, holding it up.)* Yes... Snuff!... The exquisite delight of tickling my nostrils with a pinch of the divine powder!... *(About to open the snuffbox, resisting, then finally giving in.)* Even now... Why not? While I'm alone...

Coming down right, he takes a generous pinch, just as PETITFOUR *appears at the door, up center, with a bottle of wine and a lighted candle.*

RUMPSKINNE, *as he sees him, aside*: Oh my...

He quickly pockets the snuffbox but drops the pinch of snuff on the floor.

PETITFOUR: Did you drop something, monsieur?

RUMPSKINNE: Me?

PETITFOUR, *coming down right and putting the bottle on the desk*: Yes... *(Pointing.)* That... *(He joins him, bends down with the candle, and examines the snuff.)* That...

RUMPSKINNE, *bending down beside him, innocently*: Can I help?... Did you lose something?

PETITFOUR, *picking up the snuff*: Why... It looks like... *(Sniffing it.)* It is!... *(Disgustedly.)* It's tobacco, monsieur!... Or snuff, to be precise...

He throws it away.

RUMPSKINNE: Ah!... No doubt when mademoiselle... Your sister, monsieur... When she dropped her snuffbox...

PETITFOUR: Oh? She did?

RUMPSKINNE: Why yes... You remember...

PETITFOUR: Perhaps... *(Aside.)* Clever devil... But I'll catch him...

RUMPSKINNE: Indeed... *(Aside.)* That was close!

PETITFOUR: Well, no matter... *(Aside.)* Time to start scratching...

RUMPSKINNE: As you say... *(Aside.)* Time to watch my step...

PETITFOUR, *gesturing toward the loveseat*: Please...

RUMPSKINNE: Why, thank you... *(He moves left, to the loveseat, followed by* PETITFOUR, *gesturing.)* After you...

PETITFOUR: No need to stand on ceremony... Adelbert!

RUMPSKINNE: No... No need to stand...

He sits down, leaving PETITFOUR *standing.*

PETITFOUR, *under his breath*: Crass dolt!

RUMPSKINNE, *patting the seat next to him*: No need, monsieur… Please, make yourself comfortable.

PETITFOUR blows out the candle, puts it on the desk, returns to the loveseat, and sits down.

PETITFOUR, *with feigned joviality*: As I was saying… It's a pleasure to welcome you among my *lares et penates*, as they say…

RUMPSKINNE, *aside*: They do? *(Aloud, echoing him mechanically, nodding.)* It's a pleasure to be welcomed among your… your *lares et penates*…

PETITFOUR: Yes…

RUMPSKINNE: As they say…

PETITFOUR: My sister has informed me of the purpose of your visit. And I approve, Adelbert… *(Shaking his hand.)* I consider you my son-in-law!

RUMPSKINNE: Your sister has informed you of the purpose of my visit… And you approve, Adel… *(Catching himself.)* Monsieur de Petitfour… *(Shaking his hand.)* You consider me your son-in-law!

PETITFOUR, *aside*: The man's a bloody parrot! *(Aloud.)* I have to admit that, at first, I was less than enthusiastic…

RUMPSKINNE: Oh?

PETITFOUR: Much less, in fact…

RUMPSKINNE: But—

PETITFOUR: Rumors… How shall I put it? *(Standing up.)* Rumors about your tempestuous youth… Your unbridled passions…

RUMPSKINNE: Oh… *(Aside.)* Good try, my friend!

PETITFOUR, *continuing*: Especially your most recent… adventure!… With… With… What was her name again?

RUMPSKINNE, *with a little laugh, casually*: What's in a name, monsieur!

PETITFOUR: Your mad escapades… The fortune you lavished on her…

RUMPSKINNE: Oh…

PETITFOUR: Your debts… *(Leaning over him, confidentially.)* How much, son? You can tell me…

RUMPSKINNE: Oh…

PETITFOUR: Besides… It's all over, I'm sure. Ancient history, so to speak… *(Sitting down next to him.)* Come, come… I can keep a secret. You… *(With feigned admiration and a little poke.)* You rake!

RUMPSKINNE, *standing up*: Monsieur de Petitfour…

PETITFOUR, *standing up*: Please… "Father"…

RUMPSKINNE: Father…

PETITFOUR, *as RUMPSKINNE affects a serious air and comes downstage, pausing dramatically*: Go on… *(Joining him.)* Go on…

RUMPSKINNE: At this moment in my life… This momentous moment…

PETITFOUR, *turning aside, under his breath*: Idiot!

RUMPSKINNE: As I stand at the threshold… About to enter your family…

PETITFOUR: Yes, Adelbert? Go on… I was young once too, after all.

RUMPSKINNE: I would truly be remiss were I not to be utterly truthful and frank…

PETITFOUR, *eagerly*: Go on! Go on!

RUMPSKINNE: Were I not to confess…

PETITFOUR, *as RUMPSKINNE utters a sigh*: Yes…

RUMPSKINNE: …my love and devotion… Not to one woman, father, but to two… *(Nodding reverentially.)* To two…

PETITFOUR: Two?… To two?… *(He goes to the door, up center, opens it a crack to be sure no one is listening.)* To two, Adelbert? *(Aside.)* Now I've got him!

RUMPSKINNE: Yes, father…

PETITFOUR, *joining him*: Please… "Papá"…

RUMPSKINNE: Yes, papá… My sainted mother and my wetnurse…

PETITFOUR, *taken aback*: What? *(Aside.)* Hmm!… Maybe not…

RUMPSKINNE: Yes… Mammá and Helga…

PETITFOUR: Helga?

RUMPSKINNE: Yes… Until I was ten…

PETITFOUR: You mean, you… She… *(Making meaningful gestures about his bosom.)* Until you were ten?

RUMPSKINNE: More or less, papá… I was rather precocious. They weaned me early.

PETITFOUR: Oh? *(Coming back to the subject.)* And no other woman? Never?… Not a one?

RUMPSKINNE, *very proper*: Certainly not, monsieur! *(Correcting himself.)* Father… Papá, I mean… *(Aside.)* Thinks he'll catch me, does he?

PETITFOUR: My, my… *(Taking a snuffbox from his pocket, aside.)* Let's try something else… *(Aloud, casually holding it out.)* Would you care for a pinch?… It's Turkish… The best…

RUMPSKINNE: Oh! I say… *(About to take a pinch.)* I don't mind if I… *(Catching himself.)* Tobacco?… I should say not! The very sight of it disgusts me!

He gives a little shudder.

PETITFOUR, *to himself*: Damn! I almost had him! *(Putting his arm around him.)* Ah, Adelbert!… Son!… *(Effusively.)* I must say, I had no idea you were a man of such character… Such sterling principles…

RUMPSKINNE: One does one's best, papá.

PETITFOUR: Such… Such… *(Leading him down left, hypocritically.)* Please… You must excuse me if I let my enthusiasm carry me away. My pleasure, my joy… But… Ah, Adelbert! You're the man I've always dreamed of!

RUMPSKINNE: Oh?

PETITFOUR: For my Vitruvia, I mean… The one I hoped against hope would appear… Honest, frank… The one I despaired of ever finding… With her character, after all…

RUMPSKINNE, *anxiously*: Her character?

PETITFOUR: Yes… Don't misunderstand. She's an angel… An absolute angel, but…

RUMPSKINNE: But?

PETITFOUR: Well, no one's perfect! And sometimes… Most of the time… Almost all of the time, Adelbert… Let's just say she has her faults.

RUMPSKINNE: Mademoiselle Vitruvia? Faults?… I can't believe—

PETITFOUR, *interrupting*: Oh! I've learned to live with them, mind you. After twenty-four years one gets used to anything. Even a stubborn mule!… Even an inconsiderate, thoughtless, pig-headed mule!

RUMPSKINNE, *aside*: A pig-headed mule? *(Aloud.)* Goodness me!

PETITFOUR: You say "yes," she says "no"… You say "black," she says "white"…

RUMPSKINNE, *pretending to believe him*: Tsk tsk tsk!… *(Aside.)* Methinks he doth protest too much!

PETITFOUR: But it's better that we all know our little faults now, don't you think? Before, that is…

RUMPSKINNE: Of course, of course!… If I had any I would certainly want you to know them.

PETITFOUR: And even the big ones… Maybe I shouldn't tell you, but she's—

RUMPSKINNE: Pig-headed… You told me…

PETITFOUR: Yes… And moody… And a chatterbox… And a spendthrift… And a scold!…

RUMPSKINNE: Do tell!

PETITFOUR: Impossible to get along with!

RUMPSKINNE, *with feigned seriousness*: That's incredible, monsieur!

PETITFOUR, *correcting*: Please… "Papá"…

RUMPSKINNE: Who could ask for anything more?

PETITFOUR, *taken aback*: Who could… What?

RUMPSKINNE: Those are exactly the qualities I've always wanted in a wife! Headstrong, serious, generous…

PETITFOUR: But…

RUMPSKINNE: Not afraid to talk… With a mind of her own…

PETITFOUR, *speechless*: But… But…

RUMPSKINNE: Too rare!… All too rare!

PETITFOUR: Indeed!… *(Hypocritically.)* I'm delighted, monsieur…

RUMPSKINNE, *correcting*: Please… "Adelbert"…

They shake hands effusively.

PETITFOUR: Adelbert!

RUMPSKINNE: Papá! *(Under his breath.)* Try to trick a lawyer, will you!

PETITFOUR, *moving up center, aside*: Clever bounder! *(Aloud, to* RUMPSKINNE.*)* Well now… Please excuse me while I go see to the marriage contract.

RUMPSKINNE, *aside*: Already?

PETITFOUR, *stopping as he reaches the door, patting his pockets as if looking for something*: I say… *(*RUMPSKINNE*, still down left, gives him a quizzical look.)* You wouldn't happen to have a cigar, would you? I seem to have forgotten…

RUMPSKINNE, *reaching into a pocket, noncommittal*: Oh…

PETITFOUR, *aside, triumphantly*: Ha! Now I've got him! *(As* RUMPSKINNE *takes out a handkerchief and blows his nose, aside.)* Damn! Foiled again!

He comes down right and takes the bottle of wine and the candle from the desk.

RUMPSKINNE: Excuse me… You were saying?

PETITFOUR: Beg pardon?

RUMPSKINNE: Oh… I thought you said something.

PETITFOUR, *with a casual wave*: No, no… I'll just go see when luncheon will be ready…

RUMPSKINNE: Please… No hurry on my account…

PETITFOUR, *at the desk, taking paper, pen, and ink, aside*: And send off a note to Buzenval!… He's an ugly runt, but at least he's not clever! *(Moving up right, aloud to* RUMPSKINNE, *nodding.)* Son…

Hands full, he exits.

RUMPSKINNE, *watching him go, sitting in the armchair, right*: Well! Try as you may, Monsieur Petitfour… *(Correcting himself, sarcastically.)* Monsieur de Petitfour!… I'd say I handled myself rather nicely!… An excellent performance, if I do say so myself!… Most convincing… Except when he offered me a pinch and I almost forgot! *(Chuckling.)* Not quite up to snuff, as they say!… But who can blame me? My second vice, after all… And when your nostrils are itching, is there anything more divine? Like now… Ah! *(Standing up and taking his snuffbox from his pocket.)* This very minute… *(Looking around to make sure he is alone.)* What's the harm?

As he opens the box and takes a pinch, VITRUVIA *enters, up center, holding a bouquet of flowers.*

VITRUVIA, *calling offstage*: Yes, auntie… Right away…

RUMPSKINNE, *dropping the pinch, aside*: Blast! Again?… Vice number two just doesn't have much luck!

VITRUVIA, *noticing him*: Ah! There you are, monsieur…

She comes down left and puts the flowers into the vase on the table.

RUMPSKINNE, *aside, admiringly*: Exquisite creature… *(With a little bow.)* Mademoiselle…

VITRUVIA, *nodding*: Monsieur…

RUMPSKINNE: Ah!…. *(Obviously struggling to control his passion, to himself.)* Beware, Adelbert!… Vice number one… You mustn't… The fire… The volcano… Seething… Seething…

VITRUVIA, *overhearing*: Monsieur?

RUMPSKINNE, *continuing, to himself*: Oh! Vesuvius!… My Vesuvius!

VITRUVIA, *overhearing, correcting him*: Vitruvia, monsieur…

RUMPSKINNE, *joining her, down left, continuing*: Ah! My lava… Bubbling… Bubbling…

VITRUVIA, *misunderstanding*: Your lover, monsieur?… But… *(Aside.)* Heavens! He doesn't waste much time! *(Aloud, as* RUMPSKINNE *struggles to regain his composure.)* I'm terribly flattered…

RUMPSKINNE: My lava…

VITRUVIA: But we hardly know each other…

RUMPSKINNE, *heaving a passionate sigh*: Ah!

VITRUVIA, *aside*: A Belgian? And so passionate?

RUMPSKINNE, *growing more calm*: My… Oh, my…

VITRUVIA, *aloud*: Besides, you haven't even talked to papá. You must, you know!

RUMPSKINNE: Ah, but I have, mademoiselle! I have!… Just now…

VITRUVIA, *dejectedly*: Oh dear… Then I suppose you'll be leaving.

RUMPSKINNE: Leaving?… But why should I be leaving? I just got here!

VITRUVIA: I know, but… Tomorrow, or the next day… Papá will see to it!

RUMPSKINNE: But your father… Monsieur de Petitfour… Just now, he said… He's preparing the marriage contract at this very moment!

VITRUVIA, *with a cynical little laugh*: Oh! But that's not possible, monsieur.

RUMPSKINNE: Don't say that! It is! He told me… It has to be… *(Aside.)* The volcano… The lava… *(Aloud.)* I may have my faults. My little vices, mademoiselle… I know it's hard to believe, but when you know me better… You'll see… I do have some, you know!

VITRUVIA: Faults?… *(Quickly.)* Shhh!… I don't want to hear them!

RUMPSKINNE: But…

VITRUVIA: You're a suitor, monsieur, so of course you have faults. They all do, you know! Just ask papá… By tomorrow he'll have learned them all…

RUMPSKINNE: But…

VITRUVIA: …and you'll be on the train to Brussels!

RUMPSKINNE: But…

VITRUVIA: So you really needn't tell me. You may as well keep them to yourself.

RUMPSKINNE: But mademoiselle…

VITRUVIA: And I'll do the same. I simply won't tell you mine!

RUMPSKINNE: Your what?

VITRUVIA: My faults, monsieur… I do have some…

RUMPSKINNE: Yes, I know! I know them all! Your father told me!

VITRUVIA: He what?

RUMPSKINNE: Every last one… Why, you're inconsiderate, and thoughtless, and pig-headed…

VITRUVIA: I'm… *(Scandalized.)* Monsieur, I never—

RUMPSKINNE, *interrupting*: And a chatterbox, and moody, and a spendthrift, and a scold…

VITRUVIA: But I—

RUMPSKINNE, *smiling*: So you see? I know them all!

VITRUVIA: But that's not true! I… I hope you realized—

RUMPSKINNE: Never fear, sweet child!… Justice may be blind, but this solicitor's eyes are sharp! *(Aside.)* He won't tell me that one is old as the hills!

VITRUVIA: Then surely you didn't believe him…

RUMPSKINNE: Believe him, mademoiselle?… There's only one thing I believe… Only one… I believe that you are beautiful, and charming, and tender, and—

VITRUVIA: Oh! *(Coyly.)* But those are three things, Monsieur Adelbert!

RUMPSKINNE, *reacting, aside*: She called me… She… *(Aloud.)* Oh, mademoiselle… *(Aside.)* Her lips parted… And her sweet voice whispered: "Adelbert"… She… *(Aloud.)* You… Mademoiselle… Ah! … *(Growing passionate.)* How can I tell you?… The fire in my veins…

VITRUVIA: Monsieur?

RUMPSKINNE: The lava… Molten, seething… Ah! How can I tell you…

VITRUVIA: Tell me…?

RUMPSKINNE, *seizing her hand*: Here! This is how, mademoiselle! This is how…

He kisses her hand passionately, again and again. As he is doing so, PETITFOUR *enters, up center.*

PETITFOUR, *noticing him*: Monsieur! What in the name of—

RUMPSKINNE, *innocently*: Father?

PETITFOUR, *furiously*: Just what do you think you're—

RUMPSKINNE: Papá?

PETITFOUR, *pointing to* VITRUVIA: That is my daughter, monsieur!

RUMPSKINNE, *correcting him*: Please… "Adelbert"…

PETITFOUR, *ignoring his comment*: Unhand her, you hear?

VITRUVIA: Papá!…

PETITFOUR: Unhand her this instant!

VITRUVIA *and* **RUMPSKINNE,** *together: But papá…*

PETITFOUR, *joining them, down left, and separating them, to* RUMPSKINNE: Wretch!… I'll have your head! I'll… A duel, monsieur!…

RUMPSKINNE: A duel?

VITRUVIA, *aghast*: Oh!

RUMPSKINNE: But—

PETITFOUR, *to* VITRUVIA, *vigorously wiping her hand where* RUMPSKINNE *has kissed it*: Ah!… There, there, poor child!… I know, I know… A vile insect has sullied your petals…

RUMPSKINNE, *watching him, incredulously*: What on earth…

PETITFOUR, *continuing*: Your lovely petals…

VITRUVIA: Really, papá…

PETITFOUR: Besmirched my precious flower…

VITRUVIA: You needn't—

PETITFOUR, *interrupting*: But papá is here to make it all better!

RUMPSKINNE, *to* PETITFOUR: But monsieur… Father…

PETITFOUR, *to* RUMPSKINNE: And as for you, you reprobate…

RUMPSKINNE: But I'm going to marry her, monsieur…

PETITFOUR: What?

RUMPSKINNE: Father… Papá… The contract…

PETITFOUR: Marry her?… You?… *(Scornfully.)* A lawyer?

VITRUVIA: Papá…

PETITFOUR: And a Belgian, no less!

RUMPSKINNE, *drawing himself up to his full height*: I beg your pardon!

PETITFOUR, *gradually raising his voice during the following exchange*: You?… And my Vitruvia?… Ha ha!

RUMPSKINNE: Monsieur!

PETITFOUR: You must be mad!

VITRUVIA: Papá…

RUMPSKINNE: I object!… I object!

PETITFOUR: Objection overruled, you… you… *(Pointing left.)* Out!… You hear me? Out!

RUMPSKINNE: But—

PETITFOUR: Go pack your bag! My daughter loathes the very sight of you!

VITRUVIA, *trying to protest*: Papá!

PETITFOUR, *pointing*: Out!

VITRUVIA, *to PETITFOUR*: That's not—

PETITFOUR, *interrupting, sharply, to RUMPSKINNE*: See?… You heard her… She can't stand you!… Go pack your bag, you… you… *homunculus*!

RUMPSKINNE: Of all the… *(Losing his patience.)* Blast! *(To himself.)* They've seen the last of me!

He turns to leave, left.

VITRUVIA, *to RUMPSKINNE*: But monsieur… Adelbert… I assure you..

RUMPSKINNE exits. As he does, GRISELDE enters, up right.

GRISELDE: Good heavens! What's all the commotion?

VITRUVIA, *in tears, pointing*: It's papá! He just told Monsieur Rumpskinne to leave, and—

GRISELDE, *to PETITFOUR*: You what…?

VITRUVIA: He did! He did!

GRISELDE, *to PETITFOUR, furiously*: My protégé? My Adelbert?…

PETITFOUR: The man is a good-for-nothing!

GRISELDE: My Rumpskinne?

PETITFOUR: A ne'er-do-well!… A… A *non compos mentis!*

VITRUVIA, *weeping*: No he's not, papá! He's a Belgian!

PETITFOUR: Please, Vitruvia… Don't cry…

GRISELDE: But why, Octave?

PETITFOUR, *ignoring her, to VITRUVIA*: Besides, I'll send for Oscar de Buzenval… *(Aside.)* The ugly runt!

GRISELDE, *to PETITFOUR, angrily*: I'm speaking to you!

PETITFOUR, *to VITRUVIA, continuing*: You'll love him! He's much better than your Runtskinne… *(Correcting.)* Rump… Your Rumpskinne… You'll see…

VITRUVIA: Oh…

GRISELDE, *to PETITFOUR, insisting*: I'm asking you, Octave!… *(Emphatically.)* What did he do?

PETITFOUR, *finally replying*: Do?… What did he… The scoundrel dared kiss Vitruvia's hand! That's what he did!… And without gloves!… Can you believe it?

VITRUVIA, *still weeping*: But he was wearing gloves, papá! I'm sure…

PETITFOUR: Yes, but … but you weren't! Your hand was naked, Vitruvia! Utterly naked!… *(To GRISELDE.)* And he breathed all over it…

GRISELDE: Pfff!… Is that all?

PETITFOUR: "Is that all?"… Isn't that enough?… What would you say if he did as much to you? If he smothered your hand with his vile, vulgar kisses…

GRISELDE, *scandalized*: Octave! Really!

PETITFOUR, *aside*: She'd probably ask for more! *(Aloud.)* A hand that I've kept unsullied and undefiled…

GRISELDE: My hand?

PETITFOUR, *pointing to VITRUVIA*: Hers! Hers!… Pure and chaste, for twenty-four years… And he dared… He dared…

VITRUVIA, *still in tears*: But papá…

PETITFOUR: No! I told him to leave, and he's leaving! That's all there is to it!

GRISELDE, *angrily*: Oh?… And my opinion doesn't matter, I suppose?… Well, we'll see about that!

PETITFOUR: Griselde…

GRISELDE: If he leaves, I leave! I'll go pack my bags… We'll leave together!

She begins striding upstage, in a huff.

PETITFOUR: Griselde! Please…

GRISELDE, *stopping at the door, up center*: Talk all you want… I'm not listening!

PETITFOUR: But you can't—

GRISELDE, *interrupting*: And as for my fortune… I've a good mind to get married…

PETITFOUR: What?

GRISELDE: …and leave it to my children!

PETITFOUR, *joining her at the door*: That's impossible!… You can't…

GRISELDE, *archly*: And why not?

PETITFOUR: I mean, you wouldn't…

GRISELDE: Oh?

PETITFOUR, *cajoling*: Think of Vitruvia… My Vitruvia… Your… Our…

VITRUVIA: Auntie dear…

PETITFOUR: Think of me… You wouldn't leave your poor little Octave, would you?

GRISELDE, *weakening*: Well… I…

PETITFOUR: Then you'll stay?…

GRISELDE: That depends… If Monsieur Rumpskinne stays…

PETITFOUR grimaces.

VITRUVIA: Say yes, papá!

GRISELDE, *to PETITFOUR*: And if you apologize to him!

PETITFOUR: Me?… I'd rather be drawn and quartered!… Boiled in oil…

GRISELDE: Fine! I'll go pack my things…

She turns on her heel and begins to leave.

PETITFOUR, *running up and stopping her*: Wait!… Give me a minute… Let me think…

RUMPSKINNE's door opens and he appears on the threshold, carrying his valise.

VITRUVIA, *to PETITFOUR*: Oh, papá! It's too late! *(Pointing.)* Look!

GRISELDE, *to PETITFOUR*: Apologize… Or I leave!

RUMPSKINNE steps in, the picture of injured pride.

RUMPSKINNE: Mesdames… *(Correcting himself.)* Mesdemoiselles, I mean … *(Aside.)* Whatever… *(To PETITFOUR, as dignified as possible.)* Monsieur… Please be assured that I remain your most… *(Aside.)* dis… *(Aloud.)* obedient servant!

PETITFOUR, *dryly*: Likewise, I'm sure! *(To GRISELDE.)* There!

GRISELDE, *to PETITFOUR*: You call that an apology, Octave?

VITRUVIA: Please, papá!

PETITFOUR, *to* RUMPSKINNE, *grudgingly*: Monsieur Rumpskinne… May I have a word with you?

RUMPSKINNE: I'm listening, monsieur.

PETITFOUR, *to himself*: Lowlife!… *(Aloud.)* Are you going so soon, monsieur?

RUMPSKINNE: Indeed!

PETITFOUR: The train doesn't leave for at least half an hour. *(Pointing.)* Won't you have a seat? Make yourself comfortable…

RUMPSKINNE: Thank you just the same!… There are times, monsieur, when a man's dignity tells him: "Better discomfort with honor than dishonor with comfort!"

PETITFOUR, *nodding*: Aha…

RUMPSKINNE: A Flemish proverb, monsieur… Freely translated…

PETITFOUR: Very well… I won't insist…

He moves upstage.

GRISELDE, *to* PETITFOUR: Oh? You won't?… *(Moving up center.)* Fine! In that case, I'm leaving!

PETITFOUR, *aside*: Damn! *(Aloud, to* RUMPSKINNE.*)* Monsieur Rumpskinne… May I have another word with you?

RUMPSKINNE: I'm listening, monsieur.

PETITFOUR, *joining him, giving him a good-natured tap on the cheek*: There, there now, Adelbert… You weren't going to leave without at least joining papá de Petitfour for lunch!

GRISELDE, *categorically*: He isn't going to leave at all, Octave! Lunch or not!

VITRUVIA, *to* PETITFOUR: That's right, papá!

RUMPSKINNE: I beg to differ, mesdemoiselles. My honor has been attacked. Monsieur Petitfour… *(Correcting himself, sarcastically.)* Monsieur de Petitfour has seen fit to insult not only the legal profession, which I am privileged to represent, but my ancestry as well!

PETITFOUR: I have?

RUMPSKINNE, *to* PETITFOUR: I may reside in Belgium, monsieur, but I am a Frenchman through and through!

PETITFOUR: But… *(Quizzically.)* "Rumpskinne…"?

RUMPSKINNE: On my mother's side, my friend… *(Proudly.)* She traces her family tree back to Vercingetorix the Gaul!

PETITFOUR: Ah, so… In that case… *(To* GRISELDE, *pretending to be as amiable and impressed as possible .)* Did you hear that? Monsieur goes all the way back to Julius Caesar!… You remember… "Gallia est omnis divisa in… in…"

He tries to recall the rest.

VITRUVIA: "In partis tres," papá…

PETITFOUR: Exactly… *(To* RUMPSKINNE.*)* Now I hope we can let bygones be bygones… Son!… After all, I didn't know… I mean, who would have thought…

RUMPSKINNE, *relenting*: Well…

PETITFOUR: Now… *(Joining him, left.)* For my sake, please… *(Taking his valise.)* Let me take your valise… *(With a silly little laugh.)* Ha ha!… It rhymes! *(Repeating.)* "For my sake, please… Let me take your valise…"

He puts it down on the floor, next to the chair by the door, left.

GRISELDE, *with a sigh*: Finally!

VITRUVIA, *clapping her hands*: Oh…

GRISELDE: And just to prove that the bygones are… gone by… *(To* RUMPSKINNE, *pointing to* VITRUVIA.*)* I think you should give her a nice big kiss!

RUMPSKINNE: With the greatest of pleasure, mademoiselle!

GRISELDE: Please… "Auntie"…

PETITFOUR: What?… My daughter? My… *(As* RUMPSKINNE *crosses right and proceeds to do so.)* Oh!… *(Aside.) Maledicta!*

With barely concealed rage, he gives the chair a swift kick.

GRISELDE: What on earth…?

PETITFOUR, *trying to recover his aplomb*: Sorry! I… I tripped… *(Feigning delight.)* Well now… How happy I am… To see everyone so happy…

VITRUVIA: Oh, thank you, papá!

PETITFOUR, *to himself*: Damn! Now what do I do?

CHIQUETTE enters, up right.

CHIQUETTE: Luncheon is served.

She exits.

GRISELDE, *to* RUMPSKINNE: Come, Adelbert… Give my niece your arm. *(As he complies, to* PETITFOUR.*)* Are you coming, Octave?

PETITFOUR: In a moment…

RUMPSKINNE, VITRUVIA, and GRISELDE exit, up right, into the dining room.

PETITFOUR, *to himself*: *Eheu!*… If things continue like this, that… that Hun could actually marry my daughter, heaven help us! He's on the attack… Like the barbarians at the gates of Rome… The Goths… *(Uncertain.)* The Visi… The Ostro… *(Shrugging.)* What's the difference? One or the other… And they've got to be… He's got to be stopped, before he… before they bring down the Empire!

CHIQUETTE, *entering, up right*: Isn't monsieur going to have lunch?

PETITFOUR: No!… Don't bother me. I'm thinking.

CHIQUETTE: Oh…

PETITFOUR: Ancient history… The fall of civilization… Besides, I have no appetite.

CHIQUETTE: I'm sure it's monsieur's liver.

PETITFOUR, *ignoring her, musing*: He's got to be stopped, that's all there is to it! But how?… How, Chiquette?

CHIQUETTE: Monsieur?

PETITFOUR: How do I stop that onslaught in its tracks?

CHIQUETTE: Monsieur has to stop a train?

PETITFOUR: How do I stop that Attila?… That Alaric?… How?… How?… *(Suddenly hit by an idea.)* Ah!… Eureka! I've got it!… Of course!… You, Chiquette…

CHIQUETTE: Me, monsieur?

PETITFOUR, *pointing toward the dining room*: You see that Vandal having lunch in there?

CHIQUETTE: I thought he was a Belgian, monsieur.

PETITFOUR: Yes, well…

CHIQUETTE: Mademoiselle's intended?

PETITFOUR, *angrily*: Shhh!... Don't you dare call him that!

CHIQUETTE: Oh... I thought... *(Aside.)* What was I thinking!

PETITFOUR: Listen to me, Chiquette... I want you to make him kiss you!

CHIQUETTE: Me?... But I told monsieur... I've given up the flesh.

PETITFOUR: I know... Your vision... But only a few little pecks on the cheek... Your flesh won't mind... Besides, it's worth a gold piece...

He takes a coin from his pocket.

CHIQUETTE, *protesting*: But monsieur...

PETITFOUR: And if you don't, you're fired!

CHIQUETTE: Oh... Well... *(Taking the coin.)* In that case...

PETITFOUR: Now go do your best! I don't care how, or where, or when... Just don't stop until he kisses you. Understand?

CHIQUETTE, *examining the gold piece*: If monsieur is sure it's good.

PETITFOUR: Of course it is! *(Waving her off.)* Go on! Go on!... *(Aside.) Stupida rustica!*

CHIQUETTE, *shaking her head, moving up right, to herself*: Of all things to have to do...

She exits. A moment later GRISELDE *enters from the same door.*

GRISELDE, *standing at the door*: Really, Octave! Have you lost your mind?

PETITFOUR: Now what?

GRISELDE: Luncheon, that's what!... You can't leave the two of us alone with Monsieur Rumpskinne!

PETITFOUR, *joining her*: Oh! Don't even mention that name, Griselde! *(Hypocritically.)* After what I've just found out... I couldn't eat a thing! Not a crust, not a crumb... Not a...

GRISELDE, *alarmed*: Good heavens! What is it? Tell me...

PETITFOUR: Your Monsieur Rumpskinne is a cad! An utterly unprincipled, lascivious cad!

GRISELDE: But why—

PETITFOUR: And if you don't believe me... The satyr has been trying to seduce Chiquette!

GRISELDE: Chiquette?... Our Chiquette?

PETITFOUR: Yes!... It's bad enough to be a lecher, but... With a peasant? The lowest of the low?

GRISELDE, *agape*: I... He... That's impossible! What makes you think—

PETITFOUR, *interrupting*: I heard it from her very own lips. Not two minutes ago...

GRISELDE: Oh!

PETITFOUR: And he gave her a gold piece for brushing out his clothes.

GRISELDE, *reconsidering*: So? That just proves that he's generous. I fail to see—

PETITFOUR: And he kisses her every chance he gets... *(Smacking his lips suggestively.)* All over...

GRISELDE: What?

PETITFOUR: …the house… All over the house!… Is that generosity too, sister dear?

GRISELDE, *scandalized*: Oh! If you can prove that, Octave… Oh!…

PETITFOUR, *with a glimmer of hope*: Yes?

GRISELDE: Monsieur Rumpskinne will have seen the last of me! And the last of my niece, you can be certain of that!

RUMPSKINNE's voice can be heard in the dining room, laughing.

RUMPSKINNE'S VOICE: But why not, mademoiselle? It's only champagne!

PETITFOUR: Shhh! Here he comes… And you can bet she's with him!

GRISELDE: I never…

PETITFOUR, *motioning up left, toward the terrace door*: Quick!… Out here… We won't let him see us.

GRISELDE: To spy on him, you mean?

PETITFOUR: As Suetonius said: "It is oft behind closed doors that we find the secret of a man's passions…" *(To himself.)* Or was it Tacitus?

As they exit onto the terrace, leaving the door slightly ajar, RUMPSKINNE enters from the dining room, followed by CHIQUETTE. He is holding a bottle in one hand and a glass in the other. She is holding a feather duster. Off and on during their ensuing exchange, PETITFOUR cautiously pokes his head in, obviously straining to hear but careful not to be seen.

CHIQUETTE: Monsieur isn't going to finish the bottle, is he?

RUMPSKINNE, *hovering about her, down right, as she dusts here and there*: But it's only champagne, I told you… *(Becoming slightly tipsy, singing.)* "Wine, wine… Nectar divine… Fruit of the vine… *(Pouring a glassful.)* Oh won't you be mine…" *(Admiring her, aside.)* Pert little nose, I must say!… *(Aloud, holding up the glass.)* Tell me, where did you find one so utterly tasteful?

CHIQUETTE: Monsieur chose it.

RUMPSKINNE: What?

CHIQUETTE: The champagne, monsieur?

RUMPSKINNE: No, no… *(Drinking.)* Your nose!… Perfection itself…

CHIQUETTE: My nose?… Who knows? *(As RUMPSKINNE continues singing and humming: "Wine, wine… Nectar divine…")* I was born with it, I think…

RUMPSKINNE: Ah… *(With a smug little smile.)* Nose doubt, nose doubt… "Born with it…" *(He drinks and pours again.)* A witty reply… And your rosy cheeks, Chiquette?

CHIQUETTE, *taking the glass from him and sipping, intentionally placing her cheek close to his lips*: I was born with them too, monsieur…

RUMPSKINNE: "Them too…" *(Pausing briefly to consider.)* Ha ha!… "Them two… Them two…" Very good!… But not too long ago, I would say!

He takes the glass from her and pours again.

CHIQUETTE, *moving her cheek closer, noncommittal*: Well…

RUMPSKINNE: You can tell me! How old are you, child?

CHIQUETTE: I'll be nineteen come next cherry season.

RUMPSKINNE, *aside*: Delightful repartee!… *(Aloud.)* Cherries?… In Paris?…

CHIQUETTE: At home, monsieur… In the country…

RUMPSKINNE: Ah… And when they are ripe, we must go and pick them, you and I…

He gives her the glass and she takes another sip, edging still closer to his lips.

CHIQUETTE: Oh yes, monsieur…

RUMPSKINNE: Sweet and plump… *(Taking the glass, singing.)* "Oh won't you be mine…" *(Drinking.)* Very sweet… Very plump… And what do you want to be when you grow up?

CHIQUETTE, *very matter-of-fact*: A nun, monsieur…

RUMPSKINNE, *drawing back, gagging*: A… A…

CHIQUETTE: At least I did… *(Offering her cheek.)* Before I met monsieur, that is…

RUMPSKINNE: "Before…" *(To himself.)* Blast and double blast! *(Aloud.)* "Before…" *(Aside.)* She wants me, the little tart! *(Aloud.)* You mean, I… I pass inspection?

CHIQUETTE, *pretending to be coy*: Oh yes, monsieur!… I don't inspect much, but… The minute I saw monsieur… The minute I took his clothes off… Off to be brushed, I mean… It was like a… a punch in the belly…

RUMPSKINNE, *aside*: *Gottferdomme!*… If I could be sure… *(He goes up and looks toward the dining room, aside.)* No one… Why not?…

CHIQUETTE, *thinking he is leaving, aside*: Oh! Just when I thought—

RUMPSKINNE, *rejoining her, down right*: A punch in the belly, you say?… Then let's see what this will do to you… *(About to plant a kiss on her cheek, catching sight of PETITFOUR's and GRISELDE's heads peering out from behind the door and withdrawing quickly, to himself.)* Oh la la!… Careful, Adelbert… *(Aloud.)* My child…

CHIQUETTE, *offering her cheek, expecting a kiss*: Yes, monsieur…

RUMPSKINNE puts the bottle and glass down on the desk, takes her hand, and crosses left with her.

RUMPSKINNE, *pompously*: There are things I must tell you… Important things… Things that a beautiful and chaste young lady should know…

CHIQUETTE: Monsieur?

RUMPSKINNE: The ancients, since the dawn of time, held virtue in the highest regard. *(She gives him a quizzical look.)* The Romans erected a temple to chastity…

CHIQUETTE, *aside*: To who?

RUMPSKINNE, *continuing*: The Egyptians celebrated it too in their mysteries…

CHIQUETTE: Oh! I love mysteries, monsieur! But—

RUMPSKINNE, *forcefully*: And the Hebrews… Yes, the Hebrews themselves were wont… *(Toning down his rhetoric a bit.)* were accustomed to declare that a shameless woman was as… as… *(Struggling to find an apt metaphor.)* as a cherry without a pit!

The door, up left, opens suddenly and GRISELDE strides out, joyfully, followed by a downcast PETIFOUR.

GRISELDE, *clapping her hands*: Oh! What a perfectly lovely thought! A cherry without a pit!…

PETITFOUR, *grimacing*: Just lovely!… As old as the—

GRISELDE, *to PETITFOUR*: And you dared accuse him, Octave…

PETITFOUR, *aside*: The swine!

GRISELDE: You had the gall to say that he—

PETITFOUR, *interrupting*: Me? Since when did I...? *(Pointing to* CHIQUETTE.*)* She did! She's the one... *(Approaching* CHIQUETTE, *down left, whispering to her.)* Idiot!... Give me back my gold piece!

CHIQUETTE, *replying in a whisper, ignoring his demand*: Don't blame me, monsieur! I did my best.

She exits, up right.

GRISELDE, *joining* RUMPSKINNE, *down left*: Oh, monsieur! You're a perfect angel!

RUMPSKINNE: Please... "Adelbert"...

GRISELDE, *to* PETITFOUR: Isn't he, Octave?

PETITFOUR: Oh yes... Just perfect...

GRISELDE: Pure as the driven snow!

PETITFOUR, *aside*: Again? *(Drawing her right, in a whisper.)* That's what worries me! He's just as frigid!... No passion! That's his problem!

GRISELDE, *replying in a whisper*: Pish tush!... I'm sure that when he and Vitruvia are married... *(Just as* VITRUVIA *enters, up right.)* Ah! There you are, precious!

VITRUVIA, *coming down center*: Where did everyone go? *(With a little laugh.)* I turned my back for a moment and you all disappeared!

GRISELDE, *to* VITRUVIA: I wish you could have heard what Adelbert... what your fiancé just said!

PETITFOUR, *aside*: Over my dead body!

VITRUVIA: About what, auntie dear?

PETITFOUR, *sarcastically*: About the ancient Hebrews!... And cherries... It was brilliant! *(To* RUMPSKINNE.*)* Please, monsieur... Let's hear more! Tell my daughter about the ancient Hebrews. And cherries without pits...

VITRUVIA, *puzzled*: Cherries...?

PETITFOUR, *continuing*: Please... More about the Hebrews...

RUMPSKINNE: With pleasure... It seems that, among those wise people...

PETITFOUR, *to* VITRUVIA, *sarcastically*: You'll see...

RUMPSKINNE, *continuing*: ...there used to be a custom...

PETITFOUR, *to* VITRUVIA: The man is an encyclopedia!

RUMPSKINNE, *continuing*: ...that, when a young man asked for a maiden's hand in marriage—

PETITFOUR, *interrupting*: No, no... About the cherries, monsieur...

RUMPSKINNE, *ignoring him*: ...her father would decide immediately on the wedding-day!

GRISELDE: He's right, you know!

PETITFOUR, *protesting*: Wait! Just a minute!

GRISELDE, *to* PETITFOUR: Let's follow their example, shall we?

VITRUVIA, *clapping her hands*: Oh yes, auntie dear!... *(To* PETITFOUR.*)* Papá? Let's decide!

PETITFOUR: But...

GRISELDE: Three months?

PETITFOUR: Certainly not! That's not possible...

RUMPSKINNE: Two?

PETITFOUR: Even less!

RUMPSKINNE, *intentionally misunderstanding*: Less?… One then?

PETITFOUR: One… Why not tonight, damn it!

GRISELDE, *to* PETITFOUR, *in a whisper*: Please, Octave!… The child…

PETITFOUR, *frustrated*: Oh…

GRISELDE, *to* PETITFOUR, *aloud*: Then you decide!

PETITFOUR: Fine!… A year and a half!

RUMPSKINNE, *objecting*: A year and a half?

GRISELDE: But why…?

PETITFOUR: I… I… I have no black trousers.

GRISELDE: Now you listen to me, Octave! I don't have to tell you that I enjoy a very substantial fortune.

PETITFOUR, *aside*: Good God! Her and her fortune! *(Aloud.)* Ten months, then… We'll compromise… There! It's settled!… Ten months…

GRISELDE, **RUMPSKINNE**, *and* **VITRUVIA**, *together*: Ten months!

PETITFOUR, *to himself*: Between now and then…

GRISELDE, **RUMPSKINNE**, *and* **VITRUVIA**, *together*: But…

PETITFOUR, *continuing, to himself*: Oh, will I scratch!

GRISELDE, *to* PETITFOUR, *furiously*: You must be joking…

VITRUVIA: But papá…

RUMPSKINNE: Monsieur…

GRISELDE, *to* VITRUVIA, *leading her upstage*: Come, Vitruvia… *(Loud enough for* PETITFOUR *to hear.)* Let's let him realize what a horrid mistake he's making! *(To* PETITFOUR, *archly.)* I suggest you reconsider, Octave… If you know what I mean!

She and VITRUVIA *exit, up center, leaving* PETITFOUR *and* RUMPSKINNE *downstage.*

RUMPSKINNE, *giving* PETITFOUR *a good-natured little poke, trying to be agreeable*: Really, father… Ten months… Don't you think… I mean, it's an eternity! Practically never…

PETITFOUR, *aside*: If only…

RUMPSKINNE: My heart aches at the thought!

PETITFOUR, *coldly*: No doubt it's your liver!

He goes and sits down on the loveseat.

RUMPSKINNE, *following him*: Isn't there anything I can do?

PETITFOUR, *misinterpreting his question, dryly*: Perhaps a spirited game of billiards… It calms the digestion.

RUMPSKINNE, *incredulously*: Billiards?

PETITFOUR: That's all I can suggest.

RUMPSKINNE: But… *(Suddenly struck by a thought, sitting down next to him.)* Yes! Billiards… But on one condition…

PETITFOUR: That is…?

RUMPSKINNE: Eight months for the winner!… Eighteen if you win, and two if I do…

PETITFOUR, *aside*: Damn! If I were sure…

RUMPSKINNE, *aside*: He doesn't look hard to beat. *(Aloud, holding out his hand.)* So? You agree?

PETITFOUR, *leaving his hand in mid-air*: No… I don't think… *(Aside.)* If he suggests it you can bet he's a champion. *(Aloud.)* The same condition, but… I'd prefer a game that leaves no room for doubt.

RUMPSKINNE: Doubt? In billiards you either win or lose!

PETITFOUR: Yes, but… Sometimes… The light, the angle… No, no… No billiards…

RUMPSKINNE: What do you suggest?

PETITFOUR, *pondering for a moment, then*: Odds or evens!

RUMPSKINNE: Fine! Do you have any dice?

PETITFOUR gets up, goes to the desk, down right, takes a pair of dice from the drawer and holds them in his fist.

PETITFOUR, *returning to the loveseat and sitting down*: One roll?

RUMPSKINNE: One roll…

PETITFOUR: Good! I'll go first… What is it going to be?

RUMPSKINNE, *crossing his fingers and holding them up*: Odd!

They both bend over and PETITFOUR rolls the dice on the floor.

PETITFOUR, *triumphantly*: Aha! I win!

RUMPSKINNE, *examining the dice*: What are you talking about? Six and three… Nine!… Odd! I win!

PETITFOUR: Nonsense! *(Pointing.)* One… And two… Two dice! Two… Even!

RUMPSKINNE: But that's absurd! There are always two dice!

PETITFOUR: I must say, you're not a very good loser!

RUMPSKINNE: "Good loser" my foot!… Let's call it a draw and play it with coins.

PETITFOUR: If you insist… *(He thrusts his hand into his pocket, takes out some coins, and holds out his fist.)* Odd or even?

RUMPSKINNE: Odd!

PETITFOUR, *opening his hand and spreading the coins on the floor*: I win again!

RUMPSKINNE, *examining the coins*: You?… *(Pointing.)* Twenty centimes and one centime… Twenty-one… Odd, my friend!… Odd, odd, odd!

PETITFOUR: What kind of rules do you play by? *(Pointing.)* One coin… Another coin… Two coins! Two!… Even, monsieur!

RUMPSKINNE: Odd!

PETITFOUR: Even!

RUMPSKINNE: Odd!

PETITFOUR: Very well, let's call it a draw…

RUMPSKINNE: Of all the… All right… One last time to decide the match!… This time I go! *(He stands up, thrusts both hands in his pockets, and holds out the right.)* Odd or even?

PETITFOUR, *hesitating for a moment, finally choosing*: Odd!

RUMPSKINNE, *putting his right hand in his pocket and opening his left*: Sorry!… Two coins… Even! I win!

PETITFOUR, *standing up, objecting*: Not that hand! What do you take me for? The other one!… The other—

RUMPSKINNE: No!

PETITFOUR: Yes!

RUMPSKINNE: No!

PETITFOUR: Yes!

RUMPSKINNE: Then it's a draw…

PETITFOUR: All right… *(He heaves a sigh.)* One last time…

RUMPSKINNE: But this time be sure you know the rules!

PETITFOUR: And no cheating!

RUMPSKINNE, *putting his hand in his pocket*: I'll go…

PETITFOUR, *stopping him*: No, wait!… I have a better idea. We'll bet on the first cab that goes by.

RUMPSKINNE, *sarcastically*: On how many legs the horse has?

PETITFOUR: Ha ha!… No… On the number… They all have a number.

RUMPSKINNE: Fine! But this decides the match. The winner gets eight months. Agreed?

PETITFOUR: Agreed!… Odd or even?

RUMPSKINNE: I say… Even!

They go up left, stand at the window, take lorgnettes from their pockets, and peer out at the street.

PETITFOUR, *after a few moments of expectant waiting, spotting a cab*: Ah!… There…

They follow with their gaze as it passes.

RUMPSKINNE, *finally, in triumph*: Forty-four!… I win! I win!

PETITFOUR: But…

RUMPSKINNE: Forty-four! Even!…

PETITFOUR: But…

RUMPSKINNE: And even two fours!… One, two… *(Holding up two fingers.)* Two!… Even!

PETITFOUR: But I—

RUMPSKINNE: And even four plus four… Still even!… Even! Even!

PETITFOUR, *aside*: Ayyy!

RUMPSKINNE: I win! I win! I win!

PETITFOUR, *collapsing in a heap onto the chair by the window, muttering*: I'm ruined!… Eheu! Eheu!…

As he continues groaning and muttering his lament, GRISELDE *and* VITRUVIA *enter, up center.*

RUMPSKINNE, *joining them, excitedly*: Vitruvia… *(To* GRISELDE.*)* Mademoiselle…

GRISELDE: Please… "Auntie"…

RUMPSKINNE: You'll never guess! *(Pointing.)* Monsieur de Petitfour… Father… Papá has just agreed that we can be married in two months! Two!… You hear?

VITRUVIA: He did?

GRISELDE, *surprised*: That's odd…

RUMPSKINNE: No! Even!…

VITRUVIA, *joyously*: Oh, Adelbert…

GRISELDE: Two months?… *(To* RUMPSKINNE.*)* Why, we barely have time to buy our gowns and her trousseau!

RUMPSKINNE, *pointing to* PETITFOUR, *sarcastically*: And his black trousers!

PETITFOUR, *standing up, to himself*: It can't be…

GRISELDE: Quick, Vitruvia!… Go get our hats…

PETITFOUR, *still mumbling*: There must be a way…

VITRUVIA: What for, auntie?

GRISELDE: We'll start today! No time like the present…

VITRUVIA: Oh yes! Let's!… Let's!…

GRISELDE: And only two months…

VITRUVIA exits, right.

RUMPSKINNE: And I'll go unpack my things…

He crosses left and picks up his valise.

PETITFOUR, *aside*: He's settling in? *(Aloud to* GRISELDE, *pointing, as* RUMPSKINNE *exits.)* Griselde… He… I… *(Making a last, desperate attempt, very dramatically.)* I don't know how to tell you… But… I always hoped against hope I would never have to…

GRISELDE: Tell me what, Octave?

PETITFOUR: O God, how I hoped!… And now, after all these years… *(Shaking his head.) Fiat veritas!* … The truth will out…

GRISELDE: What is it?

PETITFOUR, *very mysteriously*: Shhh!… Wait…

He goes about checking behind the doors pretending to make sure no one is listening.

GRISELDE: What on earth…

PETITFOUR, *to himself*: Now if only she swallows it!

GRISELDE: Well?

PETITFOUR, *rejoining her*: Shhh!… *(Taking her by the hand and leading her downstage.)* The secret that I've been hiding all my life, sister dear… The terrible little secret that has been gnawing away at my heart…

GRISELDE: You, Octave?

PETITFOUR: All these years… The secret that… that makes this marriage impossible…

GRISELDE: What?

PETITFOUR: Impossible!… It… It can never be!

GRISELDE: But—

PETITFOUR: Ah!… Man is weak. And temptation is strong. Oh, how well I know!… The flesh, Griselde… The flesh…

GRISELDE, *agape*: You? The flesh…?

PETITFOUR: And… And *omnia vincit amor*, sister dear… Especially when we're young… And restless… And—

GRISELDE: Will you please—

PETITFOUR, *dramatically*: It was in Spain, Griselde… My trip… You remember? Years ago?

GRISELDE: Spain?… But you didn't go to Spain. You went to Biarritz!

PETITFOUR: No, no… I told you Biarritz… But, alas, it was Spain! Ah, how I wish it had been Biarritz! I would not now be standing here before you, confessing…

GRISELDE: Confessing?

PETITFOUR: I would not have to tell that… *(Pointing right.)* that precious, innocent flower that the man she loves… *(Aside.)* The swine!… *(Aloud.)* That he… That he can never be her husband!

GRISELDE: For heaven's sake, Octave… Tell me… Please!

PETITFOUR, *to himself*: So far, so good! *(Aloud.)* We were staying in… in Los Badayos… On a little farm… In the hacienda of… of Don Juan de Caramel y Fuentes… *(Aside.)* A little local color… *(Aloud.)* On the flowering banks of the Bidassoa…

GRISELDE: "We"?… Who, Octave?

PETITFOUR, *ignoring her question*: She had come from France to take the waters… Young, beautiful…

GRISELDE: "She"?

PETITFOUR, *continuing*: Unable to resist, poor thing… And nature, conspiring… Ah! One of those Spanish nights, Griselde! And… And suddenly, the fire!… Breaking out all around us…

GRISELDE: What fire?… Who—

PETITFOUR, *continuing*: On the Bidassoa… *(Correcting himself.)* I mean, in Don Juan de Caramel y Fuentes's hacienda… And the lightning, streaking in zigzagging flashes… *(Waxing poetic.)* Ripping the clouds, all frayed with silver…

GRISELDE: Oh my…

PETITFOUR, *continuing*: And the deafening thunder… Oh, Griselde! Do you know what Spanish thunder can be like? Have you any idea…

GRISELDE, *with a shudder*: Good heavens!

PETITFOUR: And the poor child, trembling, terrified beyond belief… So helpless… So beautiful…

GRISELDE: But—

PETITFOUR: Beautiful as a… a pomegranate tree in bloom!… What can I tell you? I was young, Griselde… So young, and… and…

GRISELDE: Octave! You didn't!

PETITFOUR: The rest isn't for your ears, sister dear. Your pure, chaste ears… *(GRISELDE stands agape.)* Suffice it to say that… *(Pointing left.)* that young man is my son!

GRISELDE, *stammering*: M-M-Monsieur Rumpskinne?… Adelbert? Your… Your…

PETITFOUR: Every inch of him…

GRISELDE: Oh! Good God in heaven!

PETITFOUR, *aside*: *Consummatum est!*

GRISELDE: But… How do you know?

PETITFOUR, *aside*: Hook, line, and sinker!

GRISELDE: How did you find out?

PETITFOUR: How? *(Almost caught short.)* Her letters… Over the years… From the moment he was born… I… But I won't bore you with all the seamy details.

GRISELDE: Letters?

PETITFOUR, *quickly, as an afterthought*: I burned them all, of course!… Besides, just to look at him… My nose, my chin.… So you see… Vitruvia, and her brother!… It's quite out of the question.

GRISELDE: Oh, never!… I should say…

PETITFOUR, *forgetting himself*: So! *(With a happy smile.)* Let's show him the door and send him on his way! And the sooner the better!

GRISELDE: But he's your son, Octave!

PETITFOUR, *recovering his aplomb*: Of course! Of course!… Ah! But he must never know! *(Hypocritically.)* This father's heart must never know the joy… the pride…

GRISELDE, *sympathetically*: Tsk tsk tsk!… Your own flesh and blood…

PETITFOUR: Ah! My flesh and blood…

GRISELDE: And my nephew!… The nephew I never knew I had…

PETITFOUR: My son!… My son!…

GRISELDE, *continuing*: …and who has a right to inherit half my fortune…

PETITFOUR: Half your… *(Quickly.)* No!… You mustn't!… You… Certainly not! *(Aside.)* So far, too good!

GRISELDE: But why?

PETITFOUR: Because… Because… *(To himself.)* She's swallowing too much! *(Aloud.)* It would make him suspect the truth, Griselde. The terrible truth that he must never know…

GRISELDE: You're right!… For his sake… For his mother's…

PETITFOUR: Ah yes… His dear mother!… The poor, pathetic waif…

He looks heavenward and, with a hypocritical sigh, crosses himself.

GRISELDE: Oh, Octave… You mean, she…

PETITFOUR, *nodding solemnly*: Of shame…

GRISELDE: But… All the letters…

PETITFOUR, *sighing*: Yes… Years and years of shame…

GRISELDE: Oh! Tsk, tsk, tsk!… The sister-in-law I never knew I had…

PETITFOUR: Now promise me, Griselde… Swear that you'll never reveal my secret!

GRISELDE: I swear, Octave!

PETITFOUR: Thank you!… Thank you, sister dear! *(Aside, with a sigh.)* At last…

The door, right, opens and VITRUVIA *enters, wearing a hat and holding another.*

VITRUVIA, *to* GRISELDE: Here's your hat, auntie dear. I'm ready…

GRISELDE, *aside*: Poor child! How can I tell her?

VITRUVIA: Now, where shall we go first?

GRISELDE: Nowhere, precious… That is, there's no need… Not now…

VITRUVIA: But you said—

GRISELDE: I know… But, not now…

She sits down in the armchair, shaking her head.

VITRUVIA, *to* PETITFOUR, *quizzically*: Papá?

PETITFOUR, *shaking his head*: Tsk tsk tsk!

VITRUVIA: But what ever is the matter?

PETITFOUR: Her rheumatism… It's going to rain. This just isn't the time…

VITRUVIA, *relieved*: Well, if that's all… *(Joining* GRISELDE.*)* Don't worry, auntie dear. Tomorrow is time enough.

The door, left, opens and RUMPSKINNE *enters.*

RUMPSKINNE: There! All unpacked…

PETITFOUR, *aside*: Not for long!

RUMPSKINNE: Now, we were saying…

PETITFOUR, *to* RUMPSKINNE: Monsieur Rump—… Adelbert… *(With feigned emotion.)* Come… Give me your hand…

RUMPSKINNE, *joining him*: Father?

GRISELDE, *standing up, to herself, as* PETITFOUR *takes* RUMPSKINNE*'s hand in his*: Oh my…

PETITFOUR: Adelbert…

He presses his hand to his lips and smothers it with kisses.

GRISELDE, *to herself*: Careful, Octave…

RUMPSKINNE: Papá…?

PETITFOUR: Ah… Son!… *(With mock emotion.)* Thank you!… Oh, thank you!

RUMPSKINNE, *aside*: Now what?

PETITFOUR, *letting go his hand*: There!… My sister has something to tell you… Son!

GRISELDE, *staring at* RUMPSKINNE*'s face, to herself*: He's right… The same nose… The same chin…

RUMPSKINNE, *to* GRISELDE: You do, auntie?

GRISELDE: I… I'm afraid so…

VITRUVIA, *alarmed*: What is it?

GRISELDE, *to* RUMPSKINNE: Monsieur Rumpskinne…

RUMPSKINNE: Please… "Adel—"

GRISELDE: My dear friend…

PETITFOUR, *aside*: Addlebrain!

GRISELDE, *emotionally*: My… My neph—

PETITFOUR, *gives several loud coughs to cover her imminent faux pas.*

VITRUVIA: Aunt Griselde? *(As* PETITFOUR *continues coughing.)* Papá…?

RUMPSKINNE, *aside*: What now, I wonder?

GRISELDE, *to* RUMPSKINNE: As heaven is my witness, I wish you nothing but the best. The very, very best… Ah, if you only knew… If only… *(As* PETITFOUR *gives a few more admonitory coughs.)* If only I could tell you… But…

RUMPSKINNE: But…?

GRISELDE: This marriage that was going to bring joy to all our hearts…

VITRUVIA: Was going…?

GRISELDE, *continuing*: …simply can never be!

RUMPSKINNE, *aside, sarcastically*: Surprise!

VITRUVIA: What?… *(To* GRISELDE.*)* What do you—

GRISELDE: Vitruvia, precious…

VITRUVIA: How can you… You? Of all people… I thought that papá… But you… Oh!

PETITFOUR, *to* VITRUVIA: Please… *(At a loss for anything to say.)* Go put away your hat…

GRISELDE, *to* VITRUVIA: If you only knew, my child…

RUMPSKINNE, *to himself*: Knew?

VITRUVIA, *angrily, to* GRISELDE: Knew?... Knew?... *(To* PETITFOUR.*)* Knew?... *(To* GRISELDE, *on the verge of tears.)* No! No!... *(To* PETITFOUR.*)* Knew?... No!... *(To* GRISELDE.*)* No! *(To* PETITFOUR.*)* No! No! No!

PETITFOUR: Vitruvia...

VITRUVIA: If you don't want me to get married, just say so!

PETITFOUR: Please!... I told you... Go put away your hat!

VITRUVIA: Oh yes! I will! And I'll never wear it again! So there!... Never! Never! Never!

She storms out, right.

RUMPSKINNE, *very properly*: My friends... I believe we have some unfinished business...

PETITFOUR, *casually*: Oh?

GRISELDE, *to* RUMPSKINNE: Monsieur...

RUMPSKINNE, *leading them both downstage, one on each side of him*: I beg your pardon... Your pardons... But... I'll thank you to explain...

PETITFOUR: Explain what, monsieur?

RUMPSKINNE, *facing each one alternately*: I believe that, in polite society, it's customary, when one shows one's guests the door, to let them know why.

GRISELDE: Ask him, monsieur...

PETITFOUR: No, no... Her...

RUMPSKINNE, *to* GRISELDE: Madame... *(Correcting.)* Mademoiselle...

GRISELDE: Please... Don't ask me...

RUMPSKINNE, *to* PETITFOUR: Monsieur...

PETITFOUR: Or me... Or me...

RUMPSKINNE *turns to one then the other, several times.*

RUMPSKINNE: In other words... *(He shakes his head back and forth, duplicating the previous gesture.)* Can it be... *(To* GRISELDE.*)* Can it be, mademoiselle... that you have reason to doubt my... my qualifications?

GRISELDE: Certainly not!

RUMPSKINNE, *to* PETITFOUR: Or that you, monsieur, have reason to find me... disagreeable?

PETITFOUR: Certainly not!

RUMPSKINNE, *losing patience*: Then will one of you please explain! A suitor has a right to be told why his suit is found unfitting... Especially one with my background, if I may say... My breeding...

PETITFOUR *and* **GRISELDE**, *together*: Monsieur...

RUMPSKINNE: Bachelor of Arts, Diplomate in Civil and Criminal Law...

PETITFOUR *and* **GRISELDE**: *Monsieur...*

RUMPSKINNE: Chief clerk in the offices of Maître Gottferdeck!... I didn't come all the way from Brussels to be made fun of!

PETITFOUR and **GRISELDE**: *Monsieur...*

RUMPSKINNE, *exasperated*: No! No! No!... Hellfire and damnation!

PETITFOUR *and* **GRISELDE**, *together: Monsieur!*

RUMPSKINNE: I've had enough, you two! I demand an explanation! *(To* GRISELDE.*)* And I'll have it, you hear? *(To* PETITFOUR.*)* I'll have it!

PETITFOUR: Never!

RUMPSKINNE: Oh?… Even if… *(Seizing him by the collar.)* Even if I have to choke it out of you!

As he proceeds to suit the action to the word, GRISELDE *attempts to stop him.*

GRISELDE, *frantically*: Monsieur!… Stop!

PETITFOUR: Aaaargh!…

GRISELDE: Stop!… For God's sake! You're… You're choking your father!

RUMPSKINNE, *letting go, agape*: My…

GRISELDE, *realizing her faux pas, clapping her hand over her mouth*: Oh…

PETITFOUR: Griselde!

RUMPSKINNE: Him?… My…

PETITFOUR, *retreating upstage, as if to leave, aside*: Goddamn! I'm done for…

RUMPSKINNE, *calling him back*: Wait!… Papá!… *(Beginning to smell a rat.)* What's this I hear?… You…? My father…?

PETITFOUR, *not knowing what to say*: Why, yes… As a matter of fact… *(Muttering.)* More or less… For the most part…

GRISELDE, *to* RUMPSKINNE: Do you remember the little farm at Los Bayados?… The hacienda…

PETITFOUR, *correcting her*: Badayos… Badayos…

RUMPSKINNE: The farm at Los Blablados?

PETITFOUR, *mumbling*: And… And… Don Juan de Caramel… y Fuentes… And your mother…

RUMPSKINNE: Ah yes… Mammá!…

GRISELDE, *to* RUMPSKINNE: So you see, monsieur… You can understand why this marriage is out of the question. Your mother and… *(Pointing to* PETITFOUR.*)* Your father…

RUMPSKINNE: How quaint!… After all these years! Who would have thought… *(To* PETITFOUR*, with open arms, pretending.)* Father, dearest…

PETITFOUR, *joining him, with an embrace*: Adelbert…

GRISELDE, *to* RUMPSKINNE: If only your mother were here to see your joy!

RUMPSKINNE: Ah! If only… *(Struck by an idea.)* But she is!… In a manner of speaking, I mean…

PETITFOUR: She is?

GRISELDE: In spirit, you dear boy… Of course…

She crosses herself.

RUMPSKINNE: In spirit, and… In this… *(He takes the miniature out of his pocket and kisses it.)* Her blessèd likeness… I've carried it since the day she was taken from me… To feel that she was always close…

GRISELDE, *touched*: Oh… Imagine, Octave…

RUMPSKINNE, *holding it out to* PETITFOUR: But now I think you should have it. Now that I have found you… *(Kissing it again.)* Now that we have, I mean…

He gives it to PETITFOUR *with a look of utter solemnity.*

PETITFOUR: I… I don't know what to say…

RUMPSKINNE: Do you recognize her… *(Emphasizing.)* papá?

PETITFOUR: Oh yes!… I do! I do!… Poor thing!… Those sparkling eyes, that delicate nose…

GRISELDE: Tsk tsk tsk!…

PETITFOUR: Those lovely full lips… My pomegranate tree in bloom… The very image of my… my… *(To* RUMPSKINNE, *casually.)* What was her name again?

RUMPSKINNE, *snatching the miniature from him, sharply*: Her name was Cleopatra… *(Sarcastically.)* papá!… Queen of Egypt, as I recall…

GRISELDE, *shocked*: What?

RUMPSKINNE: Worth nine gilders at the flea market!

PETITFOUR, *babbling*: She… My… Your… *(Abashed.)* Oh my! Oh my!

GRISELDE, *to* PETITFOUR: Octave!… You… How could you?… That night in Spain… The lightning… Don Juan de Caramel…

RUMPSKINNE: Y Fuentes!

GRISELDE: Y Fuentes!

PETITFOUR: I… I…

GRISELDE: I never!… You… *(Pinching him.)* Oh! You old scoundrel!… You…

RUMPSKINNE: No harm done!… *(Good-naturedly.)* As long as Caesar and Marc Antony don't find out!

PETITFOUR: But—

The door, right, opens and VITRUVIA *enters, in tears, still wearing her hat and carrying a valise.*

VITRUVIA: I'm leaving!

PETITFOUR, *stopping her as she moves up center*: Vitruvia!

GRISELDE, *to* VITRUVIA: Don't be silly, treasure! You're getting married!

VITRUVIA: I'm what?

GRISELDE: In two months… *(Pointing to* RUMPSKINNE.*)* And to him!

VITRUVIA, *dropping her valise*: I am?… But I thought… *(Throwing her arms about* RUMPSKINNE, *as* PETITFOUR *despondently collapses into the armchair.)* Oh! Adelbert!… *(To* GRISELDE.*)* Oh! Auntie!… Thank you! Thank you!

GRISELDE: Don't thank me, precious! Thank Cleopatra…

VITRUVIA: Who?

GRISELDE and RUMPSKINNE take her aside and try to explain, as PETITFOUR, in the armchair, shakes his head in disbelief.

PETITFOUR, *muttering sadly*: The end of the Roman Empire… The Goths…

GRISELDE, *to* VITRUVIA: Understand, love?

PETITFOUR: The Huns…

VITRUVIA, *laughing*: Not a word! Not a blessèd—

RUMPSKINNE: But we told you… Cleopatra…

They attempt once again, in a jumble of explanations and gesticulations.

PETITFOUR, *shaking his head* : The end… The end…

They continue, with appropriate exclamations, as the curtain falls.

CURTAIN.

The Unshakable Suitor, or The Matter at Hand

(Un ami acharné, 1853)

Eugène Labiche & Alphonse Jolly

Characters

DUCAMOLE, a middle-class Parisian banker with a very young wife

LEFÈVRE, his long-time professional associate and confidant

JACQUES DE CROQUETTE, a young and dashing suitor

ANTOINE, Ducamole's domestic

COLETTE, Lefèvre's marriageable daughter

Lefèvre's richly furnished interior. In the upstage wall, center, a door. On either side of it, a console table, with an empty vase on each. On the one right, an embroidery basket. In each of the side walls, upstage, a door. Down left, a fireplace. Across from it, down right, a bookcase. Right center, a table with a chair behind it, facing the audience. On it, a number of letters and a newspaper. Down left, near the fireplace, a loveseat. Down right, an armchair. On the walls, several paintings. Other elegant furnishings, here and there.

At rise, LEFEVRE *is seated at the table, right, opening a few of the letters.*

LEFEVRE, *to himself*: Now then... Let's see what these bloodsuckers want today! (*Perusing a letter.*) Whoever said it was easy being a banker! (*Shaking his head.*) Tsk tsk tsk!... Money, money, money... You would think that's all a banker had to do! Just give people money!

As he continues muttering, DUCAMOLE, *in a beige overcoat, enters, up center, obviously disturbed, brandishing an ugly bouquet.*

DUCAMOLE, *under his breath*: Another one! The eighth one this week!

LEFEVRE, *still to himself*: Do they think it grows on trees?

DUCAMOLE, *overhearing*: Trees? Not bloody likely!

LEFEVRE, *noticing him*: Oh, Ducamole...

DUCAMOLE: In hothouses, I suppose...

LEFEVRE, *quizzically*: Hothouses? (*To himself.*) Money?

DUCAMOLE, *still musing*: This time of year...

LEFEVRE: Come in... Come in...

DUCAMOLE: I have, thank you! (*Joining him, right, shaking the bouquet in his face.*) The eighth one! Eight!

LEFEVRE, *nodding absentmindedly*: Yes...

DUCAMOLE: There were seven before this.

LEFEVRE, *nodding*: Quite... That makes sense.

DUCAMOLE: Oh? I'm glad *you* think so!

LEFEVRE: I mean, seven plus one...

DUCAMOLE, *as* LEFEVRE *holds up the letter he is reading*: Of all the... Who the devil...

LEFEVRE, *misunderstanding*: New York... Those blessèd gypsum speculators!

DUCAMOLE: Oh?

LEFEVRE: Another one of their urgent requests...

DUCAMOLE: Yes... Yes... (*Taking the letter.*) Give it here. I'll take care of it myself.

LEFEVRE, *misunderstanding*: All the way to New York? Are you mad? We'll cable it.

DUCAMOLE: Of course! How else do you think...

LEFEVRE: Not until February... (*As* DUCAMOLE *puts the letter down on the table.*) They have time...

DUCAMOLE, *returning to his idée fixe, shaking the bouquet*: And so ugly to boot!

LEFEVRE: The Americans?

DUCAMOLE, *muttering*: Tea roses... Hibiscus... (*Aloud.*) Of all the middle-class... Vile... Utterly vile...

He crosses left.

LEFEVRE, *as DUCAMOLE is crossing, misunderstanding*: I wouldn't know. I've never met them.

DUCAMOLE is about to fling the bouquet into the fireplace.

DUCAMOLE, *paying him no attention, to himself*: Wait… (*Thinking better of it, under his breath.*) Maybe there's a card. There must be…

LEFEVRE, *still talking at cross-purposes*: Or are you just guessing?

DUCAMOLE: There should be one, don't you think?

LEFEVRE, *continuing his thought*: Are you just supposing that they're middle-class?

DUCAMOLE, *pricking his finger*: Ayyy!… Damnation!

LEFEVRE: Americans, after all…

DUCAMOLE, *staring at him*: What are you babbling about, Lefèvre?

LEFEVRE: Babbling? Me?… Really, partner dear! (*Aside.*) "The pot calling the kettle *back*!"… (*Aloud.*) You're hardly one to talk! Just listen to you! (*Pointing upstage.*) You haven't made sense since you came downstairs and walked through that door!

DUCAMOLE, *again about to fling the bouquet into the fireplace, but stopping*: Bah! You're right! (*Sighing.*) I know… (*Returning right, upset.*) It's just that… Who, Lefèvre?… Who the devil is sending her flowers? Every day for a week… (*At the table, pointing up toward the ceiling.*) There isn't an empty vase in my apartment! Flowers! Flowers!… The place is overrun with them! Tea roses, hibiscus… Everywhere I look… It's… It's a bloody invasion!

LEFEVRE: I say…

DUCAMOLE: Hibiscus to the left, tea roses to the right… But where are they coming from?

LEFEVRE, *offhand*: Some florist, I would think…

DUCAMOLE, *ignoring his attempt at humor*: And when I ask her… Because I did, you know… "The flowers, Eugénie…"

LEFEVRE, *nodding*: Aha…

DUCAMOLE: "You must have a devoted admirer, my love!"

LEFEVRE: And?

DUCAMOLE: Can you guess what she tells me? She says she's sending them to herself! There! What do you think of that?

LEFEVRE, *with a gesture*: Pfff!…

DUCAMOLE, *emphasizing each syllable with a rap on the table*: To-her-self, Lefèvre!… She's sending them to herself! Every day!

LEFEVRE: Well, I suppose it's not out of the—

DUCAMOLE, *cutting him off*: I like myself too, but it would never occur to me to send myself flowers! Perhaps once in a while… But every day of the week?… No… She expects me to believe a story like that? She expects me to swallow her tea roses…

LEFEVRE: Thorns and all!

DUCAMOLE: Her hibiscus… Can you imagine? (*Continuing his diatribe, shaking the bouquet.*) Well, thank you just the same! I don't! Not for a minute!… Not Jacques Ducamole… Of Ducamole and Lefèvre, Limited…

LEFEVRE, *softly, correcting*: Lefèvre and Ducamole…

DUCAMOLE: Whatever… To herself, indeed! Once in a while, I could understand… But every day? (*With a cynical little laugh.*) Ha ha ha! (*Crossing left and finally flinging the bouquet into the fireplace, apostrophizing.*) So much for you and your flowers, monsieur! Whoever you are! (*To* LEFEVRE.) One doesn't rise to the top of the Parisian banking world…

LEFEVRE: Well…

DUCAMOLE, *returning to the table*: One doesn't succeed as I have, Lefèvre, without a brain in my head!…

LEFEVRE, *pondering the ambiguity*: Oh…?

DUCAMOLE: One doesn't let himself be taken in by a wife's womanly wiles!

LEFEVRE: Taken in?… You mean… (*Standing up.*) Good heavens, Ducamole! You don't really think… (*Crossing left.*) Surely you're not *recusing* her of… of…

DUCAMOLE, *following him*: Accusing her (*Emphasizing.*) of… of… No, heaven help me! I would never accuse her.. (*Emphasizing.*) of… of—

LEFEVRE: I should hope not! Not madame…

DUCAMOLE: But that doesn't stop me from suspecting her, my friend!

LEFEVRE, *shocked*: Oh! How could you?

DUCAMOLE: "How" indeed!… (*Confidentially.*) I can tell you, but… Not a word, understand? There are times when I think I may have bitten off a little more than I can chew.

LEFEVRE: Bitten off?

DUCAMOLE: By getting married…

LEFEVRE: Come now, Ducamole…

DUCAMOLE: A… (*Hesitating.*) A man of forty-fi… (*Catching himself.*) A man of forty… And a sweet young thing of nineteen!… Well, twenty now… But she *was* nineteen.

LEFEVRE: Yes… Weren't we all…

DUCAMOLE: And a musician!… Ah! A heavenly musician…

LEFEVRE, *nodding*: From the *Observatory*…

DUCAMOLE: From…?

LEFEVRE: The *Observatory*, Ducamole … Of music… One of its brightest stars, you told me.

DUCAMOLE: Oh! If only I had listened to you! All the things you said… The words of wisdom… The advice… "Look before you leap, Ducamole!"

LEFEVRE: Well, that was before—

DUCAMOLE: But I leapt… And now it's too late! Is that what you're going to tell me?

LEFEVRE: Not at all. It's just that—

DUCAMOLE: "She's not for you," you said.

LEFEVRE, *innocently*: I did?

DUCAMOLE: If only I had listened!

LEFEVRE, *with a casual wave*: Well, we all make mistakes… "To err," as they say—

DUCAMOLE: Ah! You see? You admit it! You're telling me I erred…

LEFEVRE: But really, old man… Madame Eugénie is a… a sweet young thing! Just as you say! You couldn't have made a better choice!

DUCAMOLE: Oh? Do I detect a note of sarcasm, Lefèvre?

LEFEVRE: Sarcasm? Me? Not a bit…

DUCAMOLE: That's right! Deny it!

LEFEVRE: But I assure you—

DUCAMOLE: I distinctly heard it… "A better choice…" I did! I heard it!

LEFEVRE, *finally growing impatient*: Bah! Have it your way!… Really… (*He crosses right and sits down at the table, holding up the letters.*) We have other fish to *buy*, Ducamole!

He puts down the letters, picks up the newspaper, and begins reading.

DUCAMOLE: Of course… Change the subject… (*After a moment, crossing right.*) Tell me, Lefèvre…

LEFEVRE, *absorbed in the paper*: Hmm?

DUCAMOLE: If… If you knew anything… If you knew that my honor was… If… I mean, you would tell me, wouldn't you?

LEFEVRE: Of course… Of course…

DUCAMOLE, *after musing a moment, with a sigh, nostalgically*: It was those fingers…

LEFEVRE: Beg pardon?

DUCAMOLE: Her flying fingers… If not for them, I'd still be a bachelor! You can't imagine…

LEFEVRE: You're babbling again, old man.

DUCAMOLE: The arpeggios, the trills, the runs… Ah! She had the runs… The runs of an angel, Lefèvre… Who could forget them?… And the dramatic fortissimos, the delicate pianissimos… And for a music-lover like me… You know what music does to me. (*Dramatically.*) How it electrifies me, to the very roots of my hair!… How it plunges me into the very depths of ecstatic delight…

LEFEVRE: Well…

DUCAMOLE: You remember… Before… How passionately I would play the bagpipe for you…

LEFEVRE, *aside*: God! Who could forget?

DUCAMOLE: Here… Every Sunday…

LEFEVRE, *nodding*: Every Sunday…

He stands up, newspaper in hand.

DUCAMOLE: And how you were moved to tears by its rustic charm… Its bucolic grace…

LEFEVRE, *aside*: Ha!

DUCAMOLE: "How wonderful that would sound out in the country!" you told me. "By a rustling brook… In the noonday sun…"

LEFEVRE: Quite…

DUCAMOLE: "Why don't you go to the country, Ducamole? Go… Go… Charm the beasts, the birds…"

LEFEVRE, *aside*: The bugs…

DUCAMOLE: "Let your pipes waft their harmonies over the gentle breezes…" (*After a moment of reflection, with a hint of regret.*) Ah! If only I had listened! Tsk tsk tsk!… But no… That Sunday was the day of the piano competition. And the public was invited…

LEFEVRE: Aha… To the *Observatory*…

DUCAMOLE: To the… Yes… And there I was, completely, helplessly, totally exposed…

LEFEVRE: Oh?

DUCAMOLE: …to a bevy of talented young virtuosos… (*Reflecting, correcting himself.*) "…as" (*He pronounces "uz."*)

LEFEVRE: "Uz"?

DUCAMOLE: "Virtuos*as*," Lefèvre… Of the feminine gender… Not "os"… "as"…

LEFEVRE: No danger, I imagine! With all that virtue!

DUCAMOLE: It's a musical term…

LEFEVRE: Aha… Well… (*Eager to change the subject, pointing to the table.*) Now then, about that cable to New York…

DUCAMOLE, *ignoring him, continuing*: I listened to the first… The second… The third… All very nice, but cold… No electricity, Lefèvre… No passion, no depth of ecstatic delight…

LEFEVRE: To the roots of your hair…!

DUCAMOLE: And then, out of the blue… The beautiful, the gifted, the incomparable Eugénie!

LEFEVRE: Madame…

DUCAMOLE, *continuing*: What talent in that young artiste, my friend! That *Vivace con amore!*… The elegance, the feeling… I was smitten… Ah! What a piece! What a piece!… Needless to say, she won the first prize!

LEFEVRE: Needless… Needless…

DUCAMOLE: And there I was, so utterly overwhelmed, that I threw precaution to the winds. A few discreet questions, here and there, and in no time I knew where the delightful child lived… She and her mother… Who turned out to be her aunt, but that's another story…

LEFEVRE: Please…

DUCAMOLE: A woman rather mature in years, and… Well, I must admit, she took something of a fancy to me…

LEFEVRE: Needless to say…

DUCAMOLE: Of course, little presents now and then… Trinkets, don't you know… A basket of fruit, a Christmas goose… A horse and carriage… Baubles…

LEFEVRE: Mere trinkets… Of course…

DUCAMOLE: A holiday in the country… And I would bring my bagpipe…

LEFEVRE: Of course…

DUCAMOLE: They insisted… And we would play the most exquisite duets. Eugénie on the piano, and me on my pipes… Exquisite!

LEFEVRE: I'm sure.

DUCAMOLE: And when I realized that the winds of fate were blowing her into my arms, Lefèvre… Ah! I didn't waver for an instant.

LEFEVRE: No…

DUCAMOLE: Or quaver… Or semiquaver!

LEFEVRE: Beg pardon?

DUCAMOLE: Or even hemi-demi-semiquaver!

LEFEVRE, *on whom the humor is lost*: You're babbling again!

DUCAMOLE: And so, after all my piping, there I was… (*With a self-indulgent chuckle.*) Bagged!

LEFEVRE: Married, you mean!

DUCAMOLE: The same thing…

LEFEVRE, *sarcastically*: I must say, you're the only man I know who complains about having a beautiful, talented nineteen-year-old for a wife!

DUCAMOLE, *correcting*: Twenty…

LEFEVRE: Twenty…

DUCAMOLE: There you go again with your sarcasm, Lefèvre!

LEFEVRE: What sarcasm?

DUCAMOLE: Oh yes! Tell me I'm hearing things!

LEFEVRE: Really, Ducamole…

He gets up, crosses left, and sits down on the loveseat, turning his back and reading the paper, mumbling under his breath.

DUCAMOLE, *aside*: Even the way he sits down is sarcastic!

ANTOINE appears at the door, up center, carrying a tray with a cup.

ANTOINE, *to DUCAMOLE*: Monsieur…

DUCAMOLE: Ah! Antoine… What do you want?

ANTOINE, *coming down right*: Madame sent me down to bring monsieur this. She says he's working so hard on his accounts that she's sure he must have a headache.

DUCAMOLE, *taking the cup, sniffing*: What is it?

He begins drinking it as ANTOINE moves upstage.

ANTOINE: Hibiscus tea, monsieur.

DUCAMOLE, *spitting*: What? No tea roses?

ANTOINE, *taking him literally*: Madame didn't say, but I don't think so, monsieur.

DUCAMOLE, *gulping it down, with a grimace*: Pouah!… (*Beckoning ANTOINE to approach.*) Antoine…

ANTOINE: Monsieur?

DUCAMOLE, *replacing the cup on the plate, mysteriously*: I have something important to tell you.

ANTOINE: Monsieur?

DUCAMOLE: No need to mention this to madame, but… We're expecting a young man today… Or maybe tomorrow… Or the day after… Or some other day… Is that clear?

ANTOINE: Perfectly, monsieur! A young man… Today, or some other day…

DUCAMOLE: Yes… And he's going to bring a bouquet of flowers. And he'll ask if Monsieur Ducamole is at home. And you'll say: "No. He's traveling." Understand?

ANTOINE: Oh? Is monsieur going somewhere?

DUCAMOLE: Never mind! You just say it!… Then he'll ask if madame is at home, and you'll show him in.

ANTOINE: But isn't madame going with monsieur?

DUCAMOLE: Never mind, I said! You just show him in!

ANTOINE: But if madame is all alone…

DUCAMOLE, *insisting*: You show him in!

ANTOINE: Very good, monsieur.

He shrugs and turns to leave.

DUCAMOLE, *stopping him, impatiently*: Wait a minute!

ANTOINE: Monsieur?

DUCAMOLE: Once he comes in… (*Pointing to the ceiling.*) You stamp three times on the floor.

ANTOINE: I do?

DUCAMOLE: Nice and loud, understand?

ANTOINE: Yes, monsieur.

DUCAMOLE: And if anyone asks why, you tell them… You tell them you're killing cockroaches. Is that clear?

ANTOINE: I think so, monsieur. A young man with a bouquet of flowers… And cockroaches…

DUCAMOLE: And you don't leave the apartment for the next three days.

ANTOINE: But what if madame sends me on an errand, like she always does?

DUCAMOLE: Then you come and tell me. I'll do it myself.

ANTOINE, *coming downstage*: Good! Monsieur can go right now and buy Minou fifty sous' worth of cat food. (*He gives him a handful of coins.*) Not the kind that makes him puke though…

DUCAMOLE: What?

ANTOINE: Minou, that is… Not monsieur…

DUCAMOLE: Imbecile! (*Giving him back the coins.*) Here! You'll begin when you come back!

ANTOINE: Oh…

DUCAMOLE, *waving him off*: Now get out!… Out!

ANTOINE, *under his breath*: Bah!

He exits, up center, as DUCAMOLE *sits down at the table, right.*

DUCAMOLE, *aside*: There! I can rest a little easier. At least I have someone on the lookout. Even if it's only him!

LEFEVRE, *still on the loveseat.* By the way, Ducamole… The fifty-eight thousand francs that young Monsieur de Croquette deposited yesterday… I trust you didn't forget to post them to his new account?

DUCAMOLE: Of course not! (*Standing up.*) Do I ever? What a question!

LEFEVRE: Because clients like that—

DUCAMOLE: I know. They don't grow on trees!

LEFEVRE: Quite! (*Aside.*) Especially when he's going to marry my daughter!

DUCAMOLE: I'll have to meet him. He must be rolling in money, that one!

LEFEVRE, *aside*: Let's hope! (*Aloud.*) We should be glad that he's chosen Lefèvre and Ducamole, Limited!

DUCAMOLE, *correcting*: Ducamole and—

LEFEVRE, *impatiently*: Whatever…

DUCAMOLE: Still… (*Suspicious.*) Do you ever notice a faint scent of hibiscus when he leaves?

LEFEVRE, *standing up*: Hibiscus?... Are you... Don't tell me you're going to suspect him, of all people!

DUCAMOLE: Really, Lefèvre... If there were any reason, you would tell me, wouldn't you?

LEFEVRE: Of course I would!

DUCAMOLE, *aside*: Sarcastic!

Just then, piano music can be heard coming from upstairs.

LEFEVRE: But I assure you—

DUCAMOLE: Shhh! (*He gives a sudden shudder of delight.*) Listen! She's playing it... The piece that won the prize!... (*He hums along with it, quivering his way upstage.*) Oh! Eugénie! Eugénie!... *Vivace con amore!*... How can I resist?... The electricity... The magnetism... (*Unable to hold still.*) It... It's bigger than I am! (*Trying to resist.*) "Music hath charms," Lefèvre... And... And I'm just a "savage beast"!

LEFEVRE: Oh?

DUCAMOLE, *musing briefly*: Or is it "breast"? "Savage breast..." ? I can never remember...

LEFEVRE: Whichever...

DUCAMOLE, *at the door, up center*: Don't leave! I'll be back!... (*Apostrophizing.*) Eugénie!... Ah! Eugénie!

He exits in a rhythmic flurry of arms and legs.

LEFEVRE, *watching him go, shaking his head*: Tsk tsk tsk! Poor Ducamole! Where did he ever get such ideas? It's one thing to be a little jealous, but... (*Tapping his temple.*) But even to suspect my son-in-law?... Well , almost... If Colette would only—

As the music abruptly stops, COLETTE appears at the door, up center.

COLETTE, *interrupting his musing, entering*: Good morning, papá.

LEFEVRE, *joining her, center*: Ah! Speak of the devil, angel... You're up bright and early! But then, on a special day like this...

COLETTE: Special, papá?

LEFEVRE: Now, now... Don't tell me you've forgotten that Monsieur de Croquette is coming today to ask me for your hand!

COLETTE: Oh, that!

LEFEVRE: Yes, that!... And if you don't mind my saying, Colette, I think you could show a little more enthusiasm! The poor young man falls all over himself in front of you. As gallant as can be...

COLETTE: Yes, papá.

LEFEVRE: Never at a loss for words...

COLETTE: No papá.

LEFEVRE: Always ready to *churn* a delightful phrase...

COLETTE: Yes, papá.

LEFEVRE, *aside*: Like "fifty-eight thousand francs," for example... (*Aloud.*) He absolutely showers you with compliments. And all you can do is say "Yes, monsieur... No, monsieur..." Has the cat got your tongue?

COLETTE, *naively*: We don't have a cat, papá... The neighbors I think...

LEFEVRE: You know what I mean!

COLETTE: And besides… My friends, papá… Why, they would all make fun of me! "Colette Croquette" indeed!

LEFEVRE, *emphasizing*: *De* Croquette, child! *De*… You know what that will tell your friends? That makes up for the name! They'll be eaten up with envy!

COLETTE: Well…

LEFEVRE: Surely you can't dislike him.

COLETTE; Oh no, he's terribly nice, papá! And I can't dislike him. I really don't know him well enough. Maybe if I knew him better…

LEFEVRE: You will… You will… (*Aside.*) Once the notary draws up the marriage contract… Believe me, angel, according to all my *conformants*—

COLETTE: Your what?

LEFEVRE: My *conformants*, child… You don't just give your only daughter to a man without asking people about him! Without finding out all you can… All the important details…

COLETTE: Then do you know if he can waltz, papá?

LEFEVRE: Do I… (*Jokingly, clapping his palm to his forehead.*) That's the one thing I forgot to ask! Wouldn't you know!

COLETTE: But… It's terribly important! He has to be able to waltz! If he can't waltz… Well… Whatever will we do when we're married?

LEFEVRE: He'll think of something! Besides, you can ask him yourself. When he gets here…

COLETTE, *taken aback*: Oh!

LEFEVRE: That will give you something to say besides "yes " and "no."

COLETTE: But papá…

LEFEVRE, *moving toward the door, up right*: Now if you'll excuse me, I have some accounts to go over in the office.

COLETTE: Please! You're not going to leave me alone…

LEFEVRE: Why not? What are you afraid of?

COLETTE: But what if he comes? You said—

LEFEVRE: Then you'll ask him in. You'll have him sit down…

COLETTE: And if he talks to me?

LEFEVRE: Then you'll answer him!

COLETTE: Oh! I wouldn't dare!

LEFEVRE, *losing patience*: Good heavens, child! He's not going to eat you alive! It happens every day of the week! A young man talks to a young lady, and she answers him. What could be simpler?

COLETTE: But… But…

LEFEVRE: Because, if you don't say something sooner or later… In any one of the languages I've spent a fortune teaching you… Well, Monsieur de Croquette is going to think you don't have a brain in your head! A pretty head, angel… But with nothing inside! Is that what you want?

COLETTE: Oh no, papá!

LEFEVRE: Then talk, for heaven's sake! Open your mouth and waggle your tongue!

COLETTE: I'll try…

LEFEVRE: And in that order! Because, if you waggle your tongue first—

COLETTE, *determined*: Oh no! I'll open my mouth first… I'll talk! Really! I will!

LEFEVRE, *at the door, up right*: Good! See that you do!

He exits, up right, muttering to himself.

COLETTE, *alone, coming down right*: I will, I will, I will!… I don't want such a handsome young gentleman to think I don't have a brain in my head! (*To herself.*) He's not going to eat you alive, you know! (*Hands on hips.*) He's not! He's not!… So there!

As she stamps her foot in determination, the door, up center, opens and DE CROQUETTE, *unseen by her, appears, carrying a bouquet just like* DUCAMOLE*'s.*

DE CROQUETTE, *standing at the door for a moment, checking the apartment numbers, to himself*: Ah… Two-B… Good!

COLETTE, *overhearing, turning round*: Who—

DE CROQUETTE, *stepping inside, with a little bow, to* COLETTE: Mademoiselle… Permit me…

COLETTE, *with a little scream*: Oh!

Clapping her hand to her mouth, she goes running off, up left.

DE CROQUETTE, *scratching his head*: Now where do you suppose… (*He goes over to the door, up left, opens it, and looks out, then closes it, with a shrug.*) And this is what they call a courtship? (*Coming downstage.*) Well, this is one ship that's sailing against the wind, I'm afraid! Three months and I haven't even made her father a proposition… For her hand, I mean… Not officially, that is… He knows I'm going to. Today, in fact… (*He paces back and forth for a few moments, eventually returning down center.*) Charming young thing… Colette… Not her father… Oh, he's a very pleasant sort, but… Well… And she's certainly worth the waiting… Just one thing I'm afraid of… I hope and pray she's not a musician! (*To the audience.*) After weeks and weeks as the lapdog of a beautiful young pianist… Oh! Heaven help me! Talented, I'm sure… From the Conservatory, and all that! And pretty as a picture! But to have to listen to the same piece, day after day… And night after night!… Really! That wasn't how I'd planned to spend my evenings! (*Moving right.*) Well, enough is enough!… Or "was"… Six months, and *fini!*… The next ones were no musicians! I made sure of that! Even though I found them at the Opéra… Walking the corridors… (*With a knowing wink.*) If you know what I mean!… Each one, a delight, but not exactly the kind you marry. Not when your name is Jacques de Croquette! (*Pointing to the door, up left, with the bouquet.*) Not like this one… If I can only get her to open her mouth! At least long enough to say "I do"! And as long as she's not a musician! (*He ambles left, to the fireplace, leaning on the mantelpiece.*) Well, that's when I finally had to take a stand. It was time for this rake to… to rake up the weeds… (*Continuing, in mock lyrical tone.*) in the flower garden of my heart! (*Admiring his mot.*) Ha! Not bad!… (*Continuing.*) Time to gather up all the frilly little pink billets doux… The ones signed "Flanquine," and "Risette," and "Caboche"… With all their delicious misspellings, sweet things! (*In front of the fireplace.*) Time to burn them all in one giant bonfire… To incinerate the sinners… (*He gives a nod of self-approval.*) Poor dears!… Poor dears!… Caboche, especially… The most recent… (*With a twinge of nostalgia.*) My last… No bigger than a minute… Rue Navarin… Just around the corner… Our temple of love! (*Sitting down at one end of the loveseat.*) Ah! But what a minute!… Sixty seconds of sheer delight! Hour after hour, day after… (*Interrupting himself, correcting.*) No… Night after night… (*Reflecting.*) Well, all that is over! (*Turning toward the door, up center.*) Exit Caboche… (*Turning toward *the door, up left, reaching out his arms, still holding the bouquet.*) Enter Colette!… From today on, mademoiselle… (*To himself.*) Which explains why I may not be quite myself… (*Tapping his temple.*) A little… (*Standing up.*) Why, just now, don't you know… My head was so far up in the clouds that I went to the wrong apartment! (*Pointing to the ceiling with the bouquet.*) Three-B, of all things… Lucky I realized it before they opened the door!… It seems even my flowers are destined to go astray. That idiot florist of mine admitted that he's been making the same mistake for a week! Why, I can't imagine! "Lefèvre… Second floor," I told him, plain as day. "Two-B… Two-B…" And all he could do was nod, and say "Or not to be!" and giggle his fool head off!

He returns to the fireplace, holding the bouquet behind his back, and stands reflecting. A few moments later, the door, up center, opens and DUCAMOLE *enters.*

DUCAMOLE, *aside, noticing him*: Who…? (*Seeing the flowers.*) Aha! Another one! I knew it!… But why down here? Why not upstairs? Well, we'll see about that! (*Standing center stage, arms crossed, with a menacing look, clearing his throat.*) Ahem… Ahem… Monsieur?

DE CROQUETTE, *turning around*: Oh! I beg your pardon. I didn't know—

DUCAMOLE, *very proper*: My sincere apologies, monsieur!

DE CROQUETTE: Yes, yes… Thank you, I'm sure! (*Aside.*) Who the blazes…

DUCAMOLE: You understand, of course, that I promised myself I would remain calm…

DE CROQUETTE: Of course…

DUCAMOLE: In spite of… (*Emphasizing.*) everything…

DE CROQUETTE, *nodding*: Yes… Everything…

DUCAMOLE, *moving toward him*: So! What did you want to tell me?

DE CROQUETTE: What did I—

DUCAMOLE: I'm waiting, monsieur… Come, come… Out with it!

DE CROQUETTE: What makes you think I—

DUCAMOLE, *joining him and pointedly taking a sniff of the bouquet*: What indeed! (*With a sarcastic little laugh.*) Ha ha ha! (*Taking another big sniff.*) Ha!… (*He tries to repress a sneeze.*) Ha!… H… H… Ha!… (*Finally unable to repress it.*) Ha-tchoo!

DE CROQUETTE: Bless you! (*Aside.*) Whoever you are!

DUCAMOLE, *very matter-of-fact*: Thank you. (*After a momentary pause.*) Well? I'm waiting!… Please! There's no point in pretending. I'm quite a… a… (*Sneezing.*) Ha-tchoo!… Quite aware, monsieur…

DE CROQUETTE: Bless you!

DUCAMOLE, *as before*: Thank you.

DE CROQUETTE: Please… "Quite aware…"?

DUCAMOLE, *backing away from him and the bouquet*: Silence isn't your cup of tea, my friend… Or your bouquet of tea roses, if you don't mind my saying… (DE CROQUETTE *gives a look of utter incomprehension.*) Or hibiscus, either!

DE CROQUETTE, *confused*: No… I don't suppose…

DUCAMOLE: No!

DE CROQUETTE *looks at him quizzically for a moment, shaking his head, then shrugs and moves toward the door, up center, as if to leave.*

DE CROQUETTE: If you don't mind…

DUCAMOLE, *barring his exit*: Oh no! Oh no!... Where do you think you're going?

DE CROQUETTE: Well, I—

DUCAMOLE: Upstairs, no doubt...

DE CROQUETTE: Oh?

DUCAMOLE: Oh no! If you won't talk, I will!

DE CROQUETTE: Yes... That would be nice...

DUCAMOLE, *very sarcastic, pointing to the flowers*: Lovely, monsieur, aren't they! Such exquisite taste! The height of floral sophistication, don't you think? One would say you have a penchant for tea roses, monsieur... And hibiscus... A veritable lust, by the looks of it...

DE CROQUETTE: Well... I do rather fancy them... (*Making conversation.*) Of course, at this time of year, it's rather difficult—

DUCAMOLE: Yes... Yes... (*Aside.*) But not for him, I see!

DE CROQUETTE: And you, monsieur?

DUCAMOLE: Me? Me, you ask?... I hate them! I loathe the very sight of them!

DE CROQUETTE, *taken aback*: Oh... (*Under his breath.*) Odd chap...

DUCAMOLE: If it were up to me, I wouldn't give them house room! Of course, there are times when it isn't up to me! If you know what I mean!... In fact, any time they happen to find their way past my threshold, I... I give them to the concierge! They're just right for that incredibly vulgar taste of hers! So! What do you think of that?

DE CROQUETTE, *at a loss*: Well... It's all in the way you look at them, I suppose. Some people...

DUCAMOLE, *aside*: Do I have to spell it out for him? Stupid... (*Aloud.*) No matter... I'm sure that... that... (*Emphasizing.*) *she* will find your bouquet simply delightful!

DE CROQUETTE, *aside*: What concern is it of his?

DUCAMOLE, *continuing*: And if I say "she," monsieur... It's only because I assume that it must be for—

DE CROQUETTE, *quickly*: For myself! (*Moving right, by the table.*) I love to buy myself flowers!

DUCAMOLE, *aside*: Ha! The same story, both of them...

DE CROQUETTE: They brighten my mood...

DUCAMOLE, *aside*: Collusion!

DE CROQUETTE: Especially on these drab winter days, don't you know?

DUCAMOLE, *crossing left, aside*: What do they take me for? (*At the fireplace, aloud.*) Still, my friend... You have to admit...

DE CROQUETTE, *crossing right, eager to cut the conversation short*: Excuse me, monsieur, but... (*Putting the bouquet down on the table.*) With whom do I have the honor... I don't seem to recall...

DUCAMOLE, *with a wry little laugh*: Ha ha! With whom, indeed!... You know perfectly well "with whom," my friend.

DE CROQUETTE: I do? Well, let's pretend that I don't, shall we?

DUCAMOLE, *stuffily*: Ducamole, monsieur! Of the banking firm of Ducamole and Lefèvre, Limited...

DE CROQUETTE, *aside*: Damn! A friend of the family!...

DUCAMOLE: Senior partner…

DE CROQUETTE, *aloud, trying to redeem himself, sycophantically*: Of course! Of course! What was I thinking? Monsieur… (*Mispronouncing.*) Ducomole…

DUCAMOLE *correcting him*: Ca…

DE CROQUETTE: Ca…?

DUCAMOLE: Du-*ca*… *Ca*…

DE CROQUETTE: Du*caca*mole…

DUCAMOLE, *articulating*: Du-*ca*-mole…

DE CROQUETTE: Of course!… Monsieur Ducamole… But you're so much younger than I thought…

DUCAMOLE: Oh?

DE CROQUETTE: Madame has spoken so highly of you!

DUCAMOLE: Aha… (*Aside.*) I'm sure!

DE CROQUETTE, *aside*: A little flattery… (*Aloud.*) Your financial wizardry… Your acumen…

DUCAMOLE, *aside*: My what?

DE CROQUETTE: Why, I feel as if we're old friends, monsieur!

DUCAMOLE: Yes… Yes, but…

DE CROQUETTE: But just what was it you had in mind? I don't think you said… (*Confused.*) Or did you?

DUCAMOLE: No… Not quite… But…

DE CROQUETTE: Please… Did we have something to discuss, you and I? Feel free…

DUCAMOLE, *aside*: Why not? I'll beard the lion in his den!… (*Aloud.*) As a matter of fact… I came to speak to my associate. Our junior partner… Monsieur Lefèvre… It's rather a delicate matter, but I'm sure an old friend like you…

He puts his forefinger to his lips.

DE CROQUETTE: By all means, monsieur. I'm the very soul of discretion.

DUCAMOLE: Yes… You see, I need some advice.

DE CROQUETTE: Oh?

DUCAMOLE: Perhaps you… If you're sure you don't mind…

DE CROQUETTE: Mind?… Please… Go on… I'm delighted to be of service! Though I can't imagine..

He motions him over to the loveseat, left.

DUCAMOLE: Yes, well… (*They both sit down.*) It's just that a friend of mine… A very dear friend… (*Crossing his fingers, aside.*) This way I'm not lying at least… (*Aloud.*) We couldn't be closer…

DE CROQUETTE: Aha…

DUCAMOLE, *holding up his forefinger and thumb, scarcely separated.*) That close…

DE CROQUETTE: Aha…

DUCAMOLE: Well, he's married, this friend of mine. (*As if to explain.*) He has a wife.

DE CROQUETTE: Yes… (*Aside.*) I assume…

DUCAMOLE: And… (*Aside.*) Beard him in his den… (*Aloud, to* DE CROQUETTE.) Or is it his "lair"?

DE CROQUETTE: I beg your pardon? His what…? Whose…?

DUCAMOLE, *realizing his gaffe*: Nothing… Nothing… I was thinking out loud…

DE CROQUETTE: And your friend, monsieur…? You were saying…

DUCAMOLE: Oh! He's jealous! Very jealous!… And he has good reason to suspect that a certain young scoundrel… A twit… A dandy… A snake in the grass… Is trying to steal my wife… (*Quickly correcting himself.*) His… His wife, monsieur… From under his very nose!

DE CROQUETTE, *feigning shock*: No! His nose?

DUCAMOLE: His nose!

DE CROQUETTE: No!

DUCAMOLE, *insisting*: His nose!… But he knows, my friend! He knows!

DE CROQUETTE: Oh?

DUCAMOLE: Oh yes! He knows!

DE CROQUETTE, *nodding*: He knows…

DUCAMOLE: And he's looking for a way… My friend, that is… To get rid of the snake… The scoundrel…

DE CROQUETTE: The twit…

DUCAMOLE: Exactly! And he's asked me to help him.

DE CROQUETTE, *nodding*: I see… I see… *(A little confused)* But… Just what did you want from me, monsieur? What kind of help… I'm not quite sure…

DUCAMOLE: Well, I… You seem to be a young man of the world! I'm sure you've had an affair or two…

DE CROQUETTE, *falsely modest*: Oh…

DUCAMOLE: Perhaps even of a similar nature… Under the husband's nose, I mean!

DE CROQUETTE: Really, I—

DUCAMOLE: Don't deny it! I can tell…

DE CROQUETTE, *a little fatuously*: Well… One or two, perhaps…

DUCAMOLE: And I thought you might be able to give me some advice. (*Catching himself.*) For me to give him, that is… My friend…

DE CROQUETTE: Well… It's not your everyday request, but… I suppose if I put myself in the place of the lover…

DUCAMOLE, *correcting*: The twit! The scoundrel, you mean! Call him what he is!

DE CROQUETTE, *with a mischievous little smile*: Yes… I suppose if I put myself in his shoes, I might find something… With a little kick to it!

DUCAMOLE, *wryly*: Yes… I suppose you might… (*Pointedly.*) Perhaps something recent… Something fresh in your memory!

DE CROQUETTE, *after musing for a moment*: Of course, there was that ravishing young creature, for example…

DUCAMOLE: Yes! Tell me about that one!

DE CROQUETTE, *continuing*: …whose name wild horses wouldn't drag out of me!

DUCAMOLE: No need, I assure you! (*Aside.*) Damnation! Eugénie! It must be…

DE CROQUETTE, *continuing*: The one with an absolutely unbridled passion…

DUCAMOLE, *aside, between his teeth.* Wild horses indeed!

DE CROQUETTE, *continuing*: …for flowers… My bouquets, day after day…

DUCAMOLE, *aside*: The scum! He admits it!

DE CROQUETTE, *continuing*: The one that I almost… almost… (*Suggestively.*) Not quite, but almost…

DUCAMOLE, *aside*: Over my dead body, wretch!

DE CROQUETTE, *continuing*: …in spite of that husband of hers, don't you know!

DUCAMOLE, *aside*: I'll kill him, I swear!

DE CROQUETTE: Ah yes, her husband…

DUCAMOLE, *aside*: I'll tear him limb from limb!

DE CROQUETTE: Well, the less said about that blubberhead the better!

DUCAMOLE: Monsieur!

DE CROQUETTE: Besides, it's not polite to speak ill of the dead.

DUCAMOLE, *taken aback*: The dead? What "dead"…? Who…? (*Feeling his body here and there.*) You mean, her husband… (*Confused, aside.*) Then who the devil…

DE CROQUETTE, *musing*: Oh! That beautiful creature!

DUCAMOLE: But… But… (*Pointing toward the ceiling, to himself.*) I thought…

DE CROQUETTE: And anyway… (*With a gesture of thumb and forefinger.*) That close!… Just a little closer, and he was sprouting a pair of horns, believe me.

DUCAMOLE: Oh, I do! I do!

DE CROQUETTE, *with a sigh*: What happiness was almost mine, monsieur! (*Wistfully.*) Almost… Almost…

DUCAMOLE, *under his breath*: Swine!

DE CROQUETTE, *getting up, going to the armchair, down right*: But for some inexplicable reason, I found myself, one evening, obliged to join her and her poor fool of a husband for dinner. (*Reminiscing.*) Braised loin of goat, as I recall… "How appropriate," I told myself, with a smile!… Why there, of all places?… And with them?… Who knows? Fate, no doubt… (*Sitting down, nostalgically.*) Because… Oh, I know you're going to laugh at me, but… The sight of that happy home… That calm, peaceful little family… Those little ones hugging and kissing their mother… That father, taking my hand firmly in his… So unsuspecting… (*Emotionally, brushing away a tear.*) Ah! How ashamed I felt, monsieur, standing there… (*Reflecting for a moment.*) Well, sitting actually… There, on the very threshold of my infamous, ignominious act! And, all at once, my blood ran cold. A shudder of virtue welled up through my flesh. I put down my knife and fork…

DUCAMOLE: While he was shaking your hand?

DE CROQUETTE, *ignoring the observation*: I wiped the wine from my lips… My passionate, lustful lips…

DUCAMOLE, *under his breath*: With your napkin, I hope…

DE CROQUETTE, *continuing, getting up*: And I got up and left, resolved not to sully his honor and my own! (*Coming center.*) That, monsieur, is what you can tell your friend… Ah yes! The sight of a happy home… An honest handshake, straight from the heart, monsieur… The poor, unsuspecting husband, grasping my lascivious hand…

DUCAMOLE, *standing, joining him, center*: Yes, well… All that is very touching, but… But I think we need something a little more—how shall I say?—aggressive… More physical… I'm not… (*Catching himself.*) My friend, that is… He's not one to pussyfoot, monsieur! Violence! Violence!

DE CROQUETTE: Aha… A duel, perhaps?

DUCAMOLE: Excellent idea! (*Aside.*) I'll call his bluff, the coward! (*Aloud.*) Have you ever had one, young man?

DE CROQUETTE: A duel?... Only one... Alas!

DUCAMOLE: Were you wounded?

DE CROQUETTE: No.

DUCAMOLE, *without thinking*: Killed?... (*Quickly.*) What am I saying?

DE CROQUETTE, *very matter-of-fact*: I carved up my adversary like a turkey.

DUCAMOLE, *aside*: Dear God!

DE CROQUETTE: Fortunately, it was only a flesh wound... Well, several flesh wounds... I don't have his death on my conscience, thank heaven!

DUCAMOLE, *aside*: Hmm! That changes things a little. (*Aloud.*) Now then, young man... You were saying... "An honest handshake, straight from the heart..."

DE CROQUETTE, *completing the thought*: ...is always enough to save a man of honor from plunging into the abyss of betrayal! Because a handshake is sacred, monsieur! To deceive a man who has shaken your hand... Who has trusted you... Who has enjoyed the hospitality of your table...

DUCAMOLE: Oh?

DE CROQUETTE: Why, it's worse than a betrayal, monsieur! It's... It's the basest of treachery!

He comes down right.

DUCAMOLE: You're right!... Oh yes! How right you are!

DE CROQUETTE, *humbly*: Thank you, monsieur.

DUCAMOLE, *aside*: Well, if that's how he feels... (*Reflecting, to himself.*) As long as he shakes my hand... As long as he sees my happy home... (*As an afterthought.*) Once I get rid of all the flowers...

DE CROQUETTE: I'm sure your friend will share that opinion and profit from my experience.

DUCAMOLE, *continuing, to himself*: And once he enjoys the hospitality of my table...

DE CROQUETTE: So! I do hope I've been of some modest assistance.

DUCAMOLE: Oh, you have! (*Aside.*) Immodest, even... (*Aloud*) And I thank you... (*Catching himself.*) He... We... I mean, he thanks you... That is, he would, I'm sure, if... if...

DE CROQUETTE: Think nothing of it! Happy to oblige...

DUCAMOLE, *moving left, aside*: That's it! I'll invite him to dinner. He'll have to shake my hand! And when he does... "To deceive a man who has shaken your hand..." (*Returning down right and joining* DE CROQUETTE, *aloud.*) My friend... I trust you'll do me the honor...

DE CROQUETTE: Please?

DUCAMOLE: I said: "I trust you'll do me the honor..." The honor, monsieur...

Before he has a chance to finish the thought, COLETTE *enters, up left.*

DE CROQUETTE, *paying him no attention whatsoever*: Ah! Mademoiselle!

He quickly snatches the bouquet from the table and crosses up left to greet her.

DUCAMOLE, *continuing, in a mumble*: ...of joining Madame Ducamole and me...

COLETTE, *to* DE CROQUETTE, *timidly*: I… I do hope you'll excuse me, monsieur, for… for running off the way I did…

DUCAMOLE, *approaching* DE CROQUETTE, *trying to interrupt*: I trust…

COLETTE, *continuing*: I… I wanted to be sure to let papá know that he had a visitor.

DUCAMOLE, *still trying*: I trust…

DE CROQUETTE, *to* COLETTE: You're too kind, mademoiselle. You needn't disturb him.

DUCAMOLE, *still trying*: I trust you'll do me the honor, monsieur…

DE CROQUETTE, *continuing to ignore him, offering the bouquet to* COLETTE: Permit me, mademoiselle…

COLETTE: Oh, monsieur! For me?

DUCAMOLE, *aside*: Ha! Very clever!

COLETTE, *timidly*: They're… They're lovely… I don't…

DUCAMOLE, *aside*: He thinks that will fool me, does he?

COLETTE: I don't know what to say… You're too kind, monsieur!

DUCAMOLE, *to* COLETTE, *not without a touch of sarcasm*: He is! He's all heart, mademoiselle!

DE CROQUETTE, *with a self-effacing gesture*: Please… Really…

DUCAMOLE, *under his breath*: For her, my foot! (*Aloud, to* COLETTE, *continuing.*) A heart of gold!… (*Following her as she moves left, takes a vase from one of the console tables, puts the bouquet in it, and places it over the fireplace.*) Pure gold, mademoiselle…

DE CROQUETTE: Monsieur—

DUCAMOLE, *cutting him off, introducing, holding out his hand*: My friend…

DE CROQUETTE: You're really…

DUCAMOLE: My dear friend…

DE CROQUETTE, *ignoring it, continuing*: …too kind!

DUCAMOLE: My dear, dear friend, Monsieur… (*At a loss.*) Monsieur…

DE CROQUETTE: De Croquette…

DUCAMOLE: Of course… (*Mispronouncing.*) Monsieur de Coquette…

He holds out his hand more insistently as COLETTE *sits down on the loveseat, takes her embroidery from her pocket, and begins embroidering.*

DE CROQUETTE, *correcting*: Rr… Rr…

DUCAMOLE, *quizzically, echoing the sound*: Rr…?

DE CROQUETTE, *emphasizing*. Crrroquette…… I think you said—

DUCAMOLE: Of course… Of course… (*Holding out his hand.*) My dear, dear friend, Monsieur Croquette… (*Pointing to* COLETTE.) Mademoiselle Lefèvre…

COLETTE, *embroidering, simply*: We've met, monsieur.

DE CROQUETTE *ignoring* DUCAMOLE, *joins her on the loveseat.*

DUCAMOLE: Aha… (*To* COLETTE.) You've met my friend Croquette… (*Reluctantly withdrawing his hand, aside.*) Why won't he… (*Aloud to* COLETTE.) My bosom friend, Croquette…

DE CROQUETTE, *correcting*: De… De…

DUCAMOLE: De…?

DE CROQUETTE, *emphasizing*: *De* Croquette…

DUCAMOLE: Of course… (*Aside.*) He must have a reason!

COLETTE, *to* DE CROQUETTE, *making conversation*: Have you known Monsieur Ducamole very long, monsieur?

DE CROQUETTE: Oh… Five minutes, give or take…

DUCAMOLE, *as she reacts with surprise*: But what is time, mademoiselle? With some people, one minute is all you need…

COLETTE: I'm sure…

DUCAMOLE: A single minute… To know each other, admire each other… Friend to friend… Heart to heart… To take his hand in yours… (*Approaching* DE CROQUETTE.) Dear, dear Croquette… (*Quickly correcting himself.*) De… De… (*Holding out his hand.*) Dear, dear, de Croquette…

DE CROQUETTE, *with a little bow*: You're too kind! (*Aside.*) Damn! What a prig!

DUCAMOLE, *examining his hand, aside*: What's wrong with it? (*Sniffing it, still aside.*) It must be something… (*To* DE CROQUETTE, *left, holding it out.*) Monsieur…

DE CROQUETTE, *ignoring him, to* COLETTE: As I was saying, mademoiselle…

COLETTE stands up and crosses right, to the table, with DE CROQUETTE following.

DUCAMOLE, *trying to intercept him as he passes behind him*: Monsieur…

COLETTE rummages about the table, finds a pair of scissors, and snips a thread.

DE CROQUETTE, *to* COLETTE: It seems that your father, mademoiselle…

DUCAMOLE, *to* DE CROQUETTE: I say… I was hoping…

DE CROQUETTE: Monsieur?

COLETTE returns left and sits down on the loveseat, continuing to embroider.

DUCAMOLE, *to* DE CROQUETTE: I was hoping you would dine with Madame Ducamole and me this evening. The three of us… Nothing fancy… Just a typical dinner in our happy little home…

DE CROQUETTE: Impossible, monsieur!

He attempts to cross left to join COLETTE.

DUCAMOLE, *stopping him*: Oh?

DE CROQUETTE, *attempting again*: I have guard duty with my regiment. All day, I'm afraid…

DUCAMOLE, *stopping him again*: And after that?

DE CROQUETTE: After that?… After that I have to meet with my notary.

DUCAMOLE: Aha… And after that?

DE CROQUETTE: Then back to the regiment, monsieur! (*Aside.*) If it's any concern of his!

DUCAMOLE: Nonsense!

DE CROQUETTE, *taken aback*: I beg your pardon?

DUCAMOLE: "Nonsense," I said!… You have to eat! And you're going to join madame and me for a cozy little dinner. Just the three of us… In our happy little home… Very happy…

DE CROQUETTE, *losing patience*: Yes, you said that! Yes…

DUCAMOLE: Aha! You said "yes"! Then you agree?

DE CROQUETTE: No! I… Really, I…

DUCAMOLE: Not another word! I won't take "no" for an answer! Come, shake on it, my friend!

Hopefully, he holds out his hand, which DE CROQUETTE *again ignores.*

DE CROQUETTE: I assure you, monsieur… I'm terribly flattered, but—

DUCAMOLE: No "buts," no "buts"…

DE CROQUETTE, *crossing left, toward* COLETTE, *aside*: Damn!

DUCAMOLE, *examining his hand, to himself*: Does he think I'm a leper?

DE CROQUETTE, *aside*: The man is an insufferable leech! (*Aloud, to* DUCAMOLE.) We'll see, monsieur… (*Aside.*) I'll think of something! (*He stands for a few moments looking over* COLETTE*'s shoulder at her embroidery.*) My, my! How lovely, mademoiselle!

COLETTE: Thank you, monsieur. It's for the wedding…

DE CROQUETTE, *knowingly*: Oh?

COLETTE, *standing up*: Of a friend of mine, I mean…

DE CROQUETTE: And a very good friend, I'll bet! Someone you know especially well… Someone you're very close to… (*Moving closer.*) Someone *I'm* very close to… Am I right, mademoiselle?

COLETTE, *bashfully*: Oh, monsieur…

DUCAMOLE *comes over and, interrupting their tête-à-tête, takes* DUCAMOLE *by the arm and pulls him center.*

DE CROQUETTE, *angrily*: What are you—

DUCAMOLE: Tell me, my friend—

DE CROQUETTE: Who do you think… Monsieur Ducamole! I'll thank you—

DUCAMOLE: Please! No need!… I only wanted to ask you—-

DE CROQUETTE: What? To ask me what?

DUCAMOLE: In your regiment, my friend… Tell me… Do you carry a forty-pound pack on your back?

DE CROQUETTE: Do we… I beg your pardon! What kind of—

DUCAMOLE, *insisting*: Or heavier? Maybe fifty?

DE CROQUETTE: Monsieur! (*Breaking free, losing patience.*) Unhand me, you… (*Aside.*) A bloody leech!

DUCAMOLE: But I… It's important…

DE CROQUETTE, *suddenly inspired*. Do me a favor, will you?

DUCAMOLE, *overjoyed*: A favor? Of course, monsieur! As many as you like…

DE CROQUETTE: Just one… (*Aside.*) But a long one!

DUCAMOLE, *holding out his hand*: Your wish is my command!

DE CROQUETTE, *ignoring it*: No, no… One is quite enough… (*Under his breath.*) Anything to get rid of him!… (*Aloud.*) But a terribly important one, monsieur… (*He reaches into a pocket and pulls out a sheaf of papers.*) These letters of credit… Go cash them for me, will you?

DUCAMOLE: With pleasure!… But… Let me cash them here… (*With a little laugh.*) Ducamole and Lefèvre, Limited is still solvent you know!

DE CROQUETTE, *wagging his finger*: No, no!… Bad luck!… You know what they say! "Never put all your eggs in one basket."

DUCAMOLE: Of course…

DE CROQUETTE: "Especially one that's too close to home…"

DUCAMOLE: Oh? (*Aside.*) I didn't know the rest of it…

DE CROQUETTE: No, no!… Lots of different banks… As many as you can find… Take all the time you need. And feel free to stop and buy yourself breakfast! Lunch too, if you like…

DUCAMOLE, *taking the papers*: And you're sure that's all? Nothing else, monsieur?… Nothing else for my dear friend Coquette? (*Before* DE CROQUETTE *has a chance to correct him.*) Rr… Rr…

DE CROQUETTE: De… De…

COLETTE, *overhearing, and noticing that* DUCAMOLE *seems about to leave*: Oh my!

DUCAMOLE, *half-heartedly holding out his hand, to* DE CROQUETTE: Of course… My dear friend de Croquette…

COLETTE, *getting up, standing between them, aside*: Is he leaving me alone with him?

DE CROQUETTE, *to* DUCAMOLE, *ignoring his hand*: Nothing else… Now please! Don't waste a minute! It's terribly important, and I can't thank you enough!

DUCAMOLE: Please, don't mention it! (*Nodding to each in turn.*) Mademoiselle… Monsieur… (*After holding out his hand one more time, to no avail, he shrugs and moves upstage, muttering.*) He'll have to, sooner or later… He'll have to…

He exits, upstage.

DE CROQUETTE, *heaving a sigh of relief, aside*: At last!

COLETTE, *aside, timidly*: Oh my! Just the two of us…

DE CROQUETTE, *aloud*: Ah, mademoiselle! What a joy to be alone with you! Just you… Just me…

COLETTE: And… And papá, monsieur…

DE CROQUETTE, *confused*: Oh? (*Looking around the room.*) But… (*Moving right and looking under the table.*) But where, mademoiselle? I don't quite—

COLETTE: No, Not yet… But he'll be here any minute. (*Under her breath.*) I hope!

DE CROQUETTE, *rejoining her, left, standing by the loveseat*: Just between us, mademoiselle… If you don't mind my saying… You… You seem… How shall I say?… You seem a trifle…

COLETTE: Monsieur?

DE CROQUETTE: Well, one would almost think I frighten you.

COLETTE: Frighten me, monsieur? (*With an unconvincing little laugh.*) Ha ha ha! Heavens, no! (*Aside.*) Oh my! It shows! What can I do?

DE CROQUETTE: Mind you, I would understand if I did.

COLETTE, *naively*: You would?

DE CROQUETTE: In fact, if you want to know the truth… You make me feel a little… a little…

COLETTE: I do?

He holds out the fingers of both hands, quivering intentionally.

DE CROQUETTE: See?

COLETTE: Monsieur… You're trembling…

DE CROQUETTE: I told you!… And when two people are trembling together, it cancels itself out, if you know what I mean.

COLETTE: It does? (*Aside.*) Oh my! I almost think he's right!

DE CROQUETTE: Besides, I think we're at a point, mademoiselle, where…

COLETTE, *naively*: "Where"?

DE CROQUETTE: Where we should be finding out more and more about each other… Studying each other… Probing our tastes, our likes, our dislikes…

COLETTE: Oh yes… Probing…

DE CROQUETTE: Our innermost feelings…

COLETTE: Oh, innermost!… Yes…

DE CROQUETTE: I'm sure you must have all kinds of important things to ask me.

COLETTE: I do, monsieur! I do!… And to tell you, too…

DE CROQUETTE: Well, ask away! I'm ready to take my test.

COLETTE: And I'm ready to take mine. Please! You go first… Tell me everything!

DE CROQUETTE: But there's so little to tell! The first day I saw you, I loved you…

COLETTE, *with a little shudder*: You did?

DE CROQUETTE: And admired you, mademoiselle… Your beauty, your wit, your grace… (*He is about to embrace her.*) Your passion…

COLETTE, *avoiding him*: But that's not a test, monsieur! There have to be questions to make it a test!

DE CROQUETTE: Ah, but no question about it! I only know that you're all I think about! Day and night… Night and day…

COLETTE, *aside*: Oh my!

DE CROQUETTE: You are the one!… Only you… You and you alone, mademoiselle…

COLETTE: But… The test, monsieur… You said…

DE CROQUETTE: Ask me! Go ahead, ask me anything you like. Any one of those important questions a young lady wants her young… her young… (*Hesitating over the word.*) … lover… if I may… (COLETTE *heaves a noticeable sigh.*) …her young lover to answer!

COLETTE: And… And you promise to tell me the truth?

DE CROQUETTE: I promise!

COLETTE, *summoning up her courage*: Do you waltz, monsieur?

DE CROQUETTE, *taken aback*: Do I…?

COLETTE: Waltz… You know… (*She mimes a little three-quarter step.*) The waltz…

DE CROQUETTE, *recovering his aplomb*: Of course! What gentleman today doesn't, mademoiselle? I should say—

COLETTE: And well, monsieur?

DE CROQUETTE: Superbly! Would you care to see?

COLETTE, *jumping back*: Oh no! I didn't mean—

DE CROQUETTE: Because you know, mademoiselle… There are some unscrupulous, unprincipled cads who would take advantage of you and tell you that they can, but who can't put one foot in front of the other in a seemly manner!

COLETTE, *shocked*: No!

DE CROQUETTE: And for something as essential as the waltz… Well, I certainly want you to put your mind at ease. Come… Let me show you…

COLETTE, *resisting*: But…

Just then, one hears a waltz being played on the piano, upstairs.

DE CROQUETTE: Aha! You see? (*Pointing to the ceiling.*) Fate, mademoiselle!… Now, we mustn't let it go to waste, must we?

COLETTE: But…

He takes her hands and assumes the position.

DE CROQUETTE: Now then… The test…

COLETTE: But… In broad daylight? People will think I'm absolutely mad!

DE CROQUETTE, *looking around the room and out over the audience*: Who?… What people?… Come…

They begin waltzing to the piano music as he hums along with it.

COLETTE: Oh my…

They proceed to waltz around the room. DE CROQUETTE *is the essence of debonair grace and elegance, while* COLETTE, *trying to keep up with him, is as awkward as can be. They finally come to a stop by the table, right.*

DE CROQUETTE: Ah! Such grace! Such elegance!

COLETTE: Thank you, monsieur!

DE CROQUETTE: It's clear, mademoiselle, that you were born to waltz!… So, do I pass my test?

COLETTE: Well, I'm not sure… Perhaps if you tried again…

DE CROQUETTE: With pleasure!

They begin again. COLETTE *is just as clumsy as before. After a few moments, as they arrive down left, the door, up right, opens and* LEFEVRE *appears.*

LEFEVRE, *entering*: I'm back! (*Seeing the pair dancing.*) Good heavens! What's all this?

COLETTE, } *together*: { Papá
DE CROQUETTE, } { Monsieur!

They separate, as the music continues. COLETTE *crosses quickly, up right.*

LEFEVRE: Please! Don't stop!… Don't let me *protrude*!

COLETTE, *to* LEFEVRE, *joining him, embarrassed*: But papá… I assure you… This was only a test…

DE CROQUETTE, *to* LEFEVRE: Just a test, monsieur…

COLETTE: To see how well—

LEFEVRE: No doubt!… In three-quarter time… (*Jokingly.*) Three-fourths of a test, you mean…

COLETTE, *to* LEFEVRE, *whispering in his ear, self-confidently*: But papá, I'm not afraid of him any more!

LEFEVRE, *replying in a whisper*: So I see!

COLETTE, *continuing*: And I talked to him!… I did! Really!… I opened my mouth!

LEFEVRE, *aloud, to* DE CROQUETTE, *who is still down left*: And, as for you, young man… (*Joining him.*) It seems to me we have something to discuss, you and I.

DE CROQUETTE: Monsieur?

LEFEVRE: The little matter of a marriage…

DE CROQUETTE: Nothing would please me more!

LEFEVRE, *with mock seriousness*: After all, finding you shamelessly, intimately *contorting* with my daughter…

COLETTE: But papá…

LEFEVRE: I know, young lady! It was only a test… (*Taking* DE CROQUETTE *by the arm.*) Come… (*Pointing up right.*) We'll discuss it in my office…

DE CROQUETTE: With pleasure, monsieur…

They exit, up right.

COLETTE, *alone, watching them leave*: Oh my! What a nice young man!… He's in there now asking papá for my hand… Oh yes! He really is terribly sweet. Just the perfect husband!… And he waltzes so divinely… A lucky thing, too. Because, if he didn't… (*She tiptoes to the door, up right.*) I wonder what they're saying. (*As she is about to press her ear against the door, she stops.*) No, no! That's naughty! I mustn't!

After a brief moment of indecision, she bends over and peeks through the keyhole. As she does so, DUCAMOLE *enters, up center, in full military uniform, carrying a rifle with a bayonet, and with a monstrous pack on his back.*

DUCAMOLE: There!… Perfect…

COLETTE, *standing up suddenly*: Oh my!… Is… (*Hardly recognizing him.*) Is that you, Monsieur Ducamole?

DUCAMOLE, *mysteriously*: Shhh! Not so loud!… I want it to be a surprise!

COLETTE: Are you in the reserves too, monsieur? I didn't know…

DUCAMOLE: Not me, mademoiselle… My friend de Croquette… My dear friend de Croquette…

COLETTE: But… (*Pointing to his uniform.*) But all that, monsieur… You…

DUCAMOLE: Shhh! It's a surprise, I tell you! (*Struggling with the pack, under his breath.*) Damnation!

COLETTE, *overhearing, shocked*: Oh, monsieur!

DUCAMOLE: Sorry!… It's this pack… This bloody—

COLETTE: Monsieur!

DUCAMOLE: Sorry… I… I mean… When he comes to the regiment, I'll be there, standing guard in his place! And I'll hold out my hand, and I'll say: "There you are, old man! Surprise, surprise!…" And he'll shake my hand… He'll have to, don't you think? He'll have to shake it!

COLETTE: I suppose…

DUCAMOLE: A good, firm grip… (*Illustrating, taking her hand.*) Like this… It's the least anyone can do when someone goes to the trouble of… I mean, he'll have to shake my hand, mademoiselle. And I'll be saved!

COLETTE: Saved, monsieur? From what?

DUCAMOLE: From… (*Reflecting.*) That's true… How would you know?… Nothing… Nothing at all, mademoiselle! I just like to play soldier.

COLETTE: Oh?

DUCAMOLE: Some people… (*Pretending a command.*) 'Ten-shun!

He springs to attention and gives several salutes while struggling with the pack.

COLETTE, *laughing*: Oh, monsieur! You look so funny!

DUCAMOLE, *looking around, cautiously*: Shhh!… Where is he?

COLETTE: Monsieur de Croquette? (*Pointing up right.*) He's in there with papá. But you mustn't go in! He's having a very important conversation!

DUCAMOLE: Of course not! I told you… I want to surprise him. If he sees me… Pffft!… Now, do me a favor, will you?

He pulls a batch of papers out of his pocket.

COLETTE: If I can, monsieur.

DUCAMOLE: He asked me to cash these, but he forgot to sign them.

COLETTE, *demurely*: He must have something else on his mind, monsieur!

DUCAMOLE: Yes… (*Aside.*) Something named Eugénie, I daresay! (*Aloud.*) So, the minute he comes out, be a dear and ask him to sign them. If not…

COLETTE; Yes, monsieur.

She takes them and lays them down on the console table, up right.

DUCAMOLE, *still struggling with the pack, to himself, repeating his idée fixe*: He'll have to shake my hand! He won't have any choice! (*Aloud, coming downstage.*) I say, you wouldn't happen to know if they carry a forty or a fifty-pound pack, would you?

COLETTE: Monsieur?

DUCAMOLE: In his regiment… Their pack… You wouldn't happen to know?

COLETTE, *shaking her head*: No, monsieur. We've never talked about it.

DUCAMOLE: Oh? (*To himself.*) It seems a perfectly reasonable thing to discuss… (*Aloud.*) Because, if it's neither… There's no need… (*Struggling, under his breath.*) Damnation!… (*Shrugging.*) Oh well… Better be safe than sorry… (*To a confused* COLETTE.) He'll have to shake it, mademoiselle! He'll have to!

He exits, cautiously, on tiptoe, up center.

COLETTE, *watching him leave, bemused*: Poor Monsieur Ducamole!… I must say, he's certainly fond of Monsieur Croquette… *De*, that is… (*Reflecting.*) It really is *de* Croquette, isn't it? That's what papá said, and he would know!… Not that I care, but it would be nice… (*Looking up right, toward the console table.*) Maybe those papers… They must have his name somewhere. (*She goes up and begins scanning one of the documents.*) "Herewith… This day… Whereas… Will pay the bearer… Whereas…" (*She stops.*) Hmm! No name at all… (*She takes another one.*) Maybe this one… (*Moving down center as she reads, stopping suddenly.*) What?… (*Reading.*) "Jacques precious…" (*Speaking.*) Oh!… (*Reading.*) "I haven't laid eyes on you since you went out to buy a loaf of bread. It's been one whole week, and the bakery is just around the corner. I'm beginning to think you aren't coming back…" (*Speaking.*) Oh my! (*Reading.*) "And after all your pretty speeches! It's not very nice, you know. If we're *threw* forever…" (*Speaking.*) T-H-R-E-W?... (*Reading.*) "…please send someone to fetch your beige overcoat. It's still sitting where you left it, in the sitting room, and people are beginning to talk…" (*Speaking.*) That… That… Oh!… (*Reading.*) "But if you still want me, I'd like to spend the rest of my life with you. Just the two of us. You and me, in the *dessert.*" (*Speaking.*) Oh! Did you ever… That… (*Reading.*) "PS. If you do come back, you can throw away the bread, but please bring me a chocolate *moose*…" (*Speaking.*) Dessert indeed!… Of course! (*Reading.*) "M-O-O…" (*Speaking.*) Oh! That… That cad!… (*Reading.*) "Desperately yours, Nini Caboche…" (*Speaking.*) And after swearing just now that he loved me… That I was the only one… Well, he can go spend his life with his… his… (*Brandishing the letter.*) his Mademoiselle Caboche! Just the two of them. In the *dessert!* (*Apostrophizing.*)

We're finished, monsieur! Through!… T-H-R-U-E!... (*She throws the letter down on the floor.*) Understand? And I don't care how beautifully you waltz! I don't care!

The door, up right, opens and LEFEVRE *and* DE CROQUETTE *appear.*

LEFEVRE: So, monsieur, it's all agreed. Just a few little details…

DE CROQUETTE: Please! Call me Jacques… Father!

LEFEVRE, *taking his hand*: Welcome to the family… Son!

They stop by the table, right, vigorously shaking hands.

DE CROQUETTE, *joining* COLETTE, *down center*: Ah, mademoiselle!

COLETTE, *coldly*: Monsieur!

She turns aside, nose in the air.

DE CROQUETTE: Is… Is something wrong? You seem… I must say…

COLETTE: Say what you like!

LEFEVRE, *to* COLETTE: What is it, child?

COLETTE: What is it? I'll tell you what it is, papá! (*Sarcastically.*) I'm terribly honored by monsieur's proposal. But I'm no longer interested!

LEFEVRE: What?

DE CROQUETTE: But mademoiselle…

LEFEVRE: You can't be serious…

COLETTE: Oh, can't I?

DE CROQUETTE, *to* COLETTE: I waltz… (*To* LEFEVRE.) I passed the test!

COLETTE: Yes! But that was before this!

She picks up the letter and waves it in his face.

LEFEVRE, *to* COLETTE: Tell me…

COLETTE: Tell you?… I'll show you! Read this, papá!

She hands it to him.

DE CROQUETTE, *aside*: What in blazes…

LEFEVRE, *reading*: "Jacques precious…" (*Aside.*) Oh?

DE CROQUETTE, *aside*: Damn!… One of Caboche's letters! (*As* LEFEVRE *scans the letter quickly.*) I thought I burned them all!

LEFEVRE, *reading*: "PS. Please bring me a chocolate *moose…*"

COLETTE, *sarcastically*: Yes! M-O-O-S-E, papá!

LEFEVRE: So? (*With a shrug, continuing*). "Desperately yours, Nini Caboche."

DE CROQUETTE, *as calmly and categorically as possible*: Who?… Never heard of her!… It's not mine… (*To* COLETTE.) I assure you! It's not—

COLETTE, *interrupting, sarcastically*: Of course not, monsieur! Please—

DE CROQUETTE: Excuse me, mademoiselle, but… I assure you… I never—

COLETTE: Oh?

DE CROQUETTE: I'm sure I can explain—

COLETTE, *taking the letter back*: Don't bother! You needn't trouble yourself!

DE CROQUETTE: But… But… (*Pointing.*) That letter… Where did you get it? Who gave it to you?

COLETTE: Your friend, Monsieur Ducamole!

DE CROQUETTE, *under his breath*: The wretch! He'll pay… (*Aloud, to* COLETTE.) My friend? But I hardly—

COLETTE, *insisting, pointing to the papers on the console table, up right*: He found it in all those!… Those letters of credit… Or whatever they are…

DE CROQUETTE: Oh…

COLETTE: And that you forgot to sign, so he had to bring them back…

DE CROQUETTE, *taking the papers*: Aha! Well… That explains it, mademoiselle. Of course… (*To* LEFEVRE.) Monsieur… (*To* COLETTE.) It's all perfectly clear… Those letters of credit… (*To* LEFEVRE.) One of your clerks drew them up, monsieur. (*To* COLETTE.) Who knows how many hands they've been through? (*To* LEFEVRE.) You see? One of them must have accidentally dropped it… Of course!

LEFEVRE, *to* DE CROQUETTE, *with a broad wink*: Of course…

DE CROQUETTE, *to* COLETTE: See? It's perfectly clear!

COLETTE: Unfortunately, monsieur, it was written to you!… "Jacques precious…"

LEFEVRE, *nodding*: "Jacques"…

DE CROQUETTE: But what does that prove? There are tens of thousands of "Jacques" in Paris! "Jacques" of all ages, all professions…

LEFEVRE: "Jacques" of all trades…

COLETTE, *to* DE CROQUETTE: And your beige overcoat, monsieur?

DE CROQUETTE: So? Anyone can wear one! You see them all over. Even in the provinces…

LEFEVRE: They're terribly stylish… Very *chick*, as they say…

He moves upstage, from where he watches the following exchanges.

DE CROQUETTE, *to* COLETTE: You see?

He tries to snatch the letter from her grasp.

COLETTE, *holding tight*: Oh no! Oh no, monsieur! (*She stuffs it down her bosom.*) I'll keep it, thank you! (*Sarcastically.*) And I'll only give it up to its rightful owner!

DE CROQUETTE: But—

COLETTE: If I have the pleasure of meeting him, that is!

DE CROQUETTE: But—

COLETTE: I'm sure you can find him and bring him to me, monsieur! For someone so clever, that should be child's play! I'd give anything to see him!

DE CROQUETTE: But… But…

COLETTE: In the meantime, I have no desire to compete with your Mademoiselle… Cacoche!

LEFEVRE, *correcting*: Caboche, angel…

COLETTE turns on her heel and strides toward the door, up left.

DE CROQUETTE, *following her*: My… She's not my—

COLETTE: So there!

She exits in a huff, slamming the door.

DE CROQUETTE, *aside*: Damn! Now what… (*Aloud, to* LEFEVRE.) But you, monsieur… You believe me, don't you?

LEFEVRE: What can I say, young man? You can't blame her, you know. You should know better than to leave such things lying around.

He moves up left, toward the door.

DE CROQUETTE: But monsieur... *(Wheedling.)* Father!... I assure you...

LEFEVRE, *echoing*: "So there!" monsieur ... *(With a shrug.)* So there...

He exits, up left.

DE CROQUETTE, *alone, down center*: There?... Where? That's the question!... Where to find a Jacques with an overcoat just like mine, and broad enough shoulders to take on La Caboche to boot!... *(Furiously.)* And all because of that idiot Ducamole! *(Pacing back and forth.)* I was right! That's one consolation! I could tell the man was an idiot the minute I laid eyes on him! Oh! That wretch!... That... That...

DUCAMOLE enters, up center, huffing and puffing, still in uniform, with the pack on his back, and still carrying the rifle.

DUCAMOLE, *stumbling in, without noticing DE CROQUETTE*: Ouf!

DE CROQUETTE, *down right, surprised*: What?

DUCAMOLE, *wiping the sweat from his brow*: Damnable pack!

He goes over to the fireplace and places his rifle against the wall beside it.

DE CROQUETTE: Oh!

DUCAMOLE, *turning toward him*: Oh...

DE CROQUETTE: You!

DUCAMOLE: Monsieur de Croquette!

DE CROQUETTE: I'm so delighted to see you!

DUCAMOLE, *missing his intent*: Thank you. So am I... *(As an afterthought.)* To see *you*, I mean... *You...*

DE CROQUETTE, *seething*: You...

DUCAMOLE: You...

DE CROQUETTE, *about to explode*: You... You... Oh, you have no idea, you—

DUCAMOLE, *mildly reproachful*: Very funny, monsieur!... Ha ha ha!... See? I'm laughing...

DE CROQUETTE: I beg your pardon? What—

DUCAMOLE, *repeating*: Very funny!

DE CROQUETTE: You said that! What's funny? What? What?

DUCAMOLE: I've just been to your regiment.

DE CROQUETTE: So?

DUCAMOLE: When I got to the gate, the corporal burst out laughing and asked me if I was going to a masquerade or something... "Better put down the rifle," he tells me. "Before somebody gets hurt!" "But I need it," I tell him. "To do guard duty..." "You?..." "For my friend, de Croquette..."

DE CROQUETTE: What? What guard duty?

DUCAMOLE: Yours!

DE CROQUETTE: For—

DUCAMOLE: You told me... "I can't join you for dinner because I have guard duty tonight..."

DE CROQUETTE: But—

DUCAMOLE: And I was going to surprise you... So you wouldn't have to do it...

DE CROQUETTE: But—

DUCAMOLE: You told me so yourself!

DE CROQUETTE: But... I... (*Brutally frank.*) I told you... I told you to get you out of my hair, monsieur!

DUCAMOLE: Out of your... Oh! Really, my friend... If that's your idea of a joke, I must say... (*Torn between his feelings of pique and his sycophantism.*) I find it... I find it...

DE CROQUETTE, *approaching him*: Yes?

DUCAMOLE, *changing his tone, suddenly very cordial*: Utterly charming, monsieur! (*Forcing a little laugh.*) Ha ha ha!... The joke's on me, right? (*Holding out his hand, shaking it up and down.*) Dear, dear de Croquette!

DE CROQUETTE, *ignoring the hand, aside*: It must be a tic!

DUCAMOLE, *aside*: Damnation! What do I have to do... (*Aloud.*) Now then, since you're free... No guard duty, I mean... You'll join us for dinner, madame and me...

DE CROQUETTE: I beg your pardon...

DUCAMOLE: In our happy little home... Nothing fancy...

DE CROQUETTE, *objecting*: Monsieur...

DUCAMOLE: We'll have a delicious roast venison.

DE CROQUETTE: I can't eat venison! It gives me a rash!

DUCAMOLE: Oh dear!... (*After a moment he begins giggling.*) Oh dear!...

DE CROQUETTE: You find a rash amusing, do you?

DUCAMOLE: No, no... It's what I said... "Venison," monsieur... And then "Oh dear..." (*Still giggling.*) "Deer," monsieur... Venison... (*As* DE CROQUETTE *fails to join in his laughter.*) Well then, what do you like? Perhaps a nice ham?

DE CROQUETTE: What I like? (*Categorically.*) I like, monsieur, to dine by myself! And not to be badgered, if you don't mind my saying... That's what I like!

He sits on the loveseat, leaving DUCAMOLE *center.*

DUCAMOLE: Badgered?... No, of course not... I don't blame you for a minute, my friend... You're absolutely right...

DE CROQUETTE: Thank you!

DUCAMOLE, *after a brief pause*: So... What time shall we leave?

DE CROQUETTE: Leave? What in blazes for?

DUCAMOLE: Why, to go to the theater... They're doing *Hamlet*... With puppets...

DE CROQUETTE, *losing patience*: They're doing—

DUCAMOLE: So... What time?

DE CROQUETTE, *sharply*: No time, monsieur! No time at all!

DUCAMOLE: But... *Hamlet*... With puppets...

DE CROQUETTE: Hamlet be damned, and the puppets along with him!

DUCAMOLE: But—

DE CROQUETTE: Is that clear? No venison, no ham!... And no Hamlet!... I'm not eating with you...

DUCAMOLE, *squeezing in a few words*: And madame... Madame...

DE CROQUETTE, *continuing*: ...and I'm not going to the theater! (*Aside.*) Especially with that idiot! If not for him... (*Aloud, to* DUCAMOLE.) If not for you, monsieur... You... You...

DUCAMOLE: Me?

DE CROQUETTE, *approaching him, center, exploding*: Yes, you!... After what you've done to me, damn it!

DUCAMOLE: Done, my friend?

DE CROQUETTE: Sticking your nose in my business... Turning my life inside out...

DUCAMOLE, *to himself*: Did I do that?

DE CROQUETTE: And now I've got to find myself some good-natured dolt... Some ass... Some simpleton named Jacques!... And instead of helping me... Instead of undoing your handiwork, you stand there jabbering about venison, and ham, and... and...

DUCAMOLE: *Hamlet*, my friend... With puppets...

DE CROQUETTE: I don't suppose you have one... Maybe someone in the bank?

DUCAMOLE: A simpleton named Jacques?

DE CROQUETTE: Yes!

DUCAMOLE, *misunderstanding*: In this bank, my friend?

DE CROQUETTE: I'll pay him whatever he asks!

DUCAMOLE: But... I'm the only Jacques in Ducamole and Lefèvre, Limited....

DE CROQUETTE, *with a start*: What?... You?... Your name is Jacques?

DUCAMOLE: Of course!... Since I can remember!... The same as yours, my friend... One Jacques to another!

He holds out his hand expectantly, which DE CROQUETTE *ignores.*

DE CROQUETTE, *to himself*: Hmm! A little long in the tooth for La Caboche...

DUCAMOLE, *vainly shaking his hand up and down*: Monsieur?

DE CROQUETTE, *continuing*: But beggars can't be choosers... Can I!

DUCAMOLE, *still trying, more insistently*: Monsieur?

DE CROQUETTE, *continuing, aside*: Besides, he has a beige overcoat, as I recall. (*As* DUCAMOLE *begins moving right, dejectedly.*) Yes! We're in luck!

DUCAMOLE, *overhearing, stops in his tracks.*

DUCAMOLE: We are?

DE CROQUETTE, *aloud*: Where is your overcoat, monsieur?

DUCAMOLE, *quizzically*: My what?

DE CROQUETTE: Your overcoat!

DUCAMOLE, *aside*: Odd question!

DE CROQUETTE: You had one before. Where is it?

DUCAMOLE: Why, in my apartment... Upstairs... Where I left it... (*Pointing.*) Three-B... But...

DE CROQUETTE, *aside*: If only she's willing...

DUCAMOLE, *coming center*: Is there some reason...

DE CROQUETTE, *aside*: I'll write her a note... She'll go along with it, I'm sure...

DUCAMOLE, *as congenially as possible*: Would you like it? You're welcome to it, my friend!

DE CROQUETTE, *approaching him, laughing*: Yes! That's it!... Ha ha ha!

DUCAMOLE, *laughing too, obligingly*: It is?... Ha ha ha!

DE CROQUETTE, *aside*: A stroke of genius, I must say!... Ha ha ha!

DUCAMOLE, *nodding approval without any idea why*: Ha ha ha! Ha ha ha!

DE CROQUETTE: Ah, my dear Ducamole! Do you know what you've just done for me?

DUCAMOLE: Well… Not quite, but—

DE CROQUETTE: That overcoat of yours… It's going to save my life!

DUCAMOLE, *with a shrug, aside*: If he says so… Maybe now… (*Holding out his hand, aloud.*) Dear, dear Croquette…

DE CROQUETTE, *correcting*: De… De…

DUCAMOLE: Of course! (*Waiting in vain for him to grasp his hand.*) Dear, dear de Croquette!… Ha ha ha!… Ha ha… (*Growing discouraged..*) Dear, dear… (*Giving a final, desperate little laugh.*) Ha ha ha…

DE CROQUETTE: Now where do you suppose—

DUCAMOLE, *seizing the opportunity*: What? Are you looking for something? (*Eagerly.*) What is it? Let me help you…

DE CROQUETTE: Just something to write with… (*Rummaging about the table, right.*) Paper… A pen…

DUCAMOLE: Not there!… Let me!… (*He dashes up right, to the door.*) Don't move!… Let me… I'll be right back!

He exits.

DE CROQUETTE, *alone, to himself*: Or should I ?… Maybe not… It will take too long. And letters can be dangerous!… Ha! Don't I know!… Besides, she lives just around the corner. I'll go there myself and be back in no time. (*As he moves toward the door, up center, stopping.*) But first, the little matter of his overcoat… (*He reaches into his pocket and takes out some coins.*) Ah! It's nothing a handful of francs won't take care of…

He exits, up center, just as DUCAMOLE *returns, up right, with paper, pen, and ink.*

DUCAMOLE: There! Everything you need… And the best paper, too! (*He puts the articles down on the table and positions the armchair.*) Nothing is too good for my dear, dear… (*Suddenly realizing that he is alone.*) What?… Where the devil… Here one minute and gone the next! Just like that!… I must say… (*Tapping his temple.*) I'm beginning to wonder… He's unbalanced, that's what he is! He has guard duty, he doesn't have guard duty! He wants a pen and paper, he doesn't want a pen and paper! He has me running around all morning… And with a blasted pack on my back, no less!… Well, enough of that! Off it comes! (*He takes off the pack and lays it on the console table, up left.*) No consideration, that's his problem… No manners!… And no taste!… Those ugly flowers!… Did you ever…? (*Shaking his head.*) No taste… No taste… (*Having a second thought.*) Except in women, the young lecher!… So, where is he?… (*Gazing up at the ceiling.*) Oh! Do you suppose… (*At that moment there are several loud thumps.*) Come in! Come in!… Now who… (*There are several more thumps, even louder.*) Oh!… Upstairs… It's Antoine… He's signaling me! (*Running to the door, up center.*) Well, we'll just see… (*Stopping and coming back, down left, taking the rifle.*) I'd better take this… It's not loaded, but still…

As he is about to exit, up center, ANTOINE *enters, almost knocking him down.*

ANTOINE: I…

DUCAMOLE: Ant—

ANTOINE: Damn!

DUCAMOLE: Antoine! For goodness' sake!

ANTOINE, *regaining his aplomb*: Excuse me, but… Where is monsieur going?

DUCAMOLE, *brandishing the rifle*: Can't you see? Your signal, Antoine… A young man… Just as I said…

ANTOINE: Yes, monsieur… But he didn't have a bouquet… And he didn't ask for monsieur.

DUCAMOLE: Oh?

ANTOINE: Or madame either… And I didn't see any cockroaches.

DUCAMOLE: Bah! (*Pushing him aside.*) Out of my way!

ANTOINE: Besides, he's not up there anymore. He said something to the housekeeper, monsieur, and he gave her a handful of coins.

DUCAMOLE: He didn't!

ANTOINE: And she gave him—

DUCAMOLE: A letter?

ANTOINE: No. A bundle… A big one… All wrapped up…

DUCAMOLE, *aside, moving right*: Her picture?… Has it come to that?… Oh, God help us! Eugénie!… (*Apostrophizing.*) You… You faithless tart! (*Aloud, to* ANTOINE, *shouting.*) Out of my way!

ANTOINE, *stopping him*: Where is monsieur going?

DUCAMOLE: Upstairs… To kill my wife!

ANTOINE, *frightened*: Oh!

DUCAMOLE: On second thought, that could be fatal.

ANTOINE: Yes, monsieur…

DUCAMOLE: Besides, the law says we have to catch them in the act.

ANTOINE: That's right, monsieur…

DUCAMOLE: So I will! I'll catch them! (*Pacing back and forth, with the rifle on his shoulder.*) Oh yes! I'll catch them…

ANTOINE: If monsieur says so…

DUCAMOLE: I can wait!

ANTOINE: Does monsieur mind if I go do an errand while he's waiting?

DUCAMOLE: Don't you dare! Go upstairs and keep watching, you imbecile!

ANTOINE: Then monsieur can do it for me, like he said he would… (*Handing him some coins.*) Here… (DUCAMOLE, *absentmindedly, puts them in his pocket.*) Please take my black boots to the cobbler and tell him they've sprung a leak.

DUCAMOLE, *not listening*: Yes…

ANTOINE: And the tongues are falling out.

DUCAMOLE: Yes… Yes…

ANTOINE: And—

DUCAMOLE, *finally realizing that* ANTOINE *is talking*: Will you please stop your jabbering! That's enough!… Out! You hear?

ANTOINE: Yes, monsieur… (*He turns to leave, up center, then stops.*) And thank you, monsieur!

DUCAMOLE, *pointing to the door*: Yes, yes, yes! (*Under his breath.*) Imbecile!

ANTOINE, *at the door*: It's very good of monsieur! (*He exits, then, popping his head in, a moment later.*) It really is!

He exits.

DUCAMOLE, *impatiently*: Oh!… (*Alone, pacing.*) Now I understand why he won't shake my hand!… "A handshake is sacred!" He said so himself… Well, I'll get my revenge! I'll show him what I'm made of! (*He mimes bayoneting someone, grunting appropriately.*) There!… (*Stopping, reflecting.*) No… Too much blood… (*He grimaces in disgust.*) Yechhh!… A bullet would be cleaner… (*He takes aim at an imaginary target.*) Bang!… (*Examining the imaginary result.*) Hmm! That's still not very tidy… On second thought, maybe I'll just drag him through the courts!

He shoulders the rifle and begins pacing again, careful to avoid stepping on the imaginary corpse in front of the fireplace. A moment later, LEFEVRE *enters, up left.*

LEFEVRE, *grumbling to himself*: Impossible to make her listen to reason! They're all the same… (*Coming down, noticing* DUCAMOLE.) What the… What is he… (*Aloud.*) Ducamole!

DUCAMOLE: Ah! Lefèvre…

LEFEVRE, *wryly*: Are we expecting robbers?

DUCAMOLE: Don't mind me…

LEFEVRE, *continuing*: But… (*Indicating his uniform and rifle.*) Why all this?

DUCAMOLE: Please! I have my reasons.

LEFEVRE: I thought you were going to the exchange to see how Costa Rican coffee beans are doing.

DUCAMOLE, *stopping, sarcastically*: Don't worry, Lefèvre. They're growing, I'm sure! (*Aside.*) As if that's all I have to do!

LEFEVRE: Is something wrong, Ducamole? Is something bothering you?

DUCAMOLE: Bothering me? (*Placing the rifle against the fireplace.*) I'll tell you what's bothering me, my friend! (*Joining him, down center, taking his arm.*) What's bothering me is that Croquette of yours!

LEFEVRE, *correcting*: De… De…

DUCAMOLE, *impatiently*: Yes, yes! I know!… The man is a wretch! A scoundrel!… A… A lecher!

LEFEVRE: Oh? You mean, you've found out—

DUCAMOLE, *quickly*: Found out what?… You do know something, don't you? Tell me… You promised…

LEFEVRE: I did?… But not about—

DUCAMOLE: You did! You did!

LEFEVRE: Besides, it's just a *useful* indiscretion…

DUCAMOLE: Oh?

LEFEVRE: One of those things every young man receives… And that every young lady writes…

DUCAMOLE: Writes?

LEFEVRE: Just a silly letter…

DUCAMOLE, *aside, furiously*: They write to each other?

LEFEVRE, *continuing*: …from someone named Nini…

DUCAMOLE: What?

LEFEVRE: A tart… A *scallop*… So you see—

DUCAMOLE, *aside*: Ah! That proves it!… Eugénie!… Nini… Nini… (*Apostrophizing.*) Oh! Eugénie! Eugénie!

As he collapses onto the loveseat, distraught, DE CROQUETTE *enters, up center.*

DE CROQUETTE, *with a little bow*: Messieurs, I have the honor—

DUCAMOLE, *jumping up, approaching him*: Don't talk to me about honor, monsieur! That letter! I want it!

DE CROQUETTE: Letter?

DUCAMOLE: Immediately, you hear?

DE CROQUETTE: What letter?

LEFEVRE, *to* DUCAMOLE: But he doesn't have it!

DUCAMOLE: Then who does?

LEFEVRE: My daughter… She refuses to give it up!

DUCAMOLE: Colette?… We'll see about that! She'll give it to me! You just have to be subtle…

LEFEVRE: I've tried everything…

He moves down right as COLETTE *enters, up left.*

DUCAMOLE: Ah! (*Approaching her.*) There you are, dear child!

COLETTE: Monsieur…

DUCAMOLE: Now then, if you don't mind, I'd like that letter… (*Holding out his hand.*) From Nini… You know… Nini…

COLETTE: Impossible, monsieur! I swore not to give it to anyone except its rightful owner.

DUCAMOLE: Who is…?

COLETTE: A certain someone named Jacques! If only I could find him! (*Looking daggers at* DE CROQUETTE, *sarcastically.*) But I just can't imagine what Jacques it could be!

DUCAMOLE: Aha!… (*Getting an idea, to himself.*) Well, why not? (*Whispering to* DE CROQUETTE, *beside him, who is about to object.*) Not a word, you, or I'll drag you through every court!

DE CROQUETTE: But…

DUCAMOLE, *to* COLETTE, *who is standing by the loveseat*: Well, my child… Since I have no choice… I may as well admit it. I'm the Jacques she was writing to! The letter was meant for me!

COLETTE, } *together*: { You?
LEFEVRE, } { What?

DUCAMOLE: Now, let me have it.

DE CROQUETTE, *aside*: Bless you!

LEFEVRE, *aside*: That's the most disgusting…

DUCAMOLE, *to* DE CROQUETTE, *whispering*: Not a word, you hear?

COLETTE, *to* DUCAMOLE: But… You're married!

DUCAMOLE, *aside, ruefully*: So is she!

LEFEVRE, *to* DUCAMOLE: You're a banker, my friend!

DUCAMOLE: So?

LEFEVRE: A banker has principles! He has other interests…

DE CROQUETTE, *to* COLETTE: Well, as long as monsieur is the rightful owner…

DUCAMOLE, *naively*: I am! I am!

LEFEVRE, *continuing his diatribe*: He doesn't go cheating on his wife with other women!…

COLETTE, *to* DUCAMOLE: Then here's the letter, monsieur! (*Retrieving it from her bosom, shaking her head, aside.*) Tsk tsk tsk!… For shame!

She hands it to him.

LEFEVRE, *still continuing*: Like a common filan… filan… *philanthropist*! Every day a new one…

DUCAMOLE, *aside*: At last!

LEFEVRE: Or every night!

DUCAMOLE, *to himself*: Now let's see how far they've gone, those two!

LEFEVRE, *summing up, to* DUCAMOLE: Not a banker, my friend!

DUCAMOLE, *ignoring him, continuing, aside, as the others stand shaking their heads*: Let's see what the faithless spouse has to tell our young Romeo! (*He stands reading in silence. As he arrives at the signature, his jaw drops and he shouts out, appalled.*) Who…? Nini Caboche…? Who in the name… I don't know any Nini Caboche!… I… I thought… (*Stammering.*) She… I thought… I…

DE CROQUETTE, *aside*: Ay ay ay!

DUCAMOLE: My…

LEFEVRE, *still down right*: Then who—

DUCAMOLE, *pointing* to DE CROQUETTE: Him! It's for him!

He tries to give the letter to him.

DE CROQUETTE, *moving right, avoiding him*: Oh no! Thank you just the same! It's yours! You admitted—

DUCAMOLE: Nonsense! I'm a banker!

COLETTE: And a married man, monsieur!

DUCAMOLE, *to* DE CROQUETTE: Keep your Caboche to yourself! I don't need her!

As he throws the letter down on the floor between himself and DE CROQUETTE, ANTOINE *enters, up center, with an overcoat, all folded up, in one hand and a letter in the other.*

ANTOINE, *to* DUCAMOLE: Monsieur!

DUCAMOLE: What? What is it?

ANTOINE: A messenger just brought these for monsieur.

He lays the coat on the loveseat.

DE CROQUETTE, *aside*: Ah! Nini…

ANTOINE, *moving right, to* DUCAMOLE, *handing him the letter*: What did he say, monsieur?

DUCAMOLE: Say?… Who? What did who say?

ANTOINE: The cobbler, monsieur…

DUCAMOLE, *out of patience, at the top of his lungs*: What?

ANTOINE: About my boots… The ones that leak…

DUCAMOLE, *even louder*: About your—

ANTOINE: And that need new tongues…

DUCAMOLE: Get out of here, you imbecile! (*To himself.*) Of all the… (*To* ANTOINE, *pointing up center.*) Out, you hear? Out!

ANTOINE, *holding out his hand*: Then my twenty sous, monsieur…

DUCAMOLE: Your… (*Louder still.*) Get out of my sight!

ANTOINE, *under his breath*: Bah! Some people…

He exits, up center, grumbling.

DUCAMOLE: Did you ever… (*Opening the letter, reading.*) "You silly goose…"

DE CROQUETTE,	*together:*	Ha!
COLETTE,		Oh my!
LEFEVRE,		What?

DUCAMOLE: Really!… I'll "goose" her, the tart! (*Reading, as the others mutter their reactions.*) "You're not pretty enough for me to care if you drop me like a hot potato or not. So you've seen the last of me. I'm sending you back your overcoat. The ugly beige one. Desperately yours, Nini Caboche."

LEFEVRE,	*together:*	Indeed!
COLETTE,		Tsk tsk tsk!

DE CROQUETTE, *aside, with a sigh of relief*: Dear child!

LEFEVRE, *to* DUCAMOLE: Well, my friend… What do you say now?

DE CROQUETTE, *aside, continuing*: Just the way I dictated it!…

LEFEVRE,	*together:*	Really!
COLETTE,		For shame…

DE CROQUETTE, *aside, continuing*: And not even any spelling mistakes!

DUCAMOLE: Wait a minute! Not so fast!… "You silly goose"… (*Holding out the letter to* DE CROQUETTE.) It's for you, monsieur!… It's perfectly obvious. Who would ever dare call me—

DE CROQUETTE, *avoiding him*: Oh no! No, no, no!… For you… It's for you…

LEFEVRE, *joining* DUCAMOLE, *center*: What's the address?

DUCAMOLE: That's right… That should prove it! (*Reading.*) "For Monsieur Jacques…"

DE CROQUETTE, *reading over his shoulder*: "Ducamole"… (*Victorious.*) There! Plain as day!

COLETTE, *to* DUCAMOLE: Oh, monsieur!

LEFEVRE: I say… Not much doubt…

DUCAMOLE, *gaping in disbelief at the letter*: But… But…

COLETTE: Tsk tsk tsk! None at all!

DUCAMOLE: But…

COLETTE: How could you, monsieur?

DUCAMOLE: But…

COLETTE: For shame!

DE CROQUETTE *and* **COLETTE**, *together*: For shame!

LEFEVRE *and* **DE CROQUETTE**, *together*: For shame!

LEFEVRE, *by himself*: For shame!

He moves upstage.

DUCAMOLE: But…

COLETTE, *pointing to the other letter, still on the floor*: And that one?… She probably knows every Jacques in Paris, the… the…

DE CROQUETTE, *supplying the word that she is too timid to pronounce*: Slut, mademoiselle!

COLETTE, *covering her mouth*: Oh!

DUCAMOLE: Besides, I don't know any dancing-girls! I never—

DE CROQUETTE: Aha! You hear? He knows that she's a dancing-girl! (*To the others.*) See? That proves it!

DUCAMOLE: No, no! They're all dancing-girls!

LEFEVRE, *pointing left*: And your overcoat, my friend?

He takes it and hands it to him.

DUCAMOLE: But… It… It can't be mine! Mine is upstairs!

DE CROQUETTE, *aside*: It *was*, you mean!

DUCAMOLE: You'll see… (*Unfolding the coat, aside.*) Damnation! It does look like mine…

LEFEVRE: It's beige!

COLETTE: Very beige!

LEFEVRE: And ugly!

DUCAMOLE: Oh? I don't… I… Really…

DE CROQUETTE: As beige as can be, I'd say…

LEFEVRE, *to DUCAMOLE*: Well?

DUCAMOLE: But… It won't fit me. It's too big… Look! I'll prove it… (*He takes off the uniform jacket, throws it on the armchair, right, and puts on the coat.*) Good God! It… It fits…

LEFEVRE; And the ink stain you had on the elbow, my friend? (*Pointing.*) That one!

DUCAMOLE: But…

COLETTE: Tsk tsk tsk! A married man!

DE CROQUETTE: A banker, monsieur!… I'm shocked!

DUCAMOLE, *agape*: But… I don't understand…

He reaches into a pocket and pulls out a tasseled nightcap.

DE CROQUETTE, *to the others*: His nightcap!

COLETTE, *properly embarrassed*: Oh! Monsieur…

LEFEVRE, *to DUCAMOLE*: Please, Ducamole! (*Pointing to COLETTE.*) Show a little respect…

DUCAMOLE: But it's not mine! You'll see! It's too big… (*Confused.*) Too small… Too… (*He puts it on.*) Damnation!… It… It…

DE CROQUETTE: It…

LEFEVRE: It…

COLETTE: It…

DUCAMOLE: It…

DE CROQUETTE, LEFEVRE, *and* **COLETTE**, *together*: …fits!

DUCAMOLE: Well… Not much… Just a little… (*He takes it off and examines it.*) I… I don't understand…

He puts it back in the overcoat pocket.

COLETTE, *moving right, to the table*: If Madame Ducamole ever found out, monsieur…

DE CROQUETTE, *very matter-of-fact*: Oh, she's bound to, mademoiselle…

DUCAMOLE, *terrified*: What?

DE CROQUETTE: You can't keep this sort of thing hidden for long!

DUCAMOLE: No! Please, monsieur! *(Turning to* LEFEVRE.*)* Do something! (*To* DE CROQUETTE.) I'm begging you! (*To* LEFEVRE.) I'm your partner, Lefèvre!… Lefèvre and Ducamole!… Lefèvre and Ducamole!… (*To* DE CROQUETTE.) You can't let this happen!

DE CROQUETTE: Well…

LEFEVRE, *to* DUCAMOLE, *leading him left, with* DE CROQUETTE *on their heels*: Only if you promise us…

DUCAMOLE: Promise? Promise what?

LEFEVRE: To give up this… this vulgar Caboche creature…

DE CROQUETTE, *hypocritically*: Oh, vulgar… vulgar…

DUCAMOLE: But—

LEFEVRE: This *adulterated* harlot!

DUCAMOLE: But I already have! You read her letter!… (*Catching himself.*) What am I saying? I mean… *He* has!… Whoever… Jacques… The person she wrote to…

DE CROQUETTE *sarcastically*: Of course…

LEFEVRE, *just as sarcastically*: Of course…

DE CROQUETTE, *to* LEFEVRE, *with mock resignation*: You see? He won't… It's no use… (*To* DUCAMOLE.) Tsk tsk tsk!

COLETTE, *to* DUCAMOLE: Tsk tsk tsk!… (*To* DE CROQUETTE.) Poor Madame Ducamole!

LEFEVRE: Tsk tsk tsk!

DUCAMOLE, *in desperation*: No, no, no!… Please! I will!… (*Aside.*) Don't ask me how! (*Aloud.*) I'll… I'll scream it from the rooftops!… From here to… to New York!

LEFEVRE: No, no! We can't afford the scandal! Business is bad enough! Just let me handle it! We'll settle with her for a few thousand francs…

DUCAMOLE: Oh?

LEFEVRE: No fuss… Just charged to your account…

DUCAMOLE, *exasperated*: *My* account?

LEFEVRE: And no one will ever know…

DE CROQUETTE, *to* DUCAMOLE: Especially your wife…

DUCAMOLE: But… Isn't that a little expensive? (*Aside.*) Considering…

LEFEVRE: Really, my friend! You can't just trifle with a young lady's *infection* and…

DE CROQUETTE, *completing the thought*: … and not expect to pay the piper!

LEFEVRE, *to* DUCAMOLE: You're not just some *hollow* youth, having his first affair!

COLETTE, *to* DUCAMOLE: Unless you think your wife might have a better idea, monsieur!

DUCAMOLE: No! (*To* LEFEVRE.) Whatever you say… I just don't understand… (*Aside.*) Is it possible? Did I really cheat on her? (*Scratching his head.*) Did I…

At that moment, the piano is heard from upstairs, playing the prize composition, as before. DE CROQUETTE *and* DUCAMOLE *each react to it very differently.*

DE CROQUETTE, *appalled* } *together:* { Oh!
DUCAMOLE, *ecstatic* } { Ah!

DE CROQUETTE: Again?… That blasted piece! (*Covering his ears.*) I'd know it anywhere!

LEFEVRE: What?

DUCAMOLE, *apostrophizing*: Play, my love! Play!

DE CROQUETTE: Day in, day out! Week after week! Month after month!

DUCAMOLE, *to* DE CROQUETTE, *pointing upstairs*: My wife, monsieur… The piece that won her the prize…

LEFEVRE: At the Observatory…

DE CROQUETTE, *surprised*: What? She… The one who's playing that… that…

DUCAMOLE, *proudly*: My wife… My Eugénie…

DE CROQUETTE, *aside*: Heaven help me! It's her! (*To* DUCAMOLE.) You're a very lucky man, monsieur! (*Holding out his hand, which* DUCAMOLE *seizes and shakes vigorously.*) I… I envy you!

DUCAMOLE, *with a sigh*: Ah!… (*Reveling in an endless handshake, which* DE CROQUETTE *keeps trying, unsuccessfully, to break off.*) Thank you, monsieur! (*Aside.*) At last! (*To* DE CROQUETTE.) Now monsieur… About dinner… In my happy little home…

DE CROQUETTE, *finally succeeding*:: Why, monsieur, I'd be delighted… (*With a wink to the audience.*) With madame and you… Any time… Any time at all!

COLETTE, *interrupting, to* LEFEVRE, *pointing to* DE CROQUETTE: But papá… Didn't you and monsieur have some business to attend to?

LEFEVRE: We did, angel… And we do! (*To* DE CROQUETTE.) Come, son… A few final details…

DUCAMOLE, *stopping them*: Wait!… This calls for a celebration! The details can wait… Don't anyone move… I'll be right back…

He hurries out, up center as the others look at one another in consternation.

DE CROQUETTE: Where did he go?

LEFEVRE: What do you suppose…

The piano music stops abruptly.

COLETTE: What now, I wonder…

EUGENIE'S VOICE, *from upstairs*: Jacques, love! Where are you going with that?

The others continue with appropriate exclamations. A moment later, the upstage center door opens and DUCAMOLE *appears with a bagpipe.*

DUCAMOLE, *entering*: Did someone say something about paying the piper?… Well now…

He begins a painful rendition of "The Wedding March," which the others greet with vociferous shouts of "No! Please!," "Stop!," "Spare us!," " Not that!," "Anything but that!," etc., as the curtain falls.

CURTAIN.

Barbara of Seville

(La perle de la Canebière, 1855)

Eugène Labiche & Marc-Michel

Characters

BÉLODOR, a Parisian perfumer, not without a certain affectation of manner and speech

GODEFROY, his young, gawky, and socially inept son

ANTOINE, his brusque domestic

DOÑA BARBARA, a hot-blooded young widow from Seville

NANITA, her maid and faithful companion

MADAME DE SAINTE-POULE, a portly and very proper matron

BLANCHE, Madame de Sainte-Poule's marriageable and rather naïve daughter

A drawing room in Monsieur Bélodor's well-appointed apartment. Upstage center, a door leading outside. Doors in the walls: down right, to Godefroy's room; up right, to Bélodor's; down left, to the guest suite; up left, to the rest of the apartment. Down left, against the wall, a small writing-desk and high-backed chair. Down right, an armchair. Against the rear wall, up right, a buffet. Five other occasional chairs, here and there around the room. Other appropriate furnishings.

At rise, ANTOINE, *feather duster in hand and nose in the air, is trying to repress a sneeze.*

ANTOINE: Ah... Ah... *(Pressing the handle of the duster under his nose.)* Oh! I don't dare!... Monsieur Bélodor always tells me: "No sneezing in the salon, Antoine!"... Ah... Ah... "Sneezes are foul breaches of decorum..." Whatever that means!... That's what he says. "Foul *breeches...*" *(Scratching his head.)* Sneezes?... Breeches?... "Pants" I would understand. *(He gives several exaggerated pants.)* Pants are breeches... But sneezes?... *(Again about to sneeze.)* Ah... Ah... *(Resisting.)* Bah! Who knows what he means? The way he talks... Well, I don't care. I still wouldn't work for anyone else! He smells so pretty! The biggest perfumer in Paris, after all... In all of France... All of Europe, to hear him tell it! *(Spreading his arms out wide.)* Not big, like that... But big... Important... I could just sniff him up and down all day! Like a garden!... *(Sniffing.)* Like a... *(About to sneeze.)* Ah... Ah... *(Finally unable to resist, just as* BELODOR *enters, up right.)* Ah-tchoo!

BELODOR: Antoine!

ANTOINE, *aside*: Damn!

BELODOR: What did I tell you about sneezing in the salon?

ANTOINE: I know, monsieur... About my foul breeches... But—

BELODOR, *not listening, wagging his index finger*: Not permitted, my good man... One would think it was intentional!

ANTOINE: But—

BELODOR: An attempt to try my patience...

ANTOINE: But what could I do? It wanted to come out.

BELODOR: Yes, I'm sure... "It wanted..." *(Aside.)* Delightful personification! *(Aloud.)* And who am I to deny the desires with which Nature endowed it!

ANTOINE, *approaching*: Yes, monsieur.

BELODOR: Far be it from me to heap opprobrium upon our gentle mother! She who, despite her wisdom and tenderness... Her sagacity, Antoine...

ANTOINE: Yes, monsieur.

BELODOR, *continuing*: ...has seen fit to afflict us with the vilest of actions... Calamitous actions that cause decency to wince with chagrin...

ANTOINE: Yes, monsieur. *(Sniffing, aside, admiringly.)* Oh! Lavender, I think...

BELODOR, *continuing to pontificate*: ...but who, in her generosity, permits us to foretell their gestation and forestall their birth!

ANTOINE, *not understanding a word*: Monsieur?

BELODOR: More crassly put, Antoine, one knows when one is about to sneeze, I daresay.

ANTOINE: Yes, monsieur.

BELODOR: When *(Emphasizing.)* "*it* wants to come out," as you would put it!

ANTOINE: But... But then what, monsieur?

BELODOR: Then what?... Then one takes the key to one's bedchamber. One closes oneself inside. One pays Nature her due, as silently and discreetly as possible... After which, one returns to the bosom of polite society, with a gentle smile that betokens the realization that one has respected one's civic obligation!

ANTOINE: Oh...

BELODOR: Does that answer your question, Antoine?

ANTOINE: Yes, monsieur. Next time I'll take my key...

BELODOR: Please see that you do!

ANTOINE is about to leave, up left, but returns, holding out a letter.

ANTOINE: Oh... A letter came for monsieur. I almost forgot...

BELODOR: Yes... You were so busy breaching the rules of decorum!... Give it here!... Who on earth....? *(Opening it, and reading.)* "Moosyair..." *(To himself.)* Illiterate! *(Continuing.)* "I wish order parfoon..." *(To himself.)* How many times have I told my underlings not to encroach upon the sanctity of my home! *(Continuing.)* "Big bottle of best you sell! Most expensive..." *(To himself.)* Aha... Well... *(Continuing.)* "For when I come home, soon..." *(To himself.)* Indeed! *(Continuing.)* "Is for little woman. For wife..." *(Aside.)* How elegant! *(Continuing.)* "And P.S. also... Is for to celebrate..." *(Pocketing the letter.)* Bah! I'm sure it can wait. First things first... *(To ANTOINE.)* Now then, is my son awake?

ANTOINE: Monsieur Godefroy?... I don't know, monsieur. But a few moments ago he was snoring like a cow in heat.

BELODOR, *shocked*: Good heavens! How crude...

ANTOINE: Well... Like a bull, if you'd rather... Only probably not in heat...

BELODOR: Please! One breach of decorum *per diem* is quite sufficient!

ANTOINE, *moving down right*: Do you want me to go see?

BELODOR: Really, Antoine! You'll drive me to distraction! What did I tell you last night? Do you remember?

ANTOINE *coming back down, thinking, innocently*: To go buy the newspaper...

BELODOR: That's not what I mean! I did my utmost, for the tenth time, Antoine, to... to inculcate in you the rudimentary principles of proper service.

ANTOINE: You did?... *(Drawing closer, sniffing, aside.)* Mmm! Delicious!

BELODOR, *backing away*: For one thing, a domestic keeps his distance! He does not breathe down his employer's neck!

ANTOINE: No, no! You're right, monsieur!

BELODOR: And for another, he observes a civil form of address!

ANTOINE: A... A dress, monsieur?... Cook wears a dress, not me... I—

BELODOR: No, no, no!... Address, Antoine!... He does not keep addressing his employer as "you"! "You" this... "You" that...

ANTOINE, *laughing, naively*: You're funny, monsieur!

BELODOR: And you do not say "You're funny!" You say "Monsieur is funny!" The third person! You know what that is?

ANTOINE, *looking around*: I don't see any, monsieur.

BELODOR: Any? Any what?

ANTOINE: Any third person. There's just you and me...

BELODOR: Please! "Just *monsieur* and me..." *(Flustered.)* I mean, "monsieur and I..."

"Monsieur," do you understand? Not "you"... Never "you"... *(Frustrated.)* Good heavens!

ANTOINE: If you insist...

BELODOR, *losing patience*: "If *monsieur* insists! If..." Monsieur! Monsieur! Monsieur!

ANTOINE, *laughing*: Please! You can call me Antoine...

BELODOR: What? What did I just say?... "*Monsieur* can... Monsieur *may* call me Antoine"!

ANTOINE: Ha ha!... You?... But it's not your name!

BELODOR, *throwing up his hands, aside*: Hopeless! Utterly hopeless! *(Aloud.)* "Monsieur," I told you! You always say "monsieur" to your employers! And to all your betters!

ANTOINE, *trying to understand*: Even the ladies, monsieur?

BELODOR: Even the... *(Giving up.)* Oh!...

ANTOINE, *sniffing at a distance*: Mmm!... You smell... *(Correcting himself.)* Monsieur smells good enough to eat, monsieur!

BELODOR, *resigned*: Thank you, I'm sure!

ANTOINE: And now, monsieur... If monsieur wants me to, I'll go see if monsieur's son, Monsieur Godefroy, is awake.

BELODOR, *surprised*: Excellent! You see how easy... *(As ANTOINE is about to leave, down right.)* Wait! I need you to see to something... Two persons of the opposite sex are arriving this morning from Dunkirk, to do me the honor of their company for several days.

ANTOINE: Women, monsieur?

BELODOR: Obviously...

ANTOINE: But where are we going to stick them?

BELODOR: We're going to... *(Emphasizing.)* to *lodge* them, Antoine... *(Pointing down left.)* In the guest room... Where else? The *chambre bleue*... Fortunately, it's not occupied. So you will kindly prepare it, with the greatest solicitude and the utmost dispatch.

ANTOINE: Don't worry, monsieur.

BELODOR: Please... *(Correcting him.)* "Monsieur can rest assured..."

ANTOINE: That too...

BELODOR, *shaking his head, aside*: Hopeless! *(Aloud, to ANTOINE.)* And one other matter... You will kindly remove *Daphnis and Chloë* from the wall.

ANTOINE: I'll do what?

BELODOR: *Daphnis and Chloë*... The picture... You will take it off the wall.

ANTOINE: Oh!... The two naked people...

BELODOR: Well, almost...

ANTOINE: Tsk tsk tsk!

BELODOR: Precisely! You will take it off the wall and place it in my bedroom. It's hardly appropriate for ladies! Is that clear?

ANTOINE: Yes, monsieur.

BELODOR: And you will spray the chamber.

ANTOINE: I will?

BELODOR: Yes… With eau de toilette…

ANTOINE: Oh?

BELODOR, *misunderstanding his exclamation*: De toilette… Toilet water…

ANTOINE, *shocked*: What? Do you think… *(Catching himself.)* Does monsieur think *that's* "appropriate for ladies"?

BELODOR: Do I… Of course, my good man! Fragrance… Perfume…

ANTOINE: Aha…

BELODOR: Half iris, half violet… *(Pointing down left.)* Now go to it!

ANTOINE: Yes, monsieur.

BELODOR: Remember… Half iris, half violet…

ANTOINE, *to himself*: Or vice-versa…

He exits, down left, as GODEFROY *enters, down right.*

GODEFROY, *overhearing* BELODOR*'s last remarks*: Violet?

BELODOR: Ah! *(To himself.)* There he is…

GODEFROY: Violet, papá? *(Aside.)* Someone special…

BELODOR, *ignoring the question, looking at him sternly*: Well, young man?

GODEFROY: Papá?

BELODOR: How does one greet one's progenitor upon arising?

GODEFROY: Oh… *(Mechanically.)* Good morning, father.

BELODOR: Good morning, son.

He gives him a ceremonial kiss on the forehead.

GODEFROY: Are you expecting someone?

BELODOR, *emphasizing*: Someone from Dunkirk, Godefroy…

GODEFROY, *frightened*: Oh my! Mademoiselle Blanche… *(Aside.)* And her monster of a mother!

BELODOR: Indeed! Your intended, Godefroy… And her estimable mother, Madame de Sainte-Poule… They arrive this morning… For the reading of the nuptial contract… The official betrothal…

GODEFROY: But…

BELODOR: Tomorrow, Godefroy…

GODEFROY: But… But… So soon, papá?

BELODOR: The bridal basket has been ordered… The flowers… The notary has been engaged… So… You and I shall betake ourselves to the railway station to welcome these fine ladies. I trust I shall not have to remind you to offer your arm to madame…

GODEFROY, *objecting*: Oh no, papá!

BELODOR, *misunderstanding*: Good!

GODEFROY: No, no… I mean… No! I can't! Don't make me…

BELODOR: What? And why not, may I ask?

GODEFROY: Please… She… She frightens me! She's so big! She's a mammoth!

BELODOR: Come, come, Godefroy! *(Severely.)* A mammoth, indeed! Is that a respectful way—

GODEFROY: But… B-But she is, I tell you…

BELODOR: I'll thank you to admit that it is not that delightful lady's imposing portliness that causes you to stray from civility's path, but only that dastardly timidity of yours!

GODEFROY: Oh!

BELODOR: Admit it, young man! A character flaw…

GODEFROY, *stammering*: B-But papá… It… It's not my fault…

BELODOR, *slapping him on the back*: Come, come, Godefroy! Good grief! A little backbone!… You're not a babe in arms! Why, three months ago, didn't I send you off, all alone, to see the world?… To let some of society's graces rub off on you, as it were?… To give you the spunk that makes a young man a man?… *(As GODEFROY remains silent.)* Well? Didn't I?

GODEFROY, *timidly*: Yes, papá.

BELODOR: And a lot of good it did!

GODEFROY: Oh…

BELODOR: Especially your shameful comportment in Seville, if you recall! With that rich young widow…

GODEFROY: Doña Barbara! *(Shuddering.)* Brrr!

BELODOR: One of my most important clients!… And to do what you did…

GODEFROY: But…

BELODOR: After she extended to you the hospitality of her… her hacienda… Taking you to her bosom… In a manner of speaking…

GODEFROY, *under his breath*: That horrible woman!

BELODOR: And how do you thank her? *(Not giving him time to reply.)* I'll tell you how! You tiptoe out under cover of darkness. You go running off one night, without so much as a "by your leave…" Not even a "much obliged!" Not even a "good-bye!"

GODEFROY: But she frightened me to death, papá!

BELODOR: Bah! A pretty pickle you put me in! She was furious! And who can blame her? Scandalous, Godefroy… That's the only word! Scandalous!… Fortunately, I had the presence of mind to write her an excuse for your lamentable behavior.

GODEFROY: Papá?

BELODOR: I said that you simply had to run off before your blind, lustful passion got the better of you!

GODEFROY, *aghast*: You what?… Me? Lustful… For her?… But papá, that's not true!

BELODOR: I know, I know… I had to embroider it just a little.

GODEFROY: Embroider it? Make it up out of whole cloth, you mean!

BELODOR: Tut tut!… I had no choice. Besides, what's done is done…

GODEFROY: Oh!… When she flung herself at me every time she saw me… And called me "my pet" before we were even introduced!

BELODOR: Your pet?

GODEFROY: *Her* pet!… Hers!… Really, papá… And when she threw her arms around my neck, and slobbered kisses on me whenever I got near her…

BELODOR: I admit that she may have erred a trifle on the side of familiarity, Godefroy. Her Mediterranean blood may have bubbled up a bit.

GODEFROY: Bubbled?...Boiled, papá! Seethed!

BELODOR: And, doubtless, I ought not have invited her to come visit...

GODEFROY, *shocked*: To what?

BELODOR: ...if she ever came to Paris.

GODEFROY, *frightened*: You didn't!... Papá!

BELODOR, *defending himself*: A mere civility, son... The sort of thing our class feels obliged to say... But you need not be concerned. She knows I didn't mean it. And even if I did, there's no likelihood whatever that she will accept!

GODEFROY: Oh? How can you be sure?

BELODOR: Her soap factory... The biggest and most important in all of Spain... It keeps her in Seville, day in day out.

GODEFROY: Thank heaven for that!

BELODOR, *looking at his pocket watch*: Ah!... Madame de Sainte-Poule and her daughter will be arriving shortly. We had best not be late! Punctuality is one of the cardinal virtues.

GODEFROY: Yes, papá...

BELODOR, *inspecting him, with a leer*: What?... A green cravat?... Really, Godefroy... What has got into you? Is that how I brought you up?... A green cravat, indeed!

GODEFROY: But it's my new one, papá!

BELODOR: New? Old?... It is no less green! And that simply will not do! Under the circumstances, a white cravat is de rigueur, young man!

GODEFROY: But—

BELODOR: De rigueur!... Now go change it! And be quick!

He exits, up center.

GODEFROY, *alone, sulking*: A white cravat! Of all things... I wore a white one each time he took me to Dunkirk to visit my intended. For all the good it did!... The first time I didn't open my mouth. The second time...

He is interrupted as ANTOINE *enters, down left, carrying the picture of Daphnis and Chloë.*

ANTOINE, *shaking his head, to himself*: Practically naked!

GODEFROY, *with a start*: What?

ANTOINE: And for two ladies... Tsk tsk tsk!

GODEFROY: Antoine!

ANTOINE: It's only me, monsieur. I'm hanging Daphnis here in your father's bedroom... *(Correcting himself.)* In monsieur's father's bedroom, monsieur...

He exits, up right.

GODEFROY, *continuing where he left off*: The second time, I managed to open my mouth. But nothing would come out. The third time, we were alone in the drawing room. It was getting dark... My heart was beating... *(Reflecting.)* Of course... But pounding, I mean... And... And I finally said something... "What time is it, mademoiselle?" *(Imitating.)* "A quarter to eight." And that was that! Not another word... But I love her! I really do! It's just that... that... Love turns me to a vegetable! It puts me all in a stew! I don't know what it is...

ANTOINE *reappears, up right.*

ANTOINE, *to himself*: There!... Well hung... *(Moving toward the door, up left.)* Now to make lunch...

GODEFROY, *overhearing*: Oh, Antoine... When we eat, please don't put me beside madame. Or beside her daughter either...

ANTOINE, *aside*: Where the devil then...? *(Aloud.)* But... Doesn't monsieur like the young lady?

GODEFROY: Oh! I do! I do!... But we don't talk to each other. We just look...

ANTOINE: Do you... *(Catching himself.)* Does monsieur mean that monsieur gives mademoiselle the eye, monsieur?

GODEFROY: Oh yes! *(Standing facing him.)* I look at her when she doesn't look at me, and... And when she does, I don't. We take turns. Like this... Look at me, Antoine... *(ANTOINE obliges, and GODEFROY averts his glance.)* Now stop looking! *(ANTOINE turns aside, and GODEFROY gives him a long, tender look.)* There! Isn't that nice?

ANTOINE: Well... *(Aside.)* For someone who's cross-eyed, maybe...

GODEFROY: Not like the other one!

ANTOINE: "The other one," monsieur?

GODEFROY: The one that slobbers, and that looks at me like... Like this... *(Striking an exaggeratedly seductive pose and casting a languorous glance, in a thick accent.)* Godefroy!

ANTOINE, *with an uncomprehending shrug*: Aha...

GODEFROY, *looking at his pocket watch and changing his tone*: Good heavens! Look at the time! Papá will be furious! I'd better go get my white cravat!

He exits quickly, down right.

ANTOINE, *alone*: Who cares? Frankly, I think young monsieur... Monsieur's son... Well, if you ask me... *(Tapping his temple.)* I think he's a little...

DOÑA BARBARA'S VOICE, *offstage, outside the door, up center, calling, in a heavy Spanish accent*: Nanita!

NANITA'S VOICE, *offstage, farther off*: Sí?... You weesh, señora?

DOÑA BARBARA'S VOICE: Cone! For why you dodle?

ANTOINE, *aside*: Now who on earth...

The door, up center, opens and DOÑA BARBARA appears, standing solidly in the doorway, carrying a basket of objects, large and small, over her arm, and loaded down with baggage.

DOÑA BARBARA, *calling offstage*: Ven acá! Ven acá!...We here!... We arrive!

She strides in.

NANITA'S VOICE: Ees sleepery so, señora! I almoss break nook!

She appears, likewise loaded down, and stands awkwardly on the threshold.

ANTOINE, *to himself*: Oh my! The two ladies...

He closes the door.

DOÑA BARBARA, *aside*: Ha! Un domesteec! *(Aloud, to ANTOINE.)* Good day, domesteec! How ees you are? Ees good, I hope?... You no know me, no?

ANTOINE, *flustered*: No... No... That is... I—

DOÑA BARBARA: Ees mek good sense... You no know, becose you no nevair see!

NANITA, *giggling*: Hee hee hee!

DOÑA BARBARA: Bot moss spik moch tine mi nane here, no?… Mi nane… Doña Barbara… Weedow lady… I mek soap!

ANTOINE: Aha… Soap… *(At a loss.)* Yes… In Dunkirk…

DOÑA BARBARA, *aside*: Dungcork? What ees?

ANTOINE: So I've been told…

DOÑA BARBARA: An how he ees, Moosyair Bélodor? Ees good, jes?

ANTOINE: Oh yes… Very good… *(Correcting.)* Very well, that is… But he's not at home at the moment, madame.

DOÑA BARBARA: Por favor! No ees problema. I have moch tine…

NANITA: Hee hee hee!

ANTOINE, *looking at her, aside*: There's a pleasant one!

DOÑA BARBARA: An Moosyair Godefroy? Ees good also, jes?

ANTOINE: Oh yes… *(Aside, tapping his temple.)* A little… But… *(Aloud, pointing down right.)* If madame would like—

DOÑA BARBARA, *interrupting*: No, no, domesteec!… No for to… to… *(To NANITA.)* Cómo se dice "molestar"?

NANITA: "Deestorb," señora.

DOÑA BARBARA, *to ANTOINE:* Ees I no weesh for to deestorb. Ees I weesh for to sorprize heen!

ANTOINE: Surprise?… But they're expecting you, madame… *(Correcting himself.)* I mean, they're expecting madame, madame.

DOÑA BARBARA: Cómo? What ees you say?

ANTOINE, *pointing to NANITA*: And mademoiselle, of course… *(Aside.)* Especially!

NANITA: Hee hee hee!

ANTOINE: Why yes… Your room… Madame's and mademoiselle's room is all ready. *(Aside.)* Thank heaven I got rid of Daphnis just in time!

DOÑA BARBARA: Ah sí! Ah sí!… Por supuesto!… Thees Moosyair Bélodor he know, when I receive lettair… Thees lettair who tell me I cone for to veeseet…

ANTOINE: Aha…

DOÑA BARBARA: Ay! *(Blowing on her fingers.)* Moch hot thees lettair! Moch hot thees theen he tell to me about leettle Godefroy!

ANTOINE, *aside*: Little?

DOÑA BARBARA: You weesh maybe I rid to you?

ANTOINE, *with a casual wave, discreetly*: Oh, really, madame… I think—

DOÑA BARBARA: No, no! I no do!

ANTOINE: Of course not… I wasn't suggesting…

DOÑA BARBARA: Ees family business! Ees no for domesteec!

ANTOINE, *somewhat at a loss for words, pointing to the chairs, up left*: Wouldn't madame like to make herself comfortable?

DOÑA BARBARA: Sí, sí!… Jes!

ANTOINE, *to NANITA*: And mademoiselle, too?

NANITA: Hee hee hee!

She sits down on one of the chairs, up left, with her packages on her lap.

DOÑA BARBARA: Ees… Ees… *(Sitting down in the other chair, up left, sighing.)* No have fit! No have fit!

ANTOINE, *misunderstanding*: I beg madame's pardon... Would madame like a wider chair?

DOÑA BARBARA: What? For why you say? For why you theenk?

She settles in, with her packages on her lap as well.

ANTOINE: I... I thought madame was saying that she didn't fit. And I was asking—

DOÑA BARBARA: No "fit"!... *(Trying to correct him.)* Fit! Fit! *(Pointing to her feet.)* Ees I no can fil fit! No can fil!... So beeg ees... ees... *(To NANITA.)* Cómo se dice "viaje"?

NANITA: "Treep," señora!... Hee hee hee!

DOÑA BARBARA: Sí, sí!... So beeg ees treep...

She and NANITA each take a stocking from a pocket and they begin knitting.

ANTOINE, *finally understanding*: Aha... *(Aside.)* My God, they talk funny in Dunkirk! I never knew...

DOÑA BARBARA: So moch tine we spen!

ANTOINE: Yes... I see... Of course... Yes, it is rather long...

DOÑA BARBARA: Sí, sí!... Furst we take boat to Marseille.

ANTOINE: Marseille?... But... But...

DOÑA BARBARA: Sí! Boat... Boat... *(Continuing.)* Then tren...

ANTOINE: Tren?

DOÑA BARBARA: Tren!... Two whole day een tren, moosyair!

ANTOINE, *aside*: What? *(Aloud.)* But... That's much too long... Surely you didn't have to... *(Aside.)* From Dunkirk?... But it's only... *(Aloud.)* The boat... Marseille... The train... ? There must be a better way...

DOÑA BARBARA: No, no! Ees way! Ees way!

ANTOINE, *shrugging, aside*: Maybe it's something new... A scenic route...

DOÑA BARBARA: Ay! *(Sighing.)* Beeg treep! Beeg treep! *(To NANITA.)* No es verdad, Nanita?

NANITA: Hee hee hee!

DOÑA BARBARA: Sí! Soch beeg!... *(Putting down her knitting, to ANTOINE.)* Moosyair... You tell me... *(As NANITA puts down hers as well.)* How you call?

ANTOINE: Madame?

DOÑA BARBARA: You nane... What ees?

ANTOINE: Oh... Antoine, madame.

DOÑA BARBARA and NANITA jump up suddenly, sending their packages and knitting falling to the floor.

DOÑA BARBARA: Ay!

NANITA: Ees posseeble?

ANTOINE: What?

DOÑA BARBARA: You nane he ees Antonio?

ANTOINE: More or less... Antoine, madame...

DOÑA BARBARA: Ha! Ees beautifool coeenceedence! Concierge, een Sevilla, he have nane also Antonio! Ees preetty man!

ANTOINE: Oh?... Well...

NANITA: Sí! Bot concierge he ees beeg! *(Holding her arms out wide.)* He have beeg shodler!… I know… I measure… You, moosyair… You theen, like leettle poopy dog!

ANTOINE, *aside*: Not too damn timid if she measures the concierge!

DOÑA BARBARA: Antonio, good frien… Eef soneone, lass month, he tell me: "Señora, een three week you be een Parees… At hone of Moosyair Bélodor!"… Eef soneone he tell me thees, I tell heen: "Ha! Idiota! You be crazy fool!" Who theenk I leave Sevilla, weeth so moch soap…

ANTONIO, *puzzled*: Please?

DOÑA BARBARA, *continuing*: …so moch to mek! So moch to sell!… For whole ceety! For whole conntry! For whole… whole… *(To NANITA.)* Cómo se dice "mundo," Nanita?

NANITA: "Worl," señora… Hee hee hee!

DOÑA BARBARA, *to ANTOINE*: For whole worl!

ANTOINE: Yes… I'm sure…

DOÑA BARBARA, *sadly*: An ees so deefeecolt, moosyair! For poor weedow lady… *(Sighing.)* Dios mío… All alone…

NANITA, *suddenly very serious*: Ay ay ay!

DOÑA BARBARA, *continuing*: Seence terreeble theen she happen to mi… to mi… *(To NANITA.)* Cómo se dice "esposo"?

NANITA, *reflecting for a moment*: "Espoose" señora.

DOÑA BARBARA, *continuing, confidently*: To mi espoose…

ANTOINE: Espoose?… *(Understanding.)* Ah! Madame's spouse… Her husband…

DOÑA BARBARA: Sí!… Jes!… Bot no more!… Terreeble theen she happen… She mek me be weedow, Antonio. Twenty-one year only… So young!

ANTOINE: Tsk tsk tsk!… Twenty-one?

DOÑA BARBARA: Sí!… An sex month also…

ANTOINE: My, my… And how did madame lose him, if I may—

DOÑA BARBARA: Lose?… No lose! I know where… Bot he be eat op, Antonio!

ANTOINE, *not sure he has heard correctly*: Eaten up, madame?

DOÑA BARBARA: Jes, moosyair! Fron head to toe… Beeg! Bot all feeneesh!

NANITA, *holding up her arm*: So beeg, moosyair! I know… I measure…

ANTOINE, *aside*: Him too? *(To DOÑA BARBARA.)* Eaten up, you say?… Your husband?

DOÑA BARBARA: Sí, sí!… Mi… Mi… *(To NANITA.)* Cómo se dice "magnífico"?

NANITA: "Magneefeecent," señora… Hee hee hee!

DOÑA BARBARA: Jes! Mi magneefeecent espoose… One wik only after weddeen!

ANTOINE: No!

DOÑA BARBARA: Sí! Boat go down… Seenk…

ANTOINE: Eaten up…?

DOÑA BARBARA, *continuing*: …by Canarías… Ay! Las Canarías…

ANTOINE, *aside*: Damn big canaries!

DOÑA BARBARA: He tell to me: "Chiquita… Oceano he call to me… Sumatra… Borneo… I go…" "Bot ees Friday," I tell to heen. "Friday thorteen!… Por favor! You no go!"

ANTOINE: Of course…

DOÑA BARBARA: An I fall down… I fall down…

ANTOINE: Oh my…

DOÑA BARBARA: On knee I fall down…

ANTOINE: Oh…

DOÑA BARBARA, *continuing*: …an beg, beg, beg… Bot no use!… He stobborn! Like mole…

ANTOINE: Mole?

NANITA, *correcting her*: "Mule," señora…

DOÑA BARBARA: Like mule! Like mule!… Sí, sí! Antonio… He go on Friday… On boat… *La Doña Barbara…* He call for me thees boat…

ANTOINE: Of course…

DOÑA BARBARA: An so he go sail… Everytheen fine… Good briz…

ANTOINE: Briz?

DOÑA BARBARA: Briz… *(Illustrating.) Whoosh… Whoosh… (As he nods.)* Een… Een… *(To NANITA.)* Cómo se dice "popa," Nanita?

NANITA, *reflecting*: "Poop," señora… Hee hee hee!

DOÑA BARBARA, *to ANTOINE:* Poop, Antonio… Poop…

ANTOINE: Aha…

DOÑA BARBARA: Sí, sí!… Jes!… Jes!

She stops, seemingly overcome with emotion.

ANTOINE: Oh my… But… *(To NANITA.)* Then what happened, mademoiselle?

NANITA: Then beeg, beeg storn, moosyair… *La Doña Barbara* ees boatwreck! Uno, dos, tres… She go down, go down… Capitán he sweem to shore…

DOÑA BARBARA: Bot los canibales…

NANITA: Sí, sí! Hongry canibales…

DOÑA BARBARA, *sighing*: Ay!… Sí, sí…

NANITA: They eat heen alive!

ANTOINE: How awful!

DOÑA BARBARA: An notheen ees be left. Only shurt off hees bek! *(To NANITA.)* "Franela," Nanita… Cómo se dice?

NANITA, "Flannel," señora… *(Sighing.)* Ay ay ay!

DOÑA BARBARA: Sí, sí! Antonio… Hees flannel shurt only…

NANITA: An one sliv too they eat, moosyair!

ANTOINE: Tsk tsk tsk! *(Trying to console them.)* It takes all kinds, don't you know…

DOÑA BARBARA: Jes!… Well… *(Changing her tone.)* We all die one day! So… Eighteen month I moon.

NANITA, *correcting*: "Mourn," señora…

DOÑA BARBARA: Sí! Ees what I say, no? *(Not waiting for an answer, to ANTOINE.)* Ees now enough tine, you theenk? Eighteen month I moon.

ANTOINE: I—

DOÑA BARBARA: You theenk mi espoose he theenk ees enough, moosyair?

ANTOINE: It's really not for me to say, madame, but… Yes, quite… I should think eighteen months is more than enough. I wouldn't worry a bit if I were—

DOÑA BARBARA, *cutting him off*: Ay, Dios! You talk, talk, talk, Antonio!

ANTOINE: Madame?

DOÑA BARBARA: You tell to me roon she ees ready. Bot eenstead for to show me where, you only talk, talk, talk!

ANTOINE, *aside*: Me? *(Aloud.)* Right this way, madame.. . Anything to oblige…

He motions her toward the door, down left.

DOÑA BARBARA: Ho ho ho! *(Imitating.)* "Anytheen to oblige"! For why you talk fonny, Antonio? Ho ho ho!

NANITA: Hee hee hee!

ANTOINE picks up the packages from the floor.

ANTOINE, *to himself, but loud enough to be overheard*: Not as funny as they talk in Dunkirk, madame!

DOÑA BARBARA, *at the door, to herself*: For why ees always Dungcork he say? *(To NANITA, who is following behind her.)* For why?

ANTOINE, arms full, stands aside to let them pass, and exits after them. At the same moment, GODEFROY enters, down right, wearing a white cravat.

GODEFROY, *grumbling*: There! I hope he'll be happy! A white cravat… A dozen of the silly things, and this is the only white one! *(Looking at his pocket watch.)* Papá will be furious with me if I'm late! *(He moves to leave, up center, but stops as he reaches the door.)* Oh! What on earth do I say to her? *(Determined.)* Backbone, Godefroy! Backbone!… I'll say… I'll say… "Mademoiselle… Mademoiselle, I… I…"

BELODOR'S VOICE, *offstage, outside the door, up center*: This way, dear ladies…

GODEFROY, *with a start*: Good heavens! They're here!

BELODOR'S VOICE: Madame… Mademoiselle…

GODEFROY, *looking at his watch again*: But… The train… Oh! Papá will have my head!

He cowers in the corner, up left, trying to be as inconspicuous as possible, as MADAME DE SAINTE-POULE and BLANCHE enter, followed by BELODOR, struggling under the weight of all their luggage.

BELODOR, *to the women*: Welcome to my modest, unassuming abode.

MADAME DE SAINTE-POULE: Please… Let me relieve you, monsieur.

BELODOR: No, no! I'll not hear of it! Just make yourselves at home.

He staggers up right and puts the bags down on the floor, by the buffet.

MADAME DE SAINTE-POULE, *catching sight of GODEFROY, with a note of sarcasm*: Ah, monsieur… *(To BELODOR.)* We were afraid he might be a trifle indisposed… When he failed to greet us…

BELODOR, *joining GODEFROY, up left*: Not at all! Not at all! *(In an angry whisper, to GODEFROY.)* We shall discuss this breach of decorum later! *(To MADAME DE SAINTE-POULE, all sweetness and light.)* He has been seeing to your accommodations, madame… *(To BLANCHE.)* And mademoiselle's… *(Calling.)* Antoine!… Antoine! *(To the women, continuing.)* A veritable temple of Cupid! A shrine, if I may say…

ANTOINE enters, down left.

ANTOINE, *to BELODOR*: Monsieur? *(Noticing MADAME DE SAINTE-POULE and BLANCHE, aside.)* Oh my! Two more?

BELODOR, *to the women, pointing down left*: This way…

As the two of them go up right, about to retrieve their baggage, he stops them with a gesture.

ANTOINE, *to* BELODOR, *pointing down left, in a whisper*: Not in there, monsieur!

BELODOR, *to* ANTOINE, *apparently not hearing him, pointing to the baggage*: In the *chambre bleue,* Antoine!

ANTOINE, *taking him aside, down right, whispering*: But monsieur's guests have arrived. They're in there.

The two ladies begin moving down left.

BELODOR, *whispering*: My… Who?

ANTOINE, *whispering*: A young widow… Some giant canaries ate her husband, if I understood correctly.

BELODOR, *whispering*: What?

ANTOINE, *whispering*: A Madame Barbara, I think…

BELODOR, *repressing an anguished scream*: What?… Good grief!

MADAME DE SAINTE-POULE, *to* BLANCHE: Come, precious…

They are about to exit, down left, when BELODOR *dashes over and bars their way.*

BELODOR: No!… Not this way…

MADAME DE SAINTE-POULE: Oh? I must have misunderstood…

GODEFROY, *confused*: But…

BELODOR, *to* MADAME DE SAINTE-POULE: No doubt…

MADAME DE SAINTE-POULE: Then… Where, monsieur?

BELODOR, *pointing up right*: There!… In there!

GODEFROY, *in a whisper*: But papá…

MADAME DE SAINTE-POULE, *to* BELODOR: I do hope we're not putting you to any trouble, monsieur.

BELODOR, *as agreeably as possible*: Trouble? Not in the slightest!

MADAME DE SAINTE-POULE: Well, if you're sure… *(To* BLANCHE.*)* Come, precious… *(To* GODEFROY.*)* I can't wait to see your little temple of Cupid!

BELODOR, *to* ANTOINE, *pointing alternately to the baggage and the door, up right*: In there!… In there!

ANTOINE: Very good, monsieur…

He picks up all the baggage and follows the two women out, up right.

GODEFROY, *to himself*: In his room? What is he doing? *(To* BELODOR.*)* Papá… That's not the *chambre bleue…*

BELODOR: You think I don't know? *(Pointing down left.) She's* in there! Your… Your…

GODEFROY: My…?

BELODOR: Your Doña Barbara!

GODEFROY, *trembling*: But… But… *(Beginning to babble.)* You… You said… You told me she couldn't leave Seville… All that soap—

BELODOR: Well, I was wrong!

GODEFROY: Oh! My God!

BELODOR: I've put madame and her daughter in my room. I'll go sleep at the hotel!

GODEFROY: So will I!... Oh! *(Not knowing which way to turn.)* God help me!

ANTOINE enters, up right.

BELODOR: Thank goodness my room is presentable!

ANTOINE: Not quite, monsieur...

BELODOR: What?

ANTOINE: Your boots... *(Correcting himself.)* Monsieur's boots are on his dresser.

BELODOR: Damnation!

ANTOINE: And his toupee is on the night table.

BELODOR: The... My... *(Furious.)* You mean... You left everything? You didn't take anything out?

ANTOINE: No, monsieur... But I did hang Daphnis and Chloë in the alcove.

BELODOR: You... You dunce!... You...

ANTOINE: Excuse me, monsieur... I mean, if monsieur will excuse me, I think I'm wanted in the kitchen.

He exits, up left.

BELODOR, *pacing nervously*: Good grief!

GODEFROY: What now, papá? We can't let that... that frightful woman stay here. Send her home! Throw her out!

BELODOR, *indignantly*: Godefroy!

GODEFROY: Send her back to her soap! Make a clean breast of it...

BELODOR: Do you know what you are saying? A member of the fair sex?... There are things one simply does not do! "Throw her out," indeed!

GODEFROY: But papá! If she sees me...

DOÑA BARBARA'S VOICE, *offstage, down left, calling*: Godefroy!... Where he ees, mi Godefroy?

GODEFROY, *looking about, frantically*: Ayyy! Too late!

BELODOR: Courtesy, son! Civility!

GODEFROY: Bah!

BELODOR: Now smile! The social graces demand our most hospitable behavior!

GODEFROY, *trying to smile, but managing only a few contorted grimaces*: I can't, papá! I... I'm trying, but... I can't!

DOÑA BARBARA enters, down left, with a basket slung over her arm. NANITA follows her, hanging back in the corner.

DOÑA BARBARA, *spying GODEFROY*: Ah! There he ees, my leettle tortledove!

BELODOR, *aside*: The lady herself...

DOÑA BARBARA: I hear hees voice! I know ees heen! *(Holding our her arms to him.)* Cone! Geeve to me beeg keess, Godefroy!

BELODOR, *to himself*: Younger than I thought... *(Aloud, to DOÑA BARBARA.)* Madame... Señora...

Ignoring him, she awkwardly embraces GODEFROY, planting a resounding kiss on each cheek.

DOÑA BARBARA: So!

BELODOR, *trying to get her attention, as GODEFROY, inconspicuously as possible, wipes his cheeks with his sleeve*: I say...

DOÑA BARBARA, *finally noticing him, without releasing the squirming* GODEFROY: Ah, sí!… Jes!… Ees papá, no? *(To* NANITA, *pointing.)* Ees papá!… See? See?

NANITA: Sí! Sí!… Hee hee hee! I see…

BELODOR: Yes!… Quite… *(Forcing a smile.)* It certainly is a pleasure, I must say…

GODEFROY, *aside*: Oh, must you?

BELODOR, *continuing*: …after all these years of such a happy professional association…

DOÑA BARBARA: So! *(Releasing* GODEFROY.*)* I geeve to you beeg keess also, papá! Bot for you, one only!

She gives him a kiss on one cheek.

BELODOR, *startled*: Ah…

DOÑA BARBARA: Ees so long I weesh to meet thees man… Thees preence of vagrants!

GODEFROY, *aside*: Vagrants?

BELODOR, *to* DOÑA BARBARA, *gently correcting*: "Fragrance," madame…

DOÑA BARBARA: Sí, sí!

BELODOR: No, no… You are much too kind…

DOÑA BARBARA: No, no! Ees you kine, moosyair! *(To* NANITA, *pointing to him.)* Ees so kine!

NANITA: Hee hee hee!

DOÑA BARBARA: So kine for to eenvite! So kine for to write to me: "You cone to Parees, madame! You cone to veeseet! I eenseest!… Godefroy he eenseest!…"

GODEFROY, *to* BELODOR, *whispering*: You wrote that?

DOÑA BARBARA, *continuing*: "Godefroy he have soch beeg lost een heart for you!"

NANITA: Hee hee hee!

GODEFROY, *to* BELODOR, *whispering, furiously*: Papá!

BELODOR, *to* DOÑA BARBARA: Indeed… Indeed…

DOÑA BARBARA: An you happy, moosyair?

BELODOR: Oh… Ecstatic… Ecstatic, madame…

DOÑA BARBARA, *to* GODEFROY: An you, Godefroy? You no spik? You no say notheen?

GODEFROY, *as blandly as possible*: Did you have a good trip?

DOÑA BARBARA, *with a laugh*: Pobrecito! *(To* BELODOR.*)* Ees so teemeed, poor baby! Bot I feex! One wik weeth me, an he be change good! He be change! I promeese…

She reaches into the basket and takes out various jars.

BELODOR, *aside*: Good grief! A week?

DOÑA BARBARA: So… Here! Fron mi conntry… Ees for papá!… *(Handing them to him, one at a time.)* Oleeve… Sardine… Garleek…

BELODOR: You… You shouldn't have…

DOÑA BARBARA, *continuing*: Aceite… *(To* NANITA.*)* Cómo se dice "aceite," Nanita?

NANITA: "Oil," señora… Hee hee hee!

DOÑA BARBARA: Sí, sí! "Oil"…

BELODOR: Really…

DOÑA BARBARA: An for Godefroy… Thees…

She takes out an enormous salami and hands it to him.

GODEFROY: You're too kind…

DOÑA BARBARA, *with a knowing wink*: An ees no only theen I have for heen! (*NANITA giggles.*) Bot furst… (*To GODEFROY.*) Furst I moss spik weeth papá, Godefroy! (*Waving him off.*) Por favor, you go…

GODEFROY, *under his breath*: With pleasure…

As he is about to exit, down right, MADAME DE SAINTE-POULE enters, up right, carrying a pair of boots in her left hand and a toupee in her right.

MADAME DE SAINTE-POULE, *calling*: Antoine!… Antoine!

GODEFROY, *in a whisper, to BELODOR*: Ayyy!… Madame…

BELODOR, *in a whisper*: With my boots!

GODEFROY, *in a whisper*: And your toupee…

DOÑA BARBARA, *aside*: Who ees?

MADAME DE SAINTE-POULE, *holding up the objects, to BELODOR*: I found these trinkets in your… your little temple, monsieur.

BELODOR: Ah… Antoine's… What ever were they doing in there? He must be looking high and low… (*To GODEFROY.*) Take them, son…

GODEFROY, *holding up the salami in both arms*: How, papá?

DOÑA BARBARA, *softly, to BELODOR, pointing to MADAME DE SAINTE-POULE*: Who ees beeg one?

MADAME DE SAINTE-POULE, *overhearing*: What?

DOÑA BARBARA: Ees wet norse? (*Looking around.*) Bot where ees baby?… Ees no baby… So, for why…

BELODOR, *mumbling*: No… No… (*Loading GODEFROY's arms with the objects he is holding, and grasping the toupee MADAME DE SAINTE-POULE is holding, thinking it is her hand.*) Madame de Sainte-Poule… Our… Our dearest friend… (*Introducing.*) Señora… Doña Barbara… Our… Our dearest friend…

MADAME DE SAINTE-POULE, *still holding the boots and the toupee, with a cold nod*: Charmed, madame…

DOÑA BARBARA, *pointing to the objects*: You go house to house for to sell?

MADAME DE SAINTE-POULE: I beg your—

BELODOR, *interrupting, to DOÑA BARBARA, not knowing what to say*: Madame… Madame is independently wealthy. She—

DOÑA BARBARA: Ah! Ees for why she eat so good! For why she so… (*To NANITA.*) Cómo se dice "gorda," Nanita?

NANITA: "Fet," señora… Hee hee hee!

DOÑA BARBARA: Ees for why she so fet!

MADAME DE SAINTE-POULE, *to BELODOR, unable to believe her ears*: What did she say?

BELODOR: Nothing… It's an expression… (*Babbling.*) I… I didn't hear…

DOÑA BARBARA, *to MADAME DE SAINTE-POULE*: Good frien… You esscuse now? I cone all way fron Sevilla for to talk weeth Bélodor. So! You go now, jes?

MADAME DE SAINTE-POULE, *flustered*: I… I…

DOÑA BARBARA: Bueno!… Aye aye! Aye aye!… Bon voyage… "Steady as she go!"

MADAME DE SAINTE-POULE, *to BELODOR, quizzically*: Monsieur? What…

BELODOR, *in a whisper*: It's nothing… An expression… (*Trying to appear calm.*) Now then, It's high time we had lunch. (*To MADAME DE SAINTE-POULE.*) If your charming daughter is so disposed, madame... *(To* GODEFROY, *taking the boots and toupee and loading them onto his arms.)* Give these to Antoine, in the kitchen, and tell him that he should be more careful in the future not to leave his... his things lying about!

GODEFROY: Yes, papá.

BELODOR: And tell him to serve lunch!

DOÑA BARBARA, *to* MADAME DE SAINTE-POULE: So? You go?

MADAME DE SAINTE-POULE: Indeed!

She exits, up right, as GODEFROY, *arms full, exits, up left.*

DOÑA BARBARA, *to* NANITA: You go too, Nanita. I no need... You go help...

NANITA: Sí, señora... Hee hee hee!

She exits, giggling, up left.

DOÑA BARBARA, *center, to* BELODOR, *confronting him, hands on hips*: Ees good! We alone now, moosyair!

She takes him by the arm and leads him downstage.

BELODOR: Yes... We seem to be...

DOÑA BARBARA: Eef I cone all way fron Sevilla, moosyair... Ees no for... for... *(Looking for a convincing reason.)* to see hippopotamoose een zoo!

BELODOR: No, no... *(Making conversation.)* I wasn't aware that they had one!... In fact, I don't think they do, madame... Perhaps they used to, but... No... No more...

DOÑA BARBARA: Oh! He die, hippopotamoose?... Tsk tsk tsk! Poor theen!... Mi espoose too!

BELODOR: Who?

DOÑA BARBARA: Espoose!... Mi espoose too... *(Affecting great sadness.)* Boo-hoo... Boo-hoo... Ees for why I cone here...

BELODOR, *rather confused*: I beg your pardon, but...

DOÑA BARBARA: Sí, sí!... I no more have espoose. No more...

BELODOR: Ah... Your husband... Yes, I know...

DOÑA BARBARA: So, when you sen to me nice lettair... When you say Godefroy he have moch beeg lost for me...

BELODOR: Lust?... Well...

DOÑA BARBARA: Jes! You say!... No say ees no true! No say... You say...

BELODOR: Yes, I did... But... *(Looking down left, aside.)* Damnation! And the other one?

DOÑA BARBARA: No "bot"! You say!... So, now you ask me, no? I no be hard heart! You ask... I say "sí"!... Sí, sí!

BELODOR: "Sí, sí"?

DOÑA BARBARA, *categorically*: Sí!

BELODOR, *pretending to be delighted*: I say... What an honor! What a joy!... What a... But—

DOÑA BARBARA, *cutting him off with a huge embrace*: Papá!

As she gives him a resounding kiss, MADAME DE SAINTE-POULE *enters suddenly, up right, followed by* BLANCHE.

MADAME DE SAINTE-POULE, *noticing them, as* BLANCHE, *at the door, covers her eyes*: Oh! Pardon me!... I do hope we're not intruding!

DOÑA BARBARA: No, no! *(Releasing* BELODOR.*)* We all feeneesh!

BELODOR, *wiping his mouth on his sleeve, aside*: Good grief!

DOÑA BARBARA, *to* MADAME DE SAINTE-POULE, *moving upstage*: Ees permeet you cone back now! Ees no more have to do...

MADAME DE SAINTE-POULE: You're too kind!

BELODOR, *aside*: If only she holds her tongue!

DOÑA BARBARA, *noticing* BLANCHE: Oh! What ees that?

MADAME DE SAINTE-POULE: "That," madame? "That" is my daughter!

BELODOR, *aside*: Heaven help me!

DOÑA BARBARA: Ees preetty, madame! Ees good for to mek moch baby, no?

MADAME DE SAINTE-POULE, / **BLANCHE,** } *together*: { Madame! / What?

DOÑA BARBARA, *jovially*: Bot for thees, she need espoose! You fine for her espoose, jes?

MADAME DE SAINTE-POULE: Madame?

DOÑA BARBARA: Sí, sí!... Hosban!

MADAME DE SAINTE-POULE, *sarcastically*: Why, thank you for your concern! I have every intention... In fact, madame...

DOÑA BARBARA: Ho ho! So! Ees maybe secret, thees theen?

MADAME DE SAINTE-POULE: Hardly!

BELODOR, *aside*: Oh, my God!

MADAME DE SAINTE-POULE: Why should it be? *(As* GODEFROY *and* ANTOINE *enter, up left, carrying a dining table with a bottle of wine and set with five places, each with a wine glass .)* She's marrying—

BELODOR, *crying out in near panic*: Lunch!... Lunch! Lunch!... Everyone! ... Let's sit down! Let's sit down!

ANTOINE: Luncheon is served!

BELODOR, *shouting*: Lunch! Lunch, everybody!... Sit down! Sit down!

> GODEFROY *and* ANTOINE *place the table center.* ANTOINE *goes about taking the five occasional chairs, placing them, one on each side of the table, facing each other, and three upstage, facing the footlights. The characters sit down in the following order:* BELODOR, *right, facing* DOÑA BARBARA, *across from him, left;* MADAME DE SAINTE-POULE, BLANCHE, *and* GODEFROY, *facing forward, from right to left.*

DOÑA BARBARA, *to* GODEFROY: Cone, Godefroy! *(Indicating the space to her right.)* You seet here! *(As he sits down next to* BLANCHE.*)* Ees good you seet next to woman you marry!

BELODOR, *coughing loudly in an attempt to cover her comments*: Ahem!... Ahem!

DOÑA BARBARA: Thees breen good lock!

BELODOR: Ahem!... Ahem!...

MADAME DE SAINTE-POULE, *to* BELODOR: You told her, monsieur?

BELODOR: Well... A little... Not in so many words, mind you...

MADAME DE SAINTE-POULE: Oh?

BELODOR: I mean… We have no secrets in the soap business! We're all one big family.

DOÑA BARBARA, *calling up left*: Nanita!… Estamos listos!… Puedes servir… *(To the company.)* I have for you sorpresa! Beeg sorpresa…

NANITA enters, up left, carrying a steaming platter.

BELODOR, *taken aback, aside*: Where did she come from?

NANITA places it down on the table and moves off, right.

DOÑA BARBARA: Ees cook! I breen her for to mek… *(Searching for the word.)* for to mek magneefeecent deesh! Deesh fron hone!

She contemplates it with great pleasure, while the others, apparently repelled by its odor, try not to grimace and wince.

BELODOR, *hypocritically*: Well, it certainly looks appetizing! What is it, madame?

DOÑA BARBARA: Ees garleek feesh stew… Moch garleek… Ees for sex…

There is a moment of general quiet consternation.

MADAME DE SAINTE-POULE, BELODOR *and* **GODEFROY,** *together*: What!

BLANCHE: Mammá!

DOÑA BARBARA, *counting the settings*: Uno, dos, tres… Ah! Ees five only… Bot Nanita, she mek sex…

BELODOR, *relieved*: Oh…

DOÑA BARBARA: So… Furst soak een… een cerveza… *(To NANITA.)* Cómo se dice, Nanita?

NANITA, *beaming with pride*: "Beer," señora…

DOÑA BARBARA: Sí, sí!… Then poot moch… moch… *(Trying to remember.)* … aceite… *(Turning to NANITA.)* Cómo…

NANITA, *without giving her a chance to ask*: "Oil," señora…

DOÑA BARBARA: Sí, sí!… For why ees I forget? Ees so easy thees word. An ees so eemportant!… An then, chop feesh… *(With rapid chopping motions.)* Chop, chop, chop…

BELODOR, *pretending great interest*: Oh? What kind?

DOÑA BARBARA: Ill… Ill kine…

There is a heavy, uncomprehending hush.

BELODOR: Ill?

GODEFROY, *aside*: No doubt…

DOÑA BARBARA: Ill!… Long… Theen…

BELODOR, *comprehending*: Ah! *(Pronouncing clearly.)* Eel!… Yes… Of course… *(Turning aside with a grimace.)* Eel.

DOÑA BARBARA: Jes!

BELODOR, *to the others, authoritatively*: A great delicacy where she comes from…

DOÑA BARBARA: Sí, sí!… Bot furst you clin… Take out eentesteen…

BELODOR: Indeed!

DOÑA BARBARA: Long!… Long!…

BELODOR: I'm sure!

DOÑA BARBARA: Becose ees all kine feelth… Feelthy, deesgosteen theen een eentesteen… All kine… *(To NANITA.)* You clin good, Nanita, no?

NANITA, *right*: Oh, sí! Sí, señora! I clin! I clin!

DOÑA BARBARA: An you no forget peppair? Moch peppair?

NANITA: Oh, no, señora!… Moch… Moch…

DOÑA BARBARA: Bueno!… So! *(Holding out the platter to* MADAME DE SAINTE-POULE.*)* You tek beeg, no?

MADAME DE SAINTE-POULE: No… I… My liver…

DOÑA BARBARA: Bot ees good for leevair!

MADAME DE SAINTE-POULE: I think not… *(With as polite a gesture as she can muster.)* Thank you…

DOÑA BARBARA attempts to serve BLANCHE.

BLANCHE, *timidly*: I… I'm afraid I'm not hungry enough to do it justice, madame.

DOÑA BARBARA, *to GODEFROY*: An for Godefroy?

GODEFROY, *clutching his cheek*: I have a toothache…

DOÑA BARBARA: Bot ees good for ek-tooth… Ees good… *(Still offering.)* So! *(With a note of disappointment.)* Nobody he tek?

BELODOR: Au contraire, madame! *(Aside.)* What kind of manners… *(Aloud.)* I wouldn't deprive myself of it for the world! *(Holding out his plate to her across the table.)* Please!… A good, generous *porthión!*… *(Beaming at his mot, to the others, as she places a heaping serving on his plate.)* One should never neglect the opportunity to savor the variety of our neighbors' delicacies! *(He takes a taste.)* Why, it's… it's … *(Struggling to repress a disgusted grimace.)* Most unusual!… Very piquant…

After a courageous moment he surreptitiously spits the mouthful into his napkin.

DOÑA BARBARA: Bueno moosyair… You like… You feeneesh!

She empties the rest onto his plate.

BELODOR, *aside*: God in heaven!

DOÑA BARBARA, *replacing the platter and standing up*: So! Now, who go seen?

MADAME DE SAINTE-POULE, *puzzled, to NANITA*: "Seen," mademoiselle?

DOÑA BARBARA: Nanita?

NANITA: "Sing"…

BELODOR: Sing?

DOÑA BARBARA: Sí, sí! Seen!… Ees always, at weddeen lonch… Ees always sonebody he seen!… So! I do!

MADAME DE SAINTE-POULE, *aside*: Of all the…

There is a general mumble of surprise and restrained disapproval.

DOÑA BARBARA, *to NANITA*: Nanita! You clep!

NANITA: Sí, señora…

DOÑA BARBARA takes a position, down center.

DOÑA BARBARA, *singing and dancing, as NANITA hums along and claps in rhythm*:

"La cucaracha, la cucaracha,
Ya no puede caminar…"

BELODOR, GODEFROY, MADAME DE SAINTE-POULE, BLANCHE } *together:* {
Oh my!
What?
Madame!
Oh, Mammá!

DOÑA BARBARA, *continuing*:

"Porque le falta, porque no tiene,
Una pata para andar!"

BELODOR, *applauding, hypocritically*: Bravo!… *(Correcting himself.)* Brava! … Brava!… Oh! Bueno! Bueno!… *(Aside, to himself.)* Buena?

DOÑA BARBARA, *sitting down*: Ees preetty, no?

BELODOR: Indeed! I should say…

MADAME DE SAINTE-POULE, *sarcastically*: Utterly adorable!

DOÑA BARBARA: I know more! Bot I save for when I have weddeen!

MADAME DE SAINTE-POULE: Oh? Is madame getting married?

BELODOR, *aside*: Ayyy!

MADAME DE SAINTE-POULE, *aside*: How fortunate for the gentleman! Such talent…

BELODOR, *shouting*: Antoine! The coffee!…

DOÑA BARBARA, *replying to her*: Sí, sí! I cone fron Sevilla for thees…

BELODOR, *louder, almost desperately*: Antoine!… Antoine!

MADAME DE SAINTE-POULE: Oh?

DOÑA BARBARA: Sí, sí! I marry leettle Bélodor!

Everybody jumps up, aghast.

MADAME DE SAINTE-POULE: What?

BELODOR *and* **GODEFROY**, *together*: My God!

MADAME DE SAINTE-POULE: Well! I think we've heard enough! *(To* BELODOR.*)* Of everything, monsieur! *(To* DOÑA BARBARA.*)* Everything! *(To* BLANCHE, *pointing up right.)* Go to your room, precious!

BLANCHE: Yes, mammá.

She exits.

DOÑA BARBARA, *still seated*: Where everyone he go? *(Pouring two glasses of wine and raising one to* GODEFROY.*)* To you, Godefroy!… To me!…

GODEFROY, *weakly*: I'm not thirsty…

DOÑA BARBARA: To oss!

She stands up. NANITA *and* ANTOINE *remove the table and carry it off, up left.*

MADAME DE SAINTE-POULE, *pulling* BELODOR *quickly aside, in an angry whisper*: Just what is this I hear, monsieur?

BELODOR, *feigning utter innocence, in a whisper*: Hear, madame?

MADAME DE SAINTE-POULE, *in a whisper*: That… That person is marrying—

BELODOR, *stammering, in a whisper*: M-M-M-Me!… Yes! Me!… She's… She's marrying me!

MADAME DE SAINTE-POULE, *in a whisper*: What?… But… But she said "little Bélodor… Little…"

BELODOR, *in a whisper*: That's right! It's an expression... In the soap business, madame... They always refer to one another...

MADAME DE SAINTE-POULE, *relieved*: Ah! Well... I must say... When I first came in, I... Yes, indeed... *(To* DOÑA BARBARA.*)* Please, madame! Let me be the first...

DOÑA BARBARA: Furst?... Furst what?

MADAME DE SAINTE-POULE: The first to congratulate you on your happy marriage...

GODEFROY, *shocked*: What?

BELODOR, *panicking, calling*: Antoine!... The coffee!... How many times—

GODEFROY, *to* BELODOR: But papá...

DOÑA BARBARA, *to* MADAME DE SAINTE-POULE: Sí, sí! Ees for love I marry! *(To* GODEFROY.*)* Ees no so, leettle one?

BELODOR, *quick to answer in his place*: Yes!... Si!... Yes, little one!... *(Calling.)* Antoine!... Antoine!

ANTOINE enters, up center, carrying a wedding basket on a stand, and puts them down, center.

ANTOINE: Monsieur... *(Approaching him, taking a customary sniff, but turning away with a wince, aside.)* Oh my!... *(Putting his hand up to his nose, aloud.)* The wedding basket monsieur ordered just arrived.

He exits, up left, casting a few quizzical backward glances at BELODOR as he does.

BELODOR, *calling after him*: And the coffee, Antoine?

DOÑA BARBARA,	*going to inspect the basket, together*:	Qué hermoso!
MADAME DE SAINTE-POULE,		Oh!

BELODOR, *throwing up his hands, aside*: Now what?

DOÑA BARBARA, *calling*: Nanita!... Ven acá! Ay! Tienes que ver...!

As the two women mutter their admiration, NANITA enters, up left, and joins them.

NANITA: Oh!

MADAME DE SAINTE-POULE, *pulling a shawl from the basket part way*: Look! Pure cashmere!

DOÑA BARBARA, *pulling at a mantilla*: An thees!... Ees lace!... *(To* NANITA.*)* Irlandés, Nanita!... Cómo se dice?

NANITA: "Ireesh"... "Ireesh"...

MADAME DE SAINTE-POULE, *to* NANITA, *misunderstanding*: Indeed! Who wouldn't wish for something so lovely! *(Fingering the lace.)* It's English, I think...

NANITA: No, no!... Ireesh! Ireesh!

MADAME DE SAINTE-POULE: Yes, I'm sure you do! *(Still fingering it.)* When you get married, young lady...

DOÑA BARBARA, *to* MADAME DE SAINTE-POULE: Por favor! No for to pull like so! Eef you pull, you reep!

MADAME DE SAINTE-POULE: I beg your pardon! *(Aside.)* What business is it of hers?

DOÑA BARBARA: An eef you reep, you sew!

MADAME DE SAINTE-POULE, *ignoring her, to* BELODOR: Really, monsieur! It's too much... Too much...

DOÑA BARBARA: Ha! What for you care how moch, seelly pairson?

MADAME DE SAINTE-POULE, *angrily*: "Silly…" See here, madame… Who do you think—

BELODOR, *to* MADAME DE SAINTE-POULE: Don't mind her! It's an expression… Everyone in the soap business—

MADAME DE SAINTE-POULE: Yes… I'm sure… *(Turning her attention once again to the cashmere shawl, fingering it admiringly.)* Oh! Simply elegant… So soft… *(To* BELODOR.*)* Really, monsieur… *(Calling.)* Blanche!… Blanche, precious!… Come see…

She exits, up right.

GODEFROY, *to* BELODOR, *in a desperate whisper*: What are we going to do, papá?

DOÑA BARBARA, *picking up the basket in both hands*: Oh, sí! Ees moch preetty theen een here! *(To* GODEFROY.*)* Bot wait! You see! I breen too!… Breen moch geeft for you, Godefroy! *(Moving left with the basket, to* NANITA.*)* Ven acá, Nanita!… Ven! Ven!

BELODOR: I say… Where are you going with that?

DOÑA BARBARA: You see!… I mek for you sorpresa!

BELODOR, *aside*: Good grief! Not like the last one!

DOÑA BARBARA: Fine sorpresa for mi beauteefool Godefroy! *(As she and* NANITA *are about to leave, she stops at the door, down left, and gives* GODEFROY *a seductive little wave.)* Bye-bye, mi amor!

They exit.

GODEFROY, *gaping*: Look! They're taking it with them!… Papá…

BELODOR: I see! I see!

GODEFROY, *pointing up right*: What will *they* think? Madame and her daughter… My intended…

BELODOR, *approaching him, determined*: No!… That… That woman!… We have to find a way to get rid of her!

GODEFROY: But… Civility, papá?

BELODOR, *standing face to face*: Civility be damned!

GODEFROY, *with a grimace, backing away*: Oh!…

BELODOR, *following him*: You hear? You hear?

GODEFROY, *moving down left, covering his nose with his handkerchief*: Please, papá

BELODOR: What? What is it?

GODEFROY: You smell of garlic!

BELODOR: What?

GODEFROY: Oh, papá! You… Oh, what a wretched stench! You… You stink!

They arrive down right.

BELODOR, *furiously*: Godefroy!

MADAME DE SAINTE-POULE'S VOICE, *offstage, up right*: Come, precious…

BELODOR, *looking up right*: Ayyy!

MADAME DE SAINTE-POULE *enters, followed by* BLANCHE.

MADAME DE SAINTE-POULE: You simply won't believe your eyes… It's utterly lovely!

BLANCHE, *looking around*: Where is it, mammá?

MADAME DE SAINTE-POULE: Why, over…

BLANCHE: I don't see anything...

MADAME DE SAINTE-POULE: But... I... It... *(Pointing center.)* It was right over there... *(To BELODOR, approaching him, down left.)* I beg your pardon monsieur! Would you kindly tell me—

BELODOR, *holding her off*: No, no!... Please!... Don't come any closer!

MADAME DE SAINTE-POULE: Monsieur?

BELODOR: Keep your distance!

He moves quickly around the room, counterclockwise, trying to keep her at bay, arriving down right.

BLANCHE, *approaching him*: But monsieur... What happened to—

BELODOR, *waving her off*: You too, mademoiselle!... Stay away! Stay away!

MADAME DE SAINTE-POULE, *offended*: Really, monsieur!... *(Covering her mouth.)* Are you trying to tell us... Do we... Do we offend, monsieur?

BLANCHE, *clapping her hand to her mouth*: Oh!

BELODOR: You?... Good grief! No!... No, no, no!... Two fragrant blossoms?... A rose without thorns and a... a delicate bud?... You? Heavens, no!... *(Emphasizing.) Me*, madame!... *I* do!... That vile slime she tried to make me ingest... That... *(To himself.)* Oh! That woman!... That woman!... There has to be a way!

MADAME DE SAINTE-POULE: But that magnificent wedding basket, monsieur...

BELODOR, *moving upstage*: Don't concern yourself, madame! Just give me a moment... *(Waving her off as she approaches him.)* No, no!... Don't... Don't... *(Mumbling.)* There has to be a way... There has to...

He exits, up center. BLANCHE joins MADAME DE SAINTE-POULE upstage. At the same moment, NANITA enters, down left, with the basket.

NANITA, *to GODEFROY, who is still down right*: Moosyair! For you...

GODEFROY: Ah! There it is!

He takes it and places it on the stand, center, as NANITA exits, down left.

BLANCHE: Oh! Look, mammá!

MADAME DE SAINTE-POULE: It's about time! *(To BLANCHE.)* You have no idea, precious, what utterly lovely things... A cashmere shawl... And the most divine lace mantilla...

BLANCHE, *coming center, to GODEFROY*: Oh! Monsieur Godefroy!... You're much too kind...

GODEFROY: Not me, mademoiselle... Thank papá.

MADAME DE SAINTE-POULE, *to BLANCHE, reaching down into the basket and pulling something out*: You'll see, precious! You would think that it was embroidered by the daintiest fairy fingers! *(She keeps pulling, only to reveal a pair of man's trousers, aghast.)* What?

BLANCHE, *startled*: Mammá!

MADAME DE SAINTE-POULE: I... I never...

GODEFROY, *pulling out another pair of trousers*: Oh my! Another pair...

BLANCHE, *reaching in and pulling out a man's pipe, holding it up in disbelief*: A pipe!

MADAME DE SAINTE-POULE: What kind of ghastly joke...

GODEFROY: Who ever could have put these things...

MADAME DE SAINTE-POULE, *to* GODEFROY: Someone with a warped sense of humor, monsieur!

GODEFROY: But… But…

BLANCHE, *on the verge of tears*: I… I've never been so insulted in all my life!

GODEFROY: But mademoiselle… Madame…

BLANCHE, *thrusting the pipe into his hands*: And besides, I don't smoke!

MADAME DE SAINTE-POULE, *to* GODEFROY: All those other lovely things?… Where are they, monsieur?

GODEFROY, *not knowing which way to turn*: I don't know!… I don't know!… *(Struck by a sudden realization.)* Unless… *(Pointing down left.)* Her!… It must be…

MADAME DE SAINTE-POULE: Her?

GODEFROY: Doña Barbara!

The door, down left, opens and DOÑA BARBARA *appears, bejeweled and bedecked in finery—including the cashmere shawl and the lace mantilla—striking a dramatic pose in the doorway.*

DOÑA BARBARA: Soneone he call?

MADAME DE SAINTE-POULE, Good heavens!

BLANCHE, *dumbfounded, together*: Mammá!

GODEFROY, Ayyy!

DOÑA BARBARA *comes down center.*

GODEFROY, *aside*: I was right!

DOÑA BARBARA, *to* GODEFROY: An you, leettle one! You like weddeen geeft I breen for you? Theen fron me espoose… Mi ess-espoose…

MADAME DE SAINTE-POULE, *agog at her dress*: The cashmere…

DOÑA BARBARA: Espoose muerto…

MADAME DE SAINTE-POULE: The lace… You're wearing…

DOÑA BARBARA: Sí, sí! *(Showing off her gown.)* Preetty goon… *(Holding out her arms.)* An… An preetty brazaletes… *(Holding up her hands, turning them about.)* An reens…

MADAME DE SAINTE-POULE: Oh!

DOÑA BARBARA: Everytheen!

BLANCHE: Mammá!… Mammá!

MADAME DE SAINTE-POULE, *to* DOÑA BARBARA: How dare you, madame!

BLANCHE: Make her give them back!

MADAME DE SAINTE-POULE: Take all those off! Immediately, do you hear?

DOÑA BARBARA: You weesh I for to streep?

MADAME DE SAINTE-POULE, *approaching her, menacingly*: I… I don't care if you strip! I just want you to take off those clothes… And those… Oh! Of all the cheek… Just what do you mean parading about in my daughter's trousseau?

DOÑA BARBARA: Her torso?… What ees? What ees torso?

MADAME DE SAINTE-POULE: It's all those things that you're wearing! All those things that her fiancé… *(Pointing to* GODEFROY.*)* All those things that he—

GODEFROY, *weakly*: My father, madame… Papá…

MADAME DE SAINTE-POULE, *continuing*: All those things for her wedding!

DOÑA BARBARA, *to GODEFROY*: What she talk?... Fiancé? Fiancé?... What weddeen?

GODEFROY looks around desperately and begins edging his way upstage.

MADAME DE SAINTE-POULE, *pointing to BLANCHE*: Hers!

DOÑA BARBARA: So?... An mine? You theenk I marry maybe Napoleón?

MADAME DE SAINTE-POULE: But you're marrying Monsieur Bélodor!

BLANCHE, *to DOÑA BARBARA*: You said so yourself!

DOÑA BARBARA: Sí! Sí!... *(Pointing to GODEFROY.)* Heen! Thees Moosyair Bélodor!

MADAME DE SAINTE-POULE: Nonsense! His father!... You're marrying his father!

DOÑA BARBARA: Ha ha ha!... For why you theenk I marry old fart?

BLANCHE: What?

DOÑA BARBARA: Ha ha ha!

MADAME DE SAINTE-POULE: But... But...

GODEFROY, at the door, up right, tiptoes out, unseen, and quietly shuts the door behind him.

MADAME DE SAINTE-POULE: He told me so himself... It's all arranged...

DOÑA BARBARA: Ees fonny! Ha ha ha!... *(Categorically.)* I marry leettle one, madame!

BLANCHE: Oh! Mammá!

MADAME DE SAINTE-POULE, *to DOÑA BARBARA*: But that's impossible! *(To BLANCHE.)* She doesn't know what she's saying, precious! Tell her, Monsieur Godefroy!

DOÑA BARBARA: Sí, sí! Tell her, Godefroy!

They turn to where he had been standing.

MADAME DE SAINTE-POULE, DOÑA BARBARA, *together*: Where is he? / Where he ees?

BLANCHE: He's gone, mammá!

MADAME DE SAINTE-POULE: Gone?... But... Oh! I smell a rat! *(To DOÑA BARBARA.)* Madame...

DOÑA BARBARA: Sí?... *(Sniffing.)* I no smell...

MADAME DE SAINTE-POULE, *to BLANCHE*: If you ask me, precious... Something is very rotten in the state of Denmark!

DOÑA BARBARA: Ees maybe rat... Rat... Muerto... Rat he rot, no?

BLANCHE: Oh!

DOÑA BARBARA, *aside*: Bot een Dinamarca? *(To MADAME DE SAINTE-POULE.)* So far?... *(Aside.)* How she smell so far?

MADAME DE SAINTE-POULE: I'm beginning to suspect that someone is being made a fool of!

DOÑA BARBARA: Sí, sí!... An no een Dinamarca!... Here! Aquí!... *(To MADAME DE SAINTE-POULE.)* An ees you, señora!

MADAME DE SAINTE-POULE: Me?... You dare suggest that my daughter and I have a rival in... *(Scornfully.)* in you, madame?

DOÑA BARBARA: Een me!

MADAME DE SAINTE-POULE: Come now! Be serious!... You? *(She gives a haughty laugh.)* Ha ha ha!

DOÑA BARBARA, *angrily*: An for why ees no so? Een Sevilla ees old mi familia! Ees to Rone we go back! To Rone!

MADAME DE SAINTE-POULE: To Rome?… Well… *(Waving her away.)* Please! Don't stand on ceremony! Go back any time you like! Monsieur Godefroy loves my daughter, and that's that!

BLANCHE, *dubiously*: Does he, mammá?

DOÑA BARBARA: You daughter!… Ha ha ha! *(Pointing to* BLANCHE.*)* Thees?… Ees fonny!… Ha ha ha!… Thees peegeon?

BLANCHE: Oh!

MADAME DE SAINTE-POULE: I beg your pardon, madame!

DOÑA BARBARA: Beside, you no see lettair hees papá he sen to me…

BLANCHE: What?

MADAME DE SAINTE-POULE: What letter?

DOÑA BARBARA: Fron lass month… Lettair who tell to me how leettle one he bourn weeth flem… *(The two women look at each other quizzically.)* Weeth lost! Bourneen hot, weeth flem! Weeth pasión!

BLANCHE: Mammá!

MADAME DE SAINTE-POULE: Burning with passion? Monsieur Godefroy?

DOÑA BARBARA: Weeth hot flem of love…

BLANCHE: Oh, mammá! Please! Take me home!… This instant!

MADAME DE SAINTE-POULE: Indeed I will!… I'll not let us be made fools of another minute! *(To* DOÑA BARBARA.*)* Madame, we're returning to Dunkirk!

DOÑA BARBARA: Ah, jes! Dungcork… Always Dungcork… Sí, sí! Buen viaje!… Bon voyage! Bon voyage!

MADAME DE SAINTE-POULE: You may tell Monsieur Bélodor… *(Emphasizing.)* *Messieurs* Bélodor… that they have seen the last of us! *(To* BLANCHE.*)* Come, precious!

MADAME DE SAINTE-POULE and BLANCHE turn on their heels and exit, up right.

DOÑA BARBARA, *alone*: What she theenk? She theenk she take fron me Godefroy? Ha ha ha!… Ees mine! I kip!

ANTOINE enters hurriedly, up center.

ANTOINE: Madame!… Madame!

DOÑA BARBARA: Sí!… What ees? What ees, Antonio? For why you ron een so?

ANTOINE: A man, madame… With a sailor's cap… *(Pointing up center.)* Out there!

DOÑA BARBARA: Cómo?

ANTOINE: He says he doesn't know you… *(Correcting.)* He doesn't know, madame, I mean… And he says madame doesn't know him… But that he has to tell you something… Her… To tell her…

DOÑA BARBARA: Un marinero?

ANTOINE: Something very important…

DOÑA BARBARA: Who can be?

The door, up center, opens and BELODOR appears in the doorway. He is heavily disguised, with thick black side whiskers, a drooping mustache, big gold earrings, and a sailor's cap. His right arm is tucked into his shirt, making it appear to be missing.

BELODOR, *aside*: Perfectly convincing, if I do say so myself...

He removes his cap.

DOÑA BARBARA: Ay! Caramba!

BELODOR, *to* ANTOINE, *waving him off*: Avast, drudge!

ANTOINE: Monsieur?

BELODOR: Go lower the fo'c's'le, lad, and batten down the hatches! *(Aside.)* Or something to that effect...

ANTOINE *gives him a puzzled look.*

DOÑA BARBARA, *to* ANTOINE: So? For why you wait? Go... Go, Antonio!

ANTOINE: Very good, madame. If you're sure... *(Correcting, as* BELODOR *gives him a stern look .)* If madame is sure, I mean...

He exits, up center.

BELODOR, *to himself*: Now to dispatch her forthwith to Seville!

DOÑA BARBARA: So, moosyair! What ees? What ees?

BELODOR: Madame... I've just come half way around the world... Traversed the globe, so to speak...

DOÑA BARBARA: Oh! Ees beeg treep!... You tire... *(Offering him a chair.)* Por favor! You seet!

BELODOR: No, thank you. I'm not fatigued, I assure you.

DOÑA BARBARA: So! Now you here...

BELODOR *pauses, summoning up his nerve.*

BELODOR: Madame... You see before you the last pathetic vestige... The last relic of a noble sailing vessel... *La Doña Barbara,* madame...

DOÑA BARBARA: Ayyy! Dios mío!... Hees boat!...

BELODOR, *pretending to repress a sob*: Quite...

DOÑA BARBARA: Mi espoose!... Hees boat!... You...? You know mi espoose?

BELODOR: Please, madame!... It's too painful...

DOÑA BARBARA: Bot you tell to me...

BELODOR, *shaking his head, sadly*: Eaten alive...

DOÑA BARBARA, *nodding*: Sí... Sí...

BELODOR: And on a Friday, madame!... At least, if they were good Catholics, they would have waited a day. But—

DOÑA BARBARA: Mi pobre esposo!... I tell to heen, "You no go on Friday... An ees Friday thurteen! You wait, you wait..." Bot he no leesten! Ees stobborn mole... *(Correcting.)* Was...

BELODOR: Mule...

DOÑA BARBARA: Mule...

BELODOR: Tsk tsk tsk!

DOÑA BARBARA, *after a moment of tearful silence*: Bot he theenk of me, moosyair?

BELODOR: Oh, yes, madame! I should say!... To the very last bite!

DOÑA BARBARA, *wiping her eyes*: Ay!... Mi sweat-heart!... Pobrecito!

BELODOR: He used to say I was his right arm, madame.

DOÑA BARBARA, *dubiously*: Oh?... How can be?

BELODOR, *understanding*: That is... I was... Until they got to me too...

DOÑA BARBARA: Ah, sí…

BELODOR: Just a beginning, mind you… An appetizer, so to speak… But, lucky for me, an enemy tribe attacked, and… and in the confusion I was able to escape and… and save what was left!

DOÑA BARBARA: An mi espoose, moosyair?

BELODOR: He made me promise to bring you his dying wish.

DOÑA BARBARA: Ah, sí! Ah, sí!… An I promeese I obey!… On hees ashes, moosyair!

BELODOR: On his…

DOÑA BARBARA: Sí! I swear on hees ashes!

BELODOR: Well, they might be hard to find, but the intention—

DOÑA BARBARA: So! Geeve to me pappér.

BELODOR, *misunderstanding*: Pepper, madame?

DOÑA BARBARA: Pappér!… *Papel!…* Weeth writeen… Weeth words what he say…

BELODOR, *aside*: Damnation! *(Aloud.)* Paper?… I… I'm afraid they have no paper. They write on tree bark. And they won't let it leave the country…

DOÑA BARBARA: Ah, sí!… So! You tell to me what he say, mi espoose! Tell to me hees weesh!

BELODOR: Yes… Quite… "Strombolino," he said… That's my name, madame… Giovanni Strombolino… "Go back to Seville and find my Doña Barbara… My sweet, darling wife… Wherever she may be…

DOÑA BARBARA: Ayyy!

BELODOR, *continuing, dramatically*: "And if my memory yet lives in her breast…"

DOÑA BARBARA: Oh! Sí!… Sí!… *(Feeling her bosom.)* Eet leeve! Eet leeve!

BELODOR, *continuing*: "…then tell her she must never, never marry another, no matter what betides!"

DOÑA BARBARA: Cómo?

BELODOR: Never!… That's what he said… With his dying breath, madame…

DOÑA BARBARA: Ay! Dios mío!… Thees ees what he say?

BELODOR: As they took their last bite…

DOÑA BARBARA: Ay! Caramba!… Qué hacer? Qué hacer?… What to do, Estrombobo?

BELODOR, *correcting*: Strombolino…

DOÑA BARBARA: Ees terreeble, thees theen!

BELODOR: Be brave, madame… For him…

DOÑA BARBARA: Bot ees no for me I fil thees way! Ees for mi Godefroy… Thees weell keell heen, pobrecito!

BELODOR, *casually*: Oh well…

DOÑA BARBARA: No tell to me "oh well"! You no know mi Godefroy!

BELODOR: Just remember, madame… You swore on your husband's ashes…

DOÑA BARBARA: Ah! For why los canibales they no eat you too! For why they stop weeth arm only?

BELODOR: Me?

DOÑA BARBARA: Sí, sí! Then I no know!… No know!…

BELODOR: "No know"?

DOÑA BARBARA: No!… No know thees weesh of mi espoose, moosyair!… Eef I no know, I no have problen… I marry Godefroy!… Ay! Caramba! Los canibales!… For why they no eat you too? For why?

BELODOR: You really are much too kind!

DOÑA BARBARA: Gracias!… So, what to do? What to do? *(Striking a pose in her elegant attire.)* Weeth all thees preetty theen! Thees… Thees torso he geeve to me!

BELODOR: This…?

DOÑA BARBARA: How for to tell heen?… Soch moch love he have for me… How for to geeve news?

BELODOR: You could write him a letter, madame.

DOÑA BARBARA: Sí, sí!…

BELODOR: It would soften the blow.

DOÑA BARBARA: Ay!… Weell no be easy…. Bot moss do… Moss do…

BELODOR, *aside, with a sigh of relief*: Thank heavens!… *(Aloud, pointing to the desk, left.)* There!… Paper… A pen…

Before she can sit down at the desk, GODEFROY *enters, up right, disguised much like* BELODOR, *but pretending to lack his left arm. He is obviously a little tipsy.*

GODEFROY, *calling offstage*: Lower the mizzen! I'm coming about!… Three sheets to the wind!… *(Looking around.)* Where is she?

BELODOR, *with a start, aside*,	*together*:	Who the devil…?
DOÑA BARBARA,		Now who?

BELODOR *quickly curls up on the high-backed chair, left, hiding from view.*

GODEFROY, *aside*: Those dozen gulps of absinthe should help! *(Aloud.)* Lower the boom and splice the mainbrace!… Doña Barbara?… Where is she?

DOÑA BARBARA, *joining him, center*: Ees me, capitán!… Horself… Een flush!

GODEFROY: Ha!… So…

DOÑA BARBARA: For why you weesh?

GODEFROY, *cap in hand*: You see before you the last pathetic vestige… The last relic of a noble sailing vessel… *La Doña Barbara*, madame…

BELODOR, *aside*: Ayyy!

DOÑA BARBARA: Moosyair? *(Aside.)* Ees two patheteec vesteege? Two lass releec?

GODEFROY, *aside*: So far, so good… *(Aloud.)* Sliver my tim… Shiver…

BELODOR, *aside*: Good grief! A real one!

GODEFROY: Shiver my slim… *(To himself.)* Whatever… *(To* DOÑA BARBARA.*)* I come to bring you the last dying wish of your husband, madame.

DOÑA BARBARA: Ah! Sí, sí!… I know… No need…

GODEFROY: He wants you to be sure to take another mate… To marry again…

DOÑA BARBARA,	*together*:	Hoo-hah!… What you say?
BELODOR, *aside*,		Ayyy!… Good grief!

GODEFROY: Your concierge, madame… He says you should marry your concierge, without delay…

DOÑA BARBARA: Concierge?… Een Sevilla?

GODEFROY: Yes! The very one!

DOÑA BARBARA: Bot… He have wife, an… an sex cheeldren!

GODEFROY, *aside*: Oh!

DOÑA BARBARA, *aside*: Ha! *(Pointing left.)* Thees one he tell me no, an… *(Pointing to GODEFROY.)* Theees one he tell me jes! *(Suspiciously.)* Ees moch curioso, thees! *(To GODEFROY.)* Moosyair… *(Pointing left.)* You know heen, no?

GODEFROY: "Heen," madame?… "Hoon"?

She goes to the chair where BELODOR is huddling, drags it center, and turns it toward him.

DOÑA BARBARA: Sí, here!… You work together, no?… Sane boat!

GODEFROY, *surprised, aside*: Good God! A real one?

DOÑA BARBARA, *to BELODOR, pointing to GODEFROY*: An you know heen, moosyair! You two ees good frien, no?

BELODOR, *embarrassed*: Why… Sí!… Of course… Good friend… Same boat…

DOÑA BARBARA: Bot you no talk! For why ees you no talk?

BELODOR, *getting up, to GODEFROY, stammering*: A-A-Ahoy, mate…

GODEFROY, *stammering*: A-A-Ahoy…

BELODOR: L-L-Lower the fo'c's'le!

GODEFROY: Sh-Sh-Shiver my slivers…

BELODOR *and* **GODEFROY**, *aside, together:* Ayyy!

DOÑA BARBARA, *aside*: I theenk marineros they weesh to mek fon!

BELODOR: Excuse me, but… I've got to be weighing anchor…

GODEFROY: Me too… Coming about…

DOÑA BARBARA: Oh?

GODEFROY: All hands on deck…

He and BELODOR hurry up center, obviously eager to escape.

DOÑA BARBARA, *stopping them*: Momento, señores!… Stop!… Pliz to see you saileen pappérs, por favor!

GODEFROY, *at a loss*: Papers?

BELODOR: My papers?… *(Taking from his pocket the letter he received earlier, holding it up.)* I'm afraid this is all I was able to salvage…

DOÑA BARBARA: Oh?

BELODOR: When the boat went down, madame… Just the clothes on my back… But—

He goes to put it back in his pocket.

DOÑA BARBARA, *grabbing it out of his hand*: Geeve to me, marinero! *(She squints at the letter, holding it at arm's length, trying unsuccessfully to read it, finally calling down left.)* Nanita!… Ven acá! Ven acá!

NANITA enters, down left.

NANITA: Sí, señora?

DOÑA BARBARA, *handing her the letter*: Here! You rid!

NANITA: Señora?

DOÑA BARBARA: I no see… You see?

NANITA: Sí, sí! I see… I see…*(Giggling.)* Hee hee hee!… *(Scanning the letter quickly.)* "…parfoon… moss expenseeve… leettle woman… celebrate… becose

I… I…" *(Suddenly.)* Oh!… Ay ay ay!… No ees posseeble! Señora!… Ay, Dios! No ees posseeble!

DOÑA BARBARA: What no ees, Nanita?... What ees? What ees?

NANITA: Ees… Ees el capitán, señora!… Su esposo!… Señor… Ees leeveen! Ees no muerto!… Ees—

DOÑA BARBARA: Cómo?

NANITA, *waving the letter:* Los canibales… Los canibales, señora… They no eat!

BELODOR *and* **GODEFROY,** *repeating, together:* "They no eat"?

NANITA: Ees waiteen for you een Marseille, señora…

DOÑA BARBARA, *almost collapsing into her arms:* Ayyy! Nanita! Es verdad?… Ees true?

GODEFROY, *aside:* Can it be?

DOÑA BARBARA: Ees true?

NANITA: Sí, sí, señora!… *(Waving the letter.)* Look! Ees what he say…

DOÑA BARBARA, *taking the letter and kissing it:* Ay! Madre de Dios!… Ees leeveen! Ees leeveen, mi espoose!… Ees no be eat!

BELODOR: And you're no longer a widow, madame! *(Aside.)* Thank God! We're saved!

He and GODEFROY *both run up center, to the door, calling out.*

GODEFROY,	*together, taking off their mustaches:*	Papá!… Papá!
BELODOR,		Godefroy!… Godefroy!…

GODEFROY *and* **BELODOR,** *each turning and suddenly recognizing the other:* What?… You?… I don't believe…

DOÑA BARBARA, *recognizing them:* Ho ho!… Marineros!… So! Ees what I theenk! You for to tell beeg… beeg… *(To* NANITA.*)* Cómo se dice "mentiras," Nanita?

NANITA: "Hoodfalse," señora…

DOÑA BARBARA, *to* GODEFROY *and* BELODOR: Sí!… You try to pooll leg! Ha ha!… So!… *(Sitting in the armchair, down right, and holding out her legs.)* Here! Now you pooll good!

Before they can react, MADAME DE SAINTE-POULE *enters, up right, in a huff, followed by* BLANCHE.

MADAME DE SAINTE-POULE, *to* DOÑA BARBARA: He's all yours, madame! We're leaving! *(To* BLANCHE.*)* Come, precious…

GODEFROY,	*together:*	No! You mustn't…
BELODOR,		Please, lovely lady…

MADAME DE SAINTE-POULE,	*together:*	Who in the name of…
BLANCHE, *frightened,*		Oh! Mammá!

BELODOR: Don't you know us?

DOÑA BARBARA, *jumping up, pointing:* Ees Godefroy!

MADAME DE SAINTE-POULE *and* **BLANCHE,** *together:* Oh my!

DOÑA BARBARA, *to* BLANCHE: You take heen now, señorita! *(To* MADAME DE SAINTE-POULE.*)* I fine again mi espoose! *(Ecstatically.)* He no be eat! He no be eet!

MADAME DE SAINTE-POULE: Her what?

DOÑA BARBARA: He no be eat!

BLANCHE: Oh! I don't want him, mammá! Look! He has no arm…

BELODOR: It will grow back, mademoiselle! You have my word… *(To* GODEFROY.*)* Show her, son…

He holds up his arm.

BLANCHE: Oh!… He has one! He does have one, mammá!

GODEFROY: Of course I do, mademoiselle… *(Taking her hand.)* What ever did you think?

BLANCHE, *simply*: And… And a very nice one too…

BELODOR, *to* MADAME DE SAINTE-POULE: And so do I…

He reveals his hidden arm.

MADAME DE SAINTE-POULE: But… *(Pointing to his and* GODEFROY*'s disguises.)* Why all this?… Why this mascarade?

DOÑA BARBARA: Sí, sí! For why all thees?

BELODOR, *to* GODEFROY: Why?

GODEFROY, *to* BELODOR: Why?

BELODOR, *hesitating*: Well… When we thought that madame's husband was devoured by the cannibals…

GODEFROY, *together*: When we thought that madame's husband was devoured by the cannibals…
BELODOR, *together*: We thought that a visit from his shipmates might console her…

DOÑA BARBARA: I no onderstan…

GODEFROY: It's really very simple…

GODEFROY, *together*: We thought that a visit from his shipmates might console her…
BELODOR, *together*: When we thought he had been eaten alive, madame…

DOÑA BARBARA: Steell I no onderstan!

BELODOR: Really…

DOÑA BARBARA, *to* GODEFROY: Bot no mattair, leettle one! Ees no problen! You be ogly marinero!

GODEFROY: Madame?

DOÑA BARBARA: Mi espoose he ees more preetty!

GODEFROY: Oh well…

NANITA, *holding up her hand*: Ees so beeg!… Like so!… I know… I measure…

DOÑA BARBARA: Sí, sí, Nanita! Eef canibales no eat!

GODEFROY and BELODOR force a little laugh.

MADAME DE SAINTE-POULE, *to* BLANCHE, *pointing to* BELODOR: Actually, monsieur is rather fetching as a sailor!

She approaches him and looks him up and down, approvingly.

DOÑA BARBARA, *to* NANITA: What mean thees, Nanita? Thees "fetcheen"? What mean…

NANITA: "Guapo," señora… *(With a wink in* BELODOR*'s direction)* Beauteefool, señor…

BELODOR, *modestly*: Well… Really, I….

He mumbles a few indistinguishable objections

NANITA: Wait, señor… I go measure… Hee hee hee!…

DOÑA BARBARA, *laughing along with her*: Sí, sí!… Sí, sí!…

As BELODOR *stands mumbling,* BLANCHE *joins* GODEFROY*, smiling coyly, as they all join in the laughter, which continues as the curtain falls.*

CURTAIN.

Smotherly Love: a Passion Play

(Le premier pas, 1862)

Eugène Labiche & Alfred Delacour

Characters

MAURICE DÉSARNAUX, an intelligent but cynical nineteen-year-old

BADINIER, a well-meaning but rather tactless neighbor

DOCTOR VOUZON, an old friend of the Désarnaux family, with solid bourgeois values

JEAN, a domestic

MADAME DÉSARNAUX, Maurice's obsessively doting mother

CÉLINE, Madame's niece, as unselfish as she is lovely

LILI, Badinier's high-spirited and somewhat flighty wife

A middle-class drawing room. In the upstage center wall, a double door opening onto a vestibule. Doors up and down left; the former, in an angled corner, leading to Madame Désarnaux's room, the latter to her son Maurice's. Between the two doors, close to the wall, a table with writing paraphernalia and a bell. Up right, the door to the rest of the apartment. Down right , a fireplace with a mirror on the wall above it. Right center, a loveseat; left center, an armchair. Other appropriate furnishings.

At rise, CELINE *is seated in the armchair, embroidering. After a moment,* MADAME DESARNAUX *enters, up left, as* JEAN *enters, up center, out of breath.*

MADAME DESARNAUX, *to* JEAN, *joining him, up center*: Ah! There you are, Jean! Have you been to the doctor's?

JEAN: Yes, madame. Up six floors… And down six floors too…

MADAME DESARNAUX, *impatiently*: Yes… And was he at home?

JEAN: Yes, madame. He was just coming in.

MADAME DESARNAUX: And you asked him to hurry?

JEAN: He said he would be here as soon as he finished off one rheumatism and two bronchitises.

CELINE, *smiling, to* JEAN: "Up"… Finished "up," I think…

JEAN: Whatever…

MADAME DESARNAUX, *to* JEAN: Good… Good…

JEAN: Excuse me, madame, but… Is somebody sick?

MADAME DESARNAUX, *coming down right*: Come now, Jean! Do you have to ask?… My son… Monsieur Maurice, poor dear…

JEAN: No!… With what, madame? His liver?

MADAME DESARNAUX: If I only knew! That's just the trouble! For days now he simply hasn't been himself. And he's thin as a *railing*… Surely you've noticed…

JEAN: Well…

CELINE, *putting down her embroidery*: I have, auntie dear…

JEAN, *aside*: Not really…

MADAME DESARNAUX: And I'm as worried as can be!

CELINE: Me too, auntie…

JEAN, *aside*: Him? Sick?

MADAME DESARNAUX: I know… I know what your cousin means to you, my child. Such a dear… And a heart of gold…

CELINE: Thank you, auntie.

MADAME DESARNAUX: What?… No… I mean Maurice…

CELINE: Oh…

MADAME DESARNAUX: An absolute angel…

CELINE: Why, I don't know what I'll do if he's ill! I simply don't…

MADAME DESARNAUX: Oh! Believe me! I won't leave his side! Day and night…

CELINE: And I won't leave yours, auntie dear!

MADAME DESARNAUX: Sweet child! You couldn't be more devoted!

The doorbell rings.

JEAN: The bell, madame… That must be the doctor.

MADAME DESARNAUX: Please… Go tell Monsieur Maurice… (*To* CELINE.) And you, Céline… Best leave us alone. I'll tell you what the doctor says.

CELINE, *getting up*: Oh yes, auntie dear! I'll be on tenterhooks until I know! I really will…

JEAN, *aside*: Tender hooks?

He exits, down left, scratching his head, as CELINE *exits, up right.*

MADAME DESARNAUX, *to herself, watching* CELINE *leave*: Tsk tsk tsk! Poor dear… (*As* VOUZON *enters, up center.*) Ah! Doctor… (*Joining him, upstage.*) Thank heaven you've come…

VOUZON, *laying his hat and medical bag on the table, left, and coming downstage*: As fast as my old legs would carry me!… Now then, what's this I hear? Someone is ill… (*Jovially.*) And without my permission?

MADAME DESARNAUX, *following him*: I'm afraid so…

VOUZON: Certainly not you, Marguerite! You look the very picture of health!

MADAME DESARNAUX: No, no, doctor… Maurice… For a month now it's clear that something is terribly wrong! He seems so sad, so out of sorts. Always miles away, if you know what I mean…

VOUZON, *nodding*: Aha…

MADAME DESARNAUX: Do you think it could be serious?

VOUZON: Well, we'll see. We'll have a look.

MADAME DESARNAUX: He scarcely nibbles at his food. And he seems so preoccupied. Always sad, always sighing…

VOUZON: Oh? Sighing, you say?

MADAME DESARNAUX: Yes… And for no good reason…

VOUZON: Perhaps…

MADAME DESARNAUX: And I don't think he sleeps a wink. Really, I can hear him pacing half the night. And sometimes, when I go to tuck him in, if he's not pacing, he's sitting up writing. And talking to himself! Out loud, of all things! And with a look on his face… Oh! A look full of fire…

VOUZON, *nodding sagely*: I see… I see…

MADAME DESARNAUX: I think the poor child is feverish!

VOUZON: No doubt!

MADAME DESARNAUX: Oh? Do you think it's his liver?

VOUZON, *ignoring the question*: Tell me, how old is he now? Seventeen? Eighteen?

MADAME DESARNAUX: Nineteen…

VOUZON: Aha… Well… In that case, there's no point in examining him, I'm afraid.

MADAME DESARNAUX, *alarmed*: You mean… It's that bad?

VOUZON: Not at all! In fact, I'm sure that it's nothing to worry about.

MADAME DESARNAUX: But… How can you be so sure? He doesn't eat, I'm telling you…

VOUZON, *nodding*: I know… I know…

MADAME DESARNAUX: And he talks to himself… Out loud!

VOUZON: No doubt…

MADAME DESARNAUX: Aren't those symptoms of something?

VOUZON: Indeed…

MADAME DESARNAUX: But of what? What is it?

VOUZON: Do you really want me to tell you?

MADAME DESARNAUX: Of course! How can we cure him? Please…

VOUZON, *tapping his chest*: Heartache… A classic case…

MADAME DESARNAUX, *shocked, sitting down in the armchair, left*: Oh! (*Fanning her face.*) God in heaven!… An *aneurhythm*, doctor? At his age? But how—

VOUZON, *calming her*: Now, now… Nothing of the sort!… "Heartache," I said… The young man is in love. It's as simple as that.

MADAME DESARNAUX, *jumping up, almost threateningly*: What? In love? My son?… That's absurd! He can't be!… He couldn't…

VOUZON, *trying to calm her*: Please, Marguerite… No need to get excited…

MADAME DESARNAUX, *gesticulating*: Oh? You insult my child, but I mustn't get excited?

VOUZON: Insult him? Good grief, I hardly think—

MADAME DESARNAUX, *interrupting*: He wouldn't do that to me! He wouldn't, I tell you!

VOUZON: But my dear friend… It's the way of the world! It's what every young man is supposed to do when he's nineteen years old!

MADAME DESARNAUX: Nonsense! Not my Maurice…

VOUZON: It's life! It's nature!… Come… (*Motioning to the loveseat, taking her hand.*) Sit down. I'll explain it…

MADAME DESARNAUX, *resisting, stiffly*: You needn't bother!

VOUZON, *as they sit down*: There are three stages in a young man's life. The first is when he's a baby… That delightful little bundle that lets you hold him in your arms… And cuddle him, and coddle him…. A bundle of joy…

MADAME DESARNAUX, *sentimentally*: Oh…

VOUZON: That's the honeymoon for you mothers! And you try to make it last and last, until he gets so heavy that you almost break your back. So you put him down, and… and suddenly he's not all yours anymore. His little legs dream of running here and there… Wherever he wants… With you always chasing him, never far behind…

MADAME DESARNAUX: Never…

VOUZON: Then the baby gives way to the mischievous little imp… The precious little devil who rules the roost, whose every wish is your command… And you stuff him with sweets, like a little pet poodle… And nothing is safe. He smashes your best china, goes climbing on the furniture, puts his hand in the fire, falls into the water…

MADAME DESARNAUX: Oh! How well I know…

VOUZON: So you lock him in his room, and five minutes later you find him in the cherry tree…

MADAME DESARNAUX: A maple…

VOUZON: …clambering to the top…

MADAME DESARNAUX: And tearing his clothes…

VOUZON, *nodding*: To shreds! Of course… But all he has to do is say one word… "Mammá"… And you forgive him! Because that's still what he calls you… "Mammá"…

MADAME DESARNAUX, *turning aside, in a whisper*: Mammá…

VOUZON, *getting up*: But it doesn't take long for the youngster to change. Soon he gets that faraway look. He takes care of his clothes. He combs his hair neatly... And all of a sudden you become "mother dear" when anyone is close enough to hear...

MADAME DESARNAUX: Oh...

VOUZON: And that's when the trouble begins. The third stage... The young man's turn... He seems preoccupied... He sighs... He wonders what makes the turtledoves coo...

MADAME DESARNAUX, *jumping up*: But Maurice never asked me anything of the kind! Besides, he can't stand birds!

VOUZON, *continuing*: Sometimes he writes poems. Not very good ones!

MADAME DESARNAUX: But he doesn't!

VOUZON: Well, he will, mark my words... And he's sad, and out of sorts... (*Echoing her previous words.*) "Always miles away, if you know what I mean..." It's what they sing about in songs... We medical men call it his "adolescence," Marguerite... (*Aside.*) A little late, but I'm not surprised...

MADAME DESARNAUX: Oh...

VOUZON, *aside, continuing*: And better late than never! (*Aloud.*) Yes, the critical moment in a young man's life...

MADAME DESARNAUX: But... But my Maurice is never critical... He never criticizes me... Or his cousin... Or anyone! Not even Jean!

VOUZON: No...

MADAME DESARNAUX, *continuing*: He's as sweet and agreeable as anyone could be!

VOUZON: A man would know what I mean, my friend. A man would understand...

MADAME DESARNAUX: I understand perfectly! But you're wrong, I tell you! My son is a... a good boy! He would never...

VOUZON: I don't deny it! But I was a good boy too, and I went through it...

MADAME DESARNAUX: You?... Perhaps you did. But not my Maurice! You weren't raised the way he was! With the love, the attention... With the tenderness...

VOUZON: No... I daresay...

MADAME DESARNAUX: Why, for nineteen years he hasn't been out of my sight. Not for an hour... Not for a minute!... When my poor Philippe died, I knew I was going to have to raise him by myself. Nothing else mattered. Only my Maurice...

VOUZON: I'm sure...

MADAME DESARNAUX: I found a tutor for him. A fine, upstanding family man... Married, with children... And I took him to his lessons myself, and I brought him home when they were through.

VOUZON: Admirable...

MADAME DESARNAUX: At night, I would listen to him recite his lessons... In Greek! Because I learned it just for him!

VOUZON: My compliments...

MADAME DESARNAUX: And it wasn't easy, I assure you!

VOUZON: No... Greek never is...

MADAME DESARNAUX: Later, when he finished, he wanted to study law. But I put my foot down! Not with all those things I had heard… Disturbing things… About students and… and the life they lead…

VOUZON: I see…

MADAME DESARNAUX: So I found him a position with a broker. A dear friend of Philippe's, God rest his soul… He took him under his wing, and he put him to work in a special office, between two mature clerks. One was fifty-eight and the other was sixty-two… Married men, with the highest of principles… And… And…

VOUZON, *interrupting, gently losing patience*: Needless to say, you left no stone unturned! You thought of everything, Marguerite. But when the time comes… When the hour strikes… It's like whooping cough, I'm afraid. Sooner or later, they're all going to catch it!

MADAME DESARNAUX, *misunderstanding*: But he never did!… Mumps, once… And measles… But—

VOUZON: Figuratively, dear friend!… What they catch is a… a passion… A consuming passion for a sweet young thing…

MADAME DESARNAUX: Oh!

VOUZON, *continuing*: A sweet young thing of the… If you'll pardon the expression… Of the opposite sex!

MADAME DESARNAUX, *crossing down left, in front of him, scandalized*: Impossible! (*Pointing at MAURICE's door.*) He… My… No! Not my Maurice! It can't be! (*Crossing herself.*) A woman…? Some… Some absolute stranger?

VOUZON: Well… Only at the beginning…

MADAME DESARNAUX: You're telling me that some… some tart wants to come and steal my child away? Snatch him out of my arms?

VOUZON, *with a touch of sarcasm*: Ah yes… It's a frightful thought, I know. To see that little angel… that cherub that you raised to be yours and yours alone, suddenly open his heart to another…

MADAME DESARNAUX: Oh!

VOUZON: Frightful!… Frightful!

MADAME DESARNAUX: Never!… He wouldn't…

VOUZON: Well, want to or not, I'm afraid he has no choice! Nature makes her demands…

MADAME DESARNAUX, *approaching him, right, almost angrily*: Nature?… Nature wants a young man to love his mother! That's what nature wants! (*As the door, down left, opens.*) And I know that my Maurice—

VOUZON: Shhh!

> *As he indicates with a tilt of the head that someone is coming, JEAN enters, carrying a frock coat.*

JEAN, *to MADAME DESARNAUX*: Monsieur Maurice says to tell madame that he'll be right in…

MADAME DESARNAUX: Thank you, Jean.

JEAN, *holding up the coat, continuing*: …and that he's missing a button…

MADAME DESARNAUX, *taking it*: Give it here…

JEAN: …and that he needs it so he can go out this afternoon. That's what he said I should tell madame.

MADAME DESARNAUX: Yes, Jean. I'll see to it… (*She goes through the pockets, mechanically, and takes out a slip of paper.*) What… (*Reading it.*) Oh my! It… It's a… a…

VOUZON: A poem?

MADAME DESARNAUX: Why, yes… How did you…

VOUZON: You see? What did I tell you?

MADAME DESARNAUX: Perhaps it's for me!

VOUZON, *laughing*: Oh? I hardly think so!

MADAME DESARNAUX, *reading*:

"A timid virgin's kiss, tender as spring…"

VOUZON, *slyly*: You see?

MADAME DESARNAUX, *continuing*:

"The brilliant butterfly, whose flitting wing…"

Oh my! What ever can it be?

VOUZON: The critical moment, Marguerite! Adolescence…

MAURICE enters, down left.

JEAN, *aside*: I think monsieur is becoming a man! (*Aloud, to MADAME DESARNAUX.*) If madame won't be needing me…

She waves him off, hiding the paper in her bosom, as he exits, up center.

MADAME DESARNAUX: Ah! Doctor…

VOUZON, *to MAURICE*: There you are, young man!

MAURICE: I hope you'll excuse me for keeping you waiting.

VOUZON: Not at all… Not at all… Mammá and I were just chatting about you.

MAURICE, *to MADAME DESARNAUX, nodding*: Aha… Mother dear…

VOUZON, *to MADAME DESARNAUX, in a whisper*: "Mother dear"… You hear?

MADAME DESARNAUX, *crossing left, in front of him*: Maurice, precious… Is something wrong?

MAURICE: Wrong, mother?

MADAME DESARNAUX: You always call me "mammá." Is something… Is something bothering you?

MAURICE: Goodness, no! It's just that I'm too old for that now! (*Whispering to her.*) Not when there are people… Please…

MADAME DESARNAUX: Oh… (*Whispering*) People or not… (*Aloud.*) But you still love your "mammá," don't you?

MAURICE: Of course!

MADAME DESARNAUX: And nobody else?… In the whole wide world?… (*Beginning to shed a few tears.*) Because, if you did… (*Confused.*) If you didn't, I mean… If anyone else… (*Wiping her eyes.*) I simply don't know what I would do, treasure…

MAURICE: Mother dear! What is it?

MADAME DESARNAUX: Nothing… It's nothing… (*Controlling herself.*) I… I just wanted to tell you that the doctor would like to speak with you.

MAURICE: With me?

MADAME DESARNAUX: In private…

MAURICE, *aside*: Am I sick?

MADAME DESARNAUX: I'll leave you two alone… (*Moving up left, stopping at the door.*) Just… Please… Tell him everything. No secrets! You can trust him. He's a dear, dear friend. (*Returning to MAURICE, hugging him effusively.*) Oh! Poor thing… Poor thing…

MAURICE, *surprised*: Again?… But what is it? What's the matter?

MADAME DESARNAUX, *returning up left, wiping her eyes*: Nothing, treasure… Nothing…

MAURICE, *following her*: Tell me, mammá…

MADAME DESARNAUX, *at the door, hugging him*: Oh! (*To VOUZON.*) You hear? He said… He said… (*To MAURICE, pointing to VOUZON.*) Everything, precious! Tell him everything…

She exits, leaving the door open.

VOUZON, *to MAURICE, inviting him to sit down in the armchair, as he sits on the loveseat*: Well now, you rascal… Shall we chat? Just the two of us?

MAURICE, *bemused*: With pleasure, doctor… (*Aside.*) What about? The weather?

VOUZON, *with a comical sigh*: Ah!… Beautiful, isn't she?

MAURICE: Who?… My mother?

VOUZON: Ha ha ha!… Come now! You can't fool a sly old fox like me!

MAURICE: But…

VOUZON: Your angel! The one with the blue eyes… Or brown… Or gray… You can't pull the wool over mine, young man! We doctors—

MAURICE: Excuse me, monsieur, but… Whose eyes? What angel?

VOUZON: The one you're in love with! There's no use denying—

MAURICE: Me?

VOUZON, *wagging his forefinger*: Tsk tsk tsk!… And it's only right you should be! Nature didn't give you a heart to keep it hidden in your pocket!

MAURICE: I'm sorry, doctor, but… Despite all your science, I'm afraid you're quite mistaken!

VOUZON: Nonsense!

MAURICE: Me? In love?… But that's preposterous! I wouldn't waste my time on such foolishness!

VOUZON: Such…

MAURICE: I'm young… I have my position to think about…

VOUZON: Your position?

MAURICE, *gesturing up left*: My mother, doctor…

VOUZON, *nodding*: Yes… Mammá…

MAURICE, *ignoring him, continuing*: Please keep in mind that her assets are very limited. A yearly income of some twenty thousand francs… Hardly sufficient, I'm afraid…

VOUZON: Oh? What does her yearly income have to do with it?

MAURICE: What does her… Indeed! Times have changed since you were my age, doctor! It was all well and good for you to play the sentimental troubadour… Crooning your serenades under the balconies of the tender young demoiselles…

VOUZON: True! And I'm happy to tell you—

MAURICE: In all kinds of weather… Without an umbrella!

VOUZON: And a delight it was! Believe me…

MAURICE: Then I take it, doctor, that you loved a lot, and sighed a lot…

VOUZON: Ah! I should say… (*Smiling.*) And got very wet…

MAURICE: Tell me… What's left of all that love? All those sighs? What do you have to show for them today?

VOUZON: My memories, young man…

MAURICE: And rheumatism, most likely!… But you see, I prefer to keep my health. I'm not one of your romantic young souls. I let the poets do all the singing, and I… I dream of making money! It's as simple as that!

VOUZON: Money? You love money, at your age?

MAURICE: It's not the money itself I love… But I must say, I do have a weakness for fine cigars! And when I go riding, doctor, I really can't put up with a broken down old nag, whose every gallop plays the devil with my digestion!

VOUZON: No… Of course…

MAURICE, *continuing*: Or, when I'm at the theater, I do enjoy relaxing in a comfortable seat, reserved in advance… In other words, doctor, I treat myself to the best life has to offer!

VOUZON, *aside*: At nineteen? (*Aloud.*) So I see… I must say, you do seem a trifle…

MAURICE: A trifle…?

VOUZON: Well… Egotistical, if you don't mind my saying…

MAURICE, *pretending to be offended*: Oh! That's not very kind of you!

VOUZON: It's just that… You're telling me things that… Well, frankly, I find them rather shocking!

MAURICE: I am?… Sorry… I only meant to give you a notion of my tastes. I know how precious time is, doctor, and I don't waste it on tender glances, sweet nothings, and other piddling frivolities of the sort!

VOUZON, *standing up, startled*: "Piddling…" My, my! Quite an opinion of love, I must say!… And here I thought…

MAURICE: What?

VOUZON: Nothing… Nothing… (*Aside.*) No novice, now, is he! (*Aloud.*) Come now, Maurice… Such ideas, at your age?… Surely the fire can't be out, young man! (*Going over to him, patting his chest.*) I'm sure there's something here. Something that still has feelings…

MAURICE, *laughing*: That's my purse, doctor!

VOUZON: But… (*Suddenly.*) Ah! But you write poetry, my friend!… There!

MAURICE: Me? Poetry?

VOUZON: Ha ha! Try to deny it! (*Reciting.*) "A timid virgin's kiss, tender as spring…" The poem your mother just found in your pocket…

MAURICE: Oh, that!… I found it once upon a time, and I said to myself: "This might just be useful one day… If I ever get married…" Some families are easily impressed by such sentimental drivel.

VOUZON: Indeed!… Then I take it you do intend to get married.

MAURICE: Some day, I suppose… Since nature, as you have observed, has given me a heart!… It would be rather uneconomical to waste it.

VOUZON, *growing more and more upset*: Yes! "Uneconomical"… That… That's the word!

MAURICE: I mean… Sooner or later, I'll really have to invest it.

VOUZON, *angrily*: With a mortgage of fifteen percent, I'm sure!

MAURICE, *reacting to his anger*: Goodness me, doctor! Is something wrong? Did I say—-

VOUZON: Wrong?… Not a thing! It's just that you seem to be something of a monster, my friend! No offense!

MAURICE, *with a laugh*: Now, who would take offense at that? "Chacun à son goût," as they say… Each to his own taste…

VOUZON, *sarcastically*: Thank you… I understood…

MAURICE, *standing up*: You're perfectly content living in a garret. With no lift, I imagine… Surrounded by old walnut furniture from heaven-knows-when, with a housekeeper every bit as ancient!

VOUZON: Really…

MAURICE: And you go slogging on foot, hip-deep in mud, for three francs a visit! The last of your breed in Paris, I venture to say… And most of the time you even forget to collect it!

VOUZON: I—

MAURICE: Most generous, doctor! You're a man of honor, a true gentleman. And I admire you… True, as something of a rare species, but all the same…

VOUZON, *sarcastically*: Much obliged, I'm sure!

MAURICE: But I have other ambitions, I'm afraid. My tastes run to the elegant! I love luxury. Life's little superfluities, as they say… I fancy having a fortune, and I'm working to acquire one. So, tell me, where's the harm? And how, may I ask, does that make me a… a monster?

VOUZON: Oh! Very logical, I must say!… And not very attractive!… There's only one thing you lack… A forty-year-old's experience! But you're getting there…

MAURICE: Really, doctor, there's no reasoning with you! I'm afraid you're a relic of an age gone by… (*With a little laugh.*) No offense, of course!… A museum piece, if I may say…

VOUZON: Laugh all you like! Your mother was right. You're a very sick young man… Much sicker than I thought…

MAURICE: Sick? No… Tired, perhaps… One can only spend so many sleepless nights—

VOUZON: Cavorting about at the cabarets, no doubt?

MAURICE: The cabarets? Goodness, no!… Who has time?… At my desk, my friend! With columns of figures…

VOUZON: Of course…

MAURICE: Because… Can I tell you? (*Approaching him, confidentially.*) I have an incredible project in mind. It's going to be worth millions!

VOUZON: No doubt…

MAURICE: But please… Not a word… Especially to my mother! The very word "business" would send her into a fit. She's like you…

VOUZON: Another relic…

MAURICE: Here's my plan… (*Sitting down beside him.*) I want to organize an insurance company. A mutual benefit society, you understand? To protect against all those expropriations of property nowadays… Everywhere you turn… And I'll be the director.

VOUZON: Yes, I assume… Organizing it, after all…

MAURICE: Now, this is the interesting part… All the landowners will be shareholders! For a fixed-rate, deferred redemption premium…

VOUZON, *nodding, uncomprehending*: Aha…

MAURICE: A hundred percent guaranteed!… Calculated differentially and proportionally, and based on actuarial tables that I'll be happy to explain…

VOUZON, *at a loss*: No, no, no! My head is already spinning! (*Aside.*) Good grief!

MAURICE: In fact, perhaps you could help me…

VOUZON: Me? With all that differential… proportional…

MAURICE: No, no…

VOUZON: Because, I know all the bones in the human body, but when it comes to—

MAURICE, *interrupting*: You wouldn't happen to know Monot-Lagarde, the banker, would you? I'm told he has very stubborn bunions. Perhaps he's a patient…

VOUZON: I'm afraid not. (*Wryly.*) Bunions aren't my specialty.

MAURICE: Oh… Too bad… He's precisely the man I need! He jumps into investments like this with wild abandon!

VOUZON, *aside*: With his bunions? Not too wise…

MAURICE: This is just the kind of project that would tickle his sense of adventure. Not to mention the profit!… I simply must find a way… There must be someone who knows him.

VOUZON: No doubt… (*Sarcastically.*) Someone in all of Paris, I imagine…

MAURICE, *ignoring the remark*: But who? Who can introduce me?

VOUZON, *wryly*: His podiatrist?… Really, Maurice… It hurts me to see you so… so…

MAURICE: So?

VOUZON: So misguided… So… A young man of your age… Your father was one of my dearest friends, and—

MADAME DESARNAUX appears at the door, up left, with the coat.

MAURICE: Shhh! (*Whispering.*) My mother…

He stands up.

VOUZON: Ah… (*Whispering to him.*) Later… (*Standing up, to* MADAME DESARNAUX.) Madame…

MAURICE: Mother dear…

MADAME DESARNAUX, *handing him the coat*: Here you are, precious…

MAURICE, *putting it on*: Thank you… (*Whispering.*) mammá… (*As she beams, he crosses right, posing in front of the mirror, checking the details of his appearance, then crosses down left, as if to exit.*) Well now…

MADAME DESARNAUX: Aren't you going to have lunch, treasure?

MAURICE: Goodness, no! Who has time for such things!

VOUZON: Who indeed! (*Aside.*) Not with all those actuarial tables calling…

MAURICE, *at the door to his room, down left, with a little bow:* Doctor…

VOUZON, *with a nod*: Young man…

MAURICE exits.

MADAME DESARNAUX, *approaching VOUZON, anxiously*: Well? Is it serious?… It's his liver, isn't it? Do you want me to take him to a specialist? Do you think—

VOUZON: Hardly, Marguerite… It's… It's nothing at all… Really…

MADAME DESARNAUX: Are you going to give him a prescription?

VOUZON: No need… He isn't sick… Not physically, at any rate… Get him out of Paris for a while. A good trip would do wonders. All he needs is a change of air. Take him to Italy…

MADAME DESARNAUX, *jumping to conclusions*: God in heaven! His lungs, you mean… ?

VOUZON: Nothing of the sort!

MADAME DESARNAUX: But, what you were telling me before… About his… his *assuming* passion…

VOUZON: Oh yes… He has a consuming passion, all right! A rather nasty one…

MADAME DESARNAUX, *crossing herself*: Heaven help me! (*Aside.*) Some evil woman! (*Aloud.*) You mean…

VOUZON: But we'll rout it out, madame. We'll cure him!

MADAME DESARNAUX: Oh!

VOUZON: At least, I hope so…

He takes his hat and bag from the table.

MADAME DESARNAUX: You can't be leaving? You haven't even—

VOUZON: Just a few calls… But I'll be back.

MADAME DESARNAUX: Today?

VOUZON: Today! I promise!

He exits, up center.

MADAME DESARNAUX, *alone*: A woman! … With my Maurice… But how… Who… Oh! The very idea! I… I…

JEAN appears at the door, up center.

JEAN, *announcing*: Monsieur and Madame Badinier, madame.

He exits.

MADAME DESARNAUX, *aside*: Oh! Of all times… What do *they* want? (*Changing her tone, going to greet them.*) Madame… Monsieur…

BADINIER and LILI enter, dressed for travel. She is wearing long gloves; he is carrying several valises under one arm.

BADINIER: We're not disturbing you, I hope?

MADAME DESARNAUX: Heavens no! Good neighbors are always welcome! (*Aside.*) What on earth…

LILI: You're too kind!

There is a moment of embarrassed silence.

MADAME DESARNAUX: And one sees so little of you… Stuck away up there…

LILI: Four flights…

BADINIER, *to LILI*: Unless you count the mezzanine, love… That makes five…,

Another embarrassed silence.

LILI: But since we were passing right by… On our way out, that is…

MADAME DESARNAUX: Oh? Are you leaving?

LILI: Just for the summer…

BADINIER: To the country… Chevreuse…

MADAME DESARNAUX: How nice…

Another silence.

BADINIER: Lili wouldn't dream of going anywhere else.

MADAME DESARNAUX: No…

LILI: It's so… rural.

MADAME DESARNAUX: Yes… So *rusty*, as they say…

Another silence.

LILI, *to MADAME DESARNAUX*: And you must come for a visit… If you're ever in the neighborhood…

BADINIER, *to MADAME DESARNAUX*: One never knows!

MADAME DESARNAUX, *to BADINIER*: Quite so… (*To LILI.*) You're too kind..

Another silence.

LILI: Let me give you our address… (*To BADINIER.*) Do you have our cards?… The new ones?

BADINIER, *awkwardly feeling his pockets*: Ah… I must have left them upstairs. You were in such a hurry…

LILI: Why not trot up and fetch one, Raoul?

BADINIER: Five flights, love?

LILI: Four…

BADINIER: Plus the mezzanine…

MADAME DESARNAUX, *to BADINIER*: Really, you mustn't… (*To LILI.*) Why not just jot it down on a slip of paper?

LILI: Well… The cards are so attractive!

MADAME DESARNAUX: I know, but…

BADINIER, *to MADAME DESARNAUX*: Good idea!

MADAME DESARNAUX, *to LILI*, *pointing to the table, left*: Over there, madame… A pen… Ink…

LILI, *as she sits at the table*: I really think that the cards… Oh well… (*Writing.*) "Baron Raoul de Badinier…"

MADAME DESARNAUX, *aside*: Oh?

LILI continues writing, in silence.

LILI, *stopping*: There!… (*Suddenly.*) Oh drat! Clumsy me!… Look what I've done! (*Holding up her hand.*) I've got ink on one of my fingers!… Only the little one, but still… (*To BADINIER, pointing upstairs.*) Be a dear, Raoul… My other gloves are in the second drawer… Or is it the third?

BADINIER: But Lili… We're late already! And five flights… (*Before she has a chance to object.*) Counting the mezzanine…

LILI: Oh well… (*To MADAME DESARNAUX, jovially.*) I'll just have to make a fist and hide it, wherever I go! (*Shaking her fist at BADINIER, with a laugh.*) So there! (*To MADAME DESARNAUX.*) Right, my dear?

MADAME DESARNAUX, *dour, without joining in her laughter*: Quite... Quite...

LILI: I must say... You seem a trifle... subdued. Is something wrong?

MADAME DESARNAUX, *sitting down across from her*: As a matter of fact, I'm rather concerned... It's my son...

LILI: That handsome young devil? What ever for?

BADINIER, *to* MADAME DESARNAUX: Is he ill, madame?

MADAME DESARNAUX: No... That is... I suppose I can tell you...

LILI: Of course you can! (*Taking her hand across the table.*) Neighbors are practically family, I always say. And if I had a handsome son, I would certainly tell you...

MADAME DESARNAUX: Yes, well... The doctor says... It's something about his *essence*... It's *addled,* I think he said...

LILI, *exchanging knowing glances with* BADINIER: Oh?

MADAME DESARNAUX: And he has an *assuming* passion...

LILI: Poor child!

BADINIER, *chuckling*: At his age, I should hope so!

LILI: Please, Raoul! It's no laughing matter! How he must be suffering!

MADAME DESARNAUX, *to* LILI: And he's only nineteen! Can you imagine...?

BADINIER, *sitting down on the loveseat, emphasizing*: *I* can, believe me!... Of course, with me it happened earlier. I was only seventeen. They said I was precocious.

LILI: Really! I don't think madame is interested!

BADINIER, *continuing, musing*: She worked in a pastry shop. Next door... And her husband was the cook... A beautiful brunette...

LILI: Her husband?

BADINIER: The woman, love... Ah! I could have watched her all day, icing her sweet buns. Spreading them with whipped cream... Sprinkling them with powdered sugar...

LILI: Badinier!

BADINIER: Sorry... Memories, memories... Besides, it was long before we... You and I... (*With a shrug.*) I mean...

LILI, *to* MADAME DESARNAUX: You must excuse him. He gets carried away...

BADINIER, *to* MADAME DESARNAUX: And do we know the object of the young man's passion?

MADAME DESARNAUX: I haven't the slightest idea!

LILI: He's that secretive?

MADAME DESARNAUX: His *secretion* knows no bounds, I'm afraid!

BADINIER: Oh?

LILI, *smiling*: You mean, he doesn't even confide in his mammá?

BADINIER: Of course not! *I* didn't!

LILI: Raoul!

MADAME DESARNAUX: I simply don't understand how he could meet such a... a person... He never goes anywhere. Only to his office... And he never sees any strangers but the neighbors...

LILI: Oh?... Then, you think... Someone close by? In the building, perhaps?

BADINIER: Obviously, love!

LILI, *aside*: I wonder…

MADAME DESARNAUX, *getting up*: Why, just now… I found a poem in his pocket…

LILI, *getting up, suddenly interested*: My, my!

BADINIER: That's serious! (*Laughing.*) The young rake!… (*To* MADAME DESARNAUX.) Can we see it?

LILI, *to* MADAME DESARNAUX: Yes… May we?

MADAME DESARNAUX: Well… (*She takes the paper from her bosom. The three of them come down center, with* LILI *peering at it over her shoulder.*) I suppose… (*Reading.*)

"A timid virgin's kiss, tender as spring;
The brilliant butterfly, whose flitting wing
Slips 'twixt the fragrant, blooming phlox…"

BADINIER: "Flocks"?… Of what? Sheep?

LILI: No, no… "Phlox"… The flower… *P, h…*

BADINIER: Oh…

MADAME DESARNAUX, *continuing*:

"The sounds that echo from the vaulted naves…"

BADINIER: "Knaves"? Who…? What's knavish about them? And how can a young man be "vaulted"?

LILI: No, no… "Naves"… In a church… No *k*…

BADINIER: Aha…

MADAME DESARNAUX, *continuing*:

"The rhythmic sounding of the pounding waves
Over the wetly weeping rocks…"

BADINIER, *aside*: Vile!

MADAME DESARNAUX, *to* LILI: Please! I can't… (*In tears.*) You read it… I can't bear to…

LILI: Tsk tsk tsk!… (*Reading.*)

"The nightingale, whose voice to nature warbles
An ode; the brooklet that its murmur burbles,
As through the fluttering reeds it flows…"

BADINIER: "Warbles"? "Burbles"?… That doesn't even rhyme!

LILI: It doesn't have to… It's modern!

(*Continuing.*)

"The concerts sung aloft in heaven's height;
The gentle swish of angels' wings in flight…
Fairer your name than all of those!"

BADINIER, *aside*: Absolutely vile!

LILI, *carried away*: Ah! A young man's first love!… Is there anything sweeter?

MADAME DESARNAUX: But…

LILI: And his first poem! (*To* BADINIER.) How tender!

BADINIER: Like the one I wrote for my little sugar tart! Only mine was better! (*Reciting.*)

"Cupid, the god of love, has burned my soul,

And, day and night, I cry: 'Fire! Fire! Help! Help!'"

LILI: It doesn't rhyme!

BADINIER: There's more, but that's all I can remember. Give me a minute…

LILI: Please, Raoul! We're not interested in your silly little ditty! (*To* MADAME DESARNAUX.) Are we, madame?

MADAME DESARNAUX, *hardly following the conversation, absorbed in her own thoughts*: What? (*Taking back the paper, to* LILI.) You see? No name… Not the slightest indication… It could be any woman!

BADINIER: Or every one!… Every Mimi, and Gigi, and Lili for miles around…

LILI: What?

BADINIER: Nothing personal, love… In fact, even every Fifi, now that I think of it!

LILI: Oh?

BADINIER: Or one especially!… You don't suppose…?

LILI: *Our* Fifi?

MADAME DESARNAUX, *to* BADINIER: You mean, your… (*With a note of scorn.*) Your domestic?

LILI, *to* BADINIER: Really!

BADINIER: Well, why not? She's a sweet little thing! And easy… And—

LILI: Easy?… Oh! Badinier!… You're disgusting!

MADAME DESARNAUX: A… A maid?

BADINIER: But lots of people start on the bottom and… (*With a wry wink and appropriately suggestive gestures.*) and work their way up!

LILI: Revolting!

BADINIER: Besides, it *could* be Fifi. She's pretty, and she lives in the building… I'd bet anything…

LILI: Lots of pretty women live in the building!

BADINIER, *aside*: They do?

CELINE enters, up right.

CELINE, *to* MADAME DESARNAUX: Well, auntie dear? (*Noticing the others.*) Ah! Madame Badinier… Monsieur…

LILI, *giving her a kiss*: Céline, my child…

BADINIER, *giving her a kiss on one cheek*: Mademoiselle…

He kisses her on the other cheek as well, as LILI *looks daggers at him.*

CELINE, *to* MADAME DESARNAUX: What did the doctor have to say? I'm on pins and needles…

LILI, *aside*: Oh?

CELINE, *continuing*: Poor thing! (*Emotionally.*) I won't breathe easy until you tell me, auntie.

MADAME DESARNAUX, *to herself*: Good heavens! Do you suppose…?

LILI, *aside*: I wonder…

CELINE, *to* MADAME DESARNAUX: Is he… Is Maurice…

MADAME DESARNAUX, *to herself*: Is it possible? Is she…

CELINE: Tell me!… Please, auntie dear!

MADAME DESARNAUX, *archly*: There's no need to be concerned, Céline! Your cousin… Monsieur Maurice is not in any danger.

CELINE, *with a sigh of relief*: Oh! Thank you… I was simply beside myself…

LILI, *aside*: Indeed!

MADAME DESARNAUX: Yes… (*Aside.*) So it seems… (*Aloud.*) But you needn't be! And, if I may offer you a word of advice…

CELINE, *taken aback at her tone:* Auntie?

MADAME DESARNAUX: I suggest that you express your concern with a little more discretion! Such outbursts are unseemly. A young lady doesn't wear her heart *in a sieve*, as they say!

BADINIER, *aside:* She what?

CELINE: But what did I—

She is interrupted by MAURICE, *calling offstage.*

MAURICE'S VOICE: Jean!… Jean!

MADAME DESARNAUX, *aside*: Oh!… (*Aloud, to* CELINE, *waving her off, up right.*) Go on! Go on!… Go practice your piano, young lady!

CELINE, *at a loss*: But…

MADAME DESARNAUX: There's no need for him to trip over you at every turn!

CELINE: No, auntie…

BADINIER, *to* MADAME DESARNAUX: But… In the same apartment, madame?

CELINE, *to herself, moving up right*: What is she hiding from me, I wonder?

LILI, *to* BADINIER, *in a whisper*: Mind your business, you! It's none of our concern!

BADINIER, *with a shrug*: I say…

CELINE, *to herself, at the door*: I simply must speak with the doctor myself…

She exits as MAURICE *enters, down left, gloves and hat in hand.*

MAURICE, *calling offstage*: And be sure not to disturb anything on my desk! I'll be back… (*As he lays his hat on the table, left, and begins putting on his gloves, noticing* BADINIER *and* LILI.) Ah! Madame… Monsieur…

BADINIER: Good morning! (*With a wink, in a whisper.*) Sly devil!

He gives him a little nudge.

MAURICE: Monsieur? (*Aside.*) What on earth…?

BADINIER, *aside*: It's our Fifi! No doubt about it…

LILI, *to* MADAME DESARNAUX, *in a whisper*: The poor child! I see what you mean. How piqued he looks!

MADAME DESARNAUX, *replying in a whisper, pointing up right*: It's his cousin, I'm sure. She must be the one…

LILI, *in a whisper*: You think…? Then again…

MADAME DESARNAUX: You'll see… (*Joining* MAURICE, *down left.*) Maurice, treasure…

MAURICE, *arranging his gloves*: Mother dear?

MADAME DESARNAUX: I… I don't think I told you… I have some delightful news…

MAURICE, *unmoved*: Oh?

MADAME DESARNAUX: Your cousin… Céline… She's getting married, precious!

MAURICE, *buttoning his gloves*: Good for her!… Is the young man rich?

MADAME DESARNAUX: Oh yes… Very…

MAURICE, *indifferently*: Good… (*Crossing right, at the mirror.*) That's what counts these days…

MADAME DESARNAUX, *aside*: So much for her!

LILI, *aside*: She's certainly not the one….

BADINIER, *to the two women, in a whisper*: Let me try… (*Aloud, to* MAURICE.) Maurice…

MAURICE, *primping*: Monsieur?

BADINIER: I have some pleasant news for you too… You know Fifi?… Upstairs?

MAURICE: Your domestic?

BADINIER: Our… Yes, our… She's getting married.

MAURICE: How nice… (*Aside.*) It's an epidemic! (*Aloud, to* BADINIER.) So?

BADINIER, *disappointed*: So I thought… I thought that you—

MAURICE, *still at the mirror*: And who's the fortunate spouse?

BADINIER: A… A fireman!

MAURICE, *laughing*: Good luck!… No money there!

BADINIER, *aside*: Damn! Not her either…

MADAME DESARNAUX: Maurice, precious… Come thank madame and monsieur for stopping in to say goodbye.

MAURICE, *to* LILI, *pretending disappointment*: What? You're leaving?… So soon?

LILI, *aside*: So soon? (*Aloud.*) For Chevreuse… Only for the summer…

BADINIER: It's not the end of the earth!

LILI, *to* MAURICE: And… Perhaps you'll come visit…

BADINIER, *to* MAURICE: There's a train every hour.

MAURICE, *politely*: What a lovely idea…

MADAME DESARNAUX, *to* LILI: You're too kind… But we're leaving too.

LILI: Oh?

MADAME DESARNAUX: We're taking a little trip, Maurice and I.

MAURICE, *surprised*: We are?

MADAME DESARNAUX: Italy… Rome… I've been dying to go for years.

BADINIER: How nice!

MAURICE, *to* MADAME DESARNAUX: But…

MADAME DESARNAUX: There's so much to see… The Coliseum, the *sixteen chapels*…

MAURICE, *objecting*: But mother dear, I… I can't leave now! It's out of the question!

MADAME DESARNAUX: What?

MAURICE: Not for a million! There's simply no way…

BADINIER, *whispering, to* MADAME DESARNAUX: Whoever she is, she's certainly got her hooks in him!

MADAME DESARNAUX, *to* MAURICE: We'll discuss it later, treasure.

LILI, *sighing, aside*: Ah… Young love!

BADINIER, *awkwardly taking out his pocket watch*: My my! Look at the time! (*To* LILI.) Come… We'll be late. Ten more visits, fifteen minutes each… We have just enough time before the three o'clock train. We'll start with Monot-Lagarde, next door…

MAURICE, *still at the mirror, with a start*: What?… (*Coming down, to* BADINIER.) You… (*To* LILI.) You know him? The banker?… *That* Monot-Lagarde?

LILI: Know him?

BADINIER: Of course! How many are there?

LILI: He's my cousin…

BADINIER: He's our cousin…

MAURICE, *drawing* LILI *down right, away from the others, in a whisper*: Ah, madame… If you only knew my feelings… I…

BADINIER, *to* MADAME DESARNAUX: Our first cousin…

LILI, *startled, to* MAURICE, *in a whisper*: Shhh!… Please…

MADAME DESARNAUX, *unimpressed, to* BADINIER: Aha…

MAURICE, *to* LILI, *continuing*: We have to talk, you and I!

LILI, *to* MAURICE: What are you saying?

BADINIER, *to* MADAME DESARNAUX, *continuing, pointing to* LILI: Her uncle's son…

MAURICE, *to* LILI: Here, madame!… In twenty minutes! It can't wait!… Please!

BADINIER: Her father's brother…

LILI, *to* MAURICE: A rendez-vous, monsieur?

MADAME DESARNAUX, *replying to* BADINIER: How interesting…

MAURICE, *to* LILI: My future depends on it! My happiness…

LILI: Young man…

MAURICE: My life…

BADINIER, *continuing, to* MADAME DESARNAUX, *with a laugh*: Yes… He's the rich one in the family!

LILI, *to* MAURICE: Be careful…

MAURICE: You're right… My mother…

MADAME DESARNAUX, *indifferently, replying to* BADINIER: Yes… No doubt…

LILI, *down right, aside, as* MAURICE *moves left, to the table, and takes his hat*: And my husband… Good God! A… A tryst… Just like that!

MADAME DESARNAUX, *to* MAURICE: Are you leaving, precious?

LILI, *continuing, to herself*: But I won't!… Certainly not!

MAURICE, *replying to* MADAME DESARNAUX: For a moment, mother dear… Just next door…

LILI, *to herself*: What does he take me for? (*Following him upstage, with a little wave, aloud.*) Ta ta…

MAURICE, *to* MADAME DESARNAUX, *continuing*: Just to the stationer's…

MADAME DESARNAUX: But I can send Jean…

MAURICE: No need… I won't be long… (*To* LILI, *in a whisper.*) Twenty minutes! Don't fail me! (*Nodding, aloud.*) Madame… Monsieur…

He exits, up center.

MADAME DESARNAUX: That's what he said yesterday!

LILI, *misunderstanding, surprised*: What?

MADAME DESARNAUX: "I won't be long…" He went to the stationer's and he just stayed and stayed… And today—

BADINIER, *suddenly*: Eureka!… That's it!

MADAME DESARNAUX *and* **LILI**: What?

BADINIER: I know who she is! The object of his passion!…

LILI, *aside*: My God! He was watching…

BADINIER: He's in love with the stationer's wife, that's who! (*LILI heaves a sigh of relief.*) A magnificent specimen!… And a husband who reminds me of my pastry chef…

MADAME DESARNAUX: I do believe…

LILI, *to BADINIER, eager to convince him*: You're right, Raoul! It's perfectly obvious!

MADAME DESARNAUX, *continuing*: It certainly makes sense…

LILI: It does! (*To BADINIER.*) It does! (*To MADAME DESARNAUX.*) My husband is never wrong. He has an eye for such things.

BADINIER: Besides, as soon as he leaves, I'll go survey the situation. It won't take me long.

LILI: But…

BADINIER: I'll go in and pretend I'm looking for something… For sealing wax…

MADAME DESARNAUX, *to LILI*: Does your ceiling have a leak, madame?

LILI: Our…? No… No…

BADINIER, *continuing*: And I'll chat with her for a moment or two.

MADAME DESARNAUX, *to BADINIER*: And you'll come back and tell me what you find.

BADINIER: Of course…

LILI, *to BADINIER*: But why bother? It's perfectly obvious. She's the one!

BADINIER: Just being thorough, love…

LILI: And our visits? We'll be late!

BADINIER: Now, now… What's more important? A visit or two, or a young man's first love?… Come…

He takes her by the hand as best he can, despite his valises, and pulls her upstage.

LILI, *trying unsuccessfully to resist*: But… (*To MADAME DESARNAUX, with a nod.*) Madame…

BADINIER, *nodding, to MADAME DESARNAUX*: Madame… Don't worry, I'll be back!

He and LILI exit, up center.

MADAME DESARNAUX. *alone*: Oh! Of all people!… And right next door!… Stationer's wife indeed!… That… That witch!… That child-snatcher!… (*Pacing.*) But she won't get away with it! I'll see to that!… I'll… I'll go scratch her eyes out! I'll… No! Better than that! I'll send her husband a letter! An… An *ominous* one… Without my name… And on good paper, too, so he'll take it seriously… And I'll say: "Monsieur… If I were you I would watch my wife. She's a tart and a shameless hussy, and she's trying to steal the heart of someone very dear to me!… Signed: A friend…" And I'll send it with Jean… Yes, that's what I'll do!… Oh! (*Moving up left, toward the door, as CELINE enters, unseen, up right.*) Poor, dear Maurice! He's done for!… Done for!

She exits.

CELINE, *overhearing*: Done for? My cousin?

VOUZON enters, up center.

VOUZON: Hello?... Anyone home?

CELINE, *running up to him*: Ah, doctor! Thank heaven...

VOUZON: Mademoiselle?... (*Laying his hat and bag on the table, left.*) Is your cousin about? Monsieur Maurice...

CELINE: Please! Tell me the truth!... He's... He's done for, isn't he!

VOUZON, *joining her, center*: Who?

CELINE: My cousin... Maurice... Oh, I know. You don't have to pretend...

VOUZON: Who said anything of the kind?

CELINE: My aunt, monsieur... Just now... I heard her...

VOUZON: Tut tut, young lady! She's afraid that he... that your cousin...

CELINE, *jumping to conclusions*: Oh my! It's hopeless, isn't it, doctor? There's no hope, is there!

VOUZON, *leading her down right, trying to contradict her*: Not at all... Not at all...

CELINE, *misunderstanding, throwing her arms around his neck, sobbing*: Oh! I knew it!... I... I...

VOUZON, *trying to calm her*: I mean... Of course there's hope!... You said... "There's no hope!..." And I said: "Not at all..." That is, of course there is!

CELINE, *unconvinced*: I know... There's always hope... That's what you doctors say...

VOUZON: Not at all... I mean, who the deuce said—

CELINE: If you knew how frightfully worried I am! (*To herself.*) Oh! Maurice... Maurice! (*To VOUZON.*) Seeing him this way... Suffering... In pain...

VOUZON, *to himself*: I say! She's in love with the scoundrel! (*Aloud, to CELINE.*) But he isn't, I tell you!

CELINE: I'll just die of it, doctor! I simply know I will!

VOUZON, *comforting her*: Now, now, now... You won't die, I promise! And neither will he! He's fit as a fiddle, that cousin of yours! (*Attempting a pleasantry.*) And not a string out of tune!

CELINE: Please, doctor! Don't pretend...

As he tries to reassure her, down right, LILI enters, up center, stopping at the door.

LILI, *to herself*: I'll let him go visiting by himself, for all the difference it makes. (*Noticing VOUZON.*) Oh my!... The doctor... Of all times...

She moves right, unseen by CELINE.

MADAME DESARNAUX'S VOICE, *offstage*: Céline!... Céline!

CELINE: Coming, auntie!... (*To VOUZON.*) Please, doctor... Don't go... I just know you have much more to tell me.

She exits, up left.

VOUZON, *shaking his head*: Tsk tsk tsk! Poor child!... (*Noticing LILI, up right.*) Ah! Madame Badinier... What a pleasant surprise...

LILI, *hypocritically*: And you, doctor... (*To herself.*) And Maurice, on his way...

VOUZON: I trust you're well?

LILI: Fine... Fine... (*To herself.*) How do I get rid of him?

VOUZON: No little medical problems? (*Jovially.*) Nothing to keep me busy?

LILI: No... (*To herself, struck by an idea.*) Ah! Maybe... (*Aloud.*) That is, doctor... I'm really dreadfully distraught! (*Pretending to tremble.*) You can see...

She takes some smelling salts from her pocket and inhales.

VOUZON: Oh?

LILI: Just now... Around the corner... A... A terrible accident... A man, trampled by a runaway horse...

VOUZON: Good grief!

LILI: And they're calling for a doctor!

VOUZON: Please! You'll excuse me, won't you? I really should go help...

LILI, *still trembling*: Of course...

He runs to the table and retrieves his hat and bag.

VOUZON: Where, exactly?

LILI, *with a few vague gestures*: There... Out there... Down... Up...

VOUZON, *at the door, up center*: Let's hope I'm not too late!

He exits.

LILI, *watching him leave*: Good... Oh! I should never have come! (*Pacing.*) Heaven knows I didn't want to... But if I didn't, he might think I was afraid, and that could raise his hopes. This way, at least, I can try to talk him out of his mad passion. Even scold him, poor child... It's not his fault... (*Changing her mind.*) No... That would be too cruel. I won't scold him, I'll... I'll reason with him. Gently, like a sister... Like a friend... (*Down center, looking at her watch.*) Still not here?... Oh! I was wrong to come first! What ever will he think? (*After a few moments, the door, up center, opens and* MAURICE *appears on the threshold.*) Ah! Monsieur...

MAURICE, *entering*: Madame... (*Joining her, downstage.*) Let me thank you for being so prompt.

LILI, *coyly*: Really, monsieur... It was wrong of me to come! I shouldn't be here at all...

MAURICE, *excitedly*: Don't say that! Not when you're holding my happiness in your hands... My future... My life itself...

LILI, *aside, trying to control a shudder*: Oh... (*Aloud.*) Please, Maurice... Control yourself, or... or I don't know what—

MAURICE, *interrupting*: Pardon me, madame, but... Some things are so important that... that... (*At a loss for words.*) Ah! What can I say?

LILI, *to herself*: Passionate child!

MAURICE: First, you have to promise not to breathe a word of what I'm about to say. No one must know!

LILI: Of course! (*Aside.*) What does he take me for? (*Aloud, coyly.*) You mean... Just between us... You and me...

MAURICE: Exactly! (*Taking her hand.*) Come... (*Trying to lead her to the loveseat.*) Let's sit down...

LILI, *pulling her hand away*: I... I don't think so, monsieur! We can chat just as well standing up. (*Aside.*) Not as timid as I thought!

MAURICE: As you wish! (*Very business-like.*) Now then, in a word, madame... Here's the proposition.

LILI, *surprised*: The proposition?

MAURICE: You live in Paris. And, like all of us, I'm sure you have been struck by the number of demolitions…

LILI: I beg your pardon?

MAURICE: The face of the city is changing. We go to bed, madame…

LILI: What?

MAURICE, *continuing*: …and when we wake up, next morning, the floor is being pulled out from under us!

LILI, *coyly*: Well, it may *feel* that way…

MAURICE, *continuing*: Our property has been taken over… Expropriated, madame!… A fancy word for a regrettable situation!

LILI, *aside*: What a curious approach!

MAURICE: Some people profit from the phenomenon. Others are grievously wronged, madame. Cut to the very quick… Losing what they hold most dear… (*Passionately.*) Most dear, madame… Most dear, you understand?

LILI, *baffled*: Well…

MAURICE: And these are the poor souls… These are the victims of progress, as I call them. It's to them that I've been devoting my long, sleepless nights for the last two months.

LILI: It is?… But… But monsieur… Why are you telling me this? What does that have to do with… with us?

MAURICE: It's important, madame, to make you understand the pressing need for the insurance company I'm organizing.

LILI: You… You mean… Your proposition is of a… a business nature?

MAURICE: Of course! Insurance is a business! A most lucrative business… And this one will be the most lucrative of all! Just listen to my plan… I want to organize an insurance company. A mutual benefit society, you understand? To protect against all those expropriations…

LILI: Oh my…

MAURICE: Now this is the interesting part. All the landowners will be shareholders! For a fixed rate, deferred redemption premium… A hundred percent guaranteed!

LILI, *aside*: My, my, my…

MAURICE: Calculated differentially and proportionally, and based on actuarial tables that I'll be happy to explain…

LILI: No, no… Please… Numbers, figures… I'm afraid I—

MAURICE: But it's really quite simple… And terribly clever…

LILI: Yes, I'm sure, but… I confess, I was really expecting a… a confession of a somewhat different kind.

MAURICE: You were?… What kind?

LILI, *embarrassed*: Well… I rather thought that a young man of your age… Perhaps an unhappy little love affair… Tender feelings for a young cousin…

MAURICE: What?

LILI: Unrequited, as they say… Or… Or for some other woman… Even more mature… A trifle more…

MAURICE: A little love affair? Me?… Ha ha ha!… Who has the time?

LILI: At nineteen? I should think—

MAURICE: I'm through with such nonsense!

LILI, *aside*: And he tells me to my face!… (*Aloud, turning her back and moving off, right.*) I… You… (*Facing him.*) But… But precisely of what interest is your… your clever venture to me, monsieur?

MAURICE, *joining her, taking her hands*: Ah, madame! (*Excitedly.*) You… You have it in your power to be my angel… My good fairy!… My future is in your hands. (*As she pulls her hands free.*) My life—

LILI, *cynically, wiping her hands on her skirt*: Come now! You've said that, as I recall…

MAURICE: I heard you say that Monsieur Monot-Lagarde is your cousin. The banker… And…

LILI: And?

MAURICE: And I beg you… (*Passionately.*) I beseech you, madame… to help me arrange a meeting… to use your good offices…

LILI: I see!

MAURICE: Today, if possible… At four o'clock… After the Exchange closes… Or sooner, even… Now… This instant…

LILI, *trying to control here pique, with dry sarcasm*: What wouldn't I do for such a clever young man? So serious, and with such a good head on his shoulders…

MAURICE, *taking her seriously*: Ah, madame…

LILI: So poised… So perfectly self-possessed…

He seizes her hands again.

MAURICE, *kissing them feverishly*: Oh, thank you! Thank you!

LILI, *pulling them away*: Please! You needn't… I'll go speak to cousin Gustave this very minute. Just a hop, a skip, and a jump, as it were…

MAURICE: Oh! What can I say?

LILI: I won't be long.

MAURICE: How can I… (*Reflecting.*) But not a word to my mother! She—

LILI, *hardly listening*: And if he says yes… If he's willing to see you…

MAURICE: Oh! He has to, madame! My future… My life…

LILI: Yes, well… (*Pointing to the armchair.*) I'll leave my glove on that chair… (*Waving her clenched fist, controlling her obvious pique.*) Understand?

MAURICE: You're too kind… Much too kind… I'll just go throw a few figures together… My notes, my tables…

He crosses left.

LILI, *aside*: Your deferred redemption premiums…

MAURICE, *at the door, down left*: Ah, madame! I'll owe you my happiness… My fortune…

He exits.

LILI, *alone, shaking her fist*: And your future!… And your life!… (*She stands, hands on hips.*) Little monster! He thinks I'm going to take the trouble to… Oh! (*Crossing left, shaking her fist at the door.*) A beast, who has no time to let a woman twist him around her little finger!… No time to lose his heart!… Oh no! I'll take care of him! We'll just see about that! (*She sits down at the table, left, and begins writing a note, reading as she writes.*) "Dear cousin Gustave… I am writing in regard to a young man, Monsieur Maurice Désarnaux… An impertinent little fop… An insufferable twit, with no talent whatever, ill-mannered as the day is long! Please oblige me by refusing him the service he is about to request of you!" (*She pauses.*) There!… Straight and to the point… (*Writing.*) "Your affectionate cousin, Lili Badinier." (*As an afterthought.*) Ah! A postscript… "He boasts of his utter contempt for bankers, and calls them all unscrupulous bloodsuckers." That should do it!… (*She folds the letter, seals it with sealing wax, and writes the address.*) "Monsieur Gustave Monot-Lagarde…" (*Standing up.*) And my glove…

She takes off her ink-stained glove and throws it over the back of the armchair as MADAME DESARNAUX *enters, up center.*

MADAME DESARNAUX, *aside*: The stationer should have my letter by now… (*Noticing* LILI *at the table, surprised to see her.*) Madame?…

LILI: Oh!

MADAME DESARNAUX: I thought…

LILI, *embarrassed*: I… I was waiting for Monsieur Badinier. You haven't seen him, have you?

MADAME DESARNAUX: No…

LILI: Well… I'll wait for him upstairs… (*To herself.*) As soon as I find a messenger to deliver the letter…

MADAME DESARNAUX: Oh, please… Don't go… I'm simply so upset! I need someone to talk to… A *synthetic* ear…

LILI: Of course… Tsk tsk tsk! Poor thing… (*To herself.*) I'll enjoy the look on that wretch's face when he comes back from my cousin's! (*Aloud.*) Just give me a moment, madame… I won't be long, I promise!

MADAME DESARNAUX: Really, you're too kind…

She accompanies LILI *up center, and the two of them exit, leaving the stage empty for a moment.* MAURICE *enters, down left, with a bulging brief case.*

MAURICE, *to himself*: There!… Everything I want to show him… If only she can persuade him… (*Noticing the glove on the armchair.*) Ah! Her glove… So soon ?… Thank goodness!… (*He begins smothering it with kisses.*) Then it's all arranged! She… That wonderful woman…

MADAME DESARNAUX *enters, sees him kissing the glove, and overhears his last few words.*

MADAME DESARNAUX, *aside*: What?… Of all the… (*Aloud.*) Maurice!

MAURICE, *controlling himself, and throwing the glove down on the table*: Mother dear?

MADAME DESARNAUX: I… I need you to come with me. An errand…

MAURICE: Now?… But I can't… I… I have an important appointment.

MADAME DESARNAUX: Oh? And when is this "important appointment"?

MAURICE: Why… Now… This minute… (*Holding up his briefcase.*) A client…

MADAME DESARNAUX, *aside*: No doubt! (*Aloud.*) Well, your client will have to wait!

MAURICE: But mother dear… (*Moving toward the door, down left.*) I'll get my hat and I'm on my way…

MADAME DESARNAUX: Wait! (*As if announcing a portentous piece of news.*) I think I should tell you that the stationer knows… He's ready for you, Maurice!

MAURICE: The stationer?… But that's exactly where I'm going. A ledger… Some paper…

He goes to the door.

MADAME DESARNAUX, *sharply*: Maurice! I forbid you!

MAURICE: But… My future… My life… You… You don't understand…

He exits to his room.

MADAME DESARNAUX: Oh! That woman! That… That vixen!… To make him disobey his own mother!… Oh, how he must love her!… Well, we'll see…

She runs over to the door and slams it shut.

MAURICE'S VOICE, *offstage*: Mother? (*As she locks it, leaving the key in the lock.*) What are you doing?

MADAME DESARNAUX: Now let's see him keep his "important appointment"!

BADINIER enters, up center, still carrying his valises, with his hat under his arm.

BADINIER: Hello!… I'm back!

MADAME DESARNAUX: Ah! Monsieur…

BADINIER: And I've seen her! The stationer's wife…

MADAME DESARNAUX: And…?

BADINIER: Not bad… A little on the mature side, you might say… But for a beginner like Maurice…

MADAME DESARNAUX: Oh!

BADINIER: Anyway, here's what happened… I go in, and she's all alone… So I ask for some sealing wax, and we begin to chat. And I make an awful joke about my ceiling springing a leak, and going pipi all over the floor… (*He gives a foolish little giggle.*) And next thing I know, an immense giant of a man… a bloody gorilla… jumps up from under the counter and begins pounding me over the head with an enormous ledger… Accounts payable and receivable, I imagine…

MADAME DESARNAUX: Oh my!

BADINIER: It was her husband! He suspected something…

MADAME DESARNAUX: Heavens! My letter…

BADINIER: What letter?

MADAME DESARNAUX: The one I sent him telling him to keep an eye on her…

BADINIER, *sarcastically*: Thank you! I must say… (*Showing her his flattened hat.*) A perfectly good hat…

MADAME DESARNAUX: Oh… I… I don't know what to say, monsieur!… But things have gone a lot farther since you left. My Maurice had a… a *twist!*

BADINIER: A tryst? With her?

MADAME DESARNAUX: But I didn't let him go! (*Pointing down left.*) I locked him in his room.

BADINIER: And a good thing you did! That blasted ledger would have cracked his little skull!

MADAME DESARNAUX: And just now I found him kissing a lady's glove. Absolutely smothering it with kisses, monsieur!…

BADINIER, *laughing*: Romantic young fool!

MADAME DESARNAUX, *taking the glove from the table*: This one… Hers, no doubt…

BADINIER, *taking it and looking it over*: I don't know… She has a hand like a slab of beef! An eight and three quarters, at the very least… This one is a six and a quarter at the most!… (*Suddenly.*) Aaaagh! Good God!

MADAME DESARNAUX: What is it?

BADINIER, *waving the glove*: This… This ink stain on the finger!… Before… My wife… (*In a rage.*) This is her glove! My wife's…

MADAME DESARNAUX, *with a shriek*: What?

BADINIER: Oh! He'll pay!… That… That… Who does he think—

MADAME DESARNAUX: Monsieur!… Please!

BADINIER, *striding down left*: We'll just see about that!

MADAME DESARNAUX, *trying to hold him back*: But… He's just a child!

BADINIER, *at the door*: Age has nothing to do with it, madame!… My honor… My reputation… My… (*As he unlocks the door and disappears inside, leaving it open.*) Young scoundrel…

As he exits, the door, up center, opens and LILI *appears.*

MADAME DESARNAUX, *calling after him*: Monsieur Badinier!

LILI, *standing at the door*: What…

MADAME DESARNAUX, *noticing her*: Please! Don't admit a thing!… Deny it, madame! Deny it!

LILI: Deny what?

MADAME DESARNAUX: Everything!… Whatever… (*Pointing to the table.*) Your husband found your glove, madame… With ink on the finger… The one that my Maurice was smothering with kisses!… He's furious! He wants to kill him!

LILI: But—

MADAME DESARNAUX: Please! Deny it!

BADINIER *comes storming out of the room.*

BADINIER: Empty!… Not a soul!

MADAME DESARNAUX: What?

BADINIER, *crossing right, in a rage*: There's a ladder by the window. Our young Romeo escaped!

MADAME DESARNAUX, *crossing herself, aside*: Thank heaven!

BADINIER, *noticing his wife, still upstage*: Ha! There she is! The cradle-robber!… Our Juliet, long in the tooth…

LILI: Raoul!

BADINIER: You and I have to talk, madame! (*Brandishing the glove with his free hand, backing her up against the table.*) Please be good enough to explain how this glove… *your* glove… just happened to find its way into the hands of Monsieur Maurice, and how come he was smothering it with passionate kisses!

Back to the table, hands behind her back, she dips a gloved fingertip into the ink-well.

LILI: That… That glove?… But Raoul! It's not mine!

BADINIER: Oh? And this ink stain?… Remember? (*Mimicking.*) "Be a dear, Raoul… My other gloves are in the second drawer…"

LILI: But… But you didn't!… And I didn't change them! I'm still wearing that one! (*Holding up the newly stained finger.*) See?

She joins him and holds her hand up under his nose.

BADINIER, *bumbling*: But… But… (*Humbly.*) Oh my…

MADAME DESARNAUX: She's right, monsieur…

BADINIER: But… (*To* LILI.) You mean… I… Oh! How could I… (*Taking her hand in his free hand.*) Please! Forgive me, Lili! I… I'm an absolute cad… I…

LILI: There, there… Just try not to be so jealous!

BADINIER, *raising his hand*: Never!… I swear… (*Noticing that his hand is now stained with ink, with a start.*) Aaaagh!… Oh! Damnation!

LILI *and* **MADAME DESARNAUX**: What?

BADINIER, *waving his hand in her face*: That ink was wet! See?… Look at my hand!

LILI, *aside*: Oh dear…

BADINIER: You dipped your finger in the ink just now!… You… You…

LILI: But Raoul… Dearest…

BADINIER: Don't "But Raoul" me! You have a lot of explaining to do! (*Awkwardly grasping her arm.*) And the sooner the better…

As LILI *tries to wave a little goodbye to* MADAME DESARNAUX, *they exit, up center.*

MADAME DESARNAUX, *alone*: Good heavens, what a scene!… Now what? Monsieur Badinier will have to avenge his honor! That means… (*With a shudder.*) God help me! A duel!… Oh!… No! (*She goes to the table, left, and rings the bell vigorously.*) Jean!… Jean!… (*To herself, still ringing.*) Not with my Maurice… Not a duel… Oh!

JEAN *appears at the door, up center.*

JEAN: Madame rang?

MADAME DESARNAUX: Please, Jean… As soon as Monsieur Maurice returns, you must tell him that I absolutely must speak with him! It simply can't wait… Understand?… It's terribly important! It's… Oh!

She exits, up left, sighing.

JEAN, *coming down center*: Now what's got into her, I wonder!

VOUZON *enters, up center.*

VOUZON, *to himself*: What the deuce was she talking about? "A terrible accident… A man trampled by a horse…" Where? I looked… I asked everyone… (*Noticing* JEAN.) Ah!… Has Monsieur Maurice returned?

JEAN: No, monsieur.

VOUZON, *musing, to himself*: He must have been trampled to a powder and blown away!

JEAN, *overhearing*: Oh no, monsieur. Someone would have told us.

VOUZON: What?

The door, up center, flies open and MAURICE *comes storming in.*

JEAN, *to* VOUZON, *pointing to* MAURICE: Ah! Monsieur… See? I told monsieur… He's all in one piece…

MAURICE, *brandishing his brief case*: Imbecile!… Idiot!…

JEAN, *to* MAURICE, *thinking the exclamations are directed at him*: Excuse me, monsieur… What did I—

MAURICE, *cutting him off*: Not you, dolt!

JEAN: Good… I thought—

MAURICE: Leave me alone! (*Pointing up center.*) Out, blockhead!

JEAN: I thought monsieur was insulting me…

MAURICE: Out! Out!

JEAN exits, up center.

VOUZON: What's the trouble, young man?

MAURICE, *seething*: Oh!… I went to speak to our banker friend…

VOUZON: Monot-Lagarde?

MAURICE: Yes… And he wouldn't even give me two minutes!

VOUZON, *sarcastically*: Well, time *is* money, after all…

MAURICE: And when I asked him why… (*Brandishing LILI's letter.*) He waved this in my face, and said: "So, you're the young twit!…" Oh! Madame Badinier!… How could she…? Why? Was it something I said?

VOUZON: Maybe something you didn't…

MAURICE: Bah!… And to make matters worse, my South Pacific Carborundum has absolutely plummeted!

VOUZON: Your stocks?

MAURICE: Hundreds of shares!… Worth a fortune yesterday…

VOUZON: And today?

MAURICE: Down, down, down!

VOUZON: Tsk tsk tsk!

CELINE enters, quietly, up right.

MAURICE: Not worth the paper they're printed on!… I'm ruined!

CELINE, *aside*: Oh…

MAURICE: And I owe a fortune! Five thousand francs… I could never ask my mother…

VOUZON: Not "mammá"… No…

MAURICE: Ruined!… I'm utterly ruined, I tell you!

He collapses onto the loveseat.

CELINE, *approaching*: Excuse me, cousin dear… Is that all that's troubling you?

MAURICE: All?… Isn't that enough? I'm dishonored! I'll be drawn and quartered!

CELINE: But… Maybe I can help…

MAURICE: You?

CELINE: Wait here… If it's only money you need…

She hurries out, up right.

MAURICE, *with a cynical little laugh*: Ha ha ha! Only money… (*To VOUZON.*) Now what do you suppose she's up to?

VOUZON, *standing by the loveseat*: I can't imagine. But I'm sure it's something generous. Something that you would never do, I'm sure!

MAURICE: And why do you say that?

VOUZON: Because… (*Tapping his chest.*) Because she has something here. Something called a heart, and one that still works… Not like yours, I'm afraid…

MAURICE: But… I don't understand…

VOUZON: There are many things you don't understand, Maurice. (*Moving up right, pointing to the door.*) Have you ever really given a thought to that child?

MAURICE: My cousin?

VOUZON, *continuing*: Have you ever seen the look in her eyes when they were gazing into yours? Have you ever felt her tremble when your hand touched hers?... Accidentally, of course!

MAURICE: What? But why—

VOUZON, *interrupting, coming back to the loveseat*: Why?... Because she loves you! What better reason...

MAURICE: Céline?

VOUZON: She looks up to you, poor child! She thinks you're noble, and generous, and... She thinks you have a heart!

MAURICE, *looking away*: Good heavens, doctor!... What you're telling me... It's... I... Now that you mention it...

VOUZON: Good! At least that's a start... But what is love to you? (*Standing behind the loveseat.*) It's old-fashioned. It's out of date. It was good enough for us, but... You? You've replaced it with... with South Pacific Carborundum, God help us!

MAURICE: Are you starting in again, doctor?

He gets up and moves down left.

VOUZON, *at the loveseat*: Don't worry... I won't bore you! It's just that it makes me so sad to see what you're becoming... No... What you've become!... To hear you make fun of all our old values... Bah!... I wouldn't trade my age for your youth! (*MAURICE gives a little shrug.*) Oh yes, we were silly fools to believe in such things! In love, in friendship...

MAURICE, *ironically*: In wine...

VOUZON: Why not? We sang the praises of everything good and beautiful! Of everything young, my friend...

MAURICE: Each to his taste!

VOUZON: Yes... (*Pointedly.*) "Chacun à son goût"... And unselfishness, Maurice! All for one and one for all...

MAURICE, *laughing*: How quaint!

VOUZON: Laugh all you like! If your poor father could see you...

MAURICE, *approaching him:* My father?

VOUZON: The one you never knew... A heart of gold, Maurice... My dearest friend... We grew up together, went to school together, studied medicine together... Never a sou between us, but what was money? We were friends, and that was all that mattered! How many times did one of us pawn his watch to pay for the other's?

MAURICE, *continuing to affect his cynical tone*: I'm touched...

VOUZON: Well, perhaps this will touch you a little more, my friend! (*Going over to the table, sitting down, inviting MAURICE with a gesture to do so too.*) You might want to sit down to hear me out. (*With a note of sarcasm.*) Though, of course, time is money...

MAURICE: If you insist...

He sits down across from him. Throughout VOUZON's speech, MAURICE grows noticeably more and more moved, though trying with his comments to maintain his bravado.

VOUZON: One day, your father inherited fifty thousand francs. He was in love with a beautiful young woman. Your mother… And, thanks to that fortune he was going to be able to marry her… Well, the day before the marriage contract, he learned that a fire had just destroyed my father's farm. The poor old man was ruined…

MAURICE: Wasn't he insured?

VOUZON, *ignoring the question*: Now, what would you have done in your father's place, I wonder?

MAURICE: Well, first I would have checked. Because, if he was insured…

VOUZON: Yes, well… Let me tell you… He didn't hesitate one minute. He remembered all the times when he didn't know where his next meal was coming from, and when he would share the bread that my father had sent me. So off he went, without even telling me. And he made him accept a gift that would help him to put his life back together… Twenty-five thousand francs, monsieur!

MAURICE: A gift? At no interest?

VOUZON: Then he went to your mother's family, and he told them what he had done. "My fortune is cut in half, my friends. If your daughter was marrying my money… Well, I'll simply have to let you keep her… If, on the other hand, you have confidence in me and my future, a few francs more or less shouldn't matter."

MAURICE: A few? Twenty-five thousand…

VOUZON, *continuing*: "Money can't buy love," he told them… And your mother took his hand, and she said that she was proud to share in his sacrifice…

MAURICE, *to himself*: Mammá?… She did that?

He wipes away a tear.

VOUZON: Well, they were married… No need to tell you… With no diamonds for the bride, I'm afraid… But they came later. A ring, a bracelet… For a birthday, a special occasion… When times were good… Because an honest woman's diamonds grow little by little, Maurice… Like pure crystal…

MAURICE, *softly*: I never knew that she… that they…

VOUZON: In time, I was able to pay them back what they had lent me. (*Pointedly.*) Thanks to my three francs a visit, through the mud and the rain!… But I never forgot that I owed them so much. Perhaps even my father's life…

MAURICE, *moved*: Doctor…

VOUZON, *continuing*: That's what they did for me! That's what we old-fashioned folk used to do back then… In the good old days… (*Sadly.*) And what you will never do…

MAURICE: Doctor… I…

VOUZON: Friendship… Unselfishness… (*Sarcastically.*) Just so many words!… Money is all that matters, young man!

CELINE enters, up right, carrying a little jewel-box.

CELINE, *approaching MAURICE*: Here, cousin dear… Take this…

VOUZON, *aside*: What?

CELINE: It's all I have…

MAURICE, *getting up*: What?… What are you—

CELINE: My diamonds… Well, my mother's, but…

She puts the box down on the table.

VOUZON: Oh!

MAURICE: Céline...

CELINE: I never wear them, and... and if this is all you need to save you...

MAURICE, *taking her hands, almost too moved to speak*: But... But I can't... I...

CELINE: Why not, cousin dear?

MAURICE: A... A mother's diamonds... They... They're sacred, Céline! All the work, the devotion... All the... All the love...

CELINE, *touched*: Oh!... Why... You're crying, Maurice...

MAURICE, *turning aside, with a little laugh*: I am?... Fancy that...

He wipes his eyes.

VOUZON, *to MAURICE*: Bravo, young man!... I'd say you're saved!

MAURICE: Thanks to you, Céline!

VOUZON: And in more ways than one!

MAURICE, *to CELINE*: What can I do to thank you?

VOUZON, *to MAURICE*: I can think of a way... (*Whispering to him.*) Just tell her you love her!

MAURICE: Oh yes! I do!... (*Embracing her.*) I do! I do!... I love you, Céline!

VOUZON, *with a sigh*: At last! Just like the good old days...

MAURICE, *to CELINE, as an afterthought*: But... But you're getting married, aren't you?

CELINE: Goodness me! What ever makes you think—

MAURICE: To some rich man...

CELINE: Not that I know of...

The door, up left, opens and MADAME DESARNAUX comes running in as MAURICE and CELINE hurriedly separate.

MADAME DESARNAUX, *to MAURICE, joining him, left*: Ah! There you are, treasure!

MAURICE, } *together:* { Mother dear...
CELINE, } { Auntie...

MADAME DESARNAUX, *to MAURICE*: I absolutely must speak with you! It simply can't wait!

JEAN enters, up center.

JEAN, *at the door, to MAURICE*: Ah, monsieur... Madame wanted me to tell monsieur that she absolutely must speak with him, and that it simply can't wait!

He leaves.

MAURICE: Oh?

MADAME DESARNAUX: You've got to run away! Hide... Monsieur Badinier knows everything!

MAURICE: He does? (*Puzzled.*) What, for instance?

BADINIER enters, up center, still carrying his valises, pushing LILI ahead of him, coming down right.

MADAME DESARNAUX: Oh! Too late...

LILI, *to BADINIER*: But I assure you, Raoul—

BADINIER: Enough, woman! If you have anything to say you can say it to my lawyer! (*To MAURICE.*) Young man! You're having an affair with my wife!

The following exclamations are delivered rapid-fire:

LILI: But…

VOUZON: Who…

MADAME DESARNAUX: No!

MAURICE: Me?

CELINE: Oh!

BADINIER, *to MAURICE*: You!

MAURICE: But… Monsieur Badinier! That's utterly absurd! It's preposterous!

BADINIER: Oh? Is it now?

MAURICE, *taking LILI's letter to Monot-Lagarde out of his pocket*: This should clarify the nature of my relationship with madame. (*He hands it to him.*) If you would be so good as to read it…

LILI, *appalled*: Oh my!

BADINIER: But…

LILI: Gustave didn't… He couldn't have…

BADINIER, *examining it, to LILI*: In your handwriting, madame… (*Reading.*) "Dear cousin Gustave… I am writing in regard to a young man, Monsieur Maurice Désarnaux… An impertinent little fop… An insufferable twit…"

MADAME DESARNAUX *and* **CELINE**, *scandalized*: What?

MAURICE: I'm afraid that's what it says!

BADINIER: Hmm! (*Humbly.*) I must say it's not quite what I expected!

LILI: Certainly not, Raoul! How many times do I have to tell you!

BADINIER, *to MAURICE, with a sudden change of attitude*: Well, perhaps you'll come visit us in Chevreuse after all…

LILI, *to MAURICE, in a whisper*: I do hope you'll forgive me!

MAURICE, *replying to BADINIER*: Perhaps, monsieur… (*To LILI, in a whisper.*) For what? Every word of it was true!

MADAME DESARNAUX, *confused, to MAURICE*: But precious… That *assuming* passion of yours… Who?… What?…

MAURICE: Later, mammá!

MADAME DESARNAUX, *to VOUZON, joyously, in a whisper*: Did you hear? He called me "mammá"!

MAURICE, *to MADAME DESARNAUX*: What's the difference? I'm cured!

MADAME DESARNAUX, *aside*: And whoever she is, my rival can go hang! (*To CELINE.*) Oh! I'm so happy!

CELINE: So am I, auntie!

MADAME DESARNAUX: You? Why you?

CELINE: Because you are, of course!

MAURICE, *to MADAME DESARNAUX*: I'll tell you all about it when we get to Rome! (*Inconspicuously pressing CELINE's hand.*) Or when we come back…

MADAME DESARNAUX: But I thought… You said… That matter that couldn't wait…

MAURICE: Well, it will have to!

VOUZON: Just leave that to me! (*To MAURICE, in a whisper, as they shake hands.*) Your five thousand francs… My wedding present, young man…

BADINIER, *to LILI*: I think we'd better get on with our visits.

MAURICE, *to VOUZON, in a whisper*: Oh! How can I thank you?

BADINIER, *continuing*: At this rate we'll get to Chevreuse sometime this fall!

VOUZON, *replying to* MAURICE, *in a whisper*: You have! By letting this old doctor cure you!

BADINIER, *to* MADAME DESARNAUX, *nodding*: Madame…

LILI, *to* MADAME DESARNAUX, *nodding*: Madame… Bon voyage… And do enjoy Rome…

MADAME DESARNAUX, *taking* MAURICE'*s hands in hers*: Oh! I will!… *We* will!… All those wonderful things to see… The Forum…The fountains… The Coliseum…

BADINIER, *with good-natured sarcasm*: The *sixteen chapels…*

LILI, *likewise*: Well, most of them, at any rate!

MADAME DESARNAUX: The Leaning Tower… The Alhambra… The Acropolis…

She enthusiastically continues her flawed enumeration, as the curtain falls.

CURTAIN.

A Nest Egg Well Scrambled

(Les 37 sous de M. Montaudon, 1862)

Eugène Labiche & Edouard Martin

PETITPAIN, a husband suspicious of everyone but his wife

ISIDORE, an accountant, the intended of Petitpain's daughter Angélique

VINPILLE, an old friend of Petitpain's from home, happy to enjoy his hospitality again

GROSMARTEAU, another old friend of his, an officer of the law

RICHAC, a notary, not the soul of patience

MADAME PETITPAIN, Petitpain's wife, concerned with her husband's suspicions

ANGÉLIQUE, the couple's lovely daughter, about to be married

CLAUDETTE, the Petitpains' most recent maid, not above suspicion

Petitpain's Parisian drawing room. Four doors, opening into the room: up center, double doors to a vestibule; up right, the door to the salon; down right, the door to the upstairs bedrooms; down left, the door to Petitpain's study. In the left center wall, a fireplace with all the usual furnishings. On the right center wall, a mirror and, in front of it, a table with writing paraphernalia. Up left, a small table with a bell. Right center, a loveseat. Left center, an armchair. Occasional chairs placed here and there around the room. Other appropriate furnishings.

At rise, ANGELIQUE, *elegantly dressed, is primping in front of the mirror.* CLAUDETTE, *standing behind her, is clapping her hands in admiration.* MADAME PETITPAIN *is standing by the fireplace, somewhat disconsolately.*

CLAUDETTE, to *ANGELIQUE*: Oh! Mademoiselle is pretty as a picture this morning!

MADAME PETITPAIN *utters an audible little sigh.*

ANGELIQUE: Thank you, Claudette. Just a few little touches…

CLAUDETTE: Not that she isn't every morning! But today… Oh! Today she's something special!

ANGELIQUE, *to* MADAME PETITPAIN: Mammá dearest… What's keeping papá? Doesn't he know what day this is?

MADAME PETITPAIN: He's dressing, cherub. Don't worry. We have time.

ANGELIQUE: I know, but…

MADAME PETITPAIN: The notary isn't coming till noon, and it's scarcely eleven. We have a whole hour before… (*Beginning to whimper.*) before I lose you…

ANGELIQUE: Now, now, mammá! Is that any way to talk?

MADAME PETITPAIN: My little Angélique!

CLAUDETTE, *aside*: Tsk tsk tsk!

ANGELIQUE, *to* MADAME PETITPAIN: I hope you're not going to cry when he reads the marriage contract! I couldn't stand it if you did, you know!

MADAME PETITPAIN: Certainly not! If you have to get married, love…

CLAUDETTE, *aside*: *Have* to…?

MADAME PETITPAIN: If you absolutely must… At least Monsieur Isidore is a man of means. Not like some of those fops nowadays…

ANGELIQUE: I should say! An accountant… A cashier in one of the finest shops on the Right Bank…

MADAME PETITPAIN: Twenty-five hundred francs a year…

CLAUDETTE: And lunch…

ANGELIQUE, *echoing*: And lunch, mammá…

CLAUDETTE, *under her breath, with a gesture*: Whew!

ANGELIQUE, *to* MADAME PETITPAIN: And besides, I even love him!

MADAME PETITPAIN: Bah! That won't last! I loved your father too…

ANGELIQUE, *approaching her, in a whisper*: Please, mammá! Not in front of the help…

MADAME PETITPAIN, *ignoring her objection*: I'm not only losing you, precious. What makes it worse is that I have to live here with him! All alone…

ANGELIQUE, *shocked*: Mammá!

CLAUDETTE, *aside*: And me? I'm not leaving…

MADAME PETITPAIN: A man I married for his wonderful disposition… Always cheerful, always laughing…

CLAUDETTE, *aside*: Him?

MADAME PETITPAIN: Now look at him! Moody as the day is long… Never a smile…

CLAUDETTE, *to* ANGELIQUE, *nodding, aloud*: She's right!

ANGELIQUE: Really, Claudette!

MADAME PETITPAIN, *continuing*: And suspicious of everything… The least little thing… Always skulking about… Poking here and there…

CLAUDETTE: It's true. He's forever even poking around in my drawers!

MADAME PETITPAIN, *misunderstanding, scandalized*: Your what?

ANGELIQUE, *tapping her thighs, to* CLAUDETTE, *likewise*: Your drawers?

MADAME PETITPAIN, *to* CLAUDETTE: And you let him?

ANGELIQUE: My father?

MADAME PETITPAIN, *under her breath*: Little slut!

CLAUDETTE, *to* ANGELIQUE, *correcting*: My chest, mademoiselle!

MADAME PETITPAIN, *clutching her bosom*: What?

CLAUDETTE: Of drawers… (*To* ANGELIQUE.) My chest of drawers…

MADAME PETITPAIN, *after a brief, embarrassed silence*: Oh…

ANGELIQUE: What ever can he be looking for?

MADAME PETITPAIN: Who knows? I've asked him dozens of times. I can never get a word out of him.

CLAUDETTE, *joining them, center, innocently*: Maybe he's done something horrible, madame… Some crime… (*To* ANGELIQUE.) Who knows?

ANGELIQUE: Claudette!

MADAME PETITPAIN: Bite your tongue, young lady! How can you even think such a thing?

CLAUDETTE: Well, all I know is… Whenever anyone sets foot in the house, he always asks me who they are. And those slippers of his, madame! The felt ones that he always wears inside, so no one can hear him creeping up…

ANGELIQUE: But Claudette…

CLAUDETTE: Why, just the other day, I was in the kitchen. Stirring my stew, madame… The rabbit stew that madame likes so much…

MADAME PETITPAIN, *impatiently*: Yes, yes…

CLAUDETTE: And all of a sudden there he was, standing right behind me, like a big fat cat!

ANGELIQUE: Claudette!

CLAUDETTE: And I never even heard him come in, mademoiselle! I nearly jumped out of my skin, I can tell you! And he looked at me with that angry look of his, and he said: "When a cook has a clear conscience, mademoiselle, she doesn't shake like a leaf!" (*To* MADAME PETITPAIN.) Because I was, madame! Believe me…

MADAME PETITPAIN: I do…

CLAUDETTE: "I'm not shaking, monsieur. I'm stirring," I told him. And he made me take off my shoes to see if I was hiding anything.

MADAME PETITPAIN: He what?

ANGELIQUE: Maybe he lost something. (*To* CLAUDETTE.) It's possible, you know…

CLAUDETTE: In my shoes?

The door, down right, opens quietly.

MADAME PETITPAIN, *to CLAUDETTE*: I know just what you mean. Always spying… (*PETITPAIN pokes his head in.*) Always popping up when you least expect him… Always—

The three women suddenly notice him.

ANGELIQUE, MADAME PETITPAIN. CLAUDETTE, *jumping with fright*: Ayyy!

ANGELIQUE and MADAME PETITPAIN cross quickly, left, as CLAUDETTE, fanning her face, moves up left.

PETITPAIN, *in shirtsleeves, entering*: It's only me…

ANGELIQUE: Papá!

MADAME PETITPAIN: You frightened me half to death, Gustave!

ANGELIQUE, *sighing*: Oh…

PETITPAIN, *to MADAME PETITPAIN*: Sorry, my love… You wouldn't know where my collars are, would you? I've looked high and low.

MADAME PETITPAIN, *still trembling*: Your collars, indeed!

ANGELIQUE: Really, papá!

MADAME PETITPAIN: Do you have to sneak about like a spy just to look for your collars? I never…

PETITPAIN: Now, now…

MADAME PETITPAIN: Wait here. I'll go find one.

She exits, down right, leaving the door ajar.

ANGELIQUE, *turning a cheek to him, expectantly*: Well, papá?

PETITPAIN: Well?… Well what?

ANGELIQUE: Aren't you going to give me a kiss? Especially today… Not only my birthday, but—

PETITPAIN, *tenderly*: Ah! Dear, dear Angélique!… Of course I am, my sweet! My one joy in life… (*He puckers his lips and crosses to kiss her, but stops abruptly when he sees CLAUDETTE.*) You? What are you doing here?… And why are you trembling?

CLAUDETTE: Me?

PETITPAIN: When a cook has a clear conscience she doesn't shake like a leaf!… Did you lock all the doors?

CLAUDETTE: Oh yes, monsieur! Like always…

PETITPAIN: Who came this morning? At thirteen past eight?… I heard someone… I'm sure…

CLAUDETTE: At thirteen… The milkman, monsieur.

PETITPAIN: It couldn't have been. He always comes at seven thirty-two.

CLAUDETTE: A new one, monsieur… I suppose it took him a little longer.

PETITPAIN: A new one, you say?

CLAUDETTE: Yes, but very nice, really… All smiles, he was… And… And "Bonjour, my little creampuff!…" That's what he called me! His little creampuff…

PETITPAIN: Be careful, mademoiselle! I know these milkmen… That's how they trick you! A few sweet words… And then, when your back is turned, whatever isn't tied down goes straight into their pockets!

ANGELIQUE: But papá…

PETITPAIN, *to* CLAUDETTE: Then who? I heard somebody else… At nine twenty-seven…

CLAUDETTE: The baker, monsieur… He was bringing the bread.

PETITPAIN, *suspiciously*: Again? Didn't he come yesterday?

ANGELIQUE, *to* PETITPAIN: But he comes every day!

PETITPAIN: That often? (*To* CLAUDETTE.) Why?

CLAUDETTE: If monsieur likes his bread stale, I can tell him to come once a week instead.

PETITPAIN: Yes… Perhaps…

ANGELIQUE, *losing patience*: Or not to come at all!… Really, papá! Why are you asking so many questions?

PETITPAIN: Why indeed!… (*Mysteriously.*) Have you ever lost any money, Angélique?

ANGELIQUE: Money?… (*Musing.*) No…

PETITPAIN, *to* CLAUDETTE: And you?

CLAUDETTE, *reflecting*: Well… I bet on a horse once, and he still hasn't come in!

PETITPAIN: No, no… Not "lost" like that… I mean, not been able to find it…

ANGELIQUE: Papá?

CLAUDETTE: No, monsieur. I can't say—

PETITPAIN, *interrupting*: Well, you're lucky! Both of you…

ANGELIQUE: Have you, papá?

PETITPAIN: Have I? Ha!… (*Looking at* CLAUDETTE.) There's an invisible hand in this house, Angélique.

ANGELIQUE: Oh my!

CLAUDETTE: Just a hand, monsieur?… No arm? No body?

PETITPAIN, *ignoring her remark*: One with very light fingers.

CLAUDETTE, *to* ANGELIQUE: A ghost?

PETITPAIN: But please! Not a word to your mother…

CLAUDETTE, *thinking he is talking to her*: My mother is in Toulouse, monsieur.

PETITPAIN, *ignoring her, to* ANGELIQUE: You know how terrified she is of thieves…

CLAUDETTE, *aside*: She is? How would he know?

PETITPAIN: I started to mention it to her once…

CLAUDETTE, *aside*: Oh? When, I wonder… In Toulouse?

PETITPAIN, *continuing*: …and she went all to pieces. I thought she would lose her mind…

CLAUDETTE, *aside*: Who wouldn't? A ghost, after all…

PETITPAIN, *continuing*: So since then I just keep it to myself.

CLAUDETTE, *aside*: And with just a hand…

ANGELIQUE: Of course… (MADAME PETITPAIN *can be heard approaching, down right.*) Shhh! Here she comes… Laugh! (*To* CLAUDETTE.) You too… Laugh!

The three of them stand, forcing laughs, as MADAME PETITPAIN *enters.*

MADAME PETITPAIN, *holding out several collars, to* PETITPAIN: Here you are, Gustave. Take your pick.

PETITPAIN: Ha ha ha!… Thank you, Mathilde… Ha ha ha!… (*Poking the other two to make them laugh.*) Ha ha ha!

ANGELIQUE *and* **CLAUDETTE**: Ha ha ha!

MADAME PETITPAIN, *as they all keep laughing*: My goodness! What's so funny?

PETITPAIN, *putting on a collar and giving her back the others*: What's so… Why, the new milkman, Mathilde!… You should hear what he said to Claudette this morning! (*Nudging* CLAUDETTE, *under his breath.*) Laugh, you!

CLAUDETTE, *laughing*: That's right, madame…

ANGELIQUE: Yes… You should hear…

MADAME PETITPAIN: Well, tell me. I'm all ears.

PETITPAIN: He… He said… "Bonjour, my little creampuff!"

The three break out again into gales of forced laughter, as MADAME PETITPAIN *stands watching them with a deadpan expression.*

MADAME PETITPAIN: And that's why you're splitting your sides?… I never…

CLAUDETTE: It was really very funny…

ANGELIQUE: For a milkman, mammá…

PETITPAIN, *quick to agree*: For a milkman…

MADAME PETITPAIN, *dryly, as the three continue laughing, gradually stopping*: Yes, I'm sure… (*Aside.*) He's out of his mind! (*Aloud, to* CLAUDETTE.) When you're quite able to control your hilarity, Claudette…

CLAUDETTE, *aside*: My what?

MADAME PETITPAIN: …please go help mademoiselle finish dressing.

CLAUDETTE: Very good, madame. Will I need it to help her?

MADAME PETITPAIN: Need "it"? Need what?

CLAUDETTE: What madame just said I should control… My… Whatever…

MADAME PETITPAIN, *impatiently*: Please! Just go!

CLAUDETTE, *under her breath*: I didn't even know I had one…

She and ANGELIQUE *begin moving off, down right.*

MADAME PETITPAIN, *to* PETITPAIN: And you?… I hope you're not planning to marry off your daughter in those slippers of yours! (*Under her breath.*) Did you ever…

PETITPAIN: But all my shoes squeak, Mathilde. I can never creep up on anyone…

ANGELIQUE *and* CLAUDETTE *stop at the door, down right, to listen.*

MADAME PETITPAIN: Who, for example?… And why, for goodness' sake?

PETITPAIN: Oh… No one… No reason… Just like that… Sometimes, don't you know…

ANGELIQUE, *to* CLAUDETTE, *in a whisper*: What ever does he mean, Claudette?

CLAUDETTE *shrugs, and they exit.*

PETITPAIN, *holding out his cravat, to* MADAME PETITPAIN: Here… Help me, would you?

MADAME PETITPAIN, *taking it*: With pleasure!

PETITPAIN: I'm all thumbs with these things. (*She begins knotting it around his neck.*) Ayyy! Not so tight! (*Sarcastically.*) The father of the bride should be alive when the notary reads the contract!

MADAME PETITPAIN, *aside*: Temper, temper… (*Finishing the knot.*) There!

PETITPAIN: Oh, did I tell you? I've invited two more friends.

MADAME PETITPAIN: Did you… (*Exasperated.*) You didn't! Where are we going to put them? The table is only so big…

PETITPAIN: So? If we squeeze a little… And we can set the chairs at an angle.

MADAME PETITPAIN, *aside*: Delightful! (*Aloud.*) And who, may I ask? Do I know them at least?

PETITPAIN: Of course you do. Two of my dear friends from home… Vinpille, my old friend from school, and Grosmarteau, the gendarme…

MADAME PETITPAIN: What? Why on earth…? Vinpille, of all people! We haven't laid eyes on him in at least twenty years! Or Grosmarteau either! That simpleton!

PETITPAIN: Yes, but… But now he's a brigadier. I think it's only right to congratulate him, don't you? Besides, I won't mind having an officer of the law on the premises!

MADAME PETITPAIN: What ever for?

PETITPAIN: If I told you, you wouldn't have a moment's peace, Mathilde. Believe me, you wouldn't sleep a wink!

MADAME PETITPAIN, *moving left, shaking her head*: Please, Gustave! We can't go on this way! Especially now, when we're going to be alone… Just the two of us… (*Turning aside, under her breath.*) Oh!… (*Aloud.*) I mean, now that Angélique is… is…

PETITPAIN: Please… (*Under his breath.*) Don't remind me!

MADAME PETITPAIN: But something is bothering you. I can tell…

PETITPAIN: Perhaps… A little…

MADAME PETITPAIN: Gnawing away at you… Eating you up alive…

PETITPAIN: Bah!

MADAME PETITPAIN: What is it, Gustave? I'm your wife. I have a right to know!

PETITPAIN: Know?… No, you're not strong enough, Mathilde. (*Dramatically.*) You would crumble under the weight…

MADAME PETITPAIN, *approaching him*: Is it something I've done? Or something you think I've done?… (*Struck by a sudden idea.*) Good heavens! Do you suspect…? You don't! You couldn't!

PETITPAIN: Suspect?… Who? What?

MADAME PETITPAIN, *somewhat piqued*: Who?… Me! Who else?… Do you think that I… (*At a loss for words.*) that I…

PETITPAIN: You, Mathilde?

MADAME PETITPAIN: Because, if you do, you're wrong! I swear on our daughter's grave, monsieur!

PETITPAIN, *taken aback*: Grave? What grave? She's still alive…

MADAME PETITPAIN: It's an expression… Besides, she's getting married. On the grave of her… her…

PETITPAIN: Her?

MADAME PETITPAIN: Her… Her virginity, then…

PETITPAIN: Mathilde!

MADAME PETITPAIN: I swear that I never… Never, for one moment, have I given you the slightest cause…

PETITPAIN, *realizing her intent*: No, no, no! It's nothing like that!

MADAME PETITPAIN, *moving down right, ignoring his objection*: Unless... Unless you're still brooding over that foolish bouquet some stranger sent me the day of our wedding...

PETITPAIN: Over twenty years ago? Hardly!

MADAME PETITPAIN, *not listening*: With that silly little poem...

PETITPAIN: You call that a poem? Four miserable lines that I remember to this day... (*Reciting.*)

"Love and his mother picked this fine bouquet:
A nosegay, just for you, this special day.
For, blooms that grow in Venus' garden fair,
Are meant to grace a beauty's breast fore'er!"

(*Scornfully.*) Wretched!... "Fore'er"... Pfff!

MADAME PETITPAIN: But I told you! I didn't know then who sent them, and I certainly don't know now! If that's what you're so suspicious about...

PETITPAIN: That?... Ha ha ha!... It's water under the dam... (*Correcting himself.*) Over...

MADAME PETITPAIN, *correcting him*: The bridge...

PETITPAIN: Over the bridge...

MADAME PETITPAIN: The dam...

PETITPAIN: Whatever... It's ancient history! I admit that, at the time... A young man's wedding-day, after all...

MADAME PETITPAIN: You were jealous! Don't deny it!

PETITPAIN: Of course I was! And if you had given me cause, I would have suspected everyone! I would have been upset... But not as much as I am today, with what's happening to me now!

MADAME PETITPAIN, *echoing, angrily*: "What's happening to me now... What's happening..." But what, for heaven's sake?

PETITPAIN: Nothing! With your nerves...

MADAME PETITPAIN: Gustave!

PETITPAIN: Let me go finish dressing.

MADAME PETITPAIN: Yes! Please do...

PETITPAIN, *as he goes to leave, down right*: Of course I would have been upset. But there's no comparison...

He exits.

MADAME PETITPAIN, *shaking her head*: It must be his liver... (*The doors, up center, open and* RICHAC *enters.*) Oh my, the notary...

RICHAC, *bowing, obsequiously*: Madame...

MADAME PETITPAIN, *to herself*: Already?... (*Aloud, as he kisses her hand.*) Monsieur Richac... How nice... (*A little flustered.*) I... I didn't hear you ring.

RICHAC: I didn't, madame. The door was open and I took the liberty...

MADAME PETITPAIN, *surprised*: It was? (*Aside.*) That Claudette!

RICHAC: I've come a trifle early to clarify some inheritance details with our young groom.

MADAME PETITPAIN: Our… Yes… But Monsieur Isidore isn't here. He hasn't arrived.

RICHAC: Oh?

MADAME PETITPAIN: But I'm sure he will.

RICHAC: I daresay!

MADAME PETITPAIN : Any minute…

RICHAC: Good… Good…

He shuffles from side to side, waiting to be asked to sit down.

MADAME PETITPAIN: In fact, monsieur… I'm glad you're here. There's something I'd like to discuss with you.

She motions him to the loveseat.

RICHAC, *aside*: Finally! (*He waits for her to sit down, then, joining her, aloud.*) At your service, madame!

MADAME PETITPAIN, *putting her finger to her lips*: Please! If my husband had any idea…

RICHAC: Oh? A secret?

MADAME PETITPAIN: Yes, monsieur! And he must never know!

RICHAC: I assure you…

MADAME PETITPAIN: You see… I would like to add a little something to my daughter's dowry.

RICHAC, *nodding*: I understand…

MADAME PETITPAIN: Yes… The sum of thirteen thousand five hundred and five francs…

RICHAC: And?

MADAME PETITPAIN, *misinterpreting his interrogation*: And no centimes…

RICHAC, *repeating*: The sum of thirteen thousand—

MADAME PETITPAIN, *interrupting*: Five hundred and five francs…

RICHAC: Yes, I heard you. (*Aside.*) Some sum! (*Aloud.*) A curious sum, I must say! But no matter… I can simply add it to the contract.

MADAME PETITPAIN: No, no! That will never do! My husband would find out, and with his temper…

RICHAC: I see, I see… But, if I may ask, how did you happen to acquire such a sum, madame?

MADAME PETITPAIN, *hesitating, looking for a reasonable explanation*: It… It was an inheritance, monsieur. From an old aunt… A dead one…

RICHAC: Aha…

MADAME PETITPAIN: She died…

RICHAC: Yes… I assume…

MADAME PETITPAIN: But my husband was never supposed to know.

RICHAC: That she died?

MADAME PETITPAIN: No, no… That she left me her thirteen thousand…

RICHAC: …five hundred and five francs… No centimes… I see.

MADAME PETITPAIN: Can't I simply give it to the groom, monsieur? Just like that? From me to him?

RICHAC: Impossible, madame! The gift must be acknowledged and specified in the contract. If not, it will become part of the community property. And we wouldn't want that!

MADAME PETITPAIN: We wouldn't?

RICHAC: Please! Take my word!

MADAME PETITPAIN: Then, what can I do?

RICHAC: Well, I see only one expedient, madame. You can ask a relative or a friend to contribute this sum in his name.

MADAME PETITPAIN: But *I'm* a relative…

RICHAC: Precisely, but… It's a legal technicality. Don't ask me to explain it.

MADAME PETITPAIN, *musing*: A relative or a friend… Goodness me! I don't know…

RICHAC: Think, madame… It shouldn't be difficult. (*Standing up.*) Now then, I have a few blanks to fill out on the contract. If you would be good enough to put a pen and ink at my disposal…

MADAME PETITPAIN, *standing up, pointing down left*: Of course… In Monsieur Petitpain's study…

RICHAC, *bowing*: Excellent, madame… And please be sure to send in Monsieur Isidore the moment he arrives. As I said, some inheritance details that need spelling out…

MADAME PETITPAIN: Certainly, monsieur…

RICHAC: As we say, a notary can never be too careful.

He bows again, at the door, down left, and exits.

MADAME PETITPAIN, *alone, musing*: A relative? A friend?… But who, for heaven's sake? It has to be someone with enough money to make such a gift! I can't think of a soul!

The doors, up center, open and ISIDORE *appears.*

ISIDORE, *holding out his arms*: Mother, dearest…

MADAME PETITPAIN: Monsieur!

ISIDORE: Excuse me for coming in unannounced, but the door—

MADAME PETITPAIN: It was open… I know…

ISIDORE: Besides, I'm a trifle late…

MADAME PETITPAIN, *with a wave of the hand*: Not at all, monsieur…

ISIDORE, *continuing*: …but just as I was about to leave, my employer sent for me to give me some wonderful news.

MADAME PETITPAIN: Oh?

ISIDORE: Yes… He wants to make me a partner in the firm! Imagine! Me… Not just a cashier… A partner! Think of the honor… The prestige… The—

MADAME PETITPAIN: The money…

ISIDORE: And there's only one small condition… That I invest my wife's dowry…

MADAME PETITPAIN: What?

ISIDORE: Oh, there's no danger, believe me! I know the firm like the back of my hand! As good as gold…

MADAME PETITPAIN: But…

ISIDORE: Even better!… At fifteen percent… Let me show you… (*Taking out a little notepad and pencil from his pocket, writing.*) Dowry, eighty thousand francs, at fifteen percent… That comes to twelve thousand. Plus my salary… Two thousand four hundred… That makes fourteen thousand four hundred. Plus the family's Christmas present…

MADAME PETITPAIN: I beg your pardon?

ISIDORE: I leave that blank for the moment… Sum total: an income of almost fifteen thousand francs… Say we spend five and invest ten. With interest capitalized over twenty years… (*Beginning to write again.*) Let me show you…

MADAME PETITPAIN: Not now! Please…

ISIDORE: Why not? Figures are such a joy. I just love arithmetic.

MADAME PETITPAIN: Yes, but not on your wedding-day! I should think… (*Suddenly noticing PETITPAIN's head appear at the door, down right.*) Oh!

PETITPAIN, *softly*: It's only me… I can't find my gloves, Mathilde. Where did you put them?

MADAME PETITPAIN: Your… You're impossible! You put them away yourself! In your dresser… (*Crossing right.*) Come in, for heaven's sake!

She pulls the door open.

ISIDORE: Good morning, father!

PETITPAIN: Good morning, son!. (*Mumbling, trying to justify his intrusion.*) My gloves, don't you know…

MADAME PETITPAIN, *to ISIDORE*: Please excuse me, monsieur. It's time I finished dressing. (*She moves toward the door, down right, and stops.*) Oh, before I forget… The notary wants a word with you. (*Pointing down left.*) In there…

She exits, down right.

ISIDORE: With me? How jolly… Figures, no doubt…

He moves left, about to leave.

PETITPAIN, *stopping him*: Wait!

ISIDORE: Father?

PETITPAIN: Tell me… Do you ever lose money? When you count it, I mean…

ISIDORE, *rather offended*: Me?

PETITPAIN: Is there ever any missing?

ISIDORE: I should say not! And a good thing, too! I would have to make it up out of my own pocket! A cashier, after all…

PETITPAIN: Of course… Of course… (*Waving him off.*) Well… Don't keep the notary waiting…

ISIDORE, *at the door, down left, under his breath*: Curious question!

He exits.

PETITPAIN, *alone*: Am I the only one who gets robbed?

The doors, up center, open and VINPILLE appears, carrying a valise.

VINPILLE: Well, here I am, old man! Better late than never!… These trains, don't you know…

He puts the valise down on the chair, up left, and holds out his arms to PETITPAIN.

PETITPAIN: Vinpille, my friend! How nice to see you!

VINPILLE: Du… Du…

PETITPAIN: "Dudu"?… What "dudu"…?

VINPILLE, *taking a calling card from his pocket and handing it to him, emphasizing*: *Du* Vinpille…

PETITPAIN, *reading*: "Dominique du Vinpille…" (*To* VINPILLE.) I didn't know… When…?

VINPILLE: When I had the cards printed. It didn't cost any more.

PETITPAIN: Aha… Well, well! What a pleasure…

VINPILLE: Excuse me for coming in this way. Unannounced, I mean… But the door was open…

PETITPAIN: It was?

VINPILLE, *ignoring the question, joining him, with a hug*: Petitpain!… After all these years…

PETITPAIN: Yes… But you haven't changed a day!

VINPILLE, *inspecting him*: Hmm… You have…

PETITPAIN: Oh?

VINPILLE, *changing the subject*: How good of you to invite me!… You know how I love weddings! Like yours, remember?

PETITPAIN: Of course! But I'm surprised you do… (*Aside.*) Considering how drunk—

VINPILLE: I'll never forget! Old Grosmarteau and I… The three of us! What a time!

PETITPAIN, *looking around*: Where is he? I thought he was coming with you.

VINPILLE: He was. But at the last minute… Official business… Now that he's been made a brigadier…

PETITPAIN: You mean, he's not coming?

VINPILLE: He asked me to tell you how sorry he was.

PETITPAIN: Blast!

VINPILLE: And me too! A real wag, that one… Always the life of the party… But he said he would write you a letter.

PETITPAIN: What good is a letter! I was counting on his uniform… Damn!… Well anyway, you're here. And you'll stay a few days, won't you?

VINPILLE: As many as you like! (*Laughing.*) Until you get tired of me! (*Aside.*) Or the champagne runs out!

PETITPAIN, *pointing to the valise*: Come… We're putting you upstairs, in the room next to mine.

VINPILLE, *taking the valise*: Bravo! We can talk about old times all night, over a drink!

PETITPAIN, *leading him down right*: And new times too! You can tell me everything that's happening in Saint-Etienne.

VINPILLE, *stopping*: Can I! You wouldn't believe some of the things… Do you remember old Mère Dallore? From the tobacco shop?

PETITPAIN: Of course.

VINPILLE: Well, we buried her last Wednesday.

PETITPAIN, *with a little chuckle*: Was she dead?

VINPILLE, *ignoring his remark*: And old Père Poupon? The one who got married when he was sixty-eight…

PETITPAIN: To La Floupette?

VINPILLE: Right... Well, he just had a baby, last Thursday.

PETITPAIN: No! A boy or a girl?

VINPILLE : Yes... I'm sure... One or the other...

PETITPAIN: Old Père Poupon! That's a good one! And who's the godfather?

VINPILLE: You're looking at him, old man!

PETITPAIN, *with a little laugh*: Ah! The same old Vinpille... It's good to see you. Just like old times... When I could still laugh!

VINPILLE, *putting down the valise*: What's the matter, my friend? You can't laugh anymore?

PETITPAIN: I'm afraid not.

VINPILLE: Oh? Open your mouth!

PETITPAIN: What?

VINPILLE: A man only stops laughing when he's lost all his teeth! Open up... Let me see...

PETITPAIN: Ha! I wish it were just my teeth! Oh, if you only knew...

VINPILLE: But what else...

PETITPAIN: Look... You're an old friend. I can tell you...

VINPILLE: Please...

PETITPAIN: It... It's driving me crazy. It's unbelievable... (*Confidentially.*) Vinpille, I'm being robbed!

VINPILLE: Oh? I can see that would drive you crazy, but it's certainly not unbelievable. It happens all the time nowadays.

PETITPAIN: Yes, but not like this! If somebody sneaked in, broke into my desk and made off with ten thousand francs, I would say: "Fine! Once in a lifetime... He's a thief. That's his trade, his profession! He'll never come back!" But my thief comes back every day, Vinpille! Every blessèd day, you hear me?

VINPILLE: He does?

PETITPAIN: Like someone going to his office... Good God! It's not as if he takes a lot... Just seven francs forty... Thirty-seven sous a day... But still—

VINPILLE: What? Who ever heard of such a thing? Thirty-seven sous...?

PETITPAIN: No more, no less...

VINPILLE: Of all things...

PETITPAIN: But it all adds up! And over the years...

VINPILLE: It must be an error in your accounts, old man. It's easy to make mistakes. Add too much here, subtract too much there... Forget what you spent...

PETITPAIN: Impossible! I keep track. A sou to a beggar... A sou to an organ-grinder... I write everything down! To the letter, Vinpille... And at night, when I check... Double check, triple check!... At night I'm always missing thirty-seven sous! Exactly!

VINPILLE: Odd, I must say...

PETITPAIN: Quite... Besides, it's nothing new. Ever since Angélique was born... At first I thought I was just being careless. And who had time to worry about a trifle? We had other things to think about, Mathilde and I.

VINPILLE: You mean, you suspected your daughter?

PETITPAIN: What are you talking about? A baby?

VINPILLE: But you said—

PETITPAIN: How could a baby steal thirty-seven sous from her father? Or from anyone else, for that matter?

VINPILLE: Of course! At that age they're not thinking about money. They wouldn't…

PETITPAIN: So you see what I mean… Being robbed for twenty years! Every day!… Because the scoundrel doesn't even stop on Sundays!

VINPILLE: Scandalous! You would think…

PETITPAIN: Day of rest? Not for him! Just another day!

VINPILLE: No morals, some people… To steal on a Sunday…

PETITPAIN: So you can see what it's been like. Why my nerves can't take any more…

VINPILLE, *nodding*: I can imagine…

PETITPAIN, *continuing*: Why I'm always depressed and down at the mouth… Why I don't laugh, Vinpille… Why I can't eat a thing… Why nothing agrees with me…

VINPILLE: Tsk tsk tsk…

PETITPAIN: Cabbage, shrimp, blood pudding… All the things I like…

VINPILLE, *sympathetically*: Oh! Poor Gustave!… And you haven't tried to catch the bugger?

PETITPAIN: Tried? Ha!… Dozens of times! Hundreds!… (*With a wave of the hand.*) Pfff!… He's too clever!

VINPILLE: Tsk tsk tsk!

PETITPAIN: Last night, for example… (*Pointing left.*) I left my purse above the fireplace, with nothing but a five-franc piece inside… Come… How much do you want to bet…

He crosses left and takes the purse.

VINPILLE, *laughing*: Well, let's say I bet thirty-seven sous.

PETITPAIN: Please! It's no laughing matter! (*Opening the purse.*) See? Three francs and three sous.

VINPILLE: Sixty-three sous… Plus thirty-seven makes five francs.

PETITPAIN: You see? What did I tell you? It's driving me insane!

VINPILLE: Well, at least he has principles. He left you the change.

PETITPAIN, *ignoring the pleasantry, joining him, center*: So! What do you think?

VINPILLE: Well… Could be he always spends thirty-two for his dinner, and… and treats himself to a good cigar for the other five!

PETITPAIN: Be serious, Vinpille! You must have some idea…

VINPILLE: Don't you suspect anyone?

PETITPAIN: Anyone?… Ha! Everyone! … Everyone except my wife and daughter… Just guess how many times I've changed milkmen.

VINPILLE: Four?

PETITPAIN: Sixty-three in twenty years! Five so far, this year alone!… And unless he's hiding in a bottle…

VINPILLE, *shaking his head*: No… I doubt it.

PETITPAIN: And domestics?… Maids, cooks… Can you guess how many I've fired? (*Before he can answer.*) Forty-nine! I've kept track… And I'm keeping an eye on the one I have now! I make her take off her shoes twice a day.

VINPILLE: What for?

PETITPAIN: To see if she's hiding my thirty-seven sous, damn it! But I still haven't caught her!

VINPILLE: Then she's not the one, you mean?

PETITPAIN: I don't know. I don't trust her. She has an evil look about her.

VINPILLE: Oh?

PETITPAIN: Are you good at reading faces?

VINPILLE: Very! Sometimes I amaze myself.

PETITPAIN: Good! I'll call her. You can take a look. (*He rings the bell on the table, up center.*) Just don't let her see…

VINPILLE: Don't worry, old man. I'm the soul of discretion.

CLAUDETTE enters, up right.

CLAUDETTE: Monsieur rang?

PETITPAIN: Yes, mademoiselle… This is my friend, Monsieur Vinpille. Please look him in the eye.

She complies.

VINPILLE, *aside*: Hmm! Not bad!

PETITPAIN, *in a whisper*: I bet she's hidden them in her… her… (*Caressing his bosom.*) Down there…

VINPILLE, *in a whisper*: Should I check?

CLAUDETTE, *to PETITPAIN, still staring at VINPILLE*: Should I keep looking, monsieur?

PETITPAIN: No. Just take monsieur's valise upstairs.

CLAUDETTE: Yes, monsieur.

PETITPAIN: He's in the room next to mine. The blue one.

CLAUDETTE: Very good, monsieur.

She picks up the valise and begins moving right.

PETITPAIN, *calling to her*: Wait!

CLAUDETTE, *stopping*: Please?

PETITPAIN, *very matter-of-fact*: You know, mademoiselle… In the eyes of society, the person who steals three francs forty is as guilty as the one who steals a million.

CLAUDETTE, *baffled*: Oh? I didn't know, monsieur.

PETITPAIN: Well, now you do. I just thought I should mention it.

CLAUDETTE: Thank you, monsieur… Shall I go now?

PETITPAIN, *waving her out*: Yes. Go, go, go!

VINPILLE, *patting his chest, to PETITPAIN, whispering*: You're sure you don't want me to check? Just to be sure…

CLAUDETTE exits, down right, with the valise.

PETITPAIN: You see? It's written all over her face. Can't you tell?

VINPILLE: Not really… Besides, I still think I should check.

PETITPAIN, *ignoring the remark*: You see what my life has become, Vinpille? Suspicion, suspicion… Wherever I turn… It's impossible!

VINPILLE: If I were you, one day I would put thirty-six sous in my purse, to see what happens…

PETITPAIN: I did! But the next day he took thirty-eight! I can't win!

VINPILLE: At least he's consistent, whoever he is.

PETITPAIN: Or she…

VINPILLE, *agreeing*: Or she…

PETITPAIN: Ah, Vinpille! How lucky you are not to live in this hotbed of vice and depravity!

MADAME PETITPAIN'S VOICE, *offstage*: Gustave!

PETITPAIN, *continuing, waxing melodramatic*: Not to have left Saint-Etienne… Home… The joys of nature…

MADAME PETITPAIN'S VOICE: Gustave! Your jacket…

PETITPAIN, *continuing*: To be nestled in her bosom…

VINPILLE: Whose?

PETITPAIN: Nature's… To roam her woods in peace… To frolic in her waves…

MADAME PETITPAIN'S VOICE: Gustave!

VINPILLE: Woods?… Waves?… What are you talking about? The ocean is miles away…

PETITPAIN, *confused*: I… I don't know what I'm saying… (*Calling out.*) Coming, Mathilde… (*To* VINPILLE.) Wait here. I'll be back.

He exits, down right.

VINPILLE, *alone, pacing*: And to think… I came here to enjoy myself! A fine time I'll have with him in the mood he's in! Him and his thirty-seven sous!… Suspicious! (*With a shudder.*) Brrrr!… Why doesn't he just write down in his account book, every day: "To my thief: seven francs forty…" and let it go at that! (*Stopping.*) Of course, I could go have a chat with the maid. Feel her out, so to speak… (*Pacing.*) Maybe get her to make a clean breast of it… (*Stopping again, feeling his pockets.*) What is that jingling around?… (*He reaches into one pocket and pulls out several napkin rings.*) Ah! My wedding present… A dozen napkin rings… With the inscription "Bon appétit!"… I wanted to give them one of those newfangled magic lanterns. But expensive?… Whew!… I let my wife talk me out of it. "Better give them something practical," she said. "After all, everybody eats…" "But does everybody wipe their mouth?" I asked her. "Well, if they don't, they should," she answered. So that's what I decided… And, at the price they were asking, how could I go wrong? Besides, I wrote a little poem for the bride. We always do that back home. I'll recite it when the notary reads the contract… Of course, when I say "I wrote…" I'm stretching the truth a little. Not enough to break it, mind you… I borrowed it from Grosmarteau. He wrote it for my wife's birthday. He rhymes like the rest of us talk, that brigadier of ours! A real wag, like I said… Well, thereby hangs the "tail…" (*Laughing at his own pun.*) "Wag…" "Tail…" Ha ha ha!… "No sense letting a good poem go to waste," I told myself. And I copied it out… I can't wait to hear their "oohs" and "aahs"…

MADAME PETITPAIN enters, down right, in an elegant gown, tightly corseted, obviously several sizes too small for her. She leaves the door ajar.

MADAME PETITPAIN: Goodness me! I can scarcely breathe…

VINPILLE, *under his breath, admiringly*: I say!

MADAME PETITPAIN: Ah! Monsieur Vinpille! What a pleasure…

VINPILLE, *approaching*: Likewise, I'm sure… (*Reaching out to embrace her.*) If I may, madame…

MADAME PETITPAIN: Indeed…

VINPILLE: Dear friend…

As he kisses her, first on one cheek, then the other, PETITPAIN *quietly pokes his head in the door, down right, observing.*

MADAME PETITPAIN, *catching sight of him, uttering a cry*: Oh!

VINPILLE: Beg pardon? (*Aside.*) Is it my breath?

MADAME PETITPAIN, *pointing*: Him!

VINPILLE: What?

MADAME PETITPAIN, *startled, to* PETITPAIN: You!

PETITPAIN, *entering*: It's only me…

VINPILLE, *to* PETITPAIN, *jokingly*: Just in time to catch me kissing your wife, old man!

PETITPAIN: Yes… So I see… (*To* MADAME PETITPAIN.) My stickpin, Mathilde… You wouldn't happen to know—

MADAME PETITPAIN, *fanning her face*: Of course I would! Of all the… It's in the cup above the fireplace. Where it always is!

She makes a move down right as if to exit.

PETITPAIN, *stopping her*: Don't bother… I can find it.

He exits, down right.

VINPILLE: Does he always pop up like that?

MADAME PETITPAIN: Oh!

VINPILLE: Without warning, I mean…

MADAME PETITPAIN, *sitting down on the loveseat, not without difficulty*: Really, monsieur! You don't know what it's like. You can't imagine!… And it's getting worse.

VINPILLE, *approaching her*: Tsk tsk tsk! (*Changing the subject.*) And we're going to see the pretty young bride, I hope? I have my little wedding present to give her.

MADAME PETITPAIN: Oh! You're too kind. You didn't have to…

VINPILLE : Nothing fancy, mind you… (*With a chuckle.*) No diamonds, madame! I believe in giving something practical, don't you know… "Try to be useful!" That's my motto.

MADAME PETITPAIN: Indeed… (*To herself.*) Useful?… Hmm! I wonder if he…

VINPILLE: No frills… Just be useful…

MADAME PETITPAIN, *continuing, aside*: "A friend," the notary said… Why not? (*Aloud.*) Monsieur…

VINPILLE: Madame?

MADAME PETITPAIN: I have a favor… An immense favor to ask of you…

VINPILLE: Of me?

MADAME PETITPAIN, *inviting him, with a gesture, to sit down next to her*: Please… (*As he sits down.*) But first, can I count on your discretion, monsieur?

VINPILLE: Of course, madame! A gentleman, after all… I assure you…

MADAME PETITPAIN: Discretion!

VINPILLE: "The better part of valor," as they say!

MADAME PETITPAIN, *bemused at the irrelevance of the remark*: Yes… Don't they… Well… (*She gets up and goes around checking the doors to make sure no one is listening, softly.*) Do you swear not to breathe a word to Gustave?

VINPILLE: Solemnly, madame! (*Aside.*) Don't tell me she… No! She couldn't have!… (*Aloud.*) Solemnly! (*Aside.*) I mean, who would… (*Aloud.*) You were saying? (*Aside, with a grimace.*) With her?

MADAME PETITPAIN: For twenty years, monsieur… For almost as long as Gustave and I have been married…

VINPILLE: Ah! What a wedding! I remember it as if it were yesterday!

MADAME PETITPAIN: Yes, but… Let me tell you… Since Angélique was born, I've been saving up a nest egg. In secret, monsieur…

VINPILLE: Oh?

MADAME PETITPAIN: Gustave has no idea… And it's grown now to thirteen thousand five hundred and five francs…

VINPILLE, *with a laugh*: An ostrich egg, you mean!

MADAME PETITPAIN: Perhaps it was wrong of me. But in those days all he could think about was building this, building that. First another wing, then the attic… Then a nursery for the baby… All of our savings were disappearing into bricks and mortar.

VINPILLE: Tsk tsk tsk…

MADAME PETITPAIN: So you see, monsieur… I had to do something to be sure that our daughter wouldn't grow up to be a pauper.

VINPILLE: How commendable, madame! Thrift is one of the cardinal virtues! (*Aside.*) Isn't it? (*Aloud.*) At least, it should be…

MADAME PETITPAIN: But Gustave must never know! With his suspicious nature, he would imagine all kinds of things… Frightful things… I'm sure you understand!

VINPILLE: Of course, dear lady! Of course!

MADAME PETITPAIN: And so I thought… I mean, if they came from you…

VINPILLE: From me?

MADAME PETITPAIN: Your wedding gift, monsieur… When the notary reads the contract… Thirteen thousand five hundred and five francs from our old friend, Dominique Vinpille…

VINPILLE, *handing her a card, correcting her*: Du… Du Vinpille…

MADAME PETITPAIN: Ah… I didn't know…

VINPILLE : No matter…

MADAME PETITPAIN: Oh, please! Don't say no!

VINPILLE: "No"? "No"?… Certainly not! I wouldn't dream…

MADAME PETITPAIN, *misunderstanding him*: But I'm begging you, monsieur… Monsieur du Vinpille…

VINPILLE: No need… I said: "No, I wouldn't…" Yes, that is…

MADAME PETITPAIN: What?… No? Yes?

VINPILLE: Yes… You said: "Oh, please! Don't say no!" And I said: "No? No?… Certainly not!"… That means "yes," no?… (*Aside.*) Talk about the "oohs" and "aahs" when they hear it!

MADAME PETITPAIN: Oh, thank you, monsieur! You're really too kind…

She moves upstage.

VINPILLE, *to himself*: So much for the napkin rings! Maybe I can return them… Thirteen thousand five hundred and five francs, and a poem to boot! (*As* MADAME PETITPAIN *takes a purse from her bosom, still to himself.*) Rather handsome for a man from the provinces, I would say!

MADAME PETITPAIN, *taking out a roll of bills and giving them to him*: There, monsieur… The whole sum, in bills… (*Taking out a coin*) Plus five francs…

VINPILLE: Aha… (*Quickly counting.*) Yes… Quite… Would you like a receipt?

MADAME PETITPAIN: Heavens, no! Just remember… Not a word to Gustave!

VINPILLE, *pocketing the money*: Not a word! (*Moving down left, to himself.*) This way, if they take back the napkin rings, I don't spend a thing!

As he muses, the up center doors open and a half-dozen guests of both sexes enter.

MADAME PETITPAIN: Ah! The guests…

A GUEST: Excuse us for bursting in this way… The door was open…

MADAME PETITPAIN: Not at all… How good of you to come…

As THE GUESTS *spread themselves around the room, muttering things like "I hope we're not late," "I can't wait to see her," "It's so thoughtful of you, madame," etc.,* MADAME PETITPAIN *goes up left and rings the bell on the little table. A moment later,* CLAUDETTE *enters, down right.*

CLAUDETTE: Madame rang?

MADAME PETITPAIN, *pointing to the table, right, and indicating with a gesture that it is to be placed center stage*: Please…

CLAUDETTE: Very good, madame.

As THE GUESTS *continue muttering, she places the table as indicated, with two chairs. As* CLAUDETTE *exits, up right,* ISIDORE *and* RICHAC *enter, down left.*

ISIDORE, *to* RICHAC: Good! Then we agree. I'm the sole heir. You'll be sure to put that down…

RICHAC: I have, monsieur. (*Aside.*) Not an easy one, this son-in-law!

ANGELIQUE *appears at the door, down right. As she enters,* THE GUESTS *utter appropriate exclamations of admiration: "Oh! There she is!" "Look! The bride!" "How beautiful!" etc.*

ANGELIQUE, *as* RICHAC *sits down at the table, with his briefcase on his lap*: Mesdames… Messieurs… How nice to see you…

VINPILLE, *approaching her, arms outstretched*: My child…

He gives her a hug and a kiss on both cheeks.

ISIDORE, *to* ANGELIQUE, *in a whisper*: Who the devil…?

ANGELIQUE, *replying, likewise*: I have no idea…

VINPILLE, *between kisses, to* ISIDORE: Wait till you hear how much I love you both, young man!

ISIDORE: I beg your pardon?

VINPILLE: You'll see… You'll hear! (*Pointing to* RICHAC.) When he reads my gift…

ISIDORE, *aside*: Some rich old uncle, I suppose…

VINPILLE, *aside*: May as well prepare them for it…

MADAME PETITPAIN, *looking around, to* RICHAC: Where on earth is Monsieur Petitpain? Has anyone seen—

PETITPAIN enters, down right.

PETITPAIN: Here I am, my love! (*Joining her, center, to* RICHAC.) Please excuse me…

MADAME PETITPAIN, *in an angry whisper*: Gustave! Your slippers!

PETITPAIN, *looking down, under his breath*: Blast!… Oh well… Among friends… (*Aloud, with a little bow.*) Mesdames… Messieurs… Please, won't you take your seats… Let's not keep monsieur waiting… A notary's time, don't you know…

Everyone takes a seat on the various chairs around the room. MADAME PETITPAIN sits down right, and PETITPAIN, down left.

RICHAC, *taking a document from his briefcase and reading*: "Whereas, in the presence of Maître Jean-Jacques Richac, duly accredited notary in the city of Paris…"

VINPILLE, *seated next to* MADAME PETITPAIN, *to himself*: I'll start out with the poem…

RICHAC, *continuing*: "…have appeared, on the one hand, Monsieur Isidore-Acaste Dupuis—"

VINPILLE, *standing up, interrupting*: One moment, monsieur… (*Approaching him.*) Excuse me… If you don't mind…

THE GUESTS murmur appropriate comments of surprise: "What does he want?" "What do you suppose…?" "What on earth…?" etc.

RICHAC, *taken aback*: Please?

VINPILLE: I have a poem.

RICHAC: Oh?

VINPILLE: Yes… I thought you would like to know.

THE GUESTS mutter comments like "What did he say?" "He has a poem?" "Of all things…" etc.

RICHAC, *misunderstanding, dryly*: How nice for you.

VINPILLE: No… I mean, I brought one… To recite… A poem for the bride… A little something I composed myself…

THE GUESTS react again: "My, my! He's a poet!" "He wrote a poem for her!" "How fetching!" etc.

RICHAC: Yes, but…

PETITPAIN, *to* VINPILLE: Vinpille, my friend! How thoughtful…

ISIDORE, *aside*: Is that what I'm going to hear?

PETITPAIN, *continuing*: I never guessed…

ISIDORE, *aside*: That famous gift of his?

VINPILLE: And I'll read it now, if you like.

THE GUESTS, exclaim their approval with shouts like "Oh yes!" "Please, do!" "Let us hear it!" etc.

RICHAC: But… The contract, monsieur…

PETITPAIN: It can wait a minute. If my friend went to all the trouble, I think it's only polite, after all—

THE GUESTS agree with cries of "The poem!" "Let him read it!" "Yes, yes!" etc.

VINPILLE, *taking a paper from his pocket and unfolding it, to the company*: You understand… I'm not a professional. I just let the inspiration come. And when I think of a line, I write it down, so as not to lose it.

PETITPAIN: Of course… Of course…

VINPILLE, *clearing his throat*: So… You'll see… It's supposed to be put into a bouquet of flowers, but… I didn't have time. The train was late, and—

A LADY GUEST, *passing him a bouquet she is holding*: Please! Take mine…

VINPILLE: Ah! Thank you!… I'll give it right back. (*He stands holding the bouquet in one hand and the paper in the other, pompously clearing his throat.*) So… (*Reading.*)

"Love and his mother picked this fine bouquet:
A nosegay, just for you, this special day…"

PETITPAIN, *down left, and* MADAME PETITPAIN, *down right, jumping to their feet*: What?

VINPILLE, *continuing*:

"For, blooms that grow in Venus' garden fair,
Are meant to grace a beauty's breast, fore'er."

THE GUESTS, *applauding*: Bravo! Bravo!

PETITPAIN, *aside*: But… That poem… Oh! Good God! He was the one!… Him!

MADAME PETITPAIN, *to* VINPILLE, *approaching him, in a whisper*: You mean…

PETITPAIN, *to himself*: I don't believe it!

MADAME PETITPAIN, *continuing, to* VINPILLE: It was you?

PETITPAIN, *to himself*: And he was kissing her just now!

MADAME PETITPAIN, *to herself*: Heaven help me!

VINPILLE, *to* MADAME PETITPAIN: What? Me?… Me, what?

PETITPAIN, *controlling his anger*: Oh! Of all the…

RICHAC: Yes… Well… (*Beginning again, reading.*) "Whereas, in the presence of Maître Jean-Jacques Richac—"

PETITPAIN, *to* RICHAC, *interrupting*: No!… Not now… (*Pointing to* VINPILLE.) I have to discuss something with monsieur…

THE GUESTS mutter their surprise with questions like "What did he say?" "What ever can he mean?" "What's the matter?" etc.

VINPILLE: Me?

PETITPAIN, *to the others*: In private… (*Pointing to the door, up right.*) Please! We'll just be a moment.

THE GUESTS, still muttering, leave, up right, followed by ANGELIQUE, MADAME PETITPAIN, ISIDORE, *and* RICHAC.

VINPILLE, *aside*: He must want to compliment me!

PETITPAIN, *shaking his hand vigorously*: Congratulations, Vinpille! Your poem is really terribly… gallant!

VINPILLE, *falsely modest*: Oh… It's not bad. I dashed it off this morning in the train. On the way…

PETITPAIN: Aha… This morning… Curious, I would have sworn it was older than that.

VINPILLE, *aside*: Oh my! Does he suspect…?

PETITPAIN, *sarcastically*: You seem troubled, my friend.

VINPILLE: Me?

PETITPAIN: Never mind! I'm sure we understand each other!

He takes off his gloves and slaps him in the face with them.

VINPILLE: Oh!

PETITPAIN: After the wedding... After the wedding...

VINPILLE: What?

PETITPAIN, *putting his gloves back on*: I can wait, my friend! After the wedding... (*Calling, up right.*) Maître Richac!... Monsieur!...

VINPILLE, *rubbing his cheek, as* THE GUESTS *return, up right, followed by the others*: Oh my! Oh my!

PETITPAIN: Mesdames... Messieurs... Please take your seats. We're going to continue. (*To* RICHAC, *inviting him, with a gesture, to take his seat at the table.*) Monsieur... Be so good...

VINPILLE, *sitting down next to* MADAME PETITPAIN, *down right, in a whisper*: What's got into your husband, madame?

MADAME PETITPAIN, *whispering*: Shhh! He's watching us!

VINPILLE: So?

PETITPAIN, *aside*: Blast! They're whispering to each other.

MADAME PETITPAIN, *to* VINPILLE, *whispering*: Please! This is no time...

RICHAC: With your permission I'll begin at the beginning. (*Reading, as* THE GUESTS *mutter their approval.*) "Whereas, in the presence of Maître Jean-Jacques Richac, duly accredited notary in the city of Paris, have appeared, on the one hand, Monsieur Isidore-Acaste Dupuis, cashier, employed at number nine Rue du Sentier and residing in Paris at number twelve Rue Saint-Joseph, being a major son of Monsieur Philippe-Auguste Dupuis, residing in Paris at number twenty-two Rue Rochechouart..."

PETITPAIN, *aside*: Good God! Is he going to go through the whole city?

RICHAC, *continuing*: "... and appearing on his own behalf, and, on the other hand, Mademoiselle Angélique-Marguerite Petitpain..."

VINPILLE, *aside*: I think this is the right moment...

He stands up, clearing his throat.

RICHAC, *continuing*: "...residing in Paris, at number three Rue des Moulins, being the daughter of Monsieur and Madame..."

VINPILLE, *approaching him, interrupting*: Pardon me, monsieur, if I interrupt you...

THE GUESTS *voice their surprise with a variety of exclamations: "What now?" "Again?" "What is it this time?" etc.*

RICHAC: Monsieur?

VINPILLE: But I'm sure you will agree that what I have to say is of the utmost importance.

RICHAC, *impatiently*: Really, I—

VINPILLE: Please write this down. "Whereas I, Dominique-Auguste du Vinpille, being of sane mind and sound body..."

RICHAC: Well...

VINPILLE: "…residing in Saint-Etienne at number twenty-seven Rue des Augustins, do wish to contribute to the dowry of Mademoiselle Angélique-Marguerite Petitpain…"

PETITPAIN: What?

VINPILLE: "…residing in Paris, at number three Rue des Moulins…"

RICHAC: But…

THE GUESTS voice their impatience with shouts of "Get on with it!" "We know where she lives!" "For goodness' sake!" etc.

VINPILLE: "…the sum of thirteen thousand five hundred and five francs… No centimes…"

ANGELIQUE, *jumping to her feet as PETITPAIN stands agape, and THE GUESTS "ooh" and "aah" their admiration*: What? (*To* VINPILLE.) Monsieur…

VINPILLE, *aside*: I guess that showed them!

PETITPAIN, *finding his tongue, to VINPILLE, as THE GUESTS continue to murmur their approval*: What? You… An amount like that…

MADAME PETITPAIN, *hypocritically*: My, my! How generous! (*To* VINPILLE.) You're a prince, monsieur!

ISIDORE, *to VINPILLE*: Really! I don't know how to thank you!

RICHAC: Please…

VINPILLE, *to ISIDORE*: I told you, young man, I love your bride. As much as if she were my very own daughter…

PETITPAIN: His very own…

VINPILLE, *continuing*: My own flesh and blood…

PETITPAIN, *to himself*: You don't suppose… (*To* ISIDORE.) Look at her… His eyes, his mouth…

ISIDORE: Now that you mention it… (*Aside.*) I wonder… Is it possible…

RICHAC, *impatiently, to PETITPAIN*: Monsieur?

ISIDORE, *aside*: A gift like that…

PETITPAIN, *ignoring RICHAC, aside*: Good God! Could it be…

ISIDORE: The same chin, the same brow…

PETITPAIN: My best friend…

ISIDORE, *to himself*: What difference, really…

RICHAC, *with a shrug, beginning again, reading*: "Whereas…"

PETITPAIN, *interrupting*: Pardon me, monsieur, but… I have to interrupt once more. Something has just come up…

MADAME PETITPAIN, *as THE GUESTS react with their usual exclamations of impatience*: Gustave!

ANGELIQUE: Really, papá!

PETITPAIN, *to RICHAC, pointing to VINPILLE*: I have to have a few words with monsieur…

VINPILLE: Me? Again?

PETITPAIN, *to THE GUESTS*: In private, if you don't mind… (*Pointing to the door, up right.*) Please! We'll just be a moment.

A GUEST, *to one of the others, softly*: Couldn't they go out? Why us?

RICHAC, *losing patience, to PETITPAIN*: This is highly irregular, monsieur!

PETITPAIN: Yes… (*Waving him and the others off.*) Yes… Please…

Everyone except PETITPAIN *and* VINPILLE *exit, up right, in the same order as before, muttering as usual.*

VINPILLE, *when they are alone, center*: Is there something—

PETITPAIN, *with a scarcely contained rage:* Something, Vinpille?… Something?… (*Grasping his hand.*) Yes, I daresay there's something! (*Angrily.*) Some way to thank you…

He shakes his hand vigorously.

VINPILLE: Ayyy!… You're crushing my fingers!

PETITPAIN: Such a magnificent gift… And to a total stranger…

VINPILLE, *breaking free*: Your daughter, old man? A stranger?

PETITPAIN: Yes… *My* daughter… Whom you haven't seen in twenty years… Quite a gift, I must say!

VINPILLE, *with a wave of his wounded hand*: Pfff!

PETITPAIN: My, my! A man who makes seven thousand francs a year, if he's lucky… And who still has the first sou he ever earned…

VINPILLE, *offended*: Oh!

PETITPAIN: And who lavishes thirteen thousand five hundred francs on my daughter!

VINPILLE, *correcting*: Five… Five hundred and *five…*

PETITPAIN: Yes… Quite a gift!

VINPILLE: But I… I love the child…

PETITPAIN: So I see!… Well, you can't pull the wool over my eyes, Vinpille!

VINPILLE, *thoroughly confused*: I can't?

PETITPAIN: Oh, what a blind fool I've been! And that poem… All these years!…

VINPILLE: I beg your—

PETITPAIN: Never mind! I'm sure we understand each other!

He takes of his gloves and slaps him in the face with them.

VINPILLE: Oh!

PETITPAIN: After the wedding…

VINPILLE: What?… "After…" Again?

PETITPAIN, *putting his gloves back on*: It can wait, my friend! After the wedding… My daughter's wedding, monsieur… *My* daughter's…

VINPILLE, *aside*: Who else's?

CLAUDETTE *enters, up right.*

CLAUDETTE, *to* PETITPAIN: Monsieur…

PETITPAIN, *impatiently*: What is it?

VINPILLE, *patting his bosom, to* PETITPAIN: Would you like me to check?

CLAUDETTE: The notary, monsieur. He says to tell you he thinks it's time…

PETITPAIN: Tell him… (*Suddenly.*) Take off your shoes!

CLAUDETTE, *misunderstanding*: I should tell the notary to take off his shoes?

PETITPAIN: Not him, idiot! You!

CLAUDETTE, *resigned*: If monsieur insists…

She slips off her shoes. PETITPAIN *takes them, looks inside, and gives them back.*

PETITPAIN, *waving her off*: The notary can wait!

CLAUDETTE: Yes, monsieur…

She goes to leave, up right, shoes in hand.

PETITPAIN, *stopping her, pointing to VINPILLE*: But first, go put monsieur's valise in the yellow bedroom. In the attic…

CLAUDETTE: But I put it in the blue one. Like monsieur told me…

PETITPAIN: And now I'm telling you the yellow one! (*Under his breath.*) Nice and high! (*Aloud.*) In the attic, understand?

CLAUDETTE: Yes, monsieur.

PETITPAIN, *to VINPILLE, sarcastically*: I hope you're not afraid of heights!

VINPILLE: Not at all. But I'm quite happy in the—

PETITPAIN: Or allergic to yellow…

VINPILLE: It doesn't matter… I'm color-blind…

PETITPAIN, *waving CLAUDETTE off*: Go on! Go on!

The door, up right, opens and RICHAC appears, as CLAUDETTE, shaking her head and still carrying her shoes, exits, up center.

RICHAC, *at the threshold*: Well? Are we signing the contract or not, monsieur?

PETITPAIN: Whenever you like… I was just waiting for you.

RICHAC, *in disbelief*: Oh? (*Calling out the door.*) Messieurs… Mesdames… We seem to be ready…

Everyone enters, up right, in the same order as before, muttering their usual comments and sitting down in their previous places.

PETITPAIN, *to THE GUESTS*: Please forgive the interruption…

RICHAC, *sitting at the table, reading*: "Whereas, in the presence of…"

PETITPAIN: No, no! You can skip that part! We've heard it already!

ISIDORE, *to RICHAC*: You were at the part about her dowry…

RICHAC: Yes, well… It's against all the rules, but if you insist… (*Reading.*) "The bride brings to the marriage, constituted in her own name, a dowry in the amount of eighty thousand francs…"

PETITPAIN: Fiddlesticks!

RICHAC: I beg your pardon?

PETITPAIN: "Fiddlesticks," I said!… Now that I know the truth… (*Staring at VINPILLE.*) What do you take me for?

THE GUESTS, surprised, exclaim phrases like: "The truth?" "What did he say?" "What ever does he mean?" etc.

ISIDORE: But father… (*Cajoling.*) Papá…

RICHAC, *to PETITPAIN*: But monsieur… You told me so yourself. I wrote it down just as you said…

PETITPAIN, *approaching him*: Then I have a right to cross it out!

He bends over the table and proceeds to do just that, with great savage strokes, as THE GUESTS look on in horror, with shouts of "Good heavens!" "What is he doing?" "Oh my, did you ever…" etc.

MADAME PETITPAIN: Gustave! For heaven's sake!

RICHAC, *to PETITPAIN*: Please, monsieur! I have to know the figure! What are you giving to your daughter?

PETITPAIN, *with a little sneer*: My daughter?… Not a sou! Not a centime!

THE GUESTS gasp a simultaneous "Oh!" of disbelief.

ISIDORE: No dowry?

VINPILLE, *to PETITPAIN*: That's really not enough, old man!

ISIDORE: No… Not quite…

VINPILLE: If I might be permitted a few words…

PETITPAIN: After the wedding, you! I'll thank you to shut your mouth and mind your own business!

MADAME PETITPAIN, *to PETITPAIN*: Gustave! What kind of joke…

VINPILLE, *to MADAME PETITPAIN*: Was it something I said?

PETITPAIN, *to MADAME PETITPAIN*: You too! Mind your business!

THE GUESTS utter another simultaneous "Oh!"

MADAME PETITPAIN: But it *is* my business! It is very much my business!

ISIDORE, *to PETITPAIN*: Mine too, monsieur! I thought everything was arranged.

PETITPAIN: Yes, well… Now it's unarranged! There are family secrets, young man, that should never see the light of day! (*As ISIDORE's jaw drops.*) Still, I realize that I owe you an explanation, and I'll give one to my daughter… (*Aside.*) Well, somebody's daughter! (*Aloud.*) And nobody else!

ISIDORE, *turning to MADAME PETITPAIN*: But…

PETITPAIN: Now please! Leave us alone…

RICHAC: Again?

THE GUESTS stand up, echoing his "Again?"

PETITPAIN, *waving them off, up right*: Out!… Out!… (*To ANGELIQUE, as she begins to join them.*) No! Not you…

MADAME PETITPAIN: Of all the…

PETITPAIN, *to ISIDORE, who resists*: You too… Out!

ISIDORE: Oh!

RICHAC, *to PETITPAIN*: Monsieur! This is my hundred fourteenth contract, and I have to say—

PETITPAIN: Yes… You too. (*As they all leave, up right, in the same order as before, uttering their shock and displeasure, except for VINPILLE, who lags behind.*) There!

VINPILLE, *to himself*: How much longer…?

He exits, up center.

ANGELIQUE, *who has been watching the preceding, down left, agape*: But… But…

PETITPAIN, *down right, looking at her, aside*: Look at her! The one I used to call my daughter!

ANGELIQUE: What ever is the matter?

PETITPAIN, *continuing, aside*: That mouth, those eyes… (*Aloud.*) Angélique…

ANGELIQUE: Yes, papá?

PETITPAIN, *aside*: "Papá"?… Ha! (*Aloud.*) Just call me "dear friend."

ANGELIQUE: Why in heaven…

PETITPAIN: Why? Because… I have my reasons.

He takes a handkerchief from his pocket and wipes his eyes.

ANGELIQUE: Are you crying, papá?

PETITPAIN: Please! "Dear friend!"… No, it's a cold… Just a cold… Tell me, Angélique… Tell me the truth. Do you love me?

ANGELIQUE: What a silly question! Of course I do! You're my father, aren't you?

PETITPAIN, *moving left, to the armchair, aside*: Ha! (*Aloud.*) Nothing would please me more, Angélique…

He gives her a hug and a kiss.

ANGELIQUE: "Would"?… But what's wrong, papá?

PETITPAIN: Please, mademoiselle… I told you… Just call me "dear friend"…

ANGELIQUE: "Friend"?… How can I? After all these years…

PETITPAIN, *sitting down*: Of course… Habit… Routine… (*Aside.*) She loves me out of habit! (*Taking her on his lap.*) Tell me… Be frank… When I'm next to you like this… (*Taking her hands.*) When I hold your hands… When I give you a little hug… How does it make you feel?

ANGELIQUE: "Feel," papá?

PETITPAIN, *correcting*: "Dear friend"… Please… "Dear friend"…

ANGELIQUE: I don't know… I… I feel loved, protected… When you put your arms around me, it's… it's as if I'm in a huge fortress…

PETITPAIN, *standing up, archly*: A fortress, mademoiselle? (*Aside, sarcastically.*) How tender!

ANGELIQUE, *continuing*: And nobody dares come near me!

PETITPAIN, *aside*: Not quite the voice of the blood, now is it! (*Aloud.*) And him?… Do you love him too?

ANGELIQUE: Who?

PETITPAIN: Vinpille…

ANGELIQUE, *giving him the answer she thinks he wants*: Oh yes! He's your friend, after all… Your dear friend, pa… (*Catching herself.*) dear friend… And he's so good to me. Why, just now, that lovely poem… And that perfectly magnificent wedding present! Why, Monsieur Isidore says there's even more to come. He told him so… And… And he loves mammá too!

PETITPAIN: Yes… You noticed…

ANGELIQUE: Why, I would have to be heartless not to love him, papá… (*Correcting herself.*) Dear friend, I mean… With all my heart… Want to or not…

PETITPAIN, *aside*: Now that's the voice of the blood! (*Aloud.*) Well, Angélique, it's time I explained… I'm afraid you don't know the mysteries of Parisian life!

ANGELIQUE, *naively*: Oh! I love mysteries!

PETITPAIN: You don't know that there are beasts… Wild, unprincipled beasts… Tigers, who come and lay their eggs in the nests of doves!

ANGELIQUE, *hesitating to correct him*: But… But tigers don't lay eggs, pa… dear friend…

PETITPAIN: Perhaps those reptiles shouldn't. But they do, believe me! (*Aside.*) That mouth… Those eyes… No… No doubt…

ANGELIQUE: Reptiles?

PETITPAIN, *aloud, as she grows more and more perplexed*: So you can see, mademoiselle, that now things have changed. Those eighty thousand francs… (*With a gesture.*) Pfff! Not one sou for your dowry!…

ANGELIQUE: But…

PETITPAIN: Ah! How I saved them, one at a time! For my daughter… My one joy in life… My own flesh and blood… (*Aside.*) My… His… (*Aloud.*) Always going without… Cabs? Bah! I would walk… In all kinds of weather… An umbrella was good enough! And it meant I was saving a sou for her… For… For her…

ANGELIQUE, *as he wipes away a tear*: Her?

PETITPAIN: For you… You… (*Aside.*) Whoever… (*Continuing, aloud.*) I would go to the café and bring my own sugar… (*Before she can object.*) And for supper, beef stew!… Beef stew, every day!… Oh, how I hated that damnable beef stew! But your mother thought I loved it!… "Ah! Beef stew! Yum yum yum!…" (*Weeping.*) Just for you… Just for… Just… (*Sniffling.*) So now you understand why I can't give you a dowry.

ANGELIQUE, *thoroughly confused*: I do?… But…

PETITPAIN: Ah! It's not your fault, mademoiselle. You may be the crime, but you're not the criminal…

ANGELIQUE: Papá?

PETITPAIN: The weed, but not the gardener… The bitter fruit, but not the fertilizer…

ANGELIQUE: The weed? The fruit?

PETITPAIN, *moving aside*: And as for him… (*Mimicking a dueling thrust.*) After the wedding!… (*Returning, embracing her.*) Ah, Angélique! Think kindly of the one who was your father for twenty years!

ANGELIQUE: But papá…

PETITPAIN, *pushing her away*: "Dear friend"… "Dear friend"… (*Resolutely.*) So! Now for the attic!… Yes! I'll take care of him, the wretch!

He exits, up center.

ANGELIQUE, *calling after him*: But what are you… (*As he closes the doors behind him.*) "The attic"…? "After the wedding"…?

ISIDORE, enters, up right.

ISIDORE, *approaching*: Well, what did he tell you? What was this great family secret?

ANGELIQUE: I don't know! He talked and talked, but I don't know what he said!

ISIDORE: You what?

ANGELIQUE: Or why sometimes he would call me "Angélique" and… and sometimes "mademoiselle"… Or why he would hug me one moment, and push me away the next… Or… Or why he kept saying that I mustn't call him "papá"…

ISIDORE: What should you call him? "Mammá"?

ANGELIQUE: No! "Dear friend," monsieur!

ISIDORE: And the dowry?

ANGELIQUE: "Not one sou," he said…

ISIDORE, *aside*: Damnation!

ANGELIQUE: Something about beef stew… And umbrellas…

ISIDORE: What?

ANGELIQUE: And tigers that lay eggs… And fertilizer…

ISIDORE: What are you—

ANGELIQUE, *interrupting*: But what's the difference? (*Coyly.*) You don't need money to be in love, do you?

ISIDORE, *without much conviction*: Of course not… (*To himself.*) Unless money is what you're in love with…

ANGELIQUE: Besides, we can speak to your employer. We'll tell him how much we love each other, and he'll take pity on us, I'm sure!

ISIDORE: Oh… In the business world, mademoiselle… Love is… lovely. But money is lovelier!

ANGELIQUE, *ingenuously*: It is?

ISIDORE: But what did he say? Why won't he give you your dowry?

ANGELIQUE: I told you. I didn't understand a word! First he would be hugging me, and the next minute he was pushing me away!

ISIDORE: Oh my! (*Aside.*) That brow… That chin… (*To himself.*) He must suspect…

ANGELIQUE, *overhearing*: Suspect what, monsieur?

ISIDORE: Nothing!… Nothing!… I'm afraid you don't know the mysteries of Parisian life, mademoiselle!

ANGELIQUE, *startled*: You too?

ISIDORE: But it's not your fault!

ANGELIQUE, *mechanically*: I know… I'm the weed but not the gardener. The bitter fruit… Or something like that…

VINPILLE'S VOICE, *offstage*: Ayyy!

ISIDORE: What?

CLAUDETTE'S VOICE, *angrily*: Don't you dare, monsieur!

ANGELIQUE: What on earth…

CLAUDETTE'S VOICE: I'll thank you to keep your hands to yourself, Monsieur Vinpille!

ISIDORE, *to* ANGELIQUE: Ah!… Vinpille… Maybe there's a chance… Maybe I can convince him… (*Waving her off.*) Please! Leave us alone.

ANGELIQUE: Well, if you're sure…

She exits, down right, as VINPILLE *enters, up center, rubbing his cheek.*

VINPILLE, *to himself*: Charming child!… But I don't think she's the thief. One can feel those things…

ISIDORE, *approaching him*: Monsieur…

VINPILLE: Ah… Are we starting again?… "Whereas… Whereas…"

ISIDORE: No… Monsieur Petitpain says he won't sign.

VINPILLE: What?

ISIDORE: He still refuses to give his daughter… Your… Your friend's daughter… He absolutely refuses to give her a dowry!

VINPILLE: He always was a tightwad! But still…

ISIDORE, *putting his arm around his shoulders*: And so, we… She and I… We thought that our dear friend Vinpille… Our… Her…

VINPILLE, *giving him a card, correcting*: Du… Du…

ISIDORE: Yes, of course!… Our dear, dear friend *du* Vinpille… We thought perhaps you could help us.

VINPILLE: Well, I can try. Angélique, after all…

ISIDORE, *interrupting*: I know, monsieur… I know…

VINPILLE: I'll certainly talk to him.

ISIDORE: Oh… I'm afraid that won't do any good. His mind is made up.

VINPILLE: Then… What can I do?

ISIDORE: Well, I wondered if… (*Motioning him to the loveseat.*) Please… (*As they both sit down.*) I mean… (*Pointedly.*) Since you have no children of your own… (*Aside.*) Not officially, at least…

VINPILLE, *to himself*: What is he getting at? (*Aloud.*) So?

ISIDORE: Well, we thought, Angélique and I… We thought you might give her the dowry instead—

VINPILLE, *jumping to his feet*: What?… Me?… You thought—

ISIDORE: We thought you might find it in your heart—

VINPILLE: Not in my heart, and not in my purse!

ISIDORE: But…

VINPILLE: Of all things!

ISIDORE: But flesh and blood, monsieur…

VINPILLE: Oh? What are his flesh and blood to me, damn it!

ISIDORE, *cajoling*: Really, Papá Vinpille… Your… Think of Angélique! Think of the child… Of your… Of your love, your precious memories…

VINPILLE: What memories? I haven't seen her for twenty years! Besides, I gave her thirteen thousand five hundred and five francs!

ISIDORE: Oh… A trifle, papá…

VINPILLE: And a poem! How much more—

ISIDORE: But papá…

VINPILLE, *exploding*: And I'm not your papá! (*Reaching into his pocket, taking out the napkin rings.*) Here! You can have these too! But not another centime!

ISIDORE, *examining them*: I say… They're silver plate, you know…

VINPILLE: What? You expect solid silver just to hold your dirty napkins?… Besides, you shouldn't *lick* a gift horse on the mouth! Didn't they ever teach you—

ISIDORE: Never mind! You refuse, I take it?… We can't count on you for the dowry?

VINPILLE: Certainly not!

ISIDORE: Tsk tsk tsk! (*Categorically.*) Some people stray from the path of virtue, monsieur, but are too weak to pay for their transgressions.

VINPILLE: Yes, I suppose… (*Thoroughly confused.*) But why… What does that have to do…

ISIDORE, *crossing left*: And silver plate to boot!… Tsk tsk tsk…

He exits, down left, shaking his head, taking the napkin rings with him.

VINPILLE, *calling after him*: Wait a minute! Give them back if you don't want them!… (*At the door.*) Bah!

PETITPAIN enters, up center, carrying a saw.

PETITPAIN, *to himself*: There! The attic is ready for that scoundrel! I can't wait…

VINPILLE, *noticing him*: Petitpain!… What the devil… (*Aside.*) Carpentry? On a day like this?… What a wedding!… My, my, my…

PETITPAIN: Vinpille… I have to speak to you.

VINPILLE: Oh?

PETITPAIN: Believe me, it won't be easy… A childhood friend… To do such a thing…

VINPILLE: Thing?

PETITPAIN, *reflecting for a moment*: As an adult, of course, but…

VINPILLE: What thing?

PETITPAIN: Monsieur! I demand an explanation!

VINPILLE: So do I! What are you talking about?

PETITPAIN: I know everything, my… (*Sarcastically.*) my friend!

VINPILLE, *after a brief, expectant pause*: Well? Tell me!

PETITPAIN, *down center*: Angélique is not my child!

VINPILLE, *joining him, shocked*: Good God!

PETITPAIN: Don't pretend you didn't know!

VINPILLE: When did this happen?

PETITPAIN: When she was born… When do you think?

VINPILLE: No, I mean… When did you find out?… And who—

PETITPAIN: Please! You know as well as I do!… A friend… A trusted friend…

VINPILLE: No!

PETITPAIN: A friend who shared my childhood… And much more, apparently…

VINPILLE: Tsk tsk tsk!

PETITPAIN: A friend who writes poems…

VINPILLE: You don't mean… My goodness! Grosmarteau?

PETITPAIN, *continuing*: …and who thinks he can atone for his treachery by giving her thirteen thousand five hundred and five francs!

VINPILLE, *shocked*: What?

PETITPAIN: Exactly!… You, monsieur!

VINPILLE: Me? Your daughter's father?

PETITPAIN: You, Vinpille!

VINPILLE: But… I think I would have known. Madame Petitpain is a charming creature, but… No, no… I couldn't have… No offense, Gustave, but… Really, I… I wouldn't have…

PETITPAIN: Oh? (*Miming her girth.*) Maybe not today, but twenty years ago…

VINPILLE: Even twenty years ago!… No, no… I wouldn't have…

PETITPAIN: But everything proves it! The chin, the brow… The thirteen thousand francs… No stranger would do that!

VINPILLE: Aha!… Oh, my… Of course! (*Slapping his brow.*) Now I understand! Did you ever… Well, if it's my gift… If that's your proof, old man… Discretion be damned! Promise or no promise, I'd rather tell you the truth!

PETITPAIN: Oh?

VINPILLE: Those thirteen thousand francs… It was your wife who gave them to me.

PETITPAIN: What? Mathilde…

VINPILLE: She saved them up in secret… A nest egg… For your daughter… *Your* daughter…

PETITPAIN, *speechless*: She… She…

VINPILLE: And since she was afraid to let you know, she asked me to add them to the contract in my name!

PETITPAIN, *babbling*: My wife… She… Mathilde… You mean…

VINPILLE: Exactly!

PETITPAIN: She saved… She… Oh! Is it possible? If you're telling me the truth… (*Calling up right.*) Mathilde!… Mathilde!

The door, up right, opens and RICHAC *appears.*

RICHAC: Are we ready, finally?

PETITPAIN: Not you! Not you!… My wife… Madame… (*Waving him off, sarcastically.*) "Whereas… Whereas…"

RICHAC: I never…

PETITPAIN, *calling*: Mathilde!… Mathilde!…

MADAME PETITPAIN *enters, up right, crossing* RICHAC, *who gives a little nod and goes out the same door.*

MADAME PETITPAIN: What is it, Gustave?

PETITPAIN: Come here…

MADAME PETITPAIN, *under her breath, taking a few steps toward the two men*: Oh my! What now?

PETITPAIN: Is it true that you gave monsieur here the sum of—

MADAME PETITPAIN, *terrified, interrupting*: No, no!

PETITPAIN: …thirteen thousand five hundred and five francs?

MADAME PETITPAIN: It's not true! I never did!

VINPILLE: What?

MADAME PETITPAIN, *to* PETITPAIN: Not a sou, Gustave! Not a sou!

PETITPAIN, *to* VINPILLE: Aha! Just as I thought, wretch!

VINPILLE, *to* MADAME PETITPAIN: But madame… (*To* PETITPAIN.) Let me talk to her! (*Approaching her, up right.*) It's no use denying it… The cat is out of the bag!

MADAME PETITPAIN, *playing dumb, to* PETITPAIN: Cat? (*To* VINPILLE.) What cat? (*To* PETITPAIN.) What ever does he mean, Gustave?

PETITPAIN: What ever, indeed!

MADAME PETITPAIN: It's a lie! It's a lie, I tell you!

She exits hurriedly, down left.

PETITPAIN, *to* VINPILLE: Good try, my friend!

VINPILLE: But…

PETITPAIN: A desperate attempt to cover up your shameful little escapade! But it seems that your accomplice is more honest than you!

VINPILLE: My accomplice? My… Please! I would never, I told you… Look! (*He crosses himself.*) I swear…

PETITPAIN: Don't add blasphemy to your crime! It's obvious!

VINPILLE: She is not my father!… I mean…

PETITPAIN: Besides, how could Mathilde have saved a sum like that? From the pittance I gave her? I would have noticed! If I notice a trifling thirty-seven sous, for heaven's sake…

VINPILLE, *suddenly*: Wait! That's it!… Of course!

PETITPAIN: That's what?

VINPILLE: Don't you see? Those thirty-seven sous, each day… Since your daughter was born… How old is she?

PETITPAIN: Twenty… Today, as if you didn't know!

VINPILLE: Quick! Paper!… A pen!… (*Pointing to the table, center.*) Sit down! (PETITPAIN *complies.*) Now… A few quick calculations… Hmm… Multiply twenty years by thirty-seven sous… No, thirty-seven sous by twenty years… Whichever…

PETITPAIN: How in blazes do I do that?

VINPILLE, *sitting down across from him, taking pen and paper, figuring*: Twenty times thirty-seven, times three hundred sixty-five… (*Scratching his head.*) And a quarter?… No… Forget the quarter… Times three hundred sixty-five…

PETITPAIN: Aha…

VINPILLE: And five sous to the franc… You see? Thirty-seven times three hundred sixty-five… Seven fives… Thirty-five…

PETITPAIN, *figuring, to himself*: Put down three and carry the two…

VINPILLE, *continuing*: Three times six…

Each continues, muttering to himself.

PETITPAIN: Forty-four…

VINPILLE: …and carry the four…

PETITPAIN: Three times three…

VINPILLE: Twenty-nine…

PETITPAIN: …and carry the two… Fourteen times twelve…

VINPILLE: Plus seventy-five…

PETITPAIN: Plus eighty-two… (*Aloud.*) Blast! I get forty-eight thousand, four hundred ninety-six francs.

VINPILLE: And I get sixty-three thousand and twenty-five.

PETITPAIN: We must have gone wrong somewhere.

VINPILLE: I was never good at multiplying!

PETITPAIN, *sarcastically*: Oh? Tell that to my wife!

VINPILLE: Please! You'll see… Let's try it again. Carefully, this time… Thirty-seven times twenty, times three hundred sixty-five… It has to come out right!

The door, up right, opens and RICHAC *appears.*

RICHAC: Well? Will I have to wait all day?

VINPILLE, *standing up*: The notary! We're saved! (*To* RICHAC, *pointing to the table.*) Please! Sit down…

RICHAC, *sitting down, grumbling*: Now what?

VINPILLE: Multiply thirty-seven sous a day by twenty years.

RICHAC: What? I came here to read a marriage contract, not to—

VINPILLE: Later!… First multiply thirty-seven sous by twenty years… Or vice-versa… (*To* PETITPAIN.) You too!… And me!… All three of us…

PETITPAIN, *to* VINPILLE, *out of patience*: Look! I've had enough arithmetic, and enough of your excuses!

RICHAC, *muttering*: Twenty times thirty-seven…

VINPILLE, *to* PETITPAIN: Please! Just try once more… You'll see! It's for your own good… (*Standing behind* RICHAC*, leaning the paper against his back and figuring.*) Seven plus eight…

PETITPAIN, *grumbling*: Three times seven… Twenty-one…

RICHAC, *continuing*: …times three hundred sixty-five…

VINPILLE, *to* PETITPAIN: Your own good, believe me… And your wife's… (*Figuring.*) Three times six…

PETITPAIN, *muttering*: A hundred twelve…

VINPILLE, *to* PETITPAIN: And Monsieur Isidore's… (*Aside.*) And mine! (*Figuring.*) Two times five…

RICHAC, *continuing*: Five, carry the three…

PETITPAIN: Thirty-five plus two…

VINPILLE, *to* PETITPAIN: And especially your daughter's!

RICHAC, *putting down his pen*: There!

PETITPAIN: Ah! He's got it!

RICHAC, *reading his result, categorically*: Three million seven hundred twenty-eight thousand francs!

PETITPAIN *and* **VINPILLE**: What?

RICHAC: And no centimes.

VINPILLE: Three million…? Idiot!

RICHAC, *standing up, moving left*: I beg your pardon!

ISIDORE and ANGELIQUE enter, up right, the latter hanging back, by the door.

ISIDORE, *to* RICHAC, *approaching*: Excuse me, monsieur… (*To* PETITPAIN.) Papá… The contract…?

RICHAC, *aside*: An idiot, am I?

VINPILLE, *to* PETITPAIN: Ah! Your son-in-law! An accountant… Thank heaven! (*Pushing* RICHAC *aside and having* ISIDORE *sit down in his place, addressing him.*) Multiply thirty-seven sous a day by twenty years.

ISIDORE: What?

PETITPAIN, *to* VINPILLE: Enough, for goodness' sake! And he's not my son-in-law! You're forgetting—

VINPILLE, *to* ISIDORE: Her dowry depends on it!

ANGELIQUE: Oh!

VINPILLE, *continuing*: If you want to get married, multiply, monsieur!

ISIDORE: Her dowry?

As he begins calculating, MADAME PETITPAIN enters, down left, and stands next to RICHAC.

MADAME PETITPAIN, *to* RICHAC: Well? (*To* PETITPAIN.) Gustave? (*To* ISIDORE.) Monsieur Isidore?

VINPILLE: Shhh! He's multiplying…

RICHAC, *aside*: You'll see! Three million seven hundred…

MADAME PETITPAIN, *to* VINPILLE: What is he… What are you doing?

VINPILLE: We're totaling up your account, madame.

MADAME PETITPAIN: My… *(Panicking.)* No! (*To* ISIDORE.) You mustn't! (*To* PETITPAIN.) Don't believe him, Gustave! (*To* VINPILLE.) What account? (*To* PETITPAIN.) I have no—

VINPILLE, *as* ISIDORE *puts down his pen*: Well?

ISIDORE: Thirteen thousand five hundred and five francs… No centimes…

PETITPAIN: What?

VINPILLE: Exactly!

RICHAC, *under his breath*: Nonsense!

VINPILLE, *To* PETITPAIN: Now do you understand?

MADAME PETITPAIN, *with a sigh of despair*: Oh…

PETITPAIN: Not a blasted word!

VINPILLE: Your wife was steal… (*Correcting himself.*) borrowing… She was borrowing thirty-seven sous from you… Each day…

PETITPAIN: What?

VINPILLE: Multiplied by twenty years… As a nest egg for your daughter…

RICHAC, *to* MADAME PETITPAIN, *in a whisper*: But I thought…

VINPILLE, *to* PETITPAIN: *Your* daughter, old man…

ANGELIQUE, *aside*: Oh my…

RICHAC, *to* MADAME PETITPAIN, *continuing*: But your aunt, madame? The one who died… What about her?

MADAME PETITPAIN, *replying in a whisper*: She's still dead, monsieur.

PETITPAIN: Is it possible?… (*To* MADAME PETITPAIN.) You… (*To* VINPILLE.) She… (*To* ANGELIQUE.) Your mother… (*To* MADAME PETITPAIN.) I don't believe it!

ANGELIQUE: Mammá?

MADAME PETITPAIN, *embarrassed, softly*: It's true, cherub…

PETITPAIN: Oh!… You realize I could drag you before the court, madame? Grand larceny…

MADAME PETITPAIN: Gustave…

PETITPAIN: But the shame… The notoriety… Oh! How the newspapers would lick their lips at the scandal! How they would delight in invading my home…

ANGELIQUE: But it was for me, papá!

PETITPAIN, *continuing*: …shining the glare of their light on my private life!

MADAME PETITPAIN, *pathetically*: Gustave…

PETITPAIN: Bah! I forgive you!

ANGELIQUE, *approaching him, clapping her hands*: Oh, thank you, papá!… (*Quizzically.*) "Dear friend"…?

PETITPAIN: No… "Papá," my sweet… "Papá"… (*Aside, looking at her.*) And she doesn't look like him one bit! (*Aloud, embracing her.*) Ah! What a joy it is to be a child's only father!

VINPILLE, *with a little laugh, aside*: Selfish!

PETITPAIN, *to* MADAME PETITPAIN: But why the devil only thirty-seven sous? Why not forty, while you were at it? Or fifty?

MADAME PETITPAIN: You would have noticed.

PETITPAIN: And you don't think I noticed thirty-seven? God help me! (*To VINPILLE.*) Oh, by the way, Vinpille… Be careful if you step out on the balcony in your room. Don't lean on the railing.

VINPILLE: Why not, old man?

PETITPAIN: Because I sawed through it in a moment of pique! To teach you a lesson…

VINPILLE: Ah! Thank you for telling me!

PETITPAIN: Not at all…

THE GUESTS enter, up right, in the same order as before, with cries of impatience: "Well? What about the contract?" "How long do we have to wait?" etc. As they take their places, CLAUDETTE can be heard offstage arguing with someone.

CLAUDETTE'S VOICE: But monsieur! You have to be invited!

GROSMARTEAU enters, up center, in a fancy police uniform, carrying a valise in one hand and a bouquet in the other, with CLAUDETTE on his heels.

GROSMARTEAU, *to CLAUDETTE*: Invited, child? Of course I'm invited! (*Putting down the valise.*) Look, everyone! I'm here!

PETITPAIN: Grosmarteau!

GROSMARTEAU: Excuse me for bursting in unannounced, but the door was open.

PETITPAIN: It was?

CLAUDETTE, *aside*: I could have sworn I locked it.

RICHAC, *aside*: Who the devil…?

GROSMARTEAU: Business or not, I wouldn't miss a wedding! (*To PETITPAIN.*) Especially this one! (*Shaking PETITPAIN's hand vigorously.*) Petitpain, old friend! (*Kissing MADAME PETITPAIN's hand.*) Madame… (*Holding out the bouquet to CLAUDETTE.*) And flowers for the lovely bride… (*With a chuckle.*) who thought I wasn't invited! Me!

THE GUESTS correct him with shouts of "No, not her…" "That one!" "Mademoiselle Angélique" etc.

PETITPAIN, *pointing to ANGELIQUE*: My daughter, Grosmarteau!

GROSMARTEAU: Of course, of course!… I'd know her anywhere! That neck! Those ears!… (*To ANGELIQUE.*) Mademoiselle, permit me… (*He gives her the bouquet, first taking from it a paper, which he unfolds.*) But first… (*Clearing his throat and making sure that everybody is listening.*) If I may… A little something I wrote for the occasion… *(Reading.)*

"Love and his mother picked this fine bouquet,
A nosegay, just for you, this special day…"

PETITPAIN, **MADAME PETITPAIN**, **ANGELIQUE**, *and* **ISIDORE**: What?

GROSMARTEAU, *continuing*:

"For, blooms that grow in Venus' garden fair,
Are meant to grace a beauty's breast fore'er."

PETITPAIN *and* **MADAME PETITPAIN**, *to VINPILLE*: Monsieur!

VINPILLE, *sheepishly*: Talk about your coincidences…

ISIDORE, *to PETITPAIN*: Excuse me, but aren't we forgetting something?

PETITPAIN: Son ?

ISIDORE: The contract…

As THE GUESTS *echo him with impatient shouts of "The contract, the contract!,"* RICHAC *takes his seat.*

RICHAC, *reading*: "Whereas, in the presence of..."

As he continues to read, everyone tries to shout him down with vociferous comments: "No, no!" "We've heard all that!" "Not again!" etc. He persists in reading, raising his voice as best he can, continuing despite their objections, as the curtain falls.

CURTAIN.

A Slap in the Farce

(La main leste, 1867)

Eugène Labiche & Edouard Martin

Characters

LECOUQUE, a ladies' milliner proud of his profession and cowed by his wife's temper

ANTOINE, a young artist accidentally embroiled in a Lecouque family misadventure

MADAME LECOUQUE, the irascible wife of the henpecked man of the house

CÉLINE, the couple's lovely daughter, ready for a romantic adventure

MADAME DE RIGUEUR, one of Lecouque's richest and most favorite clients

The dining room in the Lecouque household. Upstage center, a double door leading onto a vestibule. Down right and down left, two more doors. Left, a dining table and three chairs. On the table, cups and saucers, a pitcher of coffee, and the remains of lunch. Against the upstage wall, far right, a set of shelves covered with ladies' flowered hats. Close to it, by the wall, right, a work table with assorted articles: artificial flowers, ribbons, several finished hats, and a small bell. Against the upstage wall, far left, a cupboard for dishware, etc. On it, a bowl of fruit. Near the door, down right, a small desk and chair, facing the audience, with paper, inkwell, and pen. Midstage, right of center, a small loveseat. Next to it, an end table. Other appropriate furnishings— occasional chairs, pictures, etc.

At rise, LECOUQUE, MADAME LECOUQUE, and CELINE are seated around the table, left, finishing their lunch.

MADAME LECOUQUE, *to LECOUQUE, impatiently*: Well? Are you going to take all day?

LECOUQUE: My love?

MADAME LECOUQUE: With your coffee! I've never seen anyone take so long…

LECOUQUE: But it's too hot… Look…

He holds up the steaming cup.

MADAME LECOUQUE: And whose fault is that? You always want it boiling! Not one degree less!

LECOUQUE: Of course… So it can cool… *(Placing the cup under his nose.)* I love the aroma…

MADAME LECOUQUE: If you think it's a pleasure watching you sniff at it for an hour…

LECOUQUE: A real connoisseur, my love, drinks coffee twice. First with the nose, and then—

MADAME LECOUQUE, *interrupting*: Connoisseur, my foot! You're absolutely impossible!

LECOUQUE: Temper, temper, temper! *(Getting up and offering her the fruit basket on the cupboard, up left.)* Here, have a banana… It will help pass the time.

MADAME LECOUQUE: I don't want a banana! Lunch is over! I've finished!

She stands up and begins pacing back and forth.

LECOUQUE, *putting back the basket and sitting down again, aside*: Forward, march! One, two, one, two…

MADAME LECOUQUE, *stopping suddenly, looking at CELINE*: And you!… Oh!

CELINE: Me, mammá? What have I—

MADAME LECOUQUE: Sitting there, staring at your coffee, like a… like a mummy!

CELINE: But…

LECOUQUE: Really, Hildegarde…

MADAME LECOUQUE: Like father, like daughter! The two of you are impossible!

CELINE: But…

LECOUQUE: I told you…

CELINE: I can't very well pour it down papá's throat, can I? It's too hot!

MADAME LECOUQUE: Hot? Ha!… *(She picks up LECOUQUE's coffee and downs it in one gulp.)* There! That's how hot it is!

LECOUQUE: What do you think you're… That's my coffee, for heaven's sake! How many times… *(Getting up.)* If you want some, pour your own!

MADAME LECOUQUE: Don't be silly! You know I can't stomach it.

LECOUQUE: So I see…

MADAME LECOUQUE: I just wanted to show you…

LECOUQUE: Really, Hildegarde, sometimes… Now don't misunderstand… You're a wonderful woman… All kinds of fine qualities… And impeccable taste…

MADAME LECOUQUE: But…?

LECOUQUE, *attempting a little humor*: After all, you picked me…

During the ensuing dialogue, CELINE *gets up and cleans off the table, carrying off the cups, dishes, etc., exiting and reentering, left, several times.*

MADAME LECOUQUE, *aside*: Yes, didn't I!

LECOUQUE: But… Well… You do have your faults…

MADAME LECOUQUE: Oh?

LECOUQUE: I mean… You're not exactly the soul of patience…

CELINE, *still cleaning up, aside*: To say the least!

LECOUQUE: And you have been known to… to…

MADAME LECOUQUE: To…?

LECOUQUE: Your temper, my love…

MADAME LECOUQUE: My what?

LECOUQUE: You do have one, you know! You and that hand of yours!… Like lightning!… *(He gives a few quick slaps at an imaginary victim.)* You never know where it's going to land! Or why…

MADAME LECOUQUE: Well, nobody's perfect.

LECOUQUE: It's one thing when you slap me. I'm a man, I can take it… And we've got ways of getting even… But the help…

MADAME LECOUQUE: What are you talking about? What help? We don't have any help!

LECOUQUE, *pointing down right*: In the shop… Those poor girls…

MADAME LECOUQUE: Oh, that!

LECOUQUE: You go in, and… One, two, three! The least little thing, and… *(Slapping the imaginary victim again.)* Lightning strikes again!

MADAME LECOUQUE: Well, they're nothing but a pack of lazy—

LECOUQUE: Look, Hildegarde… Making artificial flowers is a very demanding job. For my hats, especially… All the detail, I mean… They were doing the best they could.

MADAME LECOUQUE: Ha!

LECOUQUE: I never should have put you in charge in the first place. That's no way to run a business!

MADAME LECOUQUE: I'm telling you… They were lazy! A slap now and then made them stay on their toes!

CELINE *reenters and stands by* LECOUQUE.

LECOUQUE, *sarcastically*: Oh, yes! Of course it did!… It made them go out on strike, that's what it made them do!

MADAME LECOUQUE: Well, good riddance!

LECOUQUE: That's what you think! Go try and find someone else to do that kind of work! And for what we pay them… Why, thanks to you and that temper of yours, we practically lost the business altogether!

MADAME LECOUQUE, *sitting down at the table, left*: Bah!

LECOUQUE, *joining her, sitting*: If I hadn't decided to let Céline take your place, I hate to think…

CELINE: That's right, mammá!

MADAME LECOUQUE, *to CELINE*: And who asked you?

LECOUQUE: Now they're treated like human beings for a change.

MADAME LECOUQUE: I'm sure!

LECOUQUE: Not that we spoil them, or anything like that… But now when they ask for a raise, at least they get a smile and a kind word. Not a slap!

MADAME LECOUQUE: And a "no," I hope!

LECOUQUE: Of course!

CELINE: Of course!

LECOUQUE: But everybody's happy, and business is just fine.

MADAME LECOUQUE: Well, temper or not… I have more important things on my mind… Much more important… *(Getting up.)* I'll be back shortly…

She begins to move toward the door, up center.

LECOUQUE: Things, Hildegarde? What things?

CELINE: Where are you going, mammá?

MADAME LECOUQUE: To the police station.

LECOUQUE: The police—

MADAME LECOUQUE: Don't worry! Only the Lost and Found…

CELINE: Did you lose something?

MADAME LECOUQUE: Yes… Last night, in the tram… I was sitting next to an absolutely insufferable individual. The most impolite…

LECOUQUE, *aside*: She lost her temper!

MADAME LECOUQUE: The most ill-mannered, insolent…

LECOUQUE, *to MADAME LECOUQUE*: Let me guess… He insulted you…

MADAME LECOUQUE: The most…

LECOUQUE: Well, what did he say?

MADAME LECOUQUE: Can you imagine? He… *(Noticing CELINE, hanging on her words.)* Céline, darling… I think you'd better go to the shop and make sure those good-for-nothings aren't twiddling their thumbs!

CELINE: Yes, mammá! *(Aside.)* I never get to hear the good parts!

She exits, right.

LECOUQUE: Well, what did this insufferable, insolent, ill-mannered young man have to say?

MADAME LECOUQUE: Young man?

LECOUQUE: Yes… I thought you said… Wasn't it a man?

MADAME LECOUQUE: Oh yes! It was a man! It most certainly was a man!

LECOUQUE: Well?

MADAME LECOUQUE: But young?… Old?… I have no idea… I never saw his face!

LECOUQUE: You what?

MADAME LECOUQUE: No… The kerosene lamps were broken and we were practically in the dark.

LECOUQUE: Of all things…

MADAME LECOUQUE: Well, all of a sudden I felt him bending over and reaching down, and… and… You'll never believe the gall…

LECOUQUE: And…?

MADAME LECOUQUE: And he put his hand on my shoes! You know… The fancy ones… With the fur…

LECOUQUE: No! *(Aside.)* It takes all kinds!

MADAME LECOUQUE: Then he began to stroke my foot. And he kept whispering: "Pretty baby, pretty baby!"

LECOUQUE, *aside*: Dark? It must have been pitch black!

MADAME LECOUQUE, *almost overhearing*: What?

LECOUQUE: Nothing, my love… Nothing… Please… Please, go on…

MADAME LECOUQUE: Well, you can just imagine!… I was absolutely furious! The nerve of some people!… I mean…

LECOUQUE: Don't tell me… Let me guess… You slapped him!

MADAME LECOUQUE: I certainly did! Wouldn't you?

LECOUQUE, *musing*: If he stroked my foot?… Yes, I suppose…

MADAME LECOUQUE: Right in the face… A good one, too… And he felt it, I can tell you!

LECOUQUE: I'm sure!

MADAME LECOUQUE: He went: "Ayyy!… My eye! My eye!…"

LECOUQUE, *aside*: Ayyy! Ayyy! Ayyy!

MADAME LECOUQUE: Well, I got up and told the conductor to stop right there! And I got off in a huff! I wasn't going to stay on that tram another minute!

LECOUQUE: I hope he refunded half your fare at least.

MADAME LECOUQUE: My fare? That was the least of my worries, believe me?

LECOUQUE: After all, six sous…

MADAME LECOUQUE: Unfortunately, I hadn't taken more than a couple of steps, when I realized that my handbag was still on my seat. With my purse inside… Full of money…

LECOUQUE: No!

MADAME LECOUQUE: Yes!… Forty-six francs, twenty-five centimes…

LECOUQUE: Damn!

MADAME LECOUQUE: I'm just hoping that somebody found it. Somebody honest, that is… Not that… that sex fiend!

LECOUQUE: Now, now, Hildegarde… Some sex fiends might be honest…

MADAME LECOUQUE: Well… That's why I'm going to the police station… Maybe somebody turned it in. *(Examining her attire for a moment.)* Hmm… I'd better put on something fancy, don't you think? They're much more polite when you come in with lots of frills…

LECOUQUE, *aside*: I never noticed.

MADAME LECOUQUE: …and when you're pretty…

LECOUQUE: Yes, my love… *(Aside.)* Go do your best!

MADAME LECOUQUE, *overhearing*: I beg your pardon?

LECOUQUE: "Oh, do get dressed!" I said… "Do get dressed!"… Of course, not that you need to… *(Slyly.)* You pretty baby!

MADAME LECOUQUE: Oh… Be quiet, you…

She exits, left.

LECOUQUE: Poor Hildegarde! For once she's right, and it costs her forty-six francs… And twenty-five centimes!… And all because some maniac falls in love with her foot!… Well, I've got other things to worry about too… Duty calls! *(He gets up, goes over to the work table, right, and takes a hat, holding it up, admiringly.)* Ah! My latest creation!… Another stunning Lecouque original!… Next week my competitors will be green with envy!… I call it "Widow's Weeds"… *(Fondling the flowers.)* Even though they're violets… Nice dark ones, of course… For widows, after all. Dark enough to be decent, but not quite enough to… *(Knowingly.)* discourage admirers!… It's bound to be all the rage. Perfect for widows with serious intentions…

The double door opens and MADAME DE RIGUEUR *strides in.*

MADAME DE RIGUEUR: Ah, monsieur! There you are!

LECOUQUE: Madame de Rigueur!… *(Aside.)* Speak of the devil! *(Aloud.)* And what can I do for my favorite customer? *(Aside,)* And one of the richest!

MADAME DE RIGUEUR: I'm looking for something very special, monsieur.

LECOUQUE: A hat?

MADAME DE RIGUEUR: Of course… But something utterly chic…

LECOUQUE: For a ball?

MADAME DE RIGUEUR: No…

LECOUQUE: A dinner?

MADAME DE RIGUEUR: No…

LECOUQUE: The theater?

MADAME DE RIGUEUR: No, no… It's rather hard to explain… Some friends are coming over this afternoon… The baroness, the countess… And some gentlemen… Writers… We're going to read poetry. It's all terribly intellectual.

LECOUQUE: Yes… I see… A literary soirée, you might say… Only in the afternoon…

MADAME DE RIGUEUR: Yes… Quite…

LECOUQUE: Well, madame, I have exactly what you're looking for! A new creation… My latest… In fact, it's so new, I'm not showing it until next week. But for you, madame… And it's perfect for widows, if you don't mind my saying… *(He shows her the hat.)* See? An inspiration, if I do say so myself!

MADAME DE RIGUEUR, *sitting on the loveseat and examining the hat*: Don't you find it a… a trifle plain?

LECOUQUE: Plain?

MADAME DE RIGUEUR: Yes… Rather undistinguished…

LECOUQUE, *taken aback*: Well, I don't think…

MADAME DE RIGUEUR: What kind of flowers are these, monsieur?

LECOUQUE: Violets… Violets, madame… Dark ones, of course… Dark enough to be decent, but not quite enough to—

MADAME DE RIGUEUR: No… No, thank you… No violets… They're much too banal!… Common… Common…

LECOUQUE, *putting the hat back on the work table*: Well… It's a matter of opinion…

MADAME DE RIGUEUR: No… I had in mind something rather more… poetic.

LECOUQUE: Yes… Yes, of course…

MADAME DE RIGUEUR: Vaguely expressive, but… but tender and… subdued…

LECOUQUE, *nodding*: Aha…

MADAME DE RIGUEUR: Something that… that sings…

LECOUQUE, *aside*: Sings?

MADAME DE RIGUEUR: Striking, but… utterly unobtrusive!… You do see what I mean, monsieur?

LECOUQUE: Oh… Perfectly!… Perfectly!

MADAME DE RIGUEUR: I was sure you would.

LECOUQUE: Perhaps a simple tiara… Tea roses, madame… With just a touch of fern… They're very poetic, and… They sing, madame… They sing…

MADAME DE RIGUEUR, *rather disdainfully*: Tea roses?

LECOUQUE: Well, dark ones… I mean, considering… Pearl grey… Or a nice navy blue…

MADAME DE RIGUEUR: Blue?.. I didn't think tea roses came in navy blue.

LECOUQUE: No… Not in the wild, as they say… But in society… In the very best salons…

MADAME DE RIGUEUR: Oh?

LECOUQUE: Yes, they're terribly chic… *(Trying to recall her words.)* Vaguely expressive, but… but tender…

MADAME DE RIGUEUR: And subdued?

LECOUQUE: Oh yes! Yes… Very…

MADAME DE RIGUEUR: Well, perhaps… Can you show me, monsieur?

LECOUQUE: Certainly! *(With a grandiose gesture toward the door. down right.)* If you'll just step into the shop, madame… I'm sure Mademoiselle Céline will be only too delighted…

MADAME DE RIGUEUR, *getting up, musing*: Navy blue tea roses… Yes, they might sing… They might…

LECOUQUE: Oh, they do, madame!… They do! But ever so discreetly… *(As* MADAME DE RIGUEUR *reaches the door, nodding,)* Madame…

MADAME DE RIGUEUR: Monsieur…

She exits.

LECOUQUE, *moving left*: Charming lady… Charming!… A little… *(He shrugs.)* But charming!

ANTOINE *appears at the double door, up center, his hair is combed over one eye, and he is carrying a lady's handbag.*

ANTOINE, *entering*: Excuse me… Madame Lecouque?

LECOUQUE: Madame…? Do I look like Madame Lecouque?

ANTOINE: No, no, monsieur… I mean… Does she live here?

LECOUQUE: Of course she does! She's my wife!

ANTOINE: Ah!… Then she must be married.

LECOUQUE: One would think so!

ANTOINE: Good! That makes things so much easier, monsieur.

LECOUQUE: It does?

ANTOINE: Oh, much!

LECOUQUE: Easier than what?

ANTOINE: I'll explain in a moment, monsieur… All in due time…

There is an awkward silence as both men eye each other.

LECOUQUE: Well?

ANTOINE: I'm returning this handbag.

LECOUQUE: You're returning… Oh my! Why didn't you say… You mean, the one Hildegarde… The one Madame Lecouque left in the tram last night?

ANTOINE: Precisely, monsieur… I took the liberty of opening it… To look inside, you understand…

LECOUQUE: Of course…

ANTOINE: I couldn't do the latter without the former.

LECOUQUE: No, no… Quite all right…

ANTOINE: And I found your name and address, monsieur… That is, madame's…

LECOUQUE: Yes… Yes…

ANTOINE: And forty-six francs, twenty-five centimes… It's all there… Down to the last centime…

He gives LECOUQUE *the handbag.*

LECOUQUE: I don't doubt it, monsieur… I'm… We're terribly grateful, madame and I. *(Aside.)* I won't insult him by offering him a reward… Just a few well-chosen words of appreciation… *(Aloud.)* It's all too rare, in this day and age, monsieur, to find someone so honest… so considerate… You're a gentleman! My congratulations!

ANTOINE: Thank you… And now that that's taken care of, we can talk about another little problem, monsieur.

LECOUQUE: We can?

ANTOINE: If I may…

LECOUQUE: Yes… Please, I insist!… What kind of problem?

ANTOINE: An affront to my honor, monsieur! Madame Lecouque, if you don't mind my saying, is rather free with her hand!

LECOUQUE, *surprised*: What?… You mean, you're the one… the man… the one she…

ANTOINE: Yes, monsieur. In the eye… As I think you can see…

He brushes back his hair, revealing a black eye.

LECOUQUE, *examining it*: My, my… Yes, I… Yes, indeed…

ANTOINE: I think I've proved my point, monsieur.

LECOUQUE: Yes, I would say… But you have to admit, you did have it coming!

ANTOINE: I did?

LECOUQUE: After all, you asked for it.

ANTOINE: Excuse me, monsieur, but… Your meaning eludes me.

LECOUQUE: Well, really!… Gentlemen don't go around stroking strange ladies' feet… Unless they get their permission, that is…

ANTOINE: Strange ladies' what?

LECOUQUE: Of course! Play dumb! I suppose you deny it!

ANTOINE: "It," monsieur?

LECOUQUE: Stroking my wife's foot last night!

ANTOINE, *dumbfounded*: What?

LECOUQUE: In the tram!

ANTOINE, *self-righteously*: I beg your pardon! I never…

LECOUQUE: Then why did you bend down? Why were you whispering sweet nothings, if I may ask…

ANTOINE, *speechless*: Sweet… Monsieur, I was stroking my dog! My pekingese… My little Chin-Chin…

LECOUQUE: Your…

ANTOINE: She was under the seat, but she wouldn't keep still. So, naturally, I bent down and tried to… You know… *(He bends down, as if patting a dog.)* "Pretty baby… Pretty baby…"

LECOUQUE: Oh my… My, my… And my wife… With her fancy shoes… The ones with the fur… She thought… She thought… *(Chuckling.)* "Pretty baby!"

He bursts out laughing.

ANTOINE: I'm glad you find it amusing, monsieur.

LECOUQUE: Amusing?.. *(Still laughing.)* It's hilarious!… Hildegarde… You thought… *(After a pause.)* Why aren't you laughing?

ANTOINE: I'm afraid I'm not amused.

LECOUQUE: Oh?

ANTOINE: You're forgetting… *(Pointing to his eye.)* My honor…

LECOUQUE: Come, come now, my friend! You don't mean to tell me… An innocent little slap… And from a pretty lady…

ANTOINE: Pretty, monsieur?

LECOUQUE: Well… ish…

ANTOINE: I beg your pardon?

LECOUQUE: Prettyish… Prettyish…

ANTOINE: Aha…

LECOUQUE: And, after all, she thought… I mean, it was all a mistake… Besides, she slaps me all the time, but do I make a fuss?

ANTOINE: She does?

LECOUQUE: Well, once in a while… She tends to be rather free with her hands!

ANTOINE: Yes, well… You, monsieur, are her husband. You have to expect it… And I assume you slap her back?

LECOUQUE: Her back?… Slap her… *(Comprehending.)* Oh, "slap her back…" No, no, monsieur! Certainly not!… I kiss her!

ANTOINE: You do?

LECOUQUE: Of course! *(Gallantly.)* A lady's slap deserves a kiss in return! Don't you agree? She's free with her hands… I'm free with my lips!

ANTOINE, *nodding*: I see… I see…

LECOUQUE, *ready to end the conversation*: Well then…

ANTOINE: Yes, monsieur… That's quite acceptable.

LECOUQUE: Please?

ANTOINE: That will be fine with me.

LECOUQUE: What will be fine with you?

ANTOINE: I'm willing to kiss your wife, monsieur.

LECOUQUE, *with a start*: You're willing to…

He laughs incredulously.

ANTOINE: As a favor, of course…

LECOUQUE: Who said anything about—

ANTOINE: Please don't misunderstand. It's not that I have any… well, lubricious designs… I've never had the pleasure of meeting Madame Lecouque… Not face to face…

LECOUQUE: No, not quite!

ANTOINE: Last night doesn't count… Her foot, I mean…

LECOUQUE: Yes…

ANTOINE: It's just that it seems like an honorable way to… How shall I say?… To resolve our affair…

LECOUQUE, *moving upstage*: Oh? Kiss my wife? Honorable?… I hardly think so!

ANTOINE: But, monsieur…

LECOUQUE: Never!… Certainly not!

ANTOINE, *crossing left*: Then I'm afraid I have no choice… I'll have to challenge you to a duel, monsieur.

LECOUQUE: Me?… Why me, for heaven's sake?

ANTOINE: Well, really! I can't very well run a sword through your wife! You wouldn't want that, I'm sure! Whereas, with you… Well…

LECOUQUE: What?

ANTOINE: I mean, you *are* her husband! The law says you're responsible.

LECOUQUE: But…

ANTOINE: And a slap, monsieur… In the face… I don't have to tell you… Besides, in front of everybody… Dozens of people…

LECOUQUE: So what? A pack of strangers… And it was dark!

ANTOINE: Not dark enough!… And they weren't all strangers either! A gentleman of my acquaintance was seated next to me, monsieur!

LECOUQUE: Oh?

ANTOINE: An associate… One of my Aix colleagues…

LECOUQUE: What difference does it make? You'll probably never see him.

ANTOINE: On the contrary, monsieur… I see him every day! I'll be the laughingstock. All our friends will know…

LECOUQUE: But… You said "ex-colleague"… I thought…

ANTOINE: Aix, monsieur… Aix-en-Provence… Near Marseille…

LECOUQUE: Oh…

ANTOINE: That's where we learned to paint… The two of us…

LECOUQUE: Paint, monsieur?… You're a painter?

ANTOINE: I daresay…

LECOUQUE: Houses?

ANTOINE: No, no… Portraits, mainly… At least, that's what everyone says I do best… *(As LECOUQUE, happy to change the subject, nods knowingly.)* They're really quite out of the ordinary.

LECOUQUE: I'm sure…

ANTOINE: If you know anyone who would like one done, they're forty francs.

LECOUQUE, *nodding*: Forty…

ANTOINE: In oils, of course…

LECOUQUE: Of course…

ANTOINE: Not exactly a fortune…

LECOUQUE: No… I should say…

ANTOINE, *after a pause, abruptly*: Well, have you decided?

LECOUQUE: On a portrait?

ANTOINE: No, no… First things first… Do I kiss your wife, or do I kill you, monsieur? It's one or the other.

LECOUQUE: But… Just like that? Kiss my… Kiss my… You have to admit, it's not every day… "May I kiss your wife, monsieur?…" Really, you have to admit…

ANTOINE, *dryly*: I admit, monsieur… Now what have you decided?

LECOUQUE, *relenting*: Well, I suppose… That is, if she doesn't mind… I mean, what's the harm, as long as you don't enjoy it…

ANTOINE: Oh, I wouldn't, monsieur… I wouldn't…

LECOUQUE: And as long as I'm watching… You understand…

ANTOINE: Quite all right… You won't disturb me.

LECOUQUE: Of course, I will have to discuss the matter first with Madame Lecouque.

ANTOINE: Certainly! I think that's only proper.

LECOUQUE: If you'll give me a few minutes… *(Indicating the loveseat.)* Please, make yourself comfortable… I won't be very long… *(Aside, leaving.)* Good God! She'll never… He strokes her foot and I ask her to kiss him!… Never!… Never in a million years…

He exits, left.

ANTOINE, *sitting down on the loveseat*: Well, it's not exactly what I had in mind, but… All things considered… I'd say I've handled the affair rather nicely!… A kiss for a slap! What could be more gallant?… And a pretty young thing… Hot-tempered, passionate… They'll love it at the club… I can just see their faces!… Tonight, at dinner… Over a glass of Saint-Emilion… Three francs a bottle… "You mean, you kissed her?…" "Yes, that's what I said! I kissed her!…" What panache!… *(Looking at his watch.)* Hmm! I wonder what's keeping her… You don't suppose she said no…

CELINE enters, right, without noticing ANTOINE, and keeps crossing left.

CELINE, *suddenly noticing him, aside*: Oh my! A man…

ANTOINE, *getting up, aside*: Well, well, well! I must say, she's worth waiting for! *(To CELINE, bowing,)* Madame…

CELINE, *aside*: Who is he, I wonder?

ANTOINE, *rather pompously*: Permit me to say how grateful I am to be the victim… The happy victim… of a momentary lapse…

CELINE, *aside*: A customer, I imagine…

ANTOINE: No hard feelings, madame… I assure you, no hard feelings… *(Gallantly,)* Especially since the remedy will amply repair any minor discomfort.

CELINE, *puzzled*: Monsieur?

ANTOINE: Oh, more than amply… Trams can be such a nuisance, but I'm really not sorry!

CELINE, *aside*: He came by tram?

ANTOINE, *aside*: Poor thing! She's so embarrassed! *(Aloud.)* Come now… A stiff upper lip… So to speak!… It won't take long…

CELINE: Monsieur?

ANTOINE: Are you ready?

CELINE: Ready? For what?

ANTOINE: To make amends, madame. After all, there's nothing that can't be mended, if we put our minds to it! *(Aside.)* Even honor!

CELINE, *moving to the work table*: Oh! You had something to be mended, monsieur? *(Aside.)* Why didn't he say so?

ANTOINE: Indeed, madame! That's one way of putting it.

CELINE, *picking up one of the hats*: This one must be yours, monsieur. It was brought in yesterday to have the lilac sewn back on.

ANTOINE: Mine?.. That?… I hardly think so… Besides, madame, I seldom wear a hat. *(Looking askance at the hat.)* Any kind of hat… Even when I'm painting…

CELINE, *replacing the hat*: Painting, monsieur?

ANTOINE: Yes, madame… Portraits, mainly… If you know anyone who would like one done… Forty francs… In oils, of course…

CELINE, *nodding*: I see… I see… *(After an embarrassed pause.)* Then… What was it you had in mind, monsieur?

ANTOINE: What was it I… You mean, he didn't tell you?

CELINE: Who, monsieur? Tell me what?

ANTOINE: Your… Monsieur Lecouque… Didn't he…

CELINE: Papá?

ANTOINE, *taken aback*: Papá?

CELINE: What did papá have to tell me, monsieur?

ANTOINE: Papá?… Papá?… *(Aside.)* Good God! It's his daughter! *(Aloud.)* Madame… Mademoiselle… He's your daughter… I mean, you're his… He's your father…

CELINE: Papá?… Of course, monsieur!

ANTOINE, *bumbling*: And you… you have a mother?

CELINE: Why, yes…

ANTOINE: And she wears shoes?

CELINE: Monsieur?

ANTOINE: Fancy ones… With fur?

CELINE: Yes, sometimes… When it's cold…

ANTOINE, *aside*: Damn! It's her mother!… She's no chicken, that's for sure! *(Aloud.)* Excuse me, mademoiselle, but… May I ask how old you are?

CELINE: Why, I'm eighteen, monsieur. But I really don't see—

ANTOINE: And your mother… How old was she when she married your father?

CELINE: I beg your pardon?

ANTOINE, *musing*: Let's say eighteen, more or less… So… Eighteen and eighteen… Thirty-six, give or take… *(Aside.)* No!… No chicken!… *(Aloud.)* Tell me, does she still have her hair?

CELINE: Monsieur?

ANTOINE: I mean, all the same color?… All still blonde?

CELINE: Brown, monsieur… But—

ANTOINE: Yes, yes… Whatever… But not grey?

CELINE: Really, I don't… *(Suddenly.)* Oh, I know, monsieur! I know why you're here!… You're a painter, and you're going to paint her portrait! Of course!

ANTOINE: Well… Not quite, mademoiselle… I'm here on a rather emotional mission…

CELINE: Emotional, monsieur?

ANTOINE: And terribly delicate…

CELINE: A delicate mission… *(Aside.)* Oh my! He must be… Of course! He's a suitor! Papá didn't tell me…

ANTOINE: I'm afraid I'd better not go into detail, but… Well, just let me say, mademoiselle, that… that I certainly hope you look like your mother!

CELINE: You do?

ANTOINE: Oh yes! Fervently!

CELINE: My goodness, monsieur… Why?

ANTOINE: Because then she would look like you, and… and…

CELINE: Yes?

ANTOINE: And… Well, it's just that… It would make things so much easier, mademoiselle.

CELINE: Monsieur?

ANTOINE: In the tram, I mean…

CELINE: In the… *(Aside.)* He's so nervous, poor thing! He doesn't know what he's saying!

ANTOINE: My Chin-Chin… My little Chin-Chin… It was dark and… The shoes…

CELINE, *aside*: Good heavens! He's babbling!

ANTOINE: No, no… I really can't go into detail… I… It's… Just believe me when I tell you that… that the more I look at you like this… the more… the more I have a feeling…

CELINE: A feeling, monsieur?

ANTOINE, *abruptly*: Could you possibly be persuaded, mademoiselle… That is, if your mother had a… a debt… Would you be willing to pay it?

CELINE: A debt? Mammá?

ANTOINE: So to speak…

CELINE: What kind? What do I have to do?

ANTOINE: Nothing, really… You just have to stand there and… *(Approaching her.)* and let me do the rest…

He takes her hand.

CELINE, *startled*: Monsieur!

ANTOINE: Just pretend I have a secret. *(Bending toward her.)* Something to whisper in your ear…

MADAME DE RIGUEUR enters, right.

MADAME DE RIGUEUR, *speaking over her shoulder, into the wings*: And today!… You won't forget!

ANTOINE, *just as he is about to kiss CELINE on the cheek*: Damn! Too late!

MADAME DE RIGUEUR: Because if not… Well… *(To CELINE, suddenly noticing her.)* You will see to it my child… Today?

ANTOINE, *aside*: "My…" Her child?

CELINE, *to MADAME DE RIGUEUR*: Yes, of course…

ANTOINE, *aside*: That's her mother? *(Looking MADAME DE RIGUEUR up and down, still aside.)* Hmm! Not too bad…

MADAME DE RIGUEUR, *to CELINE*: And the sooner the better!

ANTOINE, *aside*: My sentiments exactly! *(To MADAME DE RIGUEUR.)* Madame…

He approaches her as CELINE moves left.

MADAME DE RIGUEUR, *nodding politely*: Monsieur…

ANTOINE: No time like the present…

MADAME DE RIGUEUR: Quite…

ANTOINE: Now this won't hurt a bit…

He throws his arms around her neck and plants a kiss on her cheek. MADAME DE RIGUEUR lets out a scream.

CELINE, *looking on in horror*: Oh!

ANTOINE, *to MADAME DE RIGUEUR*: Let's let bygones be bygones, shall we?

MADAME DE RIGUEUR, *recovering her aplomb*: You… You beast! You… You…

She slaps him just as LECOUQUE appears at the door, left.

ANTOINE, *recoiling*: Again?

LECOUQUE, *entering*: Oh my! *(Solicitously, to MADAME DE RIGUEUR.)* Madame de Rigueur…

ANTOINE, *aside*: Who?

MADAME DE RIGUEUR, *to LECOUQUE*: What kind of depraved little games are you playing?

LECOUQUE: Me, madame?

MADAME DE RIGUEUR: Here! In your house! An utter stranger… A vulgar debauchee… A… A pervert!

LECOUQUE: But madame…

MADAME DE RIGUEUR, *pushing him aside*: Out of my way, monsieur! I'm taking my business elsewhere!

LECOUQUE: But… But…

MADAME DE RIGUEUR stalks out, upstage.

CELINE: Oh!

LECOUQUE, *to* ANTOINE: Now look what you've done!

MADAME DE RIGUEUR reappears at the door.

MADAME DE RIGUEUR: After I get my tiara!... This afternoon, understand?

She stalks out once again.

ANTOINE, *to* LECOUQUE: But... I thought she was your wife...

LECOUQUE: You thought... You thought...

ANTOINE: Anyway, that one doesn't count, monsieur! I mean, we agreed... Madame Lecouque ...

LECOUQUE, *not wanting* CELINE *to hear*: Yes, yes... For heaven's sake...

ANTOINE: Well? Where is she? It's time I met her.

LECOUQUE: She's not here, if you must know. She's out... At the police station...

ANTOINE: Oh... I'm sorry...

LECOUQUE: Looking for her handbag...

ANTOINE: Well then, she won't be long, considering... I can wait... I'm in no hurry... *(He looks longingly at* CELINE.*)* No hurry at all... *(To* CELINE.*)* Am I, mademoiselle?

CELINE, *coyly lowering her eyes*: I... I'm sure I don't know, monsieur...

LECOUQUE, *looking at them, back and forth, aside*: What on earth are those two up do? *(To* ANTOINE.*)* I'm sorry, monsieur... She won't be back until two, and... and we're very busy! *(To* CELINE.*)* Aren't we, Céline?

CELINE: Oh no, papá... We're not busy at all! Only Madame de Rigueur...

LECOUQUE: Yes we are! Don't contradict me!

CELINE, *naively*: We are?

LECOUQUE, *pointing toward the door, right, to* CELINE: Now you'd better get back to the shop...

CELINE: But papá...

LECOUQUE: And don't come out unless I ring for you. *(He picks up the bell on the work table and gives a little jingle.)* Understand?

CELINE, sighing, starts to leave, right.

ANTOINE, *stopping her*: No, no... You needn't... I'll go, mademoiselle... *(To* LECOUQUE.*)* Much as I hate to leave you, monsieur...

LECOUQUE: No doubt...

ANTOINE, *to* LECOUQUE: Because to know you is to... *(Turning subtly toward* CELINE.*)* to love you...

LECOUQUE: I'm sure...

ANTOINE: But I'll be back... *(To* LECOUQUE.*)* At two o'clock, monsieur... To take care of our... unfinished business...

LECOUQUE: Yes, yes...

ANTOINE, *to* CELINE, *bowing*: Mademoiselle... *(To* LECOUQUE,*)* Monsieur...

He exits, upstage.

CELINE, *after a brief pause*: Who was that nice young gentleman, papá?

LECOUQUE, *pointing to the door, upstage*: Him?

CELINE: Yes... I'm sure he's never been here before. At least, I've, never seen him!... *(Coyly.)* What could he want to speak with you about, I wonder?

LECOUQUE: Business, my dear... You heard him... Business...

CELINE, *with a note of good-natured sarcasm*: My, my! I could have sworn it was for… Well, something else!

LECOUQUE: Oh?

CELINE: Yes… Why, after all, he kissed Madame de Rigueur because he thought she was mammá! Surely that must mean something!

LECOUQUE, *trying to make light of it, shrugging*: Well… Not necessarily…

CELINE: Come now, papá… You don't have to pretend. I know all about it! Really, I do!

LECOUQUE: You do?

CELINE: Of course! Why, it's as plain as day! You didn't think you could fool me, did you? I can tell a suitor when I see one!

LECOUQUE: A suitor? Him?

CELINE: And if you must know, papá… He's really the nicest one you've ever brought to meet me!

LECOUQUE: What?

CELINE: Why, he's charming, and… and clever, and…

LECOUQUE: But… Wait just a minute…

CELINE: …and terribly attractive! Oh yes, papá! I'm sure… I'm simply sure I'm going to fall in love with him!

LECOUQUE, *aside*: That's all I need! *(Aloud.)* He's… I'm telling you… He's not a suitor!

CELINE: Tsk tsk tsk! *(Shaking her finger at him.)* Papá… Papá…

LECOUQUE: But he's not! He's… He's…

CELINE: Yes?

LECOUQUE: He's… He's just someone who rides the tram, that's all!… And… *(Deciding to tell all.)* And he stroked your mother's foot… Because he thought it was his dog…

CELINE, *incredulous*: What?

LECOUQUE: And if she doesn't let him kiss her… Just one little kiss… Then two men will be standing face to face, with drawn swords!… There! You wanted to know the truth. Now I hope you're satisfied!

CELINE, *sighing*: Really, papá! That's the most preposterous… Why on earth don't you want me to know he's a suitor?

LECOUQUE: But my dear child, I assure you… He's no such thing! I'm telling you…

CELINE, *pointing to her heart*: And this tells me that he is!

LECOUQUE: "This…"? This what?

CELINE: My heart!

LECOUQUE: Your… Your… *(At a loss for words.)* Oh… *(Beginning to lose patience,)* Get back to the shop, I told you!… And take your heart with you!

CELINE: But…

LECOUQUE, *mumbling*: Your heart… And don't come out unless I ring for you!

CELINE: Yes, papá!

She exits, right.

LECOUQUE: Her heart… That's all I need! A young good-for-nothing!… And a painter, no less! Without a sou to his name, I suppose!

MADAME LECOUQUE appears, upstage, obviously out of patience.

MADAME LECOUQUE, *entering*: Well that was a fine waste of time!

LECOUQUE: Hildegarde!

She takes off her hat and coat and lays them on one of the chairs, left.

MADAME LECOUQUE: A wild goose chase!… The police were absolutely no help at all!

LECOUQUE, *trying to get her attention*: My love…

MADAME LECOUQUE: I don't know what this city is coming to!

LECOUQUE: My love… While you were gone…

He holds up her handbag.

MADAME LECOUQUE: My… Where on earth did you…

She takes it from him, examining the contents.

LECOUQUE: A young man brought it back… A nice young man… Very nice… *(Aside.)* Now or never! *(Aloud.)* Really… Terribly nice…

MADAME LECOUQUE: How… nice! I hope you gave him a reward for his trouble.

LECOUQUE: Well, no…

MADAME LECOUQUE: Oh, Gustave! You should have… At least a franc or two…

LECOUQUE: Yes… Well… It wasn't exactly money he was after. *(Aside.)* Unfortunately! *(Aloud.)* That is…

MADAME LECOUQUE: That is…?

LECOUQUE: In fact… *(Forcing a laugh.)* You'll never believe it, Hildegarde… He's… He's the same young man…

MADAME LECOUQUE: What same young man?

LECOUQUE: The… The one you… you met last night… In the tram…

MADAME LECOUQUE: What?

LECOUQUE: Isn't that a coincidence?

MADAME LECOUQUE: Coincidence my foot! It's a scandal!

LECOUQUE, *still laughing*: "My foot." Her foot! That's a good one! Your foot…

MADAME LECOUQUE, *ignoring his remarks*: Here, in this house! That… That…

LECOUQUE: But really, Hildegarde…

MADAME LECOUQUE: And you let him… You… You mean you didn't throw him out on his ear?

LECOUQUE: But I'm telling you… He explained… It wasn't his fault. He… He thought you were his dog…

MADAME LECOUQUE: He what?

LECOUQUE: I mean, your foot… He thought your foot was his dog… His pekingese…

MADAME LECOUQUE: He thought…

LECOUQUE: On account of the fur… Your shoe… With the fur…

MADAME LECOUQUE: Now I've heard everything! And you believed him?

LECOUQUE: Well, yes… I'm sure… I mean, if you saw him you would believe him too…

MADAME LECOUQUE: Heaven forbid!

LECOUQUE: Poor chap!… He… He didn't know what to say… He was all apologies… "Oh please, monsieur!… Please, tell madame how dreadfully sorry I am…"

MADAME LECOUQUE: Indeed!

LECOUQUE: That's what he said… "Dreadfully sorry…"

MADAME LECOUQUE: Hmm!

LECOUQUE: "…and that I hope she can find it in her heart to forgive me!"

MADAME LECOUQUE, *weakening*: Oh?

LECOUQUE: Really, it was pathetic…

MADAME LECOUQUE: Well…

LECOUQUE: And after all, it wasn't his fault.

MADAME LECOUQUE: No, I suppose you're right. "To err is human…"

LECOUQUE, *relieved, sighing*: My sentiments exactly!… "And to forgive…"

MADAME LECOUQUE, *hardening her position*: Just don't let him show his face in my house again!

LECOUQUE: What?

MADAME LECOUQUE: I can't be responsible for what I might do!

LECOUQUE: But… But… He's coming back… At two o'clock… He said so…

MADAME LECOUQUE: He's what? What in heaven's name for? What possible reason…

LECOUQUE: To beg you to forgive him… To hear it from your own lips, Hildegarde… And to ask you… To ask you… *(Aside.)* Good God, she'll never…

MADAME LECOUQUE: To ask me what?

LECOUQUE: To ask you to give him… to give him… something…

MADAME LECOUQUE: And what, may I ask? *(Sarcastically.)* The reward?

LECOUQUE: No, no, my love… A… A kiss… Just a little one…

MADAME LECOUQUE, *recoiling*: I beg your… You're out of your mind! Give him a—

LECOUQUE, *interrupting*: No, no… I meant… To let him give you… To let him… You don't have to do a thing… Just stand there and let him…

MADAME LECOUQUE: Gustave! You can't be serious!

LECOUQUE: Please, Hildegarde! For me!… Just a little one…

MADAME LECOUQUE: Never! Of all the—

LECOUQUE: But why not? At your age, what's the harm? That is…

MADAME LECOUQUE, *ready to slap him, but controlling her temper*: Oh!… *(She moves upstage.)* Just like that! Kiss a man I've never met… An absolute stranger…

LECOUQUE, *as if giving her a convincing argument*: But… But he brought back your handbag!

MADAME LECOUQUE: My handbag be… *(Moving down left.)* Would I have to kiss every man who brought back my handbag?

LECOUQUE: No, no… It's just that…

MADAME LECOUQUE, *sarcastically*: Thank heavens it wasn't my valise! I can imagine…

LECOUQUE: It's just that, this one…

MADAME LECOUQUE, *regaining her composure, beginning to suspect something*: Gustave, there's more to this than meets the eye!

LECOUQUE, *innocently*: More, my love? More what?

MADAME LECOUQUE: Now stop pretending! What is this all about?

LECOUQUE, *after a pause, resigning himself, sighing*: Well, if I must… Yes, you're right… There *is* more… Much more!

He pauses again.

MADAME LECOUQUE, *waiting*: Well?

LECOUQUE: Either you kiss him or he challenges me to a duel! There! Now you know…

There is another pause while MADAME LECOUQUE *waits for him to continue.*

MADAME LECOUQUE: So?

LECOUQUE: "So?"

MADAME LECOUQUE: Is that all? A duel?… People fight them all the time!

LECOUQUE: Yes, people… But… But…

MADAME LECOUQUE: But what? Teach him a lesson! You're not afraid, are you?

LECOUQUE: Afraid? A Lecouque?… Of course I'm not afraid!… Was I afraid when I served my country? Was I afraid when I faced death in the National Guard? Every day… On weekends… No, Hildegarde! I'm not afraid!… Not for me… Not for myself… I don't care about myself… But you, Hildegarde… And Céline. *(Growing more and more emotional.)* To leave you both… defenseless, unprotected…

MADAME LECOUQUE, *softening*: Gustave…

LECOUQUE: Two waifs, alone… On this sea of degradation and corruption we call Paris… Flotsam and jetsam… My wife and my daughter…

MADAME LECOUQUE: Gustave, dearest…

LECOUQUE: And my business… The thought of leaving this nice little business, after all my work… Just when things are beginning to… Now that you're no longer… *(Abruptly changing the line of reasoning.)* I mean… At least, if I were rich… If I'd already made my fortune… Why, I wouldn't think twice… *(He makes a few heroic passes with an imaginary sword.)* Just like that! As long as I thought that you… And she…

He chokes up with emotion.

MADAME LECOUQUE, *touched*: Gustave, please…

LECOUQUE: But I know how much you both need me. I know that I still have some use on this earth…

MADAME LECOUQUE: Of course you do, dearest… Of course you do…

LECOUQUE, *simply*: Thank you…

MADAME LECOUQUE: And I want to do anything I can, believe me…

LECOUQUE: Then you mean you'll…

MADAME LECOUQUE: It's just that… Letting a strange man kiss me!… It's unheard of… It's… It's…

LECOUQUE: But I'll be there… I'll be watching…

MADAME LECOUQUE: That's even worse!

LECOUQUE: I mean, it's not as if you're doing it behind my back.

MADAME LECOUQUE, *sighing*: Still...

LECOUQUE: Really my love... You're making a mountain out of a *moleskin*. Just make believe it's New Year's Day... Or your birthday... Or something... And a gentleman comes up to you and wants to wish you—

MADAME LECOUQUE, *interrupting*: A stranger? An absolute stranger?

LECOUQUE: Well, make believe he's not! Make believe it's the... the grocer...

MADAME LECOUQUE: What?

LECOUQUE: Please, Hildegarde! For me... *(Pointing toward the door, right.)* For her... For... For us!

MADAME LECOUQUE, *sighing*: Oh, Gustave! I'll... I'll try... *(LECOUQUE heaves a sigh of relief.)* Really, I'll do my best...

LECOUQUE: Thank you, my love! I knew I could count on you.

MADAME LECOUQUE: Just give me a minute to put away my things.

She picks up her hat and coat, and exits, left.

LECOUQUE: Well... So far, so good...

ANTOINE appears at the door, upstage.

ANTOINE, *entering*: Five minutes to two!... *(Noticing LECOUQUE.)* You can see I'm prompt, monsieur.

LECOUQUE, *sarcastically*: Yes, I'm delighted!

ANTOINE: Punctuality is a virtue!... Well, is madame... Has she returned, monsieur?

LECOUQUE, *curtly*: I'll go tell her you're here.

He moves toward the door, left.

ANTOINE, *stopping him*: And mademoiselle, monsieur?

LECOUQUE: Mademoiselle who?

ANTOINE: Mademoiselle... Your daughter...

LECOUQUE: What about her?

ANTOINE: Is she at home too?

LECOUQUE: She's at work, monsieur. Just where she should be!

ANTOINE: Ah! Delightful creature... As industrious as she is beautiful!... An angel, monsieur... An angel...

LECOUQUE: Yes... Quite... *(Trying to move toward the door.)* Now, if you'll excuse me... I'll go get my wife.

ANTOINE, *holding him back*: Perhaps you would like me to paint her portrait, monsieur? A beauty like her...

LECOUQUE: My wife?... You must be joking!

ANTOINE: No, no... Your daughter... In oils, of course...

LECOUQUE: For forty francs? No thank you!

ANTOINE: For nothing, monsieur! For you, free of charge... Professional courtesy...

LECOUQUE: Thank you just the same! Not even if you pay me!

ANTOINE, *offended*: Oh...

LECOUQUE: Day after day, sitting after sitting... I have no intention of seeing you settle in!

ANTOINE: But...

LECOUQUE: Now, if you don't mind, I'll go get my wife, and you'll proceed with the business at hand! And then you'll leave!

ANTOINE: Very good, monsieur.

LECOUQUE: And for goodness' sake, remember she has something of a temper.

ANTOINE: "Something," monsieur? *(With a sardonic smile.)* You'll recall, I've been treated to rather ample proof!

LECOUQUE: Yes, well… Just don't do anything to make her lose it! No emotion… Nothing… No feeling, understand?

ANTOINE: Of course, monsieur! What do you take me for?

LECOUQUE: And whatever you do, keep your mouth shut!

ANTOINE: Indeed! You can rest assured…

LECOUQUE, *at the door, left*: No comments… Not a word…

He exits.

ANTOINE: Not a word… My lips are sealed… *(He moves right, toward the work table, sighing.)* Besides, who cares? It's not the mother I want… It's… It's that delightful creature… *(Gazing lovingly toward the door, right.)* In there… Just a few feet away… *(He begins to tremble.)* Just the thought of it makes me… Oh my! See how I'm trembling… And to think, just a ring of this bell… Just a little tinkle, and she would walk through that door… *(He goes over, about to pick up the bell, but hesitates.)* Oh no, Antoine! You mustn't… You wouldn't dare… If you do… *(He picks it up in his trembling hand and, without meaning to, makes it ring.)* Oh my! I did! *(He claps his other hand over the bell, but as soon as he removes it, he inadvertently rings it again.)* Oh…

CELINE appears at the door, right, holding a flowered tiara.

CELINE, *entering*: Did you ring for me, papá? *(Noticing ANTOINE.)* Oh, monsieur…

ANTOINE, *absentmindedly putting the bell in his pocket*: Mademoiselle…

CELINE: I thought my father…

ANTOINE: No, no… It was me… It was I… *(Bumbling.)* I mean… You must be surprised to see me, mademoiselle.

CELINE: Surprised? Not at all, monsieur! I know all about it!

ANTOINE: Oh? You do?

CELINE: Of course! Papá tried terribly hard not to let on…

ANTOINE: Yes, I should think…

CELINE, *laughing*: You should have heard him, monsieur… But I guessed… I always do, you know…

ANTOINE: "Always…" You mean, this… this has happened before?

CELINE: I should say!

ANTOINE, *aside*: My heavens! *(To CELINE.)* Very often?

CELINE: Oh yes! *(Laughing.)* I've lost count…

ANTOINE: You've lost…

CELINE: But it's always the same, monsieur… They come in and they talk with papá…

ANTOINE: And your mother…?

CELINE: Oh yes, mammá too… And I'm never supposed to know that they're asking to marry me!

ANTOINE, *with a start*: That they're asking…

CELINE: Just like you, monsieur… *(Coyly.)* But I'm not supposed to know!

ANTOINE, *nonplussed*: Just like… *(Aside.)* Now there's an idea!

CELINE: But of course, I always do!

ANTOINE: No!… You mean, we didn't fool you? You… You knew all along that… that I love you, mademoiselle? That I'm head over heels…

CELINE: Really, monsieur! It's never very hard to tell!

ANTOINE, *aside*: With all that practice!

CELINE, *very matter-of-fact*: Well, I'd better be getting back, monsieur. Papá will be angry. *(Holding up the tiara.)* He promised this for today… This afternoon…

ANTOINE, *stopping her*: What a lovely bouquet!

CELINE: It's not a bouquet, silly! It's a tiara! You wear it…

ANTOINE: Oh, of course…

CELINE: Navy blue tea roses… Papá says they have to sing…

ANTOINE, *taking the tiara, admiringly*: And to think… With your own two hands…

He kisses it.

CELINE: Monsieur! What are you doing?

ANTOINE: With your own little fingers… *(He kisses it again.)* Who wouldn't be pretty with a… *(Searching for the word.)* a *tarara* like that?… Even… *(Placing it on his own head.)* Voilà! *(CELINE begins to laugh.)* What's so funny?

CELINE: You've put it on upside down, monsieur!

ANTOINE: Upside down?… What did I tell you? Head over heels! *(CELINE, taking the tiara from his head, standing on tiptoes.)* Here… Let me… *(She sits down on the loveseat.)* Get down…

ANTOINE, *kneeling down in front of her, rather facetiously*: You see? I'm already throwing myself at your feet!

CELINE adjusts the tiara on his head.

CELINE, *laughing*: There! That's perfect! *(Just at that moment, LECOUQUE enters, left, followed by MADAME LECOUQUE, whom he is holding by the hand.)*

LECOUQUE,	*together:*	What on earth…
MADAME LECOUQUE,		Céline!

ANTOINE,	*together:*	Oh, my goodness!
CELINE,		Mammá! Papá!

ANTOINE quickly gets to his feet, still wearing the tiara.

ANTOINE, *bowing*: Madame… Monsieur…

MADAME LECOUQUE,	*together:*	What do you think you're…
LECOUQUE,		Madame de Rigueur's…

LECOUQUE pulls the tiara from ANTOINE's head.

LECOUQUE: Give me that!… Her tea roses…

MADAME LECOUQUE: Oh!

LECOUQUE: Look! They're all crumpled!

MADAME LECOUQUE, *to* CELINE: You should be ashamed of yourself, Céline!

CELINE: But…

MADAME LECOUQUE, *pointing right*: Now get back in there at once!

LECOUQUE, *handing* CELINE *the tiara*: And take care of this! They've got to sing, understand? They've got to sing!

CELINE: But mammá…

MADAME LECOUQUE: No "buts," young lady! *(Pointing.)* Out!

CELINE, *sighing*: Oh…

She grudgingly exits, right, leaving the door slightly ajar and eavesdropping, unnoticed by the others.

LECOUQUE, *after a brief pause, to* ANTOINE: Now then, monsieur… Let's proceed with the business at hand…

ANTOINE, *with a foolish little laugh*: That's rather good, monsieur…

LECOUQUE: Please?

ANTOINE: "The business at hand…" "At hand," indeed!… *(Giving himself a little slap on both cheeks.)* Very good…

MADAME LECOUQUE, *resisting the urge to slap him, aside*: Idiot!

LECOUQUE: Monsieur, don't be impertinent!

ANTOINE: Oh, sorry…

LECOUQUE: Madame is ready!

ANTOINE, *to* LECOUQUE, *whispering*: I thought you said she was pretty!

The two men continue their exchange in a whisper.

LECOUQUE: "Ish," I said… "Ish"…

ANTOINE: Even "ish"!… I mean, really…

LECOUQUE: Please, no comments… You promised…

ANTOINE: Quite… *(Aloud to* MADAME LECOUQUE *.)* Madame, first, let me assure you that I'm not what you take me for…

MADAME LECOUQUE, *offering her cheek*: Please, let's get it over with!

ANTOINE: I'm really a fine young man…

MADAME LECOUQUE: No doubt!

LECOUQUE, *aside to* ANTOINE: No speeches, I said!

ANTOINE, *to* MADAME LECOUQUE: Believe me… You'll see…

MADAME LECOUQUE, *losing patience*: Monsieur!

ANTOINE: And that's why I have the honor…

LECOUQUE: Please…

ANTOINE: …of asking for the hand of your daughter in marriage!

MADAME LECOUQUE, } *together*: { My daughter…
LECOUQUE, } *together*: { What?

MADAME LECOUQUE, *indignantly*: You?… *(She slaps him in the face.)* The nerve!

ANTOINE: Oh!

CELINE, *poking her head out, unseen by the others*: Oh dear!

MADAME LECOUQUE, *moving upstage*: That, monsieur, is the only hand you'll get!

ANTOINE, *rubbing his cheek, crossing right, fuming*: Again?… Oh no! That's the last straw! The last—

LECOUQUE: Monsieur…

ANTOINE, *to MADAME LECOUQUE*: Madame, if you weren't a lady… *(Correcting.)* A woman…

MADAME LECOUQUE: I beg your…

ANTOINE, *ranting*: A man, good God!… Is there a man in this house?

LECOUQUE, *trying to calm him*: Monsieur…

ANTOINE: You!

He gives his face a resounding slap.

CELINE, *aside*: Oh! Papá…

LECOUQUE, *furious*: You… You dare…

MADAME LECOUQUE: Gustave… He hit you!

LECOUQUE: I know, damn it! I know! *(To ANTOINE.)* Monsieur, this means a duel!

MADAME LECOUQUE, *to ANTOINE*: That's right! *(To LECOUQUE.)* Teach him a lesson!

ANTOINE: A duel, monsieur?

LECOUQUE: To the death!

MADAME LECOUQUE, *echoing*: To the death!

CELINE, *aside*: To the death?

ANTOINE: To the death?

LECOUQUE: A Lecouque, monsieur, defends his honor with his blood!

MADAME LECOUQUE, *to ANTOINE*: That's right, monsieur! His blood…

ANTOINE, *aside*: Yes… Or mine…

CELINE, *aside*: Oh my, oh my…

LECOUQUE, *very correct, to ANTOINE*: Now if monsieur will excuse me, I'll go get the weapons!

MADAME LECOUQUE, *to LECOUQUE*: Yes, Gustave… The weapons…

LECOUQUE and MADAME LECOUQUE exit, left.

ANTOINE, *alone*: Hmm! Maybe I was a little hasty…

CELINE, *bursting out from behind the door*: Well, monsieur! Very nice!

ANTOINE: Mademoiselle…

CELINE: A duel with papá! That's a fine way to ask to marry me, I must say! What ever will you do?

ANTOINE: Oh, don't worry about me! I can take care of myself!

He dramatically assumes the "en garde" position.

CELINE: Yes, but you wouldn't kill papá, I hope…

ANTOINE: Oh, I…

CELINE: Because if you did, you know… Well then, I'd never be able to marry you.

ANTOINE, *reflecting*: No… That's true…

CELINE: I mean… Never! Really!

ANTOINE: But then again, if he kills me…

CELINE: We wouldn't be much better off, monsieur, would we?

ANTOINE: No…

CELINE: You, especially…

ANTOINE: Quite!

CELINE: Of course, you could always apologize.

ANTOINE: I could do what?

CELINE: Apologizc… Tell him you're sorry…

ANTOINE: A Falsetto, mademoiselle?

CELINE: A what?

ANTOINE: A Falsetto… That's my name… My father was Italian.

CELINE: Oh, I didn't know…

ANTOINE: You want me to apologize? Swallow my pride?

CELINE: For me, monsieur… Monsieur Falsetto… That is… *(Suggestively.)* For us…

ANTOINE: Well, as long as you put it that way, I suppose…

LECOUQUE bursts in, left, carrying a tray with two cups, one white and the other blue.

LECOUQUE: All right, monsieur! *(Suddenly noticing CELINE.)* Céline! I thought I told you…

He points peremptorily toward the door, right.

CELINE, *docilely*: Yes, papá… I'm going… *(Aside, to ANTOINE, as she leaves.)* Remember… For us…

She exits, right.

LECOUQUE, *very formally*: Monsieur…

ANTOINE, *nodding*: Monsieur…

LECOUQUE: I'm sure you understand how my honor has been attacked…

ANTOINE: Well, actually, I thought we might—

LECOUQUE: …and that one of us must vanish from the face of the earth!

ANTOINE: Oh? I thought… I thought…

LECOUQUE: You thought, monsieur?

ANTOINE: That… That perhaps we might come to an… an amicable understanding…

LECOUQUE: Understanding?... A Lecouque?… Ha ha! *(Derisively.)* You must be mad!

ANTOINE: Well…

LECOUQUE: To the death, monsieur! To the death!… Now then, as the offended party I have the right to choose the weapons… I've chosen a duel with cups of milk.

ANTOINE, *bewildered, with a laugh*: What? We're going to throw milk at each other?

LECOUQUE: Don't joke, monsieur! This is serious!… We're going to drink it!

ANTOINE: What?

LECOUQUE: I've scratched the sulphur from seventy-two matches into one of these cups.

ANTOINE: Oh? Which one?

LECOUQUE, *ignoring his question*: The one who drinks it will have long, horrible convulsions, until he drops dead.

ANTOINE, *almost facetiously*: Good heavens! I've met my match!

LECOUQUE: Please! I told you… This is serious!

ANTOINE: Sorry…

LECOUQUE: Well, are you ready?

ANTOINE: Excuse me, monsieur, but… A duel is one thing, but… I'm really not thirsty…

LECOUQUE: You mean, you're afraid?

ANTOINE: No… It's just that I promised your daughter, monsieur… *(LECOUQUE gives him a quizzical look.)* I promised her I would try to settle our differences.

LECOUQUE: Impossible, monsieur! What's done is done!

He places the tray on the end table near the loveseat.

ANTOINE: Even if it meant that I… *(Clearing his throat.)* That is…

LECOUQUE, *curtly*: Unacceptable, monsieur! No apologies accepted!… Now then, I'm the offended party, so I have my choice… I take the white cup. Here, you swallow the blue one…

He turns the tray with the blue cup toward ANTOINE.

ANTOINE, *recoiling*: Ha! You're out of your mind!

LECOUQUE: You refuse?

ANTOINE: Of course I do! What do you take me for? *(Mimicking.)* "You swallow the blue one!"

LECOUQUE: That's what I said…

ANTOINE: No, thank you!… You scratch the matches, and you tell me which one to drink! That's a good one!

LECOUQUE: But…

ANTOINE: I choose the white one too! *(Turning the tray.)* Here, you swallow the blue one!

LECOUQUE: But protocol… I'm the offended—

ANTOINE: Protocol be damned!

LECOUQUE: Oh! Have you no sense of honor, monsieur? No sense… No sense…

ANTOINE: Too much sense, thank you!

LECOUQUE: I see! In other words—

ANTOINE: In other words, if you insist on this… this duel…

LECOUQUE: I do!

ANTOINE: Then I insist we let someone else do the choosing for us. A third party, monsieur… With no axe to grind…

LECOUQUE: Very well… I'll call my wife.

He goes to leave.

ANTOINE: Your… *(Stopping him.)* Oh no!… No, no, no!

LECOUQUE: Monsieur?

ANTOINE: She helped you scratch the matches! She knows… She… No, no! I'd prefer your daughter!

LECOUQUE: Céline?… Hmm!… Well… *(Aside.)* Blood is thicker than water… *(Aloud.)* I suppose… *(Aside,)* She'll make the right choice… I know she will! *(Aloud.)* All right, monsieur! My daughter!

ANTOINE: Fine!

LECOUQUE: But not a word to her, understand?

ANTOINE: Not a word!

LECOUQUE: I'll call her… *(He looks around on the work table for the bell.)* Where the devil is that bell?

ANTOINE, *looking around*: The bell, monsieur?

LECOUQUE: It's usually on the table…

ANTOINE: Yes, I remember…

He moves around, looking for the bell with LECOUQUE. *As he does so, it jingles in his pocket.*

LECOUQUE: Strange… I seem to hear it…

ANTOINE: So do I…

LECOUQUE: But I don't see it…

ANTOINE: I know I had it, but…

LECOUQUE: It must be somewhere…

ANTOINE, *stopping to listen*: Listen… It stopped…

He moves around again, stopping several times, LECOUQUE *follows him, trying to detect the source of the sound. Finally the light dawns and he stops* ANTOINE.

LECOUQUE, *pointing to the offending pocket*: Monsieur!

ANTOINE, *feeling his pocket and taking out the bell*: Now what is it doing in there?

LECOUQUE, *pulling it away*: Give me that!

He rings it. CELINE *appears at the door, right.*

CELINE: Did someone ring?

LECOUQUE: Come here, Céline…

CELINE, *joining him*: Yes, papá…

LECOUQUE: Monsieur has agreed to do us the honor of accepting a cup of milk… *(Pointing to the tray.)* Pure, delicious milk… Please be good enough to serve us.

CELINE: Then you mean… You've made up?

ANTOINE: In a manner of speaking…

CELINE, *to* ANTOINE: Which one would you like, monsieur?

LECOUQUE, *aside to* ANTOINE: Not a word!

ANTOINE, *to* CELINE, *as offhand as possible*: Oh, it really doesn't matter, mademoiselle… You decide… *(Raising his eyes to heaven, aside.)* Don't let her be a widow before she's a wife!

LECOUQUE, *to* CELINE: Yes, you decide… *(Raising his eyes, aside.)* Don't let her be an orphan!

CELINE *takes the blue cup.*

ANTOINE, } *together*: { Good God!
LECOUQUE, } { Oh my!

Both men watch uneasily as CELINE seems uncertain whom to serve first. Finally, she moves toward LECOUQUE with the cup.

LECOUQUE, *to CELINE as inconspicuously as possible, waving her off toward ANTOINE*: Pssst… Pssst…

CELINE, *to ANTOINE*: Here, monsieur… Guests first…

ANTOINE, *taking the cup, aside*: Ay ay ay!… *(Aloud.)* Thank you, mademoiselle… *(Aside.)* My angel… of death!

CELINE, *aside*: Milk in the afternoon! Of all things…

LECOUQUE, *smiling*: Our pleasure, monsieur! *(Taking the white cup and raising it.)* To your health, young man!

CELINE, *aside*: Anyway, they've made up, and that's all that matters!

ANTOINE, *raising his cup*: To yours, old friend!

He pauses.

LECOUQUE, *waiting, to ANTOINE*: Well, aren't you going to drink it?

ANTOINE: I… It's… I'm not sure I should… It's bad for my liver…

CELINE: Nonsense, monsieur! Milk is good for you!

ANTOINE, *aside*: Sometimes…

LECOUQUE, *to ANTOINE*: See? You heard her…

ANTOINE: Besides, there's a fly in it…

CELINE, *looking*: Where? In our milk?

ANTOINE: Well, I thought… I'm sure I saw one… A big one… Black…

CELINE: You couldn't have, monsieur! We don't have any!

ANTOINE: Oh… *(Aside.)* No harm in trying…

LECOUQUE: Well, bottoms up!

ANTOINE, *sardonically*: Cheers!

LECOUQUE: Chin chin, and all that…

ANTOINE, *touched, wiping away a tear*: Ah yes… Chin-Chin… My little Chin-Chin…

CELINE, *to ANTOINE*: Monsieur?

ANTOINE: My dog, mademoiselle… I was thinking about my dog…

CELINE, *aside*: His dog?

ANTOINE, *to LECOUQUE*: Excuse me, monsieur, but… Could you spare a sheet of paper?

LECOUQUE: What for?

ANTOINE: A few last minute arrangements… Before I… take my leave…

LECOUQUE: I suppose it's only right…

He goes to his desk, down right, and puts down the white cup while assembling paper, pen, and ink.

CELINE, *surprised, to ANTOINE*: Are you going somewhere, monsieur?

ANTOINE: Yes, I'm afraid so…

CELINE, *disillusioned*: But where? You told me…

ANTOINE: I'm going… I'm going, mademoiselle, where the tea roses bloom forever…

CELINE: But… I thought you were a painter, monsieur… Not a florist…

ANTOINE: Yes, I am… That is, I was… Have been… Used to be… *(Shrugging.)* Whatever…

LECOUQUE, *at the desk, to* ANTOINE: There you are, monsieur…

ANTOINE: Ah! Much obliged… *(Handing him the blue cup.)* Here, would you mind… *(He fumbles in his pocket for some coins.)* That's fifty centimes…

He gives the coins to LECOUQUE.

LECOUQUE: What for?

ANTOINE: Well, you'll have to get it notarized, and…

LECOUQUE: Oh, you didn't have to bother… *(Aside, pocketing the coins.)* Thoughtful chap!

As ANTOINE *sits down at the desk,* LECOUQUE *inadvertently raises the blue cup to his lips, stops in horror as he realizes his error, and slips it back into* ANTOINE*'s left hand as the latter begins to write with his right.*

ANTOINE, *writing*: "I, Antoine Falsetto, being of sane mind and sound body, hereby bequeath my entire estate…"

CELINE, *aside*: "Bequeath…" What on earth…

ANTOINE: "…all property and possessions to my faithful dog, Chin-Chin…"

CELINE, } *together:* { What?
LECOUQUE, } { Monsieur?

ANTOINE: "…including my annual income of twenty-five thousand francs…"

LECOUQUE, *with a start, to* ANTOINE: Your what?.. Twenty-five thousand a year?

ANTOINE, *diffidently*: Well, in round figures…

LECOUQUE: Why in heaven's name didn't you say so in the first place?

ANTOINE, *putting the cup to his lips*: And now… *(With a dramatic gaze at* CELINE.*)* Farewell…

LECOUQUE, *trying to pull the cup away*: For God's sake, don't drink that!

CELINE: But…

ANTOINE, *persisting*: My honor, monsieur! My honor…

LECOUQUE: Twenty-five thousand… *(Calling.)* Hildegarde!… *(To* CELINE.*)* Help me…

CELINE: But…

LECOUQUE, *calling*: Hildegarde! Hildegarde!

They continue the tug-of-war, as MADAME LECOUQUE *appears, left.*

MADAME LECOUQUE, *entering*: Gustave… What are you—

LECOUQUE, *aside to* MADAME LECOUQUE*, pointing to* ANTOINE: Twenty-five thousand… He has twenty-five thousand a year!

MADAME LECOUQUE, *aside to* LECOUQUE: I don't believe it!

LECOUQUE, *to* ANTOINE: Young man, my daughter is yours!

ANTOINE, *putting down the cup*: She is?

CELINE: Oh, papá…

LECOUQUE, *to* ANTOINE: You're the son I've always dreamed of!

MADAME LECOUQUE, *to* ANTOINE: A marriage made in heaven!

CELINE, *to* ANTOINE: Oh monsieur… Monsieur…

ANTOINE: I… I don't know what to say… Monsieur… Madame…

LECOUQUE: Just say "yes"!

MADAME LECOUQUE: Say "yes"!

CELINE: Yes… Say "yes"!

ANTOINE, *enthusiastically*: Yes!… Yes, yes!… *(Aside.)* It's really twenty-five hundred, but what's a zero more or less? *(To LECOUQUE.)* Father!… *(To MADAME LECOUQUE.)* Mother!…

MADAME LECOUQUE, *embracing him*: Son!

CELINE, *coquettishly*: Antoine!

ANTOINE, *aside*: They'll find out soon enough.

CELINE, *to LECOUQUE*: You see, papá! I knew it all along!

MADAME LECOUQUE, *taking ANTOINE aside, in a whisper*: When you have to talk money, son, be sure to come see me.

LECOUQUE, *to CELINE*: Knew it? Knew what?

MADAME LECOUQUE, *still whispering, to ANTOINE*: Gustave… Monsieur is an absolute zero!

CELINE, *to LECOUQUE*: That he was a suitor!

ANTOINE, *to MADAME LECOUQUE, whispering*: Fine! *(Aside.)* I can use one! *(Holding out his hand to CELINE, who joins him.)* Céline…

MADAME LECOUQUE, *to ANTOINE, aloud*: And now, son, I think we should pay our debts!

ANTOINE: Mother?

MADAME LECOUQUE: Two kisses, you dear boy! One for each slap!

They all laugh, as ANTOINE gives CELINE two kisses, one on each cheek.

ANTOINE: There!

MADAME LECOUQUE: No, no! Here I am… Over here…

ANTOINE: Oh… My mistake! It's so hard to tell the difference!

LECOUQUE stifles a guffaw.

MADAME LECOUQUE: Really? *(Kissing him.)* Why you dear, sweet boy, you! *(To LECOUQUE.)* Isn't he sweet, Gustave?

LECOUQUE: Oh, I should say, my love! *(Aside, jovially.)* A liar, but sweet!

ANTOINE, *aside to LECOUQUE, laughing*: Well… "Ish"…

LECOUQUE, *aside to ANTOINE, laughing*: "Ish…"

ANTOINE, *aloud*: There's one thing I'm sure of… I'll never stroke my Chin-Chin again in the tram… At least, not in the dark…

CELINE, *turning to LECOUQUE, puzzled*: He'll never what?

MADAME LECOUQUE, *to ANTOINE*: Your Chin-Chin indeed!… Your Chin-Chin my foot-foot!

They all laugh, except CELINE, who continues to look on quizzically.

CELINE: Will somebody please tell me what is so funny?

LECOUQUE: I told you before… Your mother, Céline…

MADAME LECOUQUE: I was sitting in the tram…

ANTOINE: And I was with my dog… My Chin-Chin, mademoiselle…

The three of them continue talking, all at once, trying to explain to a bewildered CELINE, *as the curtain slowly falls.*

CURTAIN.

A Matter of Wife and Death

(La lettre chargée, 1877)

Eugène Labiche

Characters

TIMOTHY VAN LUST, a Texas millionaire on the loose in Paris

GASTON, a verbose provincial lawyer who has difficulty proposing marriage

VIVIANE, his cousin, young at heart and hoping to become his wife

JACQUELINE, her faithful but slightly simple maid

The drawing room in Viviane's Parisian apartment. Upstage center, a double door. Down left, another door. Down right, against the wall, a sewing cabinet. Midstage, left of center, a table and chair. On the table, pen and ink, stationery, envelopes, and a bell. Midstage, right of center, a loveseat. Next to it, a small end table. Pictures, rugs, lamps, and other appropriate furnishings here and there.

At rise, GASTON *and* VIVIANE *are seated on the loveseat.* GASTON *is dozing.*

VIVIANE, *reading*:

"Now, Poet, take thy lute. Come, kiss thy muse.
Tonight the burgeoning spring is newly born;
The wild rose blooms; the breeze blows forth the news;
And feathered wagtail, waiting for the morn,
Lights on the season's first green bough and thorn.

"Now, Poet, take thy lute…"

(*She stops as* GASTON *emits a loud snore.*) Oh no! Not again!… Just look at him… (*To* GASTON, *softly.*) Gaston… Cousin dear… *(Musing.)* I must say, for a man who's come all the way from Dunkirk to ask me to marry him… Three times… Well… (*With a sweeping gesture.*) There he is! Monsieur Gaston de Courvalin, member of the bar… (*With a little laugh.*) And clearly a man with no taste for poetry!

GASTON, *mumbling in his sleep*: Exquisite… Scintillating…

VIVIANE, *shaking her head*: And that's not his only fault, I'm afraid!… Oh, nothing really serious, heaven knows… But still, sometimes it's just so annoying, I could scream!… The man has an absolute mania for big words! Really, that's what it is! A mania!… And the longer the better!… Why, he used one yesterday… I thought it would never end! He opened his mouth and it just kept coming!… "Transubstantiationalist"… Can you believe it? He simply can't speak simply… (*Laughing.*) As it were!

GASTON, *still dozing*: A rhapsody… A dithyramb…

VIVIANE: Even in his sleep, poor dear! (*Turning back to him, reading.*)

"Now, Poet, take thy lute…"

(*Getting up, to herself.*) Still, he has all kinds of excellent qualities. (*Laughing.*) A sound sleeper, for one thing!… And a heart of gold… Devoted, to a fault… (*Sighing.*) Yes, I suppose I really should marry him! I can't see any reason not to. (GASTON *emits another loud snore.*) No serious reason…Yes, this spring, I should think… If the weather holds up… (*Looking at him.*) Well, there's no sense reading to myself, I must say!

She sits down again and raps the book on the end table.

GASTON, *waking up suddenly*: Hmm?.. What?… Ah, Viviane… Concluded already?

VIVIANE: Yes… (*Wryly.*) I read quickly.

GASTON: I should say!

VIVIANE: Did you enjoy it?

GASTON: Prodigiously, my dear! Especially the termination!

VIVIANE: Beg pardon?

GASTON: The conclusion.

VIVIANE: Aha… You mean, the end?

GASTON: Why… yes…

VIVIANE, *to herself*: Case in point!

GASTON: You read so enthrallingly!

VIVIANE, *herself*: And another!

GASTON: I could sit here and listen in perpetuity!

VIVIANE, *shaking her head*: And another! (*To* GASTON, *good-naturedly.*) Oh, don't stop now! I'm sure you must have more!

GASTON: More?… More what?

VIVIANE: More of your "protracted verbiage," as someone I know might so aptly put it…

GASTON: More of my—

VIVIANE: Big words, my love! Really, it's a… a disease! You can't open your mouth without breaking out in a rash of the most long-winded, incomprehensible… (*Laughing.*) I'm afraid you're simply incurable, cousin dear!

GASTON, *somewhat abashed*: But… Why, I never… I wasn't aware… That is, I suppose it's a characteristic I've become habituated to.

VIVIANE, *interrupting, wagging her finger*: Gaston!

GASTON: I mean, a habit I've contracted…

VIVIANE: Better…

GASTON: …as a professional exigency…

VIVIANE, *aside*: Hopeless!

GASTON: We legal practitioners, after all… We do become adept at manipulating the lexicon… Even when the significance is debatable, and the concept less than pellucid…

VIVIANE, *aside, shrugging*: No doubt!

GASTON: But… (*Speaking slowly and carefully.*) But from now on I'll be careful! You'll see, I'll watch myself like a hawk! Anything to make you happy, Viviane!… Anything for the woman I want to make my wife!

VIVIANE: You're sweet!

GASTON, *still speaking with obvious care*: And as long as we're on the subject… Tomorrow it will be two weeks since I left Dunkirk. This time, that is… Because the other two times… Well, I don't have to tell you…

VIVIANE: Yes…

GASTON, *beginning to forget himself*: And I have no option but to vacate the premises and return posthaste to my juridical pursuits.

VIVIANE, *aside*: Oh my…

GASTON: But preceding my departure… Prior to my leave-taking…

VIVIANE: Yes… Before you go…

GASTON: I would esteem myself fortunate indeed…

VIVIANE, *aside*: Indeed!

GASTON: …to have some incontrovertible indication that, on this occasion, my suit will not remain infecund.

VIVIANE, *aside*: Good heavens! I don't believe it!

GASTON: When one loves as I do… Madly… Passionately…

VIVIANE, *wryly*: Oh? Is that all? "Madly…" I would have thought—

GASTON: Unswervingly… Unremittingly… Indefatigably…

VIVIANE: Aha! That's more like it!… Well, cousin dear, I appreciate the attention… (*Grandiloquently.*) But I feel it my obligation to apprise you… to render you cognizant, that is… of the fact that, while you have been engaged in "manipulating the lexicon," a rival has been endeavoring to manipulate my affection! (*Aside.*) So there!

GASTON, *with a start*: A rival? But… But that's impossible!

VIVIANE: Oh? (*With a coy little pout.*) That's not very flattering!

GASTON: I mean… (*Babbling.*) I… I've come all the way from Dunkirk… I… Who… Who is he?

VIVIANE, *resuming her usual tone*: As a matter of fact, I haven't the vaguest idea. Except that he's an American…

GASTON, *scandalized*: A what?

VIVIANE: …and that he sent me the most incredible letter, day before yesterday.

GASTON, *incredulous*: No!

VIVIANE: Yes! (*Crossing left to the table, opening the drawer and holding up some papers.*) Listen… (*Reading.*) "Dear Viviane…"

GASTON, *aside*: Impertinent!

VIVIANE, *continuing*: "You are a widow, and so am I…"

GASTON: Singular!… A widow?

VIVIANE: You know what he means… (*Reading.*) "You want to remarry, and so do I. You are in excellent health, and so am I…"

GASTON, *aside*: Presumptuous!

VIVIANE, *continuing*: "So I don't see any reason why we shouldn't get together."

GASTON: Piquant deduction, I must say!

VIVIANE, *continuing*: "I'm not enclosing my picture because it isn't very flattering. But I can be seen any time you like, for the next two days, while I'm still in Paris. Please reply in care of the Hotel De Luxe, room 124. Yours truly, Timothy Van Lust."

GASTON: Egregious!… Utterly…

VIVIANE, *reading*: "P.S., I'm an American."

GASTON: I never would have guessed!

VIVIANE, *aside*: Or even hazarded a conjecture!

GASTON: Of all things… It must be a prank, Viviane! Some buffoon's conception of a bit of jocular banter…

VIVIANE: Yes, well… If so, it's a prank in two parts.

GASTON: Two…?

VIVIANE: He sent me another letter yesterday.

GASTON: He did?

VIVIANE, *reading*: "Dear Viviane, I can't understand why you haven't replied to mine of the twenty-sixth…"

GASTON: Obviously some madman… Most likely cyclothymic…

VIVIANE: "Cyclo…" Really, Gaston!… (*Shaking her head.*) "Cyclo…"

GASTON: Sorry, my dear! It just came out…

VIVIANE: Well, my goodness!… Put it back!

GASTON: Please… I'll try to be more careful! I'll watch myself… Like a hawk…

VIVIANE: Of course…

GASTON: You'll see… (*Speaking very carefully, taking the letters.*) Here, let me have those. A friend of mine is with the local police. I'll go have a word with him.

VIVIANE: Oh… If you would…

GASTON, *gradually reverting to form*: I'm certain he'll be able to provide pertinent data regarding any foreign nationals currently residing in the vicinity…

VIVIANE, *nodding*: I'm sure…

GASTON: …resulting, no doubt, in an abundance of details…

VIVIANE, *resigned*: Yes…

GASTON: …and a veritable plethora of information concerning your Monsieur… your Mister Timothy Van Lust.

VIVIANE, *good-naturedly, sighing*: Gaston! You're impossible!

GASTON: Oh my… Did I do it again?

VIVIANE: I'm afraid so…

GASTON: I'm sorry…

VIVIANE: Good heavens! Do you think I want to marry a… a dictionary? Really, cousin dear! I'd jump out of my skin!

GASTON, *falling to his knees*: But… But I love you, Viviane!… I… I love you!

VIVIANE, *with a little laugh*: Now *that* I understand! Simple and direct…

GASTON: I… I've come all the way…

VIVIANE: Poor Gaston…

GASTON: I'll be careful… I'll watch myself…

VIVIANE: Like a hawk! I know…

GASTON: You'll see…

VIVIANE, *coyly*: Well… All right, I'll forgive you… If you promise…

GASTON, *jumping to his feet*: I do! I do!

VIVIANE: Good! Now be a dear… Run to the police station and see what you can find out about our friend…

GASTON: Instanter!

He exits, upstage.

VIVIANE, *shaking her head*: He's right… He can't help it!… Oh well, I can get used to it, I suppose. (*Getting up.*) But I really must give him an answer today! Three trips, poor thing… And all the way from Dunkirk!… I simply can't continue this perpetual vacillation… This… (*Reflecting for a moment.*) Oh my! It's contagious!

JACQUELINE enters, upstage, holding a large letter in one hand and an open register in the other.

JACQUELINE, *at the door*: Madame… There's a letter… With lots and lots of stamps…

VIVIANE: Oh? (*She takes the letter and is about to sit down at the table.*) Who on earth…

JACQUELINE, *stopping her, holding out the register*: The postman says madame has to sign…

VIVIANE signs and JACQUELINE leaves, upstage.

VIVIANE, *sitting by the table*: A registered letter?… (*Opening it.*) I wonder who… (*Reading.*) "Dear Viviane…" Oh no! Not another one!… (*Continuing.*) "I'm writing for the third time to ask you to marry me." He can't be serious!… (*Continuing.*) "I'm afraid that numbers one and two, of the twenty-sixth and twenty-seventh, may have gone astray, and I'm taking the precaution of registering number three. Please reply in care of the Hotel De Luxe, room 124." What kind of joke… Whoever he is, he's not about to give up!… Well, we'll see about that! You want a reply, my friend? All right, that's just what you'll get! And registered, no less! (*She takes a sheet of paper, pen, and ink, and begins writing.*) Direct and to the point… "Monsieur, please stop annoying me!"… There!… (*Putting the letter in an envelope, addressing it.*) "Monsieur Timothy Van Lust, room 124, Hotel De Luxe…"

She rings the bell. A moment later JACQUELINE *appears at the door, left.*

JACQUELINE: Madame?

VIVIANE, *giving her the letter*: Take this letter to the post office, will you…

JACQUELINE: Very good, madame… Then what?

VIVIANE: "Then what?"… Then come back! What do you think?

JACQUELINE: Madame doesn't want me to send the letter first?

VIVIANE: Of course I do! Take it to the post office, and send it! Then come back!

JACQUELINE: Oh…

VIVIANE: And be sure to tell the man you want to register it, Jacqueline.

JACQUELINE: Yes, madame… Before or after?

VIVIANE: Before or after what?

JACQUELINE: Before or after I send it, madame?

VIVIANE: Before, of course! (*Aside.*) Idiot! (*To* JACQUELINE, *slowly.*) You take it to the post office, then you register it, and then you send it.

JACQUELINE: Oh… (*Nodding.*) And then I come back… I see… (*Mumbling to herself.*) Take it to the post office… Register it… Send it…

She exits, upstage, and closes the door behind her.

VIVIANE, *brandishing the registered letter*: Tmothy Van Lust, indeed!… The nerve of some people! Who would ever think… An absolute stranger… A man I never met… And he has the nerve… He has the gall… (*There is a knock at the door, upstage.*) Who is it?

The door opens and VAN LUST *appears.*

VAN LUST, *entering*: Only me, ma'am…

VIVIANE, *jumping up*: Monsieur… Who on earth…

VAN LUST: The front door was open… I didn't think you'd mind…

VIVIANE: Who are you?

VAN LUST: Room 124…

VIVIANE, *sitting down again, agape*: You!… Monsieur… Mister Van Lust?

VAN LUST: In person!

VIVIANE: Why… What in heaven's name… Just what do you want, monsieur?

VAN LUST: Your answer, ma'am… To my letters…

VIVIANE: My—

VAN LUST: All three of them…

VIVIANE, *recovering her aplomb*: Yes… Well… (*Archly.*) You have it, monsieur!

VAN LUST, *puzzled*: I do?

VIVIANE: Or at least you will shortly! The postman will be delivering it rather soon, I daresay!

VAN LUST, *overjoyed*: The postman… You mean, you answered… Then what am I doing here?

VIVIANE, *aside*: Indeed!

VAN LUST, *excited*: I should be in my room. I should be there to get it. Oh my! You'll excuse me, ma'am, if I run out like this… I know it's not polite, but… Your answer, after all… I'm sorry…

He moves upstage, as if to leave.

VIVIANE, *getting up, calling him back*: Monsieur… Just a moment…

VAN LUST, *at the door*: Ma'am?

VIVIANE: Before you go… Would you mind terribly explaining… I'm really rather curious…

VAN LUST, *ingenuously*: What about?

VIVIANE: About your… your proposal, monsieur… I believe you asked me to marry you.

VAN LUST: That's right! Three times…

VIVIANE: Quite… But you see, I'm a trifle confused. I don't recall meeting you.

VAN LUST: Oh? Don't let that bother you, ma'am! You never have!

VIVIANE: No… I didn't think so…

VAN LUST: No, no… Never… Or you'd remember!

VIVIANE: Yes… But you've seen me somewhere… That's it, isn't it?… The theater? The races?

VAN LUST: Wrong again!

VIVIANE: I beg your—

VAN LUST: Never! This is the first time I've had the pleasure…

VIVIANE, *recoiling*: It is? (*Aside.*) Good God! Gaston was right! He must be mad! (*To* VAN LUST.) You mean… Never, monsieur?

VAN LUST, *categorically*: Never!

VIVIANE, *aside, anxiously*: And I'm all alone… (*Smiling wanly, to* VAN LUST.) Well… That is…

VAN LUST: I suppose you must think it's a little odd, don't you?

VIVIANE: Odd?… Why no! Why should I think… (*Aside.*) Best not upset him! (*To* VAN LUST.) Odd, monsieur?

VAN LUST: But you'll see… When I explain…

VIVIANE: Yes…

VAN LUST: Please… (*Pointing to the chair by the table.*) Have a seat…

VIVIANE: I… I'd just as soon stand, thank you.

VAN LUST, *sitting down on the loveseat*. No, no… Don't be polite!… Please! Sit down!

VIVIANE, *growing more anxious*: Of course! (*Sitting down at the table.*) If you'd rather… Whatever you say…

VAN LUST: It's really not odd at all.

VIVIANE, *trying to be agreeable*: No… No…

VAN LUST: You see, I saw you in a studio…

VIVIANE: You saw… But I thought you just told me—

VAN LUST: Your portrait, ma'am… In an artist's studio…

VIVIANE: Oh… Oh, that…

VAN LUST: And the minute I saw you… Your portrait, that is… I couldn't believe my eyes! I cried…

VIVIANE: You did?

VAN LUST: No… "Out," I mean… "Cried out"… (*Getting carried away.*) I cried: "It's Amanda!… Good Lord, it's Amanda!"

VIVIANE: A what?

VAN LUST: Miss Amanda, ma'am… The joy of my life… My angel… My wife…

VIVIANE: Oh… Miss…

VAN LUST: But late… late…

VIVIANE: Late for what?

VAN LUST: No, no… I mean, my late wife… She's dead!

VIVIANE: She's… Oh, I'm sorry… (*Aside.*) Poor thing! That must be his trouble… He's mad with grief.

VAN LUST: I got the news from America…

VIVIANE: Tsk tsk tsk!

VAN LUST: Two weeks ago…

VIVIANE, *surprised*: Two weeks?

VAN LUST: Just…

VIVIANE: And you're already thinking about remarrying, monsieur?

VAN LUST: Right!… But let me tell you why… My Amanda… There'll never be another one like her, ma'am… Never!… Looks… Brains… Feelings… She had everything!

VIVIANE: I'm sure…

VAN LUST: But stubborn, ma'am?… Like a mule!… That's why it happened! I told her not to take the train.

VIVIANE: Oh, you mean…

VAN LUST: She was crossing a bridge… A wooden one, and… Well, they just don't build bridges in America the way they ought to!

VIVIANE: My, my…

VAN LUST: Anyway, she was huffing and puffing across the bridge…

VIVIANE: Your wife, monsieur? Miss Amanda?

VAN LUST: No, no… The train…

VIVIANE: Oh…

VAN LUST: And all of a sudden, it just plain collapsed! One two three!… And the whole thing fell into the Rio Grande… Train and all…

VIVIANE: How dreadful! What a loss!

VAN LUST: You can say that again! But it could have been worse! At least she was insured.

VIVIANE: The train?

VAN LUST: No, no… My Amanda…

VIVIANE, *taken aback*: Indeed!

VAN LUST: If you marry me, ma'am, I'll insure you too!

VIVIANE: Yes… You're much too kind…

VAN LUST: Well, when I got the telegram, you can just imagine! First thing I did was go buy a ball of twine.

VIVIANE: Twine?

VAN LUST: I was crazy with grief! All I could think of was hanging myself on the spot! (*He takes a ball of twine from his pocket.*) See? I always keep it with me! I'm never without it. (*Getting up.*) Oh, it wouldn't take long, believe me! (*Looking up at the ceiling.*) A nail… A hook… (*Spotting something, pointing.*) Like that!

VIVIANE, *frightened*: Please, monsieur!… Please! Not here!

VAN LUST, *putting the twine back in his pocket*: Don't worry, ma'am! I've changed my mind… For now, that is… (*He sits down again.*) And all because I saw your portrait! It was like a miracle! I took one look and I cried: "It's Amanda!… Good Lord, it's Amanda!"

VIVIANE: Yes… I know…

VAN LUST: Because really, ma'am… Like two peas in a pod! Especially the profile… (*Getting up and going over to her.*) Excuse me… Do you mind?

He turns her head to one side.

VIVIANE, *resisting*: Monsieur…

VAN LUST, *trying again*: Please!… How else can I see what your profile looks like?

VIVIANE: But…

VAN LUST, *growing more excited*: I have to… Don't you understand? I have to…

VIVIANE, *frightened*: Of course, monsieur… Anything you say!… No need to get upset… (*Turning her head.*) There! I hope that's satisfactory!

VAN LUST, *staring*: Oh, good Lord! It's… It's… (*Taking out his handkerchief, beginning to sob.*) It's…

VIVIANE, *turning to him*: Monsieur…

VAN LUST: No, no! Don't move!

He turns her head back to one side.

VIVIANE: Oh!

VAN LUST: Just like that!… Please! Don't move!

VIVIANE: But…

VAN LUST: Let me look at you…

He sighs, sobbing.

VIVIANE, *turning to him*: But monsieur…

VAN LUST, *turning her head back*: Please!

He continues to sob.

VIVIANE, *aside*: Good heavens! I can't sit here all day just to let him cry his eyes out! (*Feeling her neck, still aside.*) Especially like this! I'm getting a stiff neck…

VAN LUST, *reaching into his pocket, very emotionally*: Here… Let me show you her picture… You'll see…

VIVIANE, *head still turned*: Yes, do! By all means…

VAN LUST, *handing it to her*: You'll see! It's unbelievable…

VIVIANE, *examining it, aside*: My goodness! Her, nose… It's all crooked…

VAN LUST: You see?

VIVIANE, *handing it back, turning to him*: Yes…

VAN LUST, *turning her head back*: Please…

VIVIANE: Very nice, I'm sure… But don't you think… The nose, I mean…

VAN LUST: Yes, you're right… Hers is prettier… But still… You have to admit, you really could be twins!

VIVIANE, *wryly*: Yes… Two peas in a pod!

VAN LUST: And when you look that much like someone… Well, it's just natural to expect that you should have some of their qualities, don't you think?

VIVIANE: No doubt!

VAN LUST: Not all of them, of course! And not always the best ones…

VIVIANE: No… (*Aside.*) Mad or not, he's insufferable!

VAN LUST: Because… No offense, ma'am, but… Between you and my Amanda… Well, you know what I mean… I'm sure you wouldn't dream of suggesting…

VIVIANE, *sarcastically, turning to him*: Heavens, no, monsieur! Why, the thought never entered my mind!

VAN LUST: My Amanda was so sweet… so simple… (*Pushing her head back to the side.*) Please…

VIVIANE, *aside*: Oh!

VAN LUST: And modest, ma'am… Modest…

VIVIANE: I'm sure!

VAN LUST: And talented! You can't imagine… Why, she spoke four languages…

VIVIANE, *aside*: All at once, I suppose!

VAN LUST: And a musician, ma'am… She was a musician…

VIVIANE: How nice…

VAN LUST: She sang… She even composed… Ah! What a voice!… Ballads, mostly… Maybe you've heard some of them… I'll sing you my favorite…

VIVIANE, *aside*: Oh no…

VAN LUST: We were sitting there one day… Just the two of us… And all of a sudden she opened her mouth… That sweet little mouth… And it just came out. I don't remember the words, but I'll never forget the tune… "La la la la…"

He sings his "la la la la" to the tune of "Frère Jacques," with exaggerated lyricism.

VIVIANE, *aside*: Indeed!

VAN LUST, *waiting for a reaction*: Well? What do you think of it?

VIVIANE: Oh, charming!… And so original!

VAN LUST, *in a sudden outburst, apostrophizing*: Ah! Amanda… Amanda… (*Beginning to sob.*) There'll never be another one like you… Never!… (*Without any transition, he throws himself at her feet.*) Please, say you'll marry me!

VIVIANE, *recoiling*: Monsieur!

VAN LUST: You'll see… I'll make you happy! (*Grasping the legs of her chair, virtually trapping her.*) I will!… You'll see! I will!… (*Growing more and more excited.*) You believe me, don't you? You… You do think I'll make you happy?

VIVIANE: Yes… I'm sure… (*Aside.*) Good God!

VAN LUST: You'll have everything… Anything your heart desires… Anything in your wildest dreams… Nothing will be too good for you… Nothing!

VIVIANE: Really, I—

VAN LUST: You can spend all the money you want... I'm rich! It doesn't matter!... You can throw it away! You can burn it! You can... (*Reaching up and turning her head to one side.*) Please...

VIVIANE: Monsieur! How much longer...

VAN LUST: That's all I ask! Marry me, and the world is yours... As long as you show me your profile now and then...

VIVIANE: "Now and then"? All day, you mean!

The door, left, opens and JACQUELINE appears.

JACQUELINE: Madame... (*Noticing VAN LUST at her feet.*) Oh, excuse me! I didn't know madame was busy! (*VAN LUST stands up.*) I'll tell the lady...

VIVIANE, *getting up*: What lady, Jacqueline?

JACQUELINE: The one from madame's charity... (*Pointing down left.*) She's waiting in there.

VIVIANE, *aside*: Thank heavens! (*To VAN LUST.*) Please excuse me, monsieur...

She begins to leave.

VAN LUST, *holding her back*: Wait! What about your answer?

VIVIANE: My... I told you... It's on the way!... Now please...

VAN LUST: And it's a "yes," ma'am, isn't it? (*Growing excited.*) It's got to be a "yes"... I don't know what I'll do if it isn't... I don't know...

VIVIANE, *trying to calm him*: Monsieur...

VAN LUST, *reconsidering*: I mean... I do know! Of course I do!... (*Taking the ball of twine from his pocket.*) There's always the twine!

VIVIANE: Please...

VAN LUST: I can change my mind again...

VIVIANE: Really... Just go back to your hotel... It's on the way, I tell you...

VAN LUST: And it's a "yes"... It's got to be!

VIVIANE, *to JACQUELINE, in a whisper*: Get rid of him, Jacqueline... But gently... The man is a raving lunatic!

VAN LUST: I can feel it in my bones...

JACQUELINE, *aside*: He is?

VIVIANE, *to JACQUELINE, in a whisper*: And don't let him back in, whatever you do!

VAN LUST: I'm sure it's a "yes"...

VIVIANE, *to JACQUELINE, still whispering*: And next time, for goodness' sake, make sure you shut the front door! (*Nodding, to VAN LUST.*) Monsieur...

She exits, left.

VAN LUST, *to JACQUELINE*: Aren't you, miss?

JACQUELINE: Aren't I what?

VAN LUST: Sure it's a "yes"...

JACQUELINE, *aside*: She's right! He's crazy! (*To VAN LUST.*) I suppose... If monsieur says so...

There is a brief, embarrassed silence.

VAN LUST: Tell me, miss... Who is she?

JACQUELINE: Who's who, monsieur?... Madame?

VAN LUST: No, no… The lady… From the charity… (*Pointing down left.*) In there…

JACQUELINE: Oh… From the orphanage, monsieur… Madame is in charge of raising money for the children.

VAN LUST: Ah! Good!… That's a good sign!… My Amanda took care of orphans too!… Little birds… But still, the thought's the same.

JACQUELINE, *aside*: Crazy!

VAN LUST, *taking out his checkbook, writing*: Here… Give her this… I'm sure she won't object to a little contribution. Is ten thousand enough?

JACQUELINE, *laughing incredulously*: Ten thousand francs, monsieur?

VAN LUST, *reconsidering*: Maybe twenty…

JACQUELINE: Why not thirty while you're at it! (*Aside.*) For all the difference it makes!

VAN LUST: You're right!… Orphans, after all… (*He finishes writing, tears out the check, and gives it to her.*) See?… Rothschild…

JACQUELINE, *aside*: Crazy, but harmless!

VAN LUST pockets his checkbook, then stands for a moment, staring at her.

VAN LUST: Well I'll be… You know, you look like her too!

JACQUELINE: I do?

VAN LUST: Like my Amanda!… Let's see… Turn your head…

JACQUELINE, *obliging*: Like this?

VAN LUST, *contemplating her profile*: Hmm!… No… I guess not… Just an illusion… (*Turning her head back.*) Sorry…

JACQUELINE: A delusion?

VAN LUST: Listen… How would you like to come to America? (*Pointing toward the door, left.*) With the two of us, I mean… When we get married…

JACQUELINE: You and the lady from the orphanage?

VAN LUST: The lady… Are you crazy?

JACQUELINE: Me? (*Aside.*) That's a good one! He's asking *me*…

VAN LUST, *pointing*: With her… Viviane…

JACQUELINE, *offhand*: Oh, I'd love to, monsieur.

VAN LUST: As soon as we get there, I'll find you a husband. What do you say to that?

JACQUELINE: Well…

VAN LUST: In fact, now that I think of it, I've got just the perfect match.

JACQUELINE, *a little facetiously*: I hope he's tall and blond, monsieur! I just love blonds.

VAN LUST: No… No… Red…

JACQUELINE: Oh? Well…

VAN LUST: All over…

JACQUELINE: What?

VAN LUST: He's an Indian!

JACQUELINE: He's a… Thank you just the same! I don't think—

VAN LUST: What's the matter? An Indian is only a white man with feathers!

JACQUELINE: Yes, well… I'll take my feathers on chickens, if you don't mind! I'd like to keep my scalp!

VAN LUST: Really, he's very nice.

JACQUELINE: I'm sure! Maybe some other time… Anyway, it's getting late, monsieur… Don't you think you should be going?

VAN LUST, *taking out his watch*: Well, now that you mention it… Besides, I have to get back to my hotel. I want to be there the minute the letter comes. The one she sent me…

JACQUELINE, *pointing down left*: Madame?

VAN LUST: Yes… Today…

JACQUELINE: With lots of stamps, monsieur?… And it had to be "registered," or something like that?

VAN LUST: Registered?

JACQUELINE: I know… I took it to the post office myself! A little while ago…

VAN LUST: You did?… You?

JACQUELINE: Me, monsieur!

VAN LUST: You mean, you took the letter… The one she wrote… The one that's going to make me the happiest man in the world…

JACQUELINE: Well…

VAN LUST, *ecstatically*: You… You angel!… You… (*Taking out his checkbook again.*) Here… Let me write you a check…

JACQUELINE, *laughing*: Oh, don't bother, monsieur! (*Aside.*) No need to waste good paper!

VAN LUST: That's nice! You're not grasping… You'll wind up in the poorhouse, but still… Very nice!

JACQUELINE, *aside*: I'll what?

VAN LUST: Well, I'm off! *(Striding quickly to the door, upstage.)* Bye-bye!

JACQUELINE, *nodding*: Monsieur…

VAN LUST, *stopping*: And remember, you don't look a thing like my Amanda!

He dashes out.

JACQUELINE, *shaking her head*: Out of his mind!

The door, left, opens and VIVIANE *appears.*

VIVIANE, *tentatively*: Is he gone, Jacqueline?

JACQUELINE: He just left.

VIVIANE: Good!

JACQUELINE: And funny? I've never seen anything like it! (*Showing her the check.*) Look! He even wrote a check for the orphanage, madame! (*Tapping her forehead, laughing*) Thirty thousand!

VIVIANE: Poor soul! You wonder how they let people like that out on the streets!

JACQUELINE: He tried to write me one too, but I wouldn't let him.

VIVIANE: Tsk tsk tsk!

JACQUELINE: And he wanted me to go to America with him… So he could marry me off to an Indian!

VIVIANE: No!

JACQUELINE: And he told me I looked like his Amanda, or something... And he said I should turn my head...

VIVIANE: You too?

JACQUELINE: And when I did, he told me I didn't look like his Amanda at all, and he called me a "delusion"...

VIVIANE: Of all things...

JACQUELINE: What's a "delusion," madame?

The door, upstage, opens suddenly and GASTON *appears.*

GASTON: Hello!

VIVIANE: Oh! Gaston...

GASTON, *entering*: I'm back...

VIVIANE: Cousin dear...

GASTON: And I've succeeded in securing considerable pertinent information regarding your Mister Timothy Van Lust.

VIVIANE: You have? Well, how nice... Of course, I don't really need it any more.

GASTON: Oh?

VIVIANE: No... I've already met him, poor thing!... He just left.

GASTON: He... You mean... He was here?

VIVIANE: Yes... (*Shaking her head, compassionately.*) Tsk tsk tsk!... It's really a terrible shame, you know...

JACQUELINE, *echoing*: Tsk tsk tsk!

GASTON, *aside*: It is?

VIVIANE: They really should put him away... Somewhere...

GASTON, *aside*: "Put him away..."?

VIVIANE: For his own good, I mean...

GASTON: What on earth for?

VIVIANE: Why, the poor man is insane! (JACQUELINE *nods assent.*) You should have heard him... You should have seen...

GASTON: What are you talking about? The individual in question is in complete possession of his faculties. There's no indication whatever that his cerebral or emotional functions have deteriorated to any appreciable degree.

JACQUELINE, *to* VIVIANE: Does monsieur mean that he's not insane, madame?

VIVIANE, *to* JACQUELINE: Yes, that's what he means! (*To* GASTON.) You're doing it again!

GASTON: I am?... Doing what?

VIVIANE: You and those big words!

GASTON: Oh... Sorry!... I wasn't thinking... (*Speaking carefully.*) I was telling you about your Mister Van Lust...

VIVIANE: Yes...

GASTON: It seems he's very clever. One of those self-made men... Captain of industry and soldier of fortune, rolled into one...

JACQUELINE, *aside*: Captain?... Soldier?...

GASTON: The kind they grow in America... You know...

JACQUELINE, *aside*: Where was his uniform, I wonder?

GASTON: And when I say "fortune"... The man is an absolute millionaire.

JACQUELINE: What?

VIVIANE, *to GASTON*: You must be joking! Him?

GASTON, *to VIVIANE*: My friend says he's worth more than forty million!

JACQUELINE: Francs?

VIVIANE: Forty million?

GASTON: At least!

JACQUELINE, *aside*: And I didn't take his check!

VIVIANE: But he can't be... That's impossible! I saw him... I talked with him... He... (*Pointing to the ceiling.*) He wanted to hang himself... With a ball of twine... He's never without it... You'd think his family would put him away!

JACQUELINE, *to GASTON*: And he wanted to marry me off to an Indian!

GASTON: That's all well and good, but... (*Beginning to forget himself.*) Notwithstanding, I assure you...

JACQUELINE, *aside, shaking her head*: Forty million...

GASTON: The facts are incontrovertible... As heretofore enunciated...

VIVIANE: Gaston!

GASTON: Oh... Oh, sorry!... I'll—

VIVIANE, *interrupting*: I know! You'll watch yourself!

GASTON: Like a hawk!

VIVIANE: I'm sure!

JACQUELINE, *aside*: Forty...

VIVIANE, *to GASTON*: You were saying...?

GASTON: Yes... (*Speaking carefully.*) My friend gave me all the information... The police have a file on him... (*Holding up his thumb and forefinger.*) This thick... He's not just some tourist. He's... He's practically a celebrity!

JACQUELINE, *aside*: Forty million...

VIVIANE, *to GASTON*: Oh?

GASTON: Why, for a time he was even president of some little country or other... You know... Over there... Where they grow all the bananas...

VIVIANE: Him? A president?

JACQUELINE: Damnation! (*Catching herself, putting her hand to her mouth.*) Oh!... (*To VIVIANE.*) Excuse me, madame... I... (*To GASTON.*) Excuse me, monsieur...

GASTON, *ignoring her, to VIVIANE*: Tell me, what did he say?

VIVIANE, *flustered*: Well... That I looked like his Amanda... His wife... That is, she was... But she drowned in a train...

GASTON: Oh?

VIVIANE: Even though she was insured... And he wants me to marry him because I look so much like her...

JACQUELINE, *aside*: A president...

GASTON, *to VIVIANE*: And you told him...?

VIVIANE: I... Well, I... I told him very politely that my answer was in a letter, and... and that if he went back to his hotel I was sure he would find it.

GASTON: You wrote him?

VIVIANE: Yes… Just after you left.

GASTON: What did you say?

VIVIANE: What did I… My goodness! If I knew he was a president…

GASTON: What?… Tell me…

VIVIANE: Not very much… Just a few words… "Monsieur, please stop annoying me!"

GASTON: Oh my… And you expect that's going to end it?… He'll be back, I assure you!

JACQUELINE, *aside*: Let's hope!

VIVIANE, *to GASTON*: No! You think…

JACQUELINE, *aside*: "Come right in, monsieur!"

GASTON, *to VIVIANE*: Of course! A man doesn't become a millionaire… forty times over… (*Beginning to forget himself.*) without evincing certain qualities of persistence and tenacity. (*VIVIANE sighs and shakes her head.*) And he most assuredly doesn't achieve the eminence of an executive incumbency like a presidency! Even over there!

VIVIANE, *sarcastically*: Most assuredly!

GASTON: No… I really envision only a single feasible expedient. I think I should go confront the gentleman *in situ*, and endeavor to convince him that the alleged resemblance between his defunct spouse and yourself is fundamentally illusory… (*Catching himself as VIVIANE stands, hands on hips, staring at him.*) Oh… Sorry, my love!… Sorry…

VIVIANE: Please! Don't stop now!… I'm almost beginning to understand you!

GASTON: I just can't help it! It's bigger than I am… (*To JACQUELINE.*) Come… You'll stand by the front door, and if he comes back you'll keep him out!

JACQUELINE, *to GASTON*: Oh? (*Aside.*) Don't be too sure!

GASTON, *to JACQUELINE*: Adamantly! Obdurately! Implacably!… Understand?

JACQUELINE: Not a blessèd word!

GASTON takes her by the hand and exits with her, upstage.

VIVIANE, *watching him go off, with a little laugh*: He's right, poor dear! He can't help it!… Oh well, it's not so awful… (*She sits down at the table.*) And our Mister Van Lust… Did you ever… Here I was, so sure that the man was crazy, and he's only an American… I have to admit, my answer could have been… well, a little more gentle… Especially for a man with millions!… And a president!… But what's done is done! And besides, I'm sure I won't be seeing him again, no matter what Gaston says!

The door, upstage, opens and JACQUELINE appears.

JACQUELINE, *announcing*: Monsieur… (*Correcting herself.*) Mister Timothy Van Lust!

VIVIANE, *getting up, surprised*: What! (*To JACQUELINE, in a whisper.*) But monsieur just told you…

JACQUELINE, *aside*: Forty million, after all!

VAN LUST enters and JACQUELINE exits.

VAN LUST, *waving VIVIANE's letter*: How could you, ma'am?… How could you…

VIVIANE: My letter!

VAN LUST: "Monsieur, please stop annoying me!" That's what it says!… And you told me… You let me think it was a "yes"…

He throws the letter down on the table.

VIVIANE, *babbling:* I… Monsieur, I never… I…

VAN LUST: So cruel, ma'am… How can anyone so beautiful be so cruel? How could you ever write me a letter like that? And registered, to boot!

VIVIANE: Mister Van Lust…

VAN LUST: One sentence… Four words…

VIVIANE: Five…

VAN LUST, *counting on his fingers:* Five…

VIVIANE: I… Excuse me. I was in a hurry…

VAN LUST: And just when I was beginning to fall in love with you…

VIVIANE: What?

VAN LUST: At first I only wanted you to marry me on account of my Amanda… Because you look so much like her… But… But now…

VIVIANE: Monsieur?

VAN LUST: But now it's because… because you're you!

VIVIANE: That's absurd! You don't even know me!

VAN LUST: But I do! Of course I do!… I know how sweet and kind you are… And charitable, and… And I know that you speak two languages…

VIVIANE: You do?

VAN LUST, *offhand:* Amanda spoke four, but… (*He shrugs.*) And I know that you love music… And that you write songs… Ballads, mostly… Just like her…

VIVIANE: Me?

VAN LUST: And that your favorite goes like this… "La la la la…"

He sings, exaggeratedly as before, to the tune of "Alouette."

VIVIANE, *stopping him:* But monsieur…

VAN LUST: You think I don't know you, ma'am. But I can tell you everything you've done for a week… Every move you've made… Every hour of every day…

VIVIANE: You… You can't be serious, monsieur! You're joking!

VAN LUST: Try me!

VIVIANE: Very well… Yesterday!

VAN LUST: Oh, yesterday's easy!… Let's see… (*Taking a little notebook from his pocket and flipping a few pages.*) Yesterday… Yes… You left the house at two thirty-five… Had yourself driven to a shop on the Rue de Rivoli, where you bought a pair of black gloves… Went visiting… First, to number forty-two Rue Saint Dominique d'Enfer, then to number thirty-three Rue de Trevise…

VIVIANE, *agape:* I don't believe it!

VAN LUST, *still referring to his notes:* At three thirty you delivered Christmas presents to some poor little children… And at four you stopped into a pastry shop… Chez Julien… For a pot of tea and two cream puffs…

VIVIANE: How on earth…

VAN LUST, *sadly:* My Amanda would have had coffee and chocolate eclairs… (*Shrugging.*) But I guess I can learn to live with tea and cream puffs!

VIVIANE: Monsieur! Will you kindly tell me precisely how you—

VAN LUST, *interrupting*: Easy!… I had you tailed…

VIVIANE, *furious*: You had me… You didn't! You wouldn't dare!

VAN LUST, *ingenuously*: Why not?

VIVIANE: A lady, monsieur? You… You had the audacity…

VAN LUST: After all, if we're getting married I thought I should get to know you.

VIVIANE: Oh!… So you had me spied on, to put it bluntly!

VAN LUST: Well, I couldn't very well do it myself, ma'am! Time is money! I came here on business… Big business… Very big…

VIVIANE: Yes, no doubt…

VAN LUST: Cotton… Cacao… Bananas… You wouldn't understand…

VIVIANE: And so you had some… some individual follow me! Some detective… Or the police…

VAN LUST: Police?… No! Nothing that crude! What do you take me for?

VIVIANE, *aside*: What, indeed!

VAN LUST: My secretary, ma'am… Very discreet… And he has a way with horses…

VIVIANE: He what?

VAN LUST: So I dressed him up, bought him a cab, and put him behind the reins.

VIVIANE: You bought him a—

VAN LUST: Yes, ma'am… First I thought I might have to buy the whole company. But then I decided one would be enough… If it was always the same one… With my secretary, that is…

VIVIANE, *incredulous*: Are you trying to tell me I've had the same driver…?

VAN LUST: Yes, ma'am… For a week…

VIVIANE: That's impossible! I would have noticed…

VAN LUST: I don't know how… He disguised himself.

VIVIANE, *outraged*: Oh!

VAN LUST: Each morning, a different wig… Or a beard… Or a mustache…

VIVIANE: I never…

VAN LUST: And to make sure that the doorman hailed him every time, he paid him three francs an hour.

VIVIANE: You bribed my doorman?

VAN LUST: "Bribed," ma'am?… No, I wouldn't say "bribed"… We employed him… And at a loss! You only paid two francs an hour for the cab!

VIVIANE, *sarcastically*: Oh! (*Taking her purse out of her pocket.*) Well, you must let me make up the difference!

VAN LUST: Now, now… No need to get nasty!

VIVIANE: I beg your pardon! (*Putting back the purse.*) I am not being nasty!

VAN LUST: One thing my Amanda didn't have was a temper!

VIVIANE: I am simply appalled, monsieur, that you would have the gall… Oh! I don't know how you do things in America, believe me… But in France, I can tell you that a man who would stoop to having a lady spied on… Well, he's certainly no gentleman!

VAN LUST, *ingenuously*: Really?… I didn't know… (*Shrugging.*) I guess you live and learn!

VIVIANE: Yes, I guess you do!

VAN LUST: Sorry…

VIVIANE, *softening*: Especially a man with an illustrious career… A government official…

VAN LUST: What?

VIVIANE: Like a president, for instance…

VAN LUST, *surprised*: Like a… What do you mean?

VIVIANE: No need to pretend, monsieur! I know…

She sits down on the loveseat.

VAN LUST: You do?

VIVIANE: Of course!

VAN LUST: Who told you?

VIVIANE: Oh, I have my sources!

VAN LUST: Spies, you mean?

VIVIANE: Hardly, monsieur!… I know all about how you were president of… of… (*With a wave of the arm.*) Over there… That country…

VAN LUST, *modestly*: Well… Just for four days… Hardly worth talking about…

VIVIANE, *with a little laugh*: Four days?

VAN LUST: It could have been longer if I wanted to have my whole cabinet shot… Two dozen or so…

VIVIANE: Oh!

VAN LUST: But Amanda didn't think I ought to…

VIVIANE: No… I shouldn't imagine…

VAN LUST: I remember… It was a Friday… And she said, in that sweet little voice of hers: "Don't do anything rash! Let's wait until tomorrow! And the next day they deposed me.

VIVIANE: No!

VAN LUST: But on Sunday I was back in office… Until Tuesday… At five o'clock… On account of the papers…

VIVIANE: The papers?

VAN LUST: The newspapers! They were against me… Every one of them! On Saturday they were all for me, but on Tuesday they were yelling about corruption, or something…

VIVIANE, *sarcastically*: Tsk tsk tsk!

VAN LUST: Anyway, when I saw that, I looked at Amanda, and I told her: "Let's skedaddle!"

VIVIANE, *quizzically*: Monsieur?

VAN LUST: "Skedaddle"… It's an American word… It means "vamoose!"

VIVIANE: Aha…

VAN LUST: So I turned in my resignation, and we took the first boat out!… And that was the end of my "illustrious career"!

VIVIANE, *laughing*: I must say…

VAN LUST, *sitting down at the table*: Well, ma'am… Now that you know the story of my life… (*Waving her letter.*) I hope you'll tell me this was all a mistake…

VIVIANE: Well, I…

VAN LUST: …and that you'll be happy to be my wife!

VIVIANE: Really, monsieur… I'm afraid… You see… You seem to be convinced that I look like your Amanda…

VAN LUST: I'll say!

VIVIANE: But that's just it! I don't!… Not really! Not if you take a good look and compare us. Why, she's so much prettier than I am… (*Correcting herself.*) She was, I mean…

VAN LUST, *sighing*: Ah…

VIVIANE: Her nose, for instance… It had such an adorable little tilt to the left…

VAN LUST: Yes…

VIVIANE: And her mouth was much more… well, majestic!

VAN LUST: Yes… Yes…

VIVIANE: And her eyes, so much less… conspicuous!… Her jaw, so much more… determined!

VAN LUST: Yes, yes… You're right…

VIVIANE: So you see…

VAN LUST: But you have to admit, the resemblance is amazing!

VIVIANE: The resem… (*She sighs, shaking her head.*) Besides, I'm afraid there's an obstacle in your path… A rather large one…

VAN LUST: Good! I'll get rid of it!

VIVIANE: I don't think so, monsieur! It's my cousin!

VAN LUST: Your what?

VIVIANE: My cousin… Monsieur Gaston de Courvalin… You see, I love him!

VAN LUST, *jumping to his feet.*) No! Don't say that!… You don't!

VIVIANE: And I'm going to be his wife.

VAN LUST: But you can't! That's impossible!

VIVIANE: He's at your hotel this very moment… To try to explain…

VAN LUST, *distraught, pacing*: But… But… You can't mean it!… Amanda… (*Correcting himself.*) I mean, Viviane … You can't be serious!… My hopes, my dreams…

VIVIANE: I'm terribly sorry, but you do understand…

VAN LUST: So! It's a "no," after all! Not a "yes"…

VIVIANE: No… (*Confused.*) Yes… That is…

VAN LUST: And that's definite? Nothing can make you change your mind?

VIVIANE, *gently*: Nothing, I'm afraid…

VAN LUST, *taking the ball of twine from his pocket*: Well, you'll only have yourself to blame!

VIVIANE, *with a start*: Monsieur! What are you doing?

VAN LUST: Don't say I didn't warn you! (*He climbs up on the chair, looking up at the ceiling.*) I'm sure I saw a nail…

He begins fashioning an improvised noose.

VIVIANE: Oh my! (*Calling.*) Jacqueline!… Jacqueline!…

The door, left, opens and JACQUELINE *rushes in.*

JACQUELINE: What is it, madame?

VIVIANE, *pointing*: Monsieur… He wants to hang himself!

JACQUELINE: Damnation! (*Catching herself.*) Oh! Excuse me...

VIVIANE: Quick! Run and get a pair of scissors!

JACQUELINE: Yes, madame!

She runs off, left.

VAN LUST, *still inspecting the ceiling*: I'm sure it was here somewhere...

VIVIANE, *hurriedly crossing right, to the sewing cabinet.*) I know I must have one...

She rummages through the drawer as VAN LUST *keeps looking for his nail.*

VAN LUST, *finally locating it*: Ah!

He tosses the noose up to the ceiling several times.

VIVIANE, *finding a pair of sewing scissors, holding it up*: There!...

JACQUELINE *comes running back in, upstage, carrying a pair of large pruning shears.*

JACQUELINE, *to* VIVIANE: This is all I could find.

She stands on one side of VAN LUST, *and* VIVIANE *on the other, instruments poised.*

VAN LUST: What are you doing?

VIVIANE: We won't let you do it, monsieur! One move, and we cut the twine!

JACQUELINE: Snip snip!

VAN LUST: You can't! That's not fair!

JACQUELINE: Snip snip!

VIVIANE, *nodding*: Snip snip!

VAN LUST: But... I have free will! I...

The door, upstage, opens and GASTON *enters.*

GASTON: Hello! I'm back!

VIVIANE, *running up to him*: Gaston!

GASTON: Your Mister Van Lust isn't in, I'm afraid.

VIVIANE: I know! He's here!... (*Pointing.*) Hanging himself!

GASTON: He is?... (*Going over to* VAN LUST.) I say, monsieur... I do hope that your resolve isn't immutable!

VAN LUST: Beg pardon?

GASTON: Irrevocable, that is... Uncommutable... Undeflectable...

VIVIANE, *to* VAN LUST: He means he hopes you'll change your mind, monsieur!

VAN LUST: Never! When my mind is made up, it's made up!

He tosses the noose up to the ceiling several more times, still unsuccessfully.

GASTON: Oh well... (*Holding out a telegram.*) Then I assume you have no inclination to peruse this dispatch...

VAN LUST: A telegram?... For me?

GASTON: It was expedited to your lodging.

VAN LUST, *jumping down, grabbing the telegram, anxiously*: Don't tell me my cotton stocks are down!... Or my cacao... (*Opening it.*) Good God! I'll be ruined!... (*Reading silently for a moment, then exclaiming.*) Oh! I don't believe it!

VIVIANE, } *together:* { What is it, monsieur?
GASTON, } { What's the matter?

VAN LUST: My Amanda... She... She... Listen!... (*Reading aloud.*) "Amanda unhurt..."

VIVIANE, GASTON, JACQUELINE, *together*: What?

VAN LUST, *reading*: "Not dead... Excuse error... Stop... Thrown into creek... Neck deep in mud... Stop... Pulled out today..."

VIVIANE: Good heavens!

VAN LUST, *reading*: "Cleaned up good as new..."

GASTON: Prodigious!

VAN LUST, *ecstatically, kissing the telegram:* Ah! You wonderful telegram!... I love you! I love you!

JACQUELINE: Did you ever...

VAN LUST, *to VIVIANE*: Sorry, ma'am, but this changes everything.

VIVIANE: Of course!

VAN LUST: I can't possibly marry you!

VIVIANE: No, I don't imagine...

VAN LUST: But if I ever do become a widower... I mean, you never know...

VIVIANE, *taking GASTON's hand, to VAN LUST*: I'm afraid I won't be available, monsieur!

GASTON, *lovingly*: Viviane!

VAN LUST, *looking GASTON up and down*: Oh, don't be too sure! Here today, gone tomorrow...

GASTON, *to VAN LUST*: Much obliged!

VAN LUST: Well, I'll be on my way...

VIVIANE: Oh... One moment, monsieur... (*Reaching into her pocket, taking out his check.*) Your check... I'm sure you want it back.

VAN LUST: Don't be silly! I'm no Indian giver!

JACQUELINE, *aside*: Him and his Indians!

VIVIANE, *to VAN LUST*: But monsieur... Thirty thousand—

VAN LUST: Please!... I insist...

JACQUELINE, *aside*: I'll take it if no one wants it!

VIVIANE: But...

VAN LUST: It's for your orphans! You can't say no!

VIVIANE: Well...

VAN LUST, *turning to JACQUELINE*: Oh, and here's something for you, miss...

He hands her his twine.

JACQUELINE: This...?

VAN LUST: It'll bring you good luck!

JACQUELINE, *aside*: So would a check!

VIVIANE: Jacqueline, see monsieur out...

VAN LUST, *at the door, upstage, nodding to VIVIANE and GASTON in turn*: Well... Bye-bye!... Au revoir!

He exits, followed by a grumbling JACQUELINE.

GASTON: And I should be getting back to Dunkirk, I imagine.

VIVIANE, *coyly*: Oh? Must you?... So soon?

She sits down on the loveseat and draws him down beside her.

GASTON: Well, not really… I suppose there are no imperious obligations that necessitate a precipitous departure on my part.

VIVIANE, *smiling, shaking her head*: Tsk tsk tsk!

GASTON, *catching himself*: Oh!… Sorry, my love… But…

VIVIANE, } *together*: { You'll watch yourself...
GASTON, } { I'll watch myself...

VIVIANE, *nodding, with a laugh*: I know, cousin dear… I know…

She picks up the book from the end table and begins reading.

"Now, Poet, take thy lute. Come, kiss thy muse.
Tonight the burgeoning spring is newly born…"

GASTON begins dozing, as the curtain slowly falls.

CURTAIN.

AFTERWORD

Finding the Funny—On Directing Farce

by Michael Clark Haney

"Louder! Faster! Funnier!" only takes you so far. This exhortation, yelled at actors by directors as far back as there has been farce on the stage, has an admirable and self-evident purpose. Yet, of all the roads to funny, this is the least effective. If "Louder! Faster! Funnier!" doesn't work, what then? As with any art, the answer is in technique.

This will be a discussion of the craft of directing farce. There is no need here for an elegant treatise of the existential nature of farce, or a disquisition on the roots of the word "farce," or an explication of the human necessity for farcical humor to leaven the all-too-serious rigors of our lives. Other writers, more learned and disciplined than I, have covered those topics in depth. Here you will find practical pointers for a director (or an actor) who is on the road to creating the frothy mix of silly, outrageous, clever, and absurd that we call Farce. Some of these techniques can be applied to any form of theater, from farce to drama. Others are unique to the style of Classic Farce represented by most of the plays contained in this volume.

First, and briefly, what exactly is Farce? At its core, the lifeblood of farce comes from the clash of opposites. Drama takes its momentum from believable plot twists and revelations. Farce takes this basic dramatic idea to its extreme, deriving its vibrancy from the abrupt and often seemingly impossible juxtaposition of opposite ideas. The world as we would like it to be, slammed up against the world as it is. The challenge for the farce director is in taking something that could seem unnatural, and creating a substantially real event in a way that allows the audience to suspend its disbelief just enough to let loose a raucous laugh.

In the Labiche/Marc-Michel play *It's All Relative,* Trébuchard desires to be married. That desire is natural and human. It is the lengths to which Trébuchard is willing (and forced) to go to achieve his dream that creates the farce. The deep and sustained laughter that well-done farce pulls out of us comes from our recognition of the humanity in the moment. As Chuck Jones (an animator and director; his most famous creations are Road Runner and Wile E. Coyote) said: "Comedy is unusual people in real situations; farce is real people in unusual situations."

Trébuchard in *It's All Relative* is a model farcical character. His overpowering motivation naturally leads to hilarious over-reaction. While it might be advisable for the actor playing Trébuchard to find "funny" things to do, even more important is for the actor to discover Trébuchard's passion. A man falling on his face is not necessarily funny—unless he's chasing his love.

Where we start the work with farce is the same as with any form of theater: study the classics. Stanislavski, Chekhov (the acting teacher, not the writer), Strasberg, Hagen, etc. Build a character, live in the moment, plumb the depths of your personal experience. That done, we can now focus on the unique challenges of Classic Farce. This discussion will be split into three sections: The Text, Farce as Contradiction, and Taking it to the Limit.

The Text

Norman Shapiro has done an excellent job adapting these plays. His challenge was to turn that which was French into English. Your challenge as the director is to take that which lives on the page in a two-dimensional form, and translate it into the three-dimensional lives of the characters on the stage. Two stylistic elements of the written form of classic farce, "suspension points" (sometimes incorrectly referred to as an ellipsis) and the character-revealing stage direction, have to be used as guides to performance—and sometimes they must be ignored. Two other elements, the aside and the monologue, are such standards of classic farce that, along with the slamming door, they are hallmarks of the genre. The director's approach to these four elements of the text —suspension points, stage directions, asides, and monologues—will be discussed in this section.

Suspension Points

In classic farce, suspension points litter the page, dropping their three dots (…) in between and after lines. The common perception of these three dots is that they mark a pause. In farce, this is rarely the case. Actually, the suspension points most often indicate a change of mental direction or the interruption of a thought. What's important here is that a new thought arrives on the scene, overcoming the old. Pauses can be deadly to comedy*. A series of contrasting, yet clearly enunciated thoughts can be hilarious. The director can use the suspension points as a guide to creating a natural flow of conversation. Each "..." becomes an interruption point, either for the character speaking, or for the character responding.

For example, at the beginning of *It's All Relative* (page 128), we find this exchange:

> **DELPHINE**, *pointing out to the patio*: That! That's the matter! (*TREBUCHARD gives a quizzical look outside.*) Fourteen this morning!... Fourteen more cigar butts...
>
> **TREBUCHARD**, *suddenly comprehending*: Oh...
>
> **DELPHINE**: Fourteen, monsieur!

The suspension points each time Delphine reiterates "Fourteen" gives the actress the opportunity to discover three different reactions to the cigar butts, in rapid succession. This has much greater comic potential than taking several pauses to mull over the mess caused by fourteen cigar butts. The suspension points after Trébuchard's "Oh..." could open the door for more mulling—but the comedy is better served if Delphine ignores his interjection and drives ahead with her discoveries.

This brings up the often-repeated observation that "acting is reacting." In the above example, it is funny if Delphine is reacting to her own thoughts; she's having a conversation with herself. (More about this when we discuss monologues.) In other exchanges, the suspension points can provide the opportunity to create lively interactions. Well-written dialogue has in it what can be called "action" words. These are the words that propel the character being spoken to into action. Natural, everyday

---

* There are, of course, exceptions to this generalization. One of the longest laughs in radio theater came from a pause. On *The Jack Benny Program,* a mugger accosted Jack Benny and demanded, "Your money or your life!" Jack Benny didn't answer. The audience, knowing that Benny's character was a notorious penny pincher, and well aware that this was a tough question for him, filled the pause with laughter. Finally, the mugger pressed Benny: "Look, bud! I said your money or your life!" And Jack Benny snapped back, "I'm thinking it over!" Uproarious laughter, and another extended and hilarious pause. (This scene was in *The Jack Benny Program,* March 28, 1948.

speech is a mess of interruptions, false starts, and misunderstandings. By making good use of action words and suspension points, the director can create a lifelike, chaotic—and often hilarious—rhythm with the characters' dialogue. In working with the actors, this can be referred to as "jumping lines." Jumping lines has the added benefit of picking up the pace. In *Pater Omnipotens* (page 236), there is this exchange:

> **VITRUVIA**, *interrupting*: Is it true what Aunt Griselde told me, papá?
>
> **PETITFOUR**: Told you?… What?
>
> **VITRUVIA**: That a new suitor arrived last night?… From Brussels…
>
> **PETITFOUR**, *sadly*: I'm afraid so, treasure… Not quite what we ordered, but…
>
> **VITRUVIA**: Ordered, papá?
>
> **PETITFOUR**: In a manner of speaking… We wanted a soprano aria, and they sent us a baritone solo… With tuba obbligato!
>
> **VITRUVIA**: "They," papá?… An aria?
>
> **PETITFOUR**: A metaphor, my love… Not at all what you would like… Take my word… Not at all…
>
> **VITRUVIA**: But… But you say that about every… *(Searching for the word.)* every metaphor who comes calling!
>
> **PETITFOUR**: Because it's always true! They're all the same. Every last one of them… Not for you… Not for my Vitruvia…

Vitruvia has a strong intention. She is excited about the prospect of a new suitor and wants the details from her father. Petitfour is equally invested in deflecting her interest. The clearest example of the use of an action word to drive the dialogue comes in the middle of this section, when Vitruvia responds to her father's line, "Not quite what we ordered, but…" She doesn't have to wait until the end of Petitfour's line to question his choice of words. If the actors jump their lines, relying on their intentions and reacting when they hear their action words, the dialogue could play as follows:

> **VITRUVIA**: Is it true what Aunt Griselde told me, papá?
>
> **PETITFOUR**: Told you?…
>
> **VITRUVIA**: That a new suitor arrived last night?Š
>
> **PETITFOUR**: What?
>
> **VITRUVIA**: From Brussels…
>
> **PETITFOUR**: I'm afraid so, treasureŠ Not quite what we ordered, butŠ
>
> **VITRUVIA**: Ordered, papá?

PETITFOUR: In a manner of speaking… We wanted a soprano aria, and they sent us a baritone solo…

VITRUVIA: "They," papá?…

PETITFOUR: With tuba obbligato!

VITRUVIA: An aria?

PETITFOUR: A metaphor, my love…

VITRUVIA: But…

PETITFOUR: Not at all what you would like… Take my word…

VITRUVIA: But you say that about every…

PETITFOUR: Not at all…

VITRUVIA: Ševery metaphor who comes calling!

PETITFOUR: Because it's always true! They're all the same. Every last one of them… Not for you… Not for my Vitruvia…

When the technique of jumping lines is applied (where appropriate) throughout the play, tremendous life and energy are created. This works best when the interplay is gradually discovered by the actors and director working together. Enforcing a rigid interpretation from the first rehearsal will be counterproductive. The actor has to be motivated by the action words, or the result will be a confusing jumble, instead of a hilarious conflagration.

This discussion brings up a note about pacing (the "faster" part of the director's exhortation): Pace comes from the actors thinking faster, not from talking faster. In practical terms, this means the actors must pick up their cues. Jumping lines, cuing reactions off of action words, will move the comedy along remarkably well.

Stage Directions

Written stage directions have always posed a challenge for directors. We rely on stage directions as a guide to the intentions of the author. When reading a play, stage directions certainly make it easier to imagine the action. However, when it comes time to rehearse, faithfulness to the written directions can impede the natural flow of dramatic movement. The directions are best used as a guide, or suggestion for the action. If during rehearsal an actor finds herself standing stage right, near the fireplace, and the stage direction reads "She sits at the dining table, stage left," you can certainly ignore that direction. Of course, if the character says, "Please join me as I sit at the dining table," then you might consider fixing the blocking.

There is a larger concern with character-revealing stage directions as they are used in farce, however. So that the reader understands the character's intention, dialogue is occasionally clarified with a direction that reveals the character's hidden motivation. *Edouard and the Chambermaid* (page 164) provides this example:

> **MADAME BEAUDELOCHE**, *to herself*: A gem!... An absolute jewel!... (*Aloud, with a note of irony, moving toward her.*) And that fireman I saw in the courtyard last night, Florestine? I would have sworn he was looking for something... Or someone...
>
> **FLORESTINE**, *defensively*: The fireman?
>
> **MADAME BEAUDELOCHE**: Rather a handsome devil...
>
> **FLORESTINE**: He... He was looking for a fire, madame! The... The neighbor next door... Her stew was burning, and... and...
>
> **MADAME BEAUDELOCHE**: Aha...
>
> **FLORESTINE**: And... *(Changing the subject.)* What shawl will madame be wearing?

Cleary, Florestine is lying. Her defensiveness is not only indicated in the stage direction "defensively," but also in the many times she interrupts herself as she tries to explain the fireman's presence. If the actor plays these lines as indicated, she is keeping the audience clued in that she's lying. She's also admitting her lie to Madame Beaudeloche—something she would never do. If Florestine is going to lie, she would be much better at it than that. A more natural, and funnier approach is to have the actress assume that the truth is that the fireman was indeed there to put out a fire. Florestine then only interrupts herself because the excitement of the event makes the telling of the tale so difficult.

Keep in mind that one of the hallmarks of farce is the humor that comes from contradiction. Since the audience can easily deduce the truth (Florestine is having an affair with a fireman), when the character contradicts that with her own truth (the fireman was battling a fire in the neighbor's stew), the audience will respond with laughter.

The Aside

Contradiction plays a role in the aside, though in a different way. When watching a play, the audience is asked to suspend its disbelief, to accept that the characters on stage are engaged in a real dialogue. With this acceptance comes permission for us to engage emotionally with the characters and to invest ourselves in what happens to them. Usually, the characters in the play help us with this by maintaining the illusion of a "fourth wall," the wall that would be there, between the stage and the audience, to complete the room the characters inhabit. And then, one of the characters "breaks" the fourth wall and turns to the audience to make a comment intended (usually) just for our ears—this is the aside.

The humor of the aside comes from two sources. The first derives from the comment itself, which often emphasizes the character's subtext, or states a truth that the character is hiding from the other characters on stage. In *It's All Relative*, Trébuchard is trying to convince Piquoiseau to meet and eventually marry Trébuchard's incredibly ugly step-daughter:

> **TREBUCHARD**, *getting up and crossing right, to get the rum*: Believe me, my friend… *(Returning and refilling* PIQUOISEAU*'s glass.)* She's not just one of your everyday beauties…
>
> **PIQUOISEAU**: No…
>
> **TREBUCHARD**: Just another pretty face…
>
> *He crosses right, picks up his glass, and pours himself a drink.*
>
> **PIQUOISEAU**: I'll drink to that!
>
> *He drinks.*
>
> **TREBUCHARD**, *drinking, aside*: So will I! *(Aloud.)* More in the classic mould, you might say… Stately… Strong features… Bold… Aggressive, if you know what I mean…
>
> **PIQUOISEAU**: Aha…
>
> **TREBUCHARD**: Especially her profile… Classic, monsieur… Classic… *(Under his breath.)* Like the Trojan Horse!… *(Aloud.)* Mind you, she's no Venus de Milo… *(Searching for another apt comparison.)* No "Winged Victory"…

Trébuchard heralds his step-daughter's beauty to Piquoiseau, and in the next moment, admits to us that she looks like a horse. The contradiction is funny in itself, and is heightened deliciously by Trébuchard's play on the definition of the word "classical." What really explodes the humor provides an example of an elemental, powerful mechanism of farce at work, a second, hidden layer of contradiction that underlies and accentuates the verbal humor. When this scene is skillfully played, we allow ourselves to commit emotionally to Trébuchard's reality (we believe his desires, we buy into his dreams). The moment that Trébuchard turns to us, the fourth wall is abruptly shattered, along with our suspension of disbelief. For that moment, Trébuchard has joined with the audience, in essence looking at himself. That both of these states (emotional investment with the character and critical analysis) can exist at the same time creates a cognitive dissonance that results in laughter.

This dance of the character in farce is a delicate balancing act between the reality of the play, and the reality of the audience. For the actor to pull it off requires commitment, timing, and focus. Most of all, and something with which the director can provide assistance, this requires clarity; the actor has to make clear and bold choices when playing an aside.

There are actually four kinds of asides: 1. To the audience; 2. To God; 3. To oneself; and, 4. To an object. Whichever type of aside the actor plays, the point is that the character is engaging in a relationship. The choice of how to play the aside springs from defining the nature of the relationship. When playing asides to the audience, for example, it can, in some circumstances, be helpful for the actor to see the audience as a friend, a helper, someone who understands. In contrast to this, it can sometimes be hilarious to make the choice that the audience is not as smart as the character. In this case, the character is always trying to bring the audience along, get them to understand the problem, explain it in a way that even this dumb audience can follow. The important thing is that the actor has made a choice of whom he or she is talking to, and what he or she wants out of the conversation.

The Monologue

The use of the word "conversation" regarding an aside is deliberate. Even if someone in the audience hasn't yelled out to Trébuchard on stage, "What do you mean, classic profile? She looks like a horse!" the actor can still respond as if he is engaged in a dialogue. This technique is most evidently useful when dealing with the monologue. In fact, when talking with actors, it is beneficial to refer to a monologue as a "dialogue with the audience," reminding the actor that the performance is about the relationship he or she has with the audience. Just because there is no one else with you on stage, does not mean that you can't be talking with someone.

When working on monologues, it is especially important to give the actor permission to slow down. There is a natural urge, when faced with a block of intimidating, unbroken text, for the actor to rush through the monologue and get it over with. Trébuchard's monologue in It's All Relative runs six pages [confirm actual printed length] and plays about as many minutes. There is no way to perform this monologue at the pace necessary for farce without breaking it down first into bite-size chunks. One way to do this is to re-write the monologue as a dialogue, inserting lines in response to what the character says, or inventing questions that will move the conversation along. The actor can then rehearse the monologue as a true dialogue. For example, Trébuchard's monologue starts like this (page 132):

TREBUCHARD, *coming downstage, to the audience*: Well, now you've seen her… Oh yes, I know what you're thinking. *(Affecting another voice.)* "Your daughter, monsieur?… You expect me to believe that that rather… mature individual…" *(In his own voice.)* I know… I know… She's fifty if she's a day! *(In the other voice.)* "Whereas you, monsieur…" *(In his own voice.)* Me? A mere twenty-nine… Give or take… *(Sighing.)* Yes, it's absolutely absurd… Absurd, but true… And all because… *(He shakes his head.)* Ah! When I think of it… All because… *(Looking at his watch.)* I still have five minutes. Let me tell you the story… The whole ugly story, from the beginning. *(Crossing right.)* I was born… *(Reconsidering.)* No… No need to go back that far. Everyone gets born sooner or later, I suppose…

In the early section of this monologue, Trébuchard creates the dialogue himself by playing several roles. For the other lines, a dialogue can be created and rehearsed:

MAN IN AUDIENCE: You didn't tell me she was that ugly.

TREBUCHARD: Well, now you've seen her—

MAN IN AUDIENCE: You can't imagine my reaction.

TREBUCHARD: Oh yes, I know what you're thinking.

TREBUCHARD AS OLDER WOMAN: Your daughter, monsieur? You expect me to believe that that rather mature individual—

TREBUCHARD: I know... I know... She's fifty if she's a day!

TREBUCHARD AS YOUNG WOMAN: And, how old are you, monsieur?

TREBUCHARD: Me? A mere twenty-nine.

WOMAN IN AUDIENCE: You don't look twenty-nine.

TREBUCHARD: Give or take.

MAN IN AUDIENCE: Your daughter's unbelievable!

TREBUCHARD: Yes, it's absolutely absurd—

MAN IN AUDIENCE: You're lying!

TREBUCHARD: Absurd, but true... And all because—

WOMAN IN AUDIENCE: Why is it so absurd?

TREBUCHARD: Ah! When I think of it... All because—

WOMAN IN AUDIENCE: Don't leave—tell us what happened!

TREBUCHARD: I still have five minutes. Let me tell you the story—

MAN IN AUDIENCE: Only the good parts—

TREBUCHARD: The whole ugly story, from the beginning. I was born—

WOMAN IN AUDIENCE: Don't get ridiculous!

TREBUCHARD: No... No need to go back that far. Everyone gets born sooner or later, I suppose.

By changing the question or comment, the director can change the tone and attitude of Trébuchard's response. By imagining the questions coming from different people in the audience, the actor will naturally move around the stage as he responds. The intimidating block of text to be rushed through, instead becomes an exciting, lively conversation.

Of course, the actor has other choices. Just as with the aside, during the monologue he or she can choose to talk to or interact with God or objects on the stage, as well as with the audience. As long as the choices are specific and the intentions clear, life and thus humor will be brought into the work.

Farce as Contradiction

When Chuck Jones described farce as "Real people in unreal situations," he highlighted the root of the comedy in farce, what I call the "inherent contradiction." Jones' juxtaposition of the words "real" and "unreal" in the same sentence is inherently contradictory. Another example of this is the oxymoron, a short phrase that is self-contradictory: "military intelligence," "jumbo shrimp," "political science." The whole phrase means one thing, but each word in the phrase contradicts the other. If a play does not include characters, actions, dialogue, and actions that are inherently contradictory, then the play is not a farce. The use of the aside and the monologue provide examples of this. Another example is in *The Unshakable Suitor,* when Ducamole and Lefèvre discuss music:

> **DUCAMOLE**: You remember… Before… How passionately I would play the bagpipe for you…
>
> **LEFEVRE**, *aside*: God! Who could forget?
>
> **DUCAMOLE**: Here… Every Sunday…
>
> **LEFEVRE**, *nodding*: Every Sunday…
>
> *He stands up, newspaper in hand.*
>
> **DUCAMOLE**: And how you were moved to tears by its rustic charm… Its bucolic grace…
>
> **LEFEVRE**, *aside*: Ha!
>
> **DUCAMOLE**: "How wonderful that would sound out in the country!" you told me. "By a rustling brook… In the noonday sun…"

There are two levels of contradiction here that create the humor. The first lies in the contrast between Lefèvre's distasteful memory of his friend's bagpipe playing and his willingness to let Ducamole believe he appreciates his skill; Lefèvre's line "Every Sunday…" sets up the contradiction when he says it with absolute joy in the memory. When

Ducamole reminds Lefèvre that he thought his bagpipe would sound wonderful "out in the country," we know Lefèvre really meant "far, far out in the country, far away from me," and we laugh. The knowledge that Lefèvre detests Ducamole's bagpipe playing contrasts with Lefèvre's lie and his friend's belief to the contrary. The tension between those two states of reality is what brings on the laughter.

The second level of contradiction derives precisely from the juxtaposition of "real" and "unreal." The audience suspends disbelief and accepts that the two friends are engaged in a real conversation in a real physical space about real events. At the same time, one of the characters has a real conversation with the actually real audience. Two conversations, two relationships, each of which is real, and each of which, by definition, makes the other unreal. Done well, this collision of realities, results in a delightful cognitive dissonance that leads to laughter.

For the director, there are several points of relevance. One is that you must embrace, indeed nourish, the inherent contradictions in farce. In the above example, Lefèvre's revulsion at the memory of his friend's bagpipe playing must be absolute. He has to hate it. Then, Lefèvre must make Ducamole believe that he greatly admires his skill. The stronger the contrast, the richer the laughter from the audience. The other point is that (as discussed in the section on asides), the actor's commitment to each conversation (the one with Ducamole and the one with the audience), must be complete, and the transition from one discourse to the other must be clear and specific. Only in creating these strong contrasts does the director allow the farce to flourish.

This idea, that the humor in farce derives from juxtaposing the strongest possible contradictions, can be applied to the physical aspects of the work as well. There is a key concept here that I refer to as the "Character as Superball." The Superball, you may recall, is a small, incredibly dense rubber ball that seems to rebound right back up to where it was dropped from. Just as with the Superball, give a character in a farce a good push in one direction, and he or she will bounce back equally hard in the other. (The Superball concept applies both to the dialogue and the physical behavior. As discussed above, Lefèvre's change in attitude from "I loathe your bagpipe playing" to "I love your bagpipe playing" is as sudden as a Superball's change in direction.)

The simplest example of the physical application of the Superball concept is in the classic spit-take, when someone takes a drink, only to immediately spit it out. A sudden reversal of movement can also derive with great effect from the strict application of the rules of etiquette, for instance, the rule that states that a man cannot sit if a woman is standing. In *Slap in the Farce,* Lecouque, a milliner, is trying to sell his rich client Madame de Rigueur a tiara decorated with tea roses (page 11 [insert actual page number]; this interchange has been shortened here for our purposes):

> **LECOUQUE:** Perhaps a simple tiara... Tea roses, madame...
> **MADAME DE RIGUEUR:** Tea roses?
> **LECOUQUE:** Yes, they're terribly chic…
> **MADAME DE RIGUEUR:** And subdued?
> **LECOUQUE:** Oh yes! Yes... Very...
> **MADAME DE RIGUEUR:** Well, perhaps... Can you show me, monsieur?
> **LECOUQUE:** Certainly!

Let's assume that Madame is already seated on the sofa, and Lecouque is standing. In order to persuade her, Lecouque sits down on the sofa with her. Just as he sits, Madame stands up, now ready to look at tea roses. Compelled by his obligation to extend every courtesy to his client, and suddenly successful with his sales pitch, Lecouque must bounce right back up out of the sofa. Adding the stage directions (and jumping a line as discussed earlicr), the scene would play this way:

> **LECOUQUE,** *standing next to the sofa*: Perhaps a simple tiara... Tea roses, madame...
> **MADAME DE RIGUEUR,** *still seated*: Tea roses?
> **LECOUQUE:** Yes, they're terribly chic…
> **MADAME DE RIGUEUR:** And subdued?
> **LECOUQUE:** Oh yes! Yes...
> **MADAME DE RIGUEUR,** *not convinced*: Well, perhaps...
> **LECOUQUE,** *sitting next her, persuasively*: Very...
> **MADAME DE RIGUEUR,** *getting up*: Can you show me, monsieur?
> **LECOUQUE,** *getting up as well*: Certainly!

Here, Lecouque is the Superball, thrown down next to Madame de Rigueur by his hope to sell her a tiara, and bounced right back up by his sudden success and his desire not to offend.

As with the aside, the humor only works when each character is totally committed to his or her action in the moment, and then totally committed to the contrasting action in the next moment. Just as the Superball doesn't know that it is about to hit the floor and rebound, so, too, Lecouque doesn't know that he will be getting up only a moment after he has sat down.

Taking It to the Limit

This total commitment on the part of the actors must also be reflected in the ferocity with which the director stages the action of the play. When a character in the farce wants something, this want must consume him or her. When the character takes action to achieve his or her goal, the action must be all-consuming. How does the director lead the actor to strong actions? By making the objective that much harder to achieve. This is true in the larger movements of the play, and reflected in the smaller details. For example, in *Mam'selle Frisette,* Gautier realizes that if he is ever to see his son he must woo Frisette. This is made difficult by the fact that Frisette hates all men, and she especially hates Gautier. He has to overcome Frisette's hatred, but he also must deal with his own revulsion of women, and of Frisette particularly. These are strong obstacles, which require strong actions. So, how is he going to win her heart? For one example, we can look at how Gautier does his best to emulate a traditional romantic gesture. From *Mam'selle Frisette* (page 48):

> GAUTIER: Wait! I've got it!… Flowers!… Of course!… But where, this time of day?… *(Looking out the window.)* Ah! *(Taking the tongs from the fireplace, right.)* The neighbor won't mind if I borrow them for a while. Besides, it's in a good cause! *(He leans out the window and plucks some unseen flowers with the tongs.)* There…

The author gives us the delightful idea that the flowers are just a little bit out of reach, hence the need for the tongs from the fireplace. Now, the director can make Gautier's immediate objective (plucking flowers) even harder to achieve. If the tongs aren't quite long enough, then Gautier has to balance on the windowsill, stretching out the tongs as far as he can. Even more, he has to wedge his leg under a chair so he won't tumble out of the window. And then, Frisette, oblivious, comes into the room, and Gautier must right himself, all the while keeping the chair from tipping over, and the flowers from falling. To extend the absurdity even further—and ignoring the stage directions—Gautier can use the tongs to formally "present" the flowers to Frisette. That Gautier treats all of this is as if it were normal will only add to the humor.

By making the immediate objective (the flowers) difficult to achieve, the director leads the actor to stronger actions, and the farce blossoms. When the text suggests something, let your imagination take the action to its limits. Explore even the smallest actions in the script and you will find comic gems that are funny enough on their own, but that, when developed to their furthest possible extent, will explode the humor.

There is another concept manifested in the above discussion, something I refer to as "ringing the changes." *Encyclopædia Britannica* explains that ringing the changes is the "traditional English art of ringing a set of tower bells in an intricate series of changes." The bell ringers attempt to play the bells in every conceivable sequence, not to produce a written melody, but to express all possible melodies, to the glory of God. This concept can be applied to farce (and the glory of Laughter), and is especially evident in the use of props. In the example from *Mam'selle Frisette,* the fire tongs are given one purpose in the text: Gautier uses them to retrieve the flowers. Ringing the changes leads us to find other ways to use the tongs, and they become an extension of Gautier's arms as he presents the flowers to Frisette.

Gautier's tongs in *Mam'selle Frisette* are not just a tool that allows Gautier to extend his reach, but also a metaphor for his struggle to find his own humanity; the tongs are a "key prop," one that is specific to Gautier's essence. The only way for Gautier to engage in the very human act of love, is to have this mechanical device as a crutch. The director should look at every key prop in the play and find other uses for it, other ways to explore the characters and their relationships.

For another example, consider Timothy Van Lust's twine in *A Matter of Wife and Death.* Van Lust is a Texas millionaire, despondent over a telegram reporting the sudden death of his wife back in America. Van Lust has come to woo Viviane, who, he has decided, is an exact replacement for his lost love. If Vivian refuses to marry Van Lust, he has determined to hang himself (from *A Matter of Wife and Death,* page 457:

> **VAN LUST**: Well, when I got the telegram, you can just imagine! First thing I did was go buy a ball of twine.
>
> **VIVIANE**: Twine?
>
> **VAN LUST**: I was crazy with grief! All I could think of was hanging myself on the spot! (*He takes a ball of twine from his pocket.*) See? I always keep it with me! I'm never without it. (*Getting up.*) Oh, it wouldn't take long, believe me! (*Looking up at the ceiling.*) A nail… A hook… (*Spotting something , pointing.*) Like that!
>
> **VIVIANE,** *frightened*: Please, monsieur!… Please! Not here!
>
> **VAN LUST,** *putting the twine back in his pocket*: Don't worry, ma'am! I've changed my mind… For now, that is…

Van Lust's pet twine works brilliantly as a metaphor for his conflicting emotions. He wants to kill himself, yet chooses a completely inappropriate tool. According to the stage directions, Van Lust takes the twine out of his pocket two more times during the course of the play, each time putting it right away again. The director might ask him or herself, what are the other ways in which the twine can be used to develop or illuminate Van Lust's character and his relationships with the others in the play? What if the ball of twine rolls free and across the floor? Who picks it up? Who gets tangled in the twine? How often can the twine be used, and for what?

So, ring the changes (to the glory of Laughter), attack these questions with commitment and ferocity, and the characters' journey through the farce will be a full, human, hilarious experience.

Conclusion

It is often said that Tragedy is cathartic, providing a way for the audience to experience life's most tragic and horrible events. We experience emotional pain vicariously through the characters' pain, suffering with the characters, and learning something about the human condition. Farce compels laughter for a similar reason, yet Farce is that much closer to our daily experience, and therefore more accessible. Farce details not the mighty and how they fall, but the meek and how they slip (and, to the meek, a slip is as great as a fall). In Tragedy, we identify with the characters because we can empathize with their emotional experiences. We are similar, in some ways, to Hamlet, the Danish prince. In Farce, however, we identify with the characters because we are the characters, or, more precisely, they are us. The experience of a great tragedy is from a distance. The experience of a great farce is from inside ourselves.

When we reward farce with uncontrollable laughter, the kind of laugher that forces us to weep and gasp for breath, we are laughing with recognition—that is me up there, exposed in my nakedness—and we are laughing with relief—thank God I'm not up there, exposed in my nakedness. The characters in a farce bumble and fall down the path of human foibles so that we don't have to.

Since it is the essential humanity of the characters in farce that allows us to laugh, it is their humanity that must be discovered, nurtured, and presented by the director and the actors. Once the truth of the characters and the reality of their situation is realized, then the comedy can flourish. The techniques we've discussed allow the director to lead the actors to a heightened performance. It is essential, however, that the techniques be servants of two masters: the first is reality; the second is comedy. The director must create a solid and very real foundation of human need and desire to support the delicate and absurd structure that is Farce. Your audience's response will be louder, the play will seem faster, and the whole experience will be much funnier.

As an Artist in Residence at Harvard University's Adams House, Michael Clark Haney directed productions of seven of Norman Shapiro's adaptations of Labiche, Feydeau, and Meilhac & Halevy farces in the Pool Theater. In Los Angeles, Michael directed Lament for the Moths, *his own adaptation of the poetry of Tennessee Williams, which also headlined the Tennessee Williams Literary Festival in New Orleans. He has directed numerous other award-winning productions, both classical and contemporary, and is a member of the Playwright/Directors Unit of the Actors Studio. He lives in Los Angeles with his wife and twin children. Comments or questions are welcome at cahaney@ca.rr.com.*